RETURN TO TUMBLEDOWN
THE FALKLANDS-MALVINAS WAR REVISITED

Mike Seear

CCCP

Critical, Cultural and Communications Press

Nottingham

2012

Return to Tumbledown: The Falklands-Malvinas War Revisited, by Mike Seear.

First published in the United Kingdom by Critical, Cultural and Comunications Press, 2012.

Publisher's website: **www.cccpress.co.uk**

ISBN 978-1-905510-39-9

Cover design by Hannibal.

Printed by The Russell Press, Nottingham.

To Alexander and Isabell
and
those who fell in the battle.

Glory

Soldier —
These are your days of glory
or are they a moment in hell?
Spent for those who say the cause is just
but ashes are ashes and dust is dust.
Those at home won't understand
how you changed from lad to man.
They're shadows at the back of your mind
where you leave things you don't want to find.
Should you tell them on the phone
that you might not be coming home?
And can you write it in a letter
that peace is good but freedom's better?

Emily Seear

Contents

Mike Seear revisits the theatre of his book's title *Return to Tumbledown: The Falklands-Malvinas War Revisited* and – the reader is warned – also a primal scene that has haunted the political, cultural, military and medical-psychiatric aftermaths of the 1982 South Atlantic conflict in the societies of the warring factions and beyond.

As a result of the impact of his first book, *With the Gurkhas in the Falklands: A War Journal*, there followed a joint undertaking with the Centre for the Study of Post-Conflict Cultures of the University of Nottingham, in which he was assisted by Dr. Eduardo Gerding, the Malvinas War Veterans' Medical Coordinator. The occasion marked the bringing together for the twenty-fifth anniversary of ex-combatants, for the first time, in face-to-face debate and remembrance. That event led to the proceedings published in *Hors de Combat: the Falklands-Malvinas Conflict in Retrospect*, edited by Mike Seear and Argentine veteran Diego García Quiroga, and brought resounding international recognition of the need for continuing re-evaluation of a clash of values, pre-suppositions, loyalties and prejudices that re-echoes whenever the inseparable but contentious terms 'Falklands' and 'Malvinas' are broached.

Long after the facts of the brief encounter, in military terms, of the seventy-four-day conflict have begun to fade from the memories of most of those not directly involved, dangerous mythologies persist, ever prey to re-visitations by politicians and opportunists, historians and writers of fiction, ready to re-appropriate the passions and indignations roused in Argentina, the United Kingdom and far from the Islands that were the epicentre of the action, actions, facts and fictions of 2 April to 14 June 1982.

Three decades on from the war there are still too many 'detailed unknowns' about how the Battle of Tumbledown was conducted by both sides, the disposition of forces on Tumbledown and, indeed, on Mount William, the decisions taken and not taken, and of the mindset and thoughts of individual key combatants. There had been too much reliance on regurgitating information from the plethora of books on the war and not enough time and energy spent in ground-breaking investigation with many of the veterans who were on that frightening, noisy-beyond-imagination and violent battlefield, where the full range of small arms and light weapons from the bayonet to the portable anti-tank gun, heavy mortars, mines, light tank cannon and guns, artillery and naval gunfire support were in constant use and the air threat was ever-present; but modern-day body armour was never used for those enduring such hell. The British still know little about the Argentine defenders, and Argentines little about their British attackers; and, in that mutual incomprehension and mistrust, language barriers and differing historical assumptions might be a greater obstacle to the former adversaries, still, than the sometimes apparently incalculable distance, cultural as well as geographical, across the Atlantic as ocean and myth.

Tumbledown was the final obstacle for the British forces to overcome in order to prevail in the war. It was the gateway into the little capital (known as 'the city' by the Argentines) of Stanley. For he who held Stanley held the Islands. It is in such a perspective that Seear evinces an all-consuming desire to discover against whom he was fighting in 1982, an urge that led him to undertake four odysseys of discovery in the period sandwiched between, and including, the twentieth and twenty-fifth anniversaries of the conflict. In this time, and with assistance from key Argentine protagonists, he built up a comprehensive network amongst veterans of the war. They gave him many nuggets of insider information about the battle which he has used in an unhesitating and unflinching narrative in order to paint a word-picture of a land battle that was, in effect, the final one of six in the war. His curiosity and determination to seek out former opponents also gave him the opportunity – no easy task – to meet and often to socialize with them and thereby attempt a form of personal reconciliation. The experience proved to be a rewarding one, but the language barrier could yet have prevented it. However, as is explained in his narrative, Seear was unusually fortunate in finding necessary interpreter expertise to meet this and so many of the other challenges that confront the writer seeking to re-engage with a former enemy on constructive terms. If achieving reconciliation between two former warring factions might be a responsibility of politicians, it nonetheless appears that this undertaking is not infrequently left to individual war veterans whose investment in understanding the past and their role in it is healthily undiminished.

To write well subjectively can be deployed to put so-called objectivity in context; not least when urgent, controlled and judicious expiation is at stake. The 'facts' of war are thereby rendered unfinished. Seear does not just return to Tumbledown; Tumbledown, through Seear's re-narrating, was, is and will be the incalculable sum of its causes, its 1982 realities, its harrowing conflict and post-conflict effects. A battle thus becomes, in the re-telling, a focal shift from post-traumatic stress to healing growth. This book is exemplary memoir, restorative memory, and memorable integrity.

The painstaking research and intelligent as well as emotional investment that has characterized Seear's previous contributions to some other-than-one-sided understanding of the British and Argentine perspectives on a conflict long-since extending beyond notions of winning and losing, here achieve ever greater penetration and resonance. Remarkable and unprecedented access to Argentine first-hand sources and participants is balanced by a scrupulous concern for evoking contemporary and subsequent British and Islander witness, testimony and recollection.

As broadly attested by those who have followed Mike Seear's unrelenting quest for personal reconstruction of a life – and the lives of many – the writing of his story has compelled him to re-open not wounds but healing processes. In this operation, restorative questioning sometimes assumes the rigour and intensity of interrogations, of others, of official and unofficial histories but, above all, of a re-constituted self. Seear's honesty is brutal. After the first shocks of reading the darkest sequences of, at times, an ostensibly private memoir, anyone committed to re-evaluating what has been labelled the last of old-style and the first of media-suffused and projected wars will take solace and find inspiration in Seear's disciplined confessional style. For his is also a testimony dependent on corroboration, consultation, cross-checking and correction.

If the military can sometimes be perceived as circumspect, at best, in the face of academic, juridical, psychiatric or, indeed, any ostensibly extraneous engagement with their worlds and 'their' wars – and undoubtedly that was the case amongst the initially cautious ex-combatants from both sides at the momentous encounter that led to *Hors de Combat: the Falklands-Malvinas Conflict in Retrospect* – Seear's latest undertaking is exemplary in crossing the bridge from a regime of however appropriate restriction into a retrospective of liberating thought and expression. For open-minded readers of this unapologetic narrative to accompany him on that trajectory will be an experience both arduous and exhilarating. They will still grasp that to follow orders and to execute in war a given mission must be prioritized. Yet they will be shown, too, that phantoms trapped, deliberately or not, in a soldier's mind, post-conflict, betray not the efficacy of that schooling whereby to show emotion in the military is a sign of weakness; rather a failure to train and to teach that it is possible to exorcise the demons of war by talking, and writing, about them. Moreover because such a dual activity creates a meaningful structure in which to locate past battlefield chaos, its therapeutic value can be immense.

To conclude, it is necessary to draw attention to that dimension of this book which, head-on, addresses what is called Post-Traumatic Stress Disorder. Amidst the overuse and under grasp of the application of the term, it is vital to differentiate – as Mike Seear does, and is able to do in a strikingly personal voice – between PTSR (Post-Traumatic Stress Reactions) and PTSD (Post-Traumatic Stress Disorder). The former is endured by the majority of those caught up in the immediate and short-term aftermath of combat. PTSD, here, is shown to be the chronic and long-term version of PTSR; that is, it does not go away but simply gets worse. Any form of post-traumatic stress can never be dismissed as a disorder *tout court*. In spite of the enormity of the suicides and the tragedies that have bedeviled the post-1982 legacy of what Jorge Luis Borges dismissed as a case of two bald men fighting over a comb, the serious possibility of reconstruction emerges in every chapter of this book. Lest anyone forget … or think, unwisely, otherwise.

A selected chronology of the 1982 Falklands-Malvinas War

Date	Event	Supplementary information
18-19 March	Argentine scrap-metal merchants land at Leith Harbour, South Georgia, and raise the Argentine national flag.	
2 April	*Operación Rosario*: Argentine troops re-take Islas Las Malvinas (Falkland Islands).	
3 April	- *Operación Azul* (Blue): Argentine Marines land at Grytviken, South Georgia. - United Nations (UN) Security Council adopts Resolution 502. - Operation Corporate: the UK Prime Minister, Mrs Margaret Thatcher, announces the dispatch of the British Task Force to recover the Islands.	
5 April	Lord Carrington resigns as UK Foreign Secretary.	Replaced by Mr Francis Pym.
6 April	The 9th Infantry Brigade (8th and 25th Infantry Regiments) commences deployment to the Islands from Comodoro Rivadavia.	- 8th Infantry Regiment to Fox Bay. - 25th Infantry Regiment to *BAM* Malvinas (Stanley) airfield.
7 April	- The Fleet replenishment ship RFA *Stromness* departs from Portsmouth with most of the Royal Marines' 45 Commando embarked. - The UK Government declares a Maritime Exclusion Zone (MEZ) of 200 miles around the Islands to come into effect at 04.00Z hours on 12 April. - Brigadier-General Mario Benjamín Menéndez assumes his appointment as Military Governor of Islas las Malvinas.	

8 April	- The 5th Marine Infantry Battalion (BIM5) commences deployment to the Islands from Río Grande.	
	- The US Secretary of State for Foreign Affairs Alexander Haig commences his diplomatic shuttle between Washington DC, London and Buenos Aires.	
9 April	The P&O liner SS *Canberra* departs Southampton with the Royal Marines' 40 and 42 Commando, and 3rd Battalion, Parachute Regiment (3 Para) embarked.	
11 April	The 10th Infantry Brigade (3rd and 6th Infantry Regiments, 7th Mechanised Infantry Regiment and a Company of the 1st Infantry Regiment) commences deployment to the Islands from Buenos Aires.	The 1st Infantry Regiment (one Company), 3rd and 6th Infantry Regiments deploy to Puerto Argentino (Stanley).
12 April	The MEZ comes into effect.	
15 April	- M Company, BIM5 deploys to Sapper Hill.	
	- N Company, BIM5 deploys to Tumbledown and Mount William.	
	- O Company, BIM5 deploys to Mount Longdon.	
16 April	The 10th Infantry Brigade is in position.	
18 April	The 7th Mechanised Infantry Regiment replaces O Company, BIM5 on Mount Longdon.	O Company becomes the BIM5 reserve at Felton Stream (near Sapper Hill).
22 April	Exercise Welsh Falcon (5th Infantry Brigade) starts at Sennybridge, Wales.	
24 April	The 3rd Infantry Brigade commences deployment to the Islands with the 5th and 12th Infantry Regiments from Comodoro Rivadavia.	- The 12th Infantry Regiment deploys to Mount Challenger (later this unit re-deploys to Goose Green, and two of its platoons reinforce Mount

		Harriet).
	-	The 5th Infantry Regiment deploys to Port Howard.
25 April	-	Operation Paraquet: Royal Marine Commando forces land at Grytviken, South Georgia and the Argentine garrison there surrenders.
	-	The P&O Roll-on/Roll-off car ferry MV *Norland* departs from Portsmouth with 2nd Battalion, Parachute Regiment (2 Para) embarked.
26 April		After being deployed initially to Patagonia from its Monte Caseros base in the northern Corrientes province to protect the Argentine border with Chile, the 4th Infantry Regiment (3rd Infantry Brigade) deploys to the Islands from Río Gallegos (in aircraft of Austral airline).
27 April	-	B and C Companies, 4th Infantry Regiment deploy to Wall Mountain.
	-	A Company, 4th Infantry Regiment deploys to the hills north of Puerto Argentino (Stanley).
29 April		The 3rd Infantry Brigade is in position.
30 April	-	The UK Total Exclusion Zone (TEZ) of 200 nautical miles around the Islands comes into effect.
	-	US President Ronald Reagan announces support for the UK.
1 May		Operation Black Buck 1: a pre-dawn bombing raid by a single RAF Vulcan bomber on *BAM Malvinas* (Stanley) airfield.

Afterwards Sea Harriers carry out the first air strikes on the same airfield and elsewhere in the Islands.

| 2 May | - | The Royal Navy (RN) submarine HMS *Conqueror* attacks and sinks the |

- Peru offers a new peace plan for resolving the crisis.
- UN offers similar services.

	Argentine cruiser ARA *General Belgrano*.	
	- Exercise Welsh Falcon ends.	
4 May	- The RN destroyer HMS *Sheffield* is hit by an Argentine air-launched Exocet missile within the TEZ and eventually sinks.	
	- Operation Black Buck 2: a second pre-dawn bombing raid by a single RAF Vulcan bomber on Stanley airfield.	
6 May		The UK Government formally accepts offer of UN mediation.
7 May	The TEZ is extended to within twelve miles of the Argentine coastline.	UN Secretary-General Javier Pérez de Cuéllar announces a new peace initiative.
12 May	- The UK decision is taken to mount a Task Force amphibious landing at San Carlos, East Falkland.	
	- The Cunard liner RMS *Queen Elizabeth 2 (QE2)* departs from Southampton with the 5th Infantry Brigade embarked.	
21 May	Operation Sutton, Phase I: the reinforced Royal Marines' 3 Commando Brigade of 4,000 men carry out an amphibious landing virtually unopposed at San Carlos, East Falkland.	- Heavy Argentine air attacks are launched against British shipping at the start of the five-day Battle of San Carlos Water between the Argentine Air Force and RN.
		- The RN frigate HMS *Ardent* is bombed, set on fire and abandoned.
		- Other British vessels are also damaged by the air attacks.
24 May	The RN frigate HMS *Antelope* sinks after an unexploded bomb on board detonates as it is being defused.	
25 May	- The RN destroyer HMS *Coventry* is attacked by Argentine aircraft and sunk.	- Argentine Air Force Commander Brigadier-General Lami Dozo sends a

	- The Cunard aircraft transport containership SS *Atlantic Conveyor* is hit and sunk by two Argentine air-launched Exocet missiles. - The Battle of San Carlos Water ends.	peace envoy to New York.
26 May	2 Para advances towards Darwin and Goose Green.	The UN Security Council adopts Resolution 505.
27 May	*QE2* and other vessels rendezvous at South Georgia to commence cross-decking of the 5th Infantry Brigade.	- 2nd Battalion, Scots Guards and 1st Battalion, Welsh Guards cross-deck to SS *Canberra*. - 1st Battalion, 7th Duke of Edinburgh's Own Gurkha Rifles cross-deck to MV *Norland*.
28 May	2 Para commences its attack on Darwin and Goose Green.	Cross-decking of the 5th Infantry Brigade is completed at South Georgia by late afternoon, and the Brigade sails for San Carlos, East Falkland.
29 May	The Argentine Goose Green garrison surrenders to 2 Para.	- Approximately 1,000 prisoners are taken at Goose Green. - 3 Para reaches Teal Inlet - 45 Commando commences its advance on Douglas.
30 May	Major-General Jeremy Moore arrives at San Carlos and assumes command of British land forces in the Islands.	45 Commando and 3 Para secure Douglas and Teal respectively.
31 May		The UN Secretary-General proposes a new peace plan.
1 June	- Operation Sutton, Phase V: the Gurkhas land at San Carlos and are flown by Chinook helicopter 'Bravo November' to Darwin. - 3 Commando Brigade forward base is established at Teal Inlet.	The 4th Infantry Regiment re-deploys to new positions at Two Sisters (C Company) and Mount Harriet (Battalion HQ and B Company).
2 June	- Remainder of the 5th Infantry Brigade land at San Carlos. - 2 Para elements are airlifted	Surrender leaflets are dropped by British aircraft over Stanley (Puerto Argentino).

	by Chinook 'Bravo November' to Bluff Cove.	
3 June	- The Gurkhas garrison Goose Green.	The US President presents a five-point peace plan to the UK Prime Minister at Versailles prior to the opening of the eighth G7 Summit on 4 June.
5 June	- O Company, BIM5 deploy to Pony's Pass. - The Scots Guards embark on HMS *Intrepid* for sea transport to the Fitzroy-Bluff Cove area	
6 June	- The Scots Guards land at Fitzroy, East Falkland and establish a base at Bluff Cove. - The Welsh Guards start their sea move to Fitzroy. - The Landings at San Carlos are completed (8,000 UK troops deployed).	5 Platoon (Marine Amphibious Engineers), N Company, BIM5 lay mines at Pony's Pass.
7 June	- The Gurkhas start moving up to Fitzroy, initially by sea, and later by helicopter.	The UN Secretary-General announces another peace plan.
8 June	The RFAs *Sir Galahad* and *Sir Tristram* are attacked by five Argentine Skyhawk aircraft whilst anchored at Port Pleasant (Bahía Agradable), near Fitzroy.	Fifty men (many from the Welsh Guards) are killed and 132 wounded. *Sir Galahad* is severely damaged. Post-war she is towed out to sea and torpedoed.
10 June	By midnight the Gurkhas are in position at Wether Ground.	
11-12 June	- 3 Commando Brigade mounts a night attack on Mount Longdon, Two Sisters and Mount Harriet. - All objectives are captured by first light on 12 June.	- 3 Para attacks Mount Longdon (defended by elements of the 7th Mechanised Infantry Regiment). - 45 Commando attacks Two Sisters (defended by elements of the 4th Infantry Regiment). - 42 Commando attacks Mount Harriet and Goat Ridge (also defended by elements of the 4th Infantry

13-14 June	-	2 Para mount a night attack on Wireless Ridge (defended by elements of the 7th Mechanised Infantry Regiment),
	-	The 5th Infantry Brigade mounts a night attack on Pony's Pass, Tumbledown, Mount William and Sapper Hill.

Regiment).

- The Scots Guards attack Pony's Pass (defended by O Company, BIM5) and Tumbledown (defended by N Company, BIM5 and B Company, 6th Infantry Regiment).
- The Gurkhas attack (unopposed) Tumbledown's north-east spur and Mount William.
- The Welsh Guards take (against minor BIM5 resistance) Sapper Hill.
- All Brigade objectives are secured by 16.00Z on 14 June.

14 June	After negotiations, Brigadier-General Mario Benjamín Menéndez surrenders all Argentine forces on East and West Falkland at 23.59Z.
20 June	The 6th Infantry Regiment embarks the icebreaker ARA *Bahía Paraiso* at Stanley, bound for Argentina.
21 June	BIM5 embarks the icebreaker ARA *Alimrante Irizar* at Stanley, bound for Argentina.
22 June	The 6th Infantry Regiment arrives at Río Gallegos, Santa Cruz province.
23 June	BIM5 arrives at Ushuaia, Tierra del Fuego province.
12 July	The UK announces that active hostilities over the Falkland Islands are regarded as having ended. Argentina does not make a similar Islas las Malvinas statement.
14 July	The Special Category Prisoners are repatriated by sea to Puerto Madryn, Argentina.
15-16 July	The Gurkhas embark the P&O transport ship SS *Uganda* and

Uganda was formerly the Task Force Hospital Ship.

	depart from Stanley on 18 July for UK.
22 July	The TEZ in place around the Islands is lifted.
31 July	The Scots Guards embark MV *Norland* at Stanley bound for Ascension Island.
9 August	The Gurkhas arrive at Southampton, and the Scots Guards arrive at Ascension Island.
10 August	The Scots Guards are flown by RAF VC-10 aircraft back to the UK, landing at RAF Brize Norton.

This self-imposed journey took six years to complete. Eighty-six people, in one way or another, assisted me on the way. I am indebted to them because, without their assistance, large, medium or small, *Return to the Tumbledown: The Falklands-Malvinas War Revisited* would not exist. All deserve an individual acknowledgement, even though there was the odd disagreement or two which I have chosen to forget.

First and foremost I must thank Bernard McGuirk who launched me on my adventure with his conception, planning and execution of that remarkable Anglo-Argentine Falklands-Malvinas War international colloquium held in November 2006 at the University of Nottingham. It was Bernard who, with his characteristic generosity, then welcomed me back after those six years. He spent four weeks in proof-reading (twice) my manuscript, provided excellent strategic advice for adjustments and then gave whole-hearted support to the publication of this, my second book, which is also the sequel to my first.

The indefatigable Eduardo Gerding was instrumental in co-ordinating the Argentine representation at Bernard's colloquium. He has also provided me with many Argentine war veteran contacts that have considerably enlarged my network and allowed me to research and write extensively with precision about the Argentine experience at the Battle of Tumbledown. Eduardo has also given me rapid high-quality interpreter and translator services. Without his gracious assistance I would have been lost during my visits to Buenos Aires and the important e-mail follow up with all those priceless veteran contacts. Neither must I forget the late Alberto Peralta Ramos for his unfailing friendship, efforts and expert guidance not only during my third visit to Buenos Aires in 2003, but also the two made in the previous year.

Likewise I am grateful to Cliff Caswell and Jack Izzard for their company and media coverage of my fourth visit to the Argentine capital in the period late-March and early-April 2007 during that emotional commemoration of the twenty-fifth anniversary of the war. Lars Weisæth also provided me with professional and personal support during this important visit. Furthermore I must thank María Isabel Clausen de Bruno for her friendship and wonderful hospitality (once again!) at her home town of General Roca in Córdoba province, and for writing and giving me a copy of her book *Entre tu mano y la mía*. To understand my letters which were eventually published in the book, she enlisted the English translation assistance of Ligia Picardi. So I must also thank Ligia for her dedication which enabled different, and potentially conflicting, cultures to meet and communicate in the most amicable manner possible. Furthermore I am indebted to Natalia Alemanno for her expert interpreter services. Without her and Eduardo Gerding the language barrier in Argentina would never have been conquered and this book not published.

The twenty-fifth anniversary year of the war in 2007 was remarkable for the many commemoration events held. I attended as many as possible and manufactured one of my own – a series of six Falklands-Malvinas War lectures on board the liner RMS *Queen Elizabeth 2*. I must thank Carol Marlow, the President of Cunard, for allowing me to do this. Then there was that memorable South Atlantic Medal Association 82 and Combat Stress organisation Pilgrimage to the Falkland Islands in November of that year. It provided the opportunity to establish contacts and gather unique material for inclusion in the second phase of this book.

Also Emily Herbert's contact information for Peter King in Stanley was much appreciated. It enabled me to catch sight of his wife's Stanley siege diary which became Chapter 12 of this book. In addition to Peter and Rosemarie, I would also like to express my gratitude to other Falkland Islanders – Lynn and Andrew Brownlee, Pat and Patrick Berntsen, Michael Butcher, Patrick Watts, Tim Miller, Phil Middleton and Jenny Cockwell – for all their assistance and contributions to this book. Not least should be mentioned Vera and Frank Leyland whose kind hospitality in Stanley for those seven remarkable days of the 2007 Pilgrimage is deeply appreciated.

The Scots Guards are well represented in this book. It took several years to carry out interviews (mainly by e-mail) and edit their powerful eye-witness accounts of the Tumbledown battle. Much of the detail has never been published before. So my five Scots Guards 'anchors', (in order of appearance) John Kiszely, Steve Cocks, Simon McNeill, Ian Morton and Steve Duffy, in addition to Billy Silver, Tony Blackburn, Steve Fleck and Theresa Davidson are all thanked for their unique stories both large and small provided during and, in most cases, after the Pilgrimage. Mike Scott has offered sage advice, information and steered me back onto the right path several times, while Simon Price, Angus Smith, George MacKenzie, Bill Nicol and Robert 'Ossie' Osborn have provided additional facts. There were also four other veterans of the war, Mike Bowles, Nicci Pugh, Gus Hales and Clive Jefferies, who gave me noteworthy contributions before, during and after the Pilgrimage. In Nicci's case I enjoyed greatly her well-organised *Uganda* twenty-fifth anniversary reunion event that took place at Southampton in April 2008.

My five 'anchors' in the Argentine phase of *Return to Tumbledown* cannot be praised enough for giving me their unstinting attention while I collected, read, edited and inserted their riveting stories into the book manuscript. It was a great pleasure to do this while, concurrently, my eyes were opened to my former protagonists' thinking and their actions prior, during and after combat. So I cannot express my gratitude enough to Diego F. García Quiroga, Eduardo Villarraza, Carlos Daniel Vázquez, Héctor Omar Miño and Esteban La Madrid. I acknowledge also information from Mario Benjamín Menéndez, Carlos Büsser, the late Carlos Hugo Robacio, Carlos Calmels, Elvio Angel Cuñe, Rubén Galliussi, Marcelo Oruezabala, Luis Lucero, Nicolás Urbieta and Esteban Pino. Finally three more Argentines should also be given a special mention. They are the two sons of Carlos Daniel Vázquez, Carlos Horacio and Guillermo 'Guille' Federico, who both gave me much assistance, as well as Eugenio Dalton for extracts from his enlightening war diary.

Lastly I must acknowledge the Gurkha representation in this book, not least my three 'anchors': David Morgan, Jeremy McTeague and Dilkumar Rai. Their stories are representative of the Gurkha war experience at three different rank levels. In addition Quentin Oates, Nigel Price, Mark Willis, David Willis and Alan Gibson have provided excellent eye-witness descriptions of their roles, while Paddy Redding reminded me of a few details that I had forgotten. Neither must Keith Robinson be forgotten. It was he who gave me the hitherto previously unknown background story, which is of historical importance, of Anglo-Nepalese relations and decision-making in

Kathmandu regarding the 7th Gurkha Rifles eventual deployment to the South Atlantic.

My ex-wife, Tove Grindhaug, also recounts her 'war' again in further (different) selection of letter extracts (compared to my first book). These were written in our family married quarter near the Gurkha barracks at Church Crookham during my absence from that UK Summer of 1982. There are also two post-war modern Florence Nightingales – one a Norwegian, Wenche Løbben, and the other a Swede, Lotte Rosenkvist – who deserve an acknowledgement for their dedicated work and informative journal entries. It was crucial also that three of my fellow officers cast their 'Gurkha' eyes over the manuscript. I am therefore indebted, once again, to David Morgan, Nigel Price and Jeremy McTeague for their proof-reading and, not least, pointing out politely where my 'war story' train had become derailed occasionally.

Three other British veterans of the war, Rod Macdonald, Chris Davies and John Roberts, are also thanked for their information; as are Scott Oliver and Pablo Valdivia (University of Nottingham), Gurkha enthusiast and Victoria Cross expert Reg Woollard, retired Norwegian Army Lieutenant-Colonel and disaster psychiatrist Pål Herlofsen, Gavin Edgerley-Harris (Archivist, Gurkha Museum, Winchester), Kevin Gorman (Archivist, Scots Guards Regimental HQ, London) and William Spencer (Principal Specialist: Military, Maritime and Transport Records, The National Archives, London).

It would also be incorrect not to acknowledge my dear wife Else for the freedom she gave me to write *Return to Tumbledown* which gradually became a cathartic obsession to expose the battle realities faced by the combatants on either side of Tumbledown's front line – and, in some cases, consequences during the aftermath.

Mike Seear
Oslo, February 2012

Three decades have swept by since my participation in arguably the greatest single-nation crisis management operation since the Second World War. As a thirty-five year-old Light Infantry officer holding the rank of Major, I was seconded at the beginning of March 1982 to the 1st Battalion, 7th Duke of Edinburgh's Own Gurkha Rifles. One month later Argentina seized the Falkland Islands. Six weeks later I was sailing with the Gurkhas on board the Cunard liner RMS *Queen Elizabeth 2* towards the South Atlantic and war. On 1 June the Battalion landed at San Carlos, East Falkland. After another fourteen days we had closed on the Tumbledown feature seized by the 2nd Battalion, Scots Guards from the defending Argentines and were nearing Mount William to initiate the war's seventh land-battle. But then, even more suddenly as it had all begun, those ten dynamic weeks of Operation Corporate came to an end. The British Task Force had prevailed.

It took twenty-one years before my first book about those events was published. *With the Gurkhas in the Falklands: A War Journal* was a story about soldiers and their decisions, actions and reactions during war, the most traumatic 'life event' of them all. My eye-witness account tried to inform honestly about 'the what, how, why, when and who' of the 1st Battalion's part in the campaign – as well as those inevitable 'warts and all'. Retired Major Nigel Price was also a 7th Duke of Edinburgh's Own Gurkha Rifles Falklands veteran who went on to complete twelve years service with the Regiment. Now a published novelist and Partner/Sales Director Asia-Pacific in a Manchester-based company which exports educational books and equipment to British and international schools worldwide, he recorded in the Regimental Association Journal:

Mike Seear has written a terrific book. While it is an extraordinary trip down memory lane for anyone who was with the battalion in 1982 and took part in the Falklands War, it has much wider appeal that takes it beyond even the casual reader of military history.

I found myself marvelling at the detail Seear has managed to glean, all of which goes to show that waiting for twenty years has paid rich dividends. The book is immeasurably better for the maturation process, painful and frustrating though this must have been for the author

The book eschews the cold objectivity of a regimental history in favour of an engagingly personal angle which, from this writer's point of view, greatly strengthens it. In effect, it pushes the book into a different league. On the one hand, the reader has almost a pocket history of the whole war, while on the other, Seear has also managed to craft an incredibly engaging story. It is personal and brutally honest. What is more, the author succeeds in conveying all of this to the layman, assisted by a useful glossary and exhaustive index. The inclusion of substantial material gained through contact with Argentine participants adds a certain feel that 'we were all in it together'.

The book is a gem and I strongly recommend it. Clearly the experience had a profound effect on Seear's subsequent life. To an extent, like the ancient mariner, he emerged a sadder but a wiser man the following morn.[1] He has achieved a remarkable degree of self-awareness, and his honesty in this regard may not sit comfortably with all readers. That said, I believe there will be many others who identify with his experiences and with the lessons he has – over the years – drawn from them. The book is from the heart, devoid of pomposity and illusion. No other factual book that I have ever read about the Gurkhas has ever achieved this.[2]

Alan Gibson was a Royal Artillery Lance-Bombardier attached to the Gurkha Battation Tactical HQ during the war. Twenty-five years afterwards he bought a copy of *With the Gurkhas in the Falklands* and subsequently wrote to me:

> It was very strange to read your book, like looking at a very powerful part of my own life through a pool of water with small ripples upon it. By this I mean that I was looking at my own very personal experiences from a distance of just a few yards away through someone else's eyes. I remember all the salient points but in a slightly different way [...] very strange, but also very therapeutic. (Does that make any sense?)[3]

To be able to give effective veteran peer support after such a life-changing event was most satisfying. Nonetheless there was not enough space in my book to document properly the totality of the Battle of Tumbledown. It is only the veterans of both sides, not historians, who can provide an accurate and detailed picture of their bloody work on that difficult terrain canalised by crags and littered with boulders. All they require is a facilitator who was also there, albeit on the periphery, to massage their thoughts into coherent written English and provide the key structure in describing their battle fought on the war's final night. It is a central theme of this sequel to my first book. Of course some had concerns, like retired Major-General Mike Scott, the former Commanding Officer of the 2nd Battalion, Scots Guards:

> I admire your efforts but do not forget that it is now nigh on twenty-seven years later and many of us, while, of course, intensely proud of our Battalion and what was achieved, have moved on. There are emotional dangers, which you will know well, of unnecessarily resurrecting chunks of the past.[4]

My answer sought to allay his fears:

> I am acutely aware of the potential emotional dangers in my 'prying' into the Battalion's fight on Tumbledown. I have the utmost respect for all who were there. However my advantage over many of those who have attempted to describe the battle is that I was a bystander on that night listening and watching everything. It is burnt into my mind. However I cannot cover all the untold stories of the battle, so my plan was to use the stories of a selected few that I met on the Pilgrimage. The latter became much more of a profound experience in the aftermath when I was exchanging all those e-mails with Lance-Corporal Simon McNeill. I must confess that, at times, I had to cope with my own battlefield nausea again as his tale was being unravelled. Together we were able to piece together the details of his remarkable story in the correct chronological sequence.[5]

But there is also another aspect. This is the extreme 'life event' nature of war and its subsequent effects and potential consequences on those who have fought in it. Retired Brigadier Rod Macdonald served with 3 Commando Brigade which also deployed to that austral war. From 1966-68 we were Officer Cadets of Inkerman Company's Intake 41 Platoon at the Royal Military Academy Sandhurst, but it would not be until thirty-nine years later that we met again at a London reunion of our platoon. He was now Senior Vice-President Sales and Business Development for a US global multi-billion dollar industry cable manufacturer.

Our conversation inevitably drifted towards the war and Rod remarked at one point, 'We lived one life up to the Falklands War. We started a new life after it was over.' He was so right. But only another war veteran can really appreciate his statement. In my case, post-war life in Norway has been a roller coaster – but it has also brought about a second marriage and two wonderful small children. So Rod's important insight has been included throughout the narrative of *Return to Tumbledown: The Falklands-Malvinas War Revisited*.

It was not until the end of 2005 after meeting Professor Bernard McGuirk at the University of Nottingham that I began my self-imposed task. The execution of Bernard's plan to assemble Scots Guards, Argentine and Gurkha veterans of the Falkland-Malvinas War and Tumbledown battle at an international colloquium at the University in November 2006, coupled with my fourth visit to Argentina in March/April 2007 and participation in the South Atlantic Medal Association 82's Pilgrimage to the Islands in November of that year, would intensify my research and writing. Scots Guards, Argentine and Gurkha perspectives of equal portions are therefore incorporated into the mix. I have also strenuously avoided regurgitating Gurkha tales from my first book. This embargo required me to trawl my network for alternative unpublished information from fellow Gurkha war veterans and other sources.

Structure is the key in this sequel which contains many eye-witness accounts of the battle. Only three Falklands-Malvinas War veterans refused to collaborate with me. Two were Argentine. The other was British. Towards the end of my writing I sent a nine-page synopsis to inquisitive Scott Oliver, a Ph.D candidate at the University of Nottingham. With clever insight, he observed how the story had been built up:

> I very much like the 'micro-historical' approach to counterbalance the 'macro-historical' way these things inevitably get reported or understood (a 'bottom-up' production of the event in ever-changing mixture with 'top-down' orders that are more a desired-for state than a description of what happened). The testimony of so many participants gives real colour to the event as an unfolding, 'open' reality, with very high stakes and much uncertainty (the constant *personal* reality of the soldier-as-man, I imagine, notwithstanding the training to subjugate personal will and identity to the collective effort/objective).

The book is divided into five phases of which *Phase I: Look Back (Not) in Anger* chronicles in a single chapter the backdrop work for Bernard McGuirk's colloquium and, thereafter, my follow-on experiences during the war's twenty-fifth anniversary year. It sets the scene for the start of my account of the Tumbledown battle in *Phase II: The Pilgrimage … and the Scots Guards' attack on Tumbledown* where the reader will traverse constantly between pilgrimage and combat separated by a twenty-five year time-span. During these five chapters, four Scots Guards pilgrims: former Lance-Corporal Simon McNeill, Lance-Corporal Steve Cocks (a Royal Army Pay Corps clerk attached to the Scots Guards), Guardsman Ian Morton and Piper Steve Duffy provide their first-hand accounts of this battle. In addition former Major John Kiszely (and now retired Lieutenant-General Sir John Kiszely), the Left Flank Company Commander, also gives his commentary and insights which underline the grim nature of the challenges that his Guardsmen had to overcome. And not least, Theresa Davidson, widow of the late Lance-Sergeant Clark Mitchell who was killed in the battle, provides her thoughts of being a Falklands 25 pilgrim. In contrast there is also a contemporary Islanders' dimension to this part of the book.

The first chapter of *Phase III: Argentine Entry and Exit* describes in detail *Operación Rosario* from the perspective of Sub-Lieutenant Diego García Quiroga. The reader will share his professionalism and excitement of being part of that operation to seize the Islands on 2 April 1982 – and then his sudden trauma, pain and suffering which nearly cost him his life. He was 'honoured and privileged' to read this end-product after my many hours of re-writing and expanding his original version. This is followed by the story of Naval Lieutenant Eduardo Villarraza, the Argentine 5th Marine Infantry Battalion's N Company Commander, and a 'big-picture' presentation of Argentine defence preparations and fighting on Tumbledown.

Then it is the turn of N Company's 4 Platoon Commander. Acting Sub-Lieutenant Carlos Daniel Vázquez with only forty-four men fought and delayed the Scots Guards for nearly seven hours. Chapter 10 describes this combat in detail as well as that of another Acting Sub-Lieutenant, Héctor Omar Miño, while the chapter's second half chronicles Vázquez's life after repatriation to Argentina.

Sir Winston Churchill once said, 'Men occasionally stumble over the truth, but most of them pick themselves up and hurry off as if nothing ever happened'. But I did not ignore the truth given to me either by British or Argentine veterans alike, and certainly not by Vázquez and manner in which the history of his platoon's battle was handled by the Argentine Navy and others. His fight on the west end of Tumbledown is complemented in the next chapter by the resistance of Sub-Lieutenant Esteban La Madrid's Argentine Army platoon at the east end. Phase IV ends with a descent into the Islands' capital of Stanley (re-named 'Puerto Argentino' by its Argentine occupiers) where the reader will follow, through siege veteran Rosemarie King's diary, the war's latter half culminating in the Tumbledown battle.

Phase IV: Gurkha Kaida *and* Josh *to Mount William via Tumbledown* reverts to the concept of three story-telling anchors. The Commandant (Commanding Officer) Lieutenant-Colonel David Morgan (mainly through edited entries from his war diary), 10 Platoon Commander Lieutenant Jeremy McTeague and 12 Platoon radio operator Rifleman Dilkumar Rai describe the preparations and advance to their ultimate objective of Mount William. Others from the Battalion and elsewhere also provide accounts of the Gurkha participation in Operation Corporate.

Three chapters are in *Phase V: Post-Conflict Cultures* which document some short- and long-term aftermaths of the Falklands-Malvinas War. The Gurkha story continues to midway in Chapter 19 where concluding personal experiences take over. I assume an 'ancient mariner' role and drill down far deeper than my first book into the personal sub-strata of post-traumatic growth and existential authority paradoxical dangers which a combat veteran can bring into the working environment of his first civilian job. Although the consequences of these are disastrous, there is a major lesson learnt (to quote Nigel Price again): 'Only in the storms are we spurred on to personal growth. And in the end, it is only personal growth that really matters'. The wheel comes full circle with an account of my third trip to Argentina in 2003 when I met Nicolás Urbieta – an Argentine soldier featured in my first book – and mutually cathartic benefits of war veteran reconciliation. Finally the *Afterword* presents three war veterans' views on the assertion that the Falklands-Malvinas is an unfinished business.

Throughout I have leant on the two and a half millennia-old wisdom of the Chinese General Sun Tzu throughout *Return to Tumbledown* – even to the extent of reproducing some of his thoughts as the chapter titles in Phase IV. His renowned treatise which contains the first known writings on the use of strategy when handling conflict, was published two centuries after his death under the original title of *Ping-far* (Military Methods). It is known today in the Western World as *The Art of War*. Sun Tzu's thirteen short chapters contain a multitude of strategic handrails as to how war can be prosecuted successfully – even in the South Atlantic of 1982. His laser conciseness and word symmetry is in a different league from that of the more fashionable but labyrinthian tome of *On War* by the nineteenth-century Prussian General Carl von Clausewitz. The battle plan must be simple.

Wherever possible I have attempted to corroborate the many combat experiences related to me, although I am aware that one or two of the protagonists' statements might be regarded as contentious. Nonetheless, I have committed myself to include them because I believe that I have been conscientiously informed by all consulted and who were present at the Battle of Tumbledown.

Notes

1. From Samuel Taylor Coleridge's *Rime of the Ancient Mariner*. Written in 1797-98, it is one of the great allegorical tales of English literature. Stopping a wedding guest on the way to a wedding ceremony, the Mariner tells him the story of a sea voyage that went horribly wrong. An unthinking act of violence against nature (due to a shortcoming in himself) brought down a curse upon the ship, and all endured subsequent hardships. He is only redeemed by an equally unthinking act, but this time one of love, and is thereafter saved. He sees sea serpents and is stunned by their beauty. Instinctively he blesses them, and that act of blessing signals his salvation. The curse is lifted and the Mariner, driven by guilt, is forced to wander the earth to tell his story and teach a lesson to those he meets. Once his tale has been, the Mariner leaves: and the wedding guest, whose reaction has turned from bemusement to impatience and fear to fascination as the Mariner's tale develops, returns home:

He went like one that that hath been stunned,
And is of sense forlorn:
A sadder and a wiser man
He rose the morrow morn.

2. *7th Duke of Edinburgh's Own Gurkha Rifles Regimental Association Journal. Edition* – No. 9/2003, p. 107.
3. E-mail dated 17 March 2009.
4. *Ibid.*
5. *Ibid.* dated 30 December 2007.

PHASE I
LOOK BACK (NOT) IN ANGER

The rush of water, to the point of tossing rocks
about. This is shih.
The strike of a hawk, at the killing snap. This is
the node.
Therefore, one skilled at battle —
His shih *is steep.*
His node is short.

Shih *is like drawing the crossbow.*
The node is like pulling the trigger.

Sun Tzu[1]

Intellectually I was in no-man's-land. Since 1984 I had lived in Norway and, job-wise, continued my crisis management consultant profession born out of the Falklands-Malvinas War's stresses and strains. My maiden book *With the Gurkhas in the Falklands: A War Journal* had been published in July 2003. But where would be my next challenge?

The answer came twenty-eight months later on 14 November 2005 when an e-mail arrived from my publisher Pen and Sword Books. It read simply: 'Professor Bernard McGuirk of the University of Nottingham has read your book. He would like you to contact him.'

With anticipation I rang the telephone number provided.

A voice answered crisply, 'Bernard McGuirk.'

'Hello. My name's Mike Seear …'

'I know who you are!' the Professor interrupted. 'I've just spent ten days filleting your book and have a proposal for you!'

He continued, 'I'm writing a book that reviews the literature, films and plays about the Falklands Conflict, and one of its chapters is about the Gurkhas. I'd like you to read it. Can you come and stay at the University for a few days before Christmas? You'll be a guest at the students' Christmas dinner and we can talk further about other matters. OK?'

There was no hesitation in my accepting his mysterious invitation. But time was of the essence, so he terminated the call abruptly. I would become used to how he handled telephone conversations, nonetheless it was a good start as his follow-up e-mail revealed: 'This afternoon's conversation was a mere confirmation of the writer whose text told me that he would be as amenable to contact as he was to being read.'

The Professor not only held the Chair of Romance Literatures and Literary Theory, in the Department of Spanish, Portuguese and Latin American Studies, but was also Head of the Postgraduate School of Critical Theory and Cultural Studies, Director of the Centre for the Study of Post-Conflict Cultures,[2] and Warden of Willoughby Hall, one of the University's Halls of Residence. So it was with trepidation four weeks later after my Oslo to London flight and viciously expensive train journey to Nottingham that I entered the main entrance of Willoughby Hall. It had always been my habit to avoid such places. Study and examinations had never been 'my thing'. However the Professor's secretary, Beverly Tribbick, seemed friendly enough and showed me to my room. A few minutes later the grey-haired academic with inquisitive eyes appeared in the doorway. He held a manuscript in one hand and a bottle of wine in the other. There were black shadows under his eyes. The author's current writing task, described to me later as his 'most important book', was obviously an intense process.

'Ah! Good to meet you, Mike,' he exclaimed. 'Sorry, I've got to leave you now as I'm lecturing shortly. But I'll be back in a couple of hours. Meanwhile here's a bottle of Argentine wine for you to relax with while reading this confidential draft chapter on the Gurkhas in my book. It's a review of a one-man show about a Malvinas War veteran who has been admitted to a psychiatric hospital. He believes the Gurkhas are still chasing him. And my thoughts about your book have also been included in the chapter!'

My generous host left as quickly as he had materialised. Tired, I lay on the bed and, ignoring the Malbec wine, read his manuscript entitled *Gurka/Gurkha* six times. The Argentine Vicente Zito Lema's play *Delirium Teatro* comprises eight texts and was first staged in the Sala Calibán, Buenos Aires, in November 1988. As an ultimate and bizarre consequence of the 1st Battalion, 7th Duke of Edinburgh's Own Gurkha Rifles' presence on the East Falkland battlefield, one of these texts is a schizo-drama entitled *Gurka* about the symptomatic 'voice in the head' of Miguel, a Malvinas War veteran who, 'from this life in flashback, the enemy, all the enemies, the absolute other, become Gurkhas; *Gurka.*' It was about the effects of extreme post-traumatic stress disorder, for example:

> I can't think of anything else. I fought in the Islands, I am a hero. Nobody forgives me for it. My own countrymen sent me to hospital and the Gurkhas swore that they'd kill me. They're just waiting for the moment, they're watching me. They're just waiting for the moment, they're watching me. At night they hid in the hospital basement. By day they disguise themselves as somebody else, even as doctors, or nurses ... But I can spot them, they smell like dead men, like spit-rags. I'm not afraid of them! I'm on red alert! I'm waiting for them! [3]

And in his hallucination roller coaster, Miguel transposed the Junta's death-squads into ultra far-fetched images of our Battalion's men. Yet he was not alone, at last, in confronting the Gurkhas in battle – even though this only occurred in his mind. Such an imaginary fight is one that other Malvinas War veterans continue to make:

> The Gurkhas have huge toothless mouths [...] Yesterday after today the Gurkhas came in a big green car. They dragged in a half-naked man, bleeding from the mouth, threw him on the ground [...] he couldn't breath. The Gurkhas trod on him in their boots, hit him with their sticks, he was weeping, they said to him: *Play the fool! Play the fool!*, and they laughed [...] The Gurkhas got back into the car, turned on the siren and left. I chased them, but I couldn't get beyond the bars. I was boxed in. Gurkhas! Gurkhas! I'm not afraid of them. Fight me head on if you're real *machos*! I'm ready for you, Gurkhas! [4]

My eyes flicked on. There was also a five-page review of my book:

Mike Seear [...] embarks upon an overdue and riveting narrative; yet his admirably concerted attempts at frank narration also simultaneously deconstruct any putting straight of the record. His account is thus, and inevitably, a re-representation of a prior representation, particularly evident in the tone of gentle humour and admiration evinced but also in his choice of certain motifs, metaphors and stylistic tropes largely absent from, say, the rendering of the facts of the Gurkha involvement in the conflict by the political historian Sir Lawrence Freedman:

The use of Nepalese troops in such a venture might be expected to raise eyebrows. According to Nott, when told by Bramall that the Gurkhas would be going, he said that this could not be done: We have frightful trouble holding things together in the United Nations and it is more than likely that the Indians will kick up a frightful fuss. It is just too risky politically to send the Gurkhas in my view.[5]

(Seear's scrupulous care for and attention to the facts will, at the end of the book, come to include a peremptory dismissal of the former Secretary of State for Defence, John Nott, in respect of his grasp and later use of the Gurkha story.)[6] For discursive evidence that would supplement and support Montanari's thesis that representations of war also kill people, it is enlightening to draw on the somewhat more than memoir of Seear. His characteristically literary style brings his rather hybrid narrative closer to that of the authors dealt with in this study than to the crisp factuality of Freedman:

Galtieri [...] gave new meaning to the expression 'The lights are on, but there's nobody at home' by pressing the button to invade the Falklands. 'That [...] is the start of the Gurkha irresistible force towards Galtieri's immovable objects on the Falklands'.

[...] The 'accident' rather than the 'cock-up' theory of war, no less than of history, is evoked in Seear's chapter 'Projecting the Image' in which he narrates the surprise of an Austrian interviewer at how 'two civilized countries were going about settling the dispute. A press-call conference turns to an effect no less powerful than any narration of combat or staging of PTSD. Some of the Gurkhas participating in the press-call bring out and start using a millstone (to sharpen their *kukris* [7]) that would come to hang heavy round the neck of history and, inseparably – for the one *is* the other – of representation. [...] It is apparent that Seear is highly alert to the degree which information is itself war; and to which media and their effects are not just social but special agents, peculiarly operative in the theatre of confrontation, pre-, intra-, and post-conflict. He remembers – and self-proclaimedly indulges – the narrative and dramatic devices of adventure stories, capturing not their irrelevance or inappropriateness but the very contrary, namely their power and thus their key operational efficaciousness. Seear [...] has, apart from his own schooling in British nation-building metaphor, the experienced Gurkhas themselves to play up and play the game of a time-honoured tactical use of information as disinformation. His clever juxtaposition of *Sun* and *Flash* media interventions sheds a blinding light on the *Vitae Lampada* pre-text of the preparation for war – pen to make and image to win? Postmodern newspaper-mogul Empire, no less than Raj nostalgia, seeks again to impose a breathless hush, be it on an enemy in trepidation or the BBC under censorship. (The pastiche plays with Sir Henry Newbolt's 'Vitae Lampada': 'There's a breathless hush on the Close tonight,/Ten to make and the match to win/A bumping pitch and a blinding light/A hour to play and the last man in'.)[8]

I was still breathless when Professor McGuirk returned. The Malbec wine was still unopened. Apologetically I told him that all my concentration had been given to his writing and supreme dexterity with the English language.

'Don't worry,' he said soothingly. 'Forget the Professor bit. My name's Bernard. Let's go and have something to eat.'

Over dinner in Willoughby Hall he revealed the main reason for inviting me. 'The twenty-fifth anniversary of the Falklands Conflict will be commemorated in 2007. In recognition of this I want to hold an international colloquium here at Nottingham in November 2006 to which Argentine and British veterans of the conflict will be invited. This would be an historic first meeting in the context of such an academic forum,' he stated unequivocally. 'Funding will be required, the main expense being to fly the Argentine veterans to the UK and accommodate them. However I am an expert in solving funding problems, but need a military man in my team: so will you assist me in organising this event?'

I readily agreed as he added, 'This will result in published proceedings out in time for the twenty-fifth anniversary.'

He did not stop. A fluent Spanish speaker, Bernard had led a UK cultural team to Argentina in 1990 after diplomatic relations had been re-established. His interest in the South Atlantic happenings of 1982 spurred him to write his current book. 'Would you be a military consultant for it?' he asked. A glutton for punishment, I accepted again.

The visit had been an Aladdin's Cave of offers to guarantee an exit out of my no-man's-land. It was sealed next evening by a Christmas dinner for 200 festive students, and I left Nottingham looking forward to November 2006. My task would be to design the programme and contact those selected to ask if they would participate. The Battle of Tumbledown fought on the night of 13-14 June 1982 was an obvious platform. It had involved four units: 2nd Battalion, Scots Guards, 1st Battalion, 7th Duke of Edinburgh's Own Gurkha Rifles, 5th Marine Infantry Battalion and B Company, 6th Infantry Regiment. I needed a contact in Argentina. My friend Dr Eduardo Gerding, the Malvinas War Veterans' Medical Co-ordinator [9] whom I met in Buenos Aires on my second visit to Argentina in December 2002, would be ideal. Eduardo was also a retired Naval Lieutenant-Commander and 5th Marine Infantry Battalion's Regimental Medical Officer during 1987-90. He agreed to my request immediately.

From 5 to 7 May I attended my first colloquium at Nottingham with the intriguing title 'Happiness and Post-Conflict Cultures'. The aim was to become acquainted with the academic atmosphere of such an event. On return to Oslo I contacted Eduardo and we began some preliminary planning. It seemed obvious that the colloquium's fulcrum should be a joint presentation by the former three Commanding Officers involved in the battle: Major-General Mike Scott, Scots Guards, Brigadier David

Morgan, 7th Gurkha Rifles, and *Contraalmirante* (Rear-Admiral) Carlos Hugo Robacio, 5th Marine Infantry Battalion. They were all retired officers with equally impressive post-military service careers. Since 1997 Mike Scott had been the Bar Council Lay Complaints Commissioner working closely with the Professional Conduct Committee, David Morgan had been the Custodian of Glastonbury Abbey and was currently heavily involved in Services charity work, and Carlos Hugo Robacio had been a Professor at the Argentine Armed Forces' War Colleges and the Joint Chiefs of Staff College.

'The Big Three' would require retired regimental back-up. Numerous veterans were contacted. Some could not attend, but finally I chose for Mike Scott his Regimental Medical Officer, Brigadier Alan Warsap; his Padre, Angus Smith; and Right Flank Company Commander, Major Simon Price. For David Morgan there was his 10 Platoon Commander, Captain Jeremy McTeague; and myself. Robacio would be supported not only by his N Company Commander on Tumbledown, *Capitán de Navío* (Naval Captain) Eduardo Villarraza, but also others from my network comprising Eduardo Gerding; *Capitán de Fragata* (Commander) Diego F. García Quiroga, a member of the Special Forces group that attacked Government House, Stanley on 2 April 1982; *Suboficial Mayor* (Warrant Officer) Nicolás Urbieta, a 4th Infantry Regiment section commander at the Battle of Two Sisters; *Teniente Primero* (Lieutenant) Jorge Daniel Pérez Grandi, Urbieta's platoon commander; and María Isabel Clausen de Bruno, an ardent supporter of the Malvinas War veterans.

I topped up this cast with the Norwegian Professor Lars Weisæth: a long-time friend who was also the world's first professor in traumatic stress; Mark Sandman, a Vietnam War Veteran and psychologist specialising in veteran peer support: Martin Reed, the First Officer of the Task Force-requisitioned P&O cruise liner SS *Canberra* (The Great White Whale) and Chairman of the South Atlantic Medal Association 82. The eighteenth person was Rebekah Wilson. She was a London barrister and one of an eight-member strong 'International Commission of Enquiry set up at the request of the Gurkha Army Ex-Servicemen's Organisation in Nepal to investigate independently the reality of the economic and social conditions of Nepali citizens who have and are serving in the Brigade of Gurkhas under the Ministry of Defence, United Kingdom, and their families'.[10]

Finally Bernard threw into this mix another three distinguished ladies: Lucrecia Escudero Chauvel, an Argentine semotician and Professor of Communication; Sophie Thonon-Wesfreid, a French Barrister at the Paris Bar responsible for bringing to court the case of the disappearance and torture of French citizens during Argentina's *La Guerra Sucia* (the Dirty War) or *El Proceso* in which the overall number of *desaparecidos* (disappeared) escalated into many thousands; [11] and María Fra Amador, an Argentine political scientist and researcher. Including Bernard and me, twenty-four persons would be programmed to make presentations in the day and a half allocated to the colloquium's second half. The entire event would last from 17-19 November. Combining two colloquiua for financial efficiency, its umbrella title became *Conflict and Post-Conflict in Latin America 200 Years On, 25 Years On*. Part I dealt with *Gender and Post-Conflict 200 Years On* that would re-think the history of Latin American Independence in terms of gender, whilst Part II *The Falklands-Malvinas Conflict 25 Years On* would focus on both the military and civil cultures of the 1982 war and its impact and aftermath in Argentina, the United Kingdom and internationally.

Bernard and I met at Cambridge University on 26 June to initiate the planning process proper. From then Eduardo and I worked hard for the next five months. E-mails were exchanged almost daily. The styles of accepting invitations differed greatly, e.g. the diplomatic strategic answer of the short, dark Robacio:

> I accept your invitation, trusting we will be able to think and listen to each other's opinions. The goal will be to enhance our relationships using reason as the proper way of reconciling our interests for the welfare of our nations.[12]

Compared to the tall, blond Scott's punchy operational response:

> Provisionally, count me in. I would definitely like to meet the old enemy. (Interestingly, many years before I was married, I had a fantastic Argentinian girlfriend, who, sensibly, returned to Argentina rather than staying with me. I wonder what would have happened had she done so!) [...] forget the General (rank), that was two lives ago! [...] I will need a bit more of an *aim* to my twenty minutes. Is it why we beat the 5 Arg Battalion? The quality of British volunteer soldiers? How my Battalion behaved before, during and after the conflict? What my plans were, what the alternatives were and why I chose to do what I did? Treatment of prisoners (Price to lead in relation to Ajax Bay special category PoWs)? Long term effects and lack of PTSD (Warsap to lead)? Would we do it again? Grateful for guidance. The good Prof should realise that I don't do deep intellectual argument, but subjects more related to the level of the mess-tin! [13]

Being an avid student of the powerful little book *The Art of War*, I was reminded of the Chinese word *shih*: power inherent in a configuration. So now 'pulling the trigger' to start the colloquium in those few unique November days would release all the *shih* energy that had been accumulated in those previous five months of planning. The aim for 'The Big Three' was to describe their regimental culture in battle during the war. The end-result differed greatly. Scott's was an understated 'broad-brush' account, Robacio's a detailed analysis of the fighting against all odds, while Morgan focused on the Gurkha soldier rather than describing their Falklands-Malvinas War operations. This perceived imbalance has been addressed by utilising my former CO's war diary in writing the penultimate phase of this book. The most thought-provoking of all presentations was arguably Jeremy McTeague's *Who Cares about the Enemy?* A former lobbyist working for UNITA to bring about an end to the civil war in Angola and currently employed in a Geneva-based philanthropic foundation, he would thank me for involving him 'in what has proved to be one of the most rewarding, stimulating and worthwhile initiatives' since his marriage.

But it was David Morgan's first-ever meeting with Robacio, his former protagonist, that gave him an absolute final confirmation of what he had long believed about his Gurkhas *vis-à- vis* all Argentine troops on the Islands during the war. They included Robacio's Marines on the Tumbledown-Mount William battlefield:

We now all know that the Argentines were afraid of us, confirmed to me by, of all people, Carlos Hugo Robacio during the colloquium. As we shook hands cordially, he remarked immediately (via an interpreter) with words to the effect of, 'Oh! Of course we were very worried about your men!'

This could have been because he thought we were an unruly rabble. But given what I knew already, I understood it to mean that his Marines were 'frightened' of us – but then I would, wouldn't I?'

However it was obvious to all who saw it right from the beginning of the war by the behaviour of the prisoners at Goose Green. The use of *kukris* was a beautiful piece of propaganda that really worked, but I prefer to think that it was much more the professionalism of our soldiers, and the unknown factor that somehow they were Mongolian supermen, that put the wind up them.

Indeed I would be prepared to go even further to say that the morale effect of having Gurkhas on the battlefield, whether they achieved anything or not, was, and still is a 'match-winner'. That effect was as true in both of the World Wars, Malaya, Borneo and the Falklands as it is in Afghanistan today.[14]

During the colloquium's social interludes Bernard successfully promoted *bonhomie* by utilising his priceless after-dinner bilingual speaking skills. The entire event was a resounding triumph, yet Mike Scott had some reservations in his New Year lead article for *The Guards Magazine*. Entitled *Face to face with the enemy*, it began with 'Readers of this Magazine who know me well will realise that I normally avoid this sort of thing at all costs' – and concluded:

I had approached this weekend with some cynicism tempered with apprehension as to exactly how we, and they, were going to behave and react to each other. I was nervous that we might be drawn into a political arena or be subjected to a 'Malvinas belongs to Argentina' campaign. I was curious that there was no Falkland Islander representation – it would have been easy enough to invite the Falkland Islands representative in London, the attractive and charismatic Sukey Cameron. Personally, I was not sure I wanted to rake over the coals again. I had managed to keep my own demons at bay and I did not want them dressing forward from their cupboards.

I need not have worried. Everyone was polite about the Malvinas; despite the Argentinian fixation, we never had to remind them that for as long as the Islanders want to remain British and refuse Argentinian rule, they can forget it. We were not politicised but happily kept to professional soldiering matters. We had respect for them and I am sure they did for us (to my eternal embarrassment, I was presented with a 5th Marine shield and a very smart pair of cuff-links!). Without exception, the Argentinians were polite, urbane, charming and, seemingly, very happy. For some, this weekend may have had a beneficial cathartic effect. My only real regret was that the programme was so packed, the translation process so laboured and the timing discipline so much more academic than military that there was no time for informal discussion. I would have enjoyed an opportunity to sit down over a drink with our opponents and really get a sense of how things had unfolded, what our hopes and fears had been and how we approached our problems.

Carlos Hugo Robacio and I parted as soldiers with mutual respect and understanding.[15]

As the colloquium co-organisor, I did not extend an invitation to any Falkland Islands representative because there could not be a disruptive political dimension to a primarily soldier-to-soldier *tête-a-tête*. There was also my investment of thirty-six hours in 'breaking the ice' with an anxious Argentine delegation immediately prior to the colloquium. We had entertained them at the University Staff Club, walked around Nottingham Castle together, ate in a restaurant, downed pints of beer at a pub while studying my map of the Tumbledown and Mount William area, and yarned about the battle. There was only one difficult moment. They were displeased that the Tristán Bauer 2004 film *Iluminados por el fuego* (Enlightened by Fire) dealing with Argentine Malvinas War veteran suicides would be screened on the colloquium's eve. Rescue came by explaining that this was not part of the official programme.

Much planning, resources and effort had been put into the colloquium. Overall the proof of the pudding was in its eating. Published eleven months later and edited by Diego and me, the book *Hors de Combat: The Falklands-Malvinas Conflict Twenty Five Years On* was an anthology of the presentations made. In its Afterword sixteen participants made highly favourable comments.

While planning the colloquium I had also compiled and sent to Bernard many of the twenty-nine pages of comments and sixty-eight of amendments for the manuscript of his unique book *Falklands-Malvinas: An Unfinished Business*. I completed these shortly after my return to Oslo. They included my thoughts on *Iluminados por el fuego*:

> The night battle scenes are poor. The terrain is open, but the Tumbledown battle took place mainly in enclosed rocky channels and amongst its crags. The British troops appear to be paratroopers (it was 2 Para who fought in the adjacent Wireless Ridge battle that same night on 13-14 June) with the paratrooper distinctive steel helmet. However it was the Scots Guards (not paratroopers) who fought in the battle against the 5th Marine Infantry Battalion. The Scots Guards also wore berets, not steel helmets, throughout the battle. Maybe the film-makers were trying to make us believe that it was actually the Gurkhas in the limited battle scenes. After all, the Gurkhas are the only British Task Force unit mentioned in the film and they did, in fact, wear steel helmets during the Tumbledown battle!
>
> Moreover after having met Robacio and Villarraza at the colloquium, I cannot believe that the 5th Marine Infantry Battalion would stake out its soldiers when they were punished for any misconduct. No wonder the Argentine delegation at the colloquium had negative thoughts about the film and did not want to see it again. It is now obvious why. They firmly believed that it was their Battalion being portrayed in this film!

Bernard's response to my work was unexpectedly contrary to the usually-held view that academic and military mindsets do not mix:

> It is well past midnight and I have spent fifteen hours finalising the text of the book, taking into consideration the totality of the remarkable double document

you have sent to me over the last few months. I have absorbed many of the suggestions and imperatives you gave me and feel that I have done so with respect both for your insights and for the style and integrity of my own approach to the representations of the 1982 war. Your work has been as remarkable as it has been meticulous and I trust that you realise that all of this and more will go into your own second book [..] I shall accompany you in this enterprise as loyally as you have followed my sometimes labyrinthine writing.

For tonight it remains for me to thank you – just as I shall do in my acknowledgement – for the supreme attention to detail and to the demands of scholarship that you, uniquely, have shown. The effects of our co-operation and friendship have been plural and staggering. Every day brings further evidence of that beautiful realisation.

Good night, comrade in post-conflict creativity and construction of a better life.[16]

Published four months later on 2 April 2007, the book's rear jacket carried my enthusiastic endorsement, 'I do believe that this is one of the most remarkable books I have ever read on the War. For this Falklands veteran it brings a new dimension to the conflict. It is a blockbuster and a remarkable piece of literature. Every Falklands-Malvinas War veteran should read it.'

Clarín, Argentina's largest daily newspaper, was more precise in its praise and described Bernard's work of five years as 'imposing' and 'the most complete and all-encompassing book study of the impact of the War in the South Atlantic on the Argentine, British and world-wide cultural production, including narrative prose, poetry, theatre, cinema, graphic humour and television'.[17] However it did not appeal to the library management in the Falkland Islands capital of Stanley. They refused to hold a copy because its title contained the taboo name 'Malvinas' and their local myopic view that the 'business *was* finished' stubbornly contradicted Bernard's realism.

Routines at home now returned to normalcy, even though I was working on a text revision for the paperback version of my first book. Concurrently planning continued with Eduardo Gerding on a detailed programme for a second joint visit (the first was made in December 2002) that Lars Weisæth and I would make to Argentina in March of next year. It represented an informal promotion of 'the Nottingham spirit' and Eduardo Gerding's forming of 'the Nottingham-Malvinas Group' for those who had participated in the colloquium. Our thirteen days there would also have an underlying theme of reconciliation.

In early December I was informed by Bernard that film and TV producer Brenda Goldblatt of Renegade Pictures, a London-based television company which had recently been formed by Alan Hayling, previously Head of Documentaries at the BBC, was 'in the process of researching a documentary on the Argentinian experience of the Falklands war'. She visited Bernard on 12 December and, during their meeting, I had a lengthy telephone conversation with her about my trip. Brenda's interest grew in recording the odyssey. But in the New Year, alas, she gave us the bad news:

I am afraid that we have been turned down all round by the broadcasters on the Falklands project. The BBC is making what appears to be an extraordinary film about the sinking of the *Coventry*, Channel 4 is making a film with Carol Thatcher and Five is not planning anything. We really did try, because we think that we would make an extraordinary documentary.[18]

At about the same time, Bernard invited Diego and me to the University of London's seminar 'Remembering the Malvinas in Argentine literature and film' to be held on 17 March. Attempting to camouflage irritation, I heard my voice many times during that day correcting some of the six presenters' distorted facts and errant assumptions about the war. The cause of my interventions was existential authority – after all, I had been there, those lecturing had not. The targetted were, no doubt, equally irritated by my oblique invitations to confront reality. One was the Argentine writer, translator and critic Carlos Gamerro whose thought-provoking presentation title was '¿'*Islas de mierda, llenas de pingüinos*' ("Bloody islands, full of penguins") (Cortázar)?: Imagining the Malvinas in fact and fiction'.[19] It stimulated me. And he wrote later:

> I took meticulous notes on every one of the interventions of Major Mike Seear. All of us had gone there to speak about or listen to *representations* of the war, yet he showed the marks, the scars, and the (literal or figurative) stumps (the meaning of war is just that: a stump of language. An amputated language). I was again surprised, too, that one night, a single night of advancing under artillery fire, not in hand-to-hand combat, just one night could change so much the life of one man and his perception of the world.
>
> I say that I was *again* surprised because I had already seen this in Argentine ex-combatants when I was interviewing them for my novel [...] Their words are the same as ours, but they do not mean the same: "cold", "bullets", "explosion", are words of a secret code. Perhaps because of that, paradoxically, it is not necessarily those who come back from the war who are its best narrators: they cannot, – they do not wish to – speak with those who *do not understand* ...[20]

In my case Gamerro was wrong. I wanted to correct what he was saying about 'my' war because of the very fact that he *did not understand*. But this cannot be done in a short conversation. Gamerro was too simplistic about that night on Tumbledown. He was unaware that we had been under artillery fire for the previous four days, and did not appreciate (but how could he?) that it was the prior ten weeks which had made a much more significant contribution to changing my life and perception of the world today. War is more than training for it, planning and fighting. It is also about coping with the fear of the unknown, (traumatic) stress, and the aftermath. Those who experience war *are* the best narrators of it – but Operation Corporate cannot be described in simple terms to those who were not members of the 1982 British Task Force. That is why I have written this sequel to my first book.

One week after the seminar I flew to Buenos Aires. Because of work commitments Lars would arrive twenty-four hours after me, however on 23 March I met up as planned with Cliff Caswell, Assistant Editor of the British Army's *Soldier* magazine, and his photographer Steve Dock. That evening we attended a dinner hosted by Jorge

Pérez Grandi in the magnificent Military Circle building. The twenty-six guests included retired Brigadier-General Mario Benjamín Menéndez, the former Governor of the Malvinas in 1982. I have never regretted more my inability to speak Spanish while seated between Robacio and Lieutenant-Colonel Mohamed Ali Seineldin, the former Commanding Officer of the 25th Infantry Regiment in the war. Also participating in *Operación Rosario*, as the Argentines say, to 'recover' the Islands on 2 April 1982, he led two unsuccessful military uprisings later: first in the northern Corrientes province in 1988 and, two years later, in Buenos Aires. Afterwards he was imprisoned for fourteen years. A devout Roman Catholic, he presented me with his book *Malvinas: un sentimiento* (*Malvinas: A Feeling*) written during his incarceration. The gift contained the inscription:

> To the dearest comrade and friend Mr Major Mike Seear, with a strong hug, I have the pleasure to deliver this humble testimony on the Malvinas War, where though we were fighting for different sides, we should recognise that we shared the last *Gentleman's War* of the twentieth century. I pray to God and Our Lady of Mercy for you and your family, for the souls of all the fallen, for the wounded and for those of us who are still alive.

I reciprocated with a copy of my book, and then took Seineldin's cue by delivering a short speech of thanks for the evening. It included an emphasis on the word 'commemoration' as opposed to 'celebration' in my regret that the Argentine Government had refused to send a representative to attend the forthcoming June London Falklands War Commemoration parade.

Heavily dependent on Eduardo Gerding's Spanish interpreter skills in Buenos Aires, Cliff and I carried out a series of interviews during the next two days with veterans of 'the other' side. First was the sympathetic Mario Benjamín Menéndez whom I had met several times before on my previous visits to Argentina. On return from the Islands he had been jailed for sixty days after publishing an 'unauthorised' 300-page post-war report. Put on trial in the Supreme Military Court in 1984 for mishandling the war, he was eventually acquitted. The retired Army officer continued to be open about his past Malvinas frustrations. Twenty-five years on they still weighed him down.

In good English he spoke with a quiet firmness, 'Before my arrival on the Islands I had been told by General Galtieri that I would be the Governor there with only 500 troops. I asked for the defence plans. But there were none. After my arrival and swearing-in, a total of four defence plans were written for the Islands. I wanted an infantry regiment and artillery battery to defend the San Carlos area (site of the initial British landings). Higher Command in Buenos Aires refused. I did not want troops on West Falkland. Again Higher Command refused. Troops were deployed there as a political symbol.'

Yet Menéndez was not the only member of his family to suffer from the defeat. 'My son also served on West Falkland at Port Howard with the 5th Infantry Regiment', he concluded. 'They were bombarded by the Royal Navy and attacked by your Harrier aircraft. He had a psychological reaction in 1989 and was diagnosed with

PTSD'.

Later that afternoon we interviewed another veteran I had met twice previously. Lieutenant-Colonel Tommy Fox, a retired artillery officer who had been directing 155mm artillery fire against the dug-in Gurkhas at Wether Ground, talked about his Malvinas War experiences as well as his later UN service in Rwanda. Tommy had aged since I had last seen him three and a half years before. Sadly at the end of the interview he fell ill, and Eduard Gerding had to accompany him to hospital. Maybe it was a reaction to resurrecting those war memories.

Next day we had conversations with Robacio and the urbane Rear-Admiral Carlos Büsser. The latter had been the Argentine Marine Corps senior officer, chief planner of the *Operación Rosario* Malvinas landing operation and Commander of the landing force, Task Force 40.1. 'I thought the Islands looked terrible on first seeing them,' he admitted to us. 'My men were ordered not to injure anyone, and fire overhead if fired upon. Our aim was to wake Governor Rex Hunt in his bed with breakfast and news that he had been captured.'

It did not work out quite like that. According to Büsser, twenty-nine Royal Marine Commandos were in the Governor's office of Government House, where Hunt had taken shelter under his desk. One of them promptly shoved the end of his rifle barrel into Büsser's stomach when the latter entered. However the Argentine officer had the presence of mind to raise his hands slowly while responding in the most English way possible, 'Good morning. I am Rear-Admiral Büsser. Pleased to meet you!'

His charm worked too, because he shook hands not only with his first aggressive host but all the other Marines in the room. After the British surrender Büsser returned to the mainland and monitored subsequent events. Later in life the Malvinas become an obsession and he wrote three books on the subject. To add to his library I gave him a copy of mine.[21]

The atmosphere of my two-hour afternoon meeting on 26 March with nine 5th Marine Infantry Battalion veterans, including six from that unit's 81mm Mortar Platoon, was captured splendidly in Cliff's subsequent *Soldier* editorial:

> It was an extraordinary sight. A former British infantry officer and more than a dozen Argentine Marine veterans talking about a war in which they fought on opposite sides – a war that claimed more than 1,000 lives.[22]
>
> It was a meeting of reconciliation that had started nervously in the lobby of a Buenos Aires hotel; a few words of introduction through an interpreter, some cautious gestures of welcome. But just a few hours later there were handshakes and hugs as the time came for them to part.
>
> These men were separated by just about every barrier imaginable – by country, hemisphere, language and politics. But what ultimately united them was their shared experience of battle. Their common military values of loyalty, respect, sacrifice and professionalism came to the fore. The reminiscences that came from both sides were remarkably similar – the sense of black humour, the comradeship and life on the wind-swept islands. And their words were almost indistinguishable – 'great courage on both sides', 'proud to fight as gentlemen', 'a war from another era' … and 'we did our job'.[23]

That evening I wrote in my diary:

> The platoon had between 400 to 600 mortar bombs at their location. It was confirmed that they had fired many bombs at the Gurkha advance along Tumbledown… here was the power of veteran reconciliation with each side telling its own story to the other. The fog of war lifted that afternoon after quarter of a century. My understanding of Spanish is nil – but I did not need to understand their language, even though Eduardo Gerding was translating for me. I saw their faces. I saw their eyes. They understood. I understood. This was also ex-combatant and veteran peer support in action. I told them that the Gurkhas trained hard for the battle against them. The Gurkhas did not underestimate their enemy. I told the Argentines that David Morgan had written they were 'a hard nut to crack' in the Battalion's Special Order of the Day issued on 10 May 1982: also that they were Marines and, by definition, must have been good troops. They appreciated that their former enemy recognised their qualities [...] Their faces lit up again. Mutual empathy and understanding of a common experience bound us together, even though we had been enemies. Civilians will never understand this phenomenon.

Cliff's stunning series of articles (for a magazine that has a monthly circulation of 90,000) on the Falklands-Malvinas War and work he did in Argentina won the British Association for Communicators in Business award for the Best Event Report on 23 May 2008. Immediately prior to this, Cliff referred to his short-listing for the award in e-mails sent to me and Eduardo. After his triumph, I received another e-mail:

> It was a true surprise to receive the [...] award [...] last Friday. The judges acknowledged the fact that the story had been told through the eyes of both sides and were extremely complimentary about the journalism. But this is not just my award. It belongs to you, Eduardo Gerding and Bernard McGuirk, as without you this story would not have been told in the magazine [...]
>
> That Sunday afternoon in the lobby of the Hotel Anexo del Centro Naval was one of the most extraordinary assignments I have ever covered, especially seeing the way the Argentine veterans reacted to you [...] The mission of reconciliation you undertook, and the images of you surrounded by your former adversaries, will live with me forever [...] The images Steve Dock took, I think, summed up the emotionally charged mood so well. I am really proud of the way it all worked out, particularly representing both sides of a story of twenty-five years ago that continues to resonate into our present. I feel as if I am a part of the story [...] And on the twenty-fifth anniversary of the war, I think it needed to be told as we remembered the men from the UK and Argentina who were in the Falklands-Malvinas War, those who died, and those who are still fighting the battle today (and) deserve to be looked after in the knowledge that they have our full understanding and respect [...] People should understand the long-term consequences of war on those we send to fight [...] and the collected memories in *Hors de Combat* make it one of the best and most-rounded books on the conflict ever produced. It is a story of men in battle, a tale of the consequences of conflict

in their later lives and an uplifting journey of veteran reconciliation in one volume. A unique collection of viewpoints from both sides, this is a compelling account of war in the South Atlantic [...] Many thanks again for all you did to get the magazine out to Argentina and for passion to see the story brought to the page.[24]

Lars and I had also planned a semi-formal platform to our mission in Argentina by giving four lectures on the war's aftermath and traumatic stress. Our first were given on 27 March to the JFK University staff in Buenos Aires assisted by Eduardo as our excellent interpreter. The media baton had been passed to BBC Radio 4's Jack Izzard who began recording a series of reports which would be compiled into an eventual broadcast to the UK on 2 April. He would interview me six times the following day with his work starting at our second lectures to a crowded lunch of 100 lady members of the Buenos Aires Womens' Forum.

I had decided not to talk about my war experiences as a Gurkha officer. After all, the Argentine capital in 1982 had been the subject of a popular song, *No bombardeen Buenos Aires* (Don't bombard Buenos Aires). Composed by Charly García, one of its thirty-six lines include the only telling reference to the British Task Force with 'The Gurkhas keep on advancing'.[25] Instead I chose the personally uncomfortable, but necessary, theme of describing what difficulties can befall a combatant post-war, exemplified by personal experiences. My ending comprised a recital of the first poem on the Falklands-Malvinas War composed by an author of renown. The haunting 'Juan López and John Ward' sonnet by the Argentine Jorge Luis Borges, was read in Spanish by Eduardo. The tactic generated applause. Afterwards two war veterans, Esteban Pino and Germán Estrada, provided their testimonies of the war, defeat and how Argentine society had rejected them afterwards. Their audience listened sympathetically. 'Pino', as he likes to be known, spoke good English and was training to be a management consultant. He had been a conscript in 2 Platoon, C Company, 3rd Infantry Regiment and deployed for a short period onto Mount William, the Gurkhas' objective, during the final forty-eight hours of the war. His and Germán's fellow veteran, Juan Casanegra, became so emotionally affected that he was unable to speak. But like me, the three had written a book about their experiences which had been published the year before.

Finally Robacio made a presentation on the war's fighting. It proved totally the wrong theme choice. At his conclusion there was an acrimonious reaction. The President remarked, 'No Islands are worth the life of a single Argentine conscript!' And some of the ladies called out vociferously in English, 'No more war! No more war!'

Next day Pino provided me with feedback (he misunderstood my Battalion appointment – I was only the lowly Operations and Training Officer):

> I don't know how to start. I just wanted to tell you that it was very important for us having met you yesterday afternoon. We felt very happy and proud. That meeting surpassed my expectations (that were huge). The leader of the Gurkhas! The 'propaganda' made us think that the Gurkhas were animals, bloodthirsty, cutting ears, etc. Could you imagine their leader?

Your presentation was not only professional, but warm. It showed a man very open-minded and with a big courage, being there with so many Argentine women! It was very sensitive to hear you telling us about your divorce, lack of job and [...] depression [...] Did you return to the Islands after the war? We didn't, but we'd love to have the possibility. We don't care a shit about having to get our passport signed by the 'Empire'. I can understand Robacio's position, but it definitely is not my case! I want to spend a night on Mount William again! [26]

We have exchanged e-mails sporadically ever since. Pino's dream was fulfilled on the Islands with his children in March 2009, and he remarked to me later, 'I took a walk from Tumbledown to Williams. Then I realised what could had happened to us [...] My visit to the Islands was something really important to me and my kids.' [27]

The same day as Pino sent his Women's Forum feedback, Lars and I travelled by bus north through the Pampas into Córdoba province en route to the country town of General Roca with its population of 3,000 and located 300 kilometres north-west of the capital. This was where María Isabel (or 'Marisa' as she is known to her friends) Clausen de Bruno lived. It was my fourth visit in five years. As usual her planning and hospitality were wonderful. Our audience consisted of nearly 150 town inhabitants and twenty-five Malvinas War veterans. As with my other three visits to Argentina Natalia Alemanno, an English school-teacher from General Roca, interpreted excellently with her concurrent Spanish version of our presentations. There was an enthusiastic response to these and my repeat reading of the Borges poem. National and local TV camera crews covered the event and I was grilled hard afterwards during the inevitable interviews. Afterwards the generous Marisa gave me a belated (and late-night) birthday party in her home which came complete, no less, with presents and a cake.

After only four hours sleep we were on the road again accompanied by Marisa and Natalia to repeat the presentations next day to 200 schoolchildren in the larger town of Oliva. My seventh and final TV interview in Argentina was given in Oliva's National Museum of the Malvinas War, ironically located in a disused railway station built by the British a century ago. Almost inevitably the female interviewer asked, 'Are the Gurkhas mercenaries?' My reply was an emphatic 'No!'

But more diplomacy was required in handling her sly parting shot, '¿*Las Malvinas son Argentinas?*' ('The Malvinas are Argentina's?') just before a lack of TV camera battery power prematurely ended my inquisition.

We returned to Buenos Aires so I could attend a low-key twenty-fifth year war anniversary commemoration ceremony on 2 April at the *Monumento a los caídos en Malvinas* (Monument for the fallen in the Malvinas) located near the city centre in Plaza San Martín and spend a pleasant final evening with Eduardo Villarraza's charming family in their apartment. Jack Izzard's six-minute news report on our activities was also broadcast late that evening in the UK. Bernard was listening – and afterwards I received his anxiety-relieving text message of 'Authentic, true, lasting', before flying back to Oslo. The same evening BBC News published Jack's article on their web-page entitled *Falklands enemies meet at last*:

This Monday marks the twenty-fifth anniversary of the Argentine invasion of the Falkland Islands. More than 900 British and Argentine soldiers died in the war that followed. Many of those who survived suffered emotional problems as a result. The BBC News website followed one of them as he went in search of his former enemies.

As he strolls through the busy streets of Buenos Aires, Mike Seear is every inch the retired British Army officer. The buttons on his blazer gleam. His regimental tie is knotted in a neat half-windsor. Twenty-five years ago, he fought for Queen and Country in the Falklands. Now he has come to Argentina on a journey of reconciliation.

'I really get a tremendous amount out of meeting the "other side" – people that I was once trying to fight and kill.'

Mike suffered post-traumatic stress after the war. He hopes that by sharing his experiences with other veterans, they will be able to heal their psychological wounds together. But these reunions can be very painful. He is close to tears as he meets Esteban, Juan and Germán; three Argentine soldiers who fought him at Tumbledown, one of the war's most infamous battles. They were artillery gunners who bombarded Mike's unit as it approached.

'Two of the shells they fired landed within ten metres of me. But they were both duds.

If they had exploded, there's no way I would be here, meeting them today. I've never met two people so closely connected to my life in the war. It's a really emotional moment.'

Many of the soldiers who survived the fighting were deeply emotionally scarred. Mike's three new friends were too ashamed to talk about their war experiences for twenty-four years. But today they can laugh and joke with their former enemy. He may have defeated them on the battlefield, but now he is helping them defeat their inner demons.

It is important to point out that Jack Izzard's article did not differentiate between post-traumatic stress disorder and post-traumatic stress reactions. It is the latter, like the majority of Falklands-Malvinas War veterans that I 'suffered' from, not the former. Back in Oslo I received the proof of my paperback in May and completed yet another text revision before travelling to London on 15 May for the Falklands War Exhibition opening at the Imperial War Museum by its Chairman, the RAF Falklands War veteran Air Chief Marshal Sir Peter Squire. There was an impressive Who's Who of British Falklands-Malvinas War personalities present. One of the first I met was former Task Force Land Commander, Major-General Sir Jeremy Moore. Of course he did not know me, but nonetheless was quick to recognise my dark green 7th Gurkha Rifles regimental tie with its striking diagonal silver *kukri* pattern. Sadly the seventy-nine year-old Royal Marine Commando officer died four months later. I had facilitated Diego's attendance which was significant for many, not least for former Falklands Governor Sir Rex Hunt whom Diego had tried to capture quarter of a century before. Accompanied by Bernard, Diego gave the event an underlying sense of reconciliation personified in the caring attitude of Baroness Margaret Thatcher. It was best remembered by her laconic 'Please don't do it again' request to my Argentine friend.

Adorned with a piratical black eye-patch, the Baroness's face covered half the front jacket of Hugh Bicheno's book *Razor's Edge: The Unofficial History of the Falklands War* which had been published as late as 2006 and had scored five optimal five-star ratings on Amazon.com.[28] This web-site's first review, written on 21 April 2006 and which fifty-nine out of sixty-three people had found helpful, carried the title 'The best account of the Falklands War'. I had read the book and was flattered that its vast twelve-page bibliography included my first book. Quite by chance, I met Hugh Bicheno that day. This military historian, who was also author of numerous other books, including the bestseller *Rebels and Redcoats*, which accompanied a four-part documentary BBC TV series presented by the distinguished military historian Professor Richard Holmes in 2003, had written at length about the Tumbledown battle in *Razor's Edge*. But Bicheno's remarks in this book about the Scots Guards officer 'chinless wonders' and their Battalion's shortcomings failed to reflect the fact that the 'chinless' ones were also the successors to their forbears at Hougoumount, the Alma, Ypres, Medenine and, not least, the Long Range Desert Group and G Squadron, Special Air Service. What 'chinless' predecessors did he think were responsible for their foundation? In my experience when push comes to shove on the battlefield, an infantry Battalion's regimental history and tradition can go a long way in making up other shortfalls.

Bicheno smiled faintly and shrugged in slight embarrassment on receiving my gentle reprimand for marking one of *Razor Edge*'s many maps with an incorrect route for the Gurkhas' advance along Tumbledown to Mount William on the war's final night. But it was just the tip of the iceberg as my later analysis of his writing on the Tumbledown battle would reveal.

My flying hours were racked up with four more events the following month. The first was attendance on 10 June at the Cunard Line-City of Southampton Falklands War Commemoration Lunch on board RMS *Queen Elizabeth 2*, the cruise liner that had transported us to the South Atlantic. I took an early flight out of Oslo that day to London, Heathrow and only just arrived at Southampton in time to meet up with the other four Gurkha Battalion representatives. During the preliminary reception in the Meridian Bar prior to a sumptuous lunch in the Queens Grill, I engaged an unknown lady in conversation. Inevitably this drifted back to those sixteen days on board *QE2* in May 1982 and a brief discussion about the public areas and whether beds had been set up there or not. It led me to tell her who I was and that three chapters in my first book had been dedicated to that surreal voyage.

'I've a few copies with me, if you're interested,' I added hesitantly.

'I'm Carol Marlow, the President of Cunard,' she replied, 'and would very much like one!'

A twenty-pound sterling note materialising from her handbag indicated that the deal was clinched much to the former Gurkha Operations and Training Officer *saheb*'s surprise. We were then led up onto the Boat Deck to view a single Harrier fighter fly-past. There I met Robert Lawrence, the Scots Guards subaltern severely wounded in the head by an Argentine sniper's bullet during the war's final day. My attempt to invite him to the Nottingham colloquium had failed, so I felt guilty on hearing that he would have liked to have participated. After lunch we were driven to the City and Holyrood Church which was burnt out in the Second World War. A touching Service of Remembrance was held in this memorial to Merchant Seamen.

Back at home I wrote a 'thank you' letter to Carol Marlow and, with pessimism, mentioned my availability to present the Gurkhas' involvement in the war within *QE2*'s enrichment lecture programme. It would be my last chance to complement a series of similar lectures I had given on board P&O's SS *Canberra* a decade before because the President of Cunard had told me that *QE2* had been sold to Dubai World and would be taken out of service in 2008.[29]

The following week I gave illustrated presentations entitled 'The Gurkhas in the Falklands War' at the National Army Museum in London on 14 June – Falklands Liberation Day – and a following day reprise at the Gurkha Museum in Winchester. Seventy-two hours later I went on parade for probably the last time in my life at the London Falklands War Commemoration parade that incorporated a drumhead service on Horseguards Parade, Whitehall. Lieutenant-General Sir John Kiszely who had fought on Tumbledown with the Scots Guards, commanded the Army section of the Parade. But the organisors failed to adhere to the regimental seniority precedence in the order of march. So there was irritation when the sixty Gurkha war veterans found themselves marching behind the Parachute Regiment, and even more by the absence of a Gurkha piper. To a degree it was offset by the poignant song *Somewhere Along the Road* sung by the thirty-year old daughter of Major Roger Nutbeem who had died in the Argentine air strike on RFA *Sir Galahad*. I thought of my daughters Victoria and Emily. They were only slightly younger than Kathryn Nutbeem in 1982.

One notable Gurkha veteran refused to parade. Lieutenant-Colonel Lester Holley's SAS background contained an aversion to such public spectacles. So he sat it out anonymously in the stands. Our marching had been preceded by a Gurkha Falkland veterans' reunion in a hired boat cruising up and down the River Thames during the morning and early afternoon, with colour provided by sari-clad Gurkha wives and food by a wonderful Gurkha *bhat* lunch. After the parade there were war stories and updates on post-war lives told over an evening glass of beer on the Tattershall Castle, a floating Thames pub known locally as 'the General Belgrano'. I have never felt more relaxed in years in that 'band of brothers' convivial company. Bernard was one of my guests. The 'cruise' had given him an opportunity to experience at close-quarters the smiling, polite, well-dressed, hospitable side of these fierce warriors' paradoxical nature – and whose battlefield reputation had caused such pain for Miguel in the Borda Psychiatric Hospital of Buenos Aires.

Another seventy-two hours later I received a copy of the following Gurkha 'thank-you' e-mail sent to Major Tim Morris, the 'cruise' organisor:

It has been exactly a month since we met for the 25th Anniversary of the Falklands Campaign event. Our gathering on 17 June was truly a great day. For me, the three hours spent on the cruise only felt like thirty minutes, it went by so quickly. On my drive back home, I tried to recall myself on the whole day itself and also the people I met. I wanted to talk to everyone present there, but due to lack of time missed out on one or two people. Thank you so much for everything you have put together to make it happen. I think I speak for all when I say, it has been a really successful and a memorable day. Given the numbers of 7GR veterans currently living in the UK and feedback from those who are in my network, it may be a good idea to make this gathering an annual event.

Salam to all *sahebs, gurujis* and brothers. It was great to see you all after such a long time. I left our programme full of joy and memories as well as with a worry. The 'worry' being that I can also be as fit and enthusiastic as our old *sahebs*, even after 25 years.

Jai Seventh (Long live the Seventh)

The author was Major (QGO) Dilkumar Rai, one of only six Gurkha Falklands War veterans still serving in the British Army. As a twenty year-old D Company Rifleman in the war, 'Dil' was the Platoon Commander's radio operator of 12 Platoon. The latter, now retired Major (QGO) Bhuwansing Limbu, had travelled from Bahrain for the London parade. Usually the Gurkha voice is absent from books written about them. However Dil's ability to express himself in written English prompted me to send him an e-mail and request his 'Nepalese Gurkha' account of his Falklands-Malvinas War experiences. In reply the Queen's Gurkha Officer who was Second-in-Command of the 2nd Infantry Training Battalion at Catterick, informed me he would retire to Nepal the following year and become an Area Welfare Officer. He agreed to provide a contribution which would complement the war experiences that had been sent to me by Jeremy McTeague. There was even more reason to include Dil in the manuscript because he was also the cousin of Rifleman Baliprasad Rai whose Falklands story had been part of my first book. Also retired from the Army, the latter had a civilian security job in Afghanistan.

Participating in a British war veterans' pilgrimage to the Falkland Islands nearly five months later was my highlight of 2007. The experience was profound and my digital camera went into overdrive during that seven-day visit: the images captured would be needed for an imminent presentation. Thirty-six hours after returning to Oslo, I was airborne again to participate in the University of Nottingham's follow-up colloquium 'Hors de Combat: Falklands-Malvinas Anniversary Retrospective' to mark the *Hors de Combat* book launch. I met my co-editor Diego again who, that summer, had moved to Geneva. Our presentation titles had been devised by Bernard. Mine was 'Look back (not) in anger', and Diego's 'Look what a year can bring'. It was a clairvoyant choice. My friend's performance was a relaxed strategic offering, whilst mine was driven by a combat veteran's raw emotions of having just returned from an exploration of his former battlefield.

Back in Oslo again I discovered that my pessimism of lecturing on board *QE2* was unfounded because my June proposal to Carol Marlow had been accepted. Three weeks later I re-joined *QE2* at Southampton as a guest lecturer on the 'Christmas Markets' North Sea cruise from 6-14 December to Hamburg, Oslo, Rotterdam, and Zeebrugge. I had prepared five lectures on 'The Gurkhas in the Falklands War' which included one about the recent Pilgrimage. My task escalated as a Force 10 storm during the initial leg prevented us from calling at the Port of Hamburg and I volunteered to create an extra Falklands War 'enrichment' lecture to assist in alleviating stressed Cruise Director David Pepper's entertainment crisis and his need to compile a subsequent new programme to keep *QE2*'s 'guests' fully occupied during their enforced extra day at sea. The weather, which had me bouncing around in my bed at night as if at the dodgems, and the programme change provided flashbacks to those continual daily changes in plan as we sailed southwards in 1982 from Ascension Island to South Georgia, only to endure similar horrendous weather for three days (minus *QE2*'s stabilisers) on board the small Hull-Rotterdam North Sea ferry MV *Norland* en route to the Falklands and San Carlos Water. My new offering focused on reconciliation and my four visits to Argentina in the past five years to meet and talk with veterans of 'the other' side.

Lecture titles of 'Joining the Gurkhas and preparing for war', 'The voyage south', 'In Goose Green and preparing for battle', 'The Battle of Tumbledown and Mount William', 'The aftermath and seeking "the other"' and 'The Pilgrimage and conclusion' ensured that the Quarter Deck's Theatre was well visited. Gurkha publicity was augmented by the video-taped lectures being shown continuously afterwards on the ship's internal TV for twelve hours. On two days I lectured twice daily: and then both were shown simultaneously on two of the seventeen TV channels available. These PowerPoint presentations that included DVD-video clips of the war and its aftermath, led to on-board sales of forty-seven copies of my first book as well as some copies of *Hors de Combat* and Bernard's book. Despite disembarking at Oslo to return home and collect another pack of books, even this re-supply proved insufficient. But it did demonstrate a high British regard for the Gurkha soldier. Nobody on board had been presented before with the true details of the Gurkhas' involvement in the Falklands-Malvinas War. It merely confirmed that writing this sequel was justified.

There was a spill-over of activity into 2008. On the twenty-sixth anniversary of the 2 April 1982 Argentine landings on the Islands, I made back-to-back presentations on the war to officer cadets at the Swedish National Defence College in Stockholm (1 April) and Danish Military Academy in Copenhagen (2 April), as well as 'opposing' cadets in their war-gaming and presentations on various aspects of the war. Since Diego wrote in his *Hors de Combat* account that the Argentine landing 'happened, contrary to several books on the war, with the use of rubber boats and shortly before midnight on 1 April', it was appropriate that my two tasks straddled both days. Instructing to a younger generation of officers about a veteran's experiences gained, mistakes made and lessons learnt was a hugely satisfying affair. This feeling was enhanced by two Danish Army officers who had been my guests at the international colloquium and their assertion that they had witnessed an historical event. The power of its *shih* gave them motivation to visit the Islands four months later.

I attended the final event of my extended twenty-fifth anniversary year on 20 April. This was the inaugural Task Force Hospital Ship HMHS *Uganda* Reunion held at Southampton. Since *Uganda* was a P&O ship which had been wrecked off Taiwan by a typhoon in the South China Sea in 1986, the main event took place on board the P&O cruise liner SS *Aurora*. However it almost seemed as if *Uganda* was present in spirit, moored nearby at the quayside where *QE2* was berthed after having just arrived back from her final world cruise.

There were 175 people present, including former Royal Navy surgeons, anaesthetists, nurses, casualties, Marine band stretcher-bearers, crew and next of kin. My qualification to participate was provided by this ship's conversion into a troop transport post-war to embark the 7th Gurkha Rifles for Southampton. Two other Gurkha Falklands veterans were present: the jovial Major Tim Morris who had been the Assault Pioneer Platoon Commander, and a disillusioned Major Paddy Redding, the Battalion Intelligence Officer. 'I get emotional when talking about the war', the latter confessed.

Former Queen Alexandra Royal Naval Nursing Service Senior Nursing Sister Nicci Pugh, who had served as an Operating Theatre Trauma Sister on board *Uganda* during the war, was the reunion co-organisor with Derek Houghton, *Uganda*'s P&O Accommodation Officer. They had spent weeks planning the event. Its detail was stunning and post-event accolade of 'a triumph' well-deserved. There was even a letter from Baroness Margaret Thatcher:

> Twenty six years ago the Hospital Ship *Uganda* departed Gibraltar for the uncertainties of the South Atlantic. Only a few days before the ship had been host to hundreds of schoolchildren cruising in the Mediterranean. She was now sailing to war. For the doctors, nurses and support staff on board, the following months would be the ultimate test of their professionalism and dedication. In the most difficult of conditions the ship became a refuge for the men who had given their all and now lay badly injured, in desperate need of life-saving treatment. Sadly, some did not make it through but what is remarkable given the circumstances is that so many patients did. As you gather to mark these months, now over a quarter of a century past, the vivid memories of the skills, the courage and the comradeship of staff and patients alike will be uppermost in your minds. For some of you, the bonds forged on *Uganda* will have survived after your return. But for all of you, those moments will remain a life-long testament to all that was achieved. Last year, at numerous events across the country, we saw that the people of Britain have not forgotten all that you did for us in that conflict. Today, again, we honour and salute you.

The climax came at the end of the gourmet lunch with the presentation of her letter in Braille to Chief Petty Officer Flight Terry Bullingham who had been blinded in an Argentine Dagger aircraft 30mm cannon attack on HMS *Antrim* during the British landings at San Carlos Water on 21 May 1982. His short speech of thanks, which included a reference to his successful 'second life' as a Braille instructor, was humbling to hear.

From the Nottingham colloquium and throughout the succeeding eighteen-month period to the *Uganda* reunion, I had participated in twenty-five war anniversary events, including six on the Pilgrimage. There were also postscripts. I returned to the University on the colloquium's second anniversary almost to the day (20 November) to share with thirty-five students and staff some of the fruits harvested from research for this book in a three-hour presentation 'What was the 1982 Falklands-Malvinas War impact on the post-conflict culture of the extraordinary little capital of Stanley?' Twenty-seven months on from the colloquium, a special e-mail was received from Bernard via María Fra Amador:

The last few months have been reasonable but the highlight was very simple. In the Government Assessment of University Departments which is announced every seven years, the Nottingham Department of Spanish Portuguese and Latin American Studies was ranked first in the United Kingdom. Achievements such as this could not be possible without the international contribution of colleagues such as yourself, Eduardo, Diego and Mike and, of course, the Nottingham-Malvinas Group, so thank you again for your input and friendship. I have no hesitation in saying that you might share this news with the group.[30]

This was most satisfying for Bernard and the University. But looking back on that twenty-fifth anniversary year of the war, it had been the Pilgrimage to the Islands and subsequent dialogue with other pilgrims who had fought there which gave me the opportunity to make a revealing retrospective examination of the Scots Guards attack on Tumbledown.

Notes

1. *The Art of War*, Chapter 5 – Shih.
2. In the New Year of 2012 this became the International Consortium for the Study of Post-Conflict Cultures, with the author accepting a nomination to become a member of its new International Advisory Board and designated Convenor of the research cluster for UK-Argentine Post-Conflict Relations.
3. *Falklands-Malvinas: An Unfinished Business.* p. 238.
4. *Ibid.*, p. 243.
5. *The Official History of the Falklands Campaign. Vol. II – War and Diplomacy*, p. 208.
6. John Nott was also a former British Army 2nd King Edward VII's Own Gurkha Rifles (The Sirmoor Rifles) officer.
7. Source of many myths, this is the famed Gurkha 'slashing' knife which is a formal part of the Gurkha soldier's equipment taken into battle.
8. *Falklands-Malvinas: An Unfinished Business.* pp. 247 and 249.
9. In 2010 Eduardo Gerding was appointed *Jefe de la División Prestaciones Médicas de la Subgerencia de Veteranos de Guerra* (Chief of the Medical Division of the War Veterans Bureau).
10. *The Gurkhas: The Forgotten Veterans*, rear jacket.
11. Also known as *Proceso de Reorganización Nacional* (Process of National Reorganisation). This was an infamous campaign waged by Argentina's military dictatorship against suspected left-wing opponents. It is estimated that about 30,000 citizens were killed, many of them became the *desaparecidos* (disappeared) of Argentina – seized by the authorities and never heard of again.
12. E-mail dated 14 September 2006.
13. *Ibid.* dated 23 June and 25 September 2006.
14. *Ibid.* dated 11 and 12 December 2011.
15. *The Guards Magazine: Journal of the Household Division*, Spring 2007, p. 5.
16. E-mail dated 26 November 2006.
17. *Clarín* dated 31 March 2007.

18. E-mail dated 15 January 2007.
19. Julio Cortázar was a famous Argentine writer of the 1960s and 1970s.
20. *Hors de Combat: The Falklands-Malvinas Conflict in Retrospect*, p. 177. (Published in June 2009, this was a revised and enlarged edition of the original *Hors de Combat: The Falklands-Malvinas Conflict Twenty Five Years On* published in 2007.)
21. In November 2009 the author was shocked by Eduardo Gerding's news that the eighty-one year-old Rear-Admiral had been one of three retired naval officers arrested for alleged human rights abuses committed at Argentina's main naval base of Puerto Belgrano during *La Guerra Sucia* (Dirty War) of 1976-83. Büsser commanded an 'anti-subversive' unit operating from this base in 1977. However he was later released from arrest.
22. The correct figure is 904 killed.
23. *Soldier, Magazine of the British Army*, June 2007, Vol. 63/06.
24. Compiled from three e-mails dated 27 and 28 April, and 26 May 2008.
25. *Falklands-Malvinas: An Unfinished Business*, p. 162.
26. E-mail dated 29 March 2007
27. *Ibid.* dated 26 April 2010.
28. By the end of 2011 another six five-star ratings had been awarded plus four four-star, one three-star and three one-star ratings.
29. The *QE2* was taken out of service in November 2008 after having been bought by Dubai World for GBP 65 million. It was intended that the liner would become a floating hotel in Dubai, but the global financial crisis and recession has postponed this plan. The *Southern Daily Echo* edition of 10 November 2011 reported that, after 1,001 days, *QE2* was still moored at Port Rashid, Dubai with 'the planned renovation plans a pipedream'.
30. E-mail dated 23 February 2009.

1.   'Breaking the ice' with the Argentine delegation prior to the University of Nottingham international colloquium, 15 November 2006.

2.   Reconciliation between the two former Commanding Officers, (left) retired *Contraalmirante* Carlos Hugo Robacio and retired Major-General Mike Scott at the University of Nottingham international colloquium, 18 November 2006.

3.   Buenos Aires, 25 March 2007 – the author with retired *Contraalmirante* Carlos Büsser, former Commander of the Argentine amphibious Task Force 40.1 which 'recovered' the Islands on 2 April 1982.

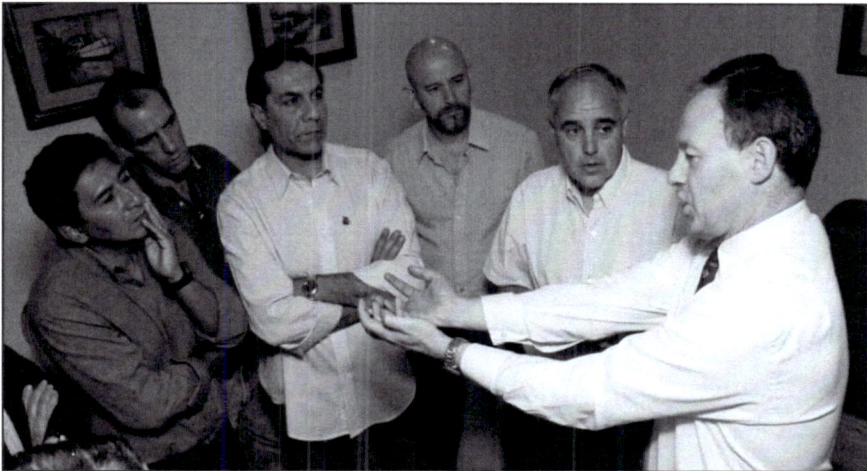

4.   '(It) was one of the most extraordinary assignments I have ever covered, especially seeing the way the Argentine veterans reacted to you [...] The mission of reconciliation you undertook, and the images of you surrounded by your former adversaries, will live with me forever [...]' (Photo by courtesy of *Soldier: Magazine of the British Army*.)

5.   The initial intensity of war veteran reconciliation, (l. to. r). Eduardo Gerding (interpreter and Malvinas War Veterans' Medical Co-ordinator), the author, Cliff Caswell (Assistant Editor, *Soldier* magazine), and Elvio Angel Cuñe (former BIM5 81mm Platoon Commander), Buenos Aires, 26 March 2007. (Photo by courtesy of *Soldier: Magazine of the British Army*.)

6.   The 'ice is broken' as the author (left) indicates on a Tumbledown map to the 81mm Mortar Platoon veterans, Buenos Aires, 26 March 2007. (Photo by courtesy of *Soldier: Magazine of the British Army*.)

7.   The reconciliation continues into its second hour. Opposite the author (r. to l.) Eduardo Villarraza and Carlos Hugo Robacio. On the author's left is Cliff Caswell and Luis Lucero (former N Company 3 Platoon Commander on Tumbledown), Buenos Aires, 26 March 2007. (Photo by courtesy of *Soldier: Magazine of the British Army*.)

8.   War veterans at the Buenos Aires Women's Forum event, (l. to r.) Esteban Pino, the author, Juan Casanegra and Germán Estrada, 28 March 2007.

9.　　The language barrier between Argentine veterans of the Battle of Darwin and Goose Green and the author being overcome by virtue of the interpreter skills of Natalia Alemanno, General Roca, 29 March 2007.

10.　　Argentine hospitality for a Gurkha Falklands-Malvinas War veteran – a belated birthday party for the author in the General Roca home of Marisa Clausen de Bruno at 1 a.m. in the morning on 30 March 2007.

11.   Crowds in front of the *Monumento a los caídos en Malvinas* (Monument for the fallen in the Malvinas) at the Plaza San Martín, Buenos Aires, 2 April 2007.

12.   The author with Bernard and Elizabeth McGuirk on board the hired Gurkha boat prior to the twenty-fifth anniversary London Falklands War Commemoration parade on Horseguards Parade, Whitehall, 17 June 2007.

13.   1st/7th Gurkha Rifles veterans prior to the London twenty-fifth anniversary Falklands War Commemoration parade, 17 June 2007. (Second from right) retired Brigadier David Morgan (the Battalion's former Commandant).

14.   Diego García Quiroga (left) and the author with a copy of *Hors de Combat* (first edition), Oslo, August 2007.

PHASE II
THE PILGRIMAGE …
AND THE SCOTS GUARDS' ATTACK ON TUMBLEDOWN

*Earth is high and low, broad and narrow, far and
near, steep and level, death and life.*
                                        – Sun Tzu [1]

I applied to become a pilgrim on 27 November 2006 for the Falklands 25 Pilgrimage
being planned by the South Atlantic Medal Association 82 (SAMA82) and Ex-Services
Mental Welfare Society (Combat Stress). The inaugural Pilgrimage for Falklands
veterans had occurred five years previously, but I had decided back in 2002 that it was
too soon for me to return to the Islands. This second opportunity from 4-14
November 2007 seemed more appropriate in terms of the twenty-fifth anniversary of
the war. But it had one drawback. The SAMA82 Internet website indicated places for
only 200 veterans. These were all the infrastructure could handle in the extraordinary
little capital of Stanley where, excluding persons present in the Falklands connected
with the military garrison, eighty-five per cent of the Islands' 2,478 population lived.
Pilgrims would be accommodated in private homes and most of the local transport
that week would be dedicated to them, with most hosts and drivers taking a week off
their annual holiday from work. However although there were indications that
veterans who had never returned to the Islands post-war would be a priority category
for the Pilgrimage, it was the figure of 200 and that pilgrims' names, with the
exception of sixty-six combat stress patients, would be drawn out of a hat that caused
me anxiety.

This was exacerbated in June next year after learning that I had been placed on the
reserve list: number ten out of forty candidates. So Plan B was to secure information
of a Royal British Legion Falklands Battlefield tour group which would arrive at the
tail-end of the Pilgrimage via Santiago, Chile and stay for ten days. This extra travel
was not the only disadvantage because, compared to the free travel and
accommodation in the Falklands 25 Pilgrimage, the Legion trip would cost nearly
£3,000 pounds sterling. However the gloom lifted somewhat when David Connett,
the publisher of the paperback version of my first book and himself a Falklands
veteran, told me that prior to the first Pilgrimage many of those selected had decided
not to travel at the last moment. In August I also noted on the SAMA82 website that
the plot had changed dramatically again – but for the better. Another fifty beds had
been found at the British Forces' Hill Side Camp in Stanley, thus enabling those on
the reserve list to qualify as pilgrims after all. Through Emily Herbert who had
attended my National Army Museum presentation on 14 June and then travelled two
months later to the Falklands to take photographs of the battlefields for her MA
degree in photography, I made contact with Peter King, the Falkland Islands
Government Secretary in Stanley. He gave me some background information and I
also circumvented the official Pilgrimage housing selection arrangements because
Peter's PA, Lynn Brownlee, was able to arrange this for me in Stanley with her
parents, Vera and Frank Leyland. The latter was a former Warrant Officer in the
Royal Artillery and – the big bonus – a Falklands battlefield tour guide.

Three weeks before my departure an e-mail arrived from Rosemarie King in Stanley. Her remarks on how she coped in the capital's siege by having faith in the powerful Gurkha 'representation of war' image, plus a copy of her war diary, were reminders of a situation I have never before or since experienced:

It is really interesting to read your e-mails to my hubby, Pete. As there was a shortage of material for the local Museum, I typed up my Diary to be included in their 25th Anniversary exhibits. Like a lot of local folk, the reputation of the Gurkhas actually got me through the seventy-four days of war. You will see that I mentioned the Gurkhas several times in my diary (the hat I knitted (and mentioned) is also in the museum!)

You may not find the diary very interesting because it is written (I was only twenty-five at the time) assuming the reader knows Stanley really well, but I hope you get an essence of the high esteem the Gurkha regiment is held, with the Gurkha reputation alone invaluable. We so look forward to meeting with you in November.

She was too modest. Her diary was riveting. The hat, knitted in red, white and blue wool, was intended for the first British soldier she saw in Stanley post-war. It was finished as we were making our final battle preparations near the western end of Goat Ridge on the war's last evening. Post-Pilgrimage Rosemarie provided me with another e-mail anecdote:

During the seventy-four days of the siege, all from our (Falklands Island Company) offices (probably eight or ten of us in total) were issued with a card to go past the Argentine guards to enter our respective offices (there were probably one or two hundred Argentines in the immediate area). Anyway, there was an Argentine Sergeant called Ricardo who called on us most days to check that we were OK. Despite one break-in, the offices were never entered into and not a thing was lost. They were therefore nice and clean for the British troops to take up floor space and office space immediately after the surrender. Ricardo spoke fluent English, was married to an English lady and had an English daughter. He met his wife whilst he was posted to Portsmouth training alongside the Royal Navy on the *Sheffield,* and used to say everyday 'just sit it out' as he had no doubt about the outcome of the situation. Imagine his distress when HMS *Sheffield* was the first ship to be hit by an Exocet missile!

They were bleak days. We could easily have had one of the horrors amongst the Argentine forces visit each day so we were pretty blessed. Anyway Ricardo seemed to disappear in the final week of the war and so we never knew if he lived or died. Then I think it was in 2002 (20th Anniversary) that an e-mail appeared in the Falkland Islands Tourism and Development portal from Ricardo looking for myself, another girl from the office and an acting policeman of the time. This was passed on to me and there was this apology for the behaviour of his country. He still sends an e-card on every special day during the year. I acknowledged the first e-mail and thanked him, but must admit not to keeping in closer touch because I prefer to leave Argentina where it is and move on. But it proves that not all

Argentines caught up in a war feel it was glory days. Most had one day of glory, realised the dire situation they were in, and seventy-three days of sheer misery.

So far my proactivity had gained some advantages. But I possessed a potential disadvantage. My four unconventional Argentine expeditions to seek and meet veterans of 'the other' side was an undertaking no other aspiring pilgrim would have considered, let alone accomplished. Nicci Pugh, who for the past five years had been heavily involved in her dedicated and complex work of organising and accompanying small groups of SAMA82 British war veterans on innumerable return trips back to the Islands, had already issued a warning to me at the end of June. It concerned one significant facet of the Islands' post-conflict culture: the still strongly negative attitude towards Argentines. This was particularly the case amongst Islanders who have remained in the Falklands since 1982. However they are steadily diminishing in number. For example only 235 people or 10.9% of the population in Stanley were 'siege veterans' and, nearly a year after the Pilgrimage, Rosemarie King informed me this figure had fallen to below ten per cent because more had died and at least another 200 people had taken up residence in the capital.

What the Islanders particularly disliked was any publicity linked into the annual big 'Commemorative Dates' of June and November. There had been a small, but unnecessary incident connected with the 14 June 2007 Falklands Liberation Day event which had been reported in a recent issue of the local *Penguin News* newspaper. Many were at the military base of Mount Pleasant Airport waiting for HRH Prince Edward and other VIPs to disembark from the aircraft that had arrived from the UK. However an Argentine was the first to leave together with Simon Weston, the badly-burnt Welsh Guardsmen from the 1982 *Sir Galahad* disaster whose medical treatment and recovery afterwards was the subject of a widely-watched BBC TV documentary. With coverage provided also by major British media such as ITV, this insensitive move was received badly and letters of disgust had been published in the *Penguin News* afterwards.

Nicci, who would also be visiting the Islands for the third time in twelve months towards the end of the Pilgrimage, had been caught in similar unthinking but well-planned manoeuvres with the Argentine press around Stanley and especially at, or following, the Remembrance Day Services which are extremely important events. Local political difficulties remained with the constant Argentine 'unfinished business' of the sovereignty issue. There were other irritations connected to the weekly Lan-Chile Airbus flight from 'the mainland' Chilean capital of Santiago, air space, logistics with cruise ships and other complex factors that caused almost daily disenchantment and disruption. A *Penguin News* Special Edition published on 14 June contained an editorial by Managing Editor Jenny Cockwell. It provided an insight into this tightly-knit patriarchal society of which, according to the 2006 Falklands Census Report,[2] eighty per cent of married men were identified as head of their household:

The day is upon us. A quarter of a century has passed since British sovereignty was secured once again over the Falkland Islands. So much has happened in that time and the Islands are now a very different place to that of two and a half decades ago, but the spirit of Islanders remains unchanged. For those who were here in 1982, the next few days will be full of memories – of both pain and jubilation – and I hope that this will prove not a time of troubles but of therapy. Over the past two weeks, and the individual anniversaries they have brought, some have finally been able to face and even talk about their war experiences and, with it, find a sense of closure. Others still have healing to do.

I was not here in 1982. I was a five year-old living in New Zealand, blissfully blind to my father's fears for his family in the Islands. However, today I call the Falklands my home and I feel deep gratitude – and yes, guilt, for the sacrifice that was made twenty-five years ago. That sacrifice means I am able to live here with my Islander husband and enjoy a happy life in a special part of the world.

The twenty-fifth mark is momentous and provides a perfect opportunity to look back at the extraordinary transformation that has taken place with pride and appreciation; it is also a time to look forward and decide how the Falklands of the future should look and feel. And, importantly, it's also a time to raise a glass in celebration. Unfortunately the shadow that existed in 1982 still remains and in recent years has become more foreboding. We have to pray the experience of war will never be repeated in these Islands: sadly though, with Argentina still intent on gaining sovereignty, there are no guarantees.

I sent a joyful e-mail to Eduardo Gerding informing him of my Pilgrimage selection. He sent a copy to a Nottingham colloquium participant, retired Royal Navy Commodore Toby Elliot who was now the Chief Executive Officer of Combat Stress and UK co-organisor of the Pilgrimage. This ex-submariner hoisted the danger signal. So retired Colonel Mike Bowles, Chairman of the UK SAMA82 Falklands 25 Pilgrimage Organising Committee, then e-mailed me on 23 August:

I know that you have seen that reserves are being called forward. In an ideal world you would have been notified personally but we are not in an ideal world on this occasion for which I apologise.

Toby Elliott has passed me a copy of an e-mail to your Argentine friends that he saw. In no way do I want to 'teach Granny to suck eggs', but may I sound a note of caution to you please? I don't think you have been back to the Islands since the conflict and therefore may not be acquainted well with any Islanders. There is an extremely hardline anti-Argentine feeling among the Islanders. They have absolutely no feeling of reconciliation amongst them. They grudgingly allow Argentine families in to visit war graves. You may well be aware of this fact and I do not intend to labour the point further here. I just wanted to alert you to my perception of the situation and to make my point about caution. It would be good to talk to you sometime about this. I do not think it would be wise to talk to Islanders at all about your collaborative ventures or the fact that you have made a number of visits there in recent years. I also think you should be similarly careful with other veterans, many of whom may still harbour feelings that would not be the same as yours and mine. In my last job in the Army I was Defence Attaché in Brazil and was good friends with a couple of Argentine Attachés. However, there will be others in the party who have not had the benefit of such social contact.

I will not rabbit on here – please come back to me with your thoughts/ reactions, etc. In the meantime I am very pleased for you that your name has finally come up. I look forward to meeting you in due course.

Coupled with Nicci's advice, forewarned was forearmed. So I replied immediately:

I am very much aware of the antagonism that the Islanders have towards Argentina. It is all indeed 'an unfinished business' as Professor Bernard McGuirk's recent book sub-title succinctly states (see SAMA82 Summer Magazine edition). I also realise that hardline feelings will also exist amongst other veterans who will be travelling south on the Pilgrimage with me. It is therefore not my intention to advertise the fact that I have travelled to Argentina four times in the past five years, met on numerous occasions Brigadier-General Menéndez or many other Argentine officers who were involved in the invasion and campaign, or have been the co-editor together with Commander (Retd.) Diego García Quiroga (the first veteran of either side to be casevaced out of the Islands on 2 April 1982) of the book *Hors de Combat: The Falklands-Malvinas Conflict Twenty-Five Years On.*

I have simply been fascinated by the Argentine state of mind over the 'Malvinas' and was determined to include an Argentine perspective in my first book published in 2003. It therefore required a piece of 'self-education' to broaden my horizons away from those few days of coming under Argentine artillery fire at Wether Ground and Tumbledown. This Argentine dimension will be further enhanced in my next book to be published in 2010, but in no way diminishes the British dimension or view. Indeed I have kept all my 1982 principles totally intact, despite making good friends in the past few years with many Argentines – both veterans and civilian non-combatants. My personal 'mission' during the Pilgrimage will be to participate fully in all events, be social and pay my respects to those who did not come back from the war at the appropriate times. I will also be observing carefully, taking notes for my next book and, not least, re-visit San Carlos, Goose Green, Wether Ground and, hopefully, walk the Gurkha Battalion Tac HQ route that we took on 14 June 1982 from the southern Sister of Two Sisters onto Tumbledown via Goat Ridge and, from there, onto Mount William. I plan to take a lot of pictures.

It will be wonderful to be able to return to the Islands after a quarter of a century (and the last time in my life). So thank you for being so patient with one Gurkha Falklands veteran. I am really looking forward to this momentous, and once in a lifetime, trip.

But like many other pilgrims, as 4 November drew closer, I was becoming anxious for another reason: a return to the site of past trauma. The questions were many. How would I cope with confronting the reality of this trauma after twenty-five years? What would the Falklands be like now? How would my fellow pilgrims think and behave? Will I find something meaningful in that harsh, yet strangely beautiful, environment that had been part of such a personal life-event? How would I react on return to the

Tumbledown-Mount William battlefield? And how would the Pilgrimage experience affect me and my future outlook on life?

It was appropriate to 'fly the flag' and travel from Oslo to London on board a British Airways flight. I made my way to the Union Jack Club adjacent to London's Waterloo Station where the pilgrims would congregate and stay overnight before travelling by coach to Gatwick Airport and specially chartered Monarch Airlines aircraft that would fly us to the Falklands. It was all made possible by a generous grant of £404,000 from the National Lottery in lieu of the British Government shirking its financial responsibility for such an important venture. I checked in with John Philips, the UK Secretary of the event. As a Warrant Officer bomb-disposal expert he had lost an arm on board HMS *Antelope* in attempting to defuse an Argentine bomb that had exploded, so it was particularly poignant to receive from him a special Pilgrimage 'Falklands 25' bag.

After gaining access to my simple but clean bedroom, I opened the bag. It contained many items, but also a paradox. Amongst the many brochures there was a ten-minute DVD-Video *The Modern Falklands* and, on its cover, a well-formulated sentence 'Falkland Islanders welcome the support of citizens and governments all over the world who share their ideals of self determination and self sufficiency, to help ensure that their future is secure'. The sentence was also on the back cover of another informative brochure on the Islands published by the Falkland Islands Government Office in London. I played the DVD in my lap-top computer. It gave a surprisingly rosy picture of the affluence of this, 'the United Kingdom's most dynamic Overseas Territory', as a direct result of the 1982 British victory. The 1986 implementation of a 150-mile economic exclusion zone around this archipelago of two large and 778 smaller islands that equate to an area just more than half the size of Wales, and subsequent international sale of fishing licenses for squid within this zone had revitalised the local economy. Investment income, agriculture, tourism and services were also principle contributors to the economy and employment, whilst potential off-shore oil reserves in the North Falkland Basin might also one day provide an additional important source of income. The self-governing Falklands, except in the areas of foreign policy and defence, were economically self-sufficient other than defence expenditure estimated at less than half of one per cent of Britain's annual defence budget.[3]

Other brochures, a *Penguin News* Special Liberation Edition and Falkland Islands Newsletter published by the Falkland Islands Association told similar stories of continuing growth and optimism. Yet there was a contrasting sombre brochure from Combat Stress. Its profound insight of the potential challenges facing many pilgrims, coupled with warnings and valuable advice, make the contents worthy of reproducing in their entirety:

> We expect that some of you will be a bit apprehensive about going back to the Falklands, but the evidence from other people who go on pilgrimages to their old battlefield is that there are real benefits to their psychological health. Many of you won't have seen or experienced the level of appreciation the Falkland Islanders have towards you and what you did to help them in 1982. They really *are* very

grateful for your sacrifices and the sacrifices of all your family and friends over the years, and of those Servicemen who did not return from the War.

Whilst you are in the Falkland Islands some of you may well experience anxiety, apprehension, sadness and grief, others will have intrusive memories, nightmares and flashbacks. Hopefully most of you will experience none of these. If you do have symptoms don't worry, it's proof that you are confronting what happened to you and that your mind is processing your different war experiences. The symptoms will improve during the Pilgrimage and may well improve your life when you get home. It is important however to look after yourself while you are there and afterwards, here are some handy tips:

Don't isolate yourself. Talk to others on the Pilgrimage, seek out old friends, talk to the Islanders, talk to Combat Stress staff. Do try to find places when you can be quiet and alone and use any relaxation techniques that you have been taught. Don't brood. If you feel angry find someone to talk to, other pilgrims or Combat Stress Staff might well be able to help. It is important to understand your anger and that you deal with it. Don't feel you have to visit the battlefields or go to the Remembrance Day Sunday Parade or the Cemeteries. You don't have to go if you don't want to and you could always ask another veteran or person to pay your respects for you. Everyone will find these events emotionally challenging. Do feel OK if you become emotional, cry or even breakdown, everybody will have similar feelings and everybody will support each other. Do find the Combat Stress staff to help you if you feel you need help when you return from the battlefields or memorial trips.

Many of you will be accommodated with the Falkland Islanders in their homes. You may find this difficult at times especially if you have problems sleeping at nights. You may be embarrassed if you wake up with a start and make a noise or sweat heavily (or even wet the bed). Our Falkland Islander hosts will understand these problems, please tell them if you need a change of bedclothes or if you want to be able to go outside in the night to smoke a cigarette. Don't forget that good communications is the best way to deal with most problems and will prevent embarrassment.

Alcohol will be quite freely available, particularly because the Falklands Islanders will want to celebrate your achievements. Try not to drink too much. Remember that some of you have had serious problems with alcohol in the past – and some in the not too distant past. We all know that while alcohol may help with problems at first, in the longer term it just makes nightmares and flashbacks more frequent and vivid, you more irritable and our hosts less appreciative of all that you did. (Also remember that cannabis has similar effects). It is important that you take your medications correctly. If you have any problems with the medication you take for psychological reasons please seek out a member of the Combat Stress staff. If you have problems with other medications that you take for physical reason, ask the Combat Stress staff to arrange for you to see a Falkland Island GP.

We hope your experience of the pilgrimage will be a positive one. Please speak to the Combat Stress staff if you are experiencing difficulties. This is your Pilgrimage. We are here to support you. Good Luck. Combat Stress Staff.

Not a Combat Stress patient, I should have nonetheless paid closer attention to these pearls of wisdom. But my eyes inevitably drifted to the packed Pilgrimage programme prior to preparing for the official cocktail reception that evening. Much detailed planning had gone into our forthcoming seven days on the Falklands. Receptions, one day trips around the Islands, overnight visits to remote areas, battlefield tours, wildlife tours, sea trips, shopping, parades, church services and more were all on the menu. It was easy to get confused and distracted, so I decided my main focus had to be on the Tumbledown and Mount William battlefield. But now it was time for the Pilgrimage's first event to take place downstairs.

Mike Bowles addressed the gathering. He had been an officer in the Royal Corps of Transport, the regiment I was commissioned into before transferring to the Light Infantry in 1971, and was a sympathetic person who had worked hard for the past two years on a voluntary basis to ensure the success of this venture. His impressive official Pilgrimage list contained 106 soldiers who outnumbered the thirty-eight marines and sixty-two sailors on it. In addition to Merchant Navy veterans, there were seventeen bereaved next of kin and eleven Combat Stress staff that would provide support to those who needed it and, in particular, to the Pilgrimage's sixty-seven Combat Stress patients. A three-man British Forces Broadcasting Service TV camera crew brought the total party strength to 253 persons. I was happy to be part of this unique band of brothers. There were 219 Task Force pilgrims. We had shared the war's dangers, but were about to experience a special journey where employment of mutual psychosocial support would replace that will to fight in re-taking the Islands twenty-five years ago. It would also be fascinating professionally because I was also a trainer for handling the aftermath of civil aviation disasters that included support to survivors and next of kin.

At 8pm the VIPs arrived, but there was only one of real significance attired in her signature blue dress. The pilgrims closed around the frail former British Prime Minister whose strategic management of that national crisis in the South Atlantic was so effective. Baroness Margaret Thatcher remains their darling, and I was determined to present my book to her. By good fortune David Connett happened to be present with his photographer. I warned him about my intentions. The photographer was then rapidly briefed to take a series of pictures whilst I, pushing into the pilgrim scrum surrounding the Iron Lady, tapped my finger on the arm of a nearby aide and showed him a copy of the book.

'No, no. She'll sign that later,' he exclaimed.

'But I want to give it to her!' I protested.

At last he understood my request, took her gently by the arm, and she turned to face me. I opened the book to my hastily scribbled standard inscription of: 'I hope you enjoy this universal story of a soldier before, during and after a war' as she listened with growing attention to my rapid explanation. Her determined chin slightly stuck out as she read the inscription carefully. Then she looked at me and in a deliberate manner intoned, 'I shall read this book not once, but twice.'

My *séance* with her had lasted not more than sixty seconds, but nonetheless it was an unforgettable personal experience with a lady who had, all those years ago, dictated my destiny and many others in the room for ten extraordinary weeks. I met others such as Rosie Elsdon, a civilian nurse on SS *Canberra*, and Jack Massey, the Gurkhas' Catering Officer in the war. Afterwards in the bar I met Emily Herbert again with Bob

Darby, a 3 Para Falklands veteran who was also the Royal British Legion's Falklands battlefield tour guide. Emily showed me the captivating results of her Falklands photography. One picture caught my eye. This was of a makeshift rock cairn memorial to two dead soldiers of the Argentine 7th Mechanised Infantry Regiment erected on the Mount Longdon battlefield most likely by fellow Argentine veterans or relatives. Following the local rules on such matters, the Islanders would have removed it by now: a mean act which most soldiers of either side would generally abhor.

The evening had been a good *hors d'oeuvre* to the official Day One of the Pilgrimage when I was up early to grab breakfast. Mike Bowles briefed us carefully on our somewhat complicated travel movements and the Pilgrimage in general, but afterwards there was an interminable wait in the lobby of the Union Jack Club for our coaches to arrive. Some pilgrims became stuck in another unreliable lift and the Fire Brigade had to rescue them, but we were serenaded by the bagpipe playing of Keith Burton. Nicknamed Paddy, he was a 40 Commando Royal Marine who suffered from PTSD and had been in therapy for the last twelve years. I also met just before my departure a worried Peter Poole, the Combat Stress Director of Welfare Services. We had been in the same Sandhurst Old College intake and had been commissioned into the Royal Corps of Transport at the same time. Peter recognised me immediately. However it took me ten embarrassingly long seconds before the penny dropped. He would not be on the Pilgrimage, but confided in me that three pilgrims who were also Combat Stress patients had gone missing.

'It's avoidance,' he explained in exasperation. 'They're worried about going back to the Islands and this is their last chance to run away from reality. I hope we find them before their coach leaves the Club.'

Fortunately they did. After a two-hour drive we arrived at Gatwick Airport for the early evening take-off. I kept myself to myself as a coping strategy for the surprising anxiety that was building up. However Paddy's bagpipes were active in providing a welcome diversion as we boarded the aircraft for the dull first leg twelve-hour flight to Rio de Janeiro. After a three-hour refuelling stop, we took off again on the final four-hour leg to the Falklands. The aircraft's Captain who came on board at Rio was Bob Tuxford. A good choice, because he was both a retired RAF Squadron-Leader and Falklands veteran, having been a Victor Tanker pilot during the war in the Operation Black Buck Vulcan bombing raids on Stanley airfield. There was noticeable tension fifteen minutes before landing as the in-cabin TV screens displayed a map of the Falklands indicating Goose Green and our flight path. Despite the strong headwind which made this leg into one of nearly six hours, Tuxford landed safely on target at Mount Pleasant Airport. It was 09.00 hours local time on the morning of 6 November.

Even though this was the start of the austral summer, there was a chill in the air as we disembarked on this Pilgrimage Day Two in this surreal moment of return – a quarter of a century after I had gazed at the Falklands slipping over the horizon from SS *Uganda*, formerly the Task Force Hospital ship, which had been converted into a troop transport for the Gurkhas' 'cruise' back to Southampton. There was also an immediate war reminder in a liberated Argentine 120mm mortar and 105mm OTO Melara pack howitzer displayed on the grass outside the small terminal building. Each of us was greeted by the Commander of British Forces Falkland Islands, Brigadier Nick Davies, and four local councillors before going through customs clearance to waiting busses and hour-long drive to Stanley. No longer that dirt track of twenty-five years ago between Darwin and Stanley, we drove along a wide tarmac road which was part of an advancing network built since the war, currently measuring over 800 kilometres.

The guide on my bus was Patrick Watts, a sixty-four year-old resident of Stanley who had been manning the Islands' radio station in the capital on the night of 1-2 April 1982. He had provided a running commentary on the Argentine landings until eventually forced to leave his place of work at gunpoint. Over the bus loudspeaker system, he told us about his courageous negotiations with the Argentines over his subsequent broadcasting work on the radio and in the TV station they installed. Of even more interest was his statement that: 'The Argentines in Stanley were scared of both the aircraft carrier HMS *Invincible* and the Gurkhas', and he became understandably emotional as he referred to us and the Islands' liberation as 'you were the boys who did it'.

There was also an excellent anecdote he had written in the *Penguin News* 'Special Liberation Edition' I had found in my Pilgrimage 'Falklands 25' bag. Late in the night of 14 June 1982 after Major-General Jeremy Moore had signed the surrender terms with Brigadier-General Mario Benjamín Menéndez, the former was entertained by Patrick in the latter's Stanley home with a supply of home-made cakes, buns and tea which, according to the Commander Land Forces Falkland Islands, otherwise known as 'Cliffy' to the troops on board *QE2*, was 'the best damned cuppa I've had since we set out'. Patrick was definitely a person to be contacted later.

Closer to Stanley, we drove past in rapid succession those war landmarks and battlefields etched forever into my mind. Indeed it was a shock to be confronted again on our left-hand side with them all. For a pilgrim who had fought there, they rolled by in a breathtaking five-minute sequence. First was the craggy Wall Mountain, then Two Sisters with its dramatic northern twin-peaked Sister overshadowing the lower and more subdued southern Sister, the long, low dinosaurian Goat Ridge with its southern slabs of rock glinting occasionally from reflections of a weak sun, the towering Mount Harriet, the sinister elongated spine of a gigantic rock fault-line which made up Tumbledown, and finally the cone-shaped dominance of Mount William. Lying behind these extraordinary features and hidden from view were Mount Longdon and Wireless Ridge. This terrain had presented us attacking British infantry with many a conundrum to crack. I understood why Sun Tzu had a fixation about terrain with three chapters in *The Art of War* primarily about the Army and its crucial utilisation of terrain in war.[4] He was so perceptive about its two alternative outcomes of 'death and life'. Get it wrong, meant death. Get it right, meant life. Perhaps my instantaneous reaction in snapping photographs of these battlefields as fast as possible was, perhaps, a first positive symptom of the Pilgrimage's therapeutic effect on offer.

Rounding Sapper Hill, site of the war's final fighting, we caught sight of the traditional red and green-roofed homes of the tiny capital in which lived 2,155 Islanders, more than double its population of 1,050 twenty-five years previously.[5] The town had also expanded accordingly. It now covered three and a half kilometres from west to east (twenty-five years before it was little more than half a mile), and 750 metres from north to south. Our final destination was the Falkland Islands Defence Force (FIDF) HQ and Drill Hall in the south-east part of the town. The building was packed with cheerful Islanders. The Governor, Mr Alan Huckle, made a speech of welcome before handing over to Gary Clement, a former Royal Marine NCO and war veteran with the Commando Logistic Regiment. He resided now in Stanley. Being the Chairman of the Falklands 25 Pilgrimage Organising Committee in the Falklands, Clement gave a quick orientation on the week's intensive programme which, he confirmed, had taken many months of planning. I counted thirty-five events – an impossibility to participate in them all. However there was a dawning awareness in me that we war veterans were, to a degree, an embodiment of Stanley's post-conflict culture. This included the battlefields we had left behind on that strangely bleak but beautiful countryside which provided the Islanders with an ever-present reminder of the conflict.

After Clement's briefing, all pilgrims met their hosts who would provide accommodation for the forthcoming week. In addition to me, Vera and Frank were to host two former Scots Guardsmen, Billy Silver and Tony Blackburn who had fought with Left Flank Company in the Tumbledown battle. The Leylands drove us west along the comparatively new Stanley by-pass along the Murray Heights. We admired the East Stanley housing development which had nearly doubled home ownership in the capital over the past decade, before turning right down Dairy Paddock Drive through the Davis Street crossroads and then left onto Brandon Road to stop outside the Leylands' comfortable bungalow at number 10.[6] They had lived in their West Stanley home ever since arriving in the Falklands eight years post-war to join their daughter, Lynn Brownlee. It lay high up on the northern slopes of the Murray Heights with uninterrupted views over Stanley Harbour and, to the west, Mount William and Tumbledown five and six kilometres distant respectively as the crow flies and, further to the west, Two Sisters.

But Brandon Road was not a good area to live during the war. Just on the western side of Dairy Paddock Road and south of Davis Street had been located three twin 30mm Hispano-Suiza anti-aircraft artillery guns and one 105mm pack howitzer. Immediately to the south, on Stanley Common, were positioned in total three 105mm pack howitzer batteries with appropriate SAM and AAA assets. Davis Street, which was parallel to Brandon Road, became so dangerous in the last two weeks of the war with constant Harrier air strikes and Royal Navy bombardments onto the Common that everybody living on the street's southern side and beyond had to be evacuated at the end of May. Also 300 metres eastwards along Davis Street near the Radio and Space Ionospheric Observatory Station (otherwise known as the Met Station), had been sited one of two 155mm howitzers located in Stanley. With a range of 20,000 metres, its main task was to engage Royal Navy warships stationed on the southern Stanley gun line bombarding Argentine positions but, throughout 12 June in conjunction with the more mobile 155mm howitzer operating lower down in the town, had conducted harassing fire missions on 3 Para after the latter had taken Mount Longdon during the night. Six more paratroopers were then killed on Longdon and Corporal Denzil Connick, the eventual founder of SAMA82, lost his left leg from a 155mm shell explosion that also badly wounded the other. After this battle a 105mm pack howitzer battery was also withdrawn from the Moody Brook area to the Racecourse where it joined another two artillery batteries of twelve 105mm pack howitzers protected by Tigercat surface-to-air missile launchers plus a 155mm CITER L33 gun sited behind nearby Sapper Hill. The Racecourse was only 300 metres from our new home.

The 155mm guns were not moved as, according to siege veteran Michael Butcher of 3A Dairy Paddock Road 'the Argentines did not have the heavy tractors necessary' to move them. Much later correspondence received from him a year after the Pilgrimage described his daily sabotage routine and the siege's final day of danger in this area of Stanley:

> As the war progressed day by day it was noticeable the Argentine transport was rattling to a halt or just driving around on steel rims. The reason for all those flat tyres was simple. I and a young boy walked around the town each day slowly emptying our pockets of thousands of small nails. It worked well [...] On the last morning we were certainly one of only two households (most other people had gone to the concrete-built police cottages and West Store) who witnessed and were in the middle of the Argentine mutiny – in our house yard alone we had some 300 Argentine troops firing at their officers and the houses. We were only fourteen feet away.

Now we were shown our peaceful bedrooms, dumped our luggage in them and Vera offered us a cup of tea. Frank had recently been in the UK for an operation on his knees which restricted his movements, a drawback for his activities as an experienced tourist. However I was flattered when he showed me his copy of my first book. We talked about the following day's activities as well as ourselves. The Leylands' two other guests were in the sixteen-man Scots Guards Pilgrimage party. The latter represented a good cross-section of six sub-units in the Battalion and obviously would be a good source of information about the Tumbledown fighting. Two pilgrims had been part of HQ Company's composite platoon that carried out a decisive diversionary attack, three had been in G Company, five in Left Flank Company (one of them – Robert 'Ossie' Osborn – was not part of the official Pilgrimage, but flew to Mount Pleasant Airport as one of the Royal British Legion battlefield tour group), three in Right Flank Company, one in the Mortar Platoon and two in the Machine-Gun Platoon. Four of these pilgrims were Combat Stress patients. After return to the UK there would be a fifth.

Billy Silver's UK civilian workplace was now at a crematorium. Pleasant and quiet, he also gave an immediate impression of being totally unflappable, just the type needed for a night-time infantry battle. My sixth-sense proved correct. Eighteen months later Major-General Mike Scott, fearing my Tumbledown battle writing would be rightly 'ill-disciplined' if I did not consult the relevant officer veteran, facilitated my contact with John Kiszely, Billy's former Company Commander in the battle. Subsequently I wrote two papers (that included forty-eight questions) about the fighting, and was gratified that the busy still-serving officer found time to answer them. He also described Billy as a 'marvellous chap – Battalion light-welterweight champion'.

On this first day of the Pilgrimage proper, Billy had been busy already. I received an update from him. 'We've been talking with Patrick Watts and have decided to go up on Tumbledown tomorrow with other Scots Guards pilgrims and also camp out the night there. That's why we've come on the Pilgrimage: to get back to Tumbledown as quickly as possible. You coming too?' he asked me.

I was torn between Billy's invitation and accompanying the planned 'round robin' four-wheel drive vehicle convoy of pilgrims around the northern and southern coastlines of East Falkland. A benchmark of the Islanders' ever-growing affluence, there were enough of these vehicles in Stanley for such a trip as their numbers had nearly sextupled from a modest 183 in 1982 to the current high of 1,023. Camping out might suck up too much of my time. There were so many other places I wanted to visit. However after much thought and indecision I choose Tumbledown. Its lure was irresistible. The forever laughing and joking Tony Blackburn gave a good enough reason why he wanted to go through with this first trip out, despite the real possibility of being caught up in forecasted bad weather.

'Well, I still get flashbacks and nightmares from it all. Don't you?' this good-natured serving prison officer asked me in his heavy Lancashire accent.

Getting back out immediately onto the original site where trauma had been caused was a good psychological battle plan, but this Falklands veteran's question about such PTSD symptoms only received my seemingly bored reply, 'Actually no, I don't.' But at least it had camouflaged my post-war reactions.

I rang Patrick Watts to confirm my attendance in the little Scots Guards convoy of vehicles going up to Tumbledown for the following day, before Frank kindly offered to give us a guided tour around the Stanley area, including the north-east peninsular where the old airport was located and which had been the target of many British air attacks during the war. However first we drove through the capital westwards towards the eastern end of Wireless Ridge to visit the remains of the Royal Marines' Moody Brook Barracks destroyed by the Argentine Special Forces on 2 April 1982. Disappointingly only the foundations were intact. Then we moved back along Ross Road to Stanley's eastern outskirts before turning north over a bridge constructed in the months after the war by Gurkha Engineers and through the little isthmus at the Canache. We parked up at Whalebone Cove where the picturesque nineteenth century wreck of the *Lady Elizabeth* with Mount William, Tumbledown, and Two Sisters in the background made a wonderful photograph. 'When working as a guide, this is the first place I bring the cruise ship tourists,' Frank assured us.

The ship was listed as one of twenty 'city attractions' in the *Penguin News Visitor Guide*. Frank then took us north to Yorke Bay. This was Red Beach for the Argentine landings on 2 April 1982. It was deceptively beautiful with sweeping white sand dunes: but the Argentines had mined the area in their preparations to counter an anticipated British landing here – and the mines had not been removed, so there was no walking on the beach that afternoon. But moving on to a nearby site we spotted a few penguins. 'Give the tourists just one opportunity to take a picture of a penguin, and their day is made,' advised Frank about the golden rule for any Falklands guide.

Driving past the old airport, we arrived back at 10, Brandon Road to tuck into the first of many excellent meals provided by Vera. Her home, reflecting Stanley's affluence, was equipped with all necessary modern conveniences.[7] Afterwards we changed into smarter clothes before attending a reception in the FIDF Drill Hall. Local gratitude and appreciation of the sacrifices made in the war and resulting suffering and scars from the experience were clearly apparent. I also met those who had provided information, or were about to, for my ongoing book project: Peter and Rosemarie King, and Lynn and Andrew Brownlee.

Also another pilgrim, the tall, bespectacled Steve Cocks, exchanged words with me. Since leaving the Army he had become a successful civilian IT consultant. But in 1982 as an eighteen year-old Royal Army Pay Corps Lance-Corporal, he had been attached to the 2nd Battalion, Scots Guards as a pay clerk. This REMF (a neutral acronym for the hideously hyperbolic military slang term of 'Rear Area Mother Fucker') as Steve described himself, had actually fought on the Tumbledown with their Right Flank Company. There was no pay clerk job for him on the Islands and so, with only thirteen weeks of initial basic infantry training under his belt, he had reverted to an infantry role. A pleasant and intelligent person, he was one of forty-two RAPC personnel who were members of the Task Force. Like me, Steve lived now in Scandinavia and owned a Stockholm flat only a short distance from the Frösundavik Head Office of Scandinavian Airlines, my former employers in Norway. Post-Pilgrimage he wrote:

> Looking back I really regret not being more 'aware' of just how monumental the events around me were. So young and so naïve. Also being Corps-attached I was never involved in any of the numerous post-mortems that those involved must have taken part in. You are the first person in twenty-five years that I have talked to about the war and shared my experiences ...[8]

On 5 June 1982 Cocks and the remainder of the Scots Guards embarked on the amphibious assault ship HMS *Intrepid* at San Carlos for their move to Bluff Cove which was occupied by 2nd Battalion, Parachute Regiment. Due to the enemy land-based Exocet missile threat, *Intrepid* would only take the Battalion to the area of Lively Island in Choiseul Sound where the Guardsmen were transferred into the ship's four flat-bottomed LCUs (Landing Craft Utility) to continue onwards to Bluff Cove. This seven-hour voyage was not to be envied. There were 150 Guardsmen packed like sardines into each landing craft. They were without shelter and it was bitterly cold. Eventually the wind rose and waves began to crash into the landing craft. These were weighed down by their heavy loads, and their scupper ports which had been designed to let water out, were frequently below the sea surface and therefore letting water in. The hapless Guardsmen were soaked. Sleep was impossible, yet there were only a minimal number of hypothermia cases. Additionally HMS *Cardiff*, a Royal Navy Type 42 guided missile destroyer which, en route to the Stanley gun line accompanied by the Type 12 frigate HMS *Yarmouth*, had just shot down in error a British Army Air Corps helicopter with a Sea Dart missile, also nearly mistook the Scots Guards landing craft for enemy. However six illuminating star shells fired by *Cardiff* established the LCUs' correct identity and thereby avoided the war's potentially biggest 'blue-on-blue' incident.

Arriving off Bluff Cove early on 6 June, the Guardsmen avoided yet another potential 'blue-on-blue' as 2 Para had not been informed of the Scots Guards transit from HMS *Intrepid*. After landing the Battalion remained static for a while and Cocks decided to lie down on the sodden ground in the driving sleet and torrential rain. Hypothermia cases began to increase alarmingly. Nonetheless he fell asleep in a puddle, only to be rudely awakened by his Company Sergeant-Major when the time came to get moving to Right Flank's position west of the settlement.

While the Scots Guards Recce Platoon engaged in reconnaissance tasks forward of the settlement to gather intelligence about the enemy, Cocks and the remainder of the Battalion began to recover from their battering by the elements. But on the afternoon of 8 June they witnessed the enemy Skyhawk fatal air strike on the Landing Ships Logistics RFAs *Sir Galahad* and *Sir Tristram* anchored at Port Pleasant. The 18,600 rounds of Scots Guards' small-arms fire directed at the ensuing series of enemy aircraft attacks were a prelude of things to come. However Cocks was not a party to putting up this 'wall of lead':

One of my 'problems' in the immediate aftermath of the Falklands was that I did not fire my rifle once. I used to ask myself over and over again if my inactions had in some way contributed to one of my mates being killed or wounded. Of course now that I am older and bolder, no longer do I ask myself these questions. But at the time it was always at the back of my mind [...] On the night of 11 June, 42 Commando assaulted Mount Harriet which we could clearly see from Bluff Cove. I stood outside the sheep pen I was sleeping in and watched the night sky lit up with tracer and flares. The ground quivered with the aftershock of artillery, mortars and shells from ships offshore. All I could think of was that we were next, though I had no real idea of just what this meant. In two days it would be our turn.

On 12 June my Colour-Sergeant, Alex Allender, gave us a briefing using a rather neat model he had made to represent Tumbledown. He was in charge of Company Echelon to which I was attached. We consisted of the original Right Flank stores personnel (Allender, Talman, Colins, Hardstaff) plus a number of attached personnel who were a couple of cooks, REME [9] mechanic, various odds and sods from Headquarters Company such as drivers (they had nothing to drive) and me. We all became 'Humpers and Dumpers' and were responsible for supplying the platoons. During the battle we would be deployed to the rear of the company with me as the 'tail-end Charlie'. My official title for the battle was 'NCO in charge of walking-wounded'. As I was a Lance-Corporal at this stage I was given the responsibility of leading any walking-wounded back to the Regimental Aid Post at Goat Ridge. Allender described in detail what was going to happen and pointed out the Company objectives Our Company, Right Flank, was to take the final third of Tumbledown.

On 13 June the Battalion was lined up in sticks of eight men and, as the helicopters landed, we leapt aboard and were whisked up to Goat Ridge. The Argentine forces had heard the movement of troops but had no direct line of sight as, by this time, they had lost their observation posts on the nearby mountains. However shells landed amongst us all day but, as they were not directed, their effect was random. We suffered our first casualty which, in typical Army humour, was laughed off as it involved one of the tough NCOs, Lance-Sergeant George, getting hit by shrapnel in his buttocks ...

Wednesday, 7 November was also Day Three of the Pilgrimage. Tony Blackburn, Billy Silver and I were joined in Stanley by three other Scots Guardsmen on our initial trip to Tumbledown. Jim Gillanders and Gordon Hoggan served with G Company whose objective, just in front of Tumbledown's western end, was a rocky knoll allegedly abandoned the night before the battle by the Argentine 5th Marine Infantry Battalion (BIM5). Gordon was in 9 Platoon which took five casualties from the subsequent shelling and, as a result of this and other extreme battle experiences, he suffered from PTSD. There was one more Guardsman present. Simon McNeill had been married only nine months before deploying to the Falklands in 1982. He was a Lance-Corporal in the Scots Guards Signals Platoon. However my eyes opened wide when he informed me seriously in his broad Scots accent, 'Aye, I was the radio operator for the Left Flank Company Commander.' He had to be an obvious target to find out more about the Tumbledown fighting. I was about to strike gold.

Guided by Patrick Watts, we drove out from Stanley in three four-wheel drive vehicles. Past Sapper Hill with Mount William looming to our front, I noticed immediately the 'Danger Mines' signs. Their white skull-and-crossbones symbol on a red background hung at regular intervals from three-strand wire fences marking the perimeter of Argentine minefields on either side of the road. My observation was reinforced by our driver. 'A cow somehow got into a minefield earlier this year,' he remarked with a wry smile, 'and the explosion could be heard back in Stanley. There was no need to take the cow to the abbatoir afterwards.'

It was surprising that of the estimated original 127 Argentine minefields in the Falklands, 101 still remained. Was lack of resources and high cost of removing them the sole argument for their continued existence? [10] The reality of the minefields had a sobering effect on visitors to the Islands travelling along this main road from Stanley to Mount Pleasant Airport, and provided an effective advertisement of Argentina's proximity: ergo – defence of the Islands *must* remain the number one priority. The minefields also played a part in the capital's post-conflict culture with minefield lore destined to be handed down from generation to generation. This was best articulated by our driver, 'So it's good the children in Stanley are aware about the dangers of these minefields through the mine and unexploded bomb briefings given to them at school up to the age of sixteen.'

However next year Rod Macdonald corrected my muted cynicism with some sound basic facts. A Royal Engineer Major, he commanded 59 Independent Commando Squadron in the war and was also a member of the Task Force planning staff for the San Carlos amphibious landings. He received a Mention in Dispatches (MID) decoration for his performance. In the immediate post-war period Rod was given the totally unrealistic and insurmountable task of clearing the Falklands' minefields. Of these he wrote to me in 2009 that:

When it comes to analysing most human events, I have always been more of a believer in cock-up rather than conspiracy. There is no effective way of wide area clearing of undetectable plastic mines. By the way, my definition of an area being cleared of mines is having the children of the person who says it is clear playing there happily. Given that, the best way to deal with mines spread over a wide area is just to fence the area off. The mines will be there for eternity. I have always felt that any army that lays undetectable plastic mines is committing a gross act of irresponsibility, polluting the land and putting others' lives at risk forever.

We arrived at the western shoulder of Mount William and parked up. I noticed the large stone run between Mount William and Tumbledown, and remembered my meeting with *Guardiamarina* (Midshipman) Marcelo Oruezabala, BIM5's 2 Platoon Commander, in Buenos Aires earlier that year. His platoon had been sited amongst the stones here, and immediately I found the remains of some of their trenches and rusting iron supports used for overhead cover in this location that Marcelo had described to me. I turned nearly 180 degrees to look south-west down towards the road we had driven along. Marcelo's men had an excellent field of fire for any 5th Infantry Brigade attack that might have been made in this direction.

Back in the vehicles, we drove up to Tumbledown and parked just south of the rocky knoll. The weather was pleasant: not the snow, Force 6 (21-26 knot) wind, minus six degrees Centigrade temperature with wind chill factor of minus twenty-two degrees centigrade endured on the war's final night. We got out and started to walk along Left Flank's route into their location where the eventual fire-fight began with the Argentine BIM5 composite 4 Platoon of twenty-eight Marines and seventeen Army soldiers including two officers. These forty-five men included the platoon commander, *Teniente de Corbeta* (Acting Sub-Lieutenant) Carlos Daniel Vázquez. Immediately behind his position we could see already the enormous slab of quartzite rock that dominated the surroundings. On the northern slopes of the 550-foot high west summit to his immediate rear was 5 Platoon comprising twenty-four Marine Amphibious Engineers, an artillery Forward Observation Officer and auxiliary conscript. The platoon commander was Acting Sub-Lieutenant Héctor Omar Miño. Some 600 metres to the rear, in the Tumbledown's centre, were fifteen Marines of a 60mm mortar section which would give indirect support fire to these two lead platoons. This meant that facing the 109-man strong Left Flank Company, and ready for battle, were eighty-six Argentine troops.

Patrick Watts was convinced the battle had started just before Left Flank's 15 Platoon and Tactical Company HQ reached a prominent peat bank some 100 metres from Tumbledown's western end. To this area he had escorted Hugh Bicheno, author of *Razor's Edge: The Unofficial History of the Falklands War* which included a detailed account of the Tumbledown battle. The former well-known Falklands War correspondent, distinguished author and newspaper editor, Sir Max Hastings, is quoted on Amazon.com from the London *Daily Mail* newspaper that Bicheno 'understand(s) how battles are fought, and explains those of the Falklands perhaps better than any other writer has done'. The book's Foreword, written by the late Professor Richard Holmes, also contained the following accolade:

The attention to terrain detail is remarkable and unparalleled. Hugh has walked and climbed all the battlefields of the war, and his own scrupulously-drawn maps make it clear that a good deal of what has been written about the fighting (sometimes by veterans, who may be forgiven if their *post hoc* reconstructions of a series of episodes and harrowing events are inexact) simply cannot be true. In the dangerous grammar of infantry battle the ground imposes its own hard rules. He is spot-on in so many of his judgments on the timeless truths of battle.[11]

With respect, his statement about veterans is disputable. How can any historian who did not fight in any battle of the war be better able to describe the combat as experienced by those who did? It is a challenge. My opinion is underscored by the *Razor's Edge* narrative in Chapter 15 – *Tumbledown/William* and another three pages in Chapter 16 – *Victory*. These are riddled with errors.[12] For example it concurred with Patrick's view by displaying a 'Photo Diagram' titled 'Left Flank Company Attack' which also had the words 'peat bank where company pinned down' overprinted on this latter feature.[13] The Scots Guards pilgrims disagreed. Before coming under Argentine fire they had moved nearly another 300 metres along Tumbledown's southern slopes.[14] So we walked on until Simon McNeill and Tony Blackburn, who had been in 14 Platoon behind the seventeen-man strong Company HQ, finally recognised this critical location. At last I understood how Left Flank had initially advanced. Not along the ridge line which many books on the war imply, but on a west-east axis further below on the southern slope. So in half an hour, this revelation revolutionised my own perceptions of the battle that had churned through my mind for twenty-five years.

Prior to the humbling business of writing about military battles, research on the ground, if possible with still-living primary sources, i.e. battle veterans, is advisable. Otherwise the author will, by necessity, commit acts of presumption. Even Sir Lawrence Freedman's massive 1,106-page *The Official History of the Falklands Campaign* published in 2005 falls into such a trap. In Volume II only six pages [15] out of its total of 849 describe the Tumbledown battle – plus Gurkha actions on that feature's north-east spur and Mount William. This one-dimensional skimpy account (including two inaccurate maps) of the only double British Battalion attack on a major Argentine unit, contains Scots Guards, Gurkha and Argentine casualty errors, and gives an erroneous impression that the Guardsmen had been in direct combat against the entire heavily Army-reinforced 5th Marine Infantry Battalion. But in the battle's main phase, Left Flank Company fought in reality against a composite force whose strength was only equivalent to that of a reinforced British platoon. To embellish his narration the political historian utilises four other publications so as to include five quotes and one comment with relevant references. Two come from my first book, one from 5 Infantry Brigade's War Diary, and three more from two other war veterans' publications.

Patrick seemed obsessed by the battle. He had been quoted in that year's June issue of *Soldier*, the Magazine of the British Army, which also contained a long article on my March visit to Buenos Aires:

For twenty years I was never interested in the war; I never read a single book about it and couldn't bring myself to listen to the tapes of my broadcast during the invasion. But recently I've started doing tours for the veterans. I think if any veteran, either Argentine or British, wants to come and clear their mind, it has to be a good thing.

He had acquired my first book of which he remarked, 'I read it non-stop on a flight to Australia. It was a most absorbing, factual account of what happened in the war. I thoroughly enjoyed it. I have recommended it to many people. For me it was important to read an account which was written by someone who was there, and saw what happened.'

The fifth-generation Falkland Islander was also a generous soul and wanted to get a fix on the site where Guardsman Derek Denholm of Left Flank's 14 Platoon had been killed instantaneously by 'Blast Injury, Multiple Shrapnel Wounds'[16] from an exploding shell. The latter's widow would arrive in the Falklands in a few weeks, and Patrick had agreed to act as her guide on a visit to the Tumbledown. Tony Blackburn was another anxiously trying to find the correct site on the ground. He failed.

However Patrick sent me better news later that month based partly on the fact that numerous wooden marker sticks or pegs with either red or orange-painted tops had been stuck into the Tumbledown battlefield post-hostilities. Each indicated a British casualty site:

> Bernie and Alistair (two locals) mentioned that Tony Blackburn had gone away unhappy because he was unable to find the rock that he was sheltering under when Guardsman Denholm was killed by a shell. Three of them were taking cover as bullets were whizzing over and above them and to the sides. He had searched but without success. The two local lads went looking around on Friday and found one of those sticks with an orange top behind a rock which was 'bollock high' as Tony put it, and which fitted the description perfectly. I had never noticed the stick there before because it was sort of under the rock and not prominently placed on top. We are sure that this was the rock because it had the flat surface which Tony had indicated and its length was about right for three men to take shelter under. This was on the south plateau just above and to the east of the slab (of rock) where Vázquez had his position below.[17] Hopefully Tony will return and we can take him to this location.[18]

But it would be Simon's comments that began to catch my imagination as his bulky frame traversed Tumbledown's southern slopes at its west end. There we found the remains of the Argentine Marine 4 Platoon's individual defensive positions.[19] Some resembled foxholes. Others were rings of rocks which had once been built up into low-walled sangars. Some were easy to locate, others not. I counted at least sixteen. A few still contained equipment, such as empty rifle magazines, pieces of clothing and rotting footwear because the battlefields have been left as they were from 1982 in memory of those soldiers that had fought for the Islanders' freedom. Indeed the poignancy of this gesture is reinforced by local regulations forbidding the smuggling of war souvenirs out of the Islands.

At the centre rear of the platoon's position was the massive twelve-metre long flat quartzite rock slab that jutted out from its surroundings at an angle of forty-five degrees. Visible from several kilometres distance to the south, the Argentines appropriately had named this 'The Wall'. Simon referred to it as 'The Ski Slope' and, at its base, Vázquez had sited his Platoon HQ where there were still sleeping bags and an orange thermos flask located in a small living space behind this huge rock. In front were the remains of three trenches. The one on the right still had a black radio cable leading back to the space behind 'The Ski Slope'.

'Must have been the command trenches,' was my educated guess to the former Left Flank radio operator as we gazed at them.

I turned to look southwards down the stunning sweep of terrain to the road two kilometres away. Vázquez had a magnificent field of fire for any British attack that might have been launched from that direction. Simon then started to talk about an Argentine officer and another badly wounded Marine he had taken prisoner. Since I had been exchanging e-mails with Vázquez earlier that year after receiving a detailed account from him of the fighting with Left Flank, my attention became focused on the Scotsman's recollections that began tumbling out. Although coherent in his explanations, the memory does play tricks after so long. So I needed clarifications and interrupted him on numerous occasions with questions. His tale would be refined considerably post-Pilgrimage in both the short- and long-term:

> Sorry for the confusion, but I am now clear in my mind. The problem is trying to transfer it onto paper. But it is only since I have visited the Falklands that all the pieces are starting to fit. I'll start from the beginning. Some of this, Mike, is me confronting things for the first time. It is only since visiting the place that I feel this is possible. All in all I can clearly remember clearing four sangars or foxholes.

A gripping story then began to emerge from this former radio operator who was twenty-two years old at the time of the battle.

Notes

1. *The Art of War*, Chapter 1 – Appraisals.
2. Nearly a year after the Pilgrimage Lynn Brownlee sent the author a series of these reports which showed the radical changes that had taken place post-conflict in the community and culture of Stanley and the Islands.
3. This figure camouflaged the per capita subsidy. Based on an annual UK defence budget of thirty-six billion pounds sterling, Falklands defence costs represented an annual sum of £180 million pounds sterling: effectively an astonishing subsidy of £72,639 pounds sterling for each of the 2,478 Islanders who did not work for the military garrison.
4. *The Art of War*, Chapter 9 – Moving the Army, Chapter 10 – Forms of the Earth, and Chapter 11 – The Nine Grounds.

5.   Falkland Islands Report of Census 1980.

6.   This was one of 585 privately owned houses out of Stanley's total of 783. Comparing the year 1982, when there were 381 houses of which 213 had been privately owned, reveals a doubling in housing over the following twenty-five years. – Falklands Islands Report of Census 1980 and Falkland Islands Census Statistics 2006.

7.   For example, there was no antiquated peat-fired cooker, a type which, in 1982, was used by 249 ex 378 Stanley households. Like the Leylands, the vast majority of houses in 2007 had gas or electricity cookers. Only eighteen peat cookers still existed because kerosene, not peat, was the preferred fuel for heating. A large flat-screen TV with a multi-channel satellite cable connection hung on my hosts' lounge wall, proof enough that ultra-modern communications technology had reached Stanley. There were 1,591 TV sets in the capital. Pre-1982 there had been none but, four years post-war, 327 – thanks primarily to the occupying Argentine forces' distribution of a large number of cut-price colour TVs to the capital's inhabitants. (Falklands Islands Reports of Census 1980 and 1986, and Falkland Islands Census Statistics 2006.)

8.   E-mail dated 28 January 2010.

9.   Royal Electrical and Mechanical Engineers.

10. During October 2009 to May 2010 a UK company, BACTEC (Battle Area Clearance, Training, Equipment and Consultancy) International, successfully completed Phase 1 of the British Foreign and Commonwealth Office's contract for clearing the minefields at Sapper Hill, Surf Bay, Goose Green and part of Fox Bay (West Falkland). Contrary to assumptions made in 1982 by various British non-Sappers that the Argentine records were inaccurate and mines laid by poorly-trained Engineers or Marines, all of which was then promptly reported by the British media at the time, experience in Phase 1 demonstrated that the Argentine records were excellent in terms of the number of mines laid, construction of the panels and location of each mine. Guy Lucas, the CEO of BATEC International who served with the Queen's Gurkha Engineers from 1968-73, and was also the former Officer Commanding 49 Explosives Ordnance Disposal Squadron in the Falklands from June to August 1982 immediately post-cessation of hostilities, informed the author that BACTEC International won the FCO Phase 2 contract which addressed the areas within the Stanley Common Minefield Fence. This work started from mid-October 2011. But BATEC had to do its work in the Stanley Common minefields without any Argentine records for this area. An Argentine Army veteran of the war, Colonel Esteban La Madrid, provided this book's author with the reason why. Although Argentine Army details of minefields laid around 'the city' had been handed over to the British in the immediate post-war period, the folder containing this vital information was promptly lost during a helicopter flight to San Carlos.

11. *Razor's Edge*, p. 27.

12. To be precise: at a conservative count there are sixty-three errors on twenty-two and a half pages. This rate of nearly three errors per page begs a simple question. Does this inaccuracy continue throughout the remainder of *Razor's Edge*?

13. *Ibid.,* p. 291.
14. From its west to east ends Tumbledown's length is 1.8 kilometres (as per the scale of my battle map used during the war). Yet the scale of the two maps in *Razor's Edge* (p. 290) incorrectly indicates Tumbledown's length as being only half of that.
15. *The Official History of the Falklands Campaign*, pp 634 to 636.
16. International Form of Medical Certificate of Cause of Death (F Med 174) signed by Surgeon-Commander Rick Jolly, RN.
17. In *Razor's Edge* (lower map – p. 290) the question mark by the assumed (and incorrect) site of where Denholm fell (and lack of his being mentioned in the narrative) indicates this was a mystery for the book's author.
18. E-mail dated 27 November 2007.
19. In *Razor's Edge* (p. 290 – lower map) the 4 Platoon position is incorrectly marked at least 200 metres too far to the east: a fact I corroborated with Vázquez eighteen months later.

Invincibility is defence.
Vincibility is attack.
Defend and one has a surplus.
Attack and one is insufficient.
— Sun Tzu [1]

McNeill's Left Flank Signals Detachment 2IC, Lance-Corporal Chris Murley who manned the forward-link Company net, and McNeill would be working together with their Company Commander, Major John Kiszely, in the twenty-one man Company HQ. Kiszely was impressed by their subsequent performance:

> Actually Simon McNeill was a new arrival to the team. My rear-link (Battalion net) radio operator, Lance-Sergeant Simpson, had been taken ill just before Tumbledown [...] and was substituted by the bold McNeill. I therefore knew McNeill less well than Lance-Corporal Murley. But he certainly did not disappoint. The aim was always to keep the radio operators at one's side, but there were brief periods during the battle when I got slightly ahead of them (I was not burdened by a Clansman radio set). I am certainly hugely grateful to both of them.

However McNeill did far more than receive and transmit messages on the Battalion radio net during the fight against Vázquez's platoon. The Scotsman was ready for the challenges that lay ahead in the dark. Not only a capable radio operator, he was also a proven marksman. Like many other Signallers in the Left Flank Company and Right Flank Company Signals Detachments, he was not armed with the 9mm Sterling submachine-gun (SMG).[2] This was relatively light in weight compared to the SLR (Self-Loading Rifle),[3] and was supposed to be the standard-issue weapon to a Signaller in order to compensate for having to man-pack an additional load — his Clansman radio-set. McNeill:

> The SLR was my personal weapon of choice because I was left-handed and therefore fired it from the left shoulder. The SMG discharged its spent cartridges from the right and these tended to jump in front of my face when firing from the aim position. So I always used the SLR in my Annual Personal Weapons Test, not the SMG. I was more comfortable with this former weapon and, to be honest, always obtained very high scores.

Furthermore the path of an ejected SMG cartridge case was slightly down and backward, so mild burns could sometimes be incurred by left-hand shooters such as McNeill. But the big disadvantage with the SLR he drew from HQ Company's Armoury at Chelsea Barracks in London was its weight of five kilos with a fully-loaded magazine. However there were also major advantages. It had much greater 'stopping power' than the SMG and, even if an arm or leg got in the way of the SLR's high-velocity 7.62mm round, then the latter could cause catastrophic damage to the limb. Additionally the SLR was not so susceptible to ammunition-feed stoppages and, because of the rifle's greater weight even with an empty magazine, its fixed bayonet could be a potent weapon in close-quarter combat. Owners of the SMG were also prone to having negligent discharges. For example, in Goose Green on 5 June a British other rank was cleaning his SMG when he managed to shoot a Gurkha in the bottom three times.

Like McNeill and Murley, Lance-Corporal Steve Fleck, one of the Signallers in the Signals Detachment to Right Flank Company HQ (and now a police officer), was also armed with an SLR. He had a succinct opinion of the SMG:

> We just didn't trust the firepower of those SMGs. There was no way I was going into battle with one of those things.[4]

As events unfolded, McNeill would learn that he had made a good choice. Indeed his trusty SLR would prove to be so valuable to him that he remembered its Company registration number of 173 painted on the rifle's butt after all these years. This newest recruit to Left Flank described the battle's start:

> G Company advanced first, and then we heard the diversionary attack going in. We advanced in single file using the Goat Ridge rocks to our left as cover. I remember the Commanding Officer and Padre wishing us good luck. Then we moved into extended line with 13 Platoon on the left, Company Tactical HQ in the centre, 15 Platoon to the right, 14 Platoon in the rear together with the Company 2IC and Company HQ.

G Company had moved off sixty minutes before Left Flank to cross the start line, a wire fence, at 23.59Z hours. It was a tense manoeuvre, particularly for the point section in which there were fewer than four seventeen year-olds. They and the remainder of the Company crossed the open countryside while mortar and artillery illuminating bombs and shells slowed their progress as they froze until the flares died out. Flurries of snow hit their faces. Sporadic artillery and mortar fire added to the anxiety.

A Scots Guards diversionary attack at Pony's Pass, two kilometres to the south-west, assisted G Company in taking its objective unopposed, despite the enemy platoon commanded by Marine Acting Sub-Lieutenant Héctor Omar Miño on the nearby west summit of Tumbledown being aware of their new neighbour's arrival. The Spanish speaking voice that some in G Company heard in the rocks above belonged to one of Miño's platoon. It was fortunate that these Marine Amphibious Engineers would withdraw prematurely back to the eastern end of Tumbledown just after the initial contact was made with the Scots Guards. Not far behind G Company was Left Flank which advanced eastwards with fixed bayonets. McNeill:

> The next thing I knew we came across some of G Company who had gone firm on their objective. I spoke to Guardsman Chris Herrity who said, 'I think they've fucked off to the diversionary attack area. You can still see the fires over there where they're still smouldering.'

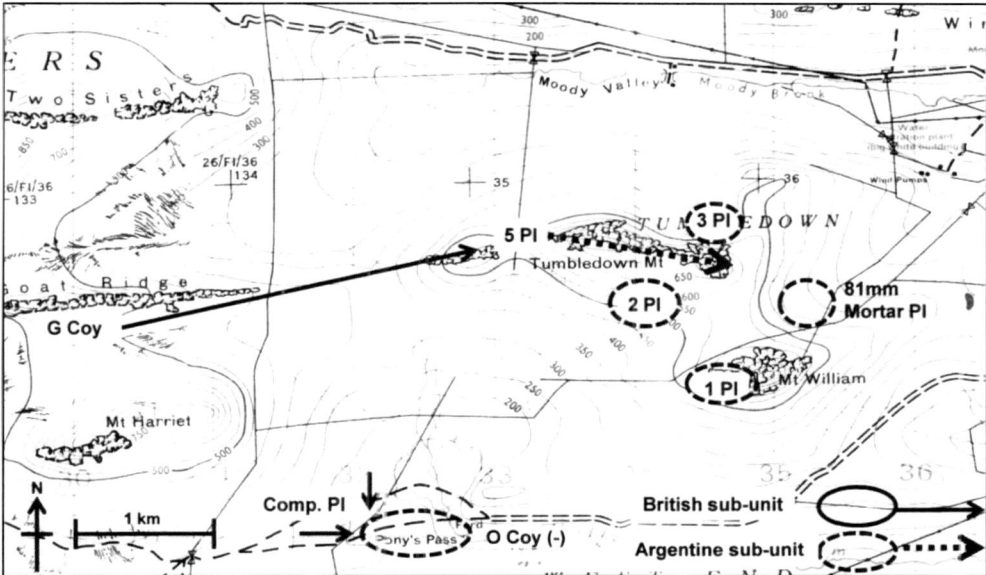

Map 1 (01.00Z-02.30Z) – Composite platoon (2SG) attacks Pony's Pass. G Company (2SG) takes the rocky knoll west of Tumbledown. 5 Platoon (BIM5) withdraws from Tumbledown's west summit to the east end.

Herrity was in 9 Platoon which would soon come under heavy artillery fire. Kiszely:

> Within Company HQ there were two similarly sized groups (about seven to eight in each), initially about perhaps thirty to forty metres apart. In my group were, I think, the Forward Observation Officer (FOO), Mortar Fire Controller (MFC), Company Sergeant Major, two radio operators, Lance-Corporal Galloway – perhaps a couple of others [...] (Galloway) was a storeman, but as an ex-Guards Para Company NCO, he was a very useful man to have around on a dark night [...] We thought that the higher ground would be defended, and 13 Platoon were advancing through it to clear it.

The Platoon Commander of 13 Platoon was Second-Lieutenant James Stuart. This platoon was on the left, Kiszely's Company HQ group was in the centre and, along the lower ground on the right, 15 Platoon commanded by Lieutenant Alastair Mitchell. Company HQ was split with the Company 2IC's group about thirty metres behind Kiszely's lead group. In depth, to the rear of the Company 2IC's group, was 14 Platoon commanded by Lieutenant Anthony Fraser.

Meanwhile behind Left Flank came Right Flank Company. The latter had crossed the start line at 01.30Z and Steve Cock's ordeal was about to begin:

> As dark fell we moved up to the start line in battle order, literally a white tape pinned to the ground, rather like the start of a race. It was at this point I found out that I would be going into the attack. At the time I was excited with the prospect

and quietly honoured, a bit like getting picked in the playground for a game of football. I carried a stretcher, SLR, 100 rounds of ammunition for my rifle and 1,000 rounds for our machine-gun in bandoliers draped over my chest and in my respirator case. Shell dressings were in every pocket and pouch and I carried a sleeping bag, not for sleeping but to keep the wounded warm. I also carried four mortar bombs that were dropped at the mortar line which we passed on moving up. My designated role was that of an ammunition mule and, once the fighting started, I was to look after the walking wounded.

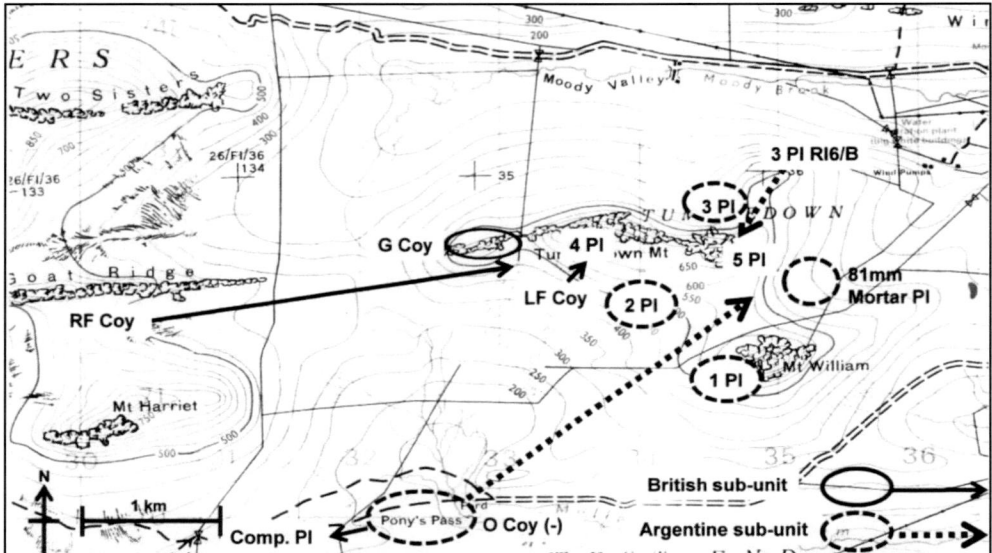

Map 2 (02.30Z-04.30Z) – Left Flank Company (2SG) engages 4 Platoon (BIM5). Composite platoon (2SG) and O Company (BIM5) withdraw from Pony's Pass. 3 Platoon (RI6/B) advances up Tumbledown's north-east spur.

Another 2007 Right Flank pilgrim was Ian Morton. In 1982 he was a twenty year-old Guardsman and 3 Platoon's sniper. More than two years post-Pilgrimage he gave me, after my request, a gripping personal story of the fighting. It began in unorthodox fashion:

The night was very cold and dark with a hint of snow in the air. My thoughts were racing with memories of all my past training and what would now be expected of me in this, my first experience of combat. I had wanted to be a soldier since a child and this was it, a chance to prove myself in combat knowing this night would remain with me forever.

As we approached the start line, I looked left and right and saw the two marker posts on which were hanging lamps with red lights. These could be seen only from our approach and not by the Argentines. Our platoon had been tabbing in single file via Goat Ridge to this location where we formed an extended line. After the enemy's direction had been pointed out, Mr Lawrence, our Platoon Commander, came over to us and said, 'Right lads, take your tin pots off and put your berets on.

Let's show these bastards who they're dealing with!'

So we changed headgear, laying out our tin pots (helmets) in a straight line. Believe it or not, we then sat on these and had a smoke break with our last cigarette before battle. Nobody spoke. Even the non-smokers had a cigarette. Although crazy, this was the best smoke break of my life. Once finished, everyone stood up and the order was given, 'Fix bayonets. Prepare to move. Move!'

Then we crossed the start line and began our advance to contact. It is difficult to explain all my many thoughts, but these did include a strange mixture of pride, dread and sense of invincibility. Nothing could stop us.

Cocks:

> We moved onto Tumbledown sometime after 11pm (02.00Z) on the night of 13 June in the middle of a snow storm. It was a silent approach as there was no pre-bombardment to warn the defences, and the first objective was seized by G Company with no fighting. As the second objective was approached the attack went 'noisy' when the Argentine 5th Marine Infantry Battalion at last realised they were under attack.

McNeill:

> We had advanced another 300 metres. I remember starting to feel the rise in the ground like we were going up a hill. You could not tell where we were in relation to the top of Tumbledown. It felt we were near the top but, in fact, we were nowhere near. Then all hell let loose as we came under heavy sustained fire. We hit the ground, took cover and returned fire.

Kiszely remarked that the enemy 'opened up with everything they had: well-planned and well-executed.' This was Vázquez's 4 Platoon. They had engaged 15 Platoon with a considerable number of semi-automatic weapons located some 200 metres to the north on 15 Platoon's left. According to Vázquez, Left Flank had made contact with his platoon at 23.15 (02.15Z).[5] The Scots Guards War Diary [6] indicates 22.30 [7] (02.30Z). But I prefer the judgement of Vázquez who was acutely aware of the precise time while personally treating a wounded Marine.

The Guardsmen of 15 Platoon immediately took cover and then Lance-Sergeant Alan Dalgleish's section attempted an immediate attack on the enemy's eastern flank (according to Vázquez it was on the centre of his position). But the section was repulsed by heavy automatic fire. It cued the start of an accurate and intense enemy artillery and mortar bombardment which was to continue throughout the night. Kiszely:

> Once we hit the ground I found myself really with nothing to do. My radio operator was giving the contact report, the two (forward) platoon commanders were gripping their platoons, the leading section commander was already ordering his section attack and I felt pretty spare really.

I remember thinking 'what the hell am I doing here? I am redundant; I have nothing to do'. A curious feeling, but it wasn't long before things started to go wrong and casualty reports started coming in.[8]

The Left Flank Company HQ and 15 Platoon had to switch direction ninety degrees to the north in order to confront the small-arms fire raking down on them from Vázquez's platoon above. Locating enemy movement at range of 100 to 200 metres through their night sights, 15 Platoon moved into firing positions to engage them. They suffered an early fatality when Guardsman Archibald Stirling was shot in the head,[9] and Sergeant Jackson – the 15 Platoon Sergeant – received a shrapnel wound during the start of probing attacks on Vázquez's eastern flank. According to the Argentine they actually reached his position at this early stage of the battle because he 'heard the distinctive sound of a Sterling submachine-gun firing at the entrance of his foxhole and saw two Scots Guardsmen, one of whom was smoking a cigarette, passing by on each side of his position'.

Meanwhile up in the crags 13 Platoon were physically separated from the remainder of Left Flank because of the lie of the terrain. In addition enemy snipers above Stuart's platoon also began to fire accurately at them with night sights superior to the British equivalent. There were four Scots Guards casualties almost immediately. Guardsman Ronnie Tanbini was killed by multiple high-velocity gunshot wounds to the pelvis and heart, Sergeant John Simeon – the 13 Platoon Sergeant – was also mortally wounded by high-velocity gunshot wounds to the legs and chest. Lance-Corporal Eyre was also wounded, and Guardsman Shaw lost one of nine lives when a 7.62mm round hit three SLR magazines in his combat jacket breast pocket. The impact knocked Shaw backwards, but the magazines protected him from any serious injury.

Company Sergeant-Major Bill Nicol had detached himself from Company HQ at the start of the Left Flank advance and was with 13 Platoon when they came under fire. He heard Sergeant Simeon shouting out that he had been hit in the thigh. Nicol:

I went forward to try and get them (Tanbini and Simeon) back under cover. Tanbini had been shot in the back and I just could not move him. I could see Sergeant Simeon, and as I went to him the fire increased. I was shot in the hand, and forced to get back.[10]

Nicol was probably hit by the same sniper that had accounted for Tanbini and Simeon. Young Second-Lieutenant Stuart needed some expert assistance. The pillar of any British Army platoon is the Platoon Sergeant. But Stuart, fresh out of Sandhurst, had just lost his at the worst possible time – the start of a battle. Fortunately the wounded Nicol was nearby. He would be awarded the Distinguished Conduct Medal (DCM) for his overall performance during the war. A central part of its citation describes his significant contribution in resolving the challenges facing Stuart:

He remained cool and calm under heavy fire encouraging and exhorting his men and, at the same time, advising one of the young platoon commanders how to defeat a seemingly impregnable enemy position.

He remained unperturbed by the weight of small arms, artillery and mortar fire thus instilling great confidence in men who might have been frightened.[11]

It was also difficult to locate people in the darkness and noise of battle, not helped by G Company engaging 13 Platoon's right-hand section with 'friendly' 66mm anti-tank rocket fire. The Platoon began to manoeuvre themselves slowly around the rear of Vázquez's platoon …

That first day of my Tumbledown research during the Pilgrimage continued. We walked westwards from where 15 Platoon and the Left Flank Company HQ had been engaged in the initial firefight to re-trace 13 Platoon's route. Billy Silver led the way. Earlier that year Patrick Watts had also escorted Lance-Sergeant Jamie Simeon, the son of 13 Platoon's Sergeant John Simeon, to the site where it was thought his father had been killed in the battle's early stages. Jamie had laid a wreath at the appropriate spot 200 metres west of 'The Ski-Slope'. Moving past this, we climbed another 100 metres eastwards up into a twenty-metre wide rock gulley below the southern side of the north-west summit. Then Patrick produced a 1994 photograph of Major Iain Dalzel-Job, the G Company Commander, which had been taken at the place we were now standing. By aligning the photograph with various boulders in the background, Patrick discovered by chance a small wooden cross concealed under some heather. Dalzel-Job had obviously placed this cross here as a memorial to mark the correct site of where Sergeant Simeon had been mortally wounded by a sniper's bullet. Guardsman Ronnie Tanbini had also been shot and killed here.

Billy led us further on. In the battle 13 Platoon had forced the Argentine snipers further up into the rocks with 84mm high-explosive anti-tank rounds, 66mm anti-tank rockets and grenades fired from M-79 grenade launchers. At a range of fifteen metres Lance-Sergeant Ian Davidson (also a 2007 pilgrim) had shot dead with his SLR the Argentine sniper who had killed Tanbini and Simeon, and wounded Nicol. Eventually Billy pointed out to us the well-concealed firing position in a rock hide from where Davidson's victim had extracted himself. Billy also showed us where he and and Davidson, who was his Section Commander, had climbed up along a natural parapet of rock fifty metres north and behind Vázquez's platoon so as to engage the Argentines with rockets fired from the throw-away 66mm Light Anti-Tank Weapon.

'There!' Billy pointed out to me modestly. 'You can see the strike marks from the 66s' explosions that are still visible on the boulders below!'

The marks were unmistakable even from a range of forty metres. Billy became thoughtful. 'In addition to the 66s, I had been issued with 100 rounds of ammunition and four hand-grenades before the battle. At the end I had only five rounds left,' he informed me.

In addition to Davidson, Billy had been busy working his 66s with Lance-Sergeant Tam McGuinness that night. There was yet another surprise. Lying on the ground and to the parapet's rear was two of these empty 66mm canisters which Billy, Davidson and McGuiness had discarded more than twenty-five years before. I seized the chance and took a photograph of the slightly bemused former Guardsman holding one of these 66mm canisters …

Together the rifle sections of McGuiness and Davidson began dealing with the sniper threat in an effective way by employing the basic infantry tactic of fire and manoeuvre. Davidson:

> He (McGuiness) moved round to the right, while I gave covering fire, and then he did the same for me. Bit by bit we were able to flush the enemy out of his sangars, but it was slow work. Still, as long as we were going up the hill, we knew we were headed in the right direction.[12]

Moving up the rocky channel in the dark with brief bursts of firing at enemy tracer fire and muzzle flashes, this was close-quarter battle under most difficult conditions, well illustrated by Stuart's observation of a bizarre situation in which a Guardsman had taken cover under a rock overhang while an enemy sniper was on its top – with both unable to engage the other. Eventually an Argentine field telephone cable was located and the Guardsmen followed this to other sniper positions even higher up. Commanded by the impressive Army *Subteniente* (Sub-Lieutenant) Oscar Silva, there were a total of five snipers from the 4th Infantry Regiment. Before the battle he had placed himself and the five out as a line of 'stops' to protect Vázquez's rear. However aided by Nicol's firing of 13 Platoon's Carl Gustav 84mm anti-tank gun, the Left Flank platoon fought all six Argentine Army soldiers and killed five of them.[13]

Subsequently McGuiness would be awarded a MID 'for his courageous action under fire and his outstanding leadership'.[14] The draft citation provides a further detailed description of the twenty-three year-old's performance:

> During the assault Lance-Sergeant McGuinness was commanding the leading Section of his Company, when they came under accurate sniper fire. Two men were wounded. With great coolness and without regard for his own safety, he moved amongst his men encouraging and steadying them. He personally fired ten anti-tank rockets at the enemy. That done, he and his men successfully overran the enemy position.

Another MID would go to twenty-seven year-old Lance-Sergeant Davidson 'for his courage under fire and selfless leadership'.[15] The draft citation documents how well Davidson's men had worked together under his command:

> During the assault Lance-Sergeant Davidson's section became pinned down by accurate sniper enemy fire. Showing a total disregard for his own safety, Lance-Sergeant Davidson moved amongst his men encouraging and steadying them. Inspired by his courageous example, they fought their way forward and destroyed two enemy positions [...]

There had been also much confusion in the dark below that southern side of the north-west summit, exemplified by Guardsman 'Ossie' Osborn's luck in escaping injury from the shrapnel of an exploding hand-grenade thrown at him, in error, by another 13 Platoon Guardsman. Osborn then clambered over the top of 'The Ski-Slope' and jumped down, only to land on top of his surprised platoon commander.[16] But despite a nightmare start, Stuart's later MID draft citation stated that he had 'demonstrated considerable qualities of character, leadership and courage under fire' during the remainder of the battle.

His platoon had also gained a considerable foothold about 150 metres to the rear of Vázquez's platoon. But the latter were imbued with a defiant morale. Guardsman George MacKenzie, the 15 Platoon HQ radio operator, recalled a few of 4 Platoon shouting in English, 'Surrender to the superior Argentine forces!' [17] The Scots Guardsmen remained quiet. Kiszely:

> We were unable to win the firefight, and therefore unable to manoeuvre. Whenever we tried, they produced a lot of pretty accurate firepower (I believe they had rather better night-sights than us – wouldn't have been hard, would it?) [...] Where we went to ground the (enemy) directed a long period of artillery and mortar fire – which caused some casualties, and made the ears ring (and the eyes blind!).

Kiszely's task was complicated by radio communications difficulties and that his artillery FOO, Captain Nicol, had become separated from him. The Gunner was in 13 Platoon's location higher up and it took time for him to re-join Kiszely who then asked for artillery fire to be brought down on the enemy in front of 15 Platoon prior to a platoon or company attack. Disorientated, Nicol was unable to produce a safe grid reference for opening fire on the enemy positions. There were also technical problems on the gun positions which caused general gunfire inaccuracy. McNeill:

> It was then that the British artillery started to fire off line and shells landed amongst us. So they had to stop. That is when there was a sort of stalemate. We were pinned down for two hours when we engaged in small-arms fire until getting artillery and mortar support back on line.

But they would be unable to make any decisive assault until more than four hours later (not the two as McNeill had perceived). Furthermore, a combination of accurate enemy small-arms, mortar and artillery fire, and a British artillery 'rogue' gun which was not firing in parallel with the other five guns of its battery and whose shells were also exploding amongst the Guardsmen, provided more than enough challenges for Kiszely. Meanwhile Cocks and the remainder of Right Flank were waiting a few hundred metres away. They had already come under 'friendly' machine-gun fire – from G Company – as they had moved into position. Steve Cocks:

> War has distinct sounds and smells that stay with me today, the smell of cordite, blood on wet grass and human excrement. The deafening thump of mortars, artillery, naval bombardment, hand grenades, machine-guns and the shouted commands as men worked their way through the rocks towards the enemy. It was

all very confusing and all you could do was hug the ground and make yourself as small as possible in the hope that somehow this would improve your chances of not being hit.

Left Flank was having a very hard time dislodging the enemy from their objective and the Battalion attack stalled. Right Flank lay on the ground in an extended line watching the tracer arcing over our heads and hitting the rocks ahead where it ricocheted in every direction. I could glimpse bodies around me and had no idea if they were alive or dead as nobody moved. It is only now that I realise they were G Company having gone firm. Somewhere on the ground between the Battalion start line and Left Flank start line I lost my gloves, not a good omen as it was freezing.

After giving Left Flank supporting fire, G Company was also hit continually by enemy mortar and artillery fire on the rocky knoll. Folklore had it that G Company were known as 'The Rabbits' because they were the smallest in the Battalion, Companies being 'sized' in the Guards. G Company would have to use their 'rabbit' expertise by digging in during the remainder of that night as it took a total of six casualties. One unlikely Left Flank Guardsman who distinguished himself in assisting casualties already in these early stages of the battle was forty-one year-old Company clothes storeman Lance-Corporal Duncan MacColl. For 'his courage under fire, and his unselfish regard for his comrades', he was later awarded a MID.[18] Its draft citation also stated:

> Disregarding his own safety Lance-Corporal MacColl went forward to administer first aid. As he was recovering a wounded colleague, along the way he also took three enemy as prisoners. Again to the fore, continuing under heavy artillery fire, he returned to recover other wounded men.

In the rocks behind Vázquez's platoon exemplary contributions were also being made by individuals such as nineteen year-old Guardsman Jim Reynolds of 13 Platoon.[19] Killed at the end of the battle, Reynolds would receive the posthumous award of the DCM. Part of its citation read:

> During the attack, Guardsman Reynolds' Platoon came under fire from a group of enemy snipers. His Platoon Sergeant was killed instantly. A confused situation developed and his Section became separated. Guardsman Reynolds immediately took command. Having located the enemy snipers he silenced several of them himself.[19]

Another to distinguish himself in this opening phase of the battle was the experienced twenty-six year-old Lance-Sergeant Clark Mitchell who had served in the Army for a decade. He was a 15 Platoon Section Commander who had climbed up onto a large boulder and, using his cumbersome first-generation image-intensification night IWS (Individual Weapon Sight) mounted on a SLR, proceeded to engage an Argentine in a sniping dual. Below at the boulder's base, MacKenzie was trying to fix his inoperative Clansman radio set. A number of other Left Flank radio operators were similarly bedevilled with this frustrating problem. It was not discovered before as no radio check had been carried out in the final battle preparations because of a fear that the transmissions would be intercepted by the enemy, thereby warning them of an imminent attack. This meant that shouted commands in the unbelievable noise, stress and confusion of a night battle became a much-used alternative method of communication.

MacKenzie was also an eye-witness to Mitchell's steely determination. 'Clark Mitchell was the bravest man I ever knew,' MacKenzie told me twenty-seven years later. Despite many enemy bullets hitting the boulder and MacKenzie urging him to take cover, Mitchell continued to fire aimed shots at his opponent. Finally he succeeded, and for some time afterwards the mortally wounded Argentine was heard to scream for his mother.

Mitchell scrambled down from his firing point and, grabbing the radio operator's webbing, pulled him away in order to rejoin the remainder of 15 Platoon behind them. His radio set abandoned, MacKenzie subsequently had to borrow a replacement from another of the Platoon's sections. But it was so cold that his frozen hands were unable to fix the throat mike around his neck, thus continuing to make subsequent radio communications a difficult task.

Meanwhile Steve Cocks was also having an unpleasant time. Left Flank had requested stretcher bearers, so fourteen men with five stretchers were sent forward by Major Simon Price, the Right Flank Company Commander. Cocks was one of them:

> Sometime later I was called to the head of the Company and, along with others in Right Flank Echelon, went forward into no-man's land to recover some wounded from the open ground below the Argentine position. As such we dropped down slightly onto the northern slopes and out of sight of the Argentines as we heard wounded calling out to us. It turned out that the 'wounded' were actually the enemy snipers in the crags above and they kept us pinned down for what seemed hours. They mimicked the cries of wounded to tempt us to come forward, which they succeeded in doing. They were brave men. To add to our discomfort our own troops in 2 Platoon had not been told that we had gone forward so they mistook us for enemy and also started firing on us. The bullets zipped all around me and I could feel the air ripple. These were not random rounds but deliberately aimed and I just knew that I was being targetted. I just froze and hugged the ground playing dead hoping the snipers would lose interest which after a minute or so they did. I could distinctly hear the Argentines taunting us in the dark and shouting insults.
>
> While being shelled and sniped I considered praying to God to spare me. But it was more lip-service. I can honestly say that having received an upbringing in which I was told to believe in God, when it came to the crunch, I put more trust in the rock in front of me and the all-concealing night. The prayer died on my lips. God was distinctly missing from the battlefield.

To add to the confusion, Right Flank's Company HQ had fired a 66mm anti-tank rocket at Lance-Corporal Catchpole of G Company who had been firing at an enemy sniper over the heads of the Right Flank stretcher-bearer party. All this served to illustrate the tightly-packed nature of the three Scots Guards rifle companies. Less the four initial fatalities, a total of 321 men were now spread over a short distance of only 500 metres either immediately due south or, the bulk of this force, west of Vázquez's isolated platoon and its supporting 60mm mortar section. The Argentines were outnumbered by more than five to one. Sun Tzu's claim that 'defend and one has a surplus: attack and one is insufficient' could not have been more graphically illustrated.

Kiszely provided a further insight into the commander's mind at such a critical time. The paramount requirement remained to win the firefight, but lack of effective indirect fire support prevented his men from doing this:

> The rogue-gun saga went on a long time [...] during it we tried some probing attacks, but with no success [...] I had the Mortar Fire Controller with me, but our mortar fire was pathetic. I believe that of the eight mortars, most were out of action due to broken bipods on the frozen ground firing at the highest charge (for long range).[21] We could have assaulted before we had won the firefight (artillery, mortars etc), and we would probably have succeeded – but my estimate at the time (and subsequently) was that our casualties killed would have been well into double figures. Would this have been worth it? I did not, and do not, believe so. Others may disagree.

He had to make a continual appreciation of his eventual assault, and every so often conferred with Lieutenant-Colonel Mike Scott:

> When he spoke to me on the radio, Colonel Mike was calm, steady and logical, but I could tell that he was under pressure from above. I told him what was happening, what I was doing about it and that we would succeed. He said something like, 'Right, you know the urgency. You're the man on the ground and I back your judgement – but don't hang about!'
>
> I had no intention of either delaying unnecessarily or, worse, of losing patience and saying 'to hell with it, let's assault' (which, I reckon would have cost us three times our casualties before were half-way up the hill). I was picking my moment and he knew it. I drew strength from his confidence in me; and I consciously used the same tone of voice on my own radio net to my Platoon and Section Commanders.
>
> [...] The longer we hung about the more chance of being hit. There was also the problem of time because I was very aware of the fact that there was a lot to be done in the Battalion after I had seized my objective. Another Company had to go through and take the remainder of Tumbledown and then both the Gurkhas and Welsh Guards had jobs to do on Mount William and Sapper Hill, which they hoped to do in darkness, and if I took too long in doing what I was doing, it could risk them having to carry out their attack in daylight. (It) could have made the disaster at Bluff Cove (Port Pleasant) look like a vicarage tea party.[22]

However the Scots Guards Commanding Officer also had to work much of the time on the Battalion radio net through Kiszely's Company HQ radio operators; and

McNeill did not have the monopoly in that respect. Scott:

> The other Left Flank radio operator I talked a lot to was Lance-Corporal Murley [...] My abiding memory of that night in dealing with Left Flank was the unusual clarity of the radio and the confidence I had in talking to John's operators, leaving him to get on with the fighting.[23]

Scott was worried and, in his mind, began to form contingency plans of going firm if Left Flank's attack failed. Another Commanding Officer, Lieutenant-Colonel Nick Vaux of 42 Commando on Mount Harriet, became engrossed by the way in which the Scots Guards' radio transmissions were being made:

> For almost all of that night I listened in on their command net, experiencing a conflicting range of feelings as the long-drawn-out ordeal took its course. To listen as someone else directed, encouraged, supported and manoeuvred his companies was riveting [...] One impression that will never fade was the timeless, Oxford English dialogue on the Scots Guards' command net. This was quite different from the crisp, varied tones of 'Four-Two', or the parachute battalions with us. But the Guards officers spoke far more than their radio operators, and always in those measured, courteous terms. In a sense I could have been eavesdropping on the 2nd Battalion, Scots Guards advancing to an attack half a century ago. Sadly, a tape-deck to record it for posterity was not at hand.[24]

Kiszely knew that the anticipated close-quarter combat was getting closer and began to prepare. He was laconic in his later description of this activity: 'I had filled my combat jacket with about a dozen grenades (mixture of L2 grenades and white phosphorous) at the bottom (of Tumbledown). I don't remember having many left at the top'.

Meanwhile men had to endure the biting cold during this excessive wait. Kiszely:

> It started to snow and people were getting very cold. One Guardsman about ten metres from me was suddenly found to be unconscious with exposure and he was dragged away by Lance-Corporal Gary Tytler, who really bullied him back to life. I remember lying there in the snow with my signaller, Lance-Corporal Murley, a great Cockney character, absolutely shivering with cold. It really became cold then, and the sensible thing to do would have been to move closer to exchange body warmth, but propriety had the upper hand until it really became so cold that we ended up pretty well in each other's arms, and I remember Murley saying to me ''ere, sir, what they gonna think if we're both killed and they find us like this?' I couldn't help laughing.[25]

McNeill shared his Company Commander's concern:

> We had taken some casualties, both from sniper fire coming from the high ground and hypothermia. I was lying beside Kiszely as I had the Battalion net on my radio.

We were starting to come under some pressure to get a move on.

Then I received confirmation that the guns and mortars were back on line and informed Kiszely.

He asked for three salvos of artillery fire for effect.

When they arrived, both the Company Commander and 15 Platoon Commander were looking at me.

I heard on the radio that the fire mission was over.

It was then Lieutenant Mitchell who asked me anxiously, 'Is that really the last one?'

'Yes,' I replied.

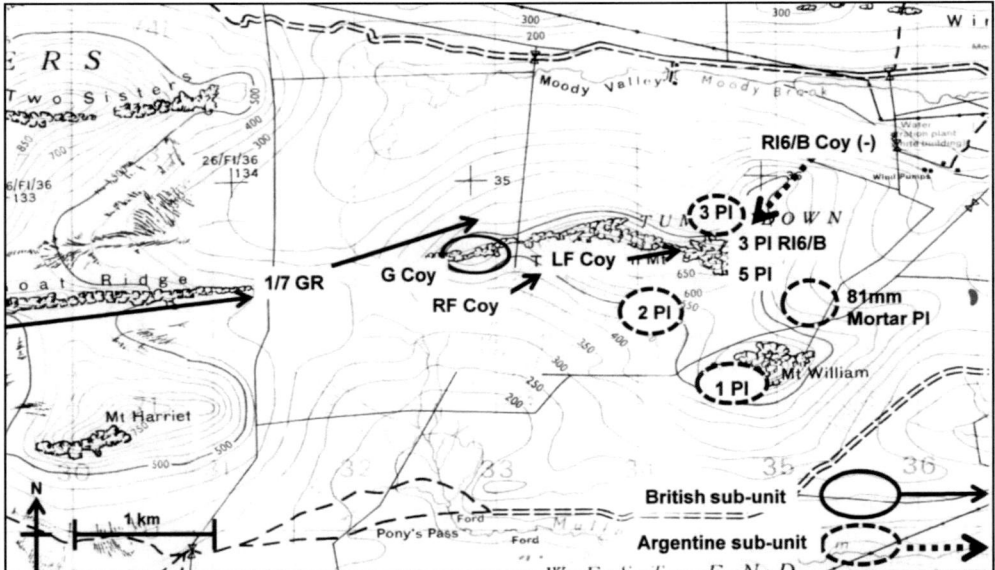

Map 3 (08.00Z-10.00Z) – Left Flank Company (2SG) assaults 4 Platoon (BIM5) and advances east to take the east summit. RI6/B Company (-) advances up the north-east spur. 1/7GR advances along Tumbledown's northern slopes.

Kiszely's battle plan was simple. With 13 Platoon providing covering fire onto the rear of the enemy platoon, 14 Platoon would move up to 15 Platoon's positions while the latter assaulted supported by Company HQ. The latter's resources would be needed because, in the dark, Lieutenant Mitchell had been only able to gather together slightly less than half his platoon for the final assault. Kiszely had told Mitchell to 'put in a platoon attack on the first ridge two or three hundred yards ahead of us'.[26] The reconstructed Scots Guards War Diary mentions 02.30 (06.30Z) [27] when this was initiated. But Kiszely recalled: 'So there we were lying there with all the shit coming in, all this artillery, until eventually [...] the rounds at last registered on target.' [28] He added that this occurred 'with two hours of darkness left'.[29]

Showtime had arrived. McNeill:

Company HQ was in the centre when Kiszely gave the command, 'Prepare to move!'

And then, 'Charge!'

But Kiszely and I had gone only about five to six paces when we realised that it was only us two who had moved forward.

So Kiszely had to shout again, 'Are you with me, Left Flank?'

Silence.

Then came a reply from the right (15 Platoon), 'Aye sir, I'm fucking with you!'

And that was it. We were off and running.

The previous near-six hours of relative inertia had come to an end at last. The radio operator would be awed by his officer's up-front leadership that would also demand from McNeill the daunting job of attempting to follow closely in Kiszely's slipstream. The latter's actions that night would earn him a Military Cross (MC) with part of its citation stating 'his outstanding leadership and heroic example was an inspiration to his men. His courage under fire was of a most exceptionally high order.' [30] This was 'I do, you do' leadership under terrifying circumstances. McNeill:

Then the momentum started as we began the charge forward.

Where's all the high-tech weapons then? I thought, this is like the Battle of Ypres and going over the top in the First World War!

There was also fear to overcome; not a fear of the enemy, but of being unable to go forward and letting others down. Nothing happened for a few seconds, but then all hell let loose. It was not very co-ordinated as individual small-arm battles were taking place. You could not see very well, i.e. it was not until you were almost upon them that you realised there was a sangar or foxhole there.

Kiszely explained:

Once we started moving, things moved pretty quickly. I would guess half an hour [...] although it seemed like about half an hour, it could have easily been longer [...] It was a 'charge' only in as much as it did not lose momentum. Yes, there were small individual actions and 'pepper-potting', and very brief moments to re-organise, but it was continuous.

Vázquez had calculated that 08.00Z was a probable start time for the final phase of his battle with Left Flank. It must have been shortly afterwards that 15 Platoon and Company HQ had made their decisive move northwards. Kiszely soon reached an enemy foxhole on this lower part of the hill. He had been firing his SLR but now, on pressing the trigger at the vital moment, experienced only the proverbial 'dead-man's click' instead of a round fired at a target. His magazine, which had contained twenty rounds, was empty. With no time to change magazines, Kiszely was forced to use his bayonet. According to McNeill, his Company Commander's action 'was the first that I had seen using his bayonet', but the radio operator would also soon become directly involved in the grim realities of such close-quarter combat.

Company HQ and 15 Platoon continued upwards side by side in an exceptionally ragged version of an extended line. They had completed the first 300 metres when Kiszely spotted 'this next ridge about two or three hundred metres up, with no activity on it (and) thought "Hell, if we can get up there, that's another ridge taken"' but admitted that he 'started rather over-involving myself in the platoon's battle and got the ones nearest to me by shouting at them and grabbing them, saying, "Come on!" But only about a dozen heard me.' [31]

The first to respond positively to this next stage of the Company Commander's inspired charge northwards to the top of the hill, and then along an eastern route up to Tumbledown's 750-foot high east summit, was MacKenzie – despite having fired all his SMG ammunition. Kiszely ran 'on to the next ridge only to find myself totally alone because those who were coming on had either lost direction or were going other places [...] but eventually in ones and twos they found me'.[32]

However McNeill presents a slightly different picture of what happened at that stage in the pitch dark as Company HQ tried, during the charge upwards, to keep pace with their fast-moving Company Commander who 'on occasions [...] found myself alone – albeit not for long':

Although the situation became disorientated, a few from Company HQ including myself, accompanied him. We were running up the hill clearing sangars and firing from the hip, but not really skirmishing. The whole climb was more a quick advance which lasted in total a maximum of thirty to forty-five minutes. I was still slightly on Kiszely's right as access to the radio was on my left, his right. It was about half-way up that we became separated. Everybody else continued to follow him. However with about four or five other Guardsmen, I had come across a sangar in which appeared to be three enemy standing in a normal firing position. One of them appeared to have some sort of rank because he possessed a side arm. I shouted down to the Guardsmen with me as I was trying to focus through the darkness. Two of them and I were trying to take these enemy prisoner, but one fired at us and wounded one of the Guardsmen with me.

So I yelled, 'Fire!' and fired two rounds from my SLR in a kneeling position at a range of twenty to thirty feet.

I can see it now as if it was yesterday. I hit an Argentine straight in the head. After a few seconds the body slumped forward against the front of his firing position.

How could I see all this clearly?

All the NCOs had been given twenty rounds of tracer, so the first four rounds in each of my magazines were tracer. Although the round hit the target so quickly, there must have been some remaining burn-time of the tracer phosphorous because the front of the Argentine's face had become illuminated in a reddish-orange dull light. There were some tiny flames around his head area and the latter seemed to glow as it took on a ghostly Halloween Jack-o-lantern appearance, except this was no hollowed-out pumpkin.[33] Being only feet away, I could clearly see his face and eyes which were open and looking right at me. Even the bullet entry hole in his forehead was visible. Post-war that face and the expression on it have become very familiar. They visit me nearly every night.

We quickly overpowered the other two enemy; only to find two more lying in the bottom of the sangar. They had given up soldiering. During this I noticed the exit wound in the rear of the dead Argentine's head. It was not pretty. A good proportion of the back of his head had been blown off and some of his brain matter was hanging out.

After the sangar was cleared, I set out to catch up with Kiszely while the wounded Guardsman began to receive first aid from someone.

McNeill then managed to re-join Kiszely at the next ridge and began to advance again up the hill. The enemy were conducting a mobile defence and withdrawing from foxhole to foxhole up the hill. So grenades had to be used frequently to clear these positions. Kiszely was to the fore with a white phosphorous grenade. Rifle fire was so heavy that, at one stage of the battle, McNeill picked up a discarded enemy FAL rifle[34] and fired it instead of his SLR in order to conserve the latter's ammunition. Those from 15 Platoon who participated in the assault were on the Company HQ's right. McNeill:

> I was now with two Guardsmen. Kiszely was to my left. I remember breathing hard, so it must have started to get steeper. Then I heard my name being called out by Kiszely who was some distance away.
>
> 'Shit, they now know my name!' I thought, as if that mattered.
>
> As I ran up to re-join him, there was a foxhole on my right. Another one of the Guardsmen with me fired into it. To be honest we received very little resistance. I just fired and did not stop running. Then I got to Kiszely and crouched down beside him behind some rocks.

It must have been just before 09.00Z. Not unsurprisingly in the heat of battle and pitch dark, Kiszely did not recognise McNeill as the Guardsman next to him. The latter had only been with the Company for only a handful of hours which was certainly not enough time for Kiszely to be acquainted with him properly. However the ever-faithful McNeill was 'without doubt' that he had caught up with his boss, ready for the next task. Unfamiliar with the art of grenade-throwing, the Battalion net rear-link radio operator was, nonetheless, about to become directly involved with his Company Commander's plan. McNeill:

> Pointing, Kiszely said, 'Look!'
>
> About ten metres in front of us were two enemy sangars some metres apart. A short burst of automatic fire came from them.[35]
>
> He handed me a grenade and said, 'You take the right one. I'll take the left.'
>
> It was difficult to make out the enemy in the dark. My grenade was the high explosive one, a Mills L2 shaped like a pineapple.
>
> Kiszely then asked, 'Ready?'
>
> 'Yes,' I replied.
>
> We pulled the pins and shouted 'Grenade!'
>
> Kiszely threw a white phosphorous grenade which landed smack bang in the

middle of his sangar.

While throwing mine I thought, don't fuck this up. Make sure you get it right! But of course my grenade landed about a foot short – and just rolled into the right sangar.

There were two detonations – and then Kiszely shouted, 'Charge!'

We got up and, with each accompanied by a Guardsman, began to run forward and fire from the hip. It was then that the Commanding Officer, Mike Scott, asked for a sitrep (situation report). I rather bluntly told him he would have to 'fucking wait'. We had a good laugh about that when we met in London for the Twenty-Fifth Anniversary Parade. Out of the corner of my left eye I saw the Company Commander with one or two others arrive at their enemy position. I never saw anybody running away from it. Three enemy were in front of me and I did not see any leave their position. If they did, they must have been quick because we got to the sangar almost immediately.

The Argie in the middle of the three was leaning motionless against the front of it. He had been killed either by the grenade or from the rounds we had fired during the attack.

I pressed my SLR trigger again, but got the dead-man's click.

My magazine was empty.

And here is another demon. That was when the bayoneting started. In fact I used my bayonet automatically. I do not know if this was instinct dictated by fear. Or that point in the battle when I lost all form of humanity. Or that my Army training had enabled me to do this. Or that I had witnessed my Company Commander doing it earlier. I simply do not know. In one way it was sort of alright, if that makes any sense. But I cannot deny that this was by far the worst experience of my life. Christ, I still feel the sensation of the bayonet going in, rather like trying to stick a knife into an orange, before hearing another person scream and watch him die in front of you. Although this only lasted seconds, the images will stay with me until the day I die – especially when the next one in that trench appeared so young.

I was about to do it to him when this Marine, with both arms held aloft above his head, looked straight into my eyes.

He was crying.

His youth and tears jolted me back into reality and start of normality. It was like coming out of a trance. After my first real enemy encounter where we had been shot at when trying to take prisoners, I had become like an animal, shooting first and asking questions later. But after the shooting, bayoneting and blowing up people and starting to get a buzz, I had suddenly now become a human again. It was a really surreal moment. I am not a religious fanatic and have questioned many times since why God put us through all that. But there was something strange about this, almost as if it were a type of divine intervention.

Why did I not just bayonet him like the other I had just done before?

Why did I pause as we looked at each other?

Why did I return to some sort of normality?

I don't know.

Then I pulled this young man from his sangar.

He fell over.

I dragged him to his feet again.

He fell again.

Cheeky bastard, I thought and kicked him. I let you live a minute ago, and now you're fucking about – plus I haven't got time for this shit!

My next thought was, I'll just kill him and keep moving on.

At that point I noticed that he kept both arms aloft, even after he had fallen. It seemed as though he was scared to move them in case I might misinterpret this as something threatening and so take the appropriate action. He never moaned, cried out in pain or said anything. He was just crying and in deep shock. It was then I noticed the black burning flesh and that, from above the knee and below, his right leg was missing.

All that remained of it was just that burning black right thigh stump.

And that smell of burning flesh was awful.

I assumed the grenade blast had blown off the missing part of his leg. However I never saw that happening. The 'amputation' could also have been caused by an exploding mortar bomb, but more likely by the grenade. I did not see blood spurting out everywhere like a fountain. With my limited night vision his charred leg was a sort of deep-black and it looked wet.[36]

My subsequent 'bandage action' would have failed the St John's Ambulance First Aid Test. I simply tied some sort of a scarf he had on him around the thigh stump. This took little more than thirty seconds. He was only a boy and definitely still alive. If he had got to our RAP and, given the good survival rate of casualties, it would be satisfying to think he had then made it home.

But there was no time to hang about. I had to hurry and catch up with Kiszely who was further up the hill. So I yelled, 'Prisoner!'

As I got up again, there was a shout in the distance of 'Keep Going Left Flank!' Maybe that was Kiszely. Everything had happened so quickly – but that black right thigh stump and burning smell have also been frequent visitors to me at night during all these years since.

One Guardsman who could have been involved later in stabilising this Argentine was 'Piper Rodgers, the Company Medic, (who) worked ceaselessly throughout the night and treated all the casualties'.[37] He would receive a Commander-in-Chief Fleet Commendation.

The estranged rear-link radio operator cum Good Samaritan hurried in his attempt to re-join Kiszely. But after only a short distance McNeill stopped:

Out of the corner of my eye I suddenly noticed on my right a large foxhole with some rocks and peat built up at the front, probably for a better firing position. It was ten to twenty metres on, and slightly behind, the position I had just attacked. This foxhole's entrance was close by me. There were two Argentines inside.

I hit the deck and shouted, 'Get down!'

Then for some reason I tried to get them to surrender by bellowing out a few Spanish words taught to us on board *QE2* during the voyage south. These were

'Mana surreba un zendo prisonaro!'or something like that.[38]

They shouted back at me. But what were they saying? So pointing my SLR and ready to fire, I yelled this time in English, 'Get out! Hands up!'

Perhaps that mysterious moment which prevented me from bayoneting the young Marine whose leg I had just blown off also accounted for my *not* firing two rounds into the first enemy to exit. I have no explanation other than to wonder if both these incidents were spiritually linked somehow. He was extremely lucky because I did not know what this Argentine was trying to do. He did not carry a rifle and had not raised his arms. So it was unclear if he was surrendering. To this day I cannot understand why I tried to talk to him rather than opening fire first. It was stupid. But fate was with us both that night. Now, I am really glad. (Mike, if you ever speak to him, tell him I am asking after him and hope he is alright.)

Smarter than the rest with better-looking gear, he appeared calm and in control, compared to the rest who were not. He talked differently than the others and, without being offensive, had a slight touch of arrogance. I knew in my own mind that this prisoner was Vázquez, even though I did not know his name at the time.

Then he said to me in English, 'I am the commander of this unit of Argentine soldiers. I have told my men to surrender.'

He looked every part the commander, but I bawled at him, 'No you fucking haven't! They're still firing at us!'

I pulled him down onto the ground, and then shouted at the foxhole opening, 'Get out now or I fire!'

The second Argentine joined me as two other Guardsmen from 15 Platoon came by. I told one of them to search the foxhole, and the other to frisk the second prisoner. Yet another Argentine was found hiding in the bottom of the foxhole. Dressed like Vázquez in newer and cleaner kit, he came out crying and shaking like a total wreck. There was no spare rifle in the foxhole. Meanwhile I searched my first prisoner.

He informed me immediately, 'I have a pistol and grenade on me.'

I found the pistol in his parka jacket pocket. It was a Colt .45 semi-automatic. In his combat trouser side pocket was the grenade.

Shit! I flapped to myself, he's a suicide bomber! [39]

When I took the grenade out several other worries crossed my mind. It's been primed! Seen nothing like this before! Don't know how it works! Therefore don't take any chances, McNeill!

So I threw it away in the darkness.

By then the three prisoners were lying in a row. I told them to put their hands on their heads and sit. Then I ordered one of the Guardsmen to stay and hand them over to the prisoner collection party of Lance-Corporal Alec Galloway.
. The other was to follow me. We had been at Vázquez's foxhole only for about a minute, so things were happening fast. As we moved off I tried to clear the Colt pistol of ammunition but, in the stress of the moment, there was a loud bang from the weapon.

My negligent discharge in the battle caused real panic.

The Guardsman with me hit the deck.

The shell-shocked prisoner moaned.

'Okay! Okay! It's only me! False alarm!' I yelled.

Then we two ran off towards the east so as to catch up with the Company Commander who was still some distance away.

In the heat of battle the latter was still unaware of what challenges his radio operator had been confronted with during the charge up the hill. It must have been just after 09.00Z. About eight enemy had been killed in the assault. Another part of Kiszely's MC citation summarised his involvement so far:

> Under fire and with a complete disregard for his own safety, he led a group of his men up a gully towards the enemy. Despite men falling wounded beside him he continued his charge, throwing grenades as he went. Arriving on the enemy position he killed two enemy with his rifle and a third with his bayonet. His courageous action forced the surrender of the remainder. His was the outstanding action in the Battalion successfully seizing its objective.[40]

Others like Lance-Sergeant Dalgleish and Lance-Corporal Gary Tytler, both of 15 Platoon, had also distinguished themselves in the assault. Each would be awarded a MID for their leadership and courage: with Tytler 'personally killing several enemy in their trenches'. Also nineteen year-old Guardsman Gary Brown of 15 Platoon was a recipient of this decoration 'for his fine example and bravery in action'. Audie Murphy might have been proud of Brown's MID draft citation:

> During the assault, Guardsman Brown's section became involved in a fierce fire fight. Disregarding his own safety, with considerable coolness he exposed himself to enemy fire and, using his machine-gun with devastating effect, killed several of the enemy. Inspired by his example, his Section fought their way through the enemy's position ...[41]

Back on the Pilgrimage we climbed higher onto Tumbledown's west summit and came across 5 Platoon's command post just as Miño had described to me in Buenos Aires seven months before. The position was virtually impregnable and had an excellent view to the west towards G Company's rocky knoll, along Moody Valley and, to the north, Wireless Ridge where 2 Para had fought their second battle of the war on the same night as the Tumbledown battle. There were also the remains of rusting iron pickets used to support overhead cover. Fifty metres east was the still intact artillery observation post of the artillery FOO Midshipman Marcelo Demarco with its built-up rock walls and two small viewing slits. Below this on the northern slopes had been located the remainder of Miño's platoon. They had all withdrawn at about 23.30 (02.30Z) to the N Company administrative area 1.5 kilometres away on the Tumbledown's eastern end,[42] leaving Left Flank to fight against forty-five Argentine combatants on the western end of the Tumbledown. Left Flank had outnumbered them by nearly three to one, thereby complying with this fundamental textbook tactical requirement for an attacking force. It also runs counter to previous official assumptions that the Scots Guards themselves had been outnumbered.

Our small party of pilgrims also continued to walk slowly along the difficult rock-strew and tufted grass ground in the direction of the eastern end where the Scots Guards' imposing iron Memorial Cross had been erected a month after the war. We were not far from the route up which Simon McNeill, the 'tail-end Charlie' of the small Scots Guards group which had been whittled down from twelve to seven men, had climbed up towards Tumbledown's east summit more than a quarter of a century before in the war ...

At that time Steve Cocks realised Right Flank's turn to enter the battle proper was fast approaching:

> After what seemed hours Left Flank were able to get some momentum going in their attack. I watched the British frigates HM Ships *Active* and *Yarmouth* on the gun line. You would see a series of flickers and then hear an incredible rushing sound as shells headed towards the Argentine positions. Then the whole mountain would quiver as they landed, gouging great holes into the earth. We eventually got the order to move up and, as we did so, mortar bombs starting to land around us and we were all showered with bits of gravel and hot shrapnel. Luckily none of us were hit but it was very disconcerting as the rounds were landing no more than four to five metres away at times. All that saved us was the soft ground as the mortars buried themselves deep before exploding.

And McNeill was also worried:

> At last I re-joined Kiszely after lagging about twenty or thirty metres behind him. Previously I had been at his side for most of the night. So that distance was quite significant. The Signal Detachment Commander must always stay close to the Company Commander. In peacetime I could have got a bollocking if not having strong reasons for being near him. I had been reasonably successful at that all night, apart from those specific reasons for becoming separated, e.g. when shooting the Argentine and capturing Vázquez.

They were all in extended line, but moving diagonally. The four on the left, including McNeill, were slowed by the steeper terrain near the high rocks. Those on the right got slightly ahead by advancing more quickly over easier going that had less cover. They swung around the rocks – and came under immediate fire as McNeill described:

> On reaching what was thought to be near the top but which was, in fact, the final false summit, we immediately came under sustained machine-gun fire from short range. The poor guys in the group ahead on the right were seen first and took the majority of fire on the initial burst as well as grenades thrown simultaneously.

According to Kiszely 'both Lance-Sergeant Mitchell and Guardsman Binnie had been hit near the bottom of the hill'. The latter was hit in his cheek by a bullet which exited from his arm. Mitchell was hit in the stomach and spine by a high-velocity bullet.

Ironically the two Guardsmen were best friends. Mitchell died in the arms of Guardsman Mick Boyes who had been trying to apply a field dressing to the latter's wound.[43]

Mitchell's 'courageous action under fire and inspiring leadership' gained him a posthumous MID: [44] however its draft citation did not match the enormity of his battle achievements:

> During the assault he personally located and killed several enemy snipers. Thereafter as he led his Section against an entrenched position, he accounted for several enemy with his rifle and grenades. A short while later, again to the fore in the assault, he was killed.

In search of a medic for Mitchell, MacKenzie ran back at least 300 metres towards the remainder of Left Flank. But at the first ridge east of Vázquez's main position which Kiszely's small group had 'sorted out three or four sangars that were there',[45] MacKenzie was stopped in his tracks by the sight of an Argentine climbing out of a foxhole and wandering towards him. Still in possession of his SMG which had empty ammunition magazines, the Scotsman decided this time that discretion was the better part of valour and promptly retreated. However the Argentine was then shot dead by Guardsman Stevie Regan.

But despite MacKenzie hearing Boyes shout of, 'He's dead!' which provided the grim news about Mitchell, he never found the location of Boyes, Mitchell or Binnie again in the dark and noise of battle. Instead he stumbled into his Company Commander. Three Guardsmen were detailed to tend Binnie and guard the few Argentines who had been taken prisoner because Kiszely had found a field telephone cable which would lead the depleted group of seven onto a third ridge before reaching their designated limit of exploitation: the east summit.

He noted that 'We arrived just before first light'. Below and four kilometres in the distance, they were mesmerized by the street lights of Stanley momentarily.[46] A curfew and black-out for the buildings was still in force, but the roads were icy and dangerous. The Argentines were transporting their casualties back from Wireless Ridge by truck, and they switched on the lights only to enable them see where they were driving.

In the burst of machine-gun fire aimed at them that followed, Kiszely had better luck than Mitchell and Binnie:

> A bullet went through my bayonet scabbard (which sits in the bottom drawer of my desk, as I write), and entered my prismatic compass (which is in the Guards Museum). I was aware at the time that a bullet had passed close to my left ear (which 'popped') but it was only afterwards that someone spotted the bullet holes and pointed them out to me.[47] This close shave happened [...] when I went on to the forward slope and went to ground. Some machine-gunner took advantage of my stupidity, and I was very lucky not to pay the price [...] just after I (or my equipment) was hit [...] Lieutenant Mitchell and Boyes were hit (Mitchell in the thigh; and Boyes badly in both legs).

McNeill thought there were several guns firing. He described the next few minutes:

> We hit the deck, crawled to cover and returned fire at the point of contact, but did not receive any back. I did not actually see where it was coming from, except it was in front of us because rounds were zipping past and hitting the ground around us all. I remember returning fire and being ordered, 'Keep going! Keep the momentum going!'
>
> About fifteen to twenty seconds and twenty-five metres later we were on the ledge looking down on Stanley. I remember lying on these flat rocks with Kiszely and a couple of others including Chris Murley, my Signals Detachment 2IC. There were rocks on either side, with quite a big drop down on the left hand side. Then it funnels in and flattens out, and stays fairly flat all the way to the end of Tumbledown. We did not go through onto the flat section. It was not until I returned to the Falklands on the Pilgrimage that I realised we were lying not far, but probably more than 300 metres, from where the Memorial Cross is located and looking at Stanley slightly to the left (if the cross is at twelve o'clock, we were looking from eleven o'clock). For twenty-five years, I thought we were at the eastern end of Tumbledown. 'Three false summits,' were Kiszely's words, I think.

Kiszely returned fire and set about giving first aid. Mitchell had been hit in the shoulder and both legs. He put his 'right hand down to touch my leg and two of my fingers went in up to the knuckles'.[48] But at the time Mitchell was unaware, like Kiszely who bandaged this leg with lesser wounds, that his left leg had also been hit and 'was completely riddled.'[49] The third casualty was Lance-Corporal Rickie Crookdake who, according to MacKenzie, had two of his fingers shot off.[50] The force of the bullet strike had spun Crookdake around.[51] All had been hit from a range of 125 metres by this enemy machine-gun and other weapons that covered the main approach to the eastern part of Tumbledown. Kiszely was acutely aware of his small group's vulnerability:

> Three of the remaining four of us were looking after the casualties, which left really one man who was fully alert to the enemy threat and I think if the counter-attack, even if it had been two or three men in an *ad hoc* group with a Corporal leading them, would have succeeded then.[52]

MacKenzie was ordered to guard the other six, then he informed Kiszely that he had no ammunition It was then the surprised Company Commander observed that 'He had an SMG, all the others had SLRs.' Running out of ammunition at the bottom of the hill, the 15 Platoon radio operator had loyally and extraordinarily participated in the charge without any possibility of defending himself. Kiszely and MacKenzie then swapped weapons because of the threatening enemy activity below them.[53] McNeill:

> We could see the Argentines re-grouping and ready for a counter-attack. There seemed an awful lot of them. The wounded were lying on the right under cover. We others were in another group close by. As we lay looking over the ridge Kiszely told us, 'Look! There's Stanley right in front of us. Those lights are Port Stanley!'

He patted my back while exclaiming, 'Well done! Well done!' and seemed to be getting quite emotional for someone not known to show his feelings. Then we carried out a hurried ammo count that included the SLR magazines of those wounded. People were calling things such as 'I've got half a mag left!' 'About sixteen rounds!

I had only three magazines, one of which was on my SLR. Both magazines in my pouch were empty. The other two I had thrown away after changing them for full ones during the charge. I took off the magazine on my SLR. By sticking a finger into the top of the magazine which was quite light in weight, I estimated there were only about five or six rounds remaining. In total we had about sixty-five to no more than 100 rounds on us.

Shit, I thought, if they charge us, now we're fucked! (Pardon my French).

Kiszely recalled that 'although we were not flush with ammunition, we were not at panic stations'. Nonetheless there was an ammunition shortage, as the tale of MacKenzie's SMG has also shown. Published thirteen years later, the next volume of the Scots Guards History of the Regiment held a contrary view on the Battalion's ammunition distribution to tackle the challenges of that dark night on Tumbledown. But its statement that 'every man finally went into battle with more than enough ammunition to enable him to do what was required' did not match reality.[54]

So in the event of an immediate enemy counter-attack on the east summit, how could Kiszely and his half-dozen unscathed and wounded Guardsmen defend it?

Notes

1. *The Art of War*, Chapter 4 – Form.
2. Sterling submachine-gun (SMG) – British-manufactured 9mm submachine-gun with a folding shoulder stock. The weapon's curved box magazine contained thirty-four 9mm calibre rounds.
3. SLR – the British Army's then standard-issue 7.62mm L1A1 Self-Loading Rifle.
4. E-mail dated 25 January.
5. During hostilities the Argentines fought in Falklands local or Whisky time. This was three hours behind the British Task Force which fought in GMT (Greenwich Mean Time) or Zulu time. Throughout the narrative all timings are in Zulu time.
6. However there was no contemporaneous Scots Guards War Diary because the Adjutant, Captain Mark Bullough, dropped his Filofax where his diary notes were recorded. It was never found again and its notes would be reconstructed from memory later (from an e-mail dated 6 August 2009 sent by Mike Scott). Scots Guards regimental 'in-house' documentation about the battle is frustratingly limited. The twenty-one page official war diary (Army Form C 2118) titled *Commander's Diary Narrative*, dated 7 May – 10 August 1982 contains only one page devoted to the Tumbledown fighting. A more detailed account was written for a Scots Guards briefing given to the UK Staff College at Camberley on 26

May 1983, with nine of its seventeen pages describing 'The Battle for Mount Tumbledown'. Another account of the battle covering twenty-four pages was also included by Charles Messenger in a draft manuscript for a Scots Guards regimental book never published. The 284-page Regimental History, *Among Friends: The Scots Guards 1956-1993* contained only a most disappointing four and a half pages about the battle's actual fighting.

7. As does *Razor's Edge* (p. 294). This was British Summer Time – four hours ahead of Falklands' local time.

8. From the Charles Messenger unpublished draft manuscript of the battle.

9. In *Razor's Edge* (p. 290 – lower map) the site where Stirling fell is incorrectly marked. In reality this was another 300 metres further to the east.

10. From the Charles Messenger unpublished draft manuscript of the battle.

11. Supplement to *The London Gazette* of Friday, 8 October 1982. Issue 49134, p. 12848.

12. From the Charles Messenger unpublished draft manuscript of the battle.

13. However *Razor's Edge* (p. 294) incorrectly states that 13 Platoon had 'ran forward to hook around Miño's northern flank, only to run into accurate rifle fire, possibly from Lucero's platoon'. This did not happen. The accompanying map and photo diagram (pp. 290 and 291) also incorrectly marked the location of the Argentine Marine 3 Platoon commanded by *Suboficial Segundo* (Second Petty Officer) Luis Jorge Lucero. The author met the latter in Buenos Aires on 25 March 2007. His platoon was not on the north-west slopes of Tumbledown, but 1.5 kilometres away and (in Eduardo Villarraza's words) 'very near the highest point on the most easterly side of Tumbledown and on a slope facing north so there could be a complete deployment of their forces facing west and covering Moody Valley with their weapons'.

14. Provoked by *Razor's Edge* (p. 298) claim that McGuinness, two other Lance-Sergeants and a platoon commander had received 'nothing' for their efforts and other comments about MoD medal 'kindergarten reasoning', the author tracked down (at the end of 2009) all the Scots Guards Battle of Tumbledown 'Recommendation(s) for Decoration, Mention in Dispatches Form S1603 (Revised 4/81)' held at the National Archives in Kew, London via the Scots Guards Regimental Archives and Ministry of Defence. The recommendations included a concise description of all the battlefield circumstances which the potential recipient had faced. This 'pen picture' provided the reason for making the MID award and was, in effect, a draft for the formal decoration citation. All the MID citations which appear in Chapters 3 and 4, and some in Chapter 5, are this 'draft citation' version. These recommendations were processed extremely rapidly through the system. All were signed by Lieutenant-General Sir Richard Trant, Land Deputy Commander-in-Chief Fleet on 7 July 1982 (little more than three weeks after the battle) and Admiral John Fieldhouse, CTF317 (the Task Force Commander). It would appear that if potential MID recipients had been forgotten, then no second chance existed of submitting more recommendations afterwards.

15. And, once again, contrary to the claim in *Razor's Edge* (p. 298) that Davidson had received 'nothing'.

16. The detail of this confused situation was provided by Osborn to the author during the *Uganda* twenty-fifth anniversary reunion at Southampton on 20 April 2008.

17. Like Kiszely, MacKenzie did not participate in the Pilgrimage. But later Kiszely gave me the telephone number of MacKenzie who is now a hotel owner in Scotland. This and other information from the former 15 Platoon HQ radio operator came from a series of telephone conversations that the author had with him on 17 and 27 May, and 31 July 2009.

18. MacColl's MID would be one of thirteen awarded to Scots Guardsmen in the battle. The recommendations for all these awards were made three weeks afterwards on 7 July.

19. *Razor's Edge* (p. 295) contrived to place the Guardsman in 15 Platoon

20. Supplement to *The London Gazette* of Friday, 8 October 1982. Issue 49134, p. 12848.

21. In fact there were a total of ten 81mm mortars in support of the Left Flank Company attack. Six were manned by the Scots Guards and four by the Gurkhas. In addition the mortar baseplates cracked and there were appalling sinkage problems as the recoil of fired mortar bombs forced the mortar 'tubes' down into the soft peat ground. From a total of six 81mm mortars only one remained operable. This had to be taken out of action frequently and re-positioned before another mortar bomb could be fired from it. The adjacent four Gurkha 81mm mortars experienced the same fate, and also only one of these was operable at the end of the battle.

22. From the Charles Messenger unpublished draft manuscript of the battle.

23. E-mail dated 17 March 2005.

24. *March to the South Atlantic: 42 Commando Royal Marines in the Falklands War*, pp. 194-95.

25. From the Charles Messenger unpublished draft manuscript of the battle.

26. *Above All, Courage*, p. 400.

27. *Razor's Edge* (p. 295) incorrectly states 02.00 (06.00Z).

28. *Above All, Courage*, p. 400.

29. *Ibid.* Kiszely gave a time modification to the author of 'a few hours'. However the author has retained the original 'two hours' because this corresponds with Vázquez's perception of when Left Flank's 'charge' began.

30. Supplement to *The London Gazette* of Friday, 8 October 1982. Issue 49134, p. 12847.

31. *Above All, Courage*, p. 401.

32. *Ibid.*

33. McNeill's description of such a visual phenomena after the relatively rare occurrence of a high-velocity 7.62mm tracer round hitting a human head at such short range was confirmed as being accurate by retired Norwegian Army Lieutenant-Colonel and disaster psychiatrist Pål Herlofsen during a telephone conversation with the author on 17 January 2012. The glow on the dead Argentine's face would have been enhanced by the night's darkness. Post-war, McNeill has experienced continual problems in attempting to describe this

bizarre effect and, as a result, people have had difficulty in understanding it.

34. FAL – *Fusil Automático Liviano*. The Argentine Marine and Army standard-issue 7.62mm self-loading light automatic assault rifle.

35. This automatic fire probably came from a FAP (*Fusil Automático Pesado*) – a heavy automatic (assault) rifle which had a bipod attached to the barrel end and a reinforced chamber for maintaining a heavier rate of fire.

36. This consequence of a Mills L2 hand-grenade exploding in such close proximity to its target was confirmed as being correct during the same telephone conversation at Note 33. McNeill's description of the 'burning black right thigh stump' was also confirmed as being accurate. The blast and resulting concussion would not only have blown off the leg, but also have caused shock, shrapnel wounds to the upper body and, most likely, internal bleeding. The left leg would have been protected to a degree from the blast against the amputated right leg, and the latter's femoral artery would have been severed. Blood from this is extremely dark red in colour and cannot be seen on a dark night. The austral winter climate gave a decided advantage to the possibility of survival because the sub-zero temperature would have slowed down the blood flow considerably.

37. Scots Guards briefing given to the UK Staff College at Camberley on 26 May 1983.

38. The correct Spanish (military) expression is '*Manos arriba! Ríndase!* (Up with your hands and give up!)'

39. It was tempting for the author to believe that McNeill's prisoner was Vázquez. But was he? There were two puzzling facts that conflicted. A lengthy e-mail sent to the author (via Eduardo Gerding) from Vázquez in 2007 containing a detailed account of the battle from his perspective indicated that the latter had held out until nearly first light at 10.00Z. And surely only officers were those armed with side arms? In April 2008 the author asked for clarification (via Eduardo Gerding again) from Commander Eduardo Villarraza who, as a *Teniente de Navío* (Naval Lieutenant), was the N Company Commander directing the Argentine defenders in the Tumbledown battle. He replied (e-mail dated 11 April 2008):

    I had a communication with Vázquez at 06.00 (09.00Z) and it was then that he told me that he could resist no longer and was going to surrender [...] It is true that officers were armed with a Colt pistol, but we were not the only ones as the Petty Officers, Corporals and conscripts used them too. I cannot recall how many of 4 Platoon carried those guns.

    This gave a much more accurate fix on the time, but the ubiquitous nature of the Colt .45 pistol in N Company was of no help at all – until McNeill explained later:

    I believe this was Vázquez's foxhole [...] Now I have absolutely no idea of timings. I never looked at my watch all night. (I can confirm though that it was no more than forty minutes or so when Kiszely and I reached the top of the Tumbledown ridgeline. Arriving there we could see Stanley below at first light.)

    At last this was confirmation that McNeill's prisoner had been indeed Vázquez.

40. Supplement to *The London Gazette* of Friday, 8 October 1982. Issue 49134, p. 12848.

41. In a telephone conversation on 24 January 2012 with George MacKenzie, the former 15 Platoon radio operator, the author was told that at Fitzroy post-hostilities Gary Brown had claimed to have taken the surrender of an Argentine who appeared to be an officer or NCO. The latter was also armed with Colt .45 with which Brown had a negligent discharge with the pistol. This could well have been the case because this type of pistol had a reasonably liberal distribution (see note 39). However the author has discounted Brown's version in the context of Vázquez's surrender because the latter stated that he was captured by three Guardsmen, two of whom were armed with SLRs and one with an SMG. Brown was a machine-gunner, and neither did he mention a third captured Argentine. McNeill does and describes this officer's traumatic stress condition in detail. This is corroborated by Vázquez. Also the pistol that Brown took was, apparently, still in a plastic wrapping. This was not so with Vázquez's which had been fired early in the battle.

42. *Razor's Edge* (p. 295) incorrectly states that: '13 Platoon retained its lodgement in the rocks to the right of Miño's position' and 'chipped away at the Argentine Sappers' resolve with anti-tank rockets and phosphorous grenades [...] at about 02.00 (05.00Z) [...] Miño, outflanked by Stuart's platoon and deserted by most of his men, abandoned his position'.

43. In *Razor's Edge* (p. 290 – lower map) the site where Mitchell fell is incorrectly marked as just east of Miño's 5 Platoon. In reality he was mortally wounded another 600 metres further on to the east.

44. And again contrary to *Razor's Edge* (p. 298) which stated Mitchell had received 'nothing'.

45. *Above All, Courage*, p. 401.

46. *Ibid.*, p. 401.

47. *Razor's Edge* (p. 296) incorrectly states that Kiszely's beret was shot off and another bullet hit one of the latter's spare magazines.

48. *The Falklands War: Then and Now*, p. 514.

49. *Ibid.*

50. *Razor's Edge* (p. 297) incorrectly states that Guardsman Reynolds was one of the seven who reached the east summit, being subsequently wounded there.

51. *The Falklands War: Then and Now*, p. 513.

52. From the Charles Messenger unpublished draft manuscript of the battle.

53. *Above All, Courage*, p. 402.

54. *Among Friends: The Scots Guards* 1956-1993, p. 147.

4   Fighting through, memorials … and endex

A victorious military is like weighing a hundred-
weight against a grain.
A defeated military is like weighing a grain
against a hundredweight.
One who weighs victory sets the people to battle
like releasing amassed water into a gorge
one thousand jen *deep.*
This is form.

– Sun Tzu[1]

At this moment of anxiety on the east summit, it was McNeill who had looked at his Company Commander:

> It was then I noticed [...] Kiszely's left pouch was ripped to shreds. That is where we discovered a bullet had hit his compass. A couple of minutes later I heard a noise from behind us. By this time it was light. I looked round and saw Right Flank led by Major Price moving in single file towards us. They were using the high rocks to the left of us. You know, the prominent ones on the high ground.
>
> It all took some bottle that night, especially the charge I have described.

The re-grouping Argentines that McNeill saw were from Army Sub-Lieutenant Esteban La Madrid's 3 Platoon of B Company, 6th Infantry Regiment (RI6). The remainder of the Left Flank Company HQ reached Kiszely's group and, a short time later, 14 Platoon arrived when Tumbledown's east summit was relatively secure. But at about 10.15Z there was another small counter-attack or, more accurately, contact with Miño's platoon. Near 14 Platoon were some of the Right Flank Guardsmen, including Cocks:

> Just then there was a big bang from a rifle grenade ten metres to my left. In the silence that followed the desperate cries of a Guardsman could be heard. Apparently he had had part of his leg blown off and was crawling around in the dark moaning and crying out looking for his leg. The effect on the rest of us waiting to attack was not good, so an educated voice of an officer asked if 'somebody could get him to shut the fuck up' as he was unnerving the chaps, something I do not think anybody would have been capable of doing.
>
> In the end he was given morphine and volunteers were called for to carry him off the mountain. I raised my hand but as we were about to go into the assault my offer was turned down. Later I heard that a stretcher party received a direct hit from a mortar bomb that killed two of the guys carrying him and blew the legs off the other two.
>
> Years later I was to discover the truth behind these events. The wounded man was Lance-Sergeant Jimmy Nash of Left Flank's 14 Platoon. The stretcher party hit was not the one that left at this time but had, in fact, headed out some time before.

Lance-Sergeant Nash was just conscious and partially hit in the face by shrapnel. Likewise Lance-Corporal Coventry also of 14 Platoon received serious shrapnel wounds, and Lance-Corporal Wilson and Guardsman Reynolds were shot. Miño's platoon quickly withdrew eastwards and off Tumbledown.[2] Guardsman Ian Morton of Right Flank's 3 Platoon:

> We were up front as the point section, so I reminded myself repeatedly of our password 'Jimmy'. This had been chosen because the Argentines had difficulty in pronouncing the letter 'J'. Likewise the Gurkhas' was 'Johnny'. To get into our final position we had to move through Left Flank: and hats off to the gunner sentry as he challenged us in the good old-fashioned way of, 'Halt! Who goes there?'
>
> Sergeant Bobby Jackson, our Platoon Sergeant, then answered, 'Johnny!' – only to correct this error immediately by adding, 'Jimmy!'. Although we enjoyed a good laugh, he almost got us all killed.
>
> Then it started to snow which pissed us off no end. As we slowly moved forward, the world suddenly seemed to erupt into madness as bullets whizzed past my head and others ripped up the ground in front. Explosions were everywhere, and the illumination sent up revealed a flickering battlefield ahead. But as a westerly wind blew the flares across it, they also created a confusing and ghostly illusion of every rock formation, crag and the mountain itself moving from left to right.
>
> On reaching our final rendezvous we went to ground. From there we had to provide Left Flank with covering fire until they had gone firm on their position. Then we could take over the assault.

McNeill:

> After the Left Flank attack, I gave an initial sitrep (situation report) to Battalion Tac HQ, the CO and Right Flank Company who were following us up ready to carry out their mission. Kiszely told me to inform Right Flank to use the high rock line on their left as cover and make their approach along that.
>
> By this time it was getting slightly lighter. Right Flank Company suddenly appeared and relieved us. Quickly we held a 'hot' Orders Group between us. I remember looking at my mate, Steve Fleck, who was in Right Flank's Signal Detachment and, as he saw me, a look of shock came across his face. It gave me a fright. I reminded him of that, but he cannot remember the moment. I can. As they were just going into action, the adrenalin must have been pumping and he had other things on his mind.
>
> Once Right Flank started their engagement there were about thirty of us waiting at our location in reserve just in case we might be needed.

The fear of the unknown was compounded by the fact that Right Flank's objective could not be viewed from the Scots Guards positions near Mount Harriet the day before because it was in dead ground to the observer. The shortfall had prevented the

Company Commander, Major Simon Price, from formulating an assault plan. Nevertheless he had not been fazed by either this or being taken off his Company Commanders Course at the School of Infantry in Warminster to deploy on Operation Corporate, and gave out at on his eve-of-battle Orders Group a much fuller than normal 'Concept of Operations' stipulating what was expected of each platoon on arrival at Tumbledown's eastern end. Such a decentralised concept is known today as 'Mission Command'. Kiszely's rapid briefing to Price made the latter realise that the quality of the enemy resistance was totally contrary to 42 Commando's information:

> I had gathered from the Commandos that all one had to do was to fire a few 66s and 84s and the Argentinians would come out with their hands up. This was quite clearly not the case.[3]

Price crawled forward to 'eyeball' the imminent Right Flank battlefield and make a crucial and rapid ground appreciation in the moon's half-light. It was a standard drill: left – the terrain sloped steeply down and was broken by rocks; centre – relatively easy but covered by fire; right – a ridge of rock pinnacles that contained a sniper threat but fell away to open ground southwards. The choice was relatively obvious: a right flanking attack into this rectangular 'box' of ground 650 metres long by 250 metres wide. First light had already arrived at 10.00Z and dawn would be at 11.00Z. So his second orders group immediately prior to the Right Flank assault lasted only a few minutes. Meanwhile 3 Platoon had been faced with another threat. Morton:

> The commanders were called forward to receive their orders. Simultaneously sentries were posted and the remainder of us ordered to dig in. But because we lay on granite, this proved an impossible task. Nonetheless, with the benefit of hindsight, it was a good decision. The temperature had dropped considerably to below freezing and everyone was wet with the snow. So I am convinced a significant number of us would have suffered from hypothermia had we not started digging.

From his vantage point McNeill noted the enemy activity below him some 250 metres distant:

> There were bodies running everywhere. I never saw any running away. They were certainly re-grouping. They seemed to be getting new instructions. I cannot give an exact figure as some were still some hidden in firing positions and we were still keeping our heads down. I suppose it looked like they were initially in total confusion and they fell back, got some ammunition, received new instructions and re-engaged in a counter-attack or defensive action. It is hard to describe what they were doing exactly as I do not think they knew themselves initially.

Cocks:
> Dawn started to approach, but still the objective for my Company had not been taken. We had to attack and quickly, otherwise daylight would see us exposed on the side of the mountain in full sight of Argentine forces in Stanley. The Company

moved into assault positions, weapons were readied, bayonets fixed and machine-gun ammunition piled up. I remember vividly the events just prior to the attack going in. There was a sense of urgency as a daylight attack across the exposed mountainside was the last thing any of us wanted. Rapid plans were made with 1 Platoon, commanded by Second-Lieutenant The Viscount James Dalrymple (now the 14th Earl of Stair), climbing into the rocks just to the left (north) so as to provide covering fire for 2 and 3 Platoons who were going to sweep around to the right (south). Company Sergeant-Major Ian Amos was rushing around making sure ammunition was placed in piles and pointing them out. We had become compressed and, as such, the Company Echelon was now deployed along with 1 Platoon. As number three on my General Purpose Machine-Gun, it was my responsibility to supply ammunition to the number two, the gunner being the number one who fires controlled bursts of a few rounds at a time. The gun is fed by a belt of ammunition and this can twist and therefore jam the gun. The job of the number two is to make sure that the linked belt of 200 rounds does not twist and jam. When the belt gets to the end, it is the job of the number two to clip another belt onto it. These were piled up in a relatively central position so that all the gun teams had access to them. My mouth went dry. This was it.

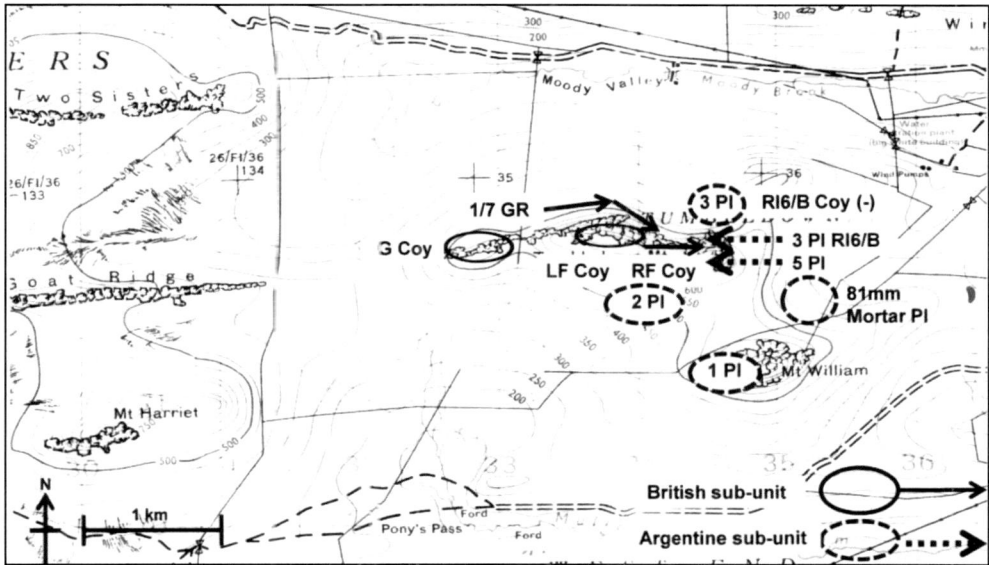

Map 4 (10.20Z-11.00Z) – Right Flank Company (2SG) moves up and assaults Tumbledown's east end. 5 Platoon (BIM5) and 3 Platoon (RI6/B) are engaged. 1/7 GR moves up behind Right Flank Company.

It was 10.30Z. No registering of artillery targets or any artillery support had occurred as it was believed incorrectly that we, the Gurkhas, were in close proximity to Right Flank. In reality, the bulk of our Battalion was still at least 200 metres to Right Flank's rear as the crow flies. Their Company HQ led by Price, together with 2 and 3 Platoons, would enter the 'box' at its south-west corner just as Sun Tzu prescribed 'like releasing amassed water into a gorge one thousand *jen* deep'. But they would have to mount their assault without artillery support. Price:

> The resulting action, to the best of my knowledge, led to the Company having to conduct the only British infantry assault on an enemy Argentine objective without any higher-level supporting fire of any type in the entire Falklands War.[4]

The first objective was 350 metres distant, a 100-metre narrow ledge of rocks running west-east on which enemy were positioned. Morton:

> Then we shook out into our assault formation and, while waiting for the order to move, checked that one full magazine fitted correctly onto our SLRs and our equipment was secure.

Cocks:

> Just as Right Flank was about to attack, the magazine on the Sergeant-Major's SLR went ping – and rounds went flying everywhere. He muttered a string of oaths and, for some reason, the tension slipped away inside me.
> Commands were given and the night erupted with small-arms fire and shouting.

Morton:

> The advance began and within seconds all hell broke loose. We broke formation to work in pairs, otherwise known as the buddy-buddy (pepper-potting) system, and continued towards our objective moving from crag to crag. The small-arms fire coming down on us was intense. I had never experienced anything like it before. But our training seemed to click into place and everyone knew what to do.

McNeill:

> We were still up at the top (near the east summit of Tumbledown) when Right Flank Company started (their attack) and the firepower from both sides could be heard which was quite heavy. Right Flank had to work hard to win the firefight and it was certainly not over in ten minutes. The Argentines were still fighting.

Another 250 metres nearer their objective, the close terrain canalised Right Flank so much that only 3 Platoon on the right and Company HQ in the centre could deploy properly. A second firebase was therefore established fifty metres south-west of the objective by half of 2 Platoon covering the assault in which there would be, surprisingly, no Scots Guards casualties. After having moved along the 'box' on its southern perimeter, 3 Platoon then turned north towards the enemy. Morton:

> I never saw any individual Argentines. We moved towards their muzzle-flashes and followed field telephone cable to their exact positions. I threw my two L2 high-explosive hand grenades at these and, after the explosions, we fought through. It was classic textbook stuff typical of the Guards.

Twenty-six year-old Captain Ian Bryden, the Company 2IC, was a relatively unsung hero of Right Flank's battle even though his subsequent MID draft citation acknowledged 'personal courage (which) was an example to all' and laconically described the first episode of his night's work:

> Captain Bryden was at the front of his Company, closing rapidly with the enemy's position. Suddenly he was confronted by three enemy. Reacting immediately and decisively, he shot and killed two of them, and overcame the third in hand to hand fighting.

Morton was also busy:

> Then I received a message that my mate, Guardsman Kev Taylor, needed me. Before becoming 3 Platoon's sniper, I was the number two on the 84mm Carl Gustav anti-tank gun with my mate Kev as the number one, and we had worked together as a team throughout most of our training at Brecon, Wales. So on hearing his request, I swallowed hard and ran at full speed towards him. Bullets were ricocheting off rock everywhere and it felt as if I could be killed at any moment.
>
> On arrival I slid down beside him and asked anxiously, 'What's wrong?'
>
> He replied, 'I just wanted to know where you were!'
>
> A feather could have knocked me down. We shared a wee grin. Then after dumping the two high-explosive 84mm rounds I had been carrying for him and knocking his beret off when slapping the side of his head, I hurried back to my position.
>
> Lying there behind a small group of rocks, I saw a target appear at twenty metres range to my front. Small-arms fire was coming from a couple of positions. As a young Guardsman inexperienced in combat, I felt that even my hand would have been shot off had it been raised. But I never knew if my target was firing at me. I took aim at it and fired.
>
> The target remained visible. I fired again.
>
> This time it vanished.
>
> I felt a massive adrenalin rush – my biggest high ever – and, in simple terms, just yearned to repeat all this. However on reaching my target's location, I puzzled over the sight before me. The Argentine was lying in the prone position, but opposite to the original direction he had been facing me.
>
> Then I understood.
>
> The Green Spot ammunition in my L42 sniper rifle had more power and accuracy for greater ranges than the standard 7.62mm round. In this case, at almost point-blank range, the increased force of the round's impact had spun him around completely. After kicking his body over I noticed half his head was missing. Only then did I realise he was dead. Oddly enough there was almost a total lack of blood. It might have been the cold that prevented the bleeding, or perhaps it was me – trying to block out the horrors of war. Until then everything had felt like an exercise. But being confronted with my enemy's body changed all that. The

reality finally sank in. This was gutter close-quarter combat taking place, not a walk in the park.

I advanced again and, at one stage, someone shouted, 'Eighty-four!' So I hit the ground instantaneously and held onto my head, only to be caught in the back-blast of the Carl Gustav shoot. It disorientated me. My ears rang and head thumped from the pressure that had sucked air from under me.

But after a few seconds I continued to press on.

Through their night sights the Scots Guards had seen the enemy beginning to withdraw. Including twenty-one year-old 3 Platoon Commander Lieutenant Robert Lawrence[5] and Bryden, a total of twelve men had assaulted the position. The subaltern's subsequent MC citation contained details of his 'outstanding example of leadership under fire and courage in the face of the enemy':

> Lieutenant Lawrence, to the fore throughout, immediately led an attack. Throwing grenades onto the enemy's position as he went, he continued in the heat of the fire fight to exhort his Platoon to follow him in the assault. His attacking group destroyed the enemy [...][6]

This first objective, a machine-gun position, was finally taken with a total of two enemy killed and four captured. Morton's kill does not appear to have been taken into account. However he would be faced with another challenge:

> Then 'Re-Org!' was shouted. On reaching a large group of rocks, two prisoners were handed down for me to guard until the arrival of the Company Sergeant Major's group. They would then take them over to be passed down the line. My heart was pumping and, because I had been taken out of the battle, fear began to creep in. I stood over both prisoners with the barrel of my L42 pointed at their heads. One was staring at me and mumbled something in Spanish. Unlike the other who was crushed in spirit and extremely afraid, he was angry and, lunging upwards with his right hand, tried to disarm me by grabbing the barrel. I pulled this backwards and then immediately thrust it forward, hitting his forehead hard. To my surprise the blow knocked him out. Adrenalin was pumping through me, filling me with rage. I wanted to kill him for his attempt on my life, but this thought soon subdued to plain anger.
>
> He was an extremely lucky man to make it off the mountain that night.

During this re-organisation pause, Price moved forward to intervene for the first time in order to regain the momentum of Right Flank's attack. Their next objective, beginning fifty metres north of the first, would be the 100-metre wide by 200-metre long 'lodgement area' located in the centre of the 'box' between Left Flank and east end of Tumbledown. Outcrops of rock there concealed La Madrid's men now engaging Right Flank. It had to be cleared before the Company could proceed eastwards. So Bryden and Lawrence began leading two groups around its western side, while another group led by the 2 Platoon Commander, Second-Lieutenant Mark Mathewson, attempted to clear the slopes below. But a second enemy machine-gun position was causing problems there on top of the rocks. This required drastic action and a second intervention by Price. Military Medals (MM) would be won by two men as a result. Guardsman Andy Pengelly of 3 Platoon:

> Tracer was streaming over our heads. I was a machine-gunner, but had already used up all my ammunition and felt a bit spare. I grabbed a grenade from someone and shinned up the Pinnacle. As I got to the top, I tried to remove the pin, but it was bent and my hands were pretty numb with the cold. Eventually I got it out and dropped it over the top. Stupidly I took a peek to see what I had done. Next moment I felt a blow in the thigh and toppled all the way down again. I'd still like to know who gave me the grenade with the bent pin.[7]

His MM citation provided more details:

> [...] he hurled a grenade and killed the sniper. As he threw the grenade he was hit and badly wounded by enemy mortar fire. His courageous action was a significant individual contribution of a high order to the success of the battle.[8]

But the enemy position remained a threat. It was then his Sergeant's turn to demonstrate 'outstanding courage under fire in the face of the enemy'. Robert Jackson's subsequent MM citation elaborated further:

> [...] discarding his rifle and armed only with grenades, he clambered forward under fire over wet and slippery rocks towards the foot of the enemy's position forty metres away. Having climbed fully fifteen metres up into the rocky crags, single-handed he attacked and destroyed the enemy's position with his grenades [...] [9]

Mathewson's group then skirted north-west around the lodgement area before moving on to the north-east corner of the 'box' in the enemy's administrative area located at Tumbledown's east end. Jackson joined Price's Company HQ group which advanced into the centre of the lodgement area where two more enemy machine-gun positions were located. One with three enemy was captured. Then Price, Jackson and Lance-Sergeant Baxter (of Company HQ) assaulted the other machine-gun hidden in a cave. They killed the machine-gunner, and captured two riflemen, one of whom was wounded.[10] Another four were captured close by.

Meanwhile Bryden's and Lawrence's groups continued to advance along the western side of this second Company objective. Another enemy was killed and, further up, one more captured. But snipers were active just north of the lodgement area and, in particular, from the administrative area 250 metres to the south-east. Guardsmen Harkness and McEnteggart were shot and wounded in the north-east of the lodgement area. A few metres further on, Lawrence was shot in the head. With covering fire provided by Lance-Sergeant McDermid and Lance-Corporal Richardson, Lance-Corporal Graham Rennie won a MID by, according to its draft citation, 'crawling forward under continuing intensive enemy machine-gun fire to rescue his Platoon Commander'. The sniper who wounded Lawrence was killed, but the subaltern would lose forty-three per cent of his brain. He had been the driving force of his platoon's battle.[11] A third and final intervention was required by Price to regain, once more, the momentum of fighting through the position. Morton became involved in resolving this stalemate situation:

> After handing over my prisoners, I returned to 3 Platoon. They were still pinned down and trying to regain the momentum by winning the firefight. It was lasting forever. Then I saw Captain Bryden approach. He asked for a volunteer to go with him. Nobody moved. So he asked again. This time I stood up and volunteered.
>
> Our two-man operation was a spur of the moment action. Targetted against the enemy position causing 3 Platoon's problems, it was vital the former be eliminated. This would allow the platoon to fight through the last known enemy position higher up and so take the mountain. However we did not know our objective on the east end of Tumbledown contained about twelve enemy – so the odds were against us from the start. Surprise would be the key to success. We made a rough guess in choosing a suitable location that might allow us to move unseen into a good final assault position.
>
> After moving off down to 3 Platoon's left behind a large rock formation, we checked our ammo and then made our way to the bottom of a sheer rock face. Taking fresh stock of the situation there, we slung our weapons over our shoulders and began to ascend the rock. It had a crevice running all the way up, so was ideal for climbing – even though we found this quite hard as our fingers were freezing. But within a couple of minutes we were peering over the top to re-assess our situation. We were a little short of the objective, but still close enough to achieve our aim. So I moved down out of sight, leaving Captain Bryden to come up with his plan.
>
> Within seconds he turned and whispered, 'Have you got any grenades?'
>
> I replied, 'I've got one White Phosphorous.'
>
> To which he ordered, 'Then give it to me!'
>
> I had held onto this since the battle's start and, having already thrown my two L2 grenades, was determined this last one would remain mine. So I replied firmly, 'I'll throw it!'
>
> Captain Bryden gave in, and I got my way. I moved back up alongside him and he pointed out my target.
>
> I had already learnt the important lessons of throwing grenades in combat. Before exploding, they had a four to seven-second delay after the fly-off lever had been released. During that first phase my platoon's assault some grenades earlier phase some grenades had been thrown back at us because of this delay. The appropriate counter-measure before throwing was therefore to count to three or four after releasing the fly-off lever. Although dangerous to the thrower, it did give him full control of the grenade.
>
> So with a big grin I pulled the pin, released the fly-off lever, counted to four and threw. It hit the rock and rolled into the target area. Immediately after the explosion there was a scream. We jumped up and began to skirmish towards the enemy. But after ten metres my rifle had a stoppage. As in training, I informed Captain Bryden. We both went to ground so my problem could be sorted out

while he gave me covering fire. But I struggled with the magazine. My L42 was camouflaged with hessian sacking cut up into small pieces to break up the rifle's outline. However because of the freezing conditions, the hessian had frozen and was jamming the magazine. My only option remaining was to discard it and hand-feed rounds into the chamber. Although this slowed my firing rate, the improvisation worked – but not for long.

I could now see the far end of Tumbledown only twenty metres away. But as I knelt down in a small crevice in the rock to give covering fire to Captain Bryden, my world suddenly exploded. There was a terrific thump in my back which threw me forward about two metres. Although hit by grenade shrapnel, I was lucky. The grenade had rolled back behind some rocks which shielded me from the main blast.

The pain was searing through me as I tried to push myself up. Everything had gone into slow motion. Getting to my knees, I looked around for Captain Bryden. It was then this red-hot glowing object homed on me at express speed. I tried to get out of the way [...] but failed. It hit me like a train and threw me forward again onto the rock. The pain was excruciating. I never thought pain could be so extreme. Every muscle in my body was in spasm as this pain of all pains ripped through it. I'm going to die, was my reflex thought.

I had been hit in the middle of my back but, because of the shot's angle, the bullet had travelled up my spine and exited at the top of my neck.

The administrative area had been the final rendezvous for La Madrid's men. But only sixteen reached this location. Leaving behind five riflemen and machine-gunner as a covering force, La Madrid and his other nine men had then withdrawn from Tumbledown. Although having no grenade to throw, Bryden nonetheless rushed towards the badly wounded Morton. He had been hit three times twenty metres or so from where the Memorial Cross now stands. Morton:

Once again someone up there must have been looking after me that night. Next I was aware of Captain Bryden turning me onto my back, grabbing my webbing yolk and dragging me into cover. The extent of my wounds was not visible. All he could see were small holes in my combat jacket and a little blood, the flow of which had been slowed considerably due to the extreme cold. It probably saved my life.

Once in cover, he injected my thigh with morphine. But being a sniper I carried about six maps on my body. Those in my lower combat trouser pocket bent the syrette's needle and so prevented the morphine from entering my system. Unaware of this, he took out a red marker pen and wrote 'M' on my forehead and time at which he assumed the drug had been administered. In reality, however, I received no pain relief until another four hours.

Sergeant Robertson of 2 Platoon assumed command of 3 Platoon and led a group from the lodgement area to the south-east corner of the 'box' to enter and occupy the administrative area.[12] Leaving behind one dead, La Madrid's covering force withdrew. Then 1 Platoon was moved up to replace the remainder of 3 Platoon in the lodgement area. Considerable time was required for the scattered Right Flank to re-organise and re-group. Another platoon-sized force of B Company, RI6 then engaged Right Flank with machine-gun fire at least 200 metres north of the latter's new position. The Guards believed this was the start of a counter-attack which did not materialise due to heavy return fire from Lance-Corporal Campbell's 1 Platoon section located on higher ground. Under heavy artillery fire from enemy and friendly guns, one shell exploded in the peat only two metres from three Guardsmen. It blew them all over, but caused no casualties. The Artillery FOO then came forward, stopped the British guns from firing on Right Flank and directed fire instead onto the escaping enemy. Later from a position midway between Moody Brook and Sapper Hill, La Madrid's depleted 3 Platoon fired at Tumbledown to support their side's general withdrawal. But the Scots Guards had taken its objective. Morton's ordeal continued however:

> Until relieved by another member of Right Flank, Captain Bryden remained with me. He saved my life. Since then I have thanked him daily in my thoughts for what he did.
> I lay on the battlefield for what seemed ages. During some shelling a voice yelled, 'Incoming!' Because of my wounds, I was unable to get into cover and could only shout back, 'Cover my head! Cover my head!' My inability to act independently had frightened me for only the second time on Tumbledown – in addition, for the first time, to feeling vulnerable and alone. But I discovered later that a piper (whose Scots Guards role in war is to act as either regimental medic or be a Machine-Gun Platoon member) was my support as he lay beside me throughout that bombardment.

The Company succeeded because it maintained the momentum of the attack despite three crises: the initial assault which had become stalled, resistance to 2 Platoon by the second enemy machine-gun nest eventually destroyed by the two individual grenade attacks, and 3 Platoon pinned down by enemy fire in the north-east part of the lodgement area after the wounding of Lawrence – all of which required the Company Commander's personal intervention. Cocks:

> It was utter mayhem and the noise was deafening and, in what seemed no time at all, the Argentines were thrown out of their last positions. All I remember of that final assault were the frantic commands being yelled and of myself crawling around collecting ammunition for our machine-gun. Our gunner was a rather old pipe-smoking Guardsman by the name of Fisher and we called him 'Pops' because he must have been in his late-twenties, maybe early-thirties, and used to call me 'Big Bird' after the character on *Sesame Street* because I was so tall. His kids loved the TV programme apparently. A driver in HQ Company who did not want promotion, Fisher was a good shot and had been given the GPMG that Echelon carried. He was very disciplined in firing controlled bursts and hammered away until the barrel glowed red hot when he had to switch to a new one, pouring water on the one that had been taken off. We soon started to run low on ammunition and I started ferrying belts of link from the central reserve to the ever-hungry gun.
> I have no idea how long the assault lasted, only that eventually we ran out of

targets and gradually the noise of battle receded. My job of being in charge of walking wounded was no longer needed as we realised that anybody wounded tonight was not going to walk off this mountain. Our Company casualties were relatively light with none killed, though some were horrendously wounded. I must admit that compared to the hours taken by Left Flank to skirmish through their part of the mountain, Right Flank's clearing of the east end was very quick. I do not think it took more than thirty to forty-five minutes.

Kiszely summed up this final phase of the battle, 'Some (of the enemy) ran away, but a few clearly stayed and carried out a limited counter-attack. (Had more done so, we would have been stuffed.) A number of the enemy stayed in position to defend the eastern end.'

My subsequent literary attempts to give structure to the battle as seen through the eyes of John Kiszely, Simon McNeill, Steve Cocks and Ian Morton cannot replace the chaotic reality. Kiszely:

> Relating what happened gives the whole thing an aura of a clear sequence of actions. There was a great deal of confusion in the dark, disorientation, flashes and bangs, sudden crises, separations of one from another, and minor actions within the whole event. From the outset, it was a case study in Clausewitzian friction – 'Everything in war is very simple, but the simplest thing is difficult [...] Countless minor incidents – the kind you can never really foresee – combine to lower the general level of performance, so that one always falls far short of the intended goal [...] Friction is the only concept that that more or less corresponds to the factors that distinguish real war from war on paper'. Not that I had ever heard of Clausewitz at the time. But when I subsequently read it, it brought home to me that Clausewitz had it spot-on.

Cocks:

> Men in my Company were awarded gallantry medals for their actions and it is often repeated in many histories of the Falklands that the Scots Guards on Tumbledown fought the best troops the Argentines had to offer and that victory was the hardest one, but it had not been cheap for, as a Battalion, we lost eight dead and forty-three wounded.[13] Thirty-odd Argentines lay dead and over 100 were wounded, as well as a number of prisoners taken.[14]

So for those on Tumbledown during that bitterly cold 14 June afternoon in 1982, relief was a trifle more than that normally felt at the end of a large military exercise or, to quote the soldiers' colloquialism, 'endex'. But the Scots Guards Regimental History over-exaggerated the number of regular Argentine Marines (there were only ten per cent in the 5th Marine Infantry Battalion) and omitted to document the involvement of a large Argentine Army Company of conscripts:

Stunned by their spectacular success in defeating a well trained battalion of regular Argentinian Marines and having fought arguably the toughest action of the whole campaign, in the immediate aftermath of the battle most people experienced understandable feeling of euphoria and relief ...[15]

And just as on 14 June 1982, it began to snow more than twenty-five years later while I took a picture of a seriously reflective Billy Silver and Simon McNeill standing either side of the near eight-foot high cross. Just over the brow and below it, we found the other Guardsmen. They wanted to camp out overnight in this small administrative area that had once been the location where the N Company Marines received their hot meals. The two rusted Argentine Marine field kitchens with regimental anchor symbols on their sides were still there. These were the only ones heated by petrol burners in this Inner Defence Zone area. Others on Wireless Ridge were wood-fired, but the drawback had been a non-availability of wood. Men from nearby Argentine units would therefore make a beeline for these two field kitchens on Tumbledown in the hope of getting a hot meal.

The Scots Guards pilgrims would be protected from the elements by a rock overhang, and Gordon Hoggan was already enthusiastically putting up his small tent provided by Patrick Watts. There could be no more intimate or therapeutic way of getting to grips with their demons from twenty-five years ago. But despite a celebratory bottle of beer from Tony Blackburn at the end of this fascinating day, I did not wish to gate-crash their regimental vigil. Wanting to visit Goose Green and San Carlos next day, I was driven back to Stanley and the Leylands' comfortable home.

Many items had been put into Falklands 25 Pilgrimage bag. One was a Cable & Wireless South Atlantic Ltd pre-paid £10 phonecard. So I was able to utilise the Falklands £5.4 million satellite telecommunications network to call my wife in Oslo before Vera's good scrambled egg and bacon breakfast on 8 November and Day Four of the Pilgrimage. Frank Leyland and I then set out in his four-wheel drive vehicle for Goose Green, a distance of 100 kilometres along the tarmac road which, in 1982, was just a dirt track. Driving to San Carlos from Stanley in those days would have taken between one to two days, depending on how many times the vehicle got bogged down and dug out.

We stopped at the Argentine War Cemetery overlooking Darwin Harbour. It was a peaceful place. The Argentine flag was not permitted to be flown there or, indeed, anywhere else on the Islands. A large white cross dominated the cemetery, and each of the 230 white grave crosses had pale blue rosary beads hung around them. The local rumour was that 234 bodies were buried there because body parts of several unidentified soldiers rest together in the same grave. Yet there were many others unidentified, personified by the Spanish words on grave stones of *Soldado Argentino Sólo Conocido Por Dios* (An Argentine Soldier Known Only To God). No Argentine body has been repatriated back to the mainland because of the Argentine sovereignty claim over Islas las Malvinas. For why should bodies be moved from one part of Argentina to another? Because of no direct air connection between Argentina and the Islands, next of kin and Malvinas War veteran visits are few. The only air route between Santiago in Chile and the Islands make such visits very expensive and therefore restricts numbers making the trip. I reflected on this sad state of affairs whilst wandering along the lines of graves. There were two tasks for me. The first was to locate and pay my veteran's respects to Sub-Lieutenant Oscar Silva's grave. I did this before my 'bridge-building' task of scooping up, as requested, a tiny portion of cemetery soil for Marisa Clausen de Bruno's Christmas present.

We continued our journey to the settlement of Goose Green via Darwin Hill. En route I walked down past another smaller memorial to two soldiers who died in the battle there to the narrow re-entrant in which the late Lieutenant-Colonel 'H' Jones's memorial was erected on the spot he had been killed. Astonishingly it was only twenty-five metres away from the trench sited on the re-entrant's opposite side that contained the eighteen year-old Argentine machine-gunner conscript, Oscar Ledesma, who killed him. I could only conclude that 'H' Jones suffered tunnel vision in carrying out his one-man assault on the Argentine trench before him, and which won him a posthumous Victoria Cross. On top of Darwin Hill was the 2 Para memorial: another simple iron cross mounted on a stone cairn. Since I was last here just after the war, the surrounding stonework had been considerably expanded and a small white perimeter fence added. Further south and lower down by the side of the Goose Green air-strip was also another stone memorial to the shot-down Sea Harrier pilot Lieutenant Nick Taylor, with small parts of his aircraft carefully incorporated into the overall design behind the headstone.

Driving into Goose Green itself the first landmark of note were the sheep shearing sheds with the letters 'POW' still daubed on their walls and roofs and which provided shelter to the many post-battle Argentine prisoners. Nobody would obliterate such a pictorial history. I located the settlement's only shop in which the Gurkha Battalion HQ had been set up. There was an unexpected personal reaction whilst walking around the small building and looking through the windows into the small office where I had kept up a hour-long running brief to Brigadier Tony Wilson during the *Sir Galahad* disaster. My emotion was not a shameful matter: it was therapeutic, but contained another hidden dimension which Nigel Price articulated perfectly in an e-mail sent four months later:

> I might be wrong, but would imagine that all sorts of other impressions and emotions can probably get caught up amongst the Falklands ones: quite simply, the general sadness at the passing of our lives. Back then we were all a quarter of a century younger. Some of us have already died in the meantime. So it must have been after all such campaigns throughout history. The oldest pass away first (generally), followed by the next oldest and so on. Look at the Great War – the nation now waits with bated breath as the last surviving participant clings to life. One by one we all slip inexorably into the darkness of a never-ending night. A pilgrimage such as you attended brings one closer to that passing of time. It must be easy to imagine being back then, in 1982, as the person one then was, so one feels sorrow and a general mourning for the time – and our youth – that has passed, never to return.

I do not mean to be maudlin, but do you not often feel this? Particularly when, say, visiting an old house, castle or other such place. Ted Hughes wrote '... the world's decay, where the wind's hands have passed'. I can imagine that walking across the bleak but strangely beautiful Falklands landscape, one could feel that decay, and mourn that, perhaps more than the specific 1982 experiences themselves.

Nigel was most perceptive. But all the impressions, emotions and pilgrims' stories would, nevertheless, become even more intense as the Pilgrimage and its special aftermath for me continued to unfold.

The population of Goose Green had been severely reduced since 1982 because many settlers had moved to Stanley for better jobs, and now the shop was only opened on a weekly basis for one hour to cater for the settlement's seventeen people. Frank located the shop owner who was a young mother, and she unlocked the door so we could look around the shop for a few minutes. It was smaller than I had visualised in my mind's eye. There were similar visits to the Community Centre where the settlement's population had been locked up by the Argentines for a month during the war, and another to the small home of Keith and Ginnie Baillie where I had stayed with four other officers for a fortnight after the war. The shepherds' bunkhouse where we had set up the Gurkha Battalion HQ after the war no longer existed. It had been demolished because of asbestos in the building.

Our next objective was San Carlos. Two kilometres out of Goose Green we stopped at Carcass Creek where I had positioned the Gurkha Battalion Tactical HQ for our first night at war on 1 June. The creek and surrounding countryside seemed much larger than then. On the south-east horizon jutted up a chimney stack which was all that remained of the dairy. Beyond it had been School House, destroyed in the Battle of Darwin and Goose Green on 28 May. But the little building on the creek's southern bank where the Battalion's first Orders Group had been held on 2 June was intact.

Back onto the main road Frank pointed out Burntside House, 2 Para's first objective in their battle, and Camilla Creek House which they had used for overnight shelter before crossing their start line. Arriving on top of the Sussex Mountains we enjoyed a panoramic view of San Carlos Water before descending to Blue Beach 2. The most photographed jetty in the Falklands was still there: the site of the Gurkhas' landing on 1 June after twenty days at sea. We arrived at the San Carlos war cemetery where seventeen British servicemen, including 'H' Jones, were buried. The rest of the British dead were repatriated to the UK post-war. By coincidence the British Minister of Veterans and Under-Secretary of State for Defence, Mr Derek Twigg, was laying a wreath, having just arrived from the UK for the remainder of the Pilgrimage. He was accompanied by the Governor of the Falklands and Mike Bowles. Afterwards we were invited for tea at Sheila and Terence McPhee's nearby home.

Living in Southampton from 1979-89, they were hounded by the media during the war. Across the bay at Wreck Point, Gerald and Doreen Dickson were the only Islanders still residing in the San Carlos area who had experienced the British landings. I talked to the Governor and Mr Twigg. Receptive to the idea of pilgrims giving him frank views on how to improve follow-up assistance to Falklands veterans who required it, Mr Twigg would be politely 'assailed' about this by some. But there was a more efficient way. So I told him about the Nottingham colloquium and asked, 'Have you received a copy of *Hors de Combat* I sent to you a month ago?'

His 'No' came as a surprise. What was his staff doing? So I promised him another copy as well as my first book.

We drove back to Stanley. Nearer the capital at Wether Ground just before Mount Harriet, Frank pointed out rock sangars on either side of the road. These must have been Gurkha-built for protection against the shelling of the Argentine 155mm gun located behind Sapper Hill.

'Do you know how Wether Ground got its name?' asked Frank.

'No,' I replied with curiosity.

'It comes from the fact that castrated rams are put out here to graze and fatten up prior to slaughter. What remains of the scrotum is tied up to wither away. Get it?'

Fortunately there was no Gurkha slaughter there back in 1982. Later I made an optimistic note in my Pilgrimage diary of 'Will visit Wether Ground later' to check out those Gurkha sangars: but, alas, lack of time prevented me.

After changing into the proscribed dark lounge suit and clutching Mr Twigg's copies of my books, I attended the second of three official receptions in Government House that evening. My secret little ambition was to find Don Bonner, the former chauffeur of 1982 Governor Rex Hunt and who had been an eye-witness to Diego García Quiroga's 2 April attack. Eighty-five pilgrims were present to enjoy a drink and the delicate finger food. No small-talk expert, I became marooned on the room's sidelines until a lady approached. We started to converse.

'So what sort of work do you do in the Islands?' I asked eventually.

'Oh, I'm the Governor's wife!' she replied.

Carpe diem!

So trying to conceal the embarrassment of my ghastly *faux pas* I asked, 'Do you know where Don Bonner's cottage is?'

She did. Quickly I manoeuvred towards the Minister of Veterans, presented him with my book gifts and slipped out to Bonner's cottage at the rear of Government House. But there was a disappointing silence to my knock on his door. At least I wandered around the nearby vegetable gardens where Diego had been shot three times by the defending Royal Marines in 1982. He had lain in the chicken run beside his mortally wounded fighting patrol commander, *Capitán de Corbeta* (Lieutenant-Commander) Pedro Edgardo Giacchino. The eventual death of '*El primer Mártir de Malvinas*' (the first martyr of the Malvinas) would be the war's first. He was also the first of eighteen Argentine servicemen to receive their country's highest military decoration for bravery, the CHVC – *Cruz 'La Nación Argentina al Heróico Valor en Combate'* ('The Argentine Nation's Cross for Heroic Valour in Combat').[16] Diego would receive the MVC – *Medalla 'La Nación Argentina al Valor en Combate'* ('The Argentine Nation's Medal for Valour in Combat').

At least the gardens were tranquil now.

I met the Leylands in Ross Road and we drove to an hour-long concert given by the red-coated Band of the Prince of Wales's Division which had been flown from the UK to provide the Pilgrimage's essential military music. It was a pleasant conclusion to this day chock full of impressions. But it was a great shame, I thought, that there were no Nepalese Gurkha pilgrims to enjoy it. So did a number of Islanders who had asked me if there were any 'real' Gurkhas on the Pilgrimage. After receiving my negative answer, their disappointed faces were, nonetheless, proof of the esteem and affection they still held for the 7th Gurkha Rifles.

After a good night's sleep who could then forget that cold sunny morning on Day Five of the Pilgrimage, 9 November, at the four war memorials of Port Pleasant and nearby settlement of Fitzroy where, so many years before, fifty men had died on board the RFAs *Sir Galahad* and *Sir Tristram* from Argentine Skyhawk air strikes? About 125 pilgrims and Islanders were in the convoy to Port Pleasant. One Pilgrimage group consisted of eighteen Welsh Guardsmen who all stood under a fluttering large Welsh flag. This morning was of great significance to them because thirty-two of their fellow-Guardsman had died on board *Sir Galahad*. The wreath-laying ceremony at the Welsh Guards Memorial was accompanied by a lament from three Scots Guards pipers.

Impossible not to be emotionally affected, the ceremony was repeated at the Royal Fleet Auxiliary Memorial on the opposite side of the little concave bay where many of the disaster's survivors had landed, and at the 16 Field Ambulance Memorial on the headland behind. There were seven former members of this unit led by white-haired Lieutenant-Colonel John Roberts. Escaping the attack by a mere ten minutes after saying goodbye to his Second-in-Command Major Roger Nutbeem and disembarking early from *Sir Galahad*, he was the one to find Nutbeem's body on return to the devastated Landing Ship Logistic.

Another of his men, Clive Jefferies, vividly described his escape during the best interview for the British Forces Broadcasting Service TV crew who were filming the Pilgrimage:

> Trying to get out of the *Sir Galahad* was very, very difficult. We were just going through a passageway. One way behind us was on fire and it was filling up with smoke, so we had to get right down almost on our hands and knees. You could feel the heat on some of the hatchways going into the tank deck, so we knew that wasn't a way out. And we got more or less to the bow of the ship and couldn't really find a way out. And we actually thought that this was it. I remember being incredibly calm at the time. I guess it was adrenalin or whatever.
>
> What had happened was that the *Galahad* had been bombed the previous week in San Carlos Water, but the bomb hadn't been fused properly and had slammed through the deck leaving a hole – and it had been covered by a tarpaulin. Now someone had obviously removed that tarpaulin and suddenly we saw some light coming down and we managed to crawl out through the bomb hole made by the Argentine bomb the previous week.
>
> When I got up onto deck by this time I think a lot of people had mostly gone, and there was hardly anyone left on board. I really started to panic so I went to go and jump over the side. I remember a Major, I think he was Royal Corps of Transport, who grabbed me by the scruff of the neck and said, 'Don't jump into the water, you'll freeze!'
>
> Many of the life rafts had already gone, and there was a young Royal Marine

Corporal who brought a Mexeflote, like a floating pontoon they used for unloading, alongside the *Galahad* and about thirty of ours got off on board that. There was quite a lot of seriously wounded on board. I also remember the ammunition on the ship was starting to explode and I don't know whether they were shells or whatever, but they were actually coming through the hull underneath us, and I was thinking we really needed to be leaving here now!

As this chap slowly took us away, it was quite difficult getting away from the *Sir Galahad* initially. I am always struck by the view I saw as we approached the shore and the thing was just well alight by this time. The majority of the casualties came ashore here. Then I remember going up to the settlement and walking into the Community Hall,[17] and I had to walk straight back out again because there was all these – smell of all these people who had been burnt. It was quite overwhelming. I just panicked and I had to just walk out again.

Then I remember seeing a lot of the Chinese crew which I hadn't actually seen on board the ship because we were only there only a day. We didn't realise that many of the crew were Hong Kong Chinese Merchant Navy guys. And they were all coming up the beach very badly burnt. And I remember finding a hose, turned it on, and they were all standing round me in a semi-circle, and I was hosing their hands down.

It was just chaotic, but we managed to get a lot of casualties away very quickly. And approximately an hour later, if you remember, a second Skyhawk came over, and I just stood up and looked up at it. I wasn't in the slightest bit bothered. And there were these paratroopers dug in behind us, 2 Para, and they opened up with everything they got. I even remember one guy, I don't know if he was a chef or something, he had an LMG,[18] basically a modern version of the Bren gun, running down the field swearing his head off and firing from the hip. It was quite, quite bizarre.[19]

A fourth wreath-laying ceremony took place at the 5th Infantry Brigade Memorial in the little settlement of Fitzroy after an incongruous and patently nervous small female trumpeter of the Band of the Prince of Wales's Division sounded the Last Post. Where, oh where, were the Scots Guards pipers? As a sense of quiet reflection took hold on everyone, tea was drunk and sandwiches and cakes munched in the compact Community Centre where Jefferies had been forced to walk out on that fateful evening twenty-five years before.

We drove back to Stanley again to rendezvous at the FIDF Drill Hall with a fifteen-vehicle convoy. This moved out to Tumbledown for another Act of Remembrance organised this time by the Scots Guards group. The weather was turning sour and snow began to fall as about forty pilgrims and Islanders arrived at the eastern end of Tumbledown. Steve would recite the poem *Ode to Tumbledown* just prior to the wreath-laying accompanied by the three Scots Guards pipers playing *The Crags of Tumbledown*.

However time was my only enemy on the Pilgrimage, so I decided rather ruthlessly not to participate. My focus was on tracking back to Vázquez's platoon position at 'The Ski Slope', and search behind it for other snipers' hides belonging to Sub-Lieutenant Oscar Silva's men on a slightly higher level of ground. En route I stumbled upon the remains of a British stretcher.

It caused me to have an instant thought.

Could this have been one of the two stretchers carrying Scots Guards' Left Flank casualties which were hit by a mortar bomb attack at 12.04Z on that last morning of the war when two stretcher-bearers were killed and another eight men wounded in the party of thirteen that included three escorts acting as a security screen …?

'Ossie' Osborn was one of them. He had just swapped places, with the stretcher-bearers becoming the Screen and the Screen becoming Bearers. Five seconds after the stretcher party re-started its journey to the Regimental Aid Post, it was hit by the enemy mortars. The person he had swapped with, Guardsman David Malcolmson, was killed. Both Osborn's legs received shrapnel wounds[20] from what he had perceived as four to six 120mm mortar bombs 'fired from a long way off'. As the Argentine 120mm mortar is not a Marine Infantry weapon, it must have been fired by an Army unit nearer the Sapper Hill area. This was probably C Company, 3rd Infantry Regiment which was tasked to cover any British advance along the Darwin-Stanley road east of Mount William.

Simon McNeill was an eye-witness of this incident. An hour or so before he had been bandaging the wounds on Lieutenant Mitchell's other leg:

We were told to move back about twenty metres to where the wounded who had been shot as we reached our final objective, were located. We withdrew, re-organised, and prepared to support Right Flank. It was then I applied a field dressing to Lieutenant Mitchell who had been shot in the thigh. I will never forget what he said after I told him, 'No probs, sir, you'll be right.'

'It's like soup,' he remarked, obviously in shock.

'What is?' I asked.

'My leg, Corporal. It's like having boiling soup poured over it,' he replied.

I thought, Christ, I could do with some! I'm freezing!

So trying to lighten the mood and take his mind off the wound, I replied, 'What flavour is it? I hope it's tomato. I'm starving!'

But my irony did not make him laugh.

Then I heard Right Flank making contact with the enemy. We were told to take cover. After what seemed like a few minutes, I heard over my radio my mate John 'Trigger' Rogers, who was Right Flank's Signals Detachment Commander and Battalion net rear-link radio operator, trying desperately to reach Battalion Tac HQ Call Sign 'Zero' with an urgent helicopter 'casevac' request. The casualty was Lieutenant Lawrence, and they had to get him out – fast. But Trigger could not get through to Tac HQ because of a dead spot in the terrain and his current location. So I climbed up amongst the rocks trying to get line of sight between Right Flank Company and Tac HQ. Then, bingo! I could hear both stations. So I said, 'Relay through me' and began to take Trigger's casevac request, relaying it word for word to Tac HQ and vice versa.

Suddenly Zero put me in direct link to Sam Drennan who was flying the chopper. He asked for a grid reference to land. Luckily I had that already from

Trigger's casevac request which had been sent to Tac HQ. But Trigger had given me this grid reference in MAPCO, the signals code we were using then, and so I sent it like that to Drennan.

His reply was most unsignal-like but an exceptionally confidant, 'Give it to me straight son. I've no fucking time to decode it. I'm going right in!'

So I deciphered it quickly, and sent it to him. Then suddenly this chopper came out of nowhere, flying about thirty feet off the ground.

Well done McNeill, I thought, your idea of a one-man relay station worked and you could get a medal for this!

It was then the 'ping-ping' began to arrive.

I had started to take enemy small arms fire because they had spotted either me or my radio aerial on top of the rocks. Then a burst of automatic fire hit the immediate area around me.

My reflex judgement was, Fuck the medal, I'm out of here!

So I scrambled down from those rocks with haste. We then were told to get back and re-group with the remainder of Left Flank in case Right Flank needed reinforcements. Although they were nearing the end of their battle, there were still snipers about and we had to take cover.

McNeill had come under fire probably from the 'stay-behind' sniper whom Falklands' folk-lore later nicknamed 'Pedro', and possibly from the machine-gun of Sergeant Héctor Echeverría who was La Madrid's Support Section Commander. The Army Air Corps Scout helicopter pilot, Captain Samuel Drennan, who was a former Scots Guards Colour Sergeant, and his air gunner and co-pilot, Lance-Corporal Julian 'Jay' Rigg, evacuated sixteen casualties during the battle 'under extremely difficult conditions. Flying under fire, over mountainous terrain, in extremely turbulent winds and heavy snow showers, Captain Drennan repeatedly put his own life at risk. His complete disregard for his own safety undoubtedly saved many lives.' [21] The only air crew that would come to the aid of those on Tumbledown under fire, Drennan and Rigg would be awarded the Distinguished Flying Cross (DFC) and a MID respectively. Their first passenger that morning had been the badly shrapnel-wounded Gurkha, Corporal Gyanbahadur Rai. One of the last was Ian Morton:

My next recollection was of being forced into a 'flying coffin'. Attached to a Scout helicopter's landing skids and complete with lid, this long box had a casualty placed into it to be then evacuated off the mountain. However I did not fit into the coffin. As they pushed in my feet, my head popped out and when they pushed in my head, my feet popped out. The bloody things were not designed for Guardsmen. So the lid was removed, I was strapped in and flew with an open top.

Initially I landed at the Advanced Dressing Station in Fitzroy, but can only remember my boots being cut off and me sipping a little tea. Later I was flown on to the Field Hospital at Ajax Bay and underwent surgery.

Unconscious for three days, I awoke to my horror in a strange place where Argentine casualties were either side of me. Convinced of having been captured, I became exceptionally agitated and tried to grab the Argentine to my right.

However a male nurse calmed me down, informing me of my location and that hostilities had ceased. I was so relieved at hearing this and of our victory. From now on it was plain sailing. I was going home.

But he was honest when I tried to prise a bigger picture out of him about his movements during Right Flank's battle:

> I was only a Guardsman and did not know which direction I [...] (or) anyone (else) moved [...] We had to fight from crag to crag in small groups. Conventional tactics did not work as everyone was separated and not in a large group controlled by the Platoon Commander. I did not even see my Section Commander Lance-Sergeant Danny McDermid during the assault. Only Danny and one other in our section were unscathed. On almost every occasion we met in Army retirement, he broke down in tears as 'all his boys got hit and not him'. The last time I heard from him he was working on the trains somewhere.[22]

When Morton was wounded his Commanding Officer had been moving up along Tumbledown from its western end to the north-east summit. Later Scott would be awarded the Distinguished Service Order (DSO), its citation revealing his performance in the battle:

> Throughout, although almost constantly under artillery fire himself, Lieutenant-Colonel Scott led his battalion in an outstanding manner. He personally directed and encouraged the leading Company Commander and his example and coolness inspired and steadied all around him. He caused artillery fire to be brought down close to his forward troops so that they were able to close with the enemy and defeat them. It was due to Lieutenant-Colonel Scott's personal determination and leadership that the Scots Guards were able to achieve a breakthrough at this vital point and so capture their main objective.[23]

However Scott was provided with an historical reminder by what he saw:

> Just before the ceasefire I made my way from Tac HQ up to Right Flank, now secure on the eastern end of Tumbledown. I was conscious more than anything else of the dead, scattered ammunition, abandoned weapons and the general filth of the battlefield. It was only then that I realized exactly what the Duke of Wellington meant when he said after Waterloo 'next to a battle lost, the greatest misery is a battle gained.'[24]

McNeill:

> The CO had joined us near the top to congratulate us. Then my Signals Detachment 2IC Chris Murley and I moved down the hill to some rocks midway between Vázquez's position and where the wounded Lieutenant Mitchell was located. We crawled under the rocks to try and keep warm. I told Chris to get out his emergency sleeping bag, the one wrapped in the little silver foil that fitted into your combat jacket pocket, and convinced him to share it. This was meant as a

kind of joke because he was a mate of mine from the Signals Platoon. However I was also the senior Lance-Corporal and had done all the survival courses. The books tell you body warmth is good. That bullshit and the joke probably saved my life. Both of us got in and tried to stay warm. After about ten minutes, I heard my name being shouted and a Guardsman pointed his SLR into the rock.

I shouted, 'It's OK! It's Left Flank!' By this time I could recognise the difference between the Argies' snub-nosed FN rifle and our longer one. Thank God it was a British one.

The runner said, 'Corporal McNeill, Kiszely's looking for you. You'd better get there quick. They need comms.'

You do not keep the Company Commander waiting, so I said to Chris, 'Come on, let's go!'

As we set off to Kiszely, little did I know that Chris was having trouble in trying to get the sleeping bag back into his Para smock pocket (for some reason he wore a Para smock) because the bag opens out one hundred times the size of the original packet. They are only meant to be used once in an emergency. The fact it was Chris who used his, probably saved my life, or at least prevented serious injury, because I had moved about ten metres away and waited for him.

It was only on turning round that I noticed a stretcher party carrying Lieutenant Mitchell whom I had bandaged earlier, coming around and over some rocks. Three Guardsmen were carrying him. I only knew one by name: young Dave Malcolmson – who, I believe, was Ronnie Tanbini's cousin. One of the others was possibly Denholm who had been shot in the arm. These two were carrying the front of the stretcher, whilst the third Guardsmen carried the rear of it on his own. So Chris threw his sleeping bag away and went back a little distance to assist. I only saw one stretcher, but not the second one.

My initial thought was, Shit, now Chris has an excuse if needed in case a bollocking is forthcoming.

The stretcher was now fifteen metres away, so I waited to see if they needed any help. I turned back again as others were shouting for me to use my radio, and that was when we started to get mortared. I heard a scream of, 'Incoming! Take cover!' before a deafening explosion threw me off my feet. I was knocked out for a couple of seconds but, on coming too, the situation had become very chaotic. Everyone was shouting to take cover. I crawled to some rocks for protection and got behind one.

Chris and the other Guardsmen at the rear of the stretcher were badly wounded. Malcolmson and Denholm[25] at the front were killed. Mr Mitchell, I think, only received shrapnel wounds to go with his shot in the leg. When I tried to stand up there was a pain in my left leg and something in my eye. I checked my leg. But there was no blood and it could be moved. Despite the situation it appeared that I was alright, although the events of the previous night and fatigue started to kick in. We also thought there was a de-escalation in the situation as the Argies withdrew in vast numbers back to Stanley. We did not expect anything else to happen and began to move away from our area that had been secured.

It just goes to show that it is never over until the fat lady sings.

Lance-Corporal Rickie Crookdake had been carried on the rear stretcher. He was not wounded by the mortar attack and, despite being hurled ten feet into the air, neither was Guardsman George MacKenzie, one of the four stretcher-bearers. Aided by Guardsman Findlay who had been wounded in the hand and using the latter's rifle as a crutch, Mitchell managed to struggle back to the Regimental Aid Post at Goat Ridge. He would be the second Left Flank platoon commander who would be awarded a MID which was for, according to its draft citation, 'outstanding courage under fire' and 'unselfish concern for his men'.[26] It would also be 15 Platoon's fifth such decoration.

Simon McNeill should also have been included in the official Tumbledown casualty statistics as British battle wounded number fifty. The mortar bomb blast had damaged his shins, and detached a tendon and dislodged a bone in his foot. But other priorities pre-occupied him:

> I had to go to where we were re-grouping and, once there, was told to get onto Battalion Tac HQ to find out what was happening. After this we were ordered to go over the positions we had fought through and look for intelligence information, prisoners, and any wounded who might have been missed. I remember seeing dead bodies lying everywhere, however we found another two Argentines hiding in separate foxholes.
>
> An image of one of them remains in my mind. As we tore the top off the foxhole he was still sitting in the bottom. There were about six of us around this particular position and yet he told us to 'Fuck off!' and then spat at us.
>
> 'Fuck, he's got a funny way of surrendering!' I thought.
>
> I had to stop two Guardsmen (one I knew very well) from hitting him with large rocks. They were not best pleased with him as he was still showing some resistance.
>
> He's either very stupid, or he's got some bottle, I thought.
>
> I was told at the Twenty-Fifth Anniversary Parade by three guys that it was me who shortly afterwards shouted out, 'There's a ceasefire!' after hearing it on my radio because Kiszely had instructed me to maintain a listening watch.

About this time Gordon Hoggan of G Company also found two enemy hiding a cave. They lunged for their weapons and the Guardsman, finding his SLR was jammed, had to bayonet one of them in the neck. Hoggan's grim end of battle experience did not end there because he also had to unzip the body bags of the Scots Guards' dead, including his best friend Malcolmson, and check their ID 'dog tags'. An hour or so before the Left Flank Company Commander had been reflecting on the night's work:

> One had a curious feeling; on the one hand one felt a tremendous sense of achievement, triumph, that one had done it. But, on the other hand, for the Company Commander to lose seven of his men killed and twenty-one wounded all in one night did come as something of a shock in the cold grey light of dawn.[27]

And in Right Flank Company Cocks was also doing his share of thinking about the life-changing event he had just been through:

As dawn approached in the immediate aftermath, a couple of dozen of us were sitting in a circle all staring blankly into nothing, utterly exhausted and all coming down from the adrenalin highs. We were covered in dirt, cordite, camouflage cream and festooned with weapons and ammunition. I distinctly remember seeing between six to eight prisoners being led away along the south part of the position and two wounded prisoners were bought hobbling to where I was sitting with the rest of 1 Platoon. Both men were about our age so they must have been young conscripts and they had gunshot wounds to the legs. They looked to be in shock and in a lot of pain and looked at us with great trepidation. Only a few minutes earlier we were trying to kill each other but now our humanity revealed itself. We sat them down and checked the dressings that had been applied before putting them in a sleeping bag and giving them a hot drink and a cigarette. They seemed to calm down and they chatted amongst themselves. None of us spoke Spanish and they did not speak any English. I often wondered what became of those two young men. I hope they made full recoveries.

It was about this time that a rumour started to circulate that there was an Argentine sniper left behind. Quite a few of the lads were running around as their blood was up and they were looking for 66mm rockets to fire at him as he was in some pretty heavy cover. They managed to get him in the end ...[28]

Back on the Pilgrimage and by 'The Ski Slope' again, I climbed to higher ground just behind Vázquez's position and, moving eastwards, found another four rock sniper hides where 13 Platoon had killed Sub-Lieutenant Oscar Silva's five Army snipers. Cocks commented later:

The events that you are writing about are so bound up in the person I am today that it feels like you are writing this book for me. I feel you are taking me on a journey through my own past and giving me glimpses into things I was unaware of at the time. For instance I have already learnt something new that I did not know before with regards the five Argentine Army snipers in the crags behind Vázquez's position. These are the guys that targetted me and hurled insults at us all night. For the first time you have given these faceless men a face. Until now they were unknown and their fate remained a mystery to me. Now I know who they were and ultimately what became of them. In my heart of hearts I had hoped that they had crawled away into the night and made it home, for I bear them no animosity. But now I know that, in fact, they were all killed and I have unknowingly visited their graves.

Battling through fog and a heavy snowfall, I arrived back at Tumbledown's east end where the Scots Guards pilgrims' Act of Remembrance had just ended. *Flashback*. The weather was reminiscent of those two horrendously cold days of survival for the majority of the Gurkhas on the battlefield in the immediate post-hostilities period.

However the Battle of Tumbledown had been three battles rolled into one. It did not only take place on Tumbledown's west and east ends, but also two kilometres to the south-west at Pony's Pass. Yet contrary to Argentina's history of the war which remains in stubborn and nonsensical denial, no enemy regimental force ever attacked BIM5's O Company located there. The responsibility for that belonged to a composite Scots Guards platoon and, although many of its members would suffer greatly for their bravery, this diversionary attack would spawn forth many benefits.

And not least, the quality of the deception, a major Sun Tzu component for success on the battlefield, was so outstanding that it has withstood the test of time. But that ought to be no surprise. The action bore the hallmark of the Special Air Service.

Notes

1. *The Art of War*, Chapter 4 – Form.
2. *Razor's Edge* (p. 299) claims that for 'the next hour or so the two groups sniped at each other across the Terrace' (a broad hollow below the summit) before Right Flank 'came up to resume the offensive'. But Miño's withdrawal and the time constraints implied that this could not have happened.
3. From the Charles Messenger unpublished draft manuscript of the battle.
4. *Hors de Combat*, p. 29.
5. *Razor's Edge* (p. 308) incorrectly assigns Lawrence as the 2 Platoon Commander while, conversely, Second-Lieutenant Mark Mathewson is given command of Lawrence's 3 Platoon.
6. Supplement to *The London Gazette* of Friday, 8 October 1982. Issue 49134, p. 12847.
7. From the Charles Messenger unpublished draft manuscript of the battle.
8. Supplement to *The London Gazette* of Friday, 8 October 1982. Issue 49134, p. 12852.
9. *Ibid.*, p. 12851.
10. Since La Madrid's platoon only possessed two heavy General Purpose Machine-Guns, the four enemy machine-gun positions mentioned so far in this account of Right Flank's attack must have been armed with the lighter FAP (*Fusil Automático Pesado*). One of La Madrid's GPMG gunners was killed further to the north of the lodgement area. The other withdrew eventually with La Madrid's platoon to Stanley.
11. *The Observer* newspaper dated 14 January 2007 alleged that Lawrence had shot fourteen enemy and bayoneted three. But this did not correspond to the Scots Guards' figures for enemy casualties of eight dead and five wounded in Right Flank's phase of the battle. La Madrid's figures were five dead and eight wounded.
12. *Razor's Edge* (p. 290 – lower map) incorrectly indicates Lawrence doing this.
13. The figure of forty-three wounded is an oft-quoted statistic in numerous books on the war including *Razor's Edge* (p. 294). However after visiting the Regimental Archives of the Scots Guards HQ in Wellington Barracks, London on 10 November 2009, the author carried out an analysis on casualties from the Battalion's Order of Battle and list of war wounded. This revealed that there were, in fact, forty-six Scots Guards wounded out of a total of forty-nine British wounded in the battle. Left Flank Company's 15 Platoon had twelve of these

casualties. The statistics were:

G Company – seven wounded.

Left Flank Company – seven killed and twenty-one wounded.

Right Flank Company – eight wounded (plus one attached Army Catering Corps NCO casualty).

Diversionary Attack Platoon – one killed and ten wounded (plus one attached Irish Guards NCO and Gunner NCO wounded). A Royal Engineer NCO was also killed. Total British Tumbledown battle fatalities were therefore nine.

14. These Argentine casualty figures have been taken from the Internet Wikipedia (free encyclopedia) site entitled 'The Battle of Mount Tumbledown'. They are dubious. Listed on the same site, the Scots Guards casualty figures of ten killed and fifty-three wounded are incorrect. Eduardo Gerding (in an e-mail dated 10 February 2012) admitted there was still an Argentine 'total reluctance to talk about this issue'. The author's research has revealed the following:

- On Tumbledown's north-east spur and/or at Moody Brook with (Jaimet's) B Company RI6 group – twelve wounded (from shellfire before nightfall).

- At Pony's Pass with the BIM5 O Company – three killed and four wounded (plus many others slightly hurt).

- On Tumbledown's west end with (Vázquez's) 4 Platoon – fifteen killed, five wounded and four missing. Ten of the fatalities and four missing were Argentine Army soldiers. By a process of deduction, thirty-six Argentines were probably captured. Certainly some time after first light on 14 June the figure of twenty-seven prisoners (including Vázquez who was believed then to be the enemy Company Commander on Tumbledown) was given to the Gurkha Battalion Tac HQ in a radio transmission by Second-Lieutenant Quentin Oates, the Gurkha liaison officer with the Scots Guards. Post-battle more Argentines were discovered still in their foxholes as described by Simon McNeill.

- On Tumbledown's centre with the 60mm mortar section – one killed and four wounded.

- On Tumbledown's east end with (Miño's) 5 Platoon and (La Madrid's) 3 Platoon (RI6/3) – one wounded (Miño) and 3 Platoon (RI6/B) – five killed and nine wounded. A Scots Guards sketch map of this area (a copy is held by the author) was drawn after the battle and shows a total of eight Argentine fatalities. Therefore another three fatalities should be added to the five from La Madrid's platoon. It is possible that either these additional three fatalities might be Marines (from shellfire?) or RI4 soldiers whom La Madrid found en route to his contact with the seven Scots Guards Left Flank Company Guardsmen on the east summit and subsequent engagement with Right Flank Company. The sketch map also shows that twelve Argentines were captured.

- On Tumbledown's north-east spur (Lucero's) 3 Platoon – one killed. This fatality was found by B Company, 1st/7th Gurkha Rifles in a sangar together with a Marine medic and two other survivors. In his book *With the*

Gurkhas in the Falklands (p. 270), the author incorrectly stated that this was a soldier from Jaimet's Company.

- In the stone runs between Tumbledown and Mount William (Oruezabala's) 2 Platoon – one wounded.
- On Mount William (Bianchi's) 1 Platoon and other attachments – no casualties except for one RI4 soldier killed.
- On withdrawal to Sapper Hill (Cuñe's) 81mm Mortar Platoon – one killed and two wounded.
- On withdrawal to Puerto Argentino (Stanley) (La Madrid's) 3 Platoon – two killed.
- On Sapper Hill BIM5 M Company (during the Welsh Guards helicopter assault on the position) – three killed.

In summary, and based on the author's research, the Argentine casualties for the Battle of Tumbledown were thirty-two killed, thirty-eight wounded and four missing plus many other O Company Marines slightly hurt. (Note that these final figures do not include the three fatalities on Sapper Hill).

15. *Among Friends: The Scots Guards 1956-1993*, p. 153.
16. Giacchino's CHVC citation read: 'For the bravery, heroism and leadership showed during *Operación Rosario*, which resulted in the recovery of the Malvinas Islands. On this occasion, Captain Giacchino led the assault on the Governor's house without opening fire against the British troops, whereby while forcing his way into the premises he was met by intense fire from the Royal Marines and was thus seriously wounded. He died in the hospital of Puerto Argentino on the same day, 2nd April 1982.'
17. It had been converted into a forward field surgical hospital with capacity to carry out two operations simultaneously while another six patients awaited their turn.
18. LMG – Light Machine-Gun (7.62mm Bren gun).
19. BFBS DVD-Video *Falklands 25: The 2007 Pilgrimage.*
20. Osborn's left leg was so badly injured it had to be amputated eight days after his arrival on board HMHS *Uganda*. He made a full recovery and, at the time of writing, is Assistant Curator of The Queen's Royal Lancers Regimental Museum at Catterick. The details of Osborn's wounding come from Nicci Pugh's book *White Ship, Red Crosses* (p. 102).
21. Supplement to *The London Gazette* of Friday, 8 October 1982. Issue 49134, p 12847.
22. E-mail dated 3 February 2010.
23. Supplement to *The London Gazette* of Friday, 8 October 1982. Issue 49134, pp. 12844 and 12845.
24. From the Charles Messenger unpublished draft manuscript of the battle.
25. However it was Guardsman Reynolds who was carrying Mitchell's stretcher together with Malcolmson. McNeill had always mistakenly thought it was Denholm, not Reynolds, who had been killed. 'That it is one of the difficulties I've had all these years later,' he explained to the author. 'Being transferred into the Company at the last moment and with only twenty-four hours to familiarise myself, meant that I did not know by name many of the people I fought with and

who were killed or wounded in front of me.' His understandable muddle motivated me to investigate further. The last part of Reynold's posthumous DCM citation stated: '[...] showing complete disregard for his own safety, he moved forward to render first aid to a wounded comrade. He himself was wounded in the hand by enemy sniper fire, but continued to aid his colleague. Whilst doing so, he was killed by enemy mortar fire.' Yet on the International Form of Medical Certificate of Cause of Death (F Med 174) signed by Royal Navy Surgeon-Commander Rick Jolly, the official medical cause of his 'Death Instantaneous' was a 'Gunshot Wound Right Chest, Large Calibre High Velocity Bullet' – while his friend Malcolmson's was 'Blast Injury, Severe Multiple Wounds Legs and Chest – Shock and Haemorrhage'. A curious puzzle indeed, but not as obvious as *Razor's Edge* (page 290 – lower map) which incorrectly indicates that the two stretcher-bearers were killed on the *north-west* slopes of Tumbledown. Of course they fell on its *south-west* slopes.

26. But just as in the cases of McGuinness, Davidson, and Clark Mitchell, *Razor's Edge* (p. 298) also incorrectly claimed that the wounded subaltern had received 'nothing' for his actions that night.

27. From the Charles Messenger unpublished draft manuscript of the battle.

28. This was 'Pedro', the same lone sniper who had been probably firing at McNeill towards the end of Right Flank's attack. 'Pedro' was eventually killed by Lance-Corporal Gary Tytler of Left Flank Company.

5   Deception and reflection

On Tumbledown in November 2007 I lost my battle with time to find the Argentine 81mm Platoon position located somewhere on the eastern saddle connecting Tumbledown and Mount William. Passing the latter on our left, we drove back down to the Stanley road, only to turn west rather than east back to the capital.

'Another Act of Remembrance is going to take place further along the road at Pony's Pass', the driver of our four-wheel drive vehicle, Patrick Watts, advised us.

This was where the Scots Guards' diversionary attack led by Major The Honourable Richard Bethell MBE, later Lord Westbury, had taken place against the eighty-nine men of BIM5's O Company commanded by Sub-Lieutenant Carlos Calmels.[2] The vehicle stopped and we got out to hurry across the grass tussock stretch of 200 metres which had been the diversionary attack battlefield quarter of a century before, to where twenty or so pilgrims and the BFBS TV crew had gathered. They stood by a small cairn on which an iron cross made from a broken Argentine entrenching tool had been mounted.

Former Pipers Steve Duffy and Peter MacInnes, who had been members of Bethell's composite platoon, had built this out of rocks taken from the position. It was located on a four-foot high peat bank where Argentine O Company sangars had once been sited. Duffy, who had also been a Recce Platoon medic employed as Bethell's radio operator for the attack, togerher with MacInnes had spent a day locating and verifying this position. These two pilgrims had also found the link for the belted General Purpose Machine-Gun 7.62mm ammunition at the place where the fire support group had been giving covering fire to the initial attack. Heads of rounds were also discovered in the peat bank, in addition to bits of blanket lying on the reverse side of the sangar positions. Duffy also picked up an Argentine Marine marked spoon which, not unreasonably, he would take back to UK as a war memento.

After the Lord's Prayer, the drone of Duffy's and Ian Davidson's bagpipes started up with a heart-wrenching lament in honour of the two who had been killed at the start of this attack ...

Bethell, who had also served with the SAS, had organised his force into three four-man assault sections from the Recce Platoon. Drill-Sergeant Wight, Sergeant Coull and Bethell commanded each of these sections which were armed with the modern version of a Bren gun. Fitted with 7.62mm barrel, this was a Light Machine-Gun (LMG) which had ammunition magazines rather than link belted ammunition. There was also a ten-man fire support group of three gun groups, each armed with two belt-fed General Purpose Machine-Guns. Commanded by Company Sergeant Major Braby, these men came from Battle Group Headquarters and A1 Echelon. The number of machine-guns was important. There would be the need for maximum firepower in order to create the most possible noise. In addition an Argentine platoon, whether it was Marine or Army, only possessed two GPMGs. Hence if they saw or heard six Scots Guards GPMGs firing simultaneously in addition to the three LMGs, then this could give the impression that a superior force was attacking them.

Other specialist support was provided by Lance-Corporal Pashley and Corporal Foran (Sappers from 9 Para Squadron Royal Engineers), Bombardier Palin (the artillery Forward Observation Officer) and Lance-Sergeant Miller (the Mortar Fire Controller). Also attached to the platoon was 4 Troop of B Squadron, The Blues and Royals. The Troop Commander was Lieutenant Mark Coreth whose mission was to provide intimate fire support with his troop's two Scimitar and two Scorpion light tanks.

Late in the afternoon of 13 June a six-man Scots Guards recce party for the diversion had moved forward to 'eyeball' their objective. It:

> quickly discovered that the Port Stanley track was mined on both sides, and only the track itself was safe [...] the recce party moved up to the 42 Commando RAP (Regimental Aid Post), which was in a red container by the side of the Port Stanley track near the west end of Mount Harriet. Leaving half the group here the remainder pushed on up the slope of Mount Harriet itself, seeing no Commando positions, but merely the odd solitary Marine. They then came under artillery fire and withdrew to the shelter of some rocks, where they could see several Argentine positions on the south side of the track, which they noted. After about one hour they were subjected to some unpleasantly close mortar fire and moved to a new position. Meanwhile the RAP had been under artillery fire, and one Welsh Guards NCO, who was riding a motor-cycle, took a direct hit. Major Bethell's group now withdrew to the RAP in rapid bounds to avoid the sporadic artillery fire and got back without mishap, apart from CSM Braby, who unwittingly chose an Argentine latrine in which to take temporary cover.[3]

The Scots Guards platoon would be outnumbered by three to one. O Company faced west with a platoon of three sections of thirteen men per section covering a frontage of 250 metres on the southern side of the Fitzroy-Stanley track. The three section positions were in a linear lay-out that did not give mutual support. There were four machine-guns co-located with this forward platoon, and two more machine-guns sited further to the rear co-located with a section of three 60mm mortars.[4] O Company HQ was seventy-five metres behind the first section position closest to the track. This section was commanded by *Cabo Primero* (Corporal) Juan Carlos Agüero:

> Fog began to develop and I realised that the visibility was going to be seriously reduced when the enemy reached our positions. At last light *Suboficial Primero* (Chief Petty Officer) Roberto Tejerina, the Company Sergeant-Major, repeated on the radio the procedure to follow in case of retreat. Basically it was:

'First phase: The third section will withdraw towards the Company's command post and from there will continue to the rendezvous area. Once there it will establish a blocking position, to cover from there the withdrawal of the rest of the company.'
'Second phase: the first section will withdraw.'
'Third phase: the second section will withdraw.'
'Final phase: the Company's support weapons.'[5]

Agüero had made a correct assumption about the visibility.

Night came and the visibility was severely reduced. There was no use in employing the night goggles, I could not see beyond 100 metres.[6]

Meanwhile the Scots Guards platoon made hurried final preparations. Time was becoming extremely short. The Orders Group had to be carried out rapidly in the dark and lacked a model of the objective, a standard requirement which would facilitate a detailed understanding of the mission. According to Duffy, the displeased Bethell commented bitterly later that it had been the worst Orders Group he had held in his military career. H-Hour was originally set for 00.30Z. But Bethell's twenty-nine man platoon was delayed in leaving their base near the RAP for thirty minutes because Welsh Guards patrols were still operating east of Mount Harriet and had to be withdrawn. Then the platoon climbed onto the Blues and Royals' light tanks and the initial start line (by 42 Commando's Alternative HQ further up the Stanley track) was crossed at 22.45Z. H-Hour had to be changed to when the first O Company positions were attacked.

Eventually the platoon was dropped off to continue their advance silently in single file towards O Company. The pitch-dark night caused navigation challenges. It was also cold and beginning to snow. At 00.45Z some enemy sangars were sighted at seventy-five metres by Bethell peering through his night IWS (Individual Weapon Sight). Just before that, Acting Sub-Lieutenant Quiroga, the original O Company Commander, had fractured his ankle and had to be replaced by *Teniente de Fragata* (Sub-Lieutenant) Carlos Calmels. Obviously this caused some disruption in O Company.

Bethell managed to get nearer to his objective. He decided that his assault sections would attack from the north. A fire base had to be established that could support the assault sections' manouevre along the front of the enemy position. This was a task for the fire support group which was dispatched south onto the right flank. So at about 01.00Z, the attack began just as G Company were crossing their start line little more than two kilometres to the north-west en route to Tumbledown.

But disaster then struck at Pony's Pass. Six-foot three-inch Drill-Sergeant Danny Wight was shot dead by an enemy Marine who fired three rounds at him from a sangar at near point-blank range. Wight went down, killed instantaneously by the first bullet, while Lance-Corporal John 'Pash' Pashley of 9 Para Squadron Royal Engineers came under fire from another sangar and was mortally wounded by a round hitting his throat. He died shortly afterwards.

However, luck had already proved to be on the side of Duffy:

We were in file, and the first that I knew were in contact with the enemy was when
a burst of automatic fire raked us. It killed Wight and Pashley and, to my
immediate front, Lance-Sergeant Denise Kincella, an Irish Guards attachment, was
shot in the head with the bullet tracking across the top of it. Simultaneously and
behind me, Lance-Corporal Tommy Owens received a gunshot wound from the
same burst. It removed most of the flesh and working parts to his upper arm. He
would be in agonising pain for many months afterwards. But somehow I escaped
injury.

   We were within twenty feet of the forward Argentine position that consisted of
approximately eight sangars with overhead protection. They were concealed in a
peat cutting bank. Caught in the open ground immediately to the front of these
sangars, we had to press home our attack quickly. A fire support group on a
peat bank fifty metres to our rear also engaged the enemy. Throughout the
diversion I anticipated an enemy counter-attack and, personally, had little
expectation of surviving the night.[7]

The assault sections attacked using firearms and hand grenades to achieve the required
'noisy' diversion. Agüero provided a 'real-time' account of his section's response:

Suddenly I hear explosions in front of our position. Private Barboza, the MAG [8]
sight operator, cries out. I put on the goggles and make out forms directly in front
of me and further to my right, where the track lies. I give the order to open fire on
them. The section answers with discipline, although Iñiguez's FAP is firing
continuously instead of just with bursts. This was to expect from his temper and
the situation. Also I open fire on the shapes.[9]

The situation was highly confused. After the initial enemy contact, Duffy was the only
uninjured man in his assault section. He described his immediate actions:

I fired my rifle into the bank to my front, and then took the LMG from wounded
Tommy Owens. On crawling forward, I found some cover in a bog pool from
where I continued to fire. My 'one in two tracer' lit up the outline of a sangar roof,
however unbeknown to me Drummer Danny Wand was directly under the lip of
the sangar and he shouted 'Stop firing!' in no uncertain way. It was only luck that
had prevented me from shooting him. Sergeant Coull then called for grenades. I
collected these from Lance-Corporal Nicholson and Piper MacInnes who were
tending the wounded, and then made my way to Sergeant Coull and Lance-
Sergeant McLintock. Being more confident in my ability with a gun, I handed over
the grenades to them. Then together with Major Bethell, they began to work their
way systematically down the line of sangars and, one by one, threw grenades into
them.

Despite return enemy fire, the platoon took the first three sangars. According to
Duffy, shadowy enemy figures were seen to leave their positions. Throughout all this
the Scotsmen were shouting; but their enemy remained strangely silent. Then the fire

support group came under heavy machine-gun fire from a southern position: but Bombardier Palin was wounded when an assault section attempted to attack it. Ten frantic minutes had passed, but Murphy's Law intervened with ammunition stoppages occurring in the machine-guns belonging to the fire support group. This was sorted out eventually and covering fire restored. But a stalemate then developed as the enemy continued to return fire.

Meanwhile 4 Troop was in a radio 'dead-spot' which meant no communications existed with Bethell. However on hearing small-arms fire at the O Company position, the troop began to move forward. They were under artillery fire when, at about 01.10Z, Coreth's Scorpion reached a huge crater in the track and turned to the north to avoid it. Immediately the Scorpion drove over an Argentine anti-tank landmine which exploded, blowing off the driver's hatch, sprockets and some road wheels, ripping the right-hand track in half, buckling the hull and lifting the engine out off its mounting.

Fortunately Coreth and his two crew members were uninjured. They evacuated their immobile Scorpion quickly and ran back twenty metres to the next tank which they climbed aboard. The explosion attracted heavy enemy shelling and the surviving three tanks carried out a tactical withdrawal by reversing fast back up the track. Communications with Bethell then returned. Although south-west of their intended firing position by more than a kilometre, 4 Troop then began to engage other enemy positions at about 01.25Z by firing their remaining Scorpion 76mm gun and two Scimitar Rarden 30mm cannon in turn. Coreth adjusted the fall of shot by running from tank to tank. The cannon's maximum range of 4,000 metres, which was nearly double that of the 76mm gun, meant it could target Mount William where (it was believed) the BIM5 81mm Mortar Platoon was located.[10] Furthermore the cannon's 30mm armour piecing tracer ammunition with its firing rate of ninety rounds per minute, as opposed to the 76mm gun's rate of only six rounds per minute, contributed to the overall 'force-multiplier' effect of the diversion and creation of an illusion at the BIM5 Battalion Command level that the overall attacking force had a strength of much more than two rifle companies.

With the Blues and Royals' spectacular tracer fire streaming across and high above the heads of Bethell's platoon towards Mount William, a foray forward was eventually made by Coull's fire support group onto O Company's position to assist with another assault on the troublesome southern enemy position. This comprised some sangars sited on top of a four-foot high peat bank. During this advance at the double into and across a dip in the ground, enemy machine-gun and rifle fire opened up from the right. Guardsman Gilmour was hit in the legs. But the support group returned fire and, after assistance was given to Gilmour, the objective was finally reached.

An impression of the confusion created by the Scots Guards attack was provided by Agüero's continued 'real-time' account:

> The Brits are approaching us without taking cover.
> Some of the shapes are falling to the ground from the effect of our fire.
> A wounded British soldier is firing his weapon in bursts from the ground.
> They use a lot of tracer bullets.
> They shout and call each other by their names.

We are facing small arms fire.
I can make out a man with a radio (much smaller than ours).
They are moving all around and I can see explosions.
I think they have encircled both my flanks and I ask the Company for fire support, because I realise that our own firing somehow has become weaker.
I receive a strong blow in the face and realise I am bleeding.[11]

Coull's fire support group gathered below the peat bank and assisted the assault group to capture the position by taking the end sangar and getting a machine-gun into it. This weapon replied effectively to the enemy fire coming from the rear while Bethell, Coull and Drummer Wand took out the remaining sangars with hand grenades. But the final sangar proved impervious to an exploding hand-grenade and Bethell ordered its occupants to surrender. The result, according to Bethell was:

a 7.62mm round through the peat bank which covered us in mud. Having received mud in the eye, the ante was put up with a white phosphorous grenade and the enemy position fell silent.[12]

And Agüero's account described the result of a probable 'white phos' grenade attack:

The enemy is pushing forward: The blanket covering me catches fire from a nearby explosion and I get burned. I manage to put the fire out, but it makes me an easy target and a bullet hits my shoulder.[13]

Then at about 02.00Z the platoon came under heavy enemy artillery fire. Its three pipers who were also trained medical assistants had been kept busy treating the wounded. Nineteen year-old Piper Peter MacInnes would be later awarded a MID 'for his bravery and unselfish regard for his colleagues'. Its citation (not draft) also described the vulnerability of his battlefield trade:

During the battle several men were killed and wounded by concentrated machine-gun fire. Soon afterwards the force came under heavy fire from mortars and artillery. Throughout this bombardment MacInnes went forward to tend the wounded and give morphine with complete disregard for his own personal safety. When time to withdraw, it was he who ensured that the wounded reached a safe area ...

The BFBS TV camera team recorded a moving ceremony on top of the four-foot high peat bank and small battlefield around it which had been lost to history for so long. The pilgrims stood at attention as a wreath was laid, the Lord's Prayer recited and the three ubiquitous Scots Guards pipers played their spine-chilling lament. Afterwards, prompted by the discovery of a few empty bullet cases lying on the ground and suspected hand-grenade in a puddle, Duffy, McNeill, Morton and Seear conducted an impromptu debriefing. Combat veterans require a further clarification of what had occurred on their battlefield. Now a Detective Inspector in the Thames Valley Police

CID, Steve Duffy had been wounded during the attack. He was Bethell's radio operator, but towards the end of the fighting had asked the Platoon Commander if he could throw his inoperative Clansman 351 radio set away. Permission to do this had been duly given because another two radios were available.

The TV crew now captured our rather disjointed discussion for posterity:

Duffy: They were all in the bank here, and there was between six and eight trenches along here. And we worked away [...] because the initial contact [...] the first burst of fire came from over there, and we were all in extended line all back [...] all the way back to that bank. And from there we worked away round this ridge taking out the trenches one by one, whilst they from the trenches behind us were firing in, and then they started calling in [...] as they started going up these trenches.

McNeill: So where did you get hit?

Duffy: Where did I get hit?

McNeill: Yeah, where?

Duffy: Oh, just over that ridge.

McNeill: That's where Bethell and you got hit there?

Duffy: Just over there. There's a flat rock. Because we heard a hand grenade come out of the trench and roll onto the rock and couldn't see it. So we just rolled up into a ball. You know, I thought it was a dud, went like that, took my hands away from my face, and it went bang!

Seear: Did you think that this attack was a successful attack?

Morton: Yes, it was. The whole idea was the Argentine force believed we were coming from that direction – towards Tumbledown. So the Battalion put in a diversionary attack to this location. When they got to here, this was as far as they got. The Drill Sergeant was killed *there* in the corner. The piper was wounded over *there* with the grenade shrapnel. Once they bugged back out again they moved back to a minefield with two of the Guardsmen ...[14]

Seear: Were you in the minefield?

Morton: No. I wasn't here. No. There were twenty-five guys in the attack, and out of the twenty-five, sixteen were wounded and two were killed ...

The grenade attack occurred at 02.15Z when Bethell and Duffy on completion of the mission gave LMG covering fire at the enemy position while the rest of the platoon withdrew to the RV (rendezvous point) with the dead and wounded. Once there, able-bodied men would be allocated to assist the wounded, and carry the dead and spare weapons. However Duffy had been carrying two 84mm HEAT (high-explosive anti-tank) rounds for the Carl Gustav anti-tank gun which Kinsella had been carrying. The piper wanted to dispatch these two rounds in the direction of the enemy and so retrieved the Carl Gustav from the wounded Lance-Sergeant. Bethell and Duffy then became an impromptu anti-tank gun crew. Their target was the O Company HQ which was on a rise in the ground further to the rear. Bethell became the number one (firer), while Duffy assumed the role as the number two (loader). The first round was duly loaded by him into gun's rear breech, and then they waited to ensure that the remainder of the platoon moved out of the gun's back-blast area. Bethell:

Sergeant Coull informed me that all were safely back in the RV when a wounded Argentinian, who had remained silent in one of the first sangars we had attacked, rolled a grenade down the side of his sangar which then rested just below Piper Duffy and me. He met his maker before the grenade exploded, wounding us both. We could both move and were able to withdraw to the RV, although there was a touch of heavy breathing from Duffy who had his lung punctured.[15]

It was Bethell who had shot and killed the Marine, the last to die in the attack. The grenade had exploded six feet away. Duffy:

Bethell took the blast through the soles of both feet and legs. I took some minor shrapnel wounds to both my shins and head, but was unlucky in that a single piece of shrapnel went between the extra magazines I had been carrying inside my smock and then into my chest.

Actual combat had lasted ninety minutes with eleven sangars attacked.[16] According to Calmels, 'Three (Marines had been) killed and four seriously wounded, but there were many others with minor injuries.' [17] But of more importance, the main aim had been achieved immediately to the west of Tumbledown. There G Company had secured virtually unopposed the rocky knoll despite their presence being detected by Miño's platoon higher up on Tumbledown's west summit. There would be also other less obvious diversionary attack synergy effects whose value was not appreciated at the time.

Meanwhile Duffy was having an uncomfortable time after the grenade explosion:

Sergeant Colin Coull, Lance-Corporal Archie Beatty and Lance-Corporal Gary Nicholson realised what had happened and returned to us immediately. I could not move and Gary gave me first aid. My webbing was removed and the Archie 'The Bear' Beatty lifted me up into a fireman's carry and then walked out of the immediate enemy area towards a rocky outcrop. Then we crossed a stile and single-strand wire fence.

At 02.30Z their trek back to 4 Troop began just as the Scots Guards Left Flank Company came under fire from Vázquez's 4 Platoon on the west end of Tumbledown. But after a short distance the situation for Bethell's platoon, now strung out in a file up to forty metres in length, was suddenly complicated by two explosions at its rear. Lance-Sergeant Miller and Guardsman Carruthers, both of whom had been carrying Gilmour, had trodden on two of the anti-personnel mines laid by Miño's Marine Amphibious Engineers nearly eight days previously. This mine type was the size of a cigarette packet and therefore exceptionally difficult to see in the dark. Both men had a foot blown off which required later leg amputations, and Lance-Sergeants McClintock, Paterson, Wolff and Lance-Corporal Mitchell all received collateral shrapnel wounds to their legs.

The explosions were a signal to the O Company Commander that the time had come to withdraw from Pony's Pass to his original position at the BIM5 Command

Post's Felton Stream location. Calmels received an authorisation to do so from the Battalion HQ. This was carried out in an orderly fashion as Bethell's platoon then came under considerable enemy artillery and mortar fire during the next forty minutes. It gave O Company effective cover as they made good their withdrawal. Calmels moved out first with two of his rifle sections and the 60mm mortars. Petty Officer Orozco followed later with his machine-guns. The latter:

> inspected the position to make sure nobody was left behind or wounded, while at the same time covering himself and the retreat of his comrades by firing a MAG (he still waits for the Navy to recognise his effort). Later, in the Quarry, he would still keep leading the wounded and stragglers towards Mount William, before rejoining his Company at the Battalion Command Post.[18]

Despite these new perils for Bethell's platoon, their effort had to be focused on rescuing those who had just been wounded. Corporal John Foran, the second 9 Para Squadron Sapper, played a critical role in this operation as the final section of his later MM citation indicated:

> Without hesitation and completely disregarding his own safety, Corporal Foran re-entered the minefield and cleared a path to his injured colleagues. Having treated them he cleared a route back out of the minefield, enabling the casualties to be evacuated.[19]

Duffy:

> I was a dead-weight, yet Archie had carried me 150 to 200 metres or more under mortar and artillery fire in the dark and over difficult terrain. He was exhausted and put me down to rest. By then I had regained some functionality and ended up at the front of the column together with Major Bethell who was in great pain from his wounds. Because of a lack of able-bodied men to carry both them and yet more spare weapons, we were forced to abandon the dead who, until this point, had been carried from the enemy position. The platoon continued to withdraw in good order despite mortar bombs and artillery shells whistling over our heads and landing to the south and west of us. The shrapnel made a surprisingly slow whirring noise through the air. It added to my despair and forced us to stand still. Lying down was not an option. My right lung had been punctured by grenade shrapnel and, by now, had collapsed. There were further shrapnel wounds to my head, eyebrow, and both lower legs.
>
> But apart from a dull ache in my chest, breathlessness and nausea, there was no pain. I was determined to get out of the minefield and set about finding an exit path with Major Bethell. We used right-angle torches to scan the ground, and illuminated anything that appeared unusual or suspicious. I am told there was some deliberation between us about what constituted 'unusual' and that I became somewhat argumentative. But I have no recollection of this. Corporal Foran did the actual clearance and put his face close to any area of concern, then used his bayonet to check the ground where we had indicated.

Rather surprisingly the enemy shelling was not targetted on the platoon itself. However it could have been that the enemy mortaring and shelling was being directed against an assumed much larger British follow-up force which was about to launch a second-wave attack against the Pony's Pass position. The platoon also had an unwelcome encounter with a Welsh Guards patrol, a situation which contained all the potential of causing a disastrous 'blue-on-blue'. But a quick exchange of passwords prevented this. Eventually after one and a half kilometres, the battered platoon that included twelve wounded [21] reached their objective at 04.30Z.[20] Including its two killed, Bethell's platoon of twenty-nine had sustained a forty-eight percent casualty rate. This was far more than the twenty-nine per cent for Left Flank Company and Right Flank Company's six per cent. In addition the diversionary attack had taken double the amount of time to complete compared to Right Flank's attack, and lasted the same ninety minutes as Left Flank's 'charge' from the bottom of Tumbledown's west end to the top of the east summit. Duffy:

> We emerged onto the Fitzroy to Stanley track and met up with Coreth's troop. Their remaining three light tanks transported us to the western side of Mount Harriet and 42 Commandos' Regimental Aid Post which had been set up in a shipping container. Then the wounded were flown by helicopter to Teal Inlet occupied by elements of 3 Commando Brigade on the north coast of East Falkland and, once there, I went under the surgeon's knife in the dining room of an Islander's home.
>
> I shall be ever grateful to Archie Beatty, Gary Nicholson and Colin Coull for returning to Major Bethell and me ...

As a postscript to this decisive action which ensured British success in the Battle of Tumbledown, a Royal Engineer arrived later that morning and removed fifty-seven anti-tank mines from the area around the demolition crater that had forced Coreth's Scorpion off the track. Bethell would also be decorated later, but only with a MID which had been recommended (draft citation) 'for his courageous action and outstanding leadership under fire'. The award was completely disproportionate to his remarkable achievement of leading a most dangerous platoon action which would cause numerous errors of judgement to be made by the Argentine Marines during the remainder of that night. The draft citation for Duffy's MID recommendation contained the words 'for his courage and resource under fire'.[22] Scott had no doubt as to the importance of the composite platoon's successful mission:

> Our diversionary attack was [...] to make the enemy think we were advancing in the track to Stanley [...] The position of O Company was irrelevant [...] We had detected the minefield in front of O Company and realised that they would cover it with fire, unless they were complete idiots. This was a very good reason for *not* coming that way.[23]

The actions of Bethell's platoon and Coreth's troop would yield other priceless dividends. This not only included the saving of life, but also the wild manipulation of

Argentine perceptions about the aim, direction and size of participating British forces. After all, Sun Tzu did stipulate 'and so the skilled general forms others yet is without form'.[24] Questions must have whirled around in Argentine minds. Was this the start of the main British advance to Stanley? Or not? If it was, then what should be the appropriate reaction? Or non-reaction?

Nearly three decades post-war Carlos Calmels was still serving in the Argentine Marine Corps with the rank of *Capitán de Navío* (Naval) Captain. Astonishingly he remained adamant about his perception of the strength of the enemy force that had attacked O Company at Pony's Pass:

> I don't think we were attacked by only twenty-nine men. We received firepower from the front and the flank, so it's obviously a fallacy to say there were only twenty-nine men. According to the amount of firepower we received [...] I think it must have been two rifle companies with almost the same amount of men (per company) that we had.[25]

So Calmels believed he was being attacked by a force of 180 men – six times the number actually involved. The former O Company Commander obviously had not taken into account that sounds and light are magnified greatly on a battlefield at night as opposed to day: a basic phenomena that I was taught when a Sandhurst Officer Cadet. Calmels's opinion could be also explained by Miño's claim that the Argentine Marine Corps did not include any diversionary attack concept in their doctrine [26] (which I have difficulty in believing). But totally misleading post-war Argentine reports that O Company 'had killed and wounded sixty British soldiers' [27] at Pony's Pass have only served to perpetuate one of the great Argentine myths of the Falklands-Malvinas War. Calmels's statement is a classic example of how Tumbledown battle facts *still* have not been reconciled between the veterans of both sides. It was frustrating that he never replied to my follow-up questions on the issue. Perhaps he felt that I was attacking his honour by suggesting O Company had been in combat with a far inferior force than originally believed. My opinion on this was uncompromising. The time was over-ripe for Calmels to be presented with the correct facts.

The BIM5 Command Post ramped up Calmels's flawed perception to the size of a regimental attack.[28] This led to N Company's 1 and 2 Platoons on Mount William and just south of Tumbledown remaining at their locations as it was deduced that there would be another British regimental thrust through Pony's Pass onto Mount William and Tumbledown. The firepower of 1 and 2 Platoon would be needed to repel this 'imminent' attack. This tactical fixation prevented the mounting later that night of a much-needed counter-attack from at least either 1 or 2 Platoon onto Vázquez's beleaguered position. It is not without reason that Sun Tzu refers to fixation as 'a calamity in employing the military'.[29]

My intense interest in this diversionary attack stemmed from that particular 1982 night when waiting with 1/7 Gurkha Rifles at the west end of Goat Ridge four kilometres north-west of Pony's Pass. I was the only member of the Battalion able to monitor the Brigade rear-link radio frequency and every unnerving report of that platoon's desperate circumstances in the minefield. Such a passive listening role cannot be recommended, particularly as we were about to go into action ourselves. At the time I prayed that none of us, Gurkha or British soldier alike, would encounter en route to our twin objectives of Tumbledown's north-east spur and Mount William that other enemy minefield (which turned out to be a dummy one – also laid by Miño) on Tumbledown's north-west slopes. And then, like Bethell's band of brothers, suffer accordingly.

Post-Pilgrimage, Simon McNeill provided me with his vested interest in this attack which had validated a key Sun Tzu tenet that 'the military is a *Tao* (Way) of deception':

There is an interesting story that I did not know about until we met up again on the Pilgrimage. I was the Signals Detachment Commander for Major Bethell of HQ Company when we were at Bluff Cove preparing for the attack. I attended the Commanding Officer's Orders Group with Major Bethell. It was during this that the CO gave the G Company Commander, Major Iain Dalzell-Job, his Company objective of taking out the suspected enemy machine-gun posts on the rocky knoll immediately to the west of Tumbledown's west end. G Company was then to go firm on the knoll. Then he said to Dalzell-Job, 'I want you to be ready to support Left Flank as they are the assault Company and may sustain most of the casualties'. (How right he proved to be.)

Then I was told to make ready for the diversionary attack in which the attack group were to total twenty-nine men, having been supplemented by some men from the Pipes and Drums and other HQ elements. I prepared the radios, briefed the Signallers and issued signals instructions. But then the attack was delayed for twenty-four hours. We were not told why. I know now: because the CO did not like the Brigadier's original plan.[30]

Next day I was told about my detachment to Left Flank in order to replace Lance-Sergeant Simpson. He was the Signals Platoon Detachment Commander for John Kiszely, but had become sick. Bethell had gone ballistic and tried to stop my transfer, but this was overruled higher up in the Battalion. Apparently they had no other qualified RSI (Regimental Signal Instructor – the qualification required for commanding a Signals Detachment.) So therefore the decision was made to sacrifice Major Bethell's Signals Detachment Commander in favour of what was perceived to be the bigger job with Left Flank. It was a decision which pissed Bethell off no end as we had worked closely together from pre-Wales training

I gave my radio to Steve Duffy, and he took my place to become Bethell's radio operator. As you know, Steve and Bethell got wounded by a grenade, and my radio, a Clansman 351, was blown up.[31] When Steve was showing me during our Pilgrimage visit where it actually happened, we had to laugh because we found a piece of this same radio he had been carrying and which I had signed for and carried after we departed UK (in 1982). So I put it in my suitcase to bring back. But we were informed about the possibility of a pilgrim who had picked up a live grenade to take home with him, and one of the local Pilgrimage organisers who runs a shipping company in the Falklands told us to hand over any souvenirs. So we had to go through all those checks at the local Customs and the radio was confiscated. Despite a promise that any such items would be forwarded on to us after being checked, this proved to be a successful bluff as nothing arrived.

For twenty-five years I thought how unlucky I was to have been sent to Left Flank. But this was not the case. Steve had a collapsed lung and it filled up with blood. Being unable to breathe properly, he had to be dragged out by Sergeant Coull and eventually taken to a Regimental Aid Post. He was lucky to survive.

And that should have been me.

However Duffy's lung healed well and he would return to piping. Later in life he also demonstrated that the regimental bond remains strong because, twelve months post-Pilgrimage, the Scotsman played his bagpipes at the wedding of the daughter of his former Commanding Officer, retired Major-General Mike Scott. Steve Duffy provided the last word on the Scots Guards diversionary attack after this account had been sent to him:

I have read the chapter and must commend you for the accuracy of the research and detail. Without direct reference you have captured the determination, discipline and fighting spirit of the Battalion. Much has been made of the Battalion's lack of battle readiness, fitness etc. However a Guards Battalion has a 'can do' attitude, probably borne out of the air of superiority transmitted from its officers that made up for deficiencies. At the time I was a very different person to what I am now and had absolute faith and belief in our collective ability and confidence in the vast majority of officers and non-commissioned ranks. We carried a burden of regimental history that simply would not allow us to fail. As you will appreciate, sheer fighting spirit grounded in effective training can achieve much ...

Everyone did what they had to do that night. I was fortunate to be recognised for my part in it, some who deserved recognition were not. Live or die, wounded, walk out without a scratch ... all was chance. I have always believed the patrol was necessary and worthwhile. Your research with the Argentines only confirms this. How the action unfolded was pretty much as expected.

Thank you for giving us a chance to give an account of our part in the bigger picture that has until now been relatively glossed over. It has been a very illuminating and strangely therapeutic experience after all this time to read accounts from the 'other side'. I apologise if I have appeared suspicious, but I have read your first book and got the feeling that your Battalion was not given the recognition it deserved. Looking back now, could it be said that there was probably a better argument for the Gurkha Battalion to take the lead on Tumbledown?

I have four sons. My eldest, William, is a school teacher. Two are at University and my youngest, Robert, at the age of nineteen is a Piper in the 1st Battalion, Scots Guards and already an Operation Herrick (Afghanistan) veteran. Your account records that action at Pony's Pass appropriately and proportionately to the outcome without glory or glamour. I am satisfied that they might read it. That is the most credit I can bestow.

I bear no hostility for the enemy. We were soldiers and did what soldiers are expected to do, even if we never really expected to...[32]

And although Ian Morton's final BFBS TV statement with its estimate of the Scots Guards composite platoon numbers and wounded statistics was historically incorrect, it paled in comparison to our e-mail dialogue much later. He had angrily misinterpreted my questions and subsequent BFBS interview (not included in the released DVD) on the Nottingham colloquium, four trips to Argentina, and communication with Robacio, Villarraza, Vázquez, Miño and other Argentine veterans. This gave him the impression of my 'disbelieving the details given about the battle and diversionary attack enemy numbers, and especially the number of enemy involved in both Left Flank and Right Flank's battles'.[33] But our further dialogue removed these misunderstandings. Morton served with the Scots Guards until 1994, reaching the rank of Sergeant. 'They were the best years of my life,' he confirmed, 'and I thank the Regiment with all my heart.' However there was a downside:

> I have been diagnosed with Combat PTSD, suffering from it for the past five years or so. This illness continues to wreck my life. It is an illness that grabs you by the throat when you are feeling low and takes you once again into a world of hurt and fear. It fills one with so much anger that you take it out on the ones you love most in the world and mentally destroy them. It keeps you awake at night with all the thoughts stowed away deep inside your head [...] of war, screams, blood, faces of the dead and dying jumping out at you from the darkness. If given the chance, it will make a recluse out of you. Not wanting to go out anywhere, your social life also becomes destroyed. All the noises and smells come back to you, no matter where you are or what you are doing. This is triggered by the smallest of things: a background noise which is very faint, but interpreted as something else which, in turn, brings all the bad memories flooding back.
>
> You are constantly wearing a mask which hides from the real world everything in your mind. So to everyone else all seems well and you appear to be the same old happy person. With some, issues become so bad that suicide is the only way out [...] I have been one of the lucky few that this has never entered my mind due to the love and support of my wife Rebecca. She is my rock and I would not be here without her. Others have not been so lucky. But for those of us who can tell the tale, the charities like Combat Stress and Talking 2 Minds have thrown the veterans a lifeline of treatment and support.
>
> PTSD never surfaced its ugly head whilst I was still serving with the Scots Guards. Matters only began to spiral downhill after my retirement which removed the security that the Regiment gave me. But not until I was together with my current wife did the situation become really bad. Until then everyone else had a problem. I was never wrong because I had been a Scots Guards Sergeant. Others were just civvies. But she made me realise the serious problem with my anger. If I did not find help, she would leave me. It was then my contact with Combat Stress occurred. The rest is history.[34]

Asking permission to publish his reply, I also described a particular post-war episode of mine. He replied in what had now become a veteran peer support initiative:

I did not know how you would react to my description of Combat PTSD. I wrote about it for two reasons. The first was to get it off my chest, just the way it is. I have amazed myself because I have never done anything like that before, but found it to be very therapeutic. However the most important reason is that this illness must be explained in simple words so people can obtain some sort of understanding of PTSD. I can assure you that every single sufferer will be nodding their heads and agreeing. Every single word written to you has been one hundred per cent fact with no exaggeration whatsoever. It would please me if you could add as much detail about PTSD as possible.

I cannot thank you enough for sharing your story with me. It gave me a little insight of what you are about.[35]

Yet despite his battlefield ordeal and its aftermath, he has no regrets. His laudable attitude is also a testament to the psychosocial support uniqueness of the British Army regimental system:

With my hand on my heart I can say that if required and able, then I would automatically do all this again. My pride for the Regiment will never change and, having met and lived briefly amongst the Falkland Islanders during the 2007 Pilgrimage, this also confirmed that everything was worth it in the end.

I am so pleased to have put all this down in words at long last. But do not misunderstand me, there were times I was back on the mountain fighting for my life. Maybe now I can start to understand why I am the way I am and, in some way, help myself get rid of all this shit going through my head every day.

To this day I will not eat corned beef unless I read the label. That sounds silly, but is how I feel. However I am actually in contact with a young Argentine who is really interested in the whole Tumbledown thing. His name is Fernando Alba. I began writing to him after he contacted me about my sale on eBay of an Argentine helmet that came from Tumbledown. He is a really nice guy and I hold no grudge. So I cannot really understand myself at times, can you? [36]

I returned to the Leylands' home. But there would be no chance to attend that evening's Royal British Legion Dance held in the pilgrims' honour. The downloading of many pictures from my digital camera into my PC laptop had to be prioritised for a Pilgrimage presentation at the University of Nottingham within forty-eight hours of arriving home in Oslo. Afterwards I discovered a personal shortfall when trying to digest the day's impressions. There was no conversation partner with whom I could discuss my experiences. With the benefit of hindsight I should have read that Combat Stress brochure more carefully and been more proactive in seeking the company of other pilgrims to prevent a 'creeping' depression. This emotionally-charged Day 5 of the Pilgrimage ended by my bedtime reading of the *Penguin News* published that morning. Jenny Cockwell's editorial contained observations about the Islanders' reactions towards us and that eternal veteran theme of PTSD:

Emotions are unbelievably running high throughout the Islands this week with the welcome arrival of the veterans and families of those who lost their lives here in

1982. It was such a pleasure to see these men and women walking around Stanley on Tuesday afternoon knowing that this visit, while it will undoubtedly be very difficult, will hopefully find them closure.

A number of veterans have been astonished at the open arms with which they have been received by the Islanders; they feel they were just here to do a job and are genuinely bewildered as to why people would want to extend such hospitality to a bunch of old servicemen. It's a very difficult feeling to describe but, at the end of the day, we all want to do as much as we can to show our gratitude for the sacrifice made for the Falklands. Words can't really sum up that debt we all feel – and I include those that weren't here in 1982, for we are only able to live here because of their efforts twenty-five years ago – and the guilt that many of these men and women are still suffering as a result of their war experiences.

Bearing that in mind, I was pleased to hear this week that the target set by the British Forces based at Mount Pleasant of raising £25,000 for Combat Stress has been achieved – and possibly exceeded. I met Toby Elliott, Chief Executive of Combat Stress, at the opening reception, and it appears this donation has far more significance than may immediately seem apparent.

This year is the first, he said, that the military have begun to actively support and campaign for PTSD charities – instead of turning a uncomfortably blind eye to this debilitating condition, something which the MoD has essentially done since its beginnings, they are finally publicly facing up to the mental trauma war can bring. We have all seen first-hand that PTSD is a treatable – if not curable – illness but it has to be diagnosed and awareness is key. This sea change is great news.

I wish the veterans a therapeutic and enjoyable week and hope you will take away good memories of the Islands and the knowledge that we will never take your sacrifices for granted.

But Day Six on 10 November was my most strenuous. It would be spent 'tabbing' [37] across that part of the Tumbledown battlefield navigated with the Gurkhas during the war's final night. After another of Vera's hearty breakfasts, she insisted on giving me some snacks to eat during the day. My twin disadvantage was the quarter of a century wait and not being able to tab with a group. Nobody would be interested in accompanying me, so it became a lonely Pilgrimage experience. Tabbing during daylight, as opposed to darkness, and actually seeing the terrain again is crucial for any combat veteran coming to terms with pent-up memories. A good parallel is aircraft accident survivors, accompanied by next of kin, re-visiting their accident site, or other disaster site survivors' visits like, more specifically, the Utøya massacre in Norway.[38] The therapeutic effect of confronting trauma's reality on the ground is greatly enhanced by being one of a group which has endured the same 'life event'.

Frank deposited me at the appropriate spot on the roadside. Mount Harriet was on my left and Mount William to my right. I tabbed up a slight incline. In the far distance was the southern Sister of the Two Sisters feature. Such was the difficult going that I had reckoned on a tab rate of just one hour per kilometre. This enabled me to get to grips again physically and mentally with the tussock grass, rock and unique multiple stone runs. The local ban on clearing Falkland battlefields of combat *bric-à-brac*, like the empty ammunition box for 84mm Carl Gustav high explosive anti-tank rounds I found 300 metres from the western end of Goat Ridge, gave a feeling of wandering in an open-air war museum.

I climbed to the top of the 500-foot ring contour where many Gurkhas had been deposited by helicopters on the eve of battle and, looking north, decided to cross the stone runs of hard quartzite blocks to the southern Sister of the Two Sisters feature where our Battalion Tactical HQ had been set up and final Orders Group held. It was only one kilometre distant. My tab over the sea of boulders required concentration, but a falcon perched on a rock nearby mocked my efforts with its off-putting 'laugh'. More than an hour was needed as I had to traverse a dozen stone runs, double the number documented in my first book. But nothing could surpass that freezing night in 1982 when every boulder was covered in ice and snow. After reaching my objective, and while the falcon's call continued to irritate, I contemplated for five long minutes that night of pre-battle nerves, shelling and star shells casting eerie shadows over the frozen terrain. Then I set out on the laborious tab back to the western end of Goat Ridge while employing my camera to capture images that might enhance presentations to Scandinavian military audiences.

At Goat Ridge I found the site where we had waited for nearly three hours while the Scots Guards were delayed by Vázquez and his men. Tabbing eastwards along the two-kilometre southern side of Goat Ridge was child's play compared to my previous stone run torture. I passed empty mortar bomb boxes and other war debris discarded by our Mortar Platoon as the incline rose gradually to a crest.

Suddenly, four kilometres distant, the 800-foot high summit of Mount William appeared.

Flashback.

Its cone-like structure was the same in daylight as then, in 1982, at night.

I tabbed on another twenty metres. Two kilometres away was Tumbledown's west summit and, below it, the huge quartzite slab of 'The Ski-Slope' came into view.

Flashback.

My mind's eye replayed those arcs of red tracer fired at the rear of Vázquez's position.

I tabbed on downhill, passing by the remains of a stretcher at the place where the Scots Guards Regimental Aid Post had waited for customers, then crossed over to the northern end of Goat Ridge and into the expansive bowl of ground below Tumbledown's west end.

That wire fence was still there.

Flashback.

It had caused quite a delay for our Battalion and now, more than a quarter of a century later, I had to climb over it once again.

Fifteen hundred metres to the north-west, was that strange 900-foot high northern Sister of the Two Sisters feature. Its T. rex tooth-shape that indicated east was a unique signpost. I re-aligned myself accordingly and then aimed off slightly towards Tumbledown's northern slopes half a kilometre away.

The sky was threateningly black.

The gradient increased. My slow tab became more laboured.

Running west to east, Moody Valley was to my left.

Drops of rain began to fall.

By the rocky knoll I looked up. The skyline was exactly identical as on that night when the odd star shell lazily illuminated the white terrain. This was it.

Flashback.

The tsunami of enemy shell and mortar bomb multiple explosions had surged towards us here.

Only luck in that next hour permitted me to write afterwards about surviving the ensuing bombardment. But to my surprise, in 2007, a few of the shell craters were still there.

A short distance further along I climbed up a narrow re-entrant to the rocky knoll's top where two women were enjoying a picnic with two children. I looked at them and felt little inclined to talk as it would be an unwelcome interruption to my tab in yesteryear. These Australian tourists tried to initiate a conversation.

'You out for a walk?' they asked.

'Yes, just looking over this part of the battlefield from the war.'

'Are you one of those war veterans then?'

They were aware of the Pilgrimage.

'Yes, I was with a British Army Gurkha Battalion in the war. And I can assure you that the night of 14 June 1982 was something totally different here compared to what you see this afternoon ...'

My voice faded as I glanced across the valley towards the south-west Gurkha objective of Mount William. Trying to describe it all was impossible.

'I've written a book about what happened,' I said, thinking this could give me an easy exit from here.

'What's the title? I'll buy it when I get back home,' asked one of my listeners. So I told her, wished them well with their Falklands holiday and tabbed back down the re-entrant to Tumbledown's northern slopes. Yet that these civilians had intruded into my 'war' tab was no bad thing. It illustrated this exotic environment had, in many ways, returned to a post-war normality.

I continued eastwards and unexpectedly found the remains of a Harrier cluster bomb unit in my path. After another 800 metres I arrived at the north-east cliffs. Long ago a herd of wild horses had stampeded over these, thus giving Tumbledown its name. Turning south, I climbed up that steep incline where once the odd hopeful enemy mortar bomb or two had exploded. Beyond the rocks where our Battalion Tactical HQ had been established, my tab continued eastwards past the eastern enemy artillery observation post which I had photographed immediately after the ceasefire. It had now collapsed into a sad pile of rocks. Then that same panorama appeared with Stanley in the distance.

Crossing over to Tumbledown's southern side, my confrontation with Mount William was a shock. It was far bigger and much more intimidating than the image stuffed into my memory. The latter's south-west shoulder was my next objective. It took time and effort to reach the site of Midshipman Carlos Ricardo Bianchi's 1 Platoon.[39] But with the exception of half a dozen semi-intact waterlogged trenches, the remainder of the nineteen I had counted twenty-five years ago were now gone. The day after 1 Platoon's withdrawal from Mount William, my curiosity had got the better of me. I had climbed into a couple of these now missing trenches that had contained two Swedish-made Bantam anti-tank missile launchers to squint through their cross-sights below onto, what was then, the southern Darwin-Stanley track. But their manual command line of sight system would have made it difficult for the firer to hit a moving target within the Bantam's 2,000 metre maximum range.

I spotted Bianchi's deeply-dug platoon command post, cleverly sited to incorporate a long protective boulder on its western wall. There were still seven stout red-rusted iron pickets in place with intertwined wire to provide a framework for overhead cover, just like other trenches in this area. With the exception of Bianchi's trench, they all had a magnificent field of fire that overlooked the broad sweep of terrain down to the road in the distance. This completed the crescent-shaped mutually-supporting defence frontline of Vázquez's 4 Platoon, Oruezabala's 2 Platoon, and Bianchi's 1 Platoon. They would have had a turkey shoot if 5 Infantry Brigade had advanced into this killing ground.

Time was pressing. I wandered down Mount William's southern slopes and met Frank Leyland at the road. We drove back to Stanley and I changed for the 'SAMA82 Service of Remembrance and Dedication of the SAMA Standard Parade' at the imposing Falklands War Liberation Monument. The pilgrims assembled on the lawn outside Government House for a group photograph and listen to the Falkland Islands Infant/Junior School pupils singing that poignant London Falklands Commemoration Parade song *Somewhere Along the Road*. Some brushed away a tear before we marched along Ross Road to the Monument behind which ran Thatcher Drive and main Government administration building known as the Secretariat. Just prior to the service start, rain began hammering down on us. Also two RAF Phantom aircraft scheduled to fly past were delayed. This was compensated by two seagulls, later nicknamed the 'Red Sparrows', flapping along the ranks of chuckling pilgrims. But only one Phantom appeared, its after-burner shooting the silver aircraft up into the low cloud base.

Afterwards we marched off to Victory Green on the seafront where two benches inscribed with the SAMA82 motto 'From the Sea, Freedom' were dedicated and presented to Stanley by Major-General Malcolm Hunt who was the President of SAMA82. This former Commanding Officer of 40 Commando in the war gave a speech of thanks to the Islanders.

It was followed by red-bereted Malcolm Simpson, the former 2 Para Regimental Sergeant-Major, stepping forward to salute His Excellency The Governor. A veteran of the Battles of Darwin and Goose Green and of Wireless Ridge, he was certainly not fazed by HE's made to measure full ceremonial dark blue uniform. Its colonial ostentatiousness was topped by the flowing white-plumed hat and general's Mameluke sword.

So with vintage RSM humour, he requested, 'Sir – Can I have your permission to fall out the veterans for liquid refreshment?'

It was granted. Then, turning to us pilgrims on parade, he ordered, 'Veterans, to the nearest public house – Dismiss!'

Most needed a drink. Other pilgrim Acts of Remembrance had been held at Mount Longdon, Pleasant Peak, and the HMS *Coventry* memorial on Pebble Island and HMS *Sheffield* memorial on Sea Lion Island. Services had also been held at sea over the sites of HM Ships *Ardent* and *Antelope*, and where HMS *Glamorgan* had been hit by a land-based Exocet missile. But liquid refreshment was not on my agenda so I returned to the Leylands. There was only time to make my daily diary entry before my head hit the pillow. To hasten sleep I carried out a count, not of Falklands' sheep, but of British war memorials seen. Including the San Carlos cemetery, my total now stood at eleven. For this simple former soldier and non-political animal, it saddened me that, apart from the Darwin cemetery, not one Argentine memorial of even modest design existed on East Falkland

'Totally disproportionate figures,' I growled to myself as sleep's mantle finally enveloped me.

Day Seven of the Pilgrimage on 11 November would be spent in Stanley. On the Pilgrimage programme was a Remembrance Sunday Service that would take place in the red-bricked Christ Church Cathedral. I had last been inside it on Sunday, 20 June 1982 at the inter-denominational memorial service for the Islands' liberation. Tomorrow's early-morning Service was most definitely an event for all pilgrims. I would not to be disappointed. Indeed the entire day would be one of unusual surprises.

Vera gave me an early breakfast and, by 8am, was ready to go. The service began in one hour. But where were the Scots Guardsmen? At last Billy and Tony materialised. Tony was barefoot and still in pyjamas. They seemed oblivious to the time of day. I became more irascible. The previous evening both had been out on town with other Scots Guards pilgrims, so maybe their keenness for a Cathedral service had been diluted accordingly. Perhaps my mood was irrational. Nonetheless it escalated to one of sheer annoyance. But I had recognised immediately this post-traumatic stress reaction that is sometimes triggered in me when confronted with a trifling matter. Besides I was no longer a serving British Army officer. The only way to handle this was by taking matters into my own hands.

So I walked out of the Leylands' home alone, down the hill via Dairy Paddock Road to the Pioneer Row junction. Ahead was Drury Street.[40] Stressing along Pioneer Row, I turned left onto Brisbane Road, then right and left onto Villiers Road. That delay all those years ago at Goat Ridge which transformed our night attack on Mount William into a potential daylight nightmare, had given me a healthy respect for time. Finally at the bottom of the hill I hurried eastwards along Ross Road to the famous Whale-Bone Arch at the Cathedral's entrance, arriving there by 8.40am.

By virtue of his profession, Steve Cocks maintained a blog on one of the more popular web-sites. After returning to Sweden, he made some observations on this about that day's Cathedral order of service as part of a daily personal Pilgrimage diary. He was not alone with his thoughts:

> With today being Remembrance Sunday, it is a packed day of ceremonies which kicked off with a 9am service down at the Cathedral. By the time I got there most of the prime seats had been taken, not that we had much chance of getting them as the lads wanted to stand outside and have a last smoke. It was already standing room inside so we were ushered into the Parish Hall where they had set up a television so we could see what was going on next door. The service itself was fairly long and did not finish until almost 10.30am. I think not enough thought was

given to the fact that not everyone is a practising Christian. Also the sermon seemed to dwell on points that were really nothing to do with why we were there, and wandered off and discussed rather political points about internal Christian wrangling. Oh, and while I am bitching, I think that the Roll of Honour should have included those who died in 1982 and not just in the First and Second World Wars as I thought that was why we were here today: to remember those who had died. There was one unplanned event, when one of the veterans walked to the front of the Cathedral and read a poem. Sadly I could not hear it, though it seemed to go down well and received a warm round of applause.

I reacted also to the lack of Task Force names being read out in addition to those on the Roll of Honour. However the congregation will remember the Service by the action of that one particular pilgrim mentioned by Steve Cocks. When Mr Derek Twigg had finished reading the lesson, Gus Hales, a former 9 Para Squadron veteran and PTSD sufferer, 'just went for it' and strode purposely up the aisle to interrupt the Church Minister poised to deliver his sermon. Gus was not on the official order of service but, in a short preamble, this Buddhist Prison Chaplain mentioned the 'humble soldier' and bereaved next of kin, two categories of war victims unmentioned during the service, and an estimated 308 British Falklands veteran post-war suicides which horrifically exceeded the figure of 255 servicemen killed during the hostilities. He underpinned his introduction by a courageous word-perfect recitation, less manuscript, of a wonderful poem he had composed for the occasion. It was a triumph. His carefully-rehearsed thoughts blazed like a beacon in the otherwise dull service:

Every year on Remembrance Sunday
I sit in the corner of a British Legion bar
dressed in blazer, shirt, regimental tie
polished shoes with my head held high.

But deep in my mind
where nobody goes
I see a wooden cross
where the wind of victory blows.

Three cheers for victory
I heard the politicians say
but they never asked me about my victory
and if they did, I would have explained it this way.

It isn't the flags or the emblems of war
or the marching of troops past the palace's door.
It isn't Mrs Thatcher on the balcony high
re-affirming her pledge to serve or die.

But it's the look and the pain on a teenager's face
as he dies for his country in a far off place.
It's the guns and the shells and the phosphorous grenades
the dead and the wounded, the freshly-cut graves.

Or a grieving wife with a fatherless child
whose young tender life will be forever defiled.
Or the alcoholic [41] soldier with a shattered mind
who takes the suicide option for some peace to find.

Well that's my victory
but no one knows,
for it's deep in my mind
where nobody goes.

There was a standing ovation for his intervention, a Pilgrimage highlight for many. Afterwards Gus received numerous congratulations and was interviewed by the BFBS TV team. I pounced at the appropriate moment.

'Could I have a copy of the poem for the book I'm writing, and background information on you?' I asked.

'Of course,' he replied as the rain continued to pour down. 'I'll give it to you in the aircraft back to UK.'

During the war Gus was a Lance-Corporal in a four-man section whose mission was to locate, collate and make available information on minefields. They became involved with mine clearance and safety at Darwin and, after being airlifted on the first Chinook helicopter flight from Goose Green to Fitzroy, stripped the Argentine reserve demolition on the bridge to Bluff Cove. There, on 2 June, they met Tim Dobbin, an Islander astute enough to record where Argentine mines had been laid around the Mount Harriet, Tumbledown and Mount William area. Returning to Fitzroy, Gus was with 2 Para during the bombing of *Sir Galahad* and *Sir Tristram*. Next day he gave a minefield briefing to the Gurkhas' D Company Commander, Major Mike Kefford before returning to other Field Engineering duties. Twenty-five years, five months and four days later he gave me a CD containing his poem recital and a note on how war can influence destiny:

Since leaving the Forces I have been an RSPCA inspector which awakened my compassion for all living beings after experiencing man's inhumanity to man. Traditional Christianity did not do it for me. I was given a book called *Seeing the Way* where a Buddhist monk called Ajahn Anando, an American Vietnam War vet who had been seriously injured in the head, had transformed suffering by developing compassion and kindness. His writings made sense, but he had died from a rare cancer caused by the metal plate in his head.

I visited the monastery where he used to be, and began to take an interest in Buddhist meditation and teachings. Since then I have developed this practice and cultivated the path of peace. I abhor violence of any sort and wish to develop myself spiritually and grow in wisdom and compassion.

Ultimately peace is the only way – an eye for an eye will make us all blind.
Mahatma Gandhi.

Steve Cock's blog described the next sequence of events that took us to West Stanley
and Cross of Sacrifice commemorating Falkland Islanders and others who gave their
lives in the two World Wars. However it was the twenty-five year-old regimental bond
between the Scots Guards pilgrims, coupled with a gunfire 'flashback' that provided
the most compelling picture:

> After the church service, we filtered out and formed up before marching to the
> Cross of Sacrifice. The Scots Guards formed our own attachment at the rear of the
> parade and, with four pipers to lead us, we followed a discrete metre or two behind
> the rest of the parade. Unlike the others we kept pace and I must say it myself we
> made an impressive sight marching along despite the rain and sleet that was by
> now falling quite heavily.
>
> On the way we did 'eyes left' to the Governor of the Falklands which again was
> rather smartly executed. At the Cross of Sacrifice we had another service with a
> wreath-laying, but as we were down on the road we did not hear anything. By this
> time the rain and sleet were still falling and we were all getting pretty cold. A two-
> gun salute was fired from Government House and the sound echoed around the
> mountains. That was an eerie noise as the last time I heard that here was all those
> years ago. 'Last Post' was played and it ended as the RAF did a fly-past. One of the
> two Phantom fighter aircraft did a very impressive victory roll at low-level over
> Stanley before punching on its after-burners and vanishing into the clouds.

The Remembrance Day Parade dismissed, giving us an opportunity to visit the nearby
1982 Memorial Wood.[42] Benches are to be found there where people can sit and
remember. Several bereaved next of kin and fellow servicemen have quietly buried
their son's or friend's keepsakes under his tree. The wood is also part of Stanley's
post-conflict culture whereby the younger generation can learn and remember in a
practical way the ultimate sacrifices made in 1982. So over the years several thousands
of daffodil bulbs have been planted, mainly by the Falklands Cub Scouts Group. More
are added each year. Many of these daffodils were still in bloom as Jack Massey and I
went searching for tree number 177 dedicated to the only Gurkha fatality. Eventually
we found it. I bent under the long branches and, by the tree's base, stuck into the
ground a small wooden cross adorned with a poppy. On the cross, two of which had
been thoughtfully included in my Falklands 25 Pilgrimage bag, I had inscribed 'To
Lance-Corporal Budhaparsad Limbu from 1/7 GR Ops/Trg Officer'. Then we
paused to remember and reflect for a few moments. This necessary task was a
privilege.

And there would be more reflections and consequent actions in the post-Pilgrimage
medium and long-term which would also lead to a surprise or two.

Notes

1. *The Art of War*, Chapter 1 – Appraisals.
2. O Company comprised one rifle platoon of forty-three men organised in three sections, and a support weapons platoon of thirty-seven men comprising one section of seventeen men armed with four MAG machine-guns and one of thirteen men with three 60mm mortars and seven men armed with two 3.5 inch *Lanzacohetes* (M-20 rocket launchers). Four men were in Company HQ co-located with one medical assistant and four stretcher-bearers. There was an intention of forming anti-aircraft patrols armed with two SAM-7 missiles. But this plan was abandoned because the SAM-7's had defective batteries. (From an e-mail dated 15 December 2011 sent by Héctor Omar Miño after a conversation with Carlos Calmels.)
3. From the Charles Messenger unpublished draft manuscript of the battle.
4. *Desde el Frente, Batallón de Infantería de Marina No. 5 (From the Front Line: 5th Marine Infantry Battalion)*, p 256 – these position details are derived from the sketch map drawn by Calmels.
5. *Ibid.*, p. 253.
6. *Ibid.*, p. 254. *Razor's Edge* (p. 293) incorrectly states that 'the O Company/Sapper group under Quiroga had been observing the British advance through passive night goggles for half an hour'.
7. This and subsequent passages describing Steven Duffy's experiences of the diversionary attack was provided to the author in an e-mail dated 27 January 2012.
8. MAG (*Mitrailleuse d'Appui Général*) – was the standard Argentine FN (*Fabrique Nationale*) 7.62mm General Purpose Machine-Gun.
9. *Desde el Frente*, p. 254.
10. In the author's first book (p. 249), the following passage had been inserted from Carlos Hugo Robacio's book *Desde el Frente* (p. 226) which was incorrectly described as being the Scots Guards' diversionary attack:

> This was a costly and incomprehensible ruse, intended to induce us into believing that the British effort would be focused on that mountain (William). This did not happen, nor did they succeed in influencing us into distracting efforts already planned. The only effect was to make us repel strongly the senseless simulated attack. The crude realism of this action, from our point of view, was that it prevented the enemy from detecting beforehand the position of O Company (-) that we had advanced north-east of Pony's Pass.

Robacio mentioned this attack in disparaging terms again at the Nottingham colloquium and claimed he had not been fooled by it. He also wrote about the attack in *Hors de Combat* (p. 56):

> Attention has to be drawn to an inexplicable diversionary attack in the direction of Mount William, which was against the pattern of doing this at night. Performed during last light on 13 June, the attacking sub-unit was (according to us) practically annihilated by fire from our defensive locations.

But there was no such British attack 'during last light on 13 June'. The only 'attack' on Mount William was the 30mm Rarden cannon fire from Coreth's 4 Troop that took place at night, more than six hours *after* last light. Having stated that, the Bethell recce party surveillance on O Company from the eastern slopes of Mount Harriet did take place a short time before 'last light' … (!).

11. *Desde el Frente*, p. 254.
12. From the Charles Messenger unpublished draft manuscript of the battle.
13. *Desde el Frente*, p. 254.
14. *The Falklands War: Then and Now* (p. 508) states that in 2002 Patrick Watts talked with 'two of the members of the diversionary raid [...] They considered that the raid was a costly farce as the actual orders did not include an assault per se, just the pinning down of the Argentines from 200 yards off [...] the whole affair has left a bitter taste with most Scots Guards veterans'. The author of *Return to Tumbledown* did not gain such an impression with the Scots Guards veterans on the Pilgrimage. On the contrary, Steven Duffy's account gives the opposite view and Ian Morton also fiercely supported the diversionary attack and its success.
15. From the Charles Messenger unpublished draft manuscript of the battle.
16. *5th Infantry Brigade in the Falklands* (p. 189) refers constantly to the Marine Amphibious Engineers of 1 Platoon as being part of O Company actively defending the Pony's Pass position. But Calmels bluntly refutes this, 'There were no Amphibious Engineers with us at the time of the attack' (e-mail dated 19 December 2011) as does Miño, the Amphibious Engineers' 1 Platoon Commander (e-mail dated 19 December 2011):
    Nothing of what's been said is true [...] Where did those versions come from? [...] I am most sorry for Mike as he must triplicate his efforts to find the truth.
17. E-mail dated 19 December 2011. *Razor's Edge* (p. 293) states incorrectly that there was 'only (one) Argentine fatality in this engagement'.
18. *Desde el Frente*, p. 253.
19. Supplement to *The London Gazette* of Friday, 8 October 1982. Issue 49134, p. 12851.
20. *Razor's Edge* (p. 293) states incorrectly that Bethell's platoon reached Coreth's location at 02.00 (06.00Z).
21. *Ibid.* (p. 294) states incorrectly that there were eleven wounded.
22. Some of the details of the diversionary attack come from the Charles Messenger unpublished draft manuscript of the battle, and eye witness accounts in *The Falklands War: Then and Now*, pp. 507-509.
23. E-mail dated 8 May 2007.
24. *The Art of War*, Chapter 6 – The Solid and the Empty.
25. E-mail dated 19 December 2011.
26. *Ibid.* dated 23 December 2011.
27. *5th Infantry Brigade in the Falklands*, p. 189.
28. *Desde el Frente*, the map opposite p. 256 depicts 1st Battalion, The Welsh Guards attacking O Company at Pony's Pass. This is also mentioned on p. 257.
29. *The Art of War*, Chapter 8 – The Nine Transformations.
30. Although the original 5 Infantry Brigade attack plan had been changed, the correct reason for this twenty-four delay was to enable logistic re-supply to take place as well as a reconnaissance of the ground.

31. Note again that this inoperative Clansman 351 radio had been thrown away by Duffy. (From two telephone conversations between Duffy and the author on 16 January and 5 February 2012.)
32. From two e-mails dated 30 January and 6 February 2012.
33. *Ibid.* dated 16 January 2010.
34. *Ibid.* dated 18 February 2010 (first).
35. *Ibid.* (second).
36. *Ibid.* dated 24 and 25 February 2010. After retirement Ian Morton became a Close Protection Operative with both the Saudi and Brunei Royal Families. A divorcee with three children, he re-married in 2007 and lives and works on his wealthy Syrian businessman employer's Oxfordshire Country Estate.
37. Tabbing – derived from the military terminology 'Tactical Advance to Battle'.
38. On 22 July 2011 thirty-two year-old Anders Behring Breivik, a white Norwegian ultra right-wing extremist, went on a shooting rampage at a Norwegian Labour Party youth camp, killing sixty-nine people and injuring another sixty-two. His victims were mainly teenagers. One month later on 19 and 20 August respectively, 600 and 1,000 survivors and next of kin returned to the island of Utøya for a meaningful group therapeutic 'confrontation with trauma's reality' and to pay their respects to the dead.
39. In December 2006 Eduardo Gerding had proposed to Bianchi that the author should visit BIM5 for twenty-four hours at their Río Grande base in Tierra del Fuego during my forthcoming trip to Argentina. Bianchi had been promoted to *Capitán de Fragata* (Commander) and would be appointed Commanding Officer of the Battalion. Initially he thought David Morgan, Jeremy McTeague and the author were Nepalese. He had many questions to ask. However such a visit was impossible as there would be many activities at the Battalion linked with the twenty-fifth anniversary of the war. It was convenient that Eduardo's suggestion had been shelved. In April 2007 Bianchi was one of seventy officers and NCOs named in a lawsuit brought by twenty-three former conscripts who made accusations that eighty alleged acts of mistreatment and torture had been committed against them during the war. A distraught Bianchi denied this, but the Navy ruthlessly removed him from his command. Robacio, his former CO, also declared in a vehement e-mail sent on 20 April to his Malvinas War '*Veteranos de nuestro glorioso BIM5*' that the accusations against his former Midshipman were false. But nearly twenty-six months later in Río Grande there was a further twist. Federal Judge Lilian Herráez found that these cases constituted crimes against humanity, although her ruling was appealed immediately (from a 9 June 2009 *Clarín* website article). Bianchi also refused to collaborate with the author in writing this book.
40. *Razor's Edge* (p. 322 – map) indicated the site of two Argentine 30mm Hispano-Suiza twin anti-aircraft artillery cannon, and an identical 'triple-A' gun emplacement another fifty metres away in a playground between Drury Street and St Mary's Walk. But siege veterans Rosemarie King and Phil Middleton would inform the author later that no such cannon had existed in either area. Indeed the local doctor Alison Bleaney had confronted the Argentine Governor

Menéndez over the need to keep the playground clear for exercising of dogs, and children and parents to use. Phil, who lived in the Historic Marine Barracks overlooking the St Mary's Walk playground, would add in a caustic e-mail to Rosemarie (copy to the author): 'Looking at (the *Razor's Edge*) map I notice that the Historic Marine Barracks has Argentine Marines admin in brackets. That's interesting as I didn't know I was sharing the building with anybody, except Rudi and Camilla'.

41. On at least one Falklands web-site publishing the poem, the author has read that the word 'alcoholic' has been replaced by 'iconic'. It is unhelpful to soften or delete any consequence of PTSD. Conversely the Combat Stress brochure in the author's Falklands 25 Pilgrimage bag addressed reality by providing pilgrims with advice on alcohol over-indulgence.

42. Designed and planted by Tim and Jan Miller of the Stanley Garden Centre to commemorate the war's tenth anniversary, it was paid for by donations from a group of commercial companies in the Falklands, including Asian companies who benefit from fishing in the economic exclusion zone. Back in 1992 the wood had been on the edge of the capital. But now it was 'in-town' due to the expansion of Stanley, with Tim and Jan maintaining this living memorial on behalf of the Falkland Islands Government. They deliberately used a variety of trees, some slower growing than others to give a 'woodland' effect. Macrocarpa and various types of Pine are the most predominant amongst the 255 trees, many of which are now more than ten feet high, representing each British Task Force member killed in action. The name plaques are grouped into Navy, Army, Air Force, Merchant Navy etc. There are also a few trees planted in memory of some of the veterans who have committed suicide due to PTSD, and a special Annexe planted in 2000 where there is a named tree for all service personnel killed whilst serving in the post-war Falklands Garrison: a total of forty-five deaths in the eighteen years up to 2000. A high price is paid for enduring freedom.

One must take it whole when contending for
all-under-heaven.
Thus the military is not blunted and advantage
can be whole.

– Sun Tzu[1]

Next month Steve Cocks shared his post-war experiences with me. The ups and downs of his post-traumatic growth would give a context to his Stanley Remembrance Sunday. But first he and the remainder of the Scots Guards had to endure a twenty-four hour wait post-battle before helicopters arrived to fly them back to the comparative luxury of Fitzroy:

> The 14 June was spent up on the mountain trying to keep warm and out of the wind and snow. For some unknown reason I decided not to go looking around the battlefield. There were nearly forty dead men in and around the rocks nearby, but I just stayed where I was. I am very grateful to have spared myself the distressing sights.
>
> I do not remember how we got from Tumbledown to Fitzroy, but it could have only been by helicopter. We spent three days in the sheep pens sleeping, eating, talking, and in my case playing scrabble with a small traveller's edition owned by Sergeant Oates. I do remember somebody dropping one of the tiles through the slats of the floor and being made to crawl under the pen to retrieve it through decades of accumulated sheep droppings. It is a testament to how dirty we were that nobody noticed the smell.
>
> From there we moved to Stanley and straight onto the MV *St Edmund* where we had a couple of rests and our first hot shower since arriving. I will always be grateful for the naval party who looked after us, from greeting us with a rum ration, for washing our clothes, and making such a fuss of us with the almost unlimited beer ration and Mars bars.

Five days later on board the ship during the post-war 'blue period', he wrote a laconic aerogramme to his parents:

> I thought I'd better drop you a line to tell you how I am. By this time you should have received my radiogram telling you that I'm all right. Well I am, unlike many of the lads who have trench foot or frostbite in their feet.
>
> As you are well aware, the Argies have packed it in, and about time too. I don't know if you know but the Scots Guards lost eight dead and countless wounded. My Company had nine wounded altogether which is not a lot considering it was our Company that booted the last of the Argentine Marines off the position.
>
> Well this is something I never want to do again in a hurry, and there are certainly some experiences that I especially do not want to relive. The Falklands themselves are wet and cold and very uninviting. Why the Argies were willing to lose thousands of men for it is beyond me!

We landed at San Carlos on 2 June after transferring from the *QE2* to the *Canberra* at South Georgia. We spent three days there without even seeing an Argie plane. We then moved to Bluff Cove which is on the East coast about nineteen kilometres from Stanley. We dug in and did nothing but shoot down two Skyhawks which were responsible for the bombing of the Welsh Guards at Fitzroy.[2]

After a week at Bluff Cove we attacked and took Tumbledown. That night was the most frightening time of my life. And at least three times I can now honestly say that I have been shelled, mortared and shot at by both British forces and Argentinian.

After the battle we stacked the dead in piles and after that we were flown back to Fitzroy where we spent four days in a sheep pen. I am now on the *St Edmund* which is a British Rail North Sea Ferry.

Well, how was your holiday in Spain Mum, and how was your boating holiday Dad? I have had a wonderful holiday in the Falklands. Hopefully I will be back for my birthday but that is only speculation.

Hope to see you very soon. Can't wait to see the house now that you have been working on it. All my love to all of you.

However there was still work to do before returning to the UK. So on 22 June eight days after the battle, Right Flank Company was detailed for a new task. Cocks:

My nineteenth birthday was spent in guarding prisoners of war. One group was left on the Islands. This comprised 593 Special Category prisoners held at Ajax Bay and who lived in primitive conditions (for a week) inside the bomb-damaged refrigeration plant. The group consisted of Brigadier-General Menéndez, pilots, officers and other specialist troops. They were considered to be key personnel and would not be released until the Argentines had formally recognised that hostilities were at an end. This was legally questionable as Article 118 of the Geneva Convention states that POWs must be 'repatriated without delay after the cessation of active hostilities'.

On 23 June the Scots Guards Right Flank Company took over guarding the prisoners from the Royal Marines. They were kept apart in five large rooms as each group did not like each other very much. There was a room for officers, one for senior NCOs and three for the *chicos* (the other ranks). The officers were very correct in their manner, disciplined and quiet. They said mass regularly and sat in small groups and chatted. The senior NCOs were very sullen and withdrawn and, as their room was to one side, we had little contact with them. The *chicos* were noisy and happy that the war had ended. They made ingenious things out of old tin cans and bits of rubbish. One group that sat by the main guard post had quite a decent chess set. We did not have a Spanish speaker amongst us so one of the conscripts, 'George', volunteered to interpret. He had a lot of fun as he was responsible for choosing the ever-popular fatigue parties.

We had a visit from the Red Cross. Three representatives turned up and looked at the conditions. They were very upset with the lack of showers and demanded that we provide washing facilities. The fact that no-one had access to washing conditions did not seem to matter and so Major Price, Right Flank's Company Commander, held a meeting with our REME armourer and some 9 Para Squadron Engineers who were staying with us. In the end they placed a plastic water bowser on top of an old shed and diverted an Antarctic stream into it. Then four Scots Guards with hard brooms were positioned around the shed while groups of naked prisoners were marched across the snow in sub-zero temperatures and given a cold shower and scrubbed with the brooms. I guess the Geneva Convention does not mention that the water had to be hot, and I must say the Red Cross was not very popular for ordering us to give them a wash.[3]

The Battalion was eventually relieved, and we came home in August 1982 to be given six weeks' leave. I spent most of that time getting drunk and trying to get back into my old life. But I had changed forever, never to be the same person again. The immediate after-effect of the Falklands was a feeling of inadequacy about what I had done. I thought I had not done enough as a soldier and would often ask myself, 'Why had I survived?' I lost the ability to communicate with people of my own age unless they were soldiers. My civilian friends lived an alien life which I had no way of relating to. All they worried about were their grades at school, yet I had seen my mates shot and blown to pieces.

The first year after the war was a time of adjustment. I would regularly get drunk. Alcohol was a good way of running away from the events I had been through, although I did not realise this at the time. At the end of the year, the Army decided it was time for me to move on. So I was posted to the Queen's Own Highlanders in Northern Ireland. It was just before leaving London that I met my future wife who, as a practising Buddhist, saved my life by taking me under her wing. Although it was to be another ten years before I started to chant, she has been a huge influence on me. Her compassion and love was so strong that I stopped drinking and, at Christmas 1983, we got engaged. I went back to Northern Ireland from where I phoned her each night.

I tried to settle down in my new unit, but found it very hard to fit in. The Queen's Own Highlanders had actually been on the way to the Falklands when the Argentine surrender was signed. So they missed out on the action and had just spent the last year clearing up the battlefields. They were very disappointed at this and the fact they had not been given the medal awarded all the troops who had fought in the campaign. They did not take too kindly to me as I wore the medal ribbon on my uniform, thereby acting as a visual reminder. I missed the Guards, my mates, my *fiancée* and this was made even worse by the death of my best friend from the Guards in a Cyprus car crash. As a result I had a huge character clash with my superior officer. It was a battle destined to be lost, so I applied to leave the Army. Instead, one week before my wedding, they offered me the chance to move back to the UK. My Buddhist pacifist *fiancée* was not terribly pleased. She was told to 'chant about it', and proceeded to do this for ten hours. We married in May 1984.

I was posted to the UK to be trained as a computer programmer, and then for the next four years worked with the Army computer systems. In 1988 I retired from the Army and set up a computer consultancy. I became obsessed with trying to achieve success, and threw myself into my consultancy working insane hours. In my first year I commuted 40,000 miles. In 1990 I won a contract to provide my services to a Swedish company and we moved to Stockholm. The next five years was a rollercoaster of software deadlines and deliveries as I tried to keep up with the team I was working with. They were incredibly talented and, once again, my feelings of inadequacy surfaced. My answer to this was to work even harder.

I kept things together until 1995 when I emotionally collapsed due to burn out, coupled with the fact that my safety net was removed when the office was shut down and my contract terminated. For years I had avoided so many things in my life by just working harder. Now that I had no more work there was nowhere to turn and no answer to my predicament – until my wife at last convinced me to start chanting. At first it was just for five minutes, but almost immediately I felt something shift within me. It was as though a huge weight had been lifted from my shoulders because, at last, I had a vehicle with which my demons could be confronted. No longer forced to burden myself in guilt, I have been able to look at the events of my life in a much more compassionate way, and now have come to terms with my past.

For years my wife had observed that I had no spiritual side to myself. I was so focused on materialism that I could not appreciate the world around me. As I had been raised a Christian, and having witnessed the contradictions of the Falklands at such a young age, this was not surprising. I think as human-beings we need something to believe in and, for many, this equates to believing in something external to ourselves. A belief in God, your friends, money – there are as many things to believe in as there are humans. What Buddhism has taught me is to believe in myself. It has given me the strength to tell myself I did not fail to prove my manhood in some animalistic blood ritual of death. I have, at last, come to terms with the fact that my survival on that battlefield was not due to cowardice, but more to do with my good fortune, my Karma.

I will never forget the Falklands because it has played a huge part in forging the person that I am today. It has been twenty-five years, but for me it still feels like yesterday. My Buddhist mentor President Ikeda wrote:

> War brings only suffering and misery to ordinary people, to families and mothers. It is always nameless and unknown people who suffer and moan amidst the mud and flames. In war, human life is used as a means to an end, an expendable commodity. It is said that it takes twenty years of peace to make a man, but only twenty seconds to destroy him. This is why we must always oppose war – neither engaging in it ourselves nor permitting others to do so. All rivalries and conflicts must be resolved, not through power, but with wisdom and through dialogue.

But Gordon O'Leary, another attached RAPC pay clerk fighting with the Scots Guards in the war, did not enjoy such a happy ending. He committed suicide in 1993. Steve had vague recollections that O'Leary was involved in helping clear up the Tumbledown battlefield and burying the dead.

I stayed overnight at Steve's and his wife's Stockholm flat at the end of March 2008 on the eve of my Falklands-Malvinas War presentation at the Swedish National Defence College. That Christmas he sent an e-mail about the long-term benefit of his pilgrimage:

> Hard to think that it's now been a year since the Pilgrimage. Life has been good to me that last year and I must say I feel quite different now. For me the Falklands is now something that happened to me twenty-five years ago and I do not find myself wondering about myself so much anymore. So many of us have suffered in our own ways that no longer do I find myself wondering if I was the only one. It sounds stupid, but knowing that others are out there is a comfort. Just wish I could get to them easier.

And in January 2010 he contacted me again about an idea of writing about his war experiences and those of six other 'REMF' RAPC personnel serving with front-line units such as the Welsh Guards, 2 Para and 3 Para. Tumbledown lives on in his mind:

> It has been an interesting journey the last couple of years finding out what happened all those years ago and talking to fellow veterans. I have really enjoyed hearing from you and your own experiences and of course your continued investigations around the fighting on Tumbledown. I often thought that the Tumbledown battle has never really been documented properly and I still think that the story has yet to be told in its entirety (especially if you also factor in BIM5) ...

Steve had been forthcoming with his war and aftermath.[4] But it was not so easy for Simon McNeill. I met him after the Stanley Remembrance Day Parade at the FIDF Drill Hall where an impressive curry lunch had been served. I took the chance and asked him, 'Would you tolerate being interviewed for my book?'

He agreed. Our subsequent conversation would trigger a coda for the Pilgrimage that made its total experience profoundly meaningful.

Buffeted by wind and rain, Simon McNeill and I walked to Brandon Road where Vera fortified us with a hot cup of tea. Our two-hour conversation plunged into a morass of confused detail about Left Flank's battle and his experiences. Frank was listening but his well-meaning remark 'Well, I guess that's crossed the 't's and dotted the 'i's' could not have been more inaccurate. McNeill's explanations had simply thrown up more questions than answers. However six months later, his e-mails would begin to reveal the details of his Tumbledown combat [5] and post-war return to a 'normal' life:

> After the battle we spent another very uncomfortable twenty-four hours on Tumbledown before being flown by helicopter back to Fitzroy. Lance-Sergeant Simpson, the original Left Flank Signals Detachment Commander, had returned to the Company and so I decided to revert immediately to HQ Company. Like the rest of the Battalion, we were all accommodated in the sheep-shearing sheds. Next

day the Left Flank 2IC, Captain Grimston, found me and said that my performance had impressed the Company Commander. Having fought well with Left Flank, I had earned the right to stay with them if that was my wish. It was a generous gesture. But my inner loyalty belonged elsewhere. This was to the Signals Detachment which I had commanded since the beginning of operations and therefore wanted to continue in that job. So the 2IC's offer was politely refused.

After another night or so in the sheep-shearing sheds, we went on board MV *St Edmund* for some rest and to get warm. It was then everybody started to suffer from the frostbite on their feet. Now that was painful, but it made the pain in my left leg soon go away. After seven days on board, I was sent to Stanley as the Rear-Link Signals Detachment Commander, whilst the Battalion was deployed to Port Howard. With a couple of days walking on the leg, it became too painful. So I went to Stanley Hospital and got some painkillers. The leg was bandaged and I was told to rest it.

Then with several weeks of very little exercise the pain in the leg died down. On the way back to the UK on board *Norland* via Ascension Island, the pain started to get so bad that I had to go sick. I saw the Medical Officer and Colour-Sergeant Baird who said to me, 'You're going to have to be casevaced on a chopper to Ascension Island where you are going into the American Hospital for about seven weeks until you're fit to fly back.'

He then shut the door and said, 'Or you could just rest the leg, stop running about on it, go home, go on leave and we'll sort it out when we get back.'

He then winked at me.

I thought, 'Fuck that American Hospital, I'm going home.'

The leg is still not better today and I have permanent disability with it, but hey, I got to go home!

There was also another item that he had to contend with on board *Norland* – Vázquez's Colt .45 semi-automatic pistol. McNeill:

I was going to keep it as a souvenir until Special Investigations Branch personnel of the Royal Military Police boarded the ship just prior to us catching RAF trooping flights from Ascension back to the UK. They warned us that they had caught other troops returning home to the UK with Argentine weapons in their possession, and there would be serious consequences if such items of kit were discovered on us.

'So this is your last chance to get rid them,' they told us menacingly.

This resulted in about twenty-five of us going out on deck later that night and throwing our war booty into the sea. Ironically it all turned out to be a bluff. Because we were the last of eight infantry units (including the Marine Commandos), to return home from the war, there were many hundreds of people from all over Scotland and England who had turned up at RAF Brize Norton to welcome us. But as for the bloody HM Customs, they were nowhere to be seen. So consequently, and much to my regret, Vázquez's pistol had been consigned to a most unnecessary and unworthy watery grave.

The pistol was also the only evidence that McNeill had taken Vázquez's surrender. And now it was gone. For three months he was an outpatient at the Queen Elizabeth Military Hospital, but then received a medically discharged from the Army in April 1983 after six years and seven months service. His next career was in the prison service from which he had now also retired. His wife, Kathleen, was twenty years of age in 1982 whilst living the first time away from home in Army married quarters at Putney. Their only child, James, was born fourteen years after the war. But Simon's left leg still caused problems. He walked with a slight limp because the tendon in his foot never healed properly. Two major operations were carried out in 2009 to remove the dislodged bone in his foot, break his ankle and heel so these could be re-set and pinned, and repair damage to his Achilles tendon caused by uneven walking ...

Billy and Tony had also arrived back in the Leylands' home. So we decided to entertain Vera and Frank at Shorty's Diner at the junction of Snake Hill and Davis Street East in East Stanley to thank them for their hospitality. After our pleasant meal we drove to Philomel Street and visited one of Stanley's six pubs for a pint of beer. Bed had to be a better option than the Victory Bar packed with locals and pilgrims. Nevertheless I sat down and admired the washing lines of Union flags festooning the ceiling while Frank bought the first round. This post-conflict cultural atmosphere reminded me of many Belfast Protestant areas during 'the Troubles' where flying Union flags was an important symbol of resistance in adversity.

A slim lady with light auburn hair was the only other person seated at my table in the corner. I had noticed her before in the two recent parades, not least because she had pinned on her coat a South Atlantic Medal mounted with an oak leaf denoting a MID decoration. This made me curious and, despite my shyness, it would be rude not to start conversing.

'Hello, we haven't met. My name's Mike. I saw you marching with the pilgrims on the parade today wearing the South Atlantic medal. What were you doing in the war?' I asked, grasping the bull by the horns in a forthright, if clumsy, manner.

'Oh, no,' she replied in the softest of Scottish accents, 'I wasn't in the war. The medal belongs to my husband who was killed on Tumbledown.'

Her few words were enough to bring those battlefield memories tumbling out again. It had suddenly become an intensely interesting, but also frightening encounter.

'Who was he?' I asked carefully. Never before had I met a Falklands widow.

'His name was Clark Mitchell. He was in the Scots Guards and died on Tumbledown just before the ceasefire at about 6am. But I don't have much more information than that.'

My mind raced through the names of the Scots Guards' battle dead. I knew them all from my research in writing my first book and being so intimately involved in assisting Bernard organise the Nottingham colloquium.

'Mitchell ... just before the ceasefire ... 6 a.m.'

I calculated the time conversion. It was 10.00Z – and therefore his death had occurred just before first light. Like a thunderclap I understood. He had to be Lance-Sergeant Mitchell who had failed to reach the north-east summit of Tumbledown after the fight against Vázquez's platoon. Our A Company Gurkhas had seen Mitchell lying in the rocks a short time later as they set up their firebase on Tumbledown to cover the B and D Gurkha Company attacks onto their respective Tumbledown north-east spur and Mount William objectives. One Gurkha had placed the Guardsman's beret over the latter's face as a mark of respect. He was safe with the Gurkhas. Some in our Battalion Tactical HQ had also seen him as the Mount William attack plan was being re-adjusted.

I became emotional as she talked about coming to terms with her husband's death, the grief, the poems written to him, and a diary commenced but ending up as a mass of scribbles. I recalled my precise location on Tumbledown immediately before first light on that 14 June morning in 1982. Having just survived the hour-long Argentine artillery and mortar bombardment, I could have been no more than 500 metres as the crow flies from Mitchell when he fell. Re-married to Billy Silver's Section Commander, Ian Davidson, Theresa was brave to have come on the Pilgrimage. I respected her strength of mind, but concluded she had been living for the past twenty-five years in a debilitating vacuum of information about the detailed circumstances of Clark Mitchell's death.

We talked for an hour before three Scots Guardsmen, including Ian, intervened by entertaining the pub with their haunting bagpipe tunes. After a while I made a request for *The Black Bear* to be played. This was a 7th Gurkha Rifles' favourite, and my abiding memory is of Gurkhas dancing wildly to this stirring tune played by the Battalion's Pipes and Drums Band on the *QE2*'s Sports Deck during the eightieth Regimental Birthday celebrations of 16 May 1982. So fortified by two pints of beer, I climbed onto a Victory Bar chair, introduced myself at the top of my voice to the assembled customers, apologised no other Gurkha was present on the Pilgrimage other than Jack Massey and myself, but asked that *The Black Bear* be played for absent Gurkha veteran friends. The pipers duly obliged.

Theresa was feeling the strain, so I did not pursue our conversation. But months later we began exchanging e-mails. My objective was to seek her permission in documenting that evening's encounter because (in her words) 'There is not enough written with reference to the ones left behind, the pain, the shock, the longing, the void left in your life that can never be filled'. She overcame her reluctance gradually and also gave an insight into her bereavement and the Scots Guards pilgrims' psychosocial support:

> When I think back to the Falklands Pilgrimage I often remember the night we met. I find it amazing that we ended up sitting together in a pub full of people. How out of the whole place we ended up sitting at the same table and that we shared such a lot of very sensitive information when we were total strangers. In a way it is almost like fate stepping in again, only this time to help me fill some of the gaps in this tragic episode of my life. I do not share information about Clark or myself easily especially with strangers, although sharing information with someone like yourself was a little different.
>
> I am not even sure if the information I gave you at the Victory is 100 per cent correct as I can only go on what I was given. The only sure thing I know is that Clark was killed on Mount Tumbledown on 14 June 1982 just before the ceasefire

around 6am approx. I am not sure if anyone really knows for certain as so much was going on. I have been told he was not alone as some of his men went to him. Was he dead or alive at that point? I do not know and really wish I did. I have so many unanswered questions and really wish someone could tell me and give me some inner peace. It all haunts me still and I will take this with me to my grave. To have loved as I loved Clark, to lose as I lost Clark, is the cruellest twist of fate. A great burden of heartache, a broken heart and a lifetime of grief is the legacy of the Falklands War for me and for so many others I am sure.

My visit to the Falklands was a heartbreaking and wonderful experience, one that I will never forget. I remember vividly Tumbledown as a desolate, ruggedly beautiful place with such a torrid history of pain, terror, death and victory: a place that changed my life forever, where fate stepped in and took from me my love. I was truly honoured to have walked that sacred ground, to have trod the battlefield on which so many lives were changed in a matter of hours. Where men had fought and fell and had gained glory, to have shared the tears of so many people, to have listened to so many stories of war, loss, pain and glory, to have spoken to, and listened to, the Falklands people and their terrible stories. To hear of the terrible wounds that men suffered and mental scars that so many of them bear to this day. It was indeed a great honour to have been part of the Pilgrimage. I laughed and cried. I made many new friends, and now have ties with people I did not even know before. We all have a bond, a very special membership to a very exclusive experience which binds us all in so many different ways, but always comes back to the same thing: the Falklands.

Simon McNeill was with me when we climbed Tumbledown on two separate occasions. On the first climb Simon was unsure of the area which Clark had taken, he knew roughly but not exactly. On the second climb we had information on the telephone from a friend who had been Clark's 2IC. He told us about the area they had been fighting in, and Simon and I climbed that route. We felt that it was as near as possible the route that Clark had taken and the area where he was killed.

Simon is a lovely man. He was a real rock for me. He gave me courage and strength as did all the other Scots Guards, including our honouree Scots Guardsman, Steve Cocks, who found me sitting on a rock crying and gave me a cuddle (the place where we believe Clark died). These guys all have such stories to tell. They were wonderful, funny, sad and tearful and I had the honour to experience all of their emotions. They all gave me so much and I was very proud to have been with them all. I will one day return to the Falklands and to the Memorial Cross on Tumbledown. I hope to meet up with all the Scots Guardsmen who were with me on Tumbledown one day soon and we can share a moment to remember all who did not come home, and I can thank them all personally for giving me strength to fulfil my dream.

I have a great admiration for all men who fought in the Falklands war. I have been honoured to know a few of them and to share their experiences. My Falklands War goes on Mike, like so many others who still battle with their demons. For me it will not end until the day I die.[6]

Monday, 12 November was the Pilgrimage's last complete day on the Islands. Time was at a premium. I decided on a final visit to the battlefield, followed by an afternoon stroll around Stanley. Both would yield surprises. After a delay at the FIDF Drill Hall, I hitched a ride in the bus that took Scots Guards and other pilgrims to Pony's Pass and Tumbledown. However I exited at Mount William in order to tab around the former Gurkha objective. On its northern slopes there were many large boulders that would have provided excellent cover for the Argentine Marines if they had slugged it out against our D Company.

Tabbing clockwise, I went down again onto the saddle that linked Mount William and Tumbledown. Would the Argentine 5th Marine Infantry Battalion's 81mm Mortar Platoon's position be visible here? My meeting eight months before in Buenos Aires with retired Mortar Platoon Commander *Suboficial Segundo* (Second Petty Officer) Elvio Angel Cuñe and some of his conscripts had left a deep impression on me. He had indicated on a map the location of his mortar base-plates from where 600 mortar bombs had been fired at us and the Scots Guards. So disappointment in not having seen everything on this battlefield, was tempered by my discovery of Cuñe's platoon position cleverly sited in dead ground and on two levels along the saddle's eastern slope. There were four large trenches on the bottom terrace, and three on the top one. The iron stakes that would have supported overhead cover were still in place.

Tabbing slowly along the position, I recalled Cuñe's interpreted Spanish words exactly: 'There were forty-seven men in my platoon. Towards the end we spiked our six mortars and moved up onto Mount William to fight as infantry. Then we were ordered to withdraw back to Sapper Hill. The British artillery was firing continuously at us during our withdrawal. Two of my men were wounded, and a third died in my arms on Sapper Hill. It was the worst day of my life.'

Happy to have made this discovery during my last foray onto the battlefield, I turned to tab back up over Mount William's north-east shoulder and down to the road below where Frank would rendezvous with me. Passing an Argentine 105mm anti-tank gun position which still contained six broken ammunition boxes stenciled in French '2 *Antitanque Cartuches*', I noted its excellent field of fire to the road. A few minutes later I sat down by the roadside and, nearby fenced-off Argentine minefield number twenty-eight, dared entertain a loose thought of returning to this battlefield for the war's thirtieth anniversary in 2012, not only with British veterans, but also Robacio, Villarraza, Vázquez, Miño, Lucero, Oruezabala, Cuñe and other Argentine Marine veterans. We would hold an 'open-air' mobile colloquium by discussing our battle preparations, the battle itself and how our lives have evolved since. It would also be an opportunity to clear up misunderstandings and misperceptions. Such a unique 'tactical exercise without troops' might provide ultimate closure. But Frank's arrival halted my day-dream.

Later I mentioned this to Mike Bowles. Surprisingly he was positive and, in the New Year, took up my 'thought' with the Falklands Islands Government Office in London. Unsurprisingly it received a veto, confirming that the exclusion of any such political dimension from the Nottingham colloquium programme had ensured its success. Generalising is a dangerous game, but I would wager good money on the supposition there are two professions many combat veterans dislike: politicians and lawyers.

On that final afternoon I visited Patrick Berntsen, the owner of the POD Gift Shop, who had received several consignments of my first book. His business was situated next to the Jetty Visitors Centre, a stone's throw from the Public Jetty of Stanley Harbour. Patrick had been working in New Zealand when Argentina invaded the Islands, but paid for his own air ticket to fly to the UK so he could offer his services as a guide for the Task Force troops. However on learning Patrick had been brought up at San Carlos and had worked a sheep shearer on virtually every Falklands farm, the authorities decided his local knowledge could be utilised more effectively by assisting the Ministry of Defence in London. So he remained on twenty-four hour call there. The only remuneration Patrick requested was a passage back down to the Islands on the first available ship after cessation of hostilities. He arrived at Stanley two months later.

Business was good for the POD Gift Shop.[7] I had a few more copies of my book to give him, and also some of *Hors de Combat: The Falklands-Malvinas Conflict Twenty-Five Years On.*

'Would you be interested in selling it?' I asked him hopefully.

Patrick took the book and looked seriously at the front cover for five seconds. He shook his head.

'Sorry, but I can't', he replied. 'If I sold that book in my shop with the name "Malvinas" in the title, then people would object.'

My writing therefore suffered the same fate as Bernard's in Stanley. It also impressed me as to the extent this vulnerable community's post-conflict culture was still affected by the war. Disappointed, I said goodbye and hurried along Ross Road. My battlefield obsession had consumed nearly all my time, leaving little to see the capital. I bought some penguin souvenirs in the Capstan Gift Shop that actually stocked my first book, gazed at the famous Upland Goose Hotel, bought a commemorative first day stamp cover of 'H' Jones at the Post Office, and strode along the seafront and past the restored Police Station which had been severely damaged in the war by a British missile. I located a building nearby in which an interesting exhibition of British newspapers covering the war had been set up by Phil Middleton, the heavily bearded proprietor. A school teacher in Stanley during the Argentine occupation, Phil was the owner now of Falklands Collectables, a company dealing in stamps, coins and other memorabilia of the Islands.

He confirmed that the Gurkhas and their *kukri* knives caused a few headaches for the Argentine garrison. 'They were supplied with information about the Nepalese soldiers mainly by the town's Spanish-speaking Chilean workers[8] who had heard about the Gurkhas on the BBC World Service,' he said obviously not adverse to enlarging on this tale.

'The Argentines compared the Gurkhas to the Indians who lived on their borders with Chile and in Corrientes, and were worried about the myth that when a Gurkha had drawn his *kukri* he could not put it back into the sheath until blood had been drawn. But they were most concerned about the Gurkhas' reputation for "sneaky-beaky" night tactics.

'In particular they fretted that their boot laces were laced diagonally, as opposed to the British boot laces which were laced straight across from left to right. The

Argentines in Stanley feared the Gurkhas so much that they thought the latter would crawl along the ground at night in order to locate Argentine v-shape laces, then immediately slash with their *kukri* upwards between the legs. This would be disastrous for their *macho* mindset.'

Sadly the Pilgrimage was nearly at an end. That evening a farewell party was held in the packed FIDF Drill Hall. There were speeches by Malcolm Hunt, Mike Bowles and Gary Clement. The Scots Guards played their bagpipes and the Welsh Guards sang. I also met Don Bonner. He was seated at a table with some other Islanders. It was Andrew Brownlee who introduced me. I mentioned Diego to the white-haired old man.

He nodded. 'Oh, yes,' he remarked quickly, 'I remember him shouting for Mr Hunt to come out of Government House on that night.'

Back at the Leyland's home, I completed packing and made the final entry in my diary. It complained that:

> The terrain and weather was terrible. Twenty-five years on I am no longer the fit thirty-five year-old who went to war. Mount William is enormous, far bigger than in 1982 – how we contemplated attacking it with only D Company is almost impossible to believe. However these strangely surreal seven November days, without being life-changing, did assist me in some ways with reliving my war experiences. But perhaps there are more questions than answers.

The following morning Billy, Tony and I thanked our hosts for their hospitality and unobtrusive understanding of our needs. We were driven back to the FIDF Drill Hall to be organised into our busses bound for Mount Pleasant Airport. Driving out of Stanley and past Sapper Hill, I looked up at the defiant Memorial Cross on the eastern end of Tumbledown where, three days before, Steve had carried out a ceremonial Gongyo (Buddhist prayer) and deposited his Juzu beads on one of the small crosses left behind by visitors to the site.

On arrival at the airport, symbol of Fortress Falklands, we checked in before eating a quick lunch in this enormous military complex. Just before boarding the aircraft I spoke for ten minutes to Brigadier Nick Davies, the Commander British Forces Falkland Islands, about my visits to Argentina and the Nottingham colloquium, and how personal contacts were established with the other side. There was some mention of a local Stanley committee that reviews Argentine matters. He listened carefully to my past attempts of nurturing, in a small way, relationships with a few Argentine veterans.

Already for some months pre-Pilgrimage I had been communicating with Carlos Daniel Vázquez, the former Argentine Marine 4 Platoon Commander in the Tumbledown battle. On return to Norway from the Islands, I e-mailed him a few photographs of his defensive positions. Later I sent an e-mail to Patrick Watts containing Vázquez's comment: 'I think that you, a British soldier, are doing for my soldiers and me that which my people did not.'

On 16 November, three days after the official Pilgrimage party had departed, Patrick and 'Ossie' Osborn, who had travelled to the Islands with the British Legion battlefield tour, returned to Tumbledown. And Patrick described to me the expectations that all veterans have on return to their site of past trauma:

I wish Vázquez could come over here and I would go to the mountain with him, because although I have walked Longdon, Wireless Ridge (Apple Pie), Two Sisters and Wall Mountain with Argentine veterans, I have never been on Tumbledown with an Argentine veteran.

(It was an) interesting visit to Tumbledown last Friday with Ossie Osborn who lost a leg in the stretcher shelling incident. He had been back five years ago but had not been able to establish the location of the incident. We spent some hours there and I took him to where those two rusty stakes are in the ground, close to where Simon said that Kiszely had thrown the grenade before charging the two positions. Do you recall seeing them?

Ossie could remember looking back down the valley and seeing Argentine soldiers milling around at the foot of William. I said we would need to crawl around and find some evidence and I found some small pieces of webbing, a few buckles and a button. Ossie then started to line up the distance between the two stretchers and slowly it came back to him. Then unbelievably I found a good size battery from a radio set hidden in the grass, and Ossie said that one of the stretcher bearers (Malcolmson) was a signaller who had his radio with him at the time they were hit! Then he started searching and found a live British round so I think it was 'BINGO'. He was elated and placed two small crosses at the exact positions of Guardsmen Reynolds' and Malcolmson's positions.[9]

Like the diversionary attack site, the location of the catastrophic stretcher incident had also been lost to history but re-discovered quarter of a century later. Patrick believed he was the only Islander who knew its position.

The pilgrims' flight back to Gatwick Airport via Rio was uneventful, just like my onward travel to Oslo. Unlike many other pilgrims, I did not return to the Union Jack Club. However Simon described the chance meeting there with his former Company Commander:

I bumped into Major Kiszely at the Union Jack Club and told him we had just arrived back, which we had a laugh about. I mentioned that I found the trenches we charged, and he confirmed there was a huge rock feature behind them. That confirms to me it was definitely those two trenches that were together under 'The Ski Slope', the ones you described as the command trenches. I told him how events unfolded and he managed to confirm pretty much how it happened. I do not think that this has ever been told in any detail before. It was just weird that I met him by chance the day after we came back. It all took some bottle that night Mike, especially the charge I have described. But without any doubt he had the most as he led from the front. I should know. I was only 1.2 metres of Clansman coaxial cable away from him. He is the bravest man I know.

But I had to chuckle. 'Major Kiszely' had become Lieutenant-General Sir John Kiszely, KCB, MC, then Director of the UK Defence Academy and, after his Army retirement in 2009, the National President of The Royal British Legion. It had been an honour to meet Simon McNeill, a classic example of a soldier inspired by his

Company Commander's leadership in battle. To his great credit McNeill was also an unusually modest man, despite being an unsung hero. His forty-eight hours with Left Flank Company on Tumbledown should have been rewarded with at least a MID decoration or maybe more. Could the lack of such a formal recognition for his outstanding work in battle have been caused, perhaps, by a simple but unforgivable matter of 'out of sight, out of mind'?

But Simon was to experience an unwelcome post-Pilgrimage postscript:

There were sixteen of the Scots Guards in the party who went down to the Falklands. It was whilst we were down there, that several of the guys noticed a couple of things about me. I was very emotional, as you can see from the Falklands 25 Pilgrimage DVD. My recollection of events was, in their view, very detailed and clear. On listening to some of their stories I knew my behaviour was similar, but I had never confronted such issues as nightmares, erratic mood swings, drinking to excess, or crying on my own.

On return in the Union Jack Club, three of the guys who know me took me to one side and advised me to get some help. After a few weeks back at home things became extremely difficult, to say the least. I could not sleep. I was up every night with nightmares. It started to affect my health. I was tired all the time, emotional, and had very bad mood swings and depression.

Most of us stayed in touch with each other after the Pilgrimage, so they kept harassing me (in a nice way) to contact Combat Stress. So I phoned them. They sent out some forms which I took weeks to fill in because I still would not accept the fact that I was ill. Things got so bad I had to go to my GP who diagnosed me with depression and PTSD. She contacted Combat Stress and was so concerned that she tried to get me into a NHS hospital. But they could not deal with me. Then there were a couple of visits from doctors, welfare officers and a representative from Combat Stress, and so I have been admitted to their facility at Audley Court, Newport, Shropshire in July for seven days treatment.

One of the contributory factors they reckon of PTSD is that prior to war or conflict individuals build up rapport, camaraderie and friendships through training, morale and teamwork etc. You know the stuff. Apparently that also builds a coping mechanism for things like PTSD, but this becomes less familiar when the situation changes and you end up with people you just about know, instead of who you would call your 'muckers'. That is what exactly happened to me. As a Signals Detachment Commander, I had trained my men, played with them, laughed and cried with them. But then the night before the battle I was transferred to Left Flank – and the rest is history.

When I returned to the UK in 1982, I was on light duties until my discharge with my leg. I also had PTSD symptoms then, but nobody knew about the condition so you just carried on regardless. On leaving the Army I was very much on my own. There was a new life to build, finding a house, paying the bills etc., you know the type of thing. So I had to push things away into the back of my mind. Because it was difficult to relate to people who were not there, I did not talk about the Falklands so much. It felt like that those I was together with might think 'oh, he's just making it all up'. So things got suppressed.

The twenty-fifth anniversary was the first time I had contact with the Battalion and met old friends. You know, you lose touch with people. Memories came back: lots of good ones. But it was not until I went back to the Falklands that the bad ones started again. Some of the guys felt it was a benefit. It was, but I did not manage to get the most out of it. Unlike some of my fellow veterans who had a head start in terms of coming to terms with things, this was my first time of understanding. I am grateful for having gone however, because the problems I had were always there, and who knows how this would have raised its ugly head one day?

Now I can start to deal with it, and I tell you something Mike, I'm going to beat this somehow. There is no way it is having any more of mine or my family's life. It may take some time, but hey, so what?

But do not misunderstand me. Returning was a very emotional and truly wonderful experience. It is one I am grateful for because of being given the opportunity to meet both old friends again and new ones. We all shared a common bond. There was the wider comradeship of Falkland Islanders and Task Force veterans, but it was the more intimate and personal bond of the Scots Guards there which helped me. They were like family. It was so good to be amongst them again. They do not know how much they helped me. I love them all.[10]

Editing his raw e-mails and then weaving them into a coherent account had been so riveting that, at times, it caused flashbacks to my own fear experienced so long ago on the Tumbledown battlefield. But just like Steve's, Ian's and Theresa's stories, I regarded this as an extension to my Pilgrimage which now lifted the whole into a profoundly new dimension. Yet there were also the details of one particular Scots Guards pilgrim's past that I much regretted failing to capture for this book. The story of Gordon Hoggan's heart-rending battle against PTSD after he retired from the Regiment a decade after the Falklands-Malvinas War appeared in an article on *The Daily Telegraph* (UK) website on 25 March 2012. It included unemployment, a broken marriage, excessive drinking, eighteen months of living rough on London streets, depression, an attempted bloody suicide and admittance to a psychiatric hospital. That he finally overcame this catalogue of terrible adversity and re-married is worthy of the utmost admiration. It is also further evidence that being a Scots Guards Tumbledown veteran provided no guarantee whatsoever against becoming a PTSD victim.

Simon McNeill acknowledged my attempts of veteran peer support for him::

I apologise for the lack of grammar and punctuation Mike, but thought it would be better to get all this down once I started. It has not been easy, but I feel it is part of the healing process. I do not think I could or would have told this to anyone who was not there, because they do not really understand. I think that was the point you were making in the comments you sent to me. I know these events to be true, although the finer details may be a bit vague, e.g. timings etc. I hope this is of some use to you. Please keep in touch, and remember when your book is published I bags one of the first signed copies from you. It would be really good if Vázquez, you and me signed one. That would go down a storm at eBay!

There was also positive feedback from him regarding Phase II of this book which had been sent for his perusal:

> I am struggling to find the right words. I am so overwhelmed. You have done a fantastic job and I thank you. I have read these chapters four times, but have never managed to finish reading them in one go. They are so emotional. It could only have been done from someone who was there on the night and at the Pilgrimage.
> I am honestly taken aback and really don't know what to say [...] I cannot wait for the rest. When I see Theresa's, Tony's, Billy's, the two Ians', Gordon's, Steve's and your name in print, it makes me so proud to have known them. I feel at one with them. They're all good people who all have had their lives affected in some way or another by events all those years ago. Well done mate.
> P.S. I really don't think I would have spoken to any other person about these events all those years ago if I did not have the respect and trust that I have for you which can only come from one veteran to another.

I would also get a Pilgrimage postscript. The Stanley grapevine had reacted quickly after learning about Mike Bowles' London visit. Patrick Watts:

> I have to admit to being very annoyed by your ludicrous suggestion that there should be a combined Argentine/British veterans visit to the Falklands in 2012. I mentioned this possibility to Gary Clement and he was most uncomplimentary about you and your aims, and the local newspaper published an item in which the local Association totally rejected any such idea. I believe that they all threatened to resign should any such proposal be seriously contemplated.
> I think that if the British vets want to lose the support, sympathy and hospitality of the Islanders then this would be the quickest and most unfortunate method of doing so. Memories of occupation, interrogation, imprisonment, loss of privileges, curfews, black-outs, searching of houses, scared and frightened children (my own daughters were ten and twelve), democratic rights etc. still linger strongly with many people – twenty-five years on. To suggest a combined visit is an insult to the Islanders who have always opened their doors with enthusiastic regularity to British veterans, and will continue to do so but NOT with Argentines alongside of them as you have suggested.
> Argentine veterans visit the Falklands in their own right and receive respect, but nothing more, from us Islanders, and that's the way it should be. If British and Argentine veterans wish to get together and exchange views then this should be done in either Britain or Argentina.[11]

I was momentarily transfixed. The referred *Penguin News* item contained a similar blunt tone of a political pre-emptive strike. Published on 15 February, it was titled 'SAMA: 'Not our pilgrimage':

> The South Atlantic Medal Association (SAMA82) has distanced itself from a rumoured joint pilgrimage which is reportedly being organised for British and Argentine veterans in 2012.

In a joint statement, Chairman of SAMA82 Tony Davies and Chairman of SAMA Falklands Gary Clement said: 'Under no circumstances while we are the respective Chairmen of SAMA82 and SAMA FI will we entertain or even discuss such a notion.'

But soon I realised that such a knee-jerk reflex action to even a whiff of reconciliation between former adversaries on Tumbledown rock and peat belonged to the quarter of a century-old war raw nerve deeply entangled in this community's otherwise thriving post-conflict culture. Indeed, months before, Nicci Pugh and Mike Bowles had warned me of this. I sympathise with the Islanders having to endure the restrictions that the Argentines placed upon them. But in Patrick's anger I also recognised that reaction which occasionally bedevils me too. Indeed traumatic stress is *the* common denominator of British and Argentine war veterans, and each party would benefit by discussing that mutual theme on the very site where it had originated. If such a low-key joint event could help British veterans come to terms with the past and diminish the impact of the trauma and stresses suffered during the war and concomitantly reduce the likelihood of suicides and other adverse effects, then would not the Islanders be helping reduce the price paid by their liberators?

In the paperback version of British veteran Vincent Bramley's *Two Sides of Hell*, a more reflective and thought-provoking sequel compared to his first book *Excursion to Hell*, one Argentine veteran of the Battle of Mount Longdon, Luis Leccese, made a similar point to Bramley in June 1993:

'I never had nightmares like some of the others, but I did have resentment towards the British. That has faded now. I'm sitting here with you, my former enemy, giving you my life story. I have a dream, even stronger now that I have met you. Before we met I always want to go back, even to fight if I had to, but a compulsion to go back. Now as we sit here I'd still love to go back but not to kill, because that would achieve nothing. I would like to go back with you and your friends from Britain and we could all walk across Longdon again in friendship and talk about it all. That would be much better than fighting again. It has been good talking with my former enemy because it has helped me see that you and your guys were just like us [...] young soldiers doing a job.' [12]

I have no axe to grind, but ours was a hugely different experience compared to that of the civilians in the besieged capital who, conversely, had to await their fate while fighting the fear of the unknown. They might embrace a crucial Sun Tzu view of 'tak(ing) it whole [... so] advantage can be whole' by assisting the Argentine veterans in their search for peace of mind. So my response to Patrick was low-key:

It was purely a thought and, of course, could never be a starter if the Islanders did not want it. It's as simple as that.

I have not pushed this to anyone except mention it to Mike Bowles after having experienced the excellent 2007 Pilgrimage. I have no 'aims' in this respect whatsoever and really do not know Gary Clement at all.

I am sorry you have been offended by this. However like the rest of the veterans I did put my life on the line in the campaign. It changed my life forever – but has not changed my principles one jot about fighting in a just cause.

He never replied. I did not pursue the matter because of my ongoing research of Argentine actions on Tumbledown and Mount William. This would be intensified by my acquisition of Carlos Hugo Robacio's 486-page book[13] on his unit's war performance. One item in the book caught my eye. Robacio alleged that in the war's final clash, forty British soldiers had been killed in two helicopters. These had crashed after being hit by gunfire from a small rearguard of his Marines on Sapper Hill. This was a gross exaggeration. Only four Marine Commandos from 40 Commando had been wounded in this incident. To claim forty fatalities placed this incident in a *Sir Galahad* and *Sir Tristram* disaster category.

Indeed British casualty figures of the war still have a life of their own in Argentina. In 2008 Eduardo Gerding forwarded to other Argentine veterans the official British casualty statistics I had sent him. Then he received a strange e-mail from Robacio:

You are contributing to the English lie of 271 dead. That is not so. I'm sorry that not even you investigated by asking my soldiers who were the ones that picked up the British casualties. Not even the nurse Corporal or the conscripts that picked up those from Sapper Hill. Do not do them more favours. The real casualties of our foes have been three times ours. Mike's work is great for his nation. I am truly sorry that they have been able to lie so much. That is not what has been known in other parts of the world.[14]

Puzzled, I replied (in Spanish) to Robacio and respectfully asked for a clarification. A year later another indirect and bizarre reply (to Eduardo again) came from Robacio:

I feel great indignation as Mike forgets that it was my men who picked up the British casualties and on land they had three times our casualties. I ask you to not collaborate with such lies. Mike is working for the good of his own country. Be careful because in your good faith you are being dragged in to give evidence of what is wrong. The worst blindness is the man who doesn't want to see.[15]

Even more perplexed, I did nothing. Three weeks later on 31 May Eduardo sent me an article in *Diario El Malvinense*, a Buenos Aires-based electronic newspaper which has a wide distribution in Argentina. Publishing the views of *Fundación Malvinas Ushuaia*,[16] the newspaper had interviewed Robacio three weeks before on 18 April:

A very important document and an interview with the person who was the BIM5 (5th Marine Infantry Battalion) Commanding Officer during the Malvinas War, gives his opinion about British casualties during the war. This interview is written by Juan Pablo Leronde. At the end of this article, you will be able to hear the interview and view some pictures.

Robacio: Things are said that are not real, not true. For example, the casualties. Everybody talks about the Argentine casualties. But do you know that British casualties were triple the Argentine casualties on land? And this is true, because I'm telling you this with the approval of the English themselves, because they invited me. I went to speak with the commander who attacked my battalion. So I can assure that English losses were triple our casualties.

Reporter: OK, your comment answers the question sent by Juan Pablo of Capital Federal. They are listening to the programme on the Web, and he is asking, 'Why does nobody trust the number of British casualties?' And there you say precisely that there are many more than the British declare. And I suppose it is for that reason that they impose for so many years a secret on their actions.

Robacio: No, but look at [...] what I am telling you about [...] the casualties [...] It was made public because there was an international congress where all the countries of Europe were represented, they were all university professors. it was held in the University of Nottingham, an encounter between English and Argentine veterans who had been in the Malvinas. And there, they acknowledged it publicly. 'We cannot write about that because they will not allow us.' But the reality of the military who were there [...] and I'm going to give you an example: General Michael Scott, who was the commander of the Scottish Battalion which attacked Tumbledown. He told me the following, 'Look, I had four companies of 150 men (in each). I cannot tell you everything of how all the companies finished up after the combat. I'm going to tell you just about one. In that company just five soldiers remained standing, twenty-seven were left dead and the others either wounded by bullets or maimed.'

So the attack was not an easy thing, and he said that he doesn't know why they paid such a high price for something that they didn't know about. He had to look a map when they told him to go to the Malvinas. The fight was very hard, it was really very bloody [...] we used practically in that war almost one hundred times the total ammunition used in the Korean War between USA and China, didn't we? So it was a very hard conflict, where two countries fought each other, one of them fought for their honour and national sovereignty, and on the other hand, the British Army came to accomplish the political objectives of a country.[17]

This was so misleading that a British response was required. So I sent an e-mail (in Spanish) to the Director of *Diario El Malvinense*, Señor Patricio Mendiondo on 15 June to inform him that the correct British war casualty figures were 255 killed and 777 wounded. He replied two days later:

We received your e-mail and forwarded it to one of our editors who wrote the paper on the casualties. He'll be getting in contact with you. On the other hand you should know that it was Robacio himself who stated what we have published on the web. Eye witness testimonies like Robacio's are not the only ones. There are a lot of accounts of soldiers as well who had to pick corpses of both sides. There have been always doubts regarding the British casualties in the Malvinas due to the fact that the official announcements were not reliable, thus we are suspicious about the number of 255. The ninety-year secrecy imposed by the British Government nurtured those doubts. I offer myself for any other doubt you may have.

My immediate response (in Spanish) re-confirmed the official British casualty figures, emphasising 'to suggest otherwise is nonsense' and that 'Robacio could not have been an eye-witness to all the British casualties in the war'. I added that there was no ninety-year secrecy act. Current British legislation imposed a thirty-year secrecy ruling on classified Government documents. This is to be reduced to twenty years. Remaining classified documents on the war pertaining to the sinking of the cruiser ARA *General Belgrano* and attempts to prevent Argentine acquisition of the Exocet missile are due to be released in 2012. All 255 British war dead names are engraved and displayed on the South Atlantic Task Force Memorial stone in the crypt of St. Paul's Cathedral, London; in the official Falklands War Chapel at Pangbourne in southern England; and on Stanley's Liberation Memorial and in its Memorial Wood. Bereaved next of kin are able to see and pay their respects at these sites. There would be absolutely no possibility of *not* including any other names of alleged British fatalities from the war. If this had happened then next of kin would generate a terrible public outcry in Britain. But it has not. There are no more names to add to the 255.[18]

As regard the British war wounded statistics I referred also to Surgeon-Commander Rick Jolly's excellent book *The Red and Green Life Machine*. But unquoted in my e-mail was Jolly's observation (that I endorse thoroughly) 'if reconciliation was to be successful, then we would have to be honest with each other, since openness and truth were the preludes to forgiveness.' [19]

Neither Mendiondo nor Leronde replied. But four months later, yet another Mendiondo article would be published by the *Fundación Malvinas Ushuaia*. Eduardo Gerding sent it to me on 1 November. The cliché that 'truth is the first casualty in war' still applies in Ushuaia twenty-seven years post-war and beyond, because Mendiondo now claimed that 1,090 British servicemen had been killed in the war. Other inaccuracies included that eighty-nine had been killed on RFA *Sir Galahad* and forty on RFA *Sir Tristram* (the combined total of 129 killed being more than double the fifty who actually died). Furthermore he claimed that 360 British servicemen had been killed on 13-14 June (the war's last night). The correct figure is twelve.[20]

It was pointless making any further comment on Mendiondo's absurdly meaningless statistics. Accuracy of military casualty figures from a war must be a sacrosanct historical matter that applies to both sides.

Although unmentioned in that final March 2008 e-mail to Patrick Watts, it would also be a mistake not to acknowledge my deeply rewarding meetings with many other Malvinas War veterans in Argentina and UK, including Robacio, and initiation of a comprehensive correspondence with Vázquez. His experiences and opinions would be thrown into my overall analysis. Any Islander battlefield tour guide worth his salt specialising in the mechanics of the Tumbledown battle would surely want to augment his knowledge so as to be fully conversant with Argentine actions on that final night of the war. It remains, arguably, the most critical turning point in the Islands' four centuries of complex history.

And if ever local permission is given (which is most unlikely) for just one battlefield site to have an Argentine war memorial erected on it, then a good candidate would be 'The Ski Slope' or 'The Wall' where so many of Vázquez's men died – because their brave fight resembled a scaled-down version of Custer's Last Stand during the 1876 Battle of Little Big Horn between the US 7th Cavalry and Lakota and North Cheyenne Indians led by Sitting Bull.

But Vázquez's fight came at the end of Argentina's 1982 military adventure. The latter's start is also important to chronicle. And Diego was part of this: a lucky man indeed to return to Argentina alive.

Notes

1. *The Art of War*, Chapter 3 – Strategy of Attack.
2. This is a myth. No Argentine aircraft were shot down by the Scots Guards over Bluff Cove that day. All aircraft returned safely to their mainland bases.
3. On 30 June the Special Category Prisoners were embarked on the SeaLink RoRo ferry MV *St Edmund* anchored off San Carlos. From 2 to 12 July *St Edmund* sailed plied slowly between Berkeley Sound and Stanley. She repatriated the Special Category Prisoners on 14 July, disembarking them at Puerto Madryn.
4. On 13 October 2011 Steve Cocks and the author each gave a two-hour presentation on the Tumbledown battle to the Swedish National Defence College in Stockholm. Afterwards Cocks commented that the author's presentation was the first briefing he had received on the precise and detailed mechanics of the battle.
5. Even as late as January 2012 with regard to the finalisation of this book's manuscript, Simon McNeill and the author exchanged many more e-mails in a most intensive two-week period which further clarified and enhanced various details of the retired Scots Guardsman's combat experiences on Tumbledown.
6. Theresa also sent to me a photograph of her memorial plaque to Clark Mitchell which, post-Pilgrimage, had been delivered to the Falklands and cemented into the rock at the base of the Memorial Cross on the eastern end of Tumbledown. The plaque's inscription was one of enduring grief:

Gone from my life, but not from my heart.
Your life a beautiful memory, your absence a silent grief.
We had no chance to say goodbye
my love for you Clark will never die.
You always had a smile to share
time to give and time to care.
Always thoughtful always kind
It was me you left behind.
Memories are treasured no-one can steal

death leaves a pain no-one can heal.
Like falling leaves the years slip by
I will love until I die.

In memory of L/Sgt Clark Mitchell
Sadly missed

Theresa

7. Pre-war only just under 2,000 tourists visited the Islands annually. That figure had exploded a quarter of a century later and there were 62,000 visitors for the 2007-08 season, with 100 cruise ships disembarking their passengers at Stanley's Public Jetty in the austral Summer season from October to April. On a few days this could boost Stanley's population considerably as Patrick's wife Pat, who had moved to the Falklands in 1986, pointed out in an e-mail sent to the author in late-2008:

> Some cruise ships of course are small, carrying less than 100 passengers, and then at the other end of the scale we have got the *Star Princess* whose capacity is 3211. On 9 March 2009 there will be three large cruise ships visiting Stanley carrying a total of 6646 passengers if full. This will triple the population of Stanley, so no doubt it will be a very busy day.

Pat's arithmetic was wrong. The cruise ships' visit on that particular day would, in fact, *quadruple* the population. What other capital in the world could boast of such a phenomenon?

8. During the war, there were only eighteen of these Chilean nationals living in Stanley. In 2007 out of the approximately 3,000 population of the Islands, half were immigrants with three prominent groups from UK (630), South Atlantic island of St Helena (153), and Chile (136). The latter will be a useful future psychological warfare asset indeed (with tongue in cheek) if British Army Gurkhas had to be deployed operationally to the Islands again in response to another Argentine military Malvinas adventure. (Statistics from the Falklands Islands Report of Census 1980 and Falkland Islands Census Statistics 2006.)

9. E-mail dated 27 November 2007.

10. Unlike Simon McNeill who was not a Combat Stress patient at the time, fifty-seven of the sixty-seven patients on the Pilgrimage participated in two questionnaire-driven exploratory studies into post-traumatic growth immediately prior to their departure to the Falklands and in the three months after their return. The Medical Director of Combat Stress, consultant psychiatrist Dr Walter Butulli, concluded that: 'The Pilgrimage was demonstrably beneficial in reduced psychiatric caseness (professional slang for 'not of clinical significance') [...] and in relation to psychological growth. More comprehensive studies would help in the understanding of the effects of pilgrimages on veterans returning to their original battlefields.' This came from the abstract of his presentation entitled '25 years on: Veterans' subjective experiences of a Falkland Islands pilgrimage – An exploratory study into post-traumatic growth' made at the Eleventh European Conference on Traumatic Stress held in Oslo from 15-18 June 2009. The author of this book attended Butulli's presentation and was most surprised to learn that military journals had actually *refused* to publish his studies. Afterwards in the question and

answer session, the author confirmed it was worth sending the pilgrims to the Islands and emphasised the importance of veteran peer support, need to pay respects to fallen fellow soldiers and personal benefits from re-visiting 'your' battlefield. Maybe all the pilgrims should have been included in Butulli's two studies. Simon McNeill is not the only Scots Guards veteran of the war receiving support from Combat Stress. As per 12 February 2008 there were another twenty-five registered with the organisation ex a grand total of 800 British veterans of this war.

11. E-mail dated 4 March 2008.
12. *Two Sides of Hell,* p. 313.
13. First published in 1996, *Desde el Frente: Batallón de Infantería de Marina No. 5 (From the Front Line: 5th Marine Infantry Battalion)* describes the unit's role and actions before, during and after the war. Robacio had presented a signed copy to Bernard McGuirk during the Nottingham colloquium, but it was not until May 2009 that the author of this book loaned it. This 2004 fourth edition copy was written in a curious military paper style with numbered sections in each chapter. The sixty-eight page account of the Tumbledown battle easily surpasses in length that of any British book on this particular event. Help was received from Pablo Valdivia, one of Bernard's colleagues, in deciphering some of the Spanish.
14. E-mail dated 15 May 2008.
15. *Ibid.* dated 18 May 2009.
16. A Foundation based in the Argentine southern town of Ushuaia with a permanent interest in the Malvinas and the war.
17. *Diario El Malvinese* article dated 29 May 2009.
18. Indeed a simple click onto Wikipedia, the Internet free encyclopedia, shows exactly the same figure of 255 in addition to the similarly correct figure of 649 Argentine fatalities.
19. *The Red and Green Life Machine,* p. 242.
20. Twenty months previously Mendiondo had based his calculations on the following strange conviction:

    The official British casualties are 255 killed and 777 wounded. We should notice the proportion between killed in action and wounded because the last is usually twice the former. Here is another trick because they mention in their list only those who were killed on the spot and not the ones who were wounded and died later as a result of those wounds. – *Diario El Malvinese* article dated 3 March 2008.

15.   'I will read this book not once, but twice.'

16.   Looking north-east from Mount Harriet towards the rocky knoll,
        Tumbledown and Mount William.

17.   Tumbledown's west end (background) viewed towards the north-east. Note the eastern end of Goat Ridge (foreground), rocky knoll (middleground) and 'the massive twelve-metre long flat quartzite rock slab that jutted out from its surroundings at an angle of forty-five degrees' half-way along the top of the crest line. The slopes below this rock slab (known by the Argentines as 'The Wall') were where Vázquez had sited his 4 Platoon.

18.   'The Wall' (BIM5) or 'The Ski Slope' (Scots Guards) at Tumbledown's west end (viewed towards the north-west) and part of the area (foreground and middleground) that Vázquez's 4 Platoon had defended against the Scots Guards' Left Flank Company.

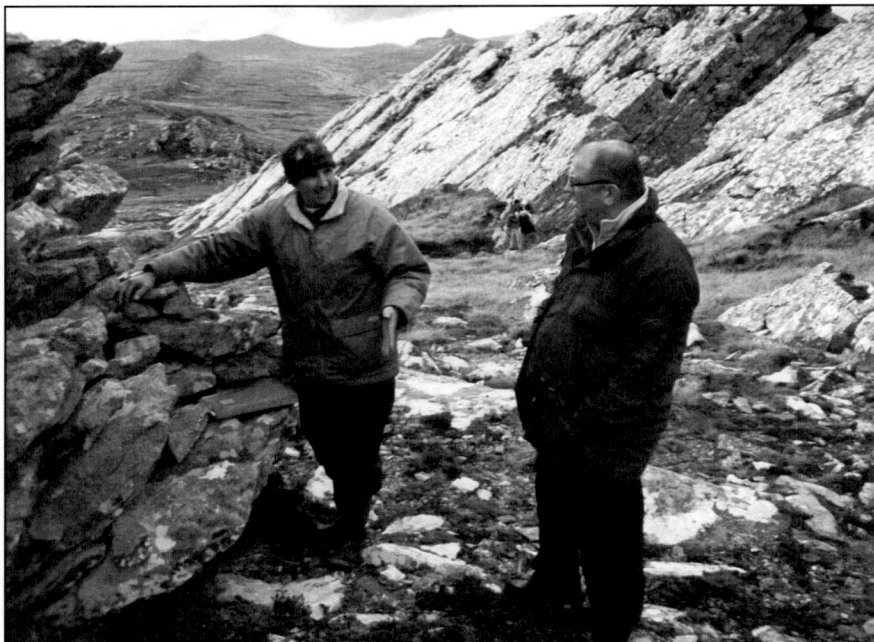

19.   Patrick Watts (left) and Simon McNeill discuss the battle on the site where Tanbini and Simeon were killed at Tumbledown's west end, 7 November 2007.

20.   'At a range of fifteen metres Lance-Sergeant Ian Davidson (also a 2007 pilgrim) had shot dead with his SLR the Argentine sniper who had killed Tanbini and Simeon, and wounded Nicol. Eventually Billy pointed out to us the well-concealed firing position in a rock hide from where Davidson's victim had extracted himself.'

21.   Climbing up to the natural parapet of rock from where Billy Silver had fired his 66s at the rear of Vázquez's 4 Platoon, 7 November 2007.

22.   'There!' Billy pointed out to me modestly. 'You can see the strike marks from the 66s' explosions that are still visible on the boulders below!'

23.   'Lying on the ground and to the parapet's rear was two of these empty 66mm canisters which Billy, Davidson and McGuiness had discarded more than twenty-five years before. I seized the chance and took a photograph of the slightly bemused former Guardsman holding one of these 66mm canisters …'

24.   'So Kiszely had to shout again, "Are you with me, Left Flank?" Silence. Then came a reply from the right (15 Platoon), "Aye sir, I'm fucking with you!" And that was it. We were off and running.'

25.   Patrick Watts standing in the remains of a 4 Platoon sangar attacked by Left Flank Company and which still contained small items of equipment, 7 November 2007.

26.   3 Platoon, Right Flank Company, 2nd Battalion, Scots Guards on board *QE2*, May 1982. (Front row, end right) Lieutenant Robert Lawrence and (second row, end right) Guardsman Ian Morton.

27.   'The Lodgement Area' (Scots Guards) or 'The Terrace' (BIM5) at Tumbledown's east end.

28.   Ian Morton returns to 'confront trauma's reality' at Tumbledown's east end on the precise site where he was badly wounded, November 2007.

29.   'And just as on 14 June 1982, it began to snow more than twenty-five years later while I took a picture of a seriously reflective Billy Silver and Simon McNeill standing either side of the near eight-foot high cross.'

30.   The remains of a BIM5 N Company field kitchen with (l. to r.) Gordon Hoggan, Simon McNeill, Tony Blackburn and Patrick Watts on Tumbledown's east end, 7 November 2007.

31.   Gordon Hoggan pitching his tent to sleep out for the night and 'confront trauma's reality' on Tumbledown's east end, 7 November 2007.

32.   The Argentine War Memorial and Cemetery at Darwin (without the Argentine national flag), 8 November 2007.

33.   'I located the (Goose Green) settlement's only shop in which the Gurkha Battalion HQ had been set up. There was an unexpected personal reaction whilst walking around the small building and looking through the windows into the small office where I had kept up a hour-long running brief to Brigadier Tony Wilson during the *Sir Galahad* disaster.'

34.   The British War Memorial and Cemetery at San Carlos (with the British Union flag), 8 November 2007.

35.   The graves of two national heros (left) Lieutenant-Colonel 'H' Jones VC, 2 Para and (right) *Subteniente* Oscar Silva MVC, RI4, 8 November 2007.

36.   16 Field Ambulance *Sir Galahad* disaster survivors at Fitzroy including Clive Jefferies (second from left) and John Roberts (centre), 9 November 2007.

37.   Steve Duffy (left) and Ian Davidson piping during the Act of Remembrance
at Pony's Pass, 9 November 2007.

38.   A section of the peat bank on which had been sited the BIM5 O Company
sangars at Pony's Pass, 9 November 2007.

39.   'Then I set out on the laborious tab back (over a dozen stone runs) to the western end of Goat Ridge (far distance) ...'

40.   'At Goat Ridge I found the site where we had waited for nearly three hours while the Scots Guards were delayed by Vázquez and his men.'

41.   'Tabbing eastwards along the two-kilometre southern side of Goat Ridge was child's play compared to my previous stone run torture.'

42.   '*Flashback*. Suddenly, four kilometres distant, the 800-foot high summit of Mount William appeared.'

43.   *Flashback.* Two kilometres away was Tumbledown's west summit and, below it, the huge quartzite slab of 'The Ski-Slope' came into view.'

44.   'I tabbed on downhill, passing by the remains of a stretcher at the place where the Scots Guards Regimental Aid Post had waited for customers, then crossed over to the northern end of Goat Ridge …'

45.   'That wire fence was still there. *Flashback*. It had caused quite a delay for our Battalion and now, more than a quarter of a century later, I had to climb over it once again.'

46.   'This was it. *Flashback*. The tsunami of enemy shell and mortar bomb multiple explosions had surged towards us here.'

47.   'But with the exception of half a dozen semi-intact waterlogged trenches (of *Guardiamarina* Carlos Ricardo Bianchi's 1 Platoon on Mount William), the remainder of the nineteen I had counted twenty-five years ago were now gone.'

48.   Steve Cocks (left) and Alex Allender outside the entrance to the 'Red and Green Life Machine' Field Hospital, Ajax Bay, November 2007. Ten days post-war, the original sign for the Field Hospital was replaced by a hastily-drawn Scots Guards regimental flag.

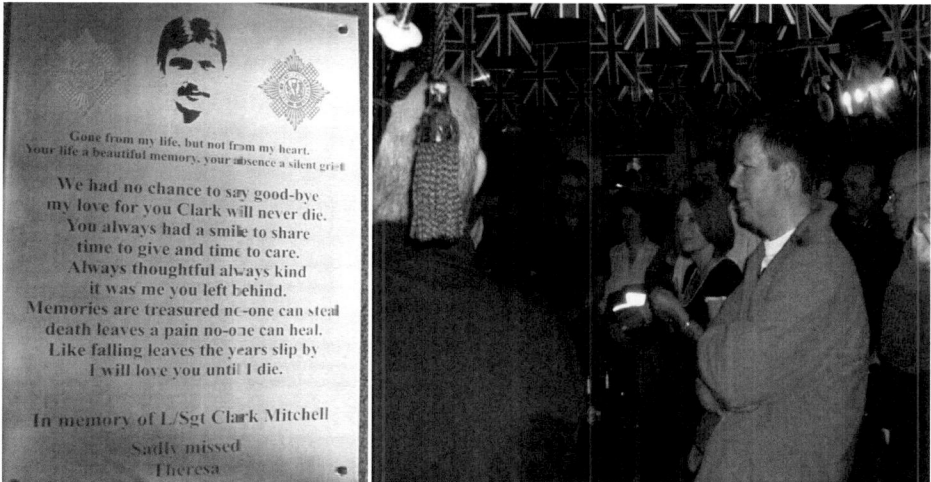

49.   Theresa Davidson (middleground centre), widow of the late Lance-Sergeant Clark Mitchell at The Victory pub, Stanley on Remembrance Sunday, 11 November 2007. Her plaque to him is cemented in place at the base of the Memorial Cross on Tumbledown.

50.   'So disappointment in not having seen everything on this battlefield, was tempered by my discovery of Cuže's (81mm Mortar Platoon) position cleverly sited in dead ground and on two levels along the saddle's eastern slope …'

PHASE III
ARGENTINE ENTRY AND EXIT

And so the method of employing the military –
When ten to one, surround them.
When five to one, attack them.
When two to one, do battle with them.
When matched, then divide them.
When fewer, then defend against them.
Thus a small enemy's tenacity
Is a large enemy's catch.

– Sun Tzu[1]

Retired *Capitán de Fregata* Diego F. García Quiroga of the Armada de la República Argentina had a liking for literature, and his English school education in Buenos Aires gave him a strong Anglophile trait. These two factors and military backgrounds undoubtedly enriched our conversations. It was usual that these contained a joke or two which, in turn, triggered characteristic whinnies of laughter from him. The mutually rewarding friendship contributed to a swift delivery, after my bold request, of his version of the Argentine Task Force deployment to recover the Malvinas. Prior to his extraordinary week which had culminated in that pivotal Friday of 2 April 1982, the dark, powerfully-built young officer had enjoyed six years of service. He had sailed in the Antarctic on both a naval cargo ship and small corvette, cruised to the USA and Europe (including a visit to Southampton to pick up the special Sea Dart missile containers mounted on Argentine Navy 42 Type frigates), patrolled in the Beagle and Magellan channels, trained for nine months in 1980 at the Mar del Plata Navy Diving School to qualify as a combat diver, and completed a one-month parachute training course near Buenos Aires.

Finally, twelve months later, he earned his 'weapons' orientation by attending the Surface Officers' School before being posted in mid-January 1982 to the *Agrupación de Buzos Tácticos* (Tactical Divers Group) at the Mar del Plata Naval Base 400 kilometres south-east of Buenos Aires. As a twenty-eight year-old *Teniente de Fregata* (Sub-Lieutenant) recently married to Alejandra, he became this unit's Operations Officer (O3) and also commanded one of its (three) operational Sections, i.e. Combat Divers, Mini-subs and Amphibious Operations. Initially he was training with the latter, but officers were expected to rotate within the year to perform a minimum of two operations with each Section. The APBT was attached to the Submarine Forces Command and considered themselves the premier Argentine Navy special operations force with their highly-qualified combat divers, underwater demolition technicians and parachutists who operated in extreme environments such as tropical, maritime and Antarctic-equivalent climates. But it was not the only Special Forces unit at Mar del Plata. There was also the *Agrupación de Comandos Anfibios* (Amphibious Commando Group). Diego explained the 'in-house' difference:

If one has to draw similarities, you could think of the *Buzos Tácticos* as the US Navy Seals. These guys are Navy blue, all the way. While not in the unit, they serve on ships and carry on with the normal life of a sailor or 'deck officer'. The *Comandos Anfibios*, on the other hand, is a unit born from within the Marines. In Argentina, the Marines are still a force within the Navy, but both are essentially different (not a difficult thing to grasp if you are a sailor). Chronologically, at least in Argentina, the *Buzos Tácticos* came first by a long way. Most of the stealth tactics the *Comandos* use today are (we like to believe) copied from ours. They do not employ them a lot, though: they are too noisy (after all, they are Marines). Again, trying to compare them to something in the US Armed Forces, you could think of them as the Recon units within the US Marines. Armed Services, being what they are, and with Argentina's Armed Services in constant need of budget improvement, spares and supplies, the fight for resources can become nasty between units that, although belonging to different Services, carry out similar operations. The result was an historical animosity between the *Buzos Tácticos* and 'our cousins'. Yet many of us still regard *Operación Rosario* as the successful event that brought these units closer together in such a fraught time.

Operación Azul (Blue), the planned re-taking of South Georgia on Saturday, 3 April 1982 was already being mounted when, on 26 March, Diego received his briefing to relieve the Duty Officer of the Day at the Mar del Plata Naval Base:

We had been training quite hard and the previous few days had been hectic with our spirits fuelled by a new tension. This affected all conversations in the base's wardroom, with a focus on analysing the scarce information received from certain operations in the South Georgias. Our CO, Lieutenant-Commander Alfredo Cufré, had been summoned up to the Puerto Belgrano Naval Base where the Naval Operational Command was located. Our unit knew that a 'star team' of *Buzos Tácticos* had been hastily put together some days before and deployed to a still secret destination. Such a procedure was not uncommon, as not all *Buzos Tácticos* in the Navy are lucky enough to serve in the unit. After receiving the special one-year training that makes them 'one of us', they are released to the Naval Detailer and go off to serve on 'normal' postings throughout the Fleet, eventually returning to the unit. Some never serve in the unit again, but only join it for special tactical exercises.

As the day's routines were coming to an end, I received a message from our CO to put the teams on standby for immediate deployment. To everybody's joy I cancelled all leave warrants right away, making myself immediately popular. Our CO arrived back soon that evening, and, as I had been already relieved from the duties of my watch to attend to 'things that mattered', he instructed me to proceed to our neighbours, the *Agrupación de Comandos Anfibios*, and make myself available to their CO, Lieutenant-Commander Sánchez Sabarots. Orders are orders and, despite the historical animosity, I went to them.

When I entered the holy 'Action Room' in the Comandos' building, their Executive Officer (XO), Lieutenant Bardi, was busily scribbling on a blackboard the list of personal equipment that men should carry for this operation, of which I still knew nothing at all. The CO was there, and he did not hesitate in announcing that, along with seven other *Buzos Tácticos* of my choice, we were to join a mixed assault group made up of *Buzos* and *Comandos* under the command of a *Comando* by the name of *Capitán de Corbeta* (Lieutenant-Commander) Pedro Edgardo Giacchino. I knew Giacchino briefly from before (he was also the XO of the 2nd Marine Infantry Battalion) and liked the guy, but had not seen him in a while. It was then I learned of *Operación Rosario* (although it did not have that name as yet), and that we were destined for the Malvinas. Such news was quite exciting, but what amazes me today was the speed in which one ignored any previous personal notion of the political issues at stake. That is what training does to you. It gets you focused on the mission, but makes you virtually blind to anything else. I still wonder if this is altogether a good thing.

There was also nothing that could be called 'patriotic' in my attitude. Indeed I was sceptical, and remain so, about the whole affair and do not recall many of us feeling very strongly about the Islands either. For me, the whole idea of fighting was a personal affair.

Information at this stage, though, was scarce. More specifics would be made known once we met Giacchino and remainder of the team in Puerto Belgrano the next day. My task was to concentrate now on picking up the men, ensure we had all the required equipment, and make it to the buses which would depart from the base at 23.00 hours.

There was clearly considerable urgency to proceed with their mission as they would be travelling most of the night to Puerto Belgrano, the largest naval base in Argentina, as it is situated some 400 kilometres south of Mar del Plata. Diego:

Back at the *Buzos Tácticos* HQ, I was debriefed by my CO. It was clear to us that, while Giacchino's assault group was to carry out a typical commando raid in which he would not need any assistance from us, some internal politics were evident in setting up the combined operation. There was actually more to it as I learnt later. Cufré was for some reason not willing then to make clear what, in retrospect, was a major shortfall in the *Comandos Anfibios'* organisation. It should be noted that being recruited from the core of Marine infantry battalions, the *Comandos Anfibios* lacked any technical skills. But this mission would need, as I would soon learn, men with navigation, communications and power-plant operating skills. In other words the mission needed us, as most of our men had undergone that type of training by serving on ships in the Fleet. It also needed somebody who could communicate in English.

The other *Buzos Tácticos* (more than forty men) would be employed in the way our field manual dictates. Operating from a submarine submerged way beyond the surge line, they would paddle and swim ashore to clear the landing beaches of obstacles and set up signals to mark the landing alleys, secure the areas near the beach and its exits to the hinterland, and wait for the main force to land on the Malvinas at first light.

Quickly I made a mental selection of the men who would accompany me. This would be no swimming contest, so I chose those whom, in my opinion, were experienced, mature and calm. These were not only the oldies, but also some of the jocks. All were tough and had been at it far longer than me. They would know how to take care of themselves and, as long as things were done according to regulations and logic, I was not interested in imposing on them my personal views with their choice of weapons. All went for the Para FAL [2] – a very reliable 7.62 mm calibre light Argentine rifle with a folding stock that was the *Buzo*'s 'sleeping companion'. I was convinced that my choice was better in picking an Argentine-manufactured *Halcón* sub-machine-gun commonly used by our police forces. It is easy to carry, has a decent firing rate and an 11.25 mm calibre round that kills what it hits.

I was going over these arrangements when Lieutenant Carlos Robbio, the unit's XO, arrived on deck. Using British terminology, Second-in-Command equates to XO. But in such a specialist and small unit this function was also required to participate in the Section Commander roulement along with the other officers. So far from having just an administrative role, the *Buzo Táctico* XO is also quite operative and works closely with the Operations Officer, his immediate subordinate. Carlos and I go way back. We started our naval life together when we entered the Naval High School as thirteen year-olds. It was 1967. He then entered the Naval Academy without pausing for a doubt, while I entertained my flower-power dreams for a couple of years more before deciding to re-enlist. Since then he was my senior in rank, and we have always been the best of friends.

Carlos was rapidly absorbing the facts, for he had been out minding his own business until called and was not yet fully aware of the details of the deployment. He had driven into the base hoping to have dinner together, and brought both our wives to say goodbye. My wife had with her two books for my trip: an annotated edition of von Clausewitz's *On War* and a pocket volume of American short stories. Little did I know that soon these were to become my contribution to counteracting somebody else's boredom on the battlefield rather than mine. We were quite busy, so dinner plans were ditched, the goodbyes hastily said there and then, and off departed the girls. Neither of them knew, and we did not say, that we were bound for the Malvinas the day afterwards.

Later that evening, the bus departure was postponed until 01.00 hours. We used a couple of hours to drive home, touch base once more with our families, and finally have dinner. At precisely 00.15 hours on 27 March, Sub-Lieutenant Bernardo Schweitzer of the *Comando Anfibio* rang our doorbell. Still with a light heart, I said my goodbyes to Alejandra and drove to the base in Bernardo's car. He was probably the only *Comando Anfibio* at that time I could refer to as a friend. His father and mine had been classmates in the Military High School before my father entered the Navy. Bernardo is a great chap, and a very capable officer. The magnitude of the mission though, and its possible outcomes, had started to cross our minds. Although no one showed any gloominess when we met at the bus, it was clear to me that those who did not know yet what we were being sucked into could easily tell that this was no exercise. Memories of 1978 and the Chilean border crisis were still fresh.[3]

We arrived at Puerto Belgrano excruciatingly early in the morning. It was cold. The trip had been uneventful, and the only thing everybody wanted badly was to fall sleep as soon as possible. This was better said than done in an old Navy bus.

While we were snoring, the submarine ARA *Santa Fé* was casting off from Mar del Plata with all the other *Buzos Tácticos* on board. She was making for a rendezvous with the Task Force at 'El Rincón', a patch of water right out of Bahía Blanca, some 30 nautical miles from Puerto Belgrano.

Once breakfast and transit accommodation were arranged for the men, the officers were summoned to attend a briefing in the Wardroom of the 2nd Marine Infantry Battalion. Giacchino was not there on my arrival, but I met Sub-Lieutenant Lugo (*Comando Anfibio*), who was serving as the Communications Officer in the 1st Marine Infantry Battalion. One year my senior in rank, he would be our Second-in-Command. Shortly afterwards Giacchino entered, trailing Sub-Lieutenant Alvárez (*Comando Anfibio*) who was the last officer to join us. Alvárez was a classmate of Robbio's, and had been the Officer Cadet in charge of my division while at the Naval Academy. We knew each other and always got along well. He was the Intelligence Officer in the 1st Marine Infantry Battalion. We were told nothing memorable at the briefing, but had now got the entire group together and Giacchino confirmed Stanley was the target. More information was to be given out as soon as we were underway.

The rest of that day was spent in arranging accommodation for us on board the ARA *Santísima Trinidad,* a British Type 42 destroyer similar to HMS *Sheffield* which was hit and sunk by one of our air-launched Exocet missiles five weeks later. We were also co-ordinating schedules, chasing misplaced equipment and reviewing checklists. Lugo and I were busy resolving these issues, while Alvárez and Giacchino attended several, endless co-ordination meetings for this first major combined military operation since our Wars of Independence from 1810-18. Somehow expecting our group to be the first out, we stacked all our things inside the helicopter hangar, leaving good space for the chopper's crew to go around in case of unexpected take-off. It was late when we collapsed on our bunks after reviewing the little information gathered by Giacchino and Alvárez, and managing to set this up – along with some pictures from the Islands and profile map of the Stanley area – on a makeshift blackboard in the cabin that the four of us were sharing.

Designated Task Force 40.1, the landing force ships consisted of the amphibious landing ship ARA *Cabo San Antonio*, two Type 42 destroyers (one of which was the flagship *Santísima Trinidad*), two frigates, a submarine, a polar vessel and a transport ship. There were 904 men in the amphibious force bound for the Malvinas. The bulk were on board the *Cabo San Antonio* which would eventually land them at Yorke Bay in the Port William area north-east of Stanley. One key sub-unit was a platoon from the 25th Infantry Regiment commanded by Lieutenant-Colonel Mohamed Ali Seineldin, my dinner table companion at the Military Circle building in Buenos Aires twenty-five years later. Although they were the 25th Infantry Regiment's Advance Party which would become the permanent garrison, their first vital task was to capture Government House. However the Special Forces would be the first to land and carry out the preliminary operation of seizing the Royal Marine barracks at Moody Brook and (Giacchino's task) various key points in the town. They would be launched from

Contralmirante (Rear-Admiral) Gualter Allara's flagship onto their target beach at Mullett Creek three kilometres south of Stanley. The aircraft carrier ARA *Veinticinco de Mayo* would be the flagship of Task Force 20 comprising all other serviceable naval ships which would give distant support to the landing force.

Whether by design or coincidence, the Argentines had followed one tenet in Sun Tzu's 'strategy of attack' to the letter. Surround the diminutive British garrison of Naval Party 8901 comprising sixty-nine Royal Marines and eleven armed Royal Navy sailors (the local small Falkland Islands Defence Force was a de facto non-combatant unit) with such overwhelming force that resistance would be pointless. Success and minimal casualties then would be guaranteed. It worked out like that too, because 'a small enemy's tenacity' did indeed become 'a large enemy's catch'. Diego:

> *Santísima Trinidad* cast off from Puerto Belgrano next day on Sunday, 28 March. She carried all the *Agrupación de Comandos Anfibios* (eighty-four men) with their CO and staff and us eight *Buzos Tácticos*. I do not remember anything special about the voyage, but then again, I am used to sailing. Everyone I have met who was there said that the Task Force went through a terrible storm which made most seasick. I do not recall it at all: one of the memories that have slipped from me, along with undoubtedly many others. My only recollection which may have a relation to this elusive storm is of an endless concern for the security outside on deck of the extraordinary amount of stacked inflatable rubber boats and equipment which had been tied down with straps and cables. Several inspection rounds were made daily to check these bundles in spite of the fact that normally, when this type of vessel is underway, circulation through external decks is forbidden.
>
> On 30 March Giacchino issued his mission orders and gave out the assault group's organisation. Altogether we numbered sixteen. This included twenty-two year-old medical assistant, Sergeant Urbina, who was a late addition and, at the time, undergoing *Comando Anfibio* training. The patrol's code name was '*Técnico*', soon to be re-named '*Techo*'. Secretly I was already fed up with all this 'typical Marine pompous gibberish' from my sailor's point of view. But the power balance was obviously dramatically tilted towards the 'greens' as we call Marines for their daily use of combat uniform instead of regular Navy blues. It was my bad luck to be so junior an officer. However I soon realised nothing could be done about it but behave and do my best.

In the landing operation twenty-one inflatable boats would be used to carry '*Técnico*' and sixty-eight *Comandos Anfibios*. The organisation of '*Técnico*' was carefully devised to ensure that a cocktail of *Buzos Tácticos* (BT) and *Comandos Anfibios* (CA) flavoured each section. Diego gave me the assault group's detailed composition. It would be divided into four sections with each allocated to a boat. The standard traffic light colour start sequence was utilised neatly to avoid any confusion in the order of march both at sea and on land. Red Section in Boat 18 was commanded by Lieutenant-Commander Giacchino. One BT, *Cabo Principal* (Sergeant) Alegre was in this section, the CA members being Sergeants Ortiz and Flores. Sub-Lieutenant Lugo commanded Orange Section in Boat 19. All his men were BTs: *Suboficial Segundo* (Second Petty Officers) Salas and López, and Sergeant Ledesma. In Boat 20 would be Green Section commanded by Diego. Sergeant Urbina was in his section as well as two BTs, Second Petty Officer Cardillo and Sergeant Gómez. Finally Boat 21 would contain Blue Section. This had the final BT representative in *Suboficial Primero* (First Petty Officer) Mansilla, together with two CAs – Second Petty Officer Gutiérrez and Sergeant Vargas. Their commander was Sub-Lieutenant Alvárez. Moreover, after the Malvinas landing, specific tasks were to be carried out by each section. Diego:

Red was to take over the Police Station at Stanley. Orange had to support Green in taking over the Power Station and keeping it running as if nothing had happened. Once this objective was secured, Orange was to support Red in its next task – seizing the Central Telephone Exchange. Blue's task was to detach itself from the assault group on the outskirts of town and set off independently to neutralise a secondary airfield lying further to the east. This was known to us as 'antenna range' because of its suspected communications capability with the UK. Intelligence was also utilised. This was contained in a set of 8 x 12cm copies of photographs that Lieutenant-Commander Gaffoglio had managed to snap while working in Stanley as Head of the Argentine Naval Transport Office. Amongst these I remember a sort of family photograph taken in, what looked like, the living room of Government House.

We spent some hours together with our respective sections planning as much as possible, and reviewing each and every movement to be taken through a built-up area suspected of being very similar to several of our towns in Patagonia. Gómez was to carry the assault group's radio. He was a promising young man, later to be commissioned as a Sub-Lieutenant one year after these events. The radio would let us keep the ships informed of our progress. This would be done by using short English phrases.

On the eve of our 1 April amphibious landing, we were informed of a drastic change in our plans. Naval Central Intelligence suspected that the English on the Islands were already aware of our approach and intentions. Thus it was decided that all of 'Techo' (now re-named) was to storm Government House so as to take the Governor, Mr Rex Hunt, hostage and then force him to broadcast a radio message to the people of Stanley. This would inform them that the town had been overpowered by Argentine forces and therefore there was no point in resisting. Every weapon in town had to be surrendered to the detachment waiting in the Town Hall, and daily chores carried out as usual. There was also a minor collateral mission. It consisted of marking a helipad on the soccer field that lay just east of Government House. This was to be the landing place for the helicopter carrying the support echelon sub-unit.

But at the time when all this information reached us, Gaffoglio and his set of photographs had been already flown off to the icebreaker ARA *Almirante Irizar*. This meant we were left with no other image of the objective than the memory of that living room photograph. Giacchino was not happy. So off he went in search of more useful intelligence, but returned only with a 'heavily-reliable intelligence report' that the place would be practically undefended. The truth is we were not even sure of where the damn residence was located, not to say of where we might find its front door!

This change of plan had an odd effect on morale because, as we neared the time for landing, there was almost a single thought in everybody's mind, 'Please let it happen! Please don't let them abort this operation!'

It was the higher state of British alert that had, in the first instance, led to Seineldin's platoon being re-directed from its original Government House objective to another: the seizure of Stanley Airport and clearance of its runway blocked by the Royal Marines.[4] Furthermore the direct action on Government House was key to taking the town with the least possible casualties on either side. But the Royal Marines prime mission on the Islands was to defend the seat of Government. So Giacchino's assault group, at less than half the strength of Sieneldin's well-prepared platoon, would discover quickly enough the wildly optimistic nature of their newly-acquired intelligence. Diego:

Spirits were still high when the *Santísima Trinidad* sailed at her minimum possible speed into the kelp-thick narrows of Port Harriet. Radar sweeps were now limited to a single sporadic pulse. She would remain at least one nautical mile off Mullett Creek. If one could have possibly checked the depths closer in, the conclusion would have been that no serious sailor with that kind of vessel ought to enter such waters as these were shallower than two times *Santísima Trinidad*'s draft. Furthermore manoeuvring space was extremely restricted because of the cove's narrowness. All lights were out. Messages were in whispers, speaker's hands cupped over listener's ear. It was dark and cold.

Supper in the Wardroom had been simple and fast. There was lots of black humour. Giacchino lamented the lack of a camera for photographs.

'Some of us might not come back', he prophesised with precision…

The destroyer heaves to. All kitted up and ready, we emerge from the lightless hangar into the freezing night. One by one, the inflatable boats are being lowered into the water. When at deck level, one man jumps into each boat ready to start the outboard engine he had previously covered with a thick dark blanket to prevent the noise being heard from ashore. One, two tugs on the engine's starter cord as soon as the boat touches the sea. If it does not start, ditch it. Another is instantly lowered to replace the valuable asset now hitting the bottom of the icy cove. I see two beautiful outboard engines go down this way.

The heavy nets for allowing the men to scramble down *Santísima Trinidad*'s side are hung out. Everything is happening with incredible swiftness. Not a sound is heard or a question asked. A complex operation is being implemented like a smooth routine. Briefly I sight the scouts setting off in a kayak. They are my good friend Bernardo Schweitzer and a *Comando Anfibio* Second Petty Officer. Using directional 'blind' torches, their task is to signal to our boats from the mouth of Mullet Creek.

Camouflaged faces are impossible to identify in the dark. I am hoping not to screw up and land in another boat other than mine. Then somebody grabs my hand, puts a piece of candy in it and whispers in my ear, 'Good luck!' It is

Lieutenant Vara, the vessel's Ordnance Officer and a caring man. There is no time for thanks. A gentle push tells me it is my turn. As swiftly as possible, I descend into the inky blackness…

Inspirationally as a career officer and member of an elite unit, I was perfectly prepared for this 'first-in' operation. It matched all the expectations belonging to my chosen life. I was a member of the prototypical 'band of brothers' and the same elation Shakespeare puts in Henry V's words before Agincourt was in the air. We were spearheading an action against an enemy I admired. My concepts of courage and duty were shaped after a mixture of Argentina's own warring tradition and many of Kipling's characters. Combat was the perfect arena to discover and test my true capabilities. The men accompanying me were as brave or, possibly, braver than me. They were perfectly honed for the mission, fit as fiddles, and happy as partygoers. I trusted them all as I had not trusted anyone before. Life was beautiful, intensity unique and everything exciting in a way never to be experienced again. It was a great moment.

With the outboard engine fired but idling, each boat was paddled back to its specific position in the row that bobbed one after the other from a length of mooring line towed behind the destroyer-cum-mothership. Once everybody was counted, we cast off from the mooring and started to power up in the wake of the leading boat. The kelp was annoyingly thick. Some of the boats' propellers became entangled in the stuff and one of their occupants had to reach with his arm underwater to remove the seaweed from the screw. Soon all hope of keeping formation vanished and I began to wonder if some of the boats would go astray.

While in this thought mode, we overtook one of the toiling crews and overheard their conversation intermingled with their swearing at the kelp. One was asking, 'Hey mate! D'you think we'll get some extra dough for this?'

He was referring to the 'supplementary salary' that the Navy pays to those sailing in latitudes further south than that of Puerto Belgrano. I did not have much to worry about, I thought, as long as our guys were reacting like this to their first war operation.

We arrived at the beach in enough disorder. My Green Section was to provide the security together with Alvárez's Blue Section while the others emerged like newborn butterflies from inside their wet suits. Soon afterwards we switched these roles. Swiftly the *Comandos* were swallowed up by the dark in their advance towards Moody Brook. Then we moved off. It was 23.14 (02.14Z) on 1 April. Somehow our assault group had landed more to the east than planned. The error prevented us from rapidly finding the fence marked on the map, so Giacchino decided to drop this reference point. Instead we started to proceed directly towards a dark bulk to the north, guessing that this must be Sapper Hill.

Marching over the soft terrain was difficult. Darkness did not assist our physical efforts although it concealed us well. Giacchino, followed by Ortiz, Alegre and Flores in the role of navigators, were up front as point section. Behind them were Orange, then Green and, at the rear, Alvárez with Blue. Although trying to focus with all my senses, I missed a step in the darkness and my knee struck a jutting-out rock. It caused formidable pain and this slowed me down. So Giacchino ordered me to change my position in the column to just behind the scouts in order not to delay the march. I felt vexed at my stupidity.

We were wary. About every fifty paces we halted. Then there was a brief wait for our scouts to whistle the all-clear. As we approached Stanley's southern outskirts, the darkness became less intense due to the blazing streetlights. Because of this, the halts became fewer. But the scouts would then take off to check the ground ahead for up to twenty minutes.

Feeling better after my fall, I returned to the head of Green Section. We were extremely close to the lower slopes of Sapper Hill when vehicle lights were spotted. These were approaching from the west on a line that lay between our current location and the hill, but still a good distance away. So Giacchino decided to continue. Running like devils towards the hill, we never stopped to look back until almost at the top. I saw the lights cruising way below my position and made sure everyone in my section had closed on me.

First light was imminent as we rested from the sprint. But to our east the streetlights' brightness seemed to indicate they were celebrating something. They sure know we're here, I thought – and then looked 1500 metres to the north. There it was! A building we all assumed to be the Governor's residence. Everything was in place. Just to its north was the flag mast. On its eastern side was the soccer field. It had a garden. We were at the correct end of town. That had to be it!

Our instructions indicated that we now had to radio a sitrep (situation report) to the ships and state our readiness to proceed – and thereafter wait (again the frightful wait!) for the affirmative response order. This also implied, conversely, that even now the whole operation could be aborted. That scenario would have forced us to creep all the way back southwards to our boats and put to sea again immediately. A dreadful thought. But Murphy was on our side because, despite several attempts, we never managed to get through to the Task Force or received any acknowledgement to our transmissions.

Indeed Murphy had been doubly benevolent to the Argentines. It was fortunate they did not reach the top of Sapper Hill because a Royal Marine single-man observation post had been deployed there since 02.00 (05.00Z). But Murphy's abstinence did not last long. Diego:

We were gathering ourselves for our advance northwards to a radio antenna located on a hillock south of, and above, Government House. Once there we would split up into our sections. Then suddenly we realised that Alvárez and Mansilla were missing from Blue. But time was against us. First light was nearer and indistinct shapes a trifle more defined. Thus reduced in number, the assault group moved off Sapper Hill. Another kilometre – and we reached the antenna. There Giacchino issued the orders we already knew by heart.

'You, Orange (Lugo), the left (west) flank is yours. Green (me), cover my movements from here while I approach the objective and recognise it. Follow when I call you.'

At only fifty percent strength, Blue was not now a viable section. Therefore the two remaining members were instructed to follow my section. Giacchino started to climb down the slope's covered approach with his section while Orange followed. They soon split, and I was unable to see Orange any more. After some ten minutes or so, I began to feel restless because of the lack of signals from Giacchino's Red. A mist made it even more difficult to spot distant figures. Smelling a rat, I set off down the slope slowly, followed closely by the rest of my section that included Blue's two orphans. We had not gone twenty metres when heavy gunfire was heard from the direction of Moody Brook. So this is the 'stealth' operation of the *Comandos Anfibios*? I thought, but checked myself immediately. And so how well do you think you're doing?

As if by magic, vehicle movement in the town began immediately. Two trucks (one which contained Royal Marines) drove towards our objective and parked at its rear. Still 400 to 500 metres away, I was positioned on relatively high ground. Everybody was hyped up. One of my men rested the barrel of his gun on a rock and, aiming at the back of the truck off-loading the Royal Marines, shouted, 'I've got them in my sights. I can easily shoot them!'

'Don't!' I ordered, sure that the range was too far for a certain hit in that murky gloom. It was also crucial to retain the advantages of surprise. They did not know we were here!

He fired. I cursed.

It was about 05.45 (08.45Z). Their initial positions out-manoeuvred, these Royal Marines had been re-deployed to Government House. At the most, thirty-one Royal Marines and Royal Navy sailors would defend Stanley's Alamo. They outnumbered Giacchino's assault group, however, by two to one. Diego:

Luckily enough we were virtually on the run towards Government House because, as soon as the Brits pinpointed our sniper, they began to return fire. While all this was happening, I heard Giacchino shouting, 'Green! Here! Hurry up!'

Checking that my guys were following behind (they were), I tried to run faster, but all the way fought a creepy notion that we could be dashing into an ambush if Giacchino was unlucky enough to spring one.

Through a frightful amount of gunfire and thud of bullets striking the ground around us, we raced towards Red and finally reached them at the south-east outer corner of a low stone white wall. This surrounded a small patch of grass at the back of the house. The soccer field was nearby. We took cover briefly in the bushes from where we fired bursts aimed in the din's general direction, hoping for a lucky hit. But the Royal Marines were shielded from us by the bushes around the house, making it impossible to see where they were actually located. Nonetheless I knew, despite being plagued by the bolt on my machine-gun jamming twice, that their movement would be discouraged by our fire.

The excitement magnified my impressions of everything happening around me: the product of unusually high amounts of adrenaline rushing through my blood. It explains the radiant surround to each of my memories.

The noise was louder.

The light brighter.

The deeds worthier.

Urbina left us shortly afterwards to run onto the soccer field 100 metres distant and convert it into a helicopter landing pad. His task there was to mark the wind direction with a pair of long johns that would resemble an arrow once the legs were spread and pegged down. Moving towards Giacchino with Cardillo closely behind, I was informed somehow that Alvárez and Mansilla of Blue had finally caught up and were trying to approach the house from its western end.

Seeing me, Giacchino snapped, 'Talk to him!'

With cupped hands over my mouth to allow my voice greater range while hoping to be heard over the din, I shouted with a voracious power, 'Mr Hunt! We are Argentine forces. The Island is taken. Amphibious vehicles have landed and are on their way towards here. Your communication lines are severed. We request that you exit the building immediately, unarmed and holding your hands up, in order to avoid greater damage. I can assure you that your rank and dignity, as well as those of all who are with you will be respected.'

There was no immediate answer.

On Giacchino's prompt, I repeated the message.

Still no answer.

'Throw them a grenade!' ordered Giacchino.

I grasped one of three M2 high-explosive hand grenades hanging from my webbing and threw it over the foliage onto the building's opposite seaward side.

Then a voice answered, 'Mr Hunt is coming out ...'

After what may have been no more than two or three minutes, but seemed an eternity in the circumstances, Giacchino lost patience and urged me to make them hurry up.

Becoming angry with these fellows inside, I yelled my increasingly parrot-like message again. It was answered this time with an increase in the rate of fire from the building and isolated shouts of, 'Don't go!' We could understand this language.

The shooting was reaching serious proportions and I glanced around looking for a clear field of fire. Flores and Alegre of Red with Ledesma of Orange were around Giacchino and me when a sudden orange-coloured blanket of light hurtled towards us. After a micro-second of idiotic surprise, I realised these were tracer rounds showering over us and pin-pointing our position for snipers as well as illuminating the direction of our attack. They came from a machine-gun firing from the edge of town – surprisingly enough, I thought – across the soccer field. To make things worst, my machine-gun jammed again after a couple of bursts of fire. I took my pistol out of its holster and swore never to trust my life again to such trash.

We hit the deck together as fast as if we had rehearsed the reaction.

Then I yelled to Giacchino, 'Sir, either we get in or they'll fry us!'

'Yeah, we should go in now,' he answered.

Simultaneously he jumped up, vaulted over the low stone wall and headed straight for the building. Immediately Cardillo charged after him. I followed suit. Behind came Flores and Ledesma. We gained entry at the first door encountered, only to find ourselves in a narrow hallway with no apparent exit except for another door close by on the right. Opening this was vital because tracer rounds were already beginning to hit the hallway's walls. Cardillo tried to kick it open, but only acquired a sore ankle. Then Giacchino swiftly drew a grenade from his webbing, smashed one of the door's panels, put his arm through the hole and felt for the key in the lock. But on opening the door from the inside only revealed a room without any further exits.

They had made a cardinal error. Rather than a Stanley Alamo rear entrance, this one belonged to a separate building – the servants' annexe. The time was now about 06.15 (09.15Z), fifteen minutes before the main Argentine landings at Yorke Bay. Diego:

> Then everything happened incredibly quickly. Retracing our steps, Giacchino went out of the building through the first door exclaiming, 'We'll have to go around!'
> I followed him immediately.
> Almost bumping into each other and instead of heading back to the stone wall, we turned right at the building's corner to enter the small grassy patch at the rear.
> I had taken two steps into this enclosure when Giacchino, who was charging forward a couple of metres in front of me, whirled round shouting, 'Christina, they got me!'
> Almost simultaneously I felt a push on my belly. It had the force of a mule's kick.
> My next recollection was of me lying against the corrugated iron sheeting of a tool-shed I had just passed on my left. I was looking at Giacchino lying there in front of me. He had been hit in the chest and was doubled up in pain.

Cardillo, Flores and Ledesma escaped from this killing area by sprinting around the rear of the main building to its west side and took refuge in the maid's quarters above the kitchen. Three hours later they would be captured there by the Stanley Alamo's defenders and thus become, albeit for only a few minutes, the war's first prisoners. Diego:

> I tried to move and felt a sudden burning pain on my right shoulder, like if my arm had been somehow chopped off from down there. Another shot, I thought, you're being too slow. My pistol slid out of my numb hand and I realised from then on that my right arm was useless for all practical purposes. In reality, and even though a bullet had hit and passed through the elbow severing the nerve and artery, this was not the wound that caused my evacuation (it could probably have been treated on the Malvinas). A much more severe gunshot wound in my lower torso where the bullet had carried away four ribs and punctured a lung, leaving a big exit opening in my back would be the reason for my return to the mainland. The hospital in Stanley could not provide the kind of surgery needed. In addition, although I was not aware of it at the time, a third British bullet had found Diego García Quiroga on 2 April. All came from different weapons.
> There were more urgent things to think about. Although feeling pleasant, an

ominous warmth grew on my lower back. Painfully [...] slowly [...] I slid down until [...] presumably [...] I lay on my back. This could only be verified by the dark sky which had now materialised directly before my eyes. Any other movement was becoming extremely difficult. Everything was happening in a weird, quieter rhythm. There was Giacchino's voice. He was trying to tell me something. But although he was very close, it was still difficult to hear anything above the din of gunfire. It finally dawned on me that he was calling for a medic. Unbeknown to both of us, Urbina had already rushed back from the soccer field and, on hearing the shouts, had tried to get through the bushes and onto the grassy patch. Then a burst of gunfire hit him in his hips and, with a cry of frustration, the unlucky Sergeant was thrown spinning onto a tree trunk. I started to call for a medic – but was later told I continued to speak in English, managing to maintain a dialogue with the Brits who had gunned us down.

'Medic! Please send a medic! We're bleeding out here!'

'OK! We will, but you've first got to tell your people to stop firing and surrender their weapons.'

'You ask too much. I can't do that, and you know it.'

'Pity then! It'll be a long morning…'

This exchange of pleasantries was repeated a couple of times more or less along the same lines. Then another voice spoke.

'That bloke at your side. He has a grenade in his hand. Tell him to put it down. I'll count to five, and then I'll shoot!'

I translated this to Giacchino. He replied, 'I can't let go of the thing. I've already removed the pin!'

I told this to the Brit, but he repeated, 'I'll count to five!'

Giacchino then removed his image-intensifying goggles from his neck, passing the leather strap over his head. He tied this around the grenade lever, leaving the grenade on the ground at his side and explained to me that he would prevent the lever from tripping by pressing his body against. It was clear that all these movements were costing him an enormous effort. But continuously he kept telling me to try and get out of the line of fire and shoot back at the windows.

The Royal Marines mistakenly believed Giacchino was pleading to be disarmed and given medical assistance so that, if they approached, he could hurl the grenade at them. This was not the case as Diego told me more than twenty-five years later, adding, 'He never pleaded for mercy. Not even to the bitter end.' The Green Section Commander's ordeal continued:

My memories of these moments, which were probably exceptionally grave and dramatic, are not very clear. But I can recall some of the things that happened and what was going through my head. They were mixed with, of course, flashes of family and personal memories and thoughts that belonged anywhere but on that patch of grass. Nevertheless there is the feeling of having seen them all from a distance through a gauze curtain. But most of my thoughts were monopolised by things happening there and then, as if having entered a reality with its own separate urgencies. Big questions like life or death were not on my mind at all. I appreciate these types of thoughts torture the minds of men unlucky enough to be under heavy shelling or bombing. This mind-shattering nightmare did not apply to me. I was incredibly lucky. My fate was as fast and clean as it can possibly be.

Behind the building I tried to loosen my belt, only to feel the stickiness of blood everywhere that was touched. I loosened the scarf around my neck, trying to move as little as possible and breathing very slowly to save as much energy as possible. My sight became blurred, then tunnelled, like the time I almost poisoned myself for lack of oxygen during a diving exercise in what seemed to be ages ago. I was dying, and it was taking too long. Perhaps I was not dying at all?

'Be aware', said Giacchino to me suddenly. 'I am close to losing consciousness. If I go, I have a grenade under my body. Tell those who lift me up that it will go off.'

He had effectively moved over, covering the grenade with his body. I entertained my thoughts by imagining what a grisly sight the two of us would make if the thing went off.

There were sounds on the grass close to my head. I moved my eyes and saw the Governor's geese – fat, white, matron-like geese – waddling clumsily around us. But they were apparently oblivious of the continuing gunfire, me and Giacchino who was breathing noisily over there. These geese were definitely out of place. I wondered what reaction open wounds could trigger on these animals. There was a lot of shouting, too.

Concurrently the drama continued elsewhere. Ignoring the incoming Royal Marines machine-gun fire, López from Orange ran across the soccer field to stop the advancing Argentine Marine column of Amtrac amphibious assault carriers on the road to Moody Brook from firing mortar bombs over Government House. Had it not been for him physically barring them by standing in front of Lieutenant-Commander Santillán's vehicle, we would have been probably blown to kingdom come.

I slid gradually from fantastic excitement into a peaceful quietness. The sun was rising quickly. Unable to move, I could still hear the voices and gunfire, but was speeding away fast.

I heard a chopper, but could not see it. The sky was blue. It was not bad to die on such a beautiful morning, among friends, lying on the grass.

It was Lugo, the Orange Section Commander, who had assumed overall command of the reduced eleven-man assault group. His revised concept of operations was most effective. Like the Scots Guards' successful diversionary attack at Pony's Pass seventy-four days later, it equated to Sun Tzu's tenet of deception that 'the military is based on guile, acts due to advantage, transforms by dividing and joining'.[5] The defenders' initial assessment of eighty attackers laying siege to Stanley's Alamo had remained unrevised prior to the arrival at about 08.20 (11.20Z) of sixty-six reinforcing *Comandos Anfibios* [6] from their fruitless mission against an unoccupied Moody Brook Barracks. Correspondingly the defenders' next assessment rose to more than double the actual total of seventy-seven enemy now surrounding their fortress.[7] At 09.20 (12.20Z) the Governor surrendered. Diego:

Sudden silence raised me from my reverie. Then I heard a voice calling Giacchino's name, 'Pedro! It's me, Tito!'

Giacchino made a movement, tried to raise his head up on his elbows and said weakly, 'Hurry up Tito, or otherwise I'm not going to make it.'

His words were followed by a lot of voices, and people materialising over us. It had taken more than ninety minutes before we could be assisted by these medics once the firing had stopped and the area was secured. By then I had reviewed my entire life several times and was still most surprised at being offered another chance.

They began to lift Giacchino up into a sort of stretcher. The moment they did this, an enormous amount of blood poured out of his parka jacket.

It made me think of waterfalls.

He sighed, fell limp into the arms of those assisting him, and was then carried into the back of a vehicle and driven to Stanley hospital.

An enormous guy suddenly appeared at my side, looking down on me. His clothes told me he was not one of us. He was a Royal Marine. I was a little confused, and felt weird rushes of pain coming from my injured back. My right arm was hurting terribly. Shortly afterwards he disappeared from my sight, and then I realised with a sinking feeling that he had crouched down. He was leaning over me, putting one hand into his combat jacket while, with the other, he was patting my chest.

This is it, I thought in an endless moment. Here comes his combat knife. This guy is going to slit open my throat without my being able to move at all. And just now, when we had made it …

The uniformed giant touched my forehead and threw a blanket over me. As in a movie, his face was off the picture and then, with no apparent transition, another face filled the limited scope of my vision. This one I knew. It was Rear-Admiral Carlos Büsser's, the top cat of the amphibious force. He was telling me something that I could not hear. But I managed to tell him, though, 'Don't touch my arm! Not my arm!'

I began to feel very faint. There was also growing desperation with an inability to draw enough breath into my lungs. I would later learn that the Brit who had leant over me had actually pulled out a morphine syringe from his pocket, injected it into my arm, and then marked my forehead with the preventive letter M (for morphine) using the fresh blood he had collected from my wet vest. Then he threw a blanket over me, for I was already shivering uncontrollably due to the loss of blood. It was also extremely cold. The fact that he made that M sign on my forehead warning others of my morphine injection undoubtedly saved me from a second morphine dose that could have been fatal. Smart. Field smart.

I do not remember being lifted into a vehicle, but can recall the hospital in Stanley.

By my side is a body. It is Giacchino's. There are three doctors around me. Two of them are female. One runs an enormous pair of scissors over my clothing. It cuts open from the boots to my neck in a single cut. One of the girls touches my hip and looks into something.

A wound there?

She makes me roll over a little, looks at me and says, 'You're through, baby.'
They confer at my side.
The diagnosis is confusing.
'You're through?' I want to ask.
Through with what?
Through with combat?
Through with life?
Through with a careless existence?
Through with what?
But I cannot speak.
I can barely breathe – and even this simple reflex is becoming more and more difficult.
I must be moved.
Nothing more they can do for me here ...

Diego was convinced that Giacchino had expired when the latter was lifted up into a blanket-cum-makeshift stretcher at Government House to be driven away in an Amtrac to the nearby King Edward VII Memorial Hospital. Nonetheless his CO was still alive – just. It was both a strange yet uplifting paradox therefore that an Anglo-Argentine medical team comprising a British female nurse, Royal Marine medic and two Argentine military doctors fought like lions in the operating theatre trying to save him. But Giacchino was defeated in his final hour-long battle while Diego's trauma continued:

My next recollection was of my stretcher being tied to the side of the chopper. Off we flew into the sky, the blades hitting the air soothingly, bound for the icebreaker-cum-hospital ship ARA *Almirante Irízar* lying at anchor in the bay.

Something then happened that I cannot recall. Months later, the discovery of a reasonably clean scar on the inside of my left arm puzzled me as to its cause. The responsible person visited me one day in hospital. He was with me on that flight, a medical officer assigned to the vessel. After realising I was losing blood extremely rapidly, he thought of giving me an in-flight blood transfusion but did not have any equipment available. So he decided to be pragmatic. Climbing over my stretcher tied to the chopper's skids, he made an incision in my arm and reached for a blood vessel. This was connected to the spout of a blood sachet and then the officer pressed the liquid into my system while simultaneously it kept pouring out through the other openings. In that short flight my saviour used three sachets. He was impressed because the massive bleeding had been due to the severing of both the radial artery in my right arm and a branch of the lung artery.

We landed on the ship. I was still tied onto the stretcher and this caused difficulties for the sailors carrying me through the narrow passages to the infirmary. So blood poured from the stretcher whenever it was tilted at every door. This also messed up the deck. Faces were talking to me, but I could not hear them. Once more I speculated about whether Diego García Quiroga was still amongst the living. One of my former classmates, Sub-Lieutenant García Neder who was now an officer on board the ship, did not recognise me initially with my face covered in camouflage cream, the bloody M, and everything else. Then suddenly he grabbed my wounded arm passionately. It hurt like hell. But being unable to speak, I could not tell him to let go. Also a *Buzo Táctico*, Lieutenant Ramiro, appeared. Praising our action and reassuring me that we would get to drink champagne together in celebration over this, he was most moved by events.

Lieutenant Dr Gatica ordered me back to the Islands after a brief inspection of my wounds. There was nothing they could do for me there. So I was awarded the dubious distinction of becoming the first serviceman on either side in the war to be evacuated from the Islands. It was easily done. Several of my *Buzo Táctico* unit, including the CO, were looking on as my stretcher went by and then lifted up the steps and into an aircraft. Their faces were grey with exhaustion. Their eyes were lowered. None spoke. None moved. Neither could I, being absolutely sure now that death had incurred. It didn't feel too bad, I thought, but those guys look really tired.

While in the Fokker F47 stripped of its cabin seats, I was saved from dying once again by someone I will always remember with gratitude, even though he is still unknown to me. Obviously entrusted to prevent me from sleeping, a deadly condition when weak and on morphine, the man achieved his mission by gently slapping my face while saying, 'Wake up, Rodríguez!'

Somehow during the flight I managed to tell him, 'I'm not Rodríguez. I'm García!'

But the guy's mindset was inflexible. Ignoring my protest, he kept on slapping me frequently and continued to insist, 'Wake up, Rodríguez!'

Perhaps it was all a dream?

On arrival at Comodoro Rivadavia we were met by a pleasant Army medical officer who accompanied us on an onward helicopter flight to the Regional Hospital. Comodoro had – and still has – a big place in my heart, because it was the place where my father used to work when he was an active logging engineer, and we used to visit him in the summers. I loved the roughness of the place, permanently wind-ridden, and the heavy smell of sea coming from the coast. But now I was feeling very faint, dizzy and tired with everything coming at me through a dense and ever darkening fog.

When my stretcher was being carried through the hospital's main entrance, I heard a muffled comment, 'It's the cyanosis!' It made me painfully aware that my appearance probably looked like hell. Suddenly I was in a dark room and noticed other people also there. It was the X-Ray Centre. Somebody asked me whether I could sit up.

'Sure,' I replied, but would have fallen on the floor had not a couple of arms reached out and laid me on the table.

'It's better lying down. It's OK like that,' one voice assured me.

They were taking pictures of my chest.

A female voice called out, 'What's this guy's name?'

Wanting this clearly on the records, I stated weakly, 'My name is Diego Fernando García Quiroga.'

Out of the ever-intensifying dark, a man's face materialised in front of me. It was a smiling, serene face of the radiologist.

'Are you a relative of Julio's?' he asked.

'He's my father," I replied.

The smile broadened at the unexpected coincidence. 'Relax,' the face said. 'I can see no damage done to the vital organs.'

As if I had been waiting for these words, somewhere inside me an electricity switch was turned off. And only on waking up more than eleven hours and two successive surgeries afterwards did this event make me reasonably sure that I was alive.

My wife and parents were there, having been flown in by the Navy. Later that day Carlos Robbio, my XO, arrived still wearing his combat dress. News of Giacchino's death and the successful result of the operation was accompanied by his presentation of a complex little piece of metal he had collected from the grassy patch behind Government House. Still in one piece, but partially bent over and with the plastic covers gone, what remained of the Swiss Army Victorinox penknife that hung from my belt in a pouch over the left groin now bore the precise hole of a 9mm bullet in its centre. Without it, my femoral artery would have been severed with the inevitable consequence that implied. So good can life be.

There was much sleeping and dreaming. When deemed strong enough, I was interviewed by some journalists at my bedside. It was a mistake. A regimen of strong painkillers had made me confused and unaware of the war's latest developments. This condition continued for some time. The Brits had already landed at San Carlos (21 May) when I was transported further north to the naval hospital in Buenos Aires. But by then I had begun reading the newspapers, only to learn from them of friends not going to come back from the war. After receiving the visit of an officer who had lost an eye in combat, I became angry with myself for being unable to return to the front. The war was certain to end soon, and my opportunity of experiencing it had vanished by being shot on D-Day. Furthermore receiving a decoration for valour was, and remains, an undeserved honour. Some tried to explain that a nation needs heroes. But those who died in the war were much braver than me.

Finally hostilities ended, but my useless right arm prevented me from returning to service. It was not until November that I was declared fit and re-joined my unit. Immediately I completed two parachute jumps to be sure about my recovery. Life went on with only a few negative post-war effects. One was that almost every new experience encountered became dull in comparison to that Malvinas fling. I write 'almost' because of my new over-sensitivity to situations and things that, before, would not have triggered a reaction from me at all. Another was that some of my memories became quite scrambled, while others have disappeared without trace. To the list can be also added enhanced scepticism, downplaying of urgency, and diminished competitive interest.

It is widely accepted that the effects of combat on men have a direct relationship with several factors: heredity, upbringing, the way in which the serviceman and his immediate group 'feel' about the war, the relations with his comrades or harmony of his private life. Some of these factors can be overshadowed by those instruments of collective influence that are used in the military such as unit discipline, structure, routines and procedural matters. I was well-equipped in these areas and this – along with my short-lived combat experience – provided no possibility of my foundations fracturing. On the contrary, my existential self has been strengthened. Along with the immediate pride of having been a part of that unique operation, I gained the satisfaction of proving my loyalty to my comrades, profession and country.

There cannot be a better deal.

Diego's tale has many postscripts. One was his inability to lend the precious smashed penknife donated to his old unit at Mar del Plata for temporary display at the 2007 Imperial War Museum Falklands War Exhibition. The disappointing *Buzos Tácticos* refusal was mitigated by an invitation to that event's opening. In addition to his Margaret Thatcher encounter, Diego was reunited with the Naval Party 8901 Royal Marines Commander whom, after the British surrender in Government House, assisted the Argentine casualties outside. In 2010 I obtained retired Major Mike Norman's e-mail address for Diego. The latter's subsequent message to him was beautifully worded: 'Though in reality that was our second meeting (in London), it was the one which gave us the opportunity to properly shake hands. I hold a warm memory of that encounter [...] how glad and thankful I (am) for having been able to meet again with fellow soldiers who I had once fought against, and confirm that our professionalism allowed us to appreciate the human beings under our uniforms.' [8]

But Diego's message also contained a mission of reconciliation. This concerned Señora Delicia Rearte de Giacchino. Now in her eighties, the Mother of Giacchino lived in Argentina's Mendoza province and, as Diego explained to Mike Norman, they had been exchanging e-mails for some time. There had been an indication that she might want to communicate with 'the British officer who was commanding the Royal Marines at Government House on that fateful morning [...] This lady is indeed a lively character, very lucid and currently very much engaged – should I also say outraged – with Argentina's political decline and the sorry corner where our country has increasingly managed to paint itself'.[9]

Mike Norman was willing to participate in any possible dialogue via Diego's translating skills. I hope this occurred. Nonetheless there would be another more personal communication after nearly twenty-eight years: an eagerly awaited letter sent to Señora Giacchino by the British nurse who had attended Pedro Giacchino's last hour on that day of days when the British lost their Falklands [...] being the extraordinary event which would, in turn, trigger the Argentine 5th Marine Infantry Battalion's preparations for deployment into the South Atlantic Theatre of Operations.

Notes

1. *The Art of War*, Chapter 3 – Strategy of Attack.
2. Para FAL – *Fusil Automático Liviano*. Exactly like the Argentine Marine and Army

standard-issue FAL rifle but with a hollow collapsible stock. The weapon is so named because it was designed for paratrooper use.

3. In late-December 1978 all Argentine military garrisons stationed along the Chilean border went to Alert 1 and the fleet was deployed on *Operación Soberanía* (Sovereignty) awaiting orders to block the Southern passages. This situation (which some consider as being Argentina's own 'Cuba missile crisis') was the climax to that year of sabre-rattling between Argentina and Chile regarding the sovereignty dispute of three islands located near the eastern mouth of the Beagle Channel. An imminent war was finally averted by Papal mediation which favoured the Chilean position. However for the Argentine military (including Diego) on the ground it meant deployment, excitement, uncertainty and a big brouhaha at higher level of command which re-examined a large number of operational procedures. The crisis also became a catalyst that rapidly enabled the military to regain awareness of its real mission after a long decade of focusing on counter-insurgency.

4. This change of plan, Giacchino's revised mission and other adjustments are contrary to *Razor's Edge* (p. 121) which incorrectly states that the original plan remained as it was because of inflexible Argentine decision-making.

5. *The Art of War*, Chapter 7 – The Army Contending.

6. Of the original sixty-eight, two dropped out during the approach march to Moody Brook. One sustained a foot injury and was assisted by the other.

7. *The Falklands War: Then and Now*, p. 35.

8. E-mail dated 23 January 2010.

9. *Ibid.*

As for the steep form –
If I occupy it first, I must occupy the high and
     yang and await the enemy.
If the enemy occupies it first, I lead the troops
     away.
Do not pursue.

– Sun Tzu[1]

Eduardo Villarraza and I had exchanged e-mails prior to the Nottingham colloquium. But his comprehensive answers[2] to my questions about Tumbledown lacked a dimension. So he and his wife Inés invited me to their Buenos Aires flat, appropriately on 2 April, during my fourth visit to Argentina in 2007. Eduardo Gerding was our interpreter. The Malvinas War veteran possessed an aura of calm. His service as a Marine Corps officer had lasted thirty-one years, including post-war appointments as Second-in-Command of the 5th Marine Infantry Battalion (BIM5) from 1991-92 and Commanding Officer of the 4th Battalion from 1995-96. After retirement in 2003 he worked for two years at the Navy Welfare Office, but was now employed in an Armed Forces welfare system.

'We've a better quality of life now with an income reduction,' commented the former *Capitán de Navío de Infantería de Marina*.

Eduardo and Inés then told me their story in the presence of their thirty year-old son Agustín and twenty-eight year-old daughter Paz who occasionally throughout the evening brought us more empanadas (patties stuffed with meat), sandwiches and drink for us. Eduardo had been first acquainted with Inés at the age of fifteen. Three years later in 1968 he enlisted into the Argentine Navy and, as a Naval Academy cadet, met her again at a party in 1970 where their romance started. Commissioned into the Marine Corps in December 1971, Midshipman Villarraza married eighteen year-old Inés the following September. Their wedding took place in the Federal Capital of Buenos Aires at the Church of San Martín de Tours, the patron saint of Buenos Aires.

The following year Eduardo, a rifle platoon commander, was promoted to Sub-Lieutenant and assumed command of an 81mm Mortar Platoon. Meanwhile she qualified as a school teacher and took specialist education to become a kindergarten teacher in 1974. Their family increased on 6 June 1976 when she gave birth to their son Agustín. But heavily pregnant again thirty months later, Inés would experience her first international crisis in the southernmost Argentine province of Isla Grande de Tierra del Fuego. This island has a north-south split with Chile possessing sixty percent in the west and Argentina the rest. Eduardo was in command of the 1st Marine Corps Brigade Reconnaissance Company equipped with six armoured and other types of vehicles in December 1978 at the climax of the Beagle Channel islands crisis with Chile. As a safety precaution Inés moved back temporarily to Buenos Aires with two year-old Agustín. Then seven weeks after the crisis had been resolved, Inés gave birth to Paz on 2 March 1979.

Comparisons between Eduardo's and my family were strikingly similar. I married Tove, my first Norwegian wife, four months before the Villarrazas' wedding; Tove also held a kindergarten teacher qualification; my daughters Victoria and Emily were, respectively, only one year younger than Agustín and Paz. The four of them would soon become children of the Falklands-Malvinas War; and both ladies would be soon sucked into the war at its worst end – maintaining their respective homes and caring for young families, while forced to endure an energy-sapping information vacuum.

Eduardo attended a Marine Officers' course in 1980 prior to being posted in February 1981 to the 5th Marine Infantry Battalion (*Bat. Ec.*) [3] at Río Grande situated on Tierra del Fuego.[4] Now a *Teniente de Navío* (Naval Lieutenant), he became the N (Nacar) Company Commander. Like other Battalion sub-units, N Company consisted of ten per cent regular personnel and ninety per cent conscripts. The Marine Corps had an advantage over the Army by inducting the conscripts on a 'trickle-feed', as opposed to block, system. This retained a degree of continuity. Regulars held nearly all N Company's key appointments, except a few which were held by conscripts because of a regular personnel shortage.[5]

Eduardo and his young family lived in a married quarter close to BIM5's camp. But they did not see too much of him in his first year with the Battalion. It would be subjected to a severe training programme devised by *Capitán de Fragata* (Commander) Carlos Hugo Robacio, the Commanding Officer, who was known throughout the Marine Corps as a powerful leader, martinet and officer of much initiative. He was determined to spend as much time as possible out of barracks to take advantage of the different environments and extreme conditions of Tierra del Fuego's sub-polar oceanic climate in which temperatures average minus four degrees Centigrade in the coldest month of June and fourteen degrees Centigrade in the warmest of January. This climate with its strong winds was, of course, similar to that of the Malvinas, as is the amount of light in the winter day which, because of Tierra del Fuego's southerly latitude, lasts only seven hours compared to the summer day of twenty. It is also a region of harsh terrain comprising steppes, mountains, dense woods of Winter's Bark and Southern Beech trees that can grow to height of twenty metres, and large lakes. The Argentine part of Tierra del Fuego was also large, possessing an area one third greater than the Malvinas, and was perfect for marine amphibious exercises because of the sea's proximity.

So Robacio's training regime throughout that year of 1981 contained multiple exercises at Battalion level which included live firing of support weapons such as 60mm, 84mm and 106mm mortars and 105mm anti-tank guns – plus artillery, naval gunfire support and strike aircraft. It culminated in the unit's programmed November efficiency inspection conducted by the Naval Infantry Command. This included a Battalion live-firing attack exercise with air strike support that was visited by Rear-Admiral Jorge Anaya, the *Comandante en Jefe* (Commander-in-Chief) *de la Armada* (Navy) *de la República Argentina*. Anaya was also a member of the three-man ruling national Military Junta and driving force behind the following year's forthcoming 'defence of our national sovereignty' in the South Atlantic. So could his interest in BIM5 be a sign that Robacio's unit already had been earmarked to participate in this special task? Certainly Anaya was already beginning to check the entire Navy's readiness and how close his Commanding Officers were aligned to his philosophy. Politics were also important in the context of the struggle for power within the Junta, and probably Anaya also wanted to secure Robacio's loyalty by paying him a special visit.[6]

Notwithstanding that, the outcome of such inspections could have immediate dire effects when matters went wrong. Typically, praise was seldom and punishment fast. But BIM5's inspection went well. It was undoubtedly the best-prepared Argentine unit for the forthcoming Malvinas land campaign. No other experienced similar 'work-up' training over such an extended period of time and in similar climatic and terrain conditions as those found on the Malvinas.

But BIM5 was not the only military unit stationed in this important strategic area of Argentina. There was also the highly important naval air base at Río Grande. During the forthcoming war this would be used by four of Argentina's November 1981 purchase of five French-manufactured Dassault-Bregeut Super Étendard strike fighter aircraft and their five AM-39 Exocet missiles. *Base Aeronaval (BAN)* Río Grande was also a potential target for the British Army's 22 Special Air Service Regiment. The local population would have every reason to fear their town's vulnerability.

Towards the end of March 1982 military activity suddenly increased and Eduardo confided to Inés, 'I think something big is about to happen.'

But no official warning was given that the Malvinas was about to be recovered by Argentina. After *Operación Rosario* was carried out successfully on Friday, 2 April, Robacio issued an order that each Company in his command was to prepare for deployment to the Islands. He was optimistic that his Battalion would be involved. In those early days, although reports were received of a British Task Force being deployed from the United Kingdom, it was perceived this would not intervene. So Robacio told his officers that their wives could visit the Islands after the Battalion's deployment. Negotiations with Britain would prevail and a 'two-flag' solution would be found to the Malvinas-Falklands dispute brought to a head by Argentina's action. After all, it was the Royal Navy which had removed the Argentine presence there in 1833 and, like his countrymen, Eduardo was convinced the Islands belonged to Argentina. He had no hesitation in believing the correctness of the Battalion's potential mission even though a military dictatorship was behind this adventure.

But Robacio also warned that Río Grande and, in particular, their camp could be subjected to air attack. This threat was not in the South Atlantic, but the west. It would be in Chile's interests that the British regained the Malvinas and so Argentina's aggressive neighbour might take advantage of the situation. Inés was mentally unprepared for this dramatic turn of events ... and suddenly on that 2 April 2007 evening in her Buenos Aires home she began to cry as those distressing memories re-surfaced. Had I been too inquisitive? But she insisted on continuing her story. Afterwards I was convinced Inés had benefitted from our therapeutic evening.

So on Sunday, 4 April 1982 the family experienced the first of a number of air raid alerts with sirens being sounded in the camp. Families were warned by Marines knocking on their windows and Eduardo hurried to the Battalion muster area. Inés perceived her five year-old son Agustín as a fifteen year-old when he helped her with three year-old Paz. Gathering up money and jewels as she believed this was a real air raid approaching, Inés cried as the three took shelter under the bed in the couple's bedroom. Although a false alarm, it had been a shock and even Paz was speechless.

Next morning the Battalion was placed on a ninety-minute notice to move. Robacio personally knew Rear-Admiral Carlos Büsser, the Commander of the Argentine landing force. The latter telephoned Robacio at 09.00 on 8 April to order BIM5's immediate deployment. Büsser and Robacio mutually agreed to maintain a direct and regular private radio communication while BIM5 was on the Islands. In all their transmissions Büsser's radio call sign would be 'Dog' and Robacio's 'Rabbit'. These gave a clue to the nature of BIM5's mission: a tenacious defence of Argentina's acquisition.

The 707-strong Battalion and its eighty tons of equipment and stores began to be flown to the Malvinas from *BAN* Río Grande by civil aircraft that afternoon for the next seventy-two hours. Concurrently in case of a Chilean attack scenario, a Marine Brigade of 2,600 men was deployed by air from the northern Puerto Belgrano Naval Base in order to fill the gap left and also beef up the naval air base's defences. Meanwhile 'three to five days' after arrival, according to Eduardo, the Battalion was assigned its positions to the immediate west of Puerto Argentino in Sector *Bronce* (Bronze). This consisted of Sapper Hill, Mount William and Tumbledown, with the (Joint) Argentine Command in Puerto Argentino issuing the definitive Defence Order on 16 April. The exception was O (Obra) Company which was initially deployed to Mount Longdon. It was relieved on 18 April by the 7th Mechanised Infantry Regiment and became the BIM5 reserve force located near the Battalion Tactical HQ Command Post at Felton Stream on the capital's outskirts three kilometres behind, and to the east of, Tumbledown's east end.[7]

The N Company location was on the southern sides of Mount William and Tumbledown. The Company's tactical area of responsibility looked west in an area between the sea coastline to the south and further north to Moody Valley. The local terrain was similar to that which the Battalion had trained across in Tierra del Fuego. But it was an enormous area for just one rifle company to cover, and should have been the entire Battalion's responsibility. The frontal distance from the north-east end of Tumbledown around the latter's west end and down to the south-east shoulder of Mount William was nearly six kilometres. In comparison British Army doctrine stated that an infantry battalion should cover a front of one kilometre. But Sapper Hill, another important feature one kilometre south-east of the BIM5 Battalion HQ, had to be occupied and so M (Mar) Company was sited there. Eduardo believed it was unsound to occupy only the high ground because the British forces would then infiltrate around and attack him from the rear. Furthermore he was convinced that any British attack would take place at night. Therefore an intermediate solution was adopted by employing mutual support between platoons and receiving further support from the Battalion.

His Company did not have problems with the distribution of fresh food supplies from Puerto Argentino. Eduardo:

Soon after our arrival we received by helicopter a field kitchen to feed the whole Company. This field kitchen works with liquid fuel, mainly kerosene, but gas and oil may be used as well. Later we received another field kitchen because other sub-units arrived and we had the task of feeding them too. With both field kitchens we were able to feed 300 men. The kitchens were placed on the east-northern side of

Tumbledown and we received a Corporal and two conscripts to manage them.

We received provisions for twenty days, e.g. noodles, rice, lentils, beans and other items suitable for stews such as onions, carrots etc. Meat was scarce and supplied in cans. We could prepare our breakfast with coffee, tea or mate and cream soups which were good as they contained fat. Flour was also received to make bread and mate. With such provisions we were able to provide the personnel three meals each day.

The field kitchen could not be turned on during the night because of the burners. We had breakfast at mid-morning, lunch at the normal time and dinner with the last daylight. Every sub-unit had a thermal container with a capacity for twenty-five or thirty rations. The meal was taken to the positions and the Commanders were in charge of distributing these to their personnel. More food was supplied to some sub-units so they could cook according to their inventive and culinary skills. Besides this each sub-unit had their combat rations which could be used when they lacked warm meals. We had combat rations for at least ten days. Although these meals were not provided in the same amount or quality, it did not affect us seriously.

Eduardo's first task was to site his three organic rifle platoons and Company HQ. Commanded by Second Petty Officer Luis Lucero, 3 Platoon was positioned to the rear on the north-east spur of Tumbledown. There the platoon could cover by fire Moody Brook Valley which stretched away to the west. Tumbledown's east end just south of 3 Platoon was a suitable place to locate his Company HQ Command Post. Attached to it, and under the HQ's command, were four men armed with two 3.5-inch *Lanzacohetes* (M-20 rocket launchers) which could be deployed to wherever a threat materialised in Eduardo's huge tactical area of responsibility. The other two platoons were sited due south of Company HQ. Eduardo:

> Taking the reference from Mount William's highest peak, 1 Platoon (Midshipman Bianchi) was situated south-west in the middle of the slope facing Mount Harriet's southern hill and the road to Goose Green [...] and was responsible for covering the incoming approach formed between Mount William and the sea. From the same topographic slope, 2 Platoon (Midshipman Oruezabala) was situated north-north-east of Mount William and south of Tumbledown facing Goat Ridge north of Mount Harriet. It covered the incoming approach between Mount William and Tumbledown [...] Both platoons were to support each other according to the location of the British attack.

Subsequently Eduardo's Marines worked hard:

> We organised our positions from mid-April until mid-June when the operation ended, and started digging our positions. The first days we slept in tents, but as days went by we dug ourselves into the ground order to shelter from the weather environment and the bombing. We barely had material to do so (tins, wood, empty fuel tanks) or anything we could find in the terrain plus stones and earth. I think the positions were well built because we had few casualties from the bombardments.

BIM5 had received a platoon of nine 12.7mm Browning Heavy Machine-Guns from the twenty-seven in the 136-man strong *Compañía de Ametralladoras de 12.7 mílimetros* which had been deployed to the Islands from the Puerto Belgrano Naval Base. A section of three guns was allocated to the Battalion Command Post's local defence, another section went to the Logistic Support Area and a third to N Company. Of the latter, two guns were allocated to 1 Platoon on Mount William and one to 3 Platoon.[8] It was a tactical error that Eduardo received so few of these guns. They would have been a good counter to the excessive frontages he had to defend and could take advantage of the excellent fields of fire that the open, rolling terrain offered. His Company also required comprehensive indirect fire support. Fortunately plenty of resources existed. A 60mm mortar section of fifteen men and three mortars were added to the Company's position, being located on the centre-east ridge of Tumbledown, and six mortars with forty-seven men of the 81mm Mortar Platoon were sited 500 metres north-east of Mount William as the crow flies, just below the saddle midway between Tumbledown and Mount William.[9] Another six mortars of the 106.6mm Mortar Platoon were positioned just west of the Felton Stream Battalion HQ Command Post and, not least, to the Command Post's eastern side were moved six 105mm howitzers of the Marine Field Artillery Battalion's B Battery.[10]

All these weapons, in addition to two Argentine Army batteries of twelve 105mm howitzers nearer the capital, had targets registered onto the west of Mount William and Tumbledown, including Mount Harriet and Two Sisters. But despite the potential lethality of these impressive indirect fire weapon resources, Eduardo still needed infantry reinforcements to close a few of the many holes in his defensive lay-out. His wishes were partially granted on 20 April with 'the arrival of the personnel which formed 4 Platoon (Acting Sub-Lieutenant Vázquez) and ameliorated the problem we had on the westernmost side of Tumbledown. However this did not end our problems'. The greatest concern was the incorrect directional focus of N Company's defence and, although later adjustments would be made, this critical flaw remained. Eduardo:

> At the beginning 1 Platoon was ordered to face south (towards the coast) and then, with the arrival of the other units, it was changed to south-west. Although the second front assigned was somewhat smaller, it was extremely wide for the Company to control. As a result the defensive system was an intermediate one which would allow us to control the heights and incoming approaches. (But) the system had no depth and was very much like an onion skin in as far as that any breach of it could easily overwhelm the defence. And that is what happened.

His thoughts coincided with those of Sun Tzu's about the steep form of terrain. Great danger would exist if the benefits of occupying 'the high and *yang*' could not be secured which, as the Argentine Marine officer had pointed out, they were not. All these defence problems had been caused by a faulty threat assessment carried out by the (Joint) Argentine Command in those first few days. It concluded that the main British attack would come from the sea by an amphibious landing on the southern coast near Puerto Argentino. The occupation by two 4th Infantry Regiment companies on Wall Mountain and Mount Challenger seven and nine kilometres respectively due west of Mount William reinforced such a judgement. Robacio disagreed. It would be a costly affair to land on a well-defended coastline and launch operations from there. He had told the Joint Argentine Command that, in his opinion, the British would seek to land on a non-defended coastline anywhere on Soledad Island (East Falkland) and their later operations would occur from the west. But his assessment unfortunately was not shared by the senior officers in Puerto Argentino.

Eduardo and Inés maintained contact with each other in this initial period by using the air mail service. Occasionally they would talk over the telephone whenever he visited Puerto Argentino. Inés would also send Eduardo cans of paté and chocolate to supplement his rations. In return, Inés would receive Eduardo's dirty socks and underpants to wash, as well as a Malvinas fern which he had dug up. Although she planted this in their garden at Río Grande, it died a year later. Meanwhile the situation had become increasingly worrying. By mid-April twelve Dagger multi-role fighter aircraft had been moved to *BAN* Río Grande from their base at Tandil. A week later four Super Étendard strike fighter aircraft with five Exocet missiles were also re-deployed to there from their Bahía Blanca base to begin final preparations for possible operations against the approaching British Task Force. With the latter's arrival in the Total Exclusion Zone, further security measures were taken:

> (The) Argentine command had moved the Super Étendards from the airbase to a number of heavily defended sand-bagged emplacements in car parks along Highway 3, close to the coast, so in effect had the SAS got there the cupboard would have been bare. The airbase's anti-aircraft defences had been reinforced early in the conflict with additional anti-aircraft artillery units, SAMs and long-range surveillance radar.[11]

This had been triggered when the shooting war began in earnest early on the morning of 1 May. Ten kilometres east of Tumbledown the RAF Vulcan bombing of the *BAM* (*Base Aerea Militar*) Malvinas airfield north of Puerto Argentino was followed, just after dawn, by a repeat performance from nine Sea Harriers. It was a wake-up call for the Argentine forces on the Malvinas. The British meant business. In mid-afternoon Eduardo observed the first of twenty-four naval gunfire support (NGS) bombardment operations that the Royal Navy would pummel Puerto Argentino's Inner and Outer Defence Zones with during the next six weeks. He spotted three ships: the 'County' Class guided missile destroyer HMS *Glamorgan*, and two Type 21 frigates HM Ships *Alacrity* and *Arrow* shelling the airfield from the southern Stanley gun line. Then the ships came under air attack themselves and were strafed by 30mm cannon fire by three Daggers – but the NGS continued into that night until 01.35Z. Only three kilometres to the east M Company's Sapper Hill was hit. Eduardo heard the bad news. One Marine was killed there and five others wounded. This dramatic day led to an immediate censorship of servicemen's private letters sent from the Malvinas, including those of Eduardo's to Inés.

However, it was the Royal Navy's torpedoing and sinking of the Argentine cruiser ARA *General Belgrano* on 2 May with massive loss of life which changed everything. The Argentine imagination was ensnared by this event: and it disregarded the successful Exocet attack by two Super Étendards from Río Grande on the Royal Navy Type 42 guided missile destroyer HMS *Sheffield* two days later. The *Belgrano* disaster led to the Argentine Navy being withdrawn to coastal waters. *BAN* Río Grande also received a reinforcement of ten Skyhawk fighter aircraft flown off the aircraft carrier ARA *Veinticinco de Mayo* thereby increasing the number of combat aircraft there to twenty-six plus two Neptune tracker aircraft. No other airbase on mainland Argentina could boast so many aircraft committed to the war.

The cruiser's demise also forced Inés to give serious consideration to these matters in which her family was now becoming even more embroiled. It was difficult to think. She had to take a decision. Maybe she had to leave her job at the school? Take Agustín out of his first grade class at school? Perhaps return to Buenos Aires? But then she remembered the 1978 Chilean threat. She was not going to live out of suitcases again with this time, not one, but two small children. So she stayed in Río Grande.

During the next nine-day period on Tumbledown, Eduardo was witness to the Royal Navy's determination. Another two night and three daytime NGS bombardment operations took place against targets around Puerto Argentino and its *BAM* Malvinas airfield The last on the afternoon of 12 May, resulted in more Argentine air attacks which damaged the Type 42 guided missile destroyer HMS *Glasgow*. Two Skyhawks were shot down. Another crashed into the sea. But Eduardo did not endure any more daytime bombardments. The final eighteen NGS operations would be carried out at night in order to interrupt his Company's and other units' precious sleep.

Inés developed a coping strategy with the stress. It was a familiar one – indeed the same being used by wives of British servicemen deployed, and being deployed, to the South Atlantic. She invited other Battalion wives to her home on a regular basis. They would pray, talk, guess about the future and go shopping together. Some wives would receive radio messages about their deployed husbands from radio hams in the Malvinas. Inés did not trust the Argentine national radio or BBC World Service, but listened instead to the Uruguayan *Radio Colonia* for news in the South Atlantic.

Daily she worked at her kindergarten class of seventeen four to five year-olds. But there was no escape from the Malvinas situation even for a few hours because all Río Grande schools had a civil defence organisation. There were air raid exercises and even Agustín remembered the blare of sirens and children taking shelter under their desks. It was forbidden for staff to listen to the radio at school as the news was affecting the children. At home the sirens agitated little Paz who, on one occasion, hid under her bed clutching the family's switched-on radio. Inés was trapped in the roller coaster circumstances and, in order to keep herself updated about Eduardo and his unit, never switched off her radio or TV.

But she would have been unaware that in the early hours of 18 May a Royal Navy Sea King helicopter had attempted to land a nine-man SAS patrol north of Río Grande. The mission, codenamed Operation Plum Duff, was to carry out a recce prior to the operation of eliminating the Super Étendards, their ten pilots and remaining three Exocets. But Plum Duff was aborted. And a heated debate began in 22 SAS regiment at Hereford as to the viability of Operation Mikado in which two

Hercules C-130 aircraft with forty-six members of B Squadron on board were to be crash-landed onto the *BAN* Río Grande airfield. With lack of appropriate detailed intelligence, the B Squadron Commander, Major John Moss, displayed moral courage when he voiced his concerns to the Director SAS, Brigadier Peter de la Billière, late Light Infantry about such a dubious high risk method of entry into the target area. The latter promptly removed Moss from his command.[12] I can only guess that the real reason for such a spiteful reaction was not so much the (wrong) perception of Moss's apparent lukewarm attitude, but more relevantly the prestige of gaining the Government's War Cabinet authorisation to carry out the Director's plan. I knew John Moss well. He was in my Sandhurst platoon and I do not know of a more loyal or solid British Army officer. Fortunately Operation Mikado, re-named by many in 22 SAS as Operation Certain Death, was eventually cancelled.

After a two-week lull the Sea Harriers started daily bombing of the Puerto Argentino *BAM* Malvinas airfield again. Eduardo's Company was more affected during 17-21 May when four nocturnal NGS bombardment operations were carried out by *Glamorgan* which liberally peppered eighty kilometres of the Soledad Island (East Falkland) south-east coast with 407 high-explosive shells and twenty-one starshell. This was a series of diversions for the British landings at San Carlos which took place on the morning of 21 May. Later that afternoon it was *BAN* Río Grande's Skyhawks which bombed and sank the Type 21 frigate HMS *Ardent*.

Inés became sick with anxiety and could not eat properly for the next three weeks. Her weight loss was eight kilos as she drank tea, not coffee, in an attempt to alleviate her worries. Meanwhile she and the other wives continued to meet. People telephoned her to ask for help in their domestic situations. Most practical problems were solved. For example, Inés's washing machine broke down one day. So she rang the BIM5 Families Officer for assistance. He arrived promptly at her home with a choice of two, but Agustín had become suspicious of anyone in uniform. So the little boy asked an oft-repeated question to his mother, 'Is he an Argentine or English soldier?'

Domestic tensions rose further when, despite many attempts of telephoning, communications were finally lost with the Battalion on Soledad Island where the Royal Navy Fleet Air Arm Sea Harriers, now reinforced with RAF GR3 Harriers, increased the intensity of their bombing operations on the Puerto Argentino airfield. These reached a crescendo in that last week of May with sixteen air strikes.

Also the Super Étendards launched more Exocet missions in this period. Two missiles destroyed the important container ship SS *Atlantic Conveyor* on 25 May. Later that night *Glamorgan* disturbed the sleep of Eduardo and his men once more by bombarding Soledad Island's south-east coast with another 146 shells. Two nights later in the early hours of 28 May N Company endured its first taste of Royal Navy NGS targeting Tumbledown. The bombardment of 209 shells fired by *Alacrity* and the Type 21 frigate HMS *Avenger* included neighbouring Sapper Hill and Mount Harriet.

This was N Company's nightmare. The five hills south-west of Puerto Argentino had a compact formation. The front three – (from west to east) Mount Harriet, Mount William and Sapper Hill – had a seven-kilometre frontage set back three kilometres from the southern coastline. The rear two were nearby. Two kilometres north-east of Mount Harriet and one north of Mount William lay Tumbledown which, in turn, was located three kilometres to the south-east of Two Sisters. Nocturnal NGS bombardment operations from the southern Stanley gun line could aim therefore at an unimpeded shooting gallery of two-tiered targets. It had also already started to become an 'area psychological neutraliser' because, no matter which target was selected, the subsequent mental effect would be equal on all defenders. But Eduardo continued his battle of finding solutions to the challenges in his defensive area.

Forty kilometres south-west, the fourteen-hour Battle of Darwin and Goose Green was being slugged out. The subsequent Argentine defeat there prompted late adjustments nearer Puerto Argentino, and the 4th Infantry Regiment withdrew from Mount Challenger and Wall Mountain to occupy Mount Harriet and Two Sisters. Apart from this, the original flawed Argentine defensive plan remained unchanged. Eduardo:

> Even after the San Carlos landing the (Argentine) Command in the Malvinas thought there would be diversionary operations from the west whilst the main attack would come from the sea on the southern coast near Puerto Argentino (Stanley). As a result of this there were many Regiments not involved in combat, and those units which occupied Mount Harriet, Two Sisters and Mount Longdon did so at the end without being able to build a defensive system.

On 30 May the Puerto Argentino area night bombardment by *Glamorgan* and Type 21 frigate *Ambuscade* preceded that day's final Super Étendard mission from BAN Río Grande. This failed, its last Exocet missing the all-important aircraft carrier HMS *Invincible*. Forty-eight hours later *Alacrity* was again pounding in 134 shells between Moody Brook and Two Sisters only three kilometres from Eduardo's N Company. Next night *Active* and *Ambuscade* went to work nearer Stanley. But a seventy-two hour respite from Royal Navy exertions occurred as high winds and rain battered down on N Company. On 5 June an adjustment of BIM5 assets was made. Eduardo:

> O Company was moved (from Felton Stream) to Pony's Pass (two kilometres south-east of Tumbledown) in order to stop any British advance from the south and, in case of an overwhelming force, to delay them while waiting for further actions [...] O Company was not a normal effective company force as it was a rifle platoon reinforced with machine-guns.[13]

The mission given to this re-deployed company would be followed to the letter. However its rigid wording did not appear to permit its reinforcing Tumbledown if any crisis might occur during a battle there. Robacio:

> We assigned O Company the task of becoming involved in a delayed combat (that is offering certain resistance for a while) and later to withdraw to their original position, as the core of the battlefield would be, and in fact was, Tumbledown.[14]

O Company had been the Battalion's reserve force. This responsibility was now assumed by M Company on Sapper Hill. C Company, 3rd Infantry Regiment was also deployed that day to the rear of Eduardo's Company between Sapper Hill and Mount William, thereby providing a further blocking force against any possible British advance. This sub-unit comprised two rifle platoons, two sections of 120mm mortars and 81mm mortars respectively and the Company HQ. In addition he received more reinforcements. A two-gun 105mm anti-tank gun section was sited on Mount William's southern slopes covering the Puerto Argentino-Darwin east-west track and, on the south-west shoulder, 1 Platoon received a Bantam Missile section of two launchers and six missiles. Furthermore twenty-four Marine Amphibious Engineers had been re-deployed to the northern side of Tumbledown's west end. They became N Company's 5 Platoon and Eduardo utilised their sapper expertise:

> Explosive traction traps were placed in N Company's defensive area, in the Tumbledown's western area and in front of 5 Platoon. Some minefields were false. They were marked in the field but contained no minefields [...] (but) the defence system kept on being an onion skin without depth or reserves.

The final nine consecutive NGS bombardment nights began in the early hours of 6 June against Eduardo's Company and, for the first time, both Tumbledown and Mount William were targetted simultaneously. The predator was the Type 12 frigate HMS *Yarmouth* which also hit Moody Brook, while the Type 42 guided missile destroyer HMS *Cardiff* took on Wireless Ridge and Sapper Hill. Their 4.5-inch guns were intimidating weapons.[15] A combined total of 438 shells fired in this particular NGS bombardment operation indicated enemy operations were approaching a climax.

The weather remained foul. Next night the war's final week started with *Ambuscade* and Type 21 frigate HMS *Active* battering Mount Harriet and area west of Stanley with another 100 shells. At least the rain had stopped at first light, but some twelve hours later *Cardiff* and *Yarmouth* poured another 198 shells onto, amongst other targets, Sapper Hill and Mount Harriet. Although ineffective regarding casualties inflicted, these bombardments were wearing down Eduardo's men mentally because of the former's unpredictability of time and targets. But on 8 June after the Argentine air strike against the RFAs *Sir Galahad* and *Sir Tristram*, Robacio became impatient to take advantage of the surprise this had caused. He wanted to mount an immediate night attack from the south-east on the Scots Guards at nearby Bluff Cove. Eduardo's Company would undoubtedly have been involved in his CO's audacious and high-risk plan.

However Robacio was thwarted because, as he pointed out years later, 'We would take breakfast during the attack, but the British would have tea with us later as nobody would step forward to give us the required logistic support. Today, with a cold head, I think that I was pretty lucky to have received no such support.' [16]

Yarmouth returned that night to pulverise Moody Brook with 124 shells. Then twenty-four hours later she repeated this task plus bombardments on the five hills less Tumbledown. This was my first night on the front at Little Wether Ground above Fitzroy, and I listened in awe at the frightening thump-thump of her shelling. Both friend and foe alike would continue to hear this disruptively intensifying Royal Navy lullaby for the next four nights. It was a driven organisation. In the small hours of 11 June *Active* and *Arrow* took on Mount Harriet once more, as well as other targets nearer Stanley, with 189 shells. As a reserve blocking force, 2 Platoon of C Company, 3rd Infantry Regiment was moved forward onto Mount William's eastern slopes.

From that day the intensity of incoming enemy artillery shelling increased and Harrier GR3s began to attack Outer and Inner Defence Zone targets, with two dropping cluster bombs on Mount Harriet. It was the prelude to 3 Commando Brigade taking the Outer Defence Zone of Mount Longdon, Two Sisters and Mount Harriet on the night of 11-12 June. *Avenger, Glamorgan* and *Yarmouth* fired 584 shells in support, while the Berkeley Sound gun line north of Stanley was used for the first time by *Arrow*'s bombardment of 238 shells on Sapper Hill and other targets further to the east. But no further British exploitation was made into the Inner Defence Zone and the 3rd Infantry Regiment platoon was withdrawn from Mount William.

On 12 June O Company at Pony's Pass observed the large file of 300 prisoners coming down from Mount Harriet following the Argentine defeat earlier that morning. The twelve-man 3 Assault Section of *Compañía de Comandos 602* was deployed into an anti-tank gun position south-west of Mount William.[17] There were also desperate attempts by Robacio to generate more reinforcements for his defensive Achilles heel on Tumbledown's west end. One asset was the 168-man strong B Company of the 6th Infantry Regiment (RI6). The Company Commander was Lieutenant Raúl Daniel Abella. Comprising three rifle platoons and a support platoon of three 81mm mortars, MAGs and dozen portable surface-to-air missiles,[18] B Company was nearly double the size of a full-strength British Army infantry rifle company. Its overall commander was Major Oscar Ramón Jaimet. Robacio:

> (It) linked the rear of Two Sisters with the troops on Longdon, and should have fallen back to Tumbledown's western salient, (but) unfortunately did this some kilometres to the east, thus weakening the anticipated plan for the defence of Tumbledown which had been already been co-ordinated and laid out. Nothing was done by higher command to correct this error, leaving those troops to cover Moody Valley.[19]

Perhaps Jaimet was encouraged to move further back to this more protected final location from N Company's *bête noire Yarmouth* which had returned to the Stanley gun line for the fifth time in order to bombard Tumbledown with the bulk of her 261 shells in a suppressive fire operation during the Mount Harriet attack.

Another sub-unit commanded by Major Guillermo Berazay, A Company of the 3rd Infantry Regiment, should also have deployed to Tumbledown's north-west slopes (where 5 Platoon was located) on the morning of 12 June. Their mission was to assist in defending that area as well as the northern part of Tumbledown further to the east. However due to ice on the road and mechanical problems with their vehicles, they never arrived but, according to Robacio, 'took up a position somewhat to the rear, two or three kilometres closer to Moody Valley'[20] on its southern slopes. Two days later Berazay's men would become sucked into the final phase of the Wireless Ridge parallel battle to Tumbledown. So this combined total of nearly 350 Army troops who could shore up this vulnerable end of Tumbledown never arrived. Moreover passage of information about such reinforcements was hopelessly defective as Vázquez, the 4

Platoon Commander, told me twenty-seven years later, 'If those plans existed I was never told about them.' [21]

Also on that day, 12 June, a pair of Harrier GR3s attacked Sapper Hill with cluster bombs, but matters would have been something else if the potentially disastrous 5th Infantry Brigade attack plan devised by another former Light Infantryman, Brigadier Tony Wilson (my former Commanding Officer) had taken place. In comparison with Major John Moss, the Scots Guards Commanding Officer, Lieutenant-Colonel Mike Scott, received a DSO rather than the sack after his moral courage in challenging Wilson's plan. Scott then promptly changed it by altering its start point and direction, and adding a diversionary attack. His initiative was followed by a second example of moral courage: this time from the Gurkha Commandant.

At the Brigade's final Orders Group held in Fitzroy, Lieutenant-Colonel David Morgan remarked that he did not think the revised attack would work. His reasoning was based on a number of factors, mainly logistic, but including the critical one that there had been no time to see the objective, let alone the ground over which the Gurkhas and Scots Guards were expected to attack. Fortunately Scott agreed and a twenty-four delay was granted. Post-war his Gurkha counterpart was awarded an OBE.

I would have participated in the original unrehearsed double-Battalion assault on Eduardo's Company in broad daylight. It would have started from the Pony's Pass area two kilometres away from Tumbledown and then moved north-east gradually uphill over ground full of impeding stone runs and devoid of cover into Eduardo's 'killing area'. This would have been raked with fire from two Browning Heavy Machine-Guns and eight General Purpose Machine-Guns in a north to east arc. After that, and totally counter to Sun Tzu's recommendation of 'battle downhill: do not ascend',[22] gradients would have increased sharply in the final 500 metres or so towards both Mount William and Tumbledown. To reach the latter would have required an adroit assault on 2 Platoon's V-shaped defensive layout in a stone run which, to its front, had been laid Miño's twenty-three grenade traction explosive traps. The scenario conjures up disturbing Somme-like images. The smooth-talking Wilson received no war decoration. He resigned his commission at the end of 1982.

The war's penultimate NGS operation targetted Sapper Hill and then, north of Tumbledown, continued its bombardment along Moody Brook during the night of 12-13 June. In a dress-rehearsal for the following night's *coup de grâce*, *Active* and *Arrow* fired 161 high explosive shells and twenty-five starshell from the northern Berkeley Sound gun line.

This reminded Eduardo of the crucial Argentine deficiencies in both naval and air fire support, but he turned his attention to finalising N Company's tactics as part of the overall Battalion defence plan. Once RI6's B Company formally came under his command, he would have 537 men available to defend his tactical area of responsibility.[23] Communications would be of key importance in such a complex defence layout. Between landline and radio links the Company signals personnel virtually tripled the number of circuits by laying out seven kilometres of field telephone cable. But this proved to be also a double-edged sword during the forthcoming battle. The cable was vulnerable to the intensive British artillery fire, and the Scots Guards would also often utilise any cable they found by following it towards the Company's defensive positions which would then be attacked. Eduardo:

> The defence of Tumbledown and Mount William was not a delaying tactic. The order was to defend the positions up to the very end and stop the British advance [...] The defensive system lacked mobility which is basic to any operation. Although the defence seemed static in appearance, counter-attacks (of M and O Company) were foreseen aimed to block the enemy's attack. Besides, defence is a temporal attitude before the assault [...] Had (the counter-attacks) happened, these forces would have been stuck on Tumbledown and would not have been able to return to their positions to have the final fight at Sapper Hill [...] As N Company's front was extremely wide and the platoons too scattered, the tactic was to keep men in their positions. If the attacking forces were overwhelming and the position could not be held, the sub-units would retreat to N Company's command post position. With our platoons gathered at such point, plus the 60mm mortars and Lucero's 3 Platoon, we could hold Tumbledown's eastern area and wait for the Battalion's counter-attack.

Next morning, on 13 June, he held his eve of battle Orders Group:

> I was sure the enemy would attack that night and that this could possibly be the last I would see some of my subordinates. But, thank God, this did not happen. I conveyed my message to them saying that the moment had now come to show what we really were and what we Marines were worth. I also said that a praiseworthy performance was expected in the hours of combat to come.[24]

But 13 June proved lucky for BIM5. It was a crisp, cold day with a sprinkling of overnight snow on the myriad of ankle-wrenching grass tussocks dotting the frozen ground. The blue sky gave ideal conditions for the RAF's maiden operational use of the 568 kilogram Laser Guided Bomb (LGB). Four air strikes using this weapon would be launched on the Argentine Marines by two pairs of Harrier GR3s. But impossible now to differentiate between incoming artillery and NGS fire, the dug-in Argentines must also have put the GR3 bombs in the same category. Certainly Eduardo, nearly two kilometres away at his Company HQ, remarked later, 'Nobody ever told me anything about those types of bombs.'[25]

His sixty-five days of preparations were complete. Only the battle remained. That evening the firing of all weapons from both sides intensified even more. Before darkness at 20.00Z, twelve men of B Company, RI6 had been wounded by British artillery fire.[26] But the initial infantry action was the enemy attack on O Company at Pony's Pass. That noise generated by the Scots Guards composite platoon deceived Eduardo in terms of numbers involved:

> O Company was subjected to an attack of at least one or two companies which were superior in number. When this company stopped the first attack and, as O Company were facing a second attack with superior forces, they were ordered to retreat to their first position (between 02.00Z to 03.00Z)[27] to act as a reserve

force. Their mission was successful as no further attacks were made during the night.

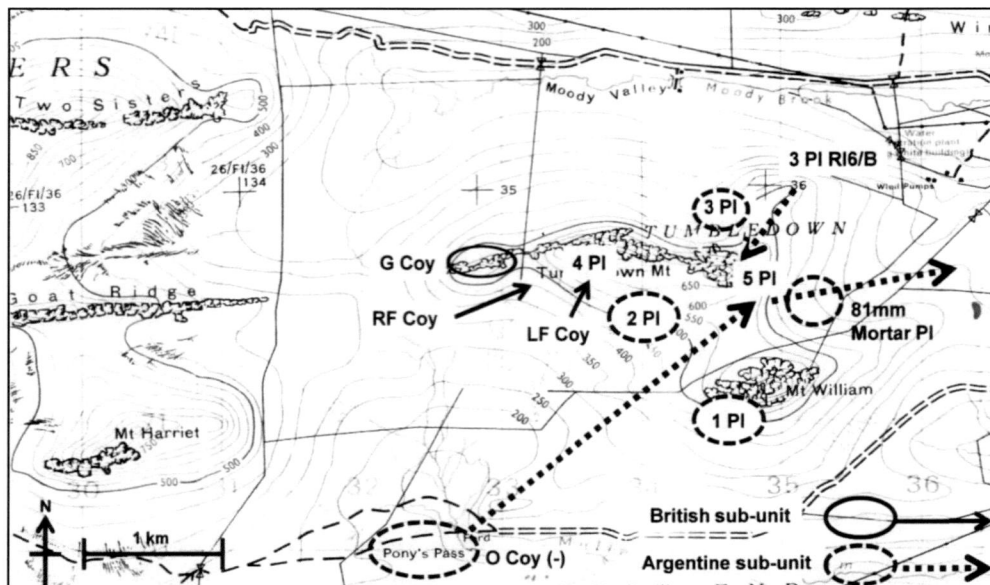

Map 5 (04.30Z-07.00Z) – Left Flank Company (2SG) continues to engage 4 Platoon (BIM5). O Company (BIM5) continues to withdraw to the Felton Stream area (Sapper Hill). 3 Platoon (RI6/B) reaches Tumbledown's east end.

However no 'second attack' materialised at Pony's Pass. O Company withdrew in two groups to the saddle between Mount William and eastern end of Tumbledown. Then at 04.30Z the order was given for the Company to pull back to Sapper Hill.[28] Perhaps some elements of O Company could have reinforced N Company which was now facing the main British thrust. But this did not happen because they were short of ammunition and burdened with their wounded. Eduardo:

> Because the attack began during the night hours I had no knowledge of the units that were attacking us. We did not know if they were Scots Guards, Gurkhas or other units. We thought at first that those attacking N Company could be a regiment. We fired with our artillery and mortars as soon as we were attacked and in those cases where we could have some type of reference [...] As things continued we required supporting fire on the incoming routes or pre-selected targets.

Operating on the Berkeley Sound gun line, three enemy frigates were to provide NGS onto Tumbledown and Mount William. Berkeley Sound was chosen so as to avoid the land-based Exocet missile threat on the southern Stanley gun line where one such missile had hit *Glamorgan* two nights previously.[29] The first arrival was, almost inevitably, *Yarmouth*. She placed out a marker buoy for the gunline, then started a bombardment of 244 shells onto N Company at 01.53Z. An early success of *Yarmouth* was the destruction of the two 105mm anti-tank guns on Mount William by fifty precise salvos. This position had been commanded by Petty Officer Celedonio Lucio Monzón. His dialogue with Robacio focused on priorities:

'Sir, all our guns have been destroyed, the concentration of naval gunfire was awesome, all our material has been rendered useless. But miraculously we have no casualties.'
'Verify whether any of our guns are still working. We're going to need them.'
'Sir, I cannot move.'
'Why?'
'I have an unexploded naval gun shell lying practically between my legs!'
'Pray to God and have a couple of your men fish you gently out of the foxhole, for you have no other chance than to keep on fighting as if you were infantry. Good luck and let me know about your new position.' [30]

The loss of these guns possibly reinforced Robacio's belief that a major British advance would occur eastwards along the Darwin to Puerto Argentino track below. *Avenger*, *Active* and *Ambuscade* joined *Yarmouth* eighty-four minutes later. *Ambuscade* provided fire support for 2 Para on Wireless Ridge, while such was the ferocity of *Active*'s 222 high-explosive shell and eight star shell bombardment in support of the Scots Guards' attack that her gun became defective fifty-seven minutes later. When the NGS operation ceased at 06.00Z, N Company had endured a total of 620 4.5-inch shells exploding on Tumbledown and Mount William.[31] No other Argentine unit in the war had been subjected either to such an intensive bombardment or being fired at by three warships simultaneously.[32]

Just after the NGS operation had begun, Miño's 5 Platoon carried out their early withdrawal from Tumbledown's west end, leaving Vázquez's 4 Platoon without support. At 03.54Z Robacio reported to the 10th Infantry Brigade HQ in Puerto Argentino that Vázquez was under 'heavy attack' from 'more than a battalion' but remained in control of the situation. Requesting that both Berazay's and Jaimet's Companies be placed under his command, Robacio was only given Jaimet's.[33] So the latter sent his 3 Platoon under command of Sub-Lieutenant Esteban La Madrid to Eduardo [34] who was now faced with the unenviable task of gathering together enough men to launch a counter-attack and relieve 4 Platoon. This meant that Miño's platoon would also have to be used.

More than an hour later Eduardo had to co-ordinate fire support for his beleaguered 4 Platoon Commander:

Vázquez asked me to fire on his position in order to hit the British troops and make them retreat. I fired, but cannot say how accurate the shots were as corrections were made and everything became quite difficult as a result of the night and heavy fire involved. I cannot say that a supporting fire mission on the Gurkhas was ever required. The supporting fire was aimed at the British troops who attacked BIM5 and not specifically against the Gurkhas.

Both N Company's 81mm and 60mm mortars fired on the 4 Platoon position and, at 05.40Z, Robacio reported to Brigade HQ that the situation was still under control. Thirty-five minutes later the Brigade Commander, Brigadier-General Oscar Luis Jofre, told Robacio to be prepared for a 'second wave' attack.[35] At 06.30Z the latter reported this had begun on Tumbledown's west end but, in reality, it had been ongoing for more than an hour. In a further radio message at 08.10Z, Robacio appeared more concerned about the threat of a British attack from Wireless Ridge to his north. Therefore in addition to Jofre ordering Jaimet to open fire with his three 81mm mortars, all artillery fire was brought to bear on this area north and west of Moody Brook.

Twenty-five minutes later Jaimet reported a stationary enemy target on Wireless Ridge and more artillery fire was called down on it. This was a distraction. Nobody, apart from Vázquez, was aware of the seriousness of his situation on Tumbledown. Robacio's information had been unclear, and at least a B Company RI6 counter-attack led by Jaimet with BIM5's O and M Companies in reserve would be required to resolve the problem.

Simultaneously Robacio informed that Vázquez was now under 'more than a battalion' attack from the west. But to the north of Tumbledown combat was perceived as being not that strong. Shortly afterwards at 08.49Z Robacio reported a major crisis, 'The enemy have taken the west end (of Tumbledown) with a massive attack and few men are resisting to the east of the (west) summit.'

When Vázquez had told Eduardo he was about to surrender, the N Company Commander ordered Lucero's 3 Platoon to advance and block Tumbledown's centre. But events had rapidly overtaken such a manouevre. The 'too little-too late' counter-attack of Miño and La Madrid had been unable to stop the British troops.

As a result Robacio asked Jaimet to mount a Company counter-attack (less 3 Platoon) to the (east) summit of Tumbledown. Jofre ordered the latter to be 'ready to move' in accordance with Robacio's requirements and organised artillery support. Ten minutes later (08.59Z) Robacio asked Brigade HQ for permission to counter-attack with M Company, providing that Jaimet's and Berazay's Companies could hold their positions. Jofre authorised Robacio's plan. But sixty minutes later (09.55Z) Robacio informed Brigade HQ he was still in his position, as did Berazay and Jaimet – but no information was forthcoming on the M Company counter-attack.

Jaimet's Command Post was one kilometre north-east of his objective. On arrival near Tumbledown's east summit at about 10.30Z he established contact with Eduardo. B Company did not have enough men to mount a counter-attack. Instead Jaimet positioned his depleted force to block the Scots Guards movements.

As dawn rose thirty minutes later Robacio informed Brigade HQ, 'Combat is continuing on Tumbledown and Mount William, but the situation is very difficult.'

Jaimet's force had opened fire on the Scots Guards. The latter returned fire. Jaimet reported he was in serious problems, but would try to assist the withdrawal of La Madrid's platoon which had been severely mauled.

Meanwhile Eduardo had been ordered to withdraw to M Company's Sapper Hill position. So after sixty-six days in the field, and with the first and second sections and gun team of 3 Platoon covering their rear, Eduardo's Company HQ and Lucero's third section evacuated Tumbledown. The remainder of 3 Platoon followed as the

81mm Mortar Platoon continued firing.

Then at 11.10Z Robacio reported, 'Now under heavy artillery and mortar fire. The Tumbledown counter-attack has failed.'

Five minutes later he added that Jaimet's Company 'is withdrawing unorganised.'

Another message arrived at 11.31Z, 'Am still trying to organise a (M Company) counter- attack. But this is difficult because the enemy is pushing my forces and we've had several losses.'

At 11.45Z Robacio reported that his troops 'from Tumbledown and William had been ejected by the enemy and were withdrawing eastwards'.[36]

During this confusion the Brigade Commander ordered, 'Those troops are to reinforce the position on Sapper Hill.'

At 12.05Z, according to Lieutenant-Colonel Eugenio Dalton of the 10th Infantry Brigade HQ, 'The day was getting clear, a weak sun began to rise among the clouds; it was a very cold and snowy morning.' O Company on Sapper Hill and remnants of Jaimet's Company now re-located near Robacio's Tactical HQ at Felton Stream were covering BIM5's withdrawal. But no information had been received for twenty minutes. So Jofre asked Robacio for an update. Their verbal exchange reflected the extreme crisis:

'Am at my Tac HQ with forty men firing at the enemy.'

'Ok. Go back to your (Main) HQ on Sapper Hill.'

'Wilco sir, as soon as my last men have passed through my position!'

'Yes, yes – but I need you at Sapper Hill now!'

Thirty minutes later Robacio reported he was withdrawing with Jaimet's Company to Sapper Hill which lay one kilometre to the south-east. The BIM5 CO added, 'They fought to the end.'

Another ninety minutes elapsed. But no ammunition re-supply was received by Robacio. Then at about 14.00Z as the Military Governor Brigadier-General Menéndez was briefing the Army Chief of Staff *Teniente General* Galtieri in an intense radio communication on the *de facto* ceasefire and imminent surrender, alarming news came that 'BIM5 had been destroyed'.

It was followed by a slightly more reassuring staff officer's update. 'BIM5 has been surrounded by the enemy and there are some helicopters around his position'.

Jofre re-established radio contact with Robacio.

'Am surrounded on the east and south,' reported the beleaguered Robacio.

So it was suggested he should withdraw 'through the north to the city'.

Thirty minutes later Jofre ordered the Brigade Recce Company to deploy south-west of the capital and give, if required, supporting fire to BIM5's withdrawal. Also the air defence unit was 'to be ready to shoot down helicopters flying close to Sapper Hill and Camber'.

The final combat radio communication to the Brigade HQ was made at 14.45Z by the Recce Company Commander, 'My Panhards (armoured cars) have arrived at our new position (close to the football field). BIM5 is withdrawing from Sapper Hill in an orderly fashion followed by British troops. They are not firing at BIM5.'

After sixty-three days N Company had exited its 'home', a veritable Dante's Inferno. The British artillery fire plan had five prime targets: Tumbledown's west end, centre, east end and north-east spur, and Mount William.[37] More than 7,000 British shells exploding within the six grid squares (six square kilometres) encompassing Tumbledown and Mount William. Add the number of mortar bombs fired by the Scots Guards, Gurkhas and 42 Commando (on Mount Harriet) in addition to Argentine shelling and mortar return fire, then Eduardo's estimate of '14,000 rounds of high-calibre weapons were fired' becomes realistic.[38]

BIM5 arrived in the capital and gathered at the *Apostadero* (Naval offices). Immediately Eduardo got to a short-wave radio set and contacted a local amateur radio ham in Río Grande. N Company's Commander cared about his men. Not only did he want to speak to Inés, there was also an important requirement to give her as many names as possible of those who had survived the battle so she could inform their next of kin in Río Grande. The radio ham immediately got into his van and drove to Inés's house. He knocked on the door and, moments later, she was inside the van speaking to Eduardo.

After a day or so the Battalion was ordered to the airport where all surrendered Argentine troops gathered. The unit was the last to leave on 21 June. Its Second-in-Command, Commander Daniel Ponce, and Eduardo were also the last Marines to embark onto the 144-ton Falkland Islands Government Motor Coaster MV *Forrest* which, in turn, cross-decked them onto the icebreaker ARA *Almirante Irízar*. There were 1,717 personnel on board her plus the crew, so a shift system had to be implemented for the use of sleeping bunks, kitchens and toilets. They departed Stanley at midnight, one week after the surrender. Thirty-six hours later the vessel arrived at Ushuaia where a logistics organisation was already in place to assist. During the late afternoon naval aircraft flew BIM5 up to Río Grande. On arrival after the twenty-minute flight, the Marines were transported by truck to their camp.

Eduardo was soon reunited with Inés. Then their telephone rang. It was Inés's mother. Excitedly she informed her daughter, 'I've just seen Eduardo on TV at Ushuaia!'

For the next twenty days BIM5 remained in camp. A medical check was carried out on all personnel and new uniforms issued to those who would continue serving. The conscripts were discharged but, strangely, no debriefings were carried out. Most traumatic stress experts will maintain that this was a serious shortfall for a vulnerable group that would now lose its collective identity in returning to civilian life as individuals. Then forty days leave was taken by the regular Marine personnel. When the regular core of BIM5 returned from leave a new draft of conscripts was received. The unit was also re-organised, re-equipped and re-armed, and thorough debriefings carried out to identify operational lessons learnt from the Malvinas campaign. In recognition of its war performance BIM5 would be awarded the MVC and, two decades later, the City of Río Grande named one of its districts 'Almirante Carlos Hugo Robacio'.[39]

It was now quite late in the Villarrazas' home. 'Do you have any final thoughts?' I asked.

Inés admitted, 'I became a changed person with new priorities in life that included a diminished attention to materialism in the long-term.'

Eduardo expressed satisfaction that N Company had accomplished its mission despite the flawed defensive system on Tumbledown which eventually fell between the two stools of the western enemy approach versus the southern.

'I also consider that the Malvinas are still Argentine and our Government should continue its struggle to recover the Islands,' was his steadfast view. 'For they are,' he concluded, 'the only factor which unites this nation.'

I looked at the Villarraza children. They had been quiet throughout the evening.

'Have you heard your parents' story about the war before?' I asked.

They replied in unison, 'Never.' And Paz exclaimed, 'It's like a movie!'

But only a portion of it had been told. My second task was to add the combat detail several years later. Perhaps one day they might read this result to gain an even better understanding of their father's 1982 Malvinas exploits.

'So would you have been able to manage in such a situation?' I asked his daughter.

But her diplomatic reply, 'The values of my generation are so much different today' neatly side-stepped my question.

Precisely one year later came a postscript. Argentina's second largest daily newspaper *La Nación* published a 'Gurkha' report written in London which included negative comments, by implication, of Eduardo's Marines on Tumbledown and Mount William. It would cause Marine Corps consternation:

> During the Malvinas War, the Argentine troops surrendered before time, because they were afraid of the Gurkhas and not as a result of any strategic causes or lack of weapons as many theories maintain. This unexpected version was explained to the journalists from *La Nación* by members of this well-known Nepalese battalion who took part in the 1982 conflict and recently demanded in Parliament a fair treatment for British military retired personnel. Just before the twenty-sixth anniversary of the military operation in which Argentina recovered during a short time its sovereignty of the Islands, different combatants said that 'the only possible reason' for which the Argentines surrendered was the panic they had in just thinking that they would have to face this force known by their lack of pity towards their enemies.
>
> Dhan Ghale, a retired soldier and his fellow men said, 'We used to comment about this amongst other British and the event cannot be explained otherwise, as we were 2,500 on board [40] in a fleet waiting to land while they were 10,000 [41] well-trained men assigned to different parts of the Islands, and even then we could beat them easily.'
>
> Braham Chantra Gru [42] said, 'We know they commented that we used a *kukri* to kill our enemies in a cruel way and even hack off their heads to destroy their morale. This stereotype was well exploited by British propaganda because it arrived just in time.' Gru believes that the Gurkhas helped to end the war faster and even spare a lot of human lives.
>
> However during their demonstration (on 19 March 2008) their pride and arrogance depicted a sharp contrast to their reality: none of those who retired before Hong Kong was returned to China in 1997 receive pensions like their British counterparts who fought in the Malvinas or previous wars. Chantra Gru

said, 'We receive a fourth of the income a British soldier received and, besides, we are not allowed to have a visa so we may stay until the end of our days in the land for which we fought.'

About fifty Gurkhas placed the medals they received as a result of their involvement in the Malvinas, Afghanistan and Kosovo in a box to be returned to Prime Minister Gordon Brown via Nick Clegg, Leader of the Liberal Democratic Party and organiser of the protest.[43]

One of them shouted his sadness and concern for having to return their medals, but he hoped such an act would help to bring the Prime Minister's attention. Other banners stated, 'We, the Gurkhas, fought as first-class soldiers, so then why are we treated like second and third-class retired personnel?' [44] In the meantime some tourists tried to get snapshots near the 2,000 demonstrators.

Eduardo responded swiftly to me. His following comments should be placed in the context of his former Commanding Officer's enlightening remark 'Of course we were very worried about your men!' to retired Brigadier David Morgan at the Nottingham colloquium:

I need to tell you something regarding the withdrawal of N Company's platoons when they were facing the Gurkhas. There is a certain myth in the province of Corrientes (well known amongst all of us who have lived in the littoral area) about the relationship of man-knife. Just as we talk about the people of Santiago del Estero with their naps,[45] so we link the people of Corrientes with the use of knives. There are a lot of jokes about it: they say that when raffles are organised in Corrientes the prizes follow this sequence: 3rd Prize: A luxurious 4 x 4 car, 2nd Prize: A big flat on the seaside, and 1st Prize: A knife!

Thus when the Gurkhas and their knives were mentioned, the answer from our conscripts and petty officers was, 'Let them come, we shall face them with our knives from Corrientes!' You should remember that Robacio was born in Corrientes and we had quite a lot of personnel from that province. That is the reason why our men were never afraid of the Gurkhas.

[...] I have said many times in Argentina and UK that our defensive position was like an onion skin, quite a wide front which could be penetrated. When 4 Platoon fell there was a blockade near the east spur of Tumbledown. Moving 1 and 2 Platoons was a certain failure and would have cost a lot of casualties as they were supposed to cross the valley between Mount William and Tumbledown. The situation here was as follows: we were facing a huge amount of troops all along the front and, on the other side (of the valley at Wireless Ridge) the Paras, who forced the withdrawal of the Argentine forces, were many kilometres to our rear. I knew through the communications that the only troops in a forward position belonged to N Company. The Army had already withdrawn to Puerto Argentino, M Company was on Sapper Hill and O Company located in the rear. These last companies were not authorised either to move or support N Company. We were quite aware that no one would be helping us.

To summarise, we knew that we had not the slightest chance of success and all that remained was to resist up to a logical point without taking an endless amount of unnecessary casualties. On the other hand it was not reasonable to withdraw without doing anything. When the attack started on the eastern end of Tumbledown things went so fast that, during the action, I was left without any communications to the platoons. As a result I could not order the withdrawal. Later they (on Mount William) were ordered by Battalion HQ to withdraw to Sapper Hill which was the Battalion rendezvous point. Personally I never knew which troops were attacking us. We could not have withdrawn because, allegedly, we were facing the Gurkhas – although at that time we did not even know who was in front of us.

The withdrawal was the result of a British attack on a very fragile defensive system without any possibility of getting help. We never knew which unit we were facing. As a result of the distance between Mount William and Tumbledown I think it would have been impossible to recognise the physical appearance of a Gurkha.[46]

Apart from the special category prisoners, including Robacio, Eduardo was the last Malvinas War veteran to depart from the Islands in June 1982. But already his 4 Platoon Commander, Acting Sub-Lieutenant Carlos Daniel Vázquez, had been repatriated to Argentina.

The root cause of his early ticket home – outstanding leadership inspiring a bloody 'do or die' resistance at Tumbledown's west end – is worthy of a close examination.

Notes

1. *The Art of War*, Chapter 10 – Forms of the Earth.
2. E-mail dated 4 October 2006.
3. *Bat. Ec. – Escuela Batallón* – School Battalion.
4. Río Grande is the commercial capital of Tierra del Fuego on the latter's east coast. It is 150 kilometres north of Ushuaia, being both the provincial capital and world's southernmost city. This is located on the Beagle Channel's northern shore. On the latter's southern shore is Chile whose border with Argentina is also only seventy-five kilometres west of Río Grande. To the north-east of Río Grande and 380 nautical miles out in the South Atlantic Ocean is Puerto Argentino (Stanley). One tenth the size of Río Grande, this is the capital of Islas las Malvinas (Falkland Islands). But according to Argentina's continuing sovereignty claim over the Malvinas, Ushuaia is also the Islands' provincial capital. Río Grande has grown considerably since 1981 when it was a relatively small town with a population of 18,000. But its geographical location between hostile Chile and the British-occupied Malvinas would make Río Grande the most vulnerable town in all Argentina during the 1982 war. Its inhabitants felt they were the meat in the middle of the front line sandwich.
5. Nearly double the size of a British Army rifle company, N Company consisted of about 175 men organised into three fifty-five man platoons. Each of these had three thirteen-man sections, a machine-gun section of nine men with two

7.62mm machine-guns, and a Platoon HQ of six men including a platoon commander, platoon sergeant, radio operators and, in some cases, a medical assistant. There were ten to fourteen men in the N Company HQ, amongst them a medical assistant, corporal (cook) and two kitchen assistants.

6. Five years later Anaya would be sentenced by a military tribunal to fourteen years in prison for 'negligence' in the conduct of the Malvinas War. He was given subsequent amnesty by President Carlos Menem. But ill-health also prevented Anaya from being interrogated in 2006 by a judge about an alleged involvement in 300 cases of kidnapping and torture of left-wing sympathisers from 1977-80 during '*El Proceso*'. The retired naval officer died in 2008.

7. *Razor's Edge* (p. 286) incorrectly assumes, 'probably on the reverse slope (between Tumbledown and Mount William) at a point central to the whole defensive scheme'.

8. *Ibid.* (p. 289) gives an incorrect allocation of three Heavy Machine-Guns to 1 Platoon, two to 2 Platoon and three to 3 Platoon.

9. *Ibid.* (p. 286 – map) incorrectly indicates that the platoon was located on the north-east shoulder of Mount William.

10. *Ibid.* incorrectly indicates that the artillery battery was located below the saddle midway between Tumbledown and Mount William.

11. *Special Forces Pilot: A Flying Memoir of the Falklands War*, p. 199.

12. *The Secret War for the Falklands: The SAS, MI6, and the War Whitehall Nearly Lost*, pp. 137-147.

13. *Razor's Edge* (p. 286) incorrectly states that 'O Company under battalion 2 i/c Major Pernias – was probably on the reverse slope at a point central to the whole defensive scheme' of Tumbledown and Mount William. Moreover Pernias was the BIM5 Operations Officer. Acting Sub-Lieutenant Quiroga was the initial O Company Commander at Pony's Pass.

14. *Desde el Frente*, p. 177.

15. *Falklands Commando*, p. 26. With a five-man Forward Observation Team from 148 Commando Forward Observation Battery Royal Artillery or a Naval Gunfire Observer on land directing the bombardment, *Yarmouth* could accurately lay down a ton of explosive in one minute from a maximum range of 18,000 metres. Her two Mark 6 guns fired from a single turret a twenty-five kilo high-explosive shell at a rate of more than one every two seconds. With its digital computer and fully automatic loading system, the single Mark 8 gun of *Cardiff* was even more accurate. Paradoxically, this was a disadvantage when shelling Eduardo's large defensive area. From a maximum range of 24,000 metres, the Mark 8 gun could fire a twenty-one kilo shell at the rate of twenty-four shells every minute. In comparison a field-artillery gun fires a sixteen kilo shell at up to four or five per minute depending on the fitness and skill of the gun crew.

16. E-mail dated 17 October 2006.

17. *Desde el Frente*, p. 213. However *Razor's Edge* (p. 287) states that on 12 June 'Pernias sent a platoon under Sub-Lieutenant Quiroga reinforced by a section of Sappers, a total of thirty-seven men, to a position in front of William, covering Ponies Pass'. This was not the case. O Company (-) had been in place at Pony's Pass already for a week. Apart from Miño and eighteen of his Marine

Amphibious Engineers assisting O Company in preparing the latter's defensive position there from 5-7 June, there was no platoon or Sappers sent to Pony's Pass on 12 June or any other day. Quiroga's correct rank was Acting Sub-Lieutenant. Also the book *5th Infantry Brigade in the Falklands* (p. 183) states incorrectly that 'Robacio (on 12 June) reinforced O Company with the 1st Amphibious Engineer Platoon, commanded by Second-Lieutenant Valdez-Zabala'. The correct platoon commander was Acting Sub-Lieutenant Héctor Omar Miño: and both he and 1 Platoon were on Tumbledown all that day (!).

18. *La Gaceta* (Argentina's fourth largest newspaper) dated 28 March 2010.
19. *Hors de Combat*, p. 26.
20. *With the Gurkhas in the Falklands*, p. 288.
21. E-mail dated 6 September 2007.
22. *The Art of War,* Chapter 9 – Moving the Army.
23. However only half of B Company (eighty-five men) was able to be deployed to the eastern end of Tumbledown in the early morning of 14 June. Hence Eduardo Villarraza had 452 men available during the battle.
24. *Hors de Combat*, p. 33.
25. E-mail dated 8 April 2010.
26. *5th Infantry Brigade in the Falklands*, p. 187.
27. War diary of Lieutenant-Colonel Eugenio Dalton, G3 (Operations), Argentine 10th Infantry Brigade HQ.
28. *Razor's Edge* (p. 293) only states that 'the O Company reserve' was sent 'to the saddle behind William'.
29. *Ibid.* (p. 288) incorrectly states that the Scots Guards Commanding Officer 'would be able to call on naval gunfire from the three 4.5-inch guns of *Yarmouth* and *Active* in the gun line to the south'.
30. *Desde el Frente,* p. 280.
31. NGS information from *Falklands War Diary: My own view from HMS Yarmouth 2 April to 28 July 1982* by Lieutenant-Commander J.D. Plummer posted on the Internet. All other NGS details in this chapter are from the book *The Royal Navy and the Falklands War*, pp. 118-332.
32. This redresses the erroneous impression in *Razor's Edge* (p. 288) that the Royal Navy guns were relatively quiet during the battle.
33. War diary of Lieutenant-Colonel Eugenio Dalton, G3 (Operations), Argentine 10th Infantry Brigade HQ.
34. Oddly, Eduardo indicated in *Hors de Combat* (p. 34) that La Madrid's Platoon was at fifty per cent strength, having only 'about twenty men' available. He was also too conservative in maintaining that the numbers of those who actually engaged in combat during 'the defence of Tumbledown [...] must have been about 100 men [...] acting in a sequential way', i.e. Vázquez's composite platoon, 60mm mortar section, and Miño's platoon, La Madrid's platoon, and a B Company, RI6 force of platoon strength. In fact the precise number of Argentine troops in direct combat against the Scots Guards on Tumbledown was 166.
35. The battle lessons learned from the previous four land battles had taught the Argentines one thing: when the British stopped attacking and the Argentines

believed the situation was under control, the former began to attack even more strongly than before. Further extracts from Lieutenant-Colonel Eugenio Dalton's war diary in this chapter describe Robacio's final actions and radio communications with the 10th Infantry Brigade HQ during the battle.

36. But nearly another three hours passed by before the 81mm Mortar Platoon and 2 Platoon pulled back onto Mount William still occupied by 2 Platoon. All 197 Argentine defenders there then withdrew to Sapper Hill, leaving behind one dead.

37. The fire plan did not include the saddle connecting Tumbledown's eastern end and Mount William which *Razor's Edge* (p. 288 and p. 290 – upper map) describes and annotates (on the map) a 'Heavily beaten zone' (of shell and mortar bomb explosions). This and the faulty map scale are misleading.

38. *Hors de Combat*, p. 34. Twenty-four hours post-battle the author, when standing on the northern slopes of Mount William, took four photographs of the entire area. On his return to the UK these were developed, enlarged, appropriately cut and glued together. The result was a magnificent near-seamless panoramic view of the terrain between Tumbledown and Mount William and further westwards towards Goat Ridge and Mount Harriet. There were an immense number of tell-tale pockmarks of shell and mortar craters everywhere. The photograph has been kept as a memento of the author's most terrifying night and day in his life. It appears on the jacket cover of this book.

39. *Razor's Edge* (p. 299) states incorrectly that Robacio received a CHVC. On the contrary he was decorated with a MVC. Its citation was: 'For being Commander of the 5th Marine Infantry Battalion during the defence of Puerto Argentino, in maintaining his unit's positions, resisting a high number of enemy attacks and continuing to fight for hours after the order to retreat had been issued.'

40. On board *QE2* were, in fact, 3,200 troops of the 5th Infantry Brigade.

41. The correct figure was 13,000 troops.

42. *La Nación* corrupted the clan surname of Gurung to Gru.

43. It was distasteful that medals were used to influence political opinion. However these were Long Service and Good Conduct Medals and not those campaign medals mentioned, including the South Atlantic Medal. Napoleon Bonaparte's maxim 'a man will fight long and hard for a piece of coloured ribbon' – still, thankfully, applies to Gurkha and other British Army soldiers. They have a fundamental need for formal war service recognition. It applies also to Argentine war veterans. During the author's second visit to Argentina in December 2002, he met some who were not only outraged by their campaign medal being awarded to them *a decade* post-war, but also that others had *still* not yet received it.

44. After hearing a challenge the following year on 27 and 28 October from the British Gurkha Welfare Society and others during a judicial review about the perceived unfairness of the British Army's Gurkha Pension Scheme which, it was alleged, breached the European Convention on European Rights and UK Race Relations Act, the British High Court ruled in favour of the Ministry of Defence. The Honourable Mr Justice Burnett's forty-three page judgement, published on 11 January 2010, was emphatic: 'Gurkhas would have been in receipt of a

Gurkha pension from normally age thirty-three by comparison with a British soldier who might have been in receipt of nothing for as long as twenty-seven years. I reject entirely the proposition that Gurkhas are less well treated.' And although British Army Gurkhas who retired before 1997 won the right of UK domicile through actress Joanna Lumley's (occasionally theatrical) interventions which contributed to the British Government's remarkable House of Commons defeat on 29 April 2009 by 267 votes to 241 after a debate on this matter, the new regulation has been difficult to implement at best, and allegedly exploited financially in an irregular way by GAESO (Gurkha Army Ex-Servicemen's Organisation) in Nepal. (From an article entitled *'Actually, Ms Lumley, you should apologise too'* published by *The Observer* newspaper dated 4 April 2010.) The author feared that this dazzling success of the actress, who is also a Gurkha British officer's daughter, would kill the goose that laid the golden egg by pricing the Gurkhas out of the British Army. However this does not appear to be the case and British Army Gurkhas continue to provide good value for money.

45. In the Argentine Province of Santiago del Estero (not its capital city), people worship the post-lunch siesta tradition. This has given rise to many Argentine jokes about these people who talk, work, play and do everything quite slowly. The weather must be partly to blame as the summer there is quite hot.

46. E-mail dated 9 April 2008.

In hills and dykes, take a position in yang.
Keep them to the right and back.
This is the advantage of the military, the assis-
tance of the earth.

– Sun Tzu[1]

They had similarities. Their Naval rank was *Teniente de Corbeta* (Acting Sub-Lieutenant). Both served with other Argentine Marine Corps units, but were attached to BIM5 as platoon commanders for the Battle of Tumbledown. And afterwards Héctor Omar Miño and Carlos Daniel Vázquez would be decorated for bravery. But there was a difference. Miño won the national CHVC,[2] and Vázquez only a much lesser Navy-sponsored MVC.[3] But after I had read their stories it was impossible not to wonder at the perverse fact that Vázquez had not received the same decoration as Miño's.

On 28 March 2007 I met the sympathetic Miño in my Buenos Aires hotel. Twice-divorced, he was still serving and held the rank of *Capitán de Navío* (Naval Captain). Accompanying him was retired *Teniente de Navío* (Lieutenant) Marcelo Oruezabala, the BIM5 2 Platoon Commander whose wartime rank was *Guardiamarina* (Midshipman). I had invited Miño to the Nottingham colloquium, but the Navy prevented him from attending. Now there was a second chance with this two-hour 'reconciliation' meeting where Eduardo Gerding was our interpreter.

The simplest way to start was to produce my map of the Tumbledown-Mount William area and explain the British perspective of the battle. Then they would tell me theirs. This procedure always worked admirably as maps are a common denominator for any soldier regardless of nationality, language or culture. There was no animosity, just a mutual desire to become acquainted and understand what we thought and did on the battlefield quarter of a century earlier. No longer were we faceless and nameless opponents. This rendezvous gave Miño the opportunity to draw sketches in my notebook of his position on the north-west summit of Tumbledown. And his explanations to me were reinforced later that year by a written account of his war experiences.[4]

The equally likeable Marcelo Oruezabala was only a bystander to the Tumbledown battle. His platoon had been dug-in amongst the stone runs midway between Tumbledown and Mount William nearly one kilometre south-east of Vázquez's platoon. Oruezabala's Marines remained static during most of the battle because they had been committed to N Company's concept of covering by fire the perceived killing ground towards the south-west into which the British advance was anticipated.

But Oruezabala had a far from peaceful time in the stone runs. Gónzalez, one of his Marines on the platoon's left flank, was wounded in the stomach by mortar shrapnel.[5] And marking on my map where they were located, Oruezabala also remarked laconically in English, 'The British shelling was so heavy during those final hours of the war that I dared not stand up. So the only way I could relieve myself was to urinate lying in my trench.'

Little more than a year later he requested information about travel authorisation to the Islands as he was planning to visit them for the first time post-war with a family member. His motive was 'to close my history in the Islands and make contact with their people'. I suggested the British Embassy in Buenos Aires could assist and then, in a later e-mail, gave him information on accommodation in Stanley as well as a digital photograph of his platoon's position north-west of Mount William.

His reply was similar to what other veterans seek regarding 'their' battlefield and past trauma, 'I liked the photo of the trench very much, but can't identify my trench. Can you send more photos please?' Unfortunately that was the only one I had taken of his position.

Eduardo had also asked four more Argentine Tumbledown veterans to attend this meeting. One who had refused was Midshipman Marcelo Demarco, the artillery Forward Observation Officer attached to Miño's 5 Platoon. He had retired from the Marine Corps in 1985. I understood his reluctance:

> About the Malvinas this is a stage of my life I want to close [...] There are certain types of memories I want to forget as they are unpleasant. As a result of this last and because there are personal motives against certain people, I don't want to talk about this issue. Please try to understand.[6]

Another accepted, but was missing that afternoon. So Eduardo rang Rubén Eduardo Galliussi. The former Acting Sub-Lieutenant who had been BIM5's 106.6mm Mortar Platoon Commander located some 1500 metres north-east of Tumbledown, was travelling on holiday. This did not prevent me from asking him, via Eduardo, about his mortar tube and mortar bomb statistics.

'He says there were six mortars,' relayed Eduardo, 'and 450 boxes of ammunition for them with two bombs in each box, i.e. 900 bombs!'

Add the 600 bombs of the BIM5 81mm Mortar Platoon with its six mortars, and this meant that the Battalion had 1,500 mortar bombs at its disposal – nearly double the Gurkhas' 800 bombs. As for Argentine and British mortars, I calculated later that a grand total of forty-four were deployed on the Tumbledown battlefield.[7]

The last two veterans were the still-serving *Capitán de Navío* Carlos Vázquez and one of his Marines, (NCO A).[8] At the top of my list of Malvinas War veterans to meet, Vázquez now worked in the Security Department of the Marine Command HQ at the Puerto Belgrano Naval Base. For some obscure reason he never received the invitation sent to him for the previous year's Nottingham colloquium. It was only in early-2009 after a lengthy series of e-mail exchanges I discovered his intense wish to attend. He was furious that, instead of him, others talked about (as he put it), 'my battle' which Robacio's book had described in great detail.[9] However the latter had, in fact, paid tribute in that book and *Hors de Combat* to the 'heroic 4 Platoon' and its commander:

> The attitude and aptitude of this platoon commander, as well as those of his men, turned them into role models. The commander, for leading his men in combat, personally engaging in greater risks and contributing with his fighting spirit, made his subordinates fight decisively. These men are an example that the Marines must treasure with pride.[10]

So my disappointment was acute when neither Vázquez nor (NCO A) materialised that afternoon in Buenos Aires. Later that year Patrick Watts gave me an anecdote about Vázquez:

> I have an excellent photo of Vázquez which was taken in the early days (of 1982) [...] when he is resting against a rock in his sun glasses etc. I believe that these films were taken from captured Argentines by British officers who then had them developed. It took us sometime to find the exact location of the photo because it was said to have been taken on Tumbledown, but it was in fact taken on the east end of Mount William. Vázquez must have been visiting there. I have accordingly named this area 'Vazquez's Rock'.[11]

One who knew Vázquez well was Diego García Quiroga:

> Vázquez was never the easiest guy to handle. I remember him very well even from the Academy, where we instantly liked each other. Loyal to the bone and fiercely honest, he could give you a bad time in front of anybody if he thought he had a point. I have reason to think that this trait together with his quick temper earned him a reputation for being 'difficult' which appears to have been exploited later by his enemies, to the point that I heard of objections raised against his promotion at the Board which decides this.
>
> Dear 'Loco', I remember him as a wild, admirable soldier and a friend to be proud of! [12]

Diego was right. Vázquez had a fiery temperament. Eduardo Gerding sent me a copy of his e-mail rejecting a British officer's comments that the Argentines had been unnecessarily led into the war by the Military Junta which was out of touch with reality, and that President Galtieri should have surrendered with honour after the Argentine defeat at the Battle of Darwin and Goose Green. His response was in the manner of an officer who had experienced hard combat:

> 4 Platoon under the command of *Teniente de Corbeta* Vázquez fought [...] on Tumbledown, only because we are soldiers and proud of calling ourselves such. We would fight again, no matter who the President of our country may be (at the time) [...] soldiers fight for their comrades [...] ask the Roman legionnaires, whether they asked who was the ruling emperor in order to fight for the Empire.[13]

However Vázquez did send, via Eduardo, an e-mail to me with a lengthy attachment. But my attention was captured initially by his *cri de coeur* explaining why (NCO A) and he were not at the hotel that afternoon. This veteran possessed a huge frustration with, he claimed, post-war official Argentine manipulation of the true historical facts regarding his platoon's battle against the Scots Guards' Left Flank Company:

> My platoon was located on the extreme western end of Tumbledown, and was the last unit that fought there against the 2nd Battalion, Scots Guards. I would have liked to attend the meeting (with you) [...] but because of important personal matters that are being considered these days about my future in the Navy, I may

not be able to be present.

I want you to know that some years ago I was interviewed by a British historian (Mr Middlebrook) who was writing an official history about the British Army in those days, and he also published a book in his country. That person knew every detail about the facts on Tumbledown.

I am sending you this report describing what the combat in my position was like or, at least, the way I saw it from my vantage point. You can be sure that this is a true re-telling of the facts, and there can only be differences in references to timetables that I may not remember precisely enough.

The total number of dead in that position amongst my platoon was seventeen,[14] a figure never recognised by the Navy since some members of the Argentine Army who had fought and died while they were under my command, were later said to have died elsewhere just because of some human meanness that arose after the war.

As you can read in the report I am sending you, my trench was the last one to fall, and it was me who talked to the Scottish officer about laying down arms [...] Unfortunately, the meanness of those who wanted to build up their own prestige on others who had really fought during the war, prevented the truth from coming out or at least distorted it. As I am the only witness alive from the officers who fought on Tumbledown, I offer my experience to answer your wonderings about it, which a friend of mine is translating because of my bad English.

I did not agree with (NCO A) being present at the meeting with you, as that man was with me during the war and I know he acted in a cowardly way, refusing to fight while he just stayed in the trench during the whole combat. That is why [...] he also has no idea about what was going on outside. However that man was decorated for bravery by Commander Robacio, even though the latter was six kilometres to the rear of my position. I mention this just for you to have an idea how little is known about the facts on Tumbledown, and I consider that to the memory of my dead and yours, we must put aside this human meanness and personal ambitions and give way to the truth which was the first casualty after the war. I am at your service for any amplification.

I highly respect the soldiers of the 2nd Battalion, Scots Guards, not only for the way they fought but also for the deferential treatment they gave me afterwards. I would like to get into touch with them again.[15]

After reading this, I was determined to use his story. A 1987 interview with Martin Middlebrook had been, as mentioned, included in the latter's subsequent book. Acquiring this, I had read his three-page account of Vázquez's combat. Apart from giving me a desire to learn more of this battle, my negative observation was that Middlebrook's abridged description lacked structure. But now nearly two decades later after a hardening of attitudes, Vázquez had sent me a much more comprehensive version. Diego did the translation. While reading its spine-chilling contents I recalled Sun Tzu's perceptive concept of 'knowing the other and knowing oneself, in one hundred battles no danger'. All aspects of the Tumbledown battle had to be penetrated. My reply was sent in late August:

In my humble estimation this is a remarkable story which lays out the facts of your engagement with the Left Flank Company of the Scots Guards with a most chilling reality. Indeed I have never seen such an account of the Tumbledown battle (as you portray it) in all the books that I have read and own on the war (and these must number more than sixty!).

Your account must be preserved for history so that future generations of soldiers can understand how a courageous platoon commander (you) goes about the business of defending a key piece of terrain against overwhelming numbers of enemy. Your leadership shines through that black night like a beacon and, I believe, all professional soldiers should learn from your experiences.

Vázquez responded immediately, and we exchanged a number e-mails in a ten-day period two months prior to the Falklands 25 Pilgrimage. In his initial e-mail to Eduardo Gerding he was pleased with my self-imposed task:

I ask you, Doctor, to please forward this e-mail to Mike, and I want to thank you and him because you are doing so much for this small piece of history. I want to tell Mike that I would be quite honoured if he includes the history of 4 Platoon, not just for me but for the silent voices of my seventeen KIA (killed in action) [16] to whom history denies their contribution. Please Doctor, tell him that I agree fully with him.[17]

And later to me:

You were very considerate with my soldiers and me [...] Thank you. The words from the enemy, were more important for me, than the words from my people. It's an honour for me, and for my soldiers, particularly for my dead soldiers, because they did not have any recognition on behalf of my country, not even from the Navy, and less still from BIM5.[18]

The result is this synthesized story of Vázquez and Miño and how they faced the Scots Guards assault. However before the Argentine seizure of the Islands on 2 April 1982, they had undergone contrasting preparations. In effect one was thoroughly trained for the mission and the other was not. Vázquez:

From 1978-79 I was a platoon commander with rank of Midshipman serving with the 2nd Marine Infantry Battalion in Puerto Belgrano. In 1980 after promotion to Acting Sub-Lieutenant I was appointed to the Amphibious Command HQ at the Mar del Plata Naval Base without having the required training. I was Platoon Commander of the Logistics Platoon. The following year I applied for the six-month Amphibious Command Course but, because of a shooting accident (a .45 bullet in the stomach), I did not attend the course and therefore did not qualify as a Commando, ending as Commander of the Amphibious Vehicles Company.

In February next year I was posted as a student to the *Escuela de Oficiales de la Armada* (Officers' Training School of the Navy) in Puerto Belgrano for the one-year Basic Course required for promotion to *Teniente de Fragata* (Sub-Lieutenant) of the Marine Corps. I was still a student when the war started two months later, but was then ordered to the Malvinas as an Advanced Air Control Officer (who guides close air strikes at the front line). On arriving in the Malvinas I was told they did not need Air Control Officers and that two other officers and I had been sent to the Islands as a mistake. Thus we were ordered to report to BIM5. One of those officers was Sub-Lieutenant Osvaldo Colombo who was eventually appointed 2IC of N Company (the Company Commander was Lieutenant Eduardo Villarraza). With my subordinate rank I was appointed 4 Platoon Commander of N Company, a platoon which did not exist then, but was formed later with ten soldiers of the Logistics Company and ten of the Battalion's Recce Platoon.

Miño was an officer in the Amphibious Engineers Company of the Argentine Marine Corps 'deployed to defend the Islands'. Unlike Vázquez, he had been training continuously with his unit for many months prior to *Operación Rosario*:

In 1981 we trained in night operations. Out of any given month we would have normal duties during one week, with the remaining three devoted to night operations. I was an officer instructor at the time. We would train in laying (exercise) mines, explosive and incendiary devices (live) and live fire with automatic weapons and grenade launchers. Our all-conscript platoons included a platoon commander with a FAL [19] a sniper with a FAP, a runner with a FAL and another Marine (known as a grenadier) with a FAL that had a grenade launcher attached.

We would begin training with a reconnaissance at sunset followed by a brief planning session, logistic re-supply and then the training exercise itself that ran from 23.00 up to 05.00 or 06.00 on the following morning. Then we had breakfast, took a nap, had lunch and began it all again. There were a few insignificant accidents, usually whilst setting explosive devices. We would always assemble with other infantry battalions and combat teams of infantry and engineers, and trained in opening passages, advancing through dangerous terrain and under low-aimed live fire from fixed MAG machine-guns, firing over our heads. We exploded Bangalore torpedoes we had made using boiler tubes from discarded naval boilers filled up with TNT that we melted or grinded. These tasks were carried out by all ranks, including officers and conscripts. In September 1981, we took part in an amphibious assault exercise with the US Marines in Punta Buenos Aires, in the province of Chubut.

Our unit was well trained, but it was not granted annual leave (which usually lasted from 20 December to 31 January). In January 1982 we were issued with night visors, residual light amplifiers and laser sights for the guns. Using Skyhawk A4Q fighter aircraft from Naval Aviation, we practised daytime close-proximity air fire support (spotting) for the launching of 250-pound bombs, using colour blankets or smoke signals for front line marking. We used 500 metres as the safety distance to the target. We also practised naval fire spotting for live naval gunfire from the cruiser ARA *General Belgrano* and the Fleet destroyers.

On 7 April, while still quartered at the Puerto Belgrano Naval Base, our effective force was 147 men. Taking one petty officer and two conscripts out (as a rear party), 144 men were flown to the Islands on 10 April.

Twenty-five year-old Vázquez's composite 4 Platoon consisted originally of twenty-four men (including the Platoon HQ). It was half the strength of a standard Marine platoon, the latter usually numbering from between fifty-two to fifty-four men. They deployed to Tumbledown on 20 April. Apart from three other patrolling missions elsewhere on the Islands that lasted six days, Vázquez remained there with his platoon for the next fifty-six days. His position was dominated to its rear by a huge slab of quartzite rock named 'The Wall'. This landmark could be used for orientation during a night battle which would be terrifyingly chaotic and noisy. Then he set about planning and establishing his defensive location. This complied with Sun Tzu's basic criteria, being 'a position in *yang* (light)' with 'the assistance of the earth':

> During those two months until my position fell, I remained there preparing it. 4 Platoon was located at the western tip of the Tumbledown heights, its front facing towards the south. The purpose of that position was to cover with flanking fire the valley that stretched to the front where, approximately 1,000-1,500 metres towards the rear (east), 1 Platoon/Midshipman Carlos Ricardo Bianchi (on Mount William) and 2 Platoon/Midshipman Marcelo Oruezabala were positioned.
>
> The platoon was deployed on a front of approximately 150 to 200 metres, and its right flank turned towards the west, covering that sector at the end of the heights (no attack was expected to come from such a steeply sloping side). The position had a depth of approximately fifty metres, including an alternate position located directly to its rear, on the topographic ridge of Tumbledown facing south, approximately thirty to fifty metres from the primary position. I never thought I would be attacked from the west in a straightforward way over my position. I believed the attack would be carried out from the west, but from the valley under my position to the south, and that such an attack would be carried out against 1 and 2 Platoon.
>
> I could count initially on two infantry rifle sections (ten men each) and a Platoon HQ, the latter commanded by me, two conscript radio operators and Lance-Corporal Amílcar Ramón Tejada. Each infantry rifle section was made up of ten men, one under (NCO A) and the other under Second Petty Officer Julio Saturnino Castillo. He would die as a hero in the fighting of 13-14 June. (NCO A) occupied Sector E (the section on my left) and Castillo Sector W (the section on my right). The left section had a 60mm mortar and a MAG machine-gun manned by Conscript 1st Class Víctor Julio Gasko. The section on the right had a FAP rifle and a MAG machine-gun. The rest of the men had Para FAL rifles.
>
> The defensive position consisted then of a primary position (already described), in addition to a considerable amount of foxholes which were turned into alternate positions, additional or simulated. These foxholes were there before, nature had made them, or else they were a product of artillery fire, etc.[20]

Twenty-seven years later Kiszely, his Scots Guards opponent, commented, 'I'm interested that Vázquez uses the word 'foxholes' (if that is the accurate translation). What I saw of their positions subsequently were, indeed, more old-fashioned foxholes than slit trenches. Very effective, too [...] I was certainly aware that that position was occupied when I got there – and in about platoon strength. They very nearly did for us.' Vázquez:

The only exception (to this mission) was during the three patrols that I volunteered to join: to Jorge Island, Sea Lion Island and Fitzroy Bridge. Those patrols did not go with my platoon. On the first two I went as the commander of an Amphibious Commando patrol. Jorge Island is located south-east off Soledad Island (East Falkland). It is very small and my mission was to recce and search for British activity. On this island was a settlement where a family lived but, on arrival, I found the ship *Penelope* at the little pier. Capturing the ship, I stayed there for twenty-four hours until an Argentine Super Puma helicopter returned for us. It was also carrying an Argentine crew to sail the ship.

On Sea Lion Island, my patrol was on board a *Prefectura Naval Argentina* (PNA) patrol vessel. There were two PNA (Coastguard) patrol vessels. Our mission was to locate a radio buoy used in air attacks on Puerto Argentino. The patrol commander was Lieutenant Imboden, an excellent soldier. We had to recce the island and find a helicopter landing site and give it security, because on that day an Army Commando Company would land and destroy the radio buoy. But they never arrived and the mission was cancelled. We returned in the afternoon on board the same ship which we had arrived. There was no contact with British troops.

The Fitzroy patrol was a static patrol near Fitzroy Bridge. I went as the commander of a regular patrol whose members did not belong to 4 Platoon. The mission was to destroy the bridge if the British Army intended to cross it. I was there for three or four days.

Miño was also busy in those initial weeks on the Islands. He worked near the capital of Puerto Argentino:

From 11 April until 11 June without missing a single day we worked on laying minefields. We were initially twenty-four (in the platoon): a Sergeant, three Corporals, nineteen conscripts and me. I had to fight two enemies: ignorance and fear. My struggle against ignorance was basically to teach my platoon that the British were coming and we would have to fight. Tough. I spoke to them about the Napoleonic Wars, the First and Second World Wars and the significance of these wars regarding the Malvinas. I said that we had a frigate (ARA *Hercules*) which was the *Sheffield*'s younger sister and that you had twenty *Sheffield*s. I told them about the aircraft carriers, the Vulcan aircraft and the Sea King helicopters. The truth is that I knew very little about the Harriers. Our task was not to act as infantry troops and even less to fight against the British infantry. We had neither the training nor the ability to do so.

We began performing general engineer tasks by laying defensive minefields (with) anti-personnel Spanish EXPAL mines,[21] Italian SB33 mines and anti-tank mines, some of which were manufactured by the Argentine Naval Ministry. We would combine them with lines of explosive traps made with hand grenades: FMMK2 (Argentine), DM51 (German) and American M67s. There were few night tasks in April. There was always a constant morning fog that allowed us to work with little risk of being detected. The minefields covered the possible landing beaches on the isthmus (east of Stanley) and the airfield perimeter. The entire Argentine defence was focused in fending off an amphibious assault from the Brits, expected to occur on the beaches near Puerto Argentino (Stanley).

Occasionally Miño visited the little 'city' and saw some of its children:

> They could not play in their streets or backyards. Every time we walked along the streets near Government House I watched the faces of one or two children looking through the windows. Everything is crazy in its own way. I asked God that nothing happened to these children [...] [22]
>
> For me, 1 May was a blessing because my struggle against ignorance was won. Next was my fight against fear. We were highly trained in night combat engineering. We had developed the ability to do things without looking and just by touch. Every day I told my platoon that if we moved as a group in a column, we would survive any possible ambush. We never stopped working. We left devices which provided us with our own security. I was always ahead because I had the experience of having practised 1980 combat formations with the 1st Marine Infantry Battalion. In the unlikely event of being attacked by coming under fire everyone should act. If the front man made it to the left, the rear men should move to the right. In any case we had to shoot and get out fast backwards or forwards. We placed out thousands of mines and hand-grenades. We were very familiar with this ammunition. During all our tasks we were never ambushed or hit either by mortar or artillery fire. We tried always to live in isolated positions. These changed five times: the last being on the top of Tumbledown.[23]
>
> Once the British landings at San Carlos were known, the defence got re-oriented, thus moving the infantry units from the peninsula (north-east of Stanley) to the heights of Two Sisters, Mount Harriet and Mount Longdon. These troops were transferred with limited equipment to fortify their new positions, i.e. no tools, no building materials, and very little time. The occupation of the assigned positions was weak with regard to the organisation of the deployment. At this stage (appx. 1-20 May), the task was to establish protective minefields at distances no further than fifty metres from the troops' defensive positions.[24] By the middle of May, the Engineers had already exhausted the existing supply of mines. It was therefore decided to use them as elements for infantry combat, as interdiction of gaps or reserve weapons [...] our platoon (1 Platoon, Marine Amphibious Engineers) was added to BIM5 and (eventually) deployed to the western side of Tumbledown. The place was a natural fortress.

Meanwhile the Argentine defeat at the Battle of Darwin and Goose Green on 28 May increased pressure on BIM5. From the end of that month, according to Vázquez,[25] the unit's command element made nightly radio calls to all Company and Platoon Commanders with shouted threats that every man disobeying orders or withdrawing without permission would be killed by artillery fire. Officers became concerned at this hysteria. It could affect morale and the will to fight. This and other matters led to the start of discussions as to when surrendering would be the best option once it appeared that continuing to fight was nonsense. This dangerous theme crept onto the agenda of formal orders groups. It made Vázquez's ensuing display of leadership and courage in battle even more remarkable. However his Company Commander, Lieutenant Eduardo Villarraza, was adamant about the state of morale:

> N Company's morale was quite good as we had received good training, and the Marines knew how to manage their weapons as well as combat techniques. The other reason in possessing a high morale was that superiors had trust in their subordinates and vice-versa. I do not remember any discipline disorder, but recall the actions of many protecting their comrades whether they were officers, petty officers or Marines alike.[26]

Miño's 5 Platoon was of similar strength to 4 Platoon, there now being a total of twenty-five men under Miño's command. At the beginning of June Miño 'had received Midshipman Demarco who was accompanied by an artillery auxiliary conscript. Demarco was to act as observer (spotter) to B Battery of the Marine Field Artillery Battalion'. The platoon started their work on 5 June, having received an urgent task early that day. They had to report to the Marine Amphibious Engineer Company HQ at Felton Stream. Nearby was the BIM5 Command Post which had deployed O Company (also located at Felton Stream) that night to Pony's Pass. The Company moved on foot with vehicles transporting their ammunition. Miño:

> O Company was the BIM5 reserve, but it had to be deployed now as a forward combat unit. Commanded by Acting Sub-Lieutenant Lieutenant Quiroga, the Company's strength was eighty-nine men. It had to leave (Felton Stream) fast and occupy the position assigned on the map. They went along the road which leads to the quarry (at Pony's Pass) far beyond Mount William. Meanwhile 5 Platoon was ordered to install obstacles (on the Pony's Pass position) in order to protect O Company. When this was co-ordinated with the Amphibious Engineers Company HQ at the latter's combat base, the platoon received two vehicles loaded with landmines, some anti-tank devices, barbed wire and stakes to mark out the area.
>
> When we arrived at Pony's Pass, O Company was anxiously waiting for these defence stores. Quiroga told us where and when he wanted the landmines laid. We started and completed the work on Sunday, 6 June. It was a race against time. The Marines were fighting all the mud you can imagine in order to prepare the defensive position while 5 Platoon laid the mines. We were no more than eighteen men. Seven laid mines, two marked out the area and five or six men armed with MAG machine-guns established a fire base nearby with a couple of men armed with rifle grenades. The mine-laying work alternated between the two sections. So when Corporal Robles's men were installing mines, Corporal Valdez's men manned the fire base. Then after a while they would switch these duties. It was the only occasion that we laid mines near the surface because part of the mined ground went through a recently-flooded lagoon. Thank God it rained cats and dogs so that the British helicopters could not see us. We heard the noise of their engine turbines (from the direction of Mount Kent).

There was no lunch that day and the mine-laying ended at 16.00 hours (19.00Z) when we ran out of mines. The minefield was 250 to 300 metres wide and no more than fifteen metres in depth. We laid out 250 Spanish EXPAL anti-personnel mines in three lines. Afterwards copies of the mine-layout plans were made inside our vehicle. Leaving the original plans with Quiroga, all of 5 Platoon withdrew from the position on 7 June. Back at the Amphibious Engineer Combat HQ the mine-layout plans were, once again, drawn up meticulously as we always did. After drying off, we returned to our position on Tumbledown.[27]

Then from Demarco's position (next day on 8 June) he reported the British landing operations (RFAs *Sir Galahad* and *Sir Tristram*) in Bahía Agradable (Port Pleasant) as well as directing other fire missions.

We saw the (ensuing) events in Bahía Agradable perfectly.[28]

Miño decided he would run a hard regime with his men and kept them busy, insisting that they made no noise. A professional defence routine was established with men cooking, ensuring their feet were clean, and sleeping. Miño:

From there I sent out five reconnaissance missions to Army positions. Four times we went out on distant reconnaissance missions. I integrated the patrols because they needed a guide to safely exit or enter through their own minefields. It was entertaining, but very hard for me because I always carried a heavy radio. On return from these missions inevitably we had to watch how careless our troops were with tell-tale fires everywhere.[29]

With no more mines available, his men constructed 300 explosive traction traps.[30] Thirty of these were laid immediately in front of his position, twenty-three in front of 2 Platoon's position just south of Tumbledown and the remainder further down Tumbledown's northern slopes into Moody Valley to link up with an anti-tank and anti-personnel minefield. Curiously they did not lay any such devices in front of 4 Platoon's southern-facing position. Had they done so, then the Scots Guards would have been confronted with a much more difficult task in their eventual attack against Vázquez's men.

Each trap comprised a trip-wire connected at both ends to either a US M-67 or German DM-51 hand-grenade. Miño was committed to his task. Hidden in his T-shirt was a map of all the booby traps and minefields he had laid. After the Argentine surrender this was handed over to Major Rod Macdonald of 3 Commando Brigade. Moreover Miño had not attempted to carry out his wildly drastic final plan. He had learned (incorrectly) that the British did not take Argentine officers prisoner in battle, and therefore was determined that, if faced with such a situation where escape was impossible, he would use one of his eight hand grenades to blow himself up. His men also laid a dummy minefield by pegging out white tape on the ground. It worked well because the Gurkhas were forced to deploy 9 Para Squadron Sappers at the head of the Battalion advance along this northerly route during the British attack. The Sappers searched for the suspected minefield by prodding the ground with long lengths of wire. Fortunately although we were quite close to the northern face of Tumbledown, none of any Miño's explosive traction traps were encountered.

Vázquez described his final defensive layout:

> 5 Platoon was deployed to a defensive position on the topographical ridge of Tumbledown's western tip. Sited northwards, the platoon's left flank closed the space that separated it and my right flank. The distance between 5 Platoon and 4 Platoon varied between twenty and fifty metres, both platoons being 'back to back' to each other with one sited northwards and other southwards.

Miño's 5 Platoon was a welcome asset for Vázquez whose below-strength platoon had been reduced at one point to only twenty-one men. One conscript was evacuated because of 'morale exhaustion'. Two others were wounded, with one failing to overcome his terror of fast-approaching combat. His inner psychological battle overwhelmed him and he was removed from 4 Platoon's position with a self-inflicted bullet wound. However another six Marine infantrymen were also brought in to reinforce his platoon, so bringing the total up to twenty-eight including Vázquez.

Then on the night of 11-12 June, the Argentine Outer Defence Zone comprising Mount Longdon, Two Sisters and Mount Harriet fell to the British and many prisoners were taken. However some Argentines managed to escape. A few hours later (Officer B) with fifteen conscripts of (Unit A) [31] from Mount Harriet, and Army Sub-Lieutenant Oscar Silva leading another fifteen men of the 4th Infantry Regiment from Two Sisters, arrived at Vázquez's position. It was a hazardous manoeuvre as the latter described, 'One of Silva's men approaching my platoon on the morning of 12 June was hit by artillery fire and died 300 metres from my position.' Miño was also busy:

> After the fall of Two Sisters and Mount Longdon, in addition to the maintenance of installed minefields, we had to guide Argentine sub-units in retreating from these features. We received strict orders to be very tolerant in using the password and avoid opening fire as there were many Argentine troops in a rather bad shape coming in. We saw from our observation post how the British helicopters lifted the artillery guns and down-loaded the ammunition. I spoke of fear. We had often seen the tremendous damage our mines or grenades did to livestock, i.e. cows and horses. It was easy for me to realise what would happen to us if we were the target. We knew that if we moved quickly then there was a chance of us surviving as a group. [32]

Then they made further preparations for the forthcoming battle. Miño:

> We divided into three sections. As a 'lover of hand-grenades' I led one. In a bag we carried six or eight US M-67 hand-grenades. Another section was led by Corporal Valdez: a 'lover of rifle grenades'. This section had three or four men, all configured as grenadiers. The third section of three men was led by Corporal Robles: a 'lover of the MAG machine-gun'. Petty Officer Ponce and 1st Corporal Sánchez did not usually go into the field because they were responsible for logistics. They and their conscripts used the FAL or FAP. We had two rifles with

telescopic sights but did not use them because of the infra-red vision system which is a beacon in the night.[33]

Meanwhile Vázquez was only 'reinforced with approximately twenty conscripts of the Argentine Army, an Army Lance-Corporal' as well as the two officers. With the impending British attack on the Inner Defence Zone, he made an assessment of these new men's fighting qualities and subsequently decided 'to send to the rear four Army conscripts who were useless for fighting'. He would remain rational in his decision-making throughout exceptionally difficult circumstances. But the correct number of Army soldiers who remained to do combat alongside his Marines was only a paltry seventeen, barely equivalent to two British Army infantry sections. Vázquez:

> Probably (Officer B) and Silva arrived at my position with many more men than I mentioned. As a matter of fact that is the way it was. But in both cases when I received them I sent their wounded to the rear and those who carried no guns (which were many). (Officer B) was in a state of panic and unable to speak [...] I assigned a group of five Army soldiers to Sub-Lieutenant Silva, with whom he occupied the centre of my alternate position on the topographical ridge of Tumbledown (some twenty metres from 5 Platoon to my rear). Their mission was to cover by fire the withdrawal of the main body of both platoons in case we could not maintain the defence of the primary position. (Officer B) did not participate in any part of the battle I describe here, since he was still in a state of shock. He remained in my foxhole until he surrendered on 14 June, curled up at my feet and uttered some words only when surrendering. Silva's troops were in better shape, and personally he kept a high morale.

Silva was, indeed, of different officer mettle. He and his platoon first spent one month on Twelve O'Clock Mount, north of Stanley. Withdrawn to the capital on 8 June, next day they were flown to Two Sisters where Silva assisted in further detailed co-ordination of defences on the South Sister. During the Battle of Two Sisters, Silva and half of his platoon occupied a southern flanking position. After this battle he led his men back to the Tumbledown, but would pay dearly for his courage during the battle there. But now, on the west end of Tumbledown, Vázquez was devising a local tactical defence plan:

> In the last days before the fighting on 13-14 June, I co-ordinated the following plans personally with Miño. Once combat began, we would both hold on to our primary positions. If my platoon could not hold its position, it would fall back towards my alternate position on the ridge of Tumbledown (thirty metres to rear) whilst protected by the fire of Silva's group. Once on the ridge, both platoons working practically back to back would try to maintain the defence of Tumbledown's western tip. If we did not succeed in this task, both would fall back towards the position held by the N Company HQ located on Tumbledown's eastern tip, some 1,800 metres to the rear. It was explicitly agreed that no platoon would fall back alone without the other.
> On Sunday 13 June in the morning with the sun shining in the sky, I went to the

N Company HQ command post to receive the last defence orders from the Company Commander (Lieutenant Villarraza). I was also representing Miño since the standard operating procedure specified that one out of every two platoon commanders should remain on the front line. At the HQ were Colombo, Jaimet, Llambias-Pravaz, but I cannot remember if it was Bianchi or Oruezabala who attended.[34]

It happened by chance that Major Jaimet [...] a pleasant and good-humoured man [...] knew Lieutenant Villarraza personally [...] They were so acquainted that Jaimet called him by his nickname '*Tuerto* (One-Eyed) Villarraza' [...] Once the orders group was finished, I returned to Tumbledown's western tip whilst the field artillery was shelling Moody Brook Valley over Tumbledown. At this time a shell dropped short and impacted near me, the strong concussion hitting me in my neck. However there were no casualties in my Company during those attacks on that day.

Vázquez arrived back at his west end position. Meanwhile 5 Platoon had been preparing for battle. Miño:

On 13 June after breakfast and having shaved, we rehearsed withdrawing to the N Company Command Post and then moved toward the positions of Acting Sub-Lieutenant Vázquez We returned to our position and then finally moved to Moody Brook Valley. Not all the platoon participated in these rehearsals. I left the radio on 'listen'. No one transmitted anything on the N Company tactical frequency. We improved the defence of two paths leading to us by placing out some booby traps. At noon we ate canned food and then slept for a while. That was our third day on alert. When darkness arrived we prepared our backpacks and weapons (in case of having) to fall back. We were silent and posted three 'listening' sentries. Everyone wanted to have the supper meal early. This was canned food and half a fried cake for each man. The silence was more visible than the black night.

Vázquez would be confronted with even more problems in this immediate pre-combat period. Concerns about the passivity of (NCO A), one of his two section commanders, led him to take a drastic decision about the latter's impending employment. Prior to this Vázquez:

relayed the received orders (of Villarraza) to Miño and reviewed with him our coordinated plan for both platoons to fall back together in case of an emergency.

I carried out some last-minute modifications in the deployment of my platoon. Firstly I placed Corporal Tejada in charge of the machine-gun to the right. Then keeping (NCO A) as my personal radio operator in my foxhole, I personally took command of the section to the left over which I had an easy visual control. The Army soldiers (with the exception of Silva, the five Army conscripts that occupied the position to our rear and (Officer B) who was psychologically disabled in my foxhole), were distributed throughout my primary defensive position, thus augmenting both infantry rifle sections of 4 Platoon.

In terms of exercising effective leadership, Vázquez had taken the correct action by keeping malcontents close to him. At 21.00Z Vázquez held a final two-hour platoon Orders Group in his foxhole 'with the commanders of the platoon's elements to review the coordination measures and predicted scheme of manoeuvre. The following were present: Silva, (Officer B), (NCO A), Castillo and Tejada'. Understandably tension was mounting in these final pre-battle hours before the anticipated British attack. It is a most terrible time, and there was a reaction from two who had been in battle two days before. Before midnight, 'there was an incident with Army (NCO C),[35] who tried to escape the position'. But Vázquez ignored what happened to him. Then another incident 'was later reported, this time an Army conscript who tried also to run from the platoon'. The primitive notion of fight, freeze or flight is derived from the animal world of predator and prey. Vázquez's men were exhibiting all three conditions. But it is a tribute to him that most in his platoon choose to fight because of the unique team bond he had created.

Then 'intense artillery fire' of seventy-five minutes duration began impacting on his position from 01.00Z. During this, the Scots Guards' G Company arrived on their objective, the rocky knoll just to the west of the two Argentine platoons. All historical accounts of the battle state that G Company remained undetected. According to Miño this was not so:

> Soon a sentry told me and Robles that he could hear voices talking in English below our positions. We threw hand grenades at them but were unable to discover the result of their explosions. A little afterwards, the voices stopped and some machine-gun fire was fired in the general direction of our positions, but did not return the fire. Nothing eventful happened. The silence returned.

Miño's men had dropped their grenades from a height of about twenty metres. But years later Vázquez complained, 'Miño never warned me about how close the English were to his position.' [36] Meanwhile 4 Platoon witnessed the Scots Guards' composite platoon diversionary attack on the Argentine Marines' O Company three kilometres to the south-west at Pony's Pass.[37] While this was being made and artillery fire continued, the Scots Guards' G Company completed taking the rocky outcrop unopposed. The combined effects of the diversionary attack and artillery fire were having the desired effect. Vázquez was kept fully occupied as the shelling:

> severed my telephone lines. I ordered Conscript Acosta to follow the cable and repair it. Although he went out of his foxhole, he soon returned saying he could not do it. I realised he was frightened and had not carried out the order because of this. I issued the same order to Tejada, who left his foxhole almost thirty metres from the platoon command post and, under intense artillery fire, followed the telephone cable until he arrived at the rock we had named 'The Wall' close to Silva's position.
>
> Then he returned, still under heavy artillery fire, and told me that it was not possible to repair the cable since it was severed in many places and some lengths were not there anymore, they having been destroyed by the shelling.

If this insurmountable communications problem was not enough, Vázquez committed himself to an urgent task in his self-imposed role of Sector E section commander whilst (NCO A), the ousted commander, remained in the relative safety of the Platoon HQ's foxhole:

> At approximately 02.00Z news was relayed to me by voice that Conscript Jorge Andrés Kihn of the section on my left had been injured by the shrapnel. Leaving my FAL rifle in the foxhole so I could run faster, I arrived at Kihn's position almost on the left end of the platoon. I found him there standing under the shelling and clutching his stomach. Pushing him into a hole with the aid of another conscript, I bandaged his wound in trying to keep his intestines from spilling out again. While I was doing this, at 02.10Z, the artillery fire stopped and almost simultaneously British infantry troops launched their assault on our position, crossing it in two waves. One wave advanced from south to north (Left Flank Company HQ, 15 and 14 Platoon) and the other (13 Platoon) from west to east. All of 4 Platoon opened fire to initiate combat that saw gunfire (eventually) mixed with hand grenades, machine-gun fire and fighting with bayonets and blows. The enemy advanced in lines, firing their weapons from their hips, aiming approximately five metres ahead and with bayonets fixed.

There was an immediate Scots Guards 15 Platoon section attack on the Argentine platoon.[38] Vázquez became directly involved in the fighting. He heard the distinctive sound of a Sterling submachine-gun firing at the entrance of his foxhole and saw two Scots Guardsmen, one of whom was smoking a cigarette, passing by on each side of his position.[39] The 4 Platoon Commander was in acute danger of being isolated from the remainder of his platoon:

> On seeing the first Englishmen who crossed over the foxhole where I was attending to Kihn, I indicated to the other conscript that he should finish the bandaging, grabbed my pistol and a hand grenade, and ran towards my foxhole at the centre of the platoon where I had left my FAL rifle and the radio with which I could direct the battle. As I was running back towards 'The Wall', I became aware that I was among the English who had then begun the assault. I fired my pistol at them as I ran amongst them until, at a certain moment, I had to play dead when an artillery star-shell exploded above and lit up the platoon. The enemy walked almost over and on both sides of me until the light faded away, and I managed to reach my position and regained control of the platoon.

The two Scots Guardsmen 'didn't react quickly enough' as they had also fired back at him in his dash back to the 4 Platoon HQ.[40] No-one was hit. Meanwhile Left Flank Company's 13 Platoon did not go over the Argentine platoon's positions, but manoeuvred around its extreme western flank to an area behind. Once there they began to engage Silva's five men who had been placed out as a line of 'stops', and establish positions from which they could fire onto the remainder of the Argentines. However Vázquez mistakenly assumed that his platoon's rear was still being guarded by 5 Platoon on the north-west slopes of Tumbledown:

Fighting was already generalised along all the front and rear areas of the platoon. The bulk of the English attackers went over us, taking positions to my rear, with many of them still remaining intermingled with us, starting then a fire-fight from distances of ten to twenty metres which, when it took too long to silence the defender, concluded with the English charging on the trenches in order to get to bayonet distance or hand to hand combat.

During that first attack, the British showed themselves very confidently. For example, one man [...] made a lone attack on one of our foxholes. It was really one-to-one combat. That kind of tactic was only used in the first rush; they did not do it later – I think it was too costly. I think the British thought it would be easy at first and they were over-confident. If they had been more and they had used more hand grenades as they came over our holes, they could have cleared us up. They used a lot of hand grenades against empty positions [...] The use of tracer by the British helped us, first to identify who were the British and, second, when the range was over thirty metres, you just had time to get your head down and take cover when it fired.[41]

On several occasions I tried to get through to Miño, but found it impossible. Being unable to communicate over the radio with him had happened previously, although we were barely fifty metres apart. At a certain moment, I noticed that I was receiving very intense fire from the rear, from where my alternate position occupied by Silva was supposed to be. Given the number of weapons that seemed to be firing from that position (included machine-guns), I assumed that Miño, on seeing what was happening, had turned his platoon about face to support me. But this fire was killing my people; a machine-gun was even beating the area behind me from thirty metres away, firing directly over my trench and making it almost impossible to take a look outside. I could not personally neutralise them, neither using my rifle nor with a couple of rifle anti-tank grenades that I fired. So I asked Conscript Victor Gasko manning the machine-gun to my left to silence it. After a while, since he had engaged in hand-to-hand fighting with the enemy that kept coming up, he returned to fire the MAG and neutralised the machine-gun.

I called my Company Commander on the radio and said: 'Tell Miño to stop supporting me! He is killing my men!'

Lieutenant Villarraza replied: 'Miño is with me.'

Thus I understood that Miño had fallen back without warning me, and also assumed that Silva and his five men were no longer there.

This also confirmed to me that we were surrounded.

About this time the 2 Platoon Commander, Midshipman Marcelo Oruezabala called Villarraza on the radio and asked him what 2 Platoon, which was still located in the stone run south-east of 4 Platoon's position, could do to support Vázquez. But Villarraza's order was 'not to move or let anyone into (2 Platoon's) position' and that there would be a counter-attack of M Company to repel the attack on Vazquez.[42]

This was another most positive, but hugely underrated, effect for the Scots Guards that emanated from their diversionary attack on Pony's Pass. It not only kept the BIM5 2 Platoon anchored in the stone runs south-east of Vázquez's position, but also prevented 1 Platoon from moving off Mount William. So Vázquez could not expect any counter-attack from these two platoons. Additionally that anticipated M Company counter-attack would never materialise.

He was not only surrounded, but also totally isolated.

Notes

1. *The Art of War*, Chapter 9 – Moving the Army.
2. Its citation was: 'For the gallantry, heroism and leadership showed during the battle of Tumbledown, where notwithstanding numerical and material disadvantage he led several counter-attacks, successfully holding the British offensive force led by the Welsh and Scots Guards, actions by which he received severe wounds and was later taken prisoner by the enemy forces.'
3. It soon became obvious that it was inefficient to wait for a consensus needed to award these decorations. The result was that each of the services (Army, Air Force and Navy) began awarding similar medals in which the prefix '*La Nación Argentina*' was conveniently modified to read '*El Ejército Argentino*', '*La Armada Argentina*' or '*La Fuerza Aérea Argentina*'. These medals are slightly different from those issued at national level because, although the ribbon is in national colours, they carry the corresponding services' emblem on their front instead of the national Shield. For the Navy this is an Admiralty anchor.
4. Enhanced by four e-mails dated 26 and 27 October, and 15 and 17 December 2011.
5. *Ibid.* dated 9 January 2012.
6. *Ibid.* dated 27 December 2006.
7. In addition to the six mortars each of the BIM5 106.6mm and 81mm Mortar Platoon, Vázquez's 4 Platoon was the only one in N Company that possessed a 60mm mortar. There was also the 60mm mortar section sited in the centre-east of Tumbledown consisting of three mortars manned by fifteen men, three 60mm mortars of O Company at Pony's Pass, two 120mm mortars and two 81mm mortars of C Company, 3rd Infantry Regiment located east of Mount William, and the three 81mm mortars of B Company, 6th Infantry Regiment west of Sapper Hill. Thus at the start of the battle the total number of Argentine mortars available was twenty-six, eight more than the British. A combined Gurkha and Scots Guards total of ten 81mm mortars was supplemented by another six of 42 Commando's. Also retired Major Mike Norman of 42 Commando told the author at the Imperial War Museum's opening of its 2007 Falklands War exhibition that a further two Argentine 120mm mortars on Mount Harriet were turned and fired onto Mount William by his unit's Marines.
8. Name deliberately deleted.
9. Seventeen pages of *Desde el Frente*'s sixty-eight about the Tumbledown fighting were earmarked for Vázquez's platoon, twelve of which being extracts from the latter's post-war combat report.
10. *Hors de Combat*, p. 26.
11. E-mail dated 22 November 2007. The black and white photo (with his name

incorrectly captioned as Valdez) is included in the 2003 book *5th Infantry Brigade in the Falklands*. Six years later the colour version of this photo was published above another of Patrick Watts leaning in similar pose against the same rock in the near atlas-sized book *The Falklands War: Then and Now* (p. 517) by Gordon Ramsey. This interesting 624-page tome also incorporated, amongst many others from twenty-four books on the war, eight extracts (the last filling four pages) from *With the Gurkhas in the Falklands* (without the author's permission, contrary to Ramsey's 'acknowledgement' that this had been given). As well as the sunglasses which had led the rock to be re-named a flippant 'Rock Star Rock' in Ramsey's book, the moustached and alert-looking young officer with 'the typically South American military demeanour' was wearing a helmet and combat waistcoat. He had the air of a leader about him. Also an account of the battle by Vázquez, regurgitated from Martin Middlebrook's 1989 book *The Fight for the 'Malvinas': The Argentine Forces in the Falklands War*, (pp. 257-260) was inserted alongside and under these photos as well as on the following page: a classic example of how post-war myths are created. After e-mailing the photo to Vázquez's eldest son on 22 January 2010, Carlos Horacio, the latter promptly informed the author, 'My dad told me that he didn't use sunglasses in the Malvinas. And that he had never been on Monte William.' The photo was of fellow-officer Midshipman Carlos Ricardo Bianchi who had a pair of RayBan sunglasses in the Malvinas and was the BIM5 Platoon Commander of 1 Platoon dug-in on Mount William. Two days later his son, Mariano, confirmed this in an e-mail to Carlos Horacio and '[...] that they had that picture at home.'

12. E-mail dated 9 January 2012.
13. *Ibid.* dated 8 May 2007.
14. The correct number of men killed was fifteen. An official document written by Vázquez in October 2004 contained the detailed breakdown by name of the men under his command who had been killed, wounded, missing and unwounded.
15. E-mail dated 25 March 2007.
16. Again, the correct number of men killed was fifteen.
17. E-mail dated 28 August 2007.
18. *Ibid.* dated 7 September 2007.
19. FAL (*Fusil Automático Liviano*) – was the Argentine standard-issue 7.62mm light automatic (assault) rifle.
20. Vázquez possessed a copy of *Razor's Edge* and, during his e-mail dialogue with the author, it was used often as a mutual reference. In two e-mails dated 7 March 2009, he commented on the inaccuracy of *Razor's Edge*'s maps (pp. 286, 290 and 291):

    Although (the chapter referring to Tumbledown) has good information, not all the things written there are true. It has many errors. For example, the drawings of the positions of the companies and platoons are wrong. They show Robacio's version of the story (also it is the official version) where he tries to cover the evident errors in the deployment and direction of his troops in his defensive positions. Particularly the positions of N Company (on p. 286) are false [...] 3 Platoon, RI6-B, O (-) Company (to the east of the Tumbledown-Mount William saddle), 6 x 105mm howitzers [...] the location of (those) units on the map are false and Miño's position is not there [...] Page 290 (3 Platoon) Lucero was not there. He was 1500 metres to the east. Near the place where in the other map (p. 290) you can read RI6-B [...] Page 290 (lower map) where you read Lucero, that was Miño's position (5 Platoon) [...] Page 291 – Both of these maps (photo diagram 31: Tumbledown) are totally wrong.

21. EXPAL – Explosivos Alaveses, the Spanish company that manufactured these mines. They were made of PVC and had no metal parts, thus making them impossible to be detected by a mine detector. About 20,000 EXPAL P-4-B and FMK-1 anti-personnel mines were laid by the Argentines in the Islands during the war.
22. E-mail dated 27 October 2011.
23. *Ibid.* dated 26 October 2011.
24. During October 2009 and May 2010 BACTEC International recovered all the 190 mines laid on Sapper Hill by Miño's 5 Platoon.
25. E-mail dated 8 March 2009.
26. *Ibid.* dated 4 October 2006.
27. E-mails dated 15 and 17 December 2011.
28. *Ibid.* dated 17 December 2011.
29. *Ibid.* dated 26 October 2011.
30. A figure of 450 '*trampas explosivas*' is given in *Desde el Frente* (p. 210).
31. Name of officer and unit deliberately deleted.
32. E-mails dated 26 October and 16 December 2011.
33. *Ibid.* dated 26 October 2011.
34. Sub-Lieutenant Marcelo Llambias-Pravaz of the 4th Infantry Regiment had already been heavily involved in the fighting. He had commanded 3 Platoon, and a number of his men had been killed and wounded both in a patrol clash with the Royal Marines and during the Two Sisters battle. Withdrawing from Two Sisters with Silva, he and his small group of men joined forces with Bianchi's 1 Platoon on Mount William. Therefore it was Oruezabala who attended that final Company Orders Group because Llambias-Pravaz would have represented Bianchi.
35. Name deliberately deleted.
36. E-mail dated 10 March 2009.
37. Twenty-five years later the author provided Vázquez with information about the Pony's Pass (not 'Ponies Pass' as in *Razor's Edge*, pp. 282, 287, 292 and 294) diversionary attack His reaction was most heated:

    Please be aware that no one in Argentina has made such a statement. Robacio says that such an attack was carried by the 1st Welsh Guards Battalion [...] Nobody in my Company ever thought that the attack of the 1st Battalion on O Company at the 5th Marine Infantry Battalion's southern flank could have been a diversionary attack. What is more, we never understood why they stopped their advance [..]

    Mike, our history is an extremely lying one. Our Army had a lot of dishonourable actions, and so it was necessary to write a particular history.

The official Army history is not true. This was similar in the case of the BIM5 history, but not for dishonourable actions (of course a few of these actions existed). In the case of BIM5, a fantasy history was made because only a few men fought in combat and the Navy needed a lot of medals. At this time there existed a conflict with the Army and Air Force about prestige in war. Political problems. Robacio gave a lot medals in his Battalion to men that did not fight. Then he needed to make a particular history, and this history was convenient for the Navy. In the Navy the old men know the truth, but the fantasy history is good for the future. Do you understand?

For example, Robacio says that 'all BIM5 fought against the Scots Guards'. You know that is not true. Robacio did not talk about the dishonourable actions in the Army, and the Army men agreed with the Robacio History. I fought on Tumbledown. Is it not strange that I did not know about the travel to England (for the Nottingham colloquium) to speak with the Scotsmen, when Robacio and Villarraza travelled?

A story near the truth is actually being prepared in the Navy. But in this history, a lot of success will not be mentioned because it is not the best for our young officers and soldiers. (From a compilation of e-mails dated 4, 6 and 10 September 2007.)

38. In an e-mail dated 7 March 2009, Vázquez commented on *Razor's Edge* (p. 290 – lower map) that: 'The Scots Guards Left Flank Company attack was in the same direction as indicated on the map, but 200 metres to the west. They attacked my platoon in the middle from the south.

39. *The Fight for the 'Malvinas': The Argentine Forces in the Falklands War.* p. 257.

40. *Ibid.*

41. *Ibid.*, pp. 258-259.

42. E-mail dated 19 October 2011.

10 Two battles and one war

Throw them where they cannot leave,
Facing death, they will not be routed.
Officers and men facing death,
*   How could one not obtain their utmost*
*   strength?*

– Sun Tzu[1]

Vázquez was both alarmed and angry at his predicament. The battle's first phase had come to an end. Two more were to follow. He was in a desperate position. Outnumbered nearly three to one by the Scots Guards Left Flank Company, 4 Platoon's rear was no longer protected by 5 Platoon. Miño and his men had watched the impressive British tracer fire (probably from the Blues and Royals Scimitar light tanks' 30mm Rarden cannon against Argentine positions on Wireless Ridge) as well as 'tracer fire on occasions on Pony's Pass in the scarce opportunities we watched from the high rocks'.[2] This fire was probably from the two Rarden cannon of Lieutenant Coreth's 4 Troop in support of the Scots Guards diversionary attack. Furthermore there was the artillery fire. Miño:

> We heard quite clearly the artillery shells whistling above us. I do not know if it was Argentine or British artillery. It seemed to me it was the British artillery, but not on us as no shell came near our position.[3]

All this and, in particular, the tracer fire 'in the valley that ends at Moody Brook' indicated to Miño that:

> we had been overwhelmed. I met one of my fears. I did not want to get isolated, and much less in the long corridor where we were located. If we were attacked from the rear of the corridor then it would be our grave [...] [4] We had practised withdrawal during the day, according to various possible routes to Villarraza to Vázquez or through the Moody Valley. We were not to fight in position as the infantry did. We did not have either this task or the ability to do so. In fact we never dug a foxhole or anything like it [...] [5]

Miño's account is contrary to Vázquez's who had stated there was a joint defence plan of the Tumbledown's west end conceived by both platoon commanders. Hence Vázquez was expecting Miño's platoon to fight in the infantry role. But a reconciliation of both officers' accounts is impossible.[6] Miño:

> I asked permission (by radio) to withdraw twice. The second time [...] come midnight (03.00Z) [7] [...] I was given authorisation by Sub-Lieutenant Colombo. We knew Tumbledown quite well. If we had been confronted by British troops then we had a good chance of survival. We moved back to N Company in an orderly fashion and passed by the abandoned 60mm mortar position where there was a

dead Marine Corporal. In the vicinity of the N Company Command Post I ordered that backpacks were to be left in a hole and went to see Lieutenant Villarraza. I was ordered by him to deploy my men as a blocking force in the vicinity of the field kitchen.[8]

Miño's premature withdrawal from the west end of Tumbledown is a little known consequence of the British advance that included the Scots Guards' diversionary attack at Pony's Pass. This was one of a number of factors that had contributed to Miño's final decision. But Vázquez's perception of Miño's action was different:

> Miño fell back a few minutes after the British attack was initiated. The attack began at 2310 hours (02.10Z) and Miño withdrew around 23.20 hours (02.20Z) [...] He did not receive orders from the Company Commander.[9] Both Petty Officer Eduardo Ponce who was with Miño [...] and Midshipman Demarco were against this decision. They told Miño he was not respecting the agreement we had previously arranged and should not leave me.
>
> It is an action that has remained in the darkness of history.[10]

Once more it is impossible to adjudicate on Vázquez's allegations except to point out that, during their later military careers, Ponce continued to work with Miño in various appointments. According to the latter Ponce never said anything about Miño's decision which was made in accordance with an assessment of the situation at the time and after receipt of an authorisation to withdraw.[11]

But for the Gurkhas this was indeed a major piece of good fortune. If 5 Platoon had continued to occupy their positions overlooking the north and north-west approaches to Tumbledown then, five hours later, they could have observed through their high-quality night viewing devices the Gurkhas' advance along this exact route. When the latter were subsequently pinned down close to the rocks of Tumbledown by heavy artillery and mortar fire for about an hour, Miño and his men could have taken advantage of this predicament by pouring down small-arms fire onto the Gurkhas from an effective range of less than 200 metres. There would have been casualties and the Gurkhas' A Company (which was leading the Battalion's advance) would have become involved in a fire-fight with Miño's platoon. This would have caused a further delay. There were also those thirty explosive traction traps laid out directly in front of Miño's position which the Gurkhas would have been forced to advance through. They would have prevailed but, because of even more casualties that might have been taken during this attack on 5 Platoon, plans would have to have been adjusted for setting up the vital Gurkha fire base on the eastern end of Tumbledown. What effect would this have had on the outcome of the battle if the Argentine Marines had elected to hold their ground on Mount William?

Fortunately all this is a 'worst-case' scenario that remains one of fiction. But now, after the withdrawal of 5 Platoon and two hours of combat for Vázquez's platoon, any average officer might have contemplated surrender. Such a thought did not enter the 4 Platoon Commander's head. On the contrary he determined something desperate had to be done. Sun Tzu would have approved. 'If quick, I survive. If not quick, I am lost. This is "death"'.[12] Vázquez:

The situation held approximately until 04.15Z when I concluded finally that we would all die due to the obvious numerical superiority of the enemy. So based on my appreciation, I ordered the mounting mechanism of the 60mm mortar manned by Conscript First Class Ramón Rotela on my left to be removed, and the fifty-four remaining bombs to be fired vertically upwards so they would fall over our position. The reason why I issued that order was that the English, who were mixed between us, had less protection than we had and therefore would have more casualties. In addition, and as best as I could, because we were still fighting hand-to-hand, I shouted and ordered the message to be passed that I wanted the mortar to fire on top of our position. The order was carried out, and the English who remained between us withdrew quickly. It was 04.30Z.

Kiszely was pithy in describing the effectiveness of Rotela's firing, 'I was certainly aware that some bastard with no shortage of ammunition was mortaring us pretty accurately for a long period of time!' Vázquez:

There began a pause in the battle, with no firing until 05.00Z.

When the platoon became aware of the withdrawal of the English, a wave of euphoria ran through all the men, and they begun to shout insults and other things.

'And singing, I remember,' remarked Kiszely, although Vázquez claimed that they 'were just shouting'. But other essential matters were demanding the Argentine officer's attention at this time:

During that lull I received the casualty reports and ammunition state, and communicated with the Battalion Commander through the Company Commander (I learnt later that the Battalion had switched over to the Company tactical channel). I explained the situation to him. The Commander asked whether I wanted to hold or fall back.

I answered, 'Sir, I do not have control of the situation, but neither do the English. If you send reinforcements, I can hold.'

He replied, '[...] all right, hold on. Reinforcements will be sent.'

The last chance for Vázquez and his platoon to withdraw from the position had now disappeared. They were committed to fight until the end. This was pure Sun Tzu methodology; the only way to 'obtain their utmost strength'.[13] Then Vázquez received more bad news:

During this pause, Silva came to me and said: 'Those who were at our back are gone.' He was referring to 5 Platoon. 'The English got us from the rear and killed my men. I was able to push forward.'

I ordered him to get himself close to the FAP which was at the centre of the section on the right and control that weapon for me. He did this. Also during this battle pause I ordered (Officer B) to take my place outside the foxhole because I needed to rest. As he was still unable to answer, I requested (NCO A) to do this. He did. The only thing we could do was to keep alert.

At that point in the battle Vázquez's casualties were relatively light with only a few wounded in addition to the five Army personnel killed.[14] The fifteen-man 60mm mortar section in the centre of Tumbledown had run out of mortar bombs and also taken casualties, including the one fatality that Miño and his men had passed by. Spiking their mortars, the ten unwounded survivors had reverted to an infantry role and joined 4 Platoon.

Meanwhile at the east end of Tumbledown, Miño was about to be tasked with a new mission. By now it must have been clear to the N Company Commander that a major British thrust was being made on the west end of Tumbledown. Authorised or not, the withdrawal of Miño's platoon had been a tactical blunder. Miño:

> For us it was a surprise that (the Scots Guards) made such a fierce attack on Vázquez. We thought (they) would take Tumbledown by bypassing Vázquez and getting to the centre. It made no sense to attack the only position on the whole of Tumbledown (which) was an objective (that) had to be defended by at least two rifle companies.[15]

However the perceived threat of a regimental attack on Pony's Pass was still alive. So 1 Platoon on Mount William and 2 Platoon in the stone runs south-east of Vázquez's position remained at these locations covering the anticipated enemy 'killing area' below them. There was no option left for Villarraza other than to attempt to plug the gaping hole in his west end defences. The Marine Amphibious Engineer Platoon Commander knew Tumbledown's terrain and so therefore his platoon, despite its sapper background, was an obvious choice for this infantry task. Miño:

> Soon the N Company Warrant Officer arrived and told me that Sub-Lieutenant Colombo wanted to see me. Outside the Command Post I saluted Colombo who ordered me to advance with an Army platoon and relieve Vázquez's position.[16]

Miño's platoon would lead this force which totalled seventy men. In the rear would be RI6 B Company's 3 Platoon under the command of Second-Lieutenant Esteban La Madrid. This unit had never been on Tumbledown before and neither had they carried out any reconnaissance on it in daylight. Therefore their knowledge of the terrain was nil. All this was yet another benefit that the Scots Guards derived from their diversionary attack on Pony's Pass. Furthermore neither Miño's nor La Madrid's platoon could communicate by radio with the N Company HQ in the event of any combat because they had no working radio batteries and had not been re-supplied with charged ones. Their mission was doomed to failure from the start.

Villarraza briefed Miño in the Command Post. Not unnaturally, the younger officer must have been most concerned and had the moral courage to make the logical point, according to Vázquez, 'that his troops were Engineers and not trained to lead a counter-attack. (But) Villarraza repeated the order (and) Miño stepped out of the Command Post to prepare'.[17] At this time La Madrid's platoon had arrived, and so the Army 3 Platoon Commander was also briefed by Villarraza. The latter had been talking with Major Oscar Jaimet. He was preparing also a platoon-sized force from his RI6 B Company group which had withdrawn from a position west of Two Sisters two nights before and was located in Moody Valley, north of Tumbledown's long north-east spur.

Back on Tumbledown's west end fifty men, less the two 'non-combatants' in Vázquez's trench and those wounded, now faced the second phase of Left Flank's assault. He reckoned it began at 05.00Z:

The British assault was repeated after intense but short-lasting artillery fire. But this time the assault came only from the southern flank (this being to the front of the platoon). There were possibly still some English troops left from the previous attack at the topographic ridge of Tumbledown, for immediately after the second assault began I started receiving also fire from the rear.

There ensued a fight with the same characteristics and intensity as the previous. The one thing that progressively began to look different, was that when previously each Scottish soldier had attacked the man who was right in front of him, in his direct path, now it was as if they had coordinated beforehand that they would be either two or three, firing from positions angling almost 180 degrees from the target and simultaneously attacking each one of us from these two or three positions. This happened after the assault wave had reached us, and the method was employed by the Scottish soldiers who were still intermingled with us. Just as in the first assault, some of them crossed over our position and moved to our rear.

I personally called on the radio to my immediate higher echelon in the chain of command and asked where the reinforcements were. They answered: 'Hold on, they are about to leave.'

Meanwhile the fighting carried on in the same way, with intense use of hand grenades by both sides and sporadic use of guided rockets/missiles fired by the Scots. One missile (possibly of the Milan type) [18] hit the machine-gun foxhole to my right, where Corporal Tejada and the machine-gun crew were. The round did not explode and the motor got consumed with the nose of the projectile buried into the wall of the foxhole. Given the short distance between opponents, the machine-guns were being fired without their support bases, right from the hip or using the trench defensive perimeter as supports.

Sub-Lieutenant Silva was constantly shouting, encouraging the soldiers who were next to him. In addition he took care to find replacements for the FAP, since at least two or probably three men of its crew were possibly killed between 05.00Z and 07.00Z. Second Petty Officer Castillo (with the section to my right), was approximately thirty metres from my position, fighting at least two Scottish soldiers who fired at him from ten or fifteen metres to his rear while sheltering behind a group of rocks. He was outside his foxhole. It was then that a Scottish soldier reached the foxhole of Conscript 1st Class Galarza (from Castillo's section) and started thrusting his bayonet into Galarza's chest. This was seen simultaneously by Castillo and machine-gun crew on the right, a foxhole apart from Galarza's. As the machine-gun swivelled to shoot the Scottish soldier, Castillo stood up and, turning towards his (mortally) wounded man, raised his gun to the shoulder and, aiming at the Scottish soldier, shouted 'Son of a bitch!' Castillo fell dead almost immediately. I was able to see that there was a big gap in his uniform around the area of the left shoulder blade.

For his outstanding bravery Castillo would receive a posthumous CHVC. But if the steadily diminishing number of men in Vázquez's platoon were to have a chance of holding their increasingly exposed position, then assistance would be required quickly. Vázquez:

> Realising I could not control the situation, and seeing now that hand-to-hand combat had become generalised again, I called personally on the radio once more. The dialogue was as follows:
> 'Where are the reinforcements?'
> 'They are on their way right now.'

On receipt of this (temporarily) encouraging information, Vázquez ratcheted up his initial tactic of using the platoon's 60mm mortar to bombard his own position. Two more calculated risks would be taken to buy more time with the other considerable Argentine indirect fire assets. He retained an admirable ability to make such ice-cool decisions in the crisis, despite mounting casualties and, in particular, the morale-crushing news of the death of a key officer who had been making a most valuable contribution to the fighting with similar extreme leadership qualities. Vázquez:

> Then I asked that the Battalion's 81mm mortars fired on my position to relieve the pressure of the attack I was receiving. They did this, but their fire did not manage to alleviate the situation.
> The combat continued with equal intensity. At approximately 06.00Z, an Army conscript came to me from the position of Sub-Lieutenant Silva. I was then busy with the attack on the left sector of the platoon, and this man whose name I never knew said to me: '*Capitán*, my *Subtieniente* has been hit.'
> 'Where was he hit?' I asked.
> He answered, 'He was hit in the chest, on the left side, and there's a lot of blood coming out from his mouth.'
> I assumed the Sub-Lieutenant had died. I ordered the conscript to try and return to his foxhole or get to any other he might be able to reach (there were English soldiers scattered between our foxholes, protected behind boulders and who had got mixed amongst us). I never knew what happened to that soldier.

Silva had picked up one of the wounded machine-gunners, taking the Marine to safety through heavy fire. With one of his soldiers, probably the same that reported the Army officer's death to Vázquez, Silva then returned to his position where he was killed.[19] Vázquez:

> The pressure was too strong and, assessing once again that we did not stand a chance, I asked my Commander to use field artillery on my position. I thought it was only a matter of time until all of us got killed. Lieutenant Ubaldo Pagani (BIM5 artillery officer) asked on the radio for my position's location.
> I became infuriated and told him that I had been in the same place since two months ago and it was just now that he was asking about it. I called him names. After a long while I received a radio call saying that artillery was going to fire on my position. I answered that I would make the corrections.[20]

Another who became involved in this fire mission was the 3 Platoon Commander, Second Petty Officer Luis Jorge Lucero. Dug-in at the north-eastern end of Tumbledown, his men were covering Moody Valley. However his task was difficult as both sides' artillery were engaging targets simultaneously. Lucero:

> The (Battalion) HQ asked me to adjust the fire onto Vazquez's position. I was confused then. I noticed the artillery was shooting short so I requested them to fire at a longer range. I was told then that they had not begun shooting yet. The reason was that this fire was coming from the British side.[21]

Vázquez was watching for the fall of shot:

> I never saw the first salvo.
> The second fell far away and I radioed an important correction.
> Finally they switched over to effective fire, beating all of the platoon's area.
> Although I tried again to warn my men to try and take cover, that warning did not reach most of them. It was impossible to keep effective communications by shouting out orders, because the continuity of the platoon's line had been already broken more than an hour before. This was due as much as to the effect of both our own casualties as well as the English soldiers' presence between the foxholes.
> After the war, an officer of the Airborne Artillery Group of the Argentine Army (whose codename was GATO 10) made some comments in the presence of Chaplain Commander Luis Manceñido, saying that he had personally listened to my request for artillery fire. Also if my memory serves me right, I think that a battery of the Argentine Army also fired their guns on my position. Although the artillery fire was accurate, it did not have the effect of the previous bombardment because, at that stage of events, there were already many English soldiers occupying our own foxholes. When one of ours got killed, they would remove the corpse and take the dead man's place in the now vacant foxhole. They also got in the few simulated or empty foxholes.

Kiszely concurred with Vázquez's judgement of this shelling, 'There was some indirect fire, but I don't think it affected us much.' Vázquez:

> Once again I got on the radio to Battalion and/or Company command, asking for reinforcements.
> They answered again, 'They already are on their way.'
> I asked about their recognition signal because I was facing a 360-degree front and they could then be met by friendly fire.
> They answered, 'Keep cool, you'll make them out!'

There appeared to be a number of other sub-units which might have been deployed to reinforce the beleaguered 4 Platoon. One was Lucero's 3 Platoon. But Vázquez was aware of the limitations:

The problem was that (this platoon) was in a static position (from) where the defence never moved reserve forces or positioned troops [...] we did not use them for reinforcing or counter-attacking Tumbledown's west spur.[22]

But matters were not going well either at Tumbledown's east end. The environment there was not conducive for preparing to go into battle. Men had to be briefed, a re-supply of ammunition made and magazines filled. Already it had been a long, dark night which was bitterly cold with frequent flurries of snow. The strong westerly wind not only increased the chill factor considerably, but cut straight into fatigued defenders' faces. Furthermore the unrelenting enemy naval gunfire and artillery bombardments had psychologically drained most to extremes. 'Ask of me anything but time, I will lose a man but never a moment' was a vital Napoleon Bonaparte maxim that did not exist here in this crucial situation. Time kept ticking by, but the advance of the counter-attack force had still not begun so, according to Vázquez, 'Villarraza called Miño once again [...] and asked why his orders had not been followed. Miño replied that he could not gather together all his and Sub-Lieutenant La Madrid's men. Villarraza repeated the order and Miño left again to prepare [...] [23]

On Sapper Hill there was also M Company which could have been deployed eastwards as reinforcements. Vázquez:

> Robacio ordered Lieutenant Binotti's M Company to get ready to counter-attack from Sapper Hill towards Tumbledown. That order was never carried out [...] The truth is that   [...] an order for a counter-attack was never issued and Argentine troops were never deployed towards Tumbledown.[24]

Left Flank Company began their final assault on Vázquez's position just before 08.00Z. Vázquez:

> Combat continued [...] the machine-gun to my right informed me that it had run out of rounds, or that the barrel was obstructed, I cannot remember exactly. I started progressively to lose contact with each end of the platoon, particularly with the right one which had been most punished. I began to notice that I was losing control of the platoon. At that time I was aware of an increase of pressure from our Scottish attackers [...]
>
> Between 08.00Z and 10.00Z, each remaining man was fighting alone for his foxhole. The possibility of mutual support had become almost non-existent, and my orders were not followed anymore. Again, and almost despairing, I personally called Battalion Command asking for reinforcements. They answered, 'They should be making contact with you at any moment.'
>
> Around (0.900Z),[25] the situation was as follows: there was almost no weapon fire, nobody followed my orders, I could see a few English among us and that the only remaining foxholes were the one to my right and the one to my left (both of these were double foxholes), and there was no support fire. At that time [26] I called my superior echelon (Company Commander/Battalion Commander) and had the following dialogue:
>
> 'Nobody is following my orders. I have no way to tell whether they are all dead,

have fallen prisoner to the enemy or simply do not want to obey me. There is almost no fighting now. I can hear the English shouting but cannot find out what is happening, nor understand what they say. Where are the reinforcements?'

'Hold on. They're already leaving for there.'

I uttered insults, tore the handset from the radio and threw myself down onto the bottom of the trench. As I had been speaking on the radio, I felt a violent underground explosion very close to my foxhole. Soon I learnt that the English had reached the foxhole on my left and thrown a phosphorous hand grenade inside it, which forced its two occupants to leave the foxhole trying to escape in spite of severe burns on their bodies. One of them was also hit in the back with shots from a Sterling submachine-gun as he ran out. All this was happening while I was on the radio.

I asked (NCO A) what he thought was our best possible next step and he said, 'I don't know sir, you're the one in command here.'

Vázquez added later, 'Although (NCO A) did not refuse to fight, he remained in the foxhole during the whole combat without firing a single shot. He froze. Only thirty-six men fought. Of those thirty-six, seventeen were KIA (killed in action), and five were wounded [...] Wounded and unharmed men were taken prisoner.' [27] The Argentine officer was about to meet his captor Lance-Corporal Simon McNeill who had shot, hand-grenaded and bayoneted his way en route to the 4 Platoon Commander's foxhole.[28] Vázquez:

I decided to take a peek outside and see what was happening. As I started to climb out from the foxhole, I met three English soldiers who were right at its top, apparently waiting for me to appear. Two of them were carrying FALs and one had a Sterling (submachine-gun). They were kneeling, aiming at me with their weapons, fifty centimetres from my face. Keeping both my hands on the edge of the foxhole, I lowered my head and said to (NCO A), 'I'm going to step out. If they kill me they'll also kill you, so you just take hold of my weapon and kill them before they do.'

I left the foxhole with my hands up, identified myself as the one in command of all the men who were fighting in that sector and requested permission to speak with my men.

They granted this, and climbing onto the defence mound dug around my position, I shouted, 'Listen here, 4 Platoon, I am Sub-Lieutenant Vázquez. The combat has ended. Lay down your weapons and approach my foxhole. Stay calm, lives are going to be respected.'

Only six men came forward.[29]

All the area was scattered with English personal equipment, there were dead and injured who screamed and started receiving first aid.

Not surprisingly, given the stress of battle, McNeill had a slightly different perception of what happened then:

He did not do it in quite the way he describes, i.e. 'I want to speak to my men' [...] But that is a small point. Let him remember it the way he describes, I think he has earned that one. I never saw six men come forward but, to be fair, could not hang around. I had to catch up then with the Company Commander

As described earlier, McNeill did re-join Kiszely and the other five Scots Guardsmen who were to climb the east summit eventually.[30] But some of Vázquez's platoon had been able to fall back and continue fighting. This group included Conscript Jorge Sánchez. His account and circumstantial evidence points to the probability that he killed Mitchell and wounded Guardsman Binnie:

Many of my comrades became prisoners, others were also wounded. I had a single clip (of ammunition) left while standing in my foxhole. I could see bulky shapes gathering to attack my position (and) decided to get out. In doing this I fired the whole clip. It was a surprise for my enemies. I could see many who fell, but they reacted quickly and began to pursue me. I was trying to get to 2 Platoon's position as it had not yet begun to fight. As I was running down the hill I heard an explosion and fell, but found that I had no wounds and kept on running. About fifty metres behind somewhere several of the Scots were after me. I could hear machine-gun bursts passing over my head.

Another grenade exploded close by and I felt as if a big hand had stopped me by throwing me upwards. My eyes were full of dust and mud, but I felt no pain nor could feel blood anywhere on my body. I started to run again and was able to escape my pursuers in the darkness. I arrived at the positions of 2 Platoon and desperately shouted that I was an Argentine of 4 Platoon. Fortunately they did not shoot me, and shortly afterwards I received another gun to continue the combat.[31]

It must have been when Left Flank Company began their final assault on Vázquez's platoon that the Argentine counter-attack force departed from Tumbledown's east end. Three fatally slow hours had passed since Villarraza's initial briefing. Miño:

Demarco and I were ahead of the platoon. As we advanced, having already covered some 600-800 metres, those of us wearing night vision goggles made out a group of men reclining against a stone wall. We stopped and heard somebody on the left asking who we were in English. Midshipman Marcelo Demarco, who spoke very good English, answered that we were Argentines. The second time he spoke we threw three hand grenades. Two exploded. Immediately an exchange of hand grenades followed and we began firing at each other with our automatic weapons.[32]

Miño's contact took place by a huge rock located a short distance south of Tumbledown's east summit. It had been previously designated as the BIM5 Battalion HQ's alternative (unused) observation post.[33] The ensuing firefight with the Scots Guards Left Flank 14 Platoon was at a point-blank range of ten metres.[34] Vázquez believed that 'before arriving at that place, Sub-Lieutenant La Madrid's soldiers ran away, so when he arrived he was just with the Engineers. Nobody from the Army stayed with him'.[35] On the contrary, this was not so. La Madrid had begun to engage targets on the east summit – and his platoon would also become involved in the fighting. Miño:

I had the impression that we were being fired at by two or three light rifles and a MAG. Corporal José Horacio Robles, a member of our platoon, was firing with his machine-gun from its bipod stand. Corporal Valdez, aided by two fusiliers, was firing rifle grenades. We took cover behind a rock. At my side Midshipman Demarco was vomiting. Tracer fire went over our heads. They came at first from a single sector, but then the Brits positioned a second fire base and the rounds started coming from different directions.

Sometime during this, an explosion knocked me down and stunned me. When I came to, I moved over to Corporal Sánchez and ordered him to go to the N Company Command Post and tell them we were in combat. I told Petty Officer Eduardo Ponce to fall back to the blocking position with the conscripts who had taken cover from the fire. Our firing had practically ceased. Corporal Valdez had six or seven conscripts with him. Corporal Robles was isolated with two conscripts. I grabbed Midshipman Demarco's hand and told him to try and get to the N Company's Command Post. Robles lay and fired his machine-gun, and two conscripts were calmly firing as well. One machine-gun fired first, and then the other. Bullet strikes kicked up the snow like perfect shafts of light. Carrying two machine-gun belts of ammunition and keeping down, I crawled to where Robles was and told him to lift his machine-gun from its position. The two conscripts gathered up some of the loose ammunition on the ground and we four crawled out, one after the other, from that unprotected position. No automatic weapons were being fired at us then, but we could feel artillery fire coming in very close. Completely wet from sweat, we managed to get safely into cover and somehow found Valdez and his conscripts. Corporal Sánchez then returned and told me that there was nobody in the N Company Command Post.

Dawn was breaking and tracer fired far above us. Once we arrived at the blocking position, I counted that all the Marines were in. Two of our conscripts had light injuries. Corporal Robles had sustained a severe blow, and I was still unaware of the shrapnel in my leg. We gathered our backpacks and part of the ammo (machine-gun belts and hand grenades) and in file moved down Tumbledown to the BIM5 Battalion Command Post. Our radio communications were useless, due both to jamming interference and a lack of batteries already as from 13 June. It was when I stumbled on the snow and put my hand on the ground to get up again, that I touched my blood. I had been wounded, but did not know where or how badly. The only thing I wanted was to get to a hospital quickly. When on the road we met Ponce and Demarco. All in the platoon were all alive and well, wore helmets and carried their weapons. We did not know exactly what had we done. What everyone saw that morning was kept to ourselves and we never talked about it. [36]

Miño's battle and war was over. Nearly three decades later he asked that this postscript be added:

> (I want) to thank the conscripts who were with me. All they did was of unmatched quality. Their professional work saved lives. The landmines were exactly where they were supposed to be nearly thirty years later. They grew up in a hard environment. You may count on me if there is anything I can do to mitigate the pain caused. Even today [...] I cannot find the proper way to address the British families who lost a son, a brother or a father.[37]

As first light began to appear just after 10.00Z on 14 June 1982, the captured Vázquez was escorted further down the western end of Tumbledown. Because of his officer status he was taken to the Scots Guards Commanding Officer Lieutenant-Colonel Mike Scott in the Battalion Tactical HQ. This had moved up some time before from Goat Ridge and was now located at an outcrop of rock in the saddle between G and Left Flank Companies. After arrival there, Scott and his team had been subjected to some perilously close enemy shelling. But now as Right Flank Company's assault was about to start just before 10.30Z, some rapid intelligence was needed off Vázquez, such as a map showing the positions of his men. Until he talked to the six-foot four-inch Anti-Tank Platoon Commander Captain Jeremy Campbell-Lamerton (of rugby fame) who spoke Spanish, Vázquez was uncooperative. According to Scott, 'He then realised, that for him, the war was over.' But with the benefit of hindsight, Scott's observation requires a correction. It was Vázquez's *battle* that was over. Once back in Argentina his war would continue.

McNeill had every right to be concerned about 4 Platoon's will to fight. A tiresome sniper was still firing in the direction of Tac HQ. Campbell-Lamerton told Vázquez to get out into the open in the gully by the HQ and order this man to stop otherwise they would have to do something about it. Apparently although Vázquez initially refused, the Scots Guards officer's determined face changed the BIM5 officer's mind and, with trepidation, he moved courageously out into the gully to shout up at the rocks where the sniper was located.[38] Scott provided another version in that this 'did not prove necessary as the culprit either buggered off or surrendered'. Perhaps the latter saw also the Scots Guards Operations Officer, Captain Tim Spicer, armed with his CO's personal M-79 grenade launcher coming up the rocks to hunt for the sniper.[39] At least one Guardsman had been hit by him. This was G Company's Gordon Hoggan, who was badly wounded in the side of his body wound from a bullet ricochet off a rock. But Vázquez was more concerned with his platoon:

> I asked the senior-ranking Scottish officer to let me inspect the foxholes, for it was possible that they still held some of my wounded men. This he would not permit, saying that they would take care of that afterwards. I was only allowed to go over the dead bodies of those men who were out of the foxholes. Regrettably, none of the identity tags of the Argentine Army soldiers were engraved with their data, for which I was never able to complete the death roll of the platoon.
>
> The same British officer took to me to where the body of Conscript Héctor Cerles lay. He was lying on his back, his right arm raised and a hand grenade in it.

It took me a while to realise that he was dead. I removed the grenade from his grasp and threw it down on the ground.

Vázquez believed, incorrectly, that his platoon had been attacked throughout the night by the entire Scots Guards battalion plus some Gurkhas:

> After the war, through a British officer who took part in this attack, I learnt that the (first) assault was carried out by a Company of the 2nd Battalion, Scots Guards, with some elements of the Gurkha Regiment. The second assault at 05.00Z was executed by another Company of the Scottish Battalion, and the third assault (approximately at 07.00Z) by the third Company of that unit.[40]

Vázquez described his perception of BIM5's final actions:

> Nobody ordered the withdrawal of BIM5, but the N and M Company Commanders, Lieutenant Villarraza and Lieutenant Binotti (the original M Company Commander, Lieutenant Cionchi, was replaced on 13 June at night by Binotti because the former said 'he was sick'), withdrew of their own will. At approx. 0700Z-0800Z on 14 June, N Company positions were left without any commanders to give orders, and they started a disorganised withdrawal towards the city of Puerto Argentino when they saw the approach of British soldiers from the west end of Tumbledown. When the Scots Guards arrived at the N Company HQ (on the east side of Tumbledown), the HQ members withdrew to Puerto Argentino with 3 Platoon. But 1 and 2 Platoons did not receive any orders and they remained in their positions until the next morning, without knowing that their Company Commander was not there anymore [...] [41]

As for the RI6 B Company group commanded by Major Jaimet, there were more harsh words about them from Vázquez:

> During the night (of the battle) Major Jaimet told Lieutenant Villarraza, '*Tuerto, esto no da para más, vayámonos a la mierda* (One-Eyed, this is all over, let's get the shit out of here).' Villarraza did not pay any attention to him, but Jaimet left Tumbledown with the rest of his Company. Neither he nor his troops were ever involved in combat.[42]

However the indignant Vázquez was again mistaken because the platoon-sized force led by Jaimet *did* reach a position just north of Tumbledown's east end and, at dawn, exchanged fire with a platoon of the Scots Guards Right Flank Company. But it was all too little and too late. Jaimet was a realist, not a coward. The Scots Guards held the high ground exactly in accordance with Sun Tzu's view of how the victorious army should retain the advantage of position 'in sum, the army likes the high and hates the low, values *yang* and disdains *yin*'.[43] So Jaimet concentrated instead on ensuring that the remnants of La Madrid's platoon managed to withdraw eastwards from Tumbledown, whereupon Jaimet's force followed suit. Vázquez placed the BIM5 general withdrawal into perspective:

What Robacio describes as an organised BIM5 withdrawal to Puerto Argentino was, in fact, the withdrawal of a Company that was never engaged in combat (M Company). Lieutenant Koch received the order to cover the Company while they were withdrawing. At that moment, Koch saw two British helicopters at 1,000 metres from his position. He opened fire with two machine-guns (MAG), hitting one of them while it was on the ground. This was the last action in combat from BIM5.[44]

Captain Ian Bryden collected the prisoners and walking wounded and took them back to the Regimental Police and RAP. They were then moved back to Fitzroy. There, in this immediate post-combat period, Vázquez was subjected to alleged shameful abuse from certain other British troops:

> All the survivors of 4 Platoon were taken behind the British lines, first to a first aid post for the wounded, and then to a Prisoners Transitory Area located in Fitzroy and finally to San Carlos (at Ajax Bay) to another prisoner camp [...] at the first aid post for the wounded my people were recognised by troops of the Scottish Battalion, who ordered all mistreatment to stop immediately [...] it was at this same camp where I was inconsiderately hit by airborne officers and later questioned. When I refused to give information, I was put before a mock firing squad that fired blanks at me. All this took place before the Scots arrived at the place.

But so impressed with the treatment he received from his battlefield captors, Vázquez commented that, 'During and after the war, I received more deference and respect from the Scots Guards than from my country and the Argentine Navy.' [45] He and 1,120 other prisoners were rapidly repatriated to Argentina. They embarked aboard the P & O liner SS *Canberra* before dark on 15 June, sailing the following day from San Carlos Water to Stanley. There another 3,046 prisoners were embarked. *Canberra* sailed for Argentina on 18 June, arriving the next day at Puerto Madryn. Vázquez was immediately transported to the Almirante Marcos Zar Naval Air Base at Trelew and debriefed there by Naval Intelligence officers. Returning to Puerto Belgrano, he was subjected to another debriefing by senior officers and officers at the Command Building of the Naval Infantry before rejoining the same course at the Officers Training School that he had been on prior to mobilisation. There was an interview with the Director of the Basic Course about his unique battle experiences, but some of his instructors must have considered him a 'threat' to their own professional knowledge on war-fighting. He had become, in many respects, far better qualified than them. He had done it. They had not. But strangely one item was missing. There had been no formal BIM5 requirement for him to submit either a combat report about his actions on Tumbledown, or fitness reports on the performance of personnel under his command during the war. Despite requesting instructions from Robacio and being told that such reports were not required, with characteristic determination Vázquez nonetheless wrote and submitted them through his chain of command.

What happened next tested Vázquez's mettle to the utmost. He was ordered to the Head of the Naval Infantry's office and, during the subsequent interview, told that the content of his report reflected badly on the Marines' image. An invitation was extended to review and rewrite it in different terms. Vázquez refused. He continued to wage this war for the true facts concerning his surviving and dead men of 4 Platoon. After all, his report only repeated what had been told to all those who had debriefed him. Twice more he was interviewed by the same Rear-Admiral. Twice more he refused the same invitation. His mindset was unshakeable. The Rear-Admiral could not have been aware of the effect that Tumbledown combat had on Vázquez's existential authority.

The Acting Sub-Lieutenant then courageously repeated his report's content at a conference held in the Officers' Training School of the Navy at which the Commander, Naval Operations was present as well as a large number of officers. Later Vázquez became outraged on learning that (NCO A) had been awarded a Navy-sponsored MVC, despite his lack-lustre performance on Tumbledown and adverse fitness report. Protesting to Robacio about this perverse decoration, Vázquez was told the 'error' would be corrected, but then later informed it would not be possible after all. Done was done.

More anger was generated by the fact that (Officer B), the other 'non-combatant' in Vázquez's foxhole, and Jaimet, the reserve Commanding Officer of the RI6 B Company group, had both been awarded an MVC. Then, long after his medal had been awarded, Vázquez received the text of its accompanying citation. This wrongly stated that he had withdrawn his platoon from the west end of Tumbledown during the battle, thereby giving a totally distorted picture of the resistance made there. Furthermore the citation of Second Petty Officer Castillo's decoration did not depict the heroic circumstances in which he died, and Sub-Lieutenant Oscar Silva's citation to his posthumous MVC weirdly indicated that Silva had died in action on 11 June at Mount Harriet. Vázquez was infuriated. The Army officer had been killed in combat when under *his* command. But again all Vázquez's requests were turned down.

The British media were interested in the exploits of Argentina's hero of the Tumbledown battle. In 1984 Vázquez appeared before a BBC TV team at a ranch in Buenos Aires province. There, in the presence of a Naval Intelligence officer, he met a Scots Guards officer who had fought on Tumbledown. They discussed the battle which included aspects from Vázquez's combat report. Three years later when a Sub-Lieutenant at the Naval Military Academy, he was interviewed by Martin Middlebrook in the Edificio Libertad (Navy HQ in Buenos Aires). Four senior Argentine officers were present. All that Vázquez said about the Tumbledown battle was corroborated by the well-informed British historian. The latter even corrected Vázquez about the timings of actions carried out by his platoon in the battle. He never read Middlebrook's subsequent book, but twenty years later I sent Vázquez the relevant extracts. His opinion was forthright:

This is how the Navy created this story for public opinion, and for the 'competition' between the three different services [...] for merit in war: a story where an entire Marine Battalion of heroes appears to be fighting under Commander Robacio's orders. The truth is that only fifty men of the 5th Marine Infantry Battalion engaged in combat: 4 Platoon and a section (10 men) of Obra Company.[46] Due to the fact that this version of the history was politically convenient for the Argentine Navy and, even knowing it was not true, they accepted and turned it into the official version.

[...] Even though after the Malvinas War I held a high prestige with the officers and non-commissioned officers of the Navy for my actions during the war and, based on the fact that my peers know the true story about the 5th Marine Infantry Battalion, those actions were not revealed and always concealed. Many times during my career I have written official papers explaining the real facts. But the Army never paid attention to them. Even though they have told me in person that I was right in my arguments, knowledge about the truth would only cause damage to the institutional image because the official version of the war did not match the real facts.[47]

Vázquez become a father in 1986. His wife, Guadalupe, gave birth to Carlos Horacio and, six years later, his second son Guillermo Federico. His career progressed and he was appointed the Argentine Defence Attaché to Bolivia in the late-1990s. María Paz, his daughter, was born in Bolivia in 2000 before he assumed command of BIM5 in Río Grande. I was able to establish contact with his eldest son much later (in March 2009). Carlos Horacio, who was a Midshipman in the Argentine Navy, gave me this insight to his father's second battle:

Sometimes my dad takes a lot of time to reply your e-mails [...] because he feels sad and does not want to write at that moment (most of the times). I am writing to you so you do not think that he does not write because he does not want to help you or he is mad at you.

The Malvinas is an extremely sensitive topic for him [...] Try to place yourself a second in his shoes. It is like if you made a heroic act in combat, and all your prestige and merit for doing that is divided between a lot of people that did not do anything, or were cowards.

In 2002, twenty years after the war, my dad was BIM5's CO. In the ceremony for the twentieth anniversary more or less twenty war veterans came to me (some of them knew I was his son, but not all of them) and told me a lot of things about the war. They said a lot of bad things about [...] other (officers). And they talked about my dad like if he was God. One of them, I cannot remember his name, was an Army radio operator. He had one eye, four missing fingers and a missing leg due to the artillery fire. I spent a lot of time with him. He told me that night he heard all the radio communications at Tumbledown. He said that he cannot believe why my dad did not kill all the people telling lies about Tumbledown (and) making false stories that never existed, when 'the reality is that they ran away when they saw the first British soldier, but your father stayed over there until the British took him out from his trench without ammo'.

That day I felt the same way that my dad did, the frustration of knowing that an entire Battalion took the glory of just one platoon. And people from 4 Platoon that never engaged in combat or ran away received more tribute than the soldiers who stayed there fighting. I felt very bad.

I hope that with this e-mail you can understand why my dad feels disappointed every time somebody talks to him about Malvinas or you write to him. That is the reason why he takes a long time to write to you. He wants to help you with the book, but sometimes he feels very bad and does not want to talk about it with anybody when he is in that mood, not even myself.[48]

The Argentine Navy should have listened to Vázquez and taken the appropriate corrective actions. But his existential authority and continuing complaints, even to Admiral Jorge Godoy, the Chief of Staff of the Argentine Navy,[49] in October 2004 had no effect:

> After the war I lived through different phases of my life. First I trusted my superior officers while waiting during those months for somebody to ask me for a report about what happened during the battle. When I realised nobody was going to ask me for that and everyone was telling a very different story, I sent the reports without waiting for my superiors to ask me for them.
>
> Since that moment I lived many years without trusting my superiors in the Navy, and that affected also my personal life. So I started a part of my life when I tried to forget everything, because that was the only way to proceed day after day with a 'real story' that was not real about what happened during the war. At that time I kept suffering bitterness and disappointments each time that, inside and outside the Navy, I was confronted with allegedly historical texts of authors who claimed for themselves underserved merits, ignoring the true leading roles of the men who did them. About that, I want to say that the 2nd Battalion, Scots Guards was stopped for eight hours[50] in hand-to-hand combat by a platoon, not the entire BIM5 as everyone says.
>
> Despite that I kept silent, trusting that someday the Navy would tell the true story of what happened, and at least give correct recognition to the soldiers who gave the Marine Corps the prestige that it has today. Notwithstanding that, the years went by without any news. I watched the strengthening of the historical version which ignores the main characters while assigning the merits of 4 Platoon to other people. 4 Platoon was the only main unit involved in the biggest infantry battle that the Marine Corps ever had since its creation.
>
> Assuming the responsibility I have for being the leader of the people who served in 4 Platoon at Tumbledown and, for what I consider to be also a moral duty at the end of my naval career, it is my duty to try and do justice to those who gave more than duty required and which the Navy did not recognise.

But neither did he succeed in his request that the correct recognition be given to four extremely brave 4 Platoon men, despite writing convincing 'citations' for them.[51] It is a paradox that post-traumatic growth, although a 'good news' story compared to PTSD despair, can also lead to a dangerous personal situation as Argentina's hero of the Tumbledown battle was about to experience. Working in an intelligence unit at the Almirante Marcos Zar Naval Base in Trelew, he was probably now (wrongly) perceived as a threat to the establishment. Vázquez:

In 2006, an official investigation was started against me in Trelew for having started presumed internal political intelligence activities, ordered by the High Command, whereby I was accused of wrongly developing a public function. This resulted in my not being assigned command of a first-class unit, as appropriate for my rank. The Navy did nothing to show that I was just obeying orders given by its High Staff. What is worse they tried to make me responsible for following those orders.[52]

I sympathised with his predicament. He gave me a final summary of the in-fighting amongst the various Services of the Argentine Armed Forces in the aftermath of the war and the way in which the war's history was recorded:

I think that sometimes I assume you know things that I take for granted and are not familiar with you back there in Norway. After the war in Argentina, fights developed between the military institutions because of the prestige among each Service. Once the war ended, the Service that lost more prestige was the Army. And the most prestigious one was the Air Force. The Navy's prestige was affected in a bad way especially because of the Fleet participation. But the Naval Aviation had a good development (in fact, superior to that of the Air Force) as did the Marines with BIM5 (due to the combat at Tumbledown). The fights for prestige between them involved the following actions in each Service: they tried to hide cowardly actions [...] modified the story of the operations during the war [...] made up false heroic stories [...] turned regular facts into heroic stories [...] invented a lot of non-existent actions to give military decorations [...] books were written with false heroic stories [...] and they made an official version of the story that has nothing to do with reality. For example, you can read in the official Army version of (the 6th Infantry Regiment) B Company counter-attack led by Major Jaimet, and [...] see in the drawings that he reached the western end of Tumbledown and rescued me and my platoon.

Why am I telling you this? Because you are trying to compare things that I have lived with that are based on facts given by these false versions of the war.

Mike, I think distance and acknowledgment of the real facts that occurred in Argentina after the war do not allow you to understand that you might be the only Englishman having access to these [...] facts that were hidden from public knowledge, including the Argentine public. I am tired of reading lies in Argentina and that is the reason for my interest in letting you know all this. Because here it is impossible to discuss the official version due to the institutional and personal exposure this would involve.[53]

And a crystal-clear opinion of Robacio's book:

What (Robacio) says about N Company, BIM5 is incomplete [...] The (stated) magnitudes of the engagements are not true, nor are the roles played by other sub-units and companies who are portrayed as having played a much larger role than the one they had. (He) presents facts as having implicitly taken place, where in reality they never did. (He) twists timetables, thus extending the time of actions that lasted for half an hour and making them appear as lasting for three or four hours. (By) doing this he modifies the magnitude of engagements.[54]

And a postscript, after I sent him final drafts of this and the previous chapter:

While it was great to hear from you, and you have allowed me to meet your family with that beautiful photo that you sent us, sometimes is not easy for me to answer you and talk about what happened in the war because it leads me to remember what was done by my comrades after the war in distorting the story. That gives me a pain that I prefer to forget while I can [...]

I felt a deep satisfaction to see, perhaps for the first time, the truth written of what happened on Tumbledown [...] and thank you for respecting and believing in the things I told you. I imagine it would not have been easy at a distance to ascertain the truth among so many different versions you have had to compare. From [...] both chapters, I think you have made a good approximation to what I believe is the truth [..] and wish that it spreads as it deserves to my country, and particularly to Argentina's Navy which is what most interests me.

It is my belief that a soldier is always looking for the recognition of their comrades. I think this has always been the case. In war one does one's duty so as not to fail one's comrades. The flag is too far from one to die for it. We just die for our comrades, and all we ask in return is recognition from them who are the only ones able to understand the sacrifice [...] the Navy, because it suited them better at that time, took this recognition from me. I have a great pain that will accompany me until the last day of life.

Have you ever read the *Ode to Tumbledown*? It was written by a Scots Guardsman.[55] That is recognition. It was also recognition the way that the Scots Guards treated me after the battle. Also Army officers from Chile sent me invitations to talk about the war and gave me a present in recognition. I had been told that in the War College of the Chilean Navy they study that battle. All those things are recognition. But my Navy did not do anything. It is cruel.[56]

His youngest son, 'Guille' (Guillermo Federico), also wrote to me several years later and gave a most disturbing update on Argentina's hero of the Tumbledown battle:

I want to thank you for writing to my father. He is going through a really hard time (you surely know what am I talking about) and apart from your wonderful holidays, letting my father know you are interested in him and sending him every year a Christmas card, makes him realise that he's not alone and not a fool after all the things that have happened. You make him feel better with himself.[57]

Thanks for all you are doing for my father (telling the truth about the Falklands/Malvinas) and for all the wonderful things you said about him. It makes me proud to be his son. My dad's trial in which he is charged with illegal internal political intelligence activities, i.e. counter-intelligence, begins in March 2012. The Commander of the Navy at the end of (2011) has been retired too and is involved in the trial that concerns my father. The entire promotion (group) of my father and two more below his were retired too.

My father knew he was going to be retired from the Navy soon, but the main problem is the trial (he can go to jail) and what the economic problems of being retired will mean when living on fifty percent of his salary. At the moment he is just trying to enjoy his retirement, but it will get hard in a month. Let us hope everything goes fine, because with this Government ruling, I can only expect a bad future for us military people.[58]

The Tumbledown combat and utter frustration rages on for Vázquez. It includes the prospect of having to fight one more major battle in his life. Carlos Daniel Vázquez is an Argentine Marine at heart and an exceptionally brave man. So from one Falkland-Malvinas veteran to another I wish him the best of luck.

But back in 1982 there *was* also brave resistance made by Sub-Lieutenant Esteban La Madrid's 3 Platoon of B Company, RI6 just before that 14 June dawn on the east end of Tumbledown. And he will tell the complete story of their bloody fight, which contains many hitherto untold details.

Notes

1. *The Art of War*, Chapter 11 – The Nine Grounds.
2. E-mail dated 23 January 2012.
3. *Ibid.*
4. E-mail dated 26 October 2011.
5. *Ibid.* dated 18 January 2012.
6. The author's only comment is reserved for the apparent (and incongruous) non-infantry training of conscript Argentine Marine Amphibious Engineers prior to the war. In comparison British Army doctrine demanded (and still does) that all its regular soldiers undergo basic infantry training regardless of the nature of their future military careers and trades. Hence Steve Cocks, who was a Royal Army Pay Corps Lance-Corporal, fought in the Scots Guards Right Flank Company as an infantry soldier. Furthermore the delay imposed on the Scots Guards Left Flank Company's in making their final all-out attack on Vázquez's platoon was causing major concern at the 5th Infantry Brigade Tactical HQ on Mount Harriet. Therefore a contingency plan was already in the embryo stage of being formed whereby, in the event of a stalemate on Tumbledown, 9 Parachute Squadron, Royal Engineers would be converted to an infantry company with a mission to participate in a second attack on Tumbledown (and Vázquez's position) during the following night of 14/15 June. Unlike Miño's Marine Amphibious Engineer platoon, both are great examples of the British Army regular soldier's and Royal Engineers' flexibility.
7. The local time of midnight (03.00Z) comes from Miño's original detailed account sent to the author shortly after the latter's fourth visit to Argentina in March/April 2007.
8. E-mail dated 26 October 2011.
9. As Miño stated, he received an authorisation to withdraw from Sub-Lieutenant

Colombo, the N Company 2IC.

10. E-mails dated 10 September 2007 and 10 March 2009. Robacio (*Desde el Frente*, pp 260, 264, 278, and 288) is misleading about Miño's actions in these first hours of combat. He states that between 01.30Z to 02.00Z Miño's 5 Platoon was attacked by the Gurkhas. The fighting is alleged to have continued until Miño was ordered to withdraw between 04.00Z to 04.30Z. This never happened. The Gurkhas were still four kilometres away on the western end of Goat Ridge in their Forming Up Point and did not move out until 05.00Z.

11. E-mail dated 18 January 2012.

12. *The Art of War*, Chapter 11 – The Nine Grounds.

13. *Ibid.*

14. *The Fight for the 'Malvinas': The Argentine Forces in the Falklands War*, p. 258.

15. E-mail dated 27 October 2011.

16. *Ibid.* dated 26 October 2011.

17. E-mail dated 10 March 2009.

18. No Milan missiles were used. It was a LAW 66mm rocket that malfunctioned.

19. *5th Infantry Brigade in the Falklands*, p. 196.

20. *Razor's Edge* (pp. 288 and 292) is misleading in its claim that Vázquez 'had the utmost difficulty persuading his own gunners and mortar men to fire on his position'.

21. E-mail dated 29 May 2006.

22. *Ibid.* dated 6 September 2007.

23. *Ibid.* dated 10 March 2010.

24. Vázquez was insistent about the alleged non-existent Argentine Army combat. He based his view on the opinion of the N Company 2IC, Sub-Lieutenant Osvaldo Colombo. The latter would become a Rear-Admiral and Commander of the Argentine Marine Corps: he had been also a Naval Military Academy classmate of Diego García Quiroga. It is strange Colombo ignores the true historical facts, but perhaps this had something to do with the Marine Corps disdain of the Army. In an e-mail dated 21 April 2009, Vázquez informed the author:

> A few days ago I asked Rear-Admiral Osvaldo Colombo, and he is sure there was no combat at the east end of Tumbledown. He fell back with the last men that were there from the Company HQ. He told me that the British arrived at the east end and started shooting over their heads, while the Argentine soldiers fell back. He is sure, with the exception of soldiers firing while falling back, that nobody made any resistance at the east end.

It took the author time and effort to persuade Vázquez that La Madrid's platoon had actually fought against the Scots Guards Right Flank Company.

25. E-mail dated 6 September 2009.

26. Vázquez's account incorrectly states 10.00Z. As mentioned in Chapter 3, his final radio conversation with his N Company Commander occurred at 09.00Z.

27. These figures are incorrect. Forty-five men (less the two 'non-combatants' in Vázquez's foxhole) fought – fifteen were killed, five were wounded and four went missing. Ten of those killed were Army soldiers. Another ten Marines from

the 60mm mortar section on the centre of Tumbledown reinforced Vázquez's platoon midway through the battle. *Razor's Edge* (p. 296) incorrectly gives the casualty figures as 'eight of (Vazquez's) men dead, (and) five wounded'.

28. *Razor's Edge* (p. 296) also incorrectly states: 'Vazquez surrendered at dawn'. In reality this occurred two hours before.

29. *Ibid.* also incorrectly states: 'four men responded'.

30. *Ibid.* also incorrectly states: 'With Miño's men gone and Vázquez's left behind, it must have been Silva's orphaned men who made the Scots fight for every inch of the defile to the summit, killing Lance-Sergeant Mitchell and wounding several others.' However Silva's five men had died at least five hours before.

31. *Desde el Frente*, p. 314.

32. E-mail dated 26 October 2011.

33. From an e-mail (dated 1 March 2009) sent by Vázquez. Guardsman Fisher, the machine-gunner to whom Steve Cocks had supplied ammunition during Right Flank's attack would, a short time later, use this particular rock as cover. Cocks also took a photo of it during the Falklands 25 Pilgrimage and, sixteen months later, located the rock on Google Earth for the author.

34. From the author's conversation with Miño in Buenos Aires on 28 March 2007:

35. E-mail dated 10 March 2009.

36. *Ibid.* dated 26 October 2011.

37. *Ibid.* dated 27 October 2011. Miño retired from the Marine Corps on 30 December 2011.

38. *Razor's Edge* (p. 309-310) gives the misleading impression that the location of this sniper (later killed by Left Flank Company) was confined to the east end of Tumbledown.

39. This and the previous paragraph are based partly on two e-mails dated 13 and 14 March 2009 from Mike Scott.

40. The author corrected (by e-mail) Vázquez's alleged sighting of Gurkhas in the first assault. In an e-mail dated 4 September 2007, he replied:

   In the first of those three attacks I saw short soldiers mixed among the Scots who had oriental features. If you say they were not Gurkhas I guess you must be right. In the following two attacks I saw no more soldiers with such features. I was attacked solely by the Scots Guards. When I was taken prisoner a British officer told me that the Guards received a Gurkha reinforcement.

   The 'Gurkha reinforcement' was A Company. It remained in reserve to the Scots Guards and never actually reinforced them during the battle.

41. E-mail dated 8 March 2009.

42. *Ibid.* dated 6 May 2010.

43. *The Art of War*, Chapter 9 – Moving the Army.

44. E-mail dated 8 March 2009.

45. *Ibid.* dated 7 March 2009.

46. To be more precise, if the Argentine Army soldiers are excluded from 4 Platoon's Order of Battle and 60mm mortar section of fifteen men are added, then only thirty-seven Marine infantrymen (less NCO A) engaged the Scots Guards in direct combat on Tumbledown. To this figure should be added O

Company at Pony's Pass. The author disagrees with Vázquez and is convinced there were considerably more than just ten O Company Marines involved in direct combat with the composite Scots Guards platoon.

47. E-mail dated 12 February 2009.

48. *Ibid.* dated 28 March 2009.

49. British equivalent: Admiral of the Fleet.

50. This is incorrect. Vázquez's platoon delayed Left Flank Company for about six and a half hours.

51. These 'citations' read:

Sub-Lieutenant Oscar Silva: Although his original unit had retreated the previous day, he asked to join a Marine platoon to continue fighting. Resisting two enemy attacks in hand-to-hand bayonet fighting, he was constantly an example to his soldiers until he died from enemy fire.

Second Corporal Amílcar Tejada: Checked out a telephone line (when) under enemy artillery fire (and) assumed the role of section commander when the original commander died. He was an example to his soldiers without care for his life in resisting three enemy hand-to-hand attacks by bayonet, enduring enemy artillery fire, and only surrendered when he ran out of ammunition and (on) being ordered (to do so) by his platoon commander.

Conscript Ramón Rotela: As chief of the mortar, he obeyed his platoon commander in firing fifty-four bombs onto his own position without consideration for his own safety. He resisted three British assaults in hand-to-hand bayonet fighting while enduring overwhelming fire from his own artillery. He surrendered his position only after exhausting his ammunition and following the orders of his platoon commander.

Conscript Pablo Rodríguez: Although wounded in the leg by gunfire the previous day, he said nothing in order not to give problems to the platoon although knowing that he could be evacuated. He stayed in his position fighting all the night until he was wounded again, and fell unconscious while resisting three British attacks under artillery fire.

52. E-mail dated 27 February 2009. The investigation into domestic spying by the Navy [...] was spurred by a criminal complaint presented by the Centre for Legal and Social Studies think-tank and a young seaman who had refused to take part in the illegal espionage. An intelligence unit at the Almirante Marcos Zar naval base in south Argentine was found to have a file on the-then President Néstor Kirchner detailing his political activities as far back as the 1970s. (*MercoPress, South Atlantic News Agency*, Montevideo, 4 January 2012.) On 23 December 2011 by way of Decree 247, President Cristina Fernández de Kirchner and Defence Minister Arturo Puricelli, accepted the request for the 'voluntary removal' of Admiral Jorge Godoy – therefore 'relieving him of his duties as Navy General' after being accused of illegal espionage (*Buenos Aires Herald,* 23 December 2011.) Prohibited by Argentina's law, the alleged practices of 'domestic intelligence' were against politicians, civic activists and human rights organisations in the years between 2003 and 2006. Admiral Godoy was eight years in the post and became famous for publicly admitting and apologizing in March 2004 for the Argentine Navy's

role and responsibility in killings, disappearances and torture during the military regime. He also accepted that the notorious Navy's Mechanical School and one of the major torture centres be converted into a Space for Memory Museum. Godoy's replacement, Rear-Admiral Carlos Paz is described as a Malvinas War veteran. However he never set foot on the Islands since he was Head of Communications for the Navy's air-wing from the Argentine mainland. On 2 and 3 January 2012, following the dismissal of Godoy (who had been Vázquez's Commander), the Argentine President purged thirty-six high-ranking officers from the Armed Forces by announcing their early retirement These comprised thirteen Army Generals, ten Air Force Brigadier-Generals and thirteen Rear-Admiral and Vice-Admirals. (Source: *MercoPress, South Atlantic News Agency*, Montevideo, 4 January 2012.)

53. *Ibid.* dated 17 March 2009.
54. *Ibid.* dated 1 October 2009.
55. The poem was written by Second-Lieutenant Mark Mathewson of 2 Platoon, Right Flank Company, 2nd Battalion, Scots Guards on the wall of a dark room in the Ajax Bay freezing plant (used as a Field Hospital and Prisoner of War Camp). Dated 20 June 1982, it commemorates the eight Scots Guardsmen who died on Tumbledown (seven fatalities) and at Pony's Pass (one fatality):

> It was the Guardsmen of the Crown
> Who scaled the heights of Tumbledown
> And fought that night a bloody fight
> To see Victory by dawn's first light.
>
> From crag to crag amongst the rock
> They skirmished on, numbed by shock.
> Through shell and mortar fire they moved
> Till at last the ground they'd proved
> Port Stanley there … just ahead,
> As they began to count their dead.
> But where the glory, where the pride,
> Of those eight brave men who died?
> They who made that lonely sacrifice
> And through each death paid the final price
> In their final heroic act
> Did surely speed the worrying armies pact
> Each one who there his life laid down
> Saved countless others from their own unknown
> So that those of you who will live to talk
> Let your pride hover as does the hawk
> And never let men these acts forget
> Nor the memory of our own dead neglect
> But once returned across the vast sea
> Remember then just what it was to be …
>
> A Scots Guardsman.

56. E-mail dated 24 January 2010.
57. *Ibid.* dated 28 January 2012.
58. *Ibid.* dated 29 January 2012

The leader sets the time of battle with them,
Like climbing high and removing the ladder.
The leader enters with them deep into the land of
the feudal lords,
Pulling the trigger.

– Sun Tzu[1]

I tracked him down via Eduardo Gerding and Jorge Pérez Grandi, a former 4th Infantry Regiment Platoon Commander and Two Sisters battle veteran whom I met during my first visit to Argentina in 2002. In our exchange of more than 150 e-mails between August 2010 and November 2011, fifty year-old *Coronel* (Colonel) Augusto Esteban Vilgré La Madrid[2] wrote about the common denominator of our past, 'I know who you are very well and the books you wrote but, unfortunately, I have not read them yet. We shared the same battles in the last days of the war on Tumbledown and Mount William, but did not come 'face to face' in the field'.

He also acknowledged (with historical imprecision) that, 'The Gurkhas were well-trained soldiers, ready to win or die for the glory of the British Empire'. Also he showed admirable respect for his former Scots Guards enemy:

Several years ago I sent an e-mail to Lieutenant-General Sir John Kiszely when he was Director of the UK Defence Academy. An NCO answered me and told me that the General was almost retired but 'will answer you soon', but I think he has never read my mail. Sometimes civilians do not understand soldiers, and in the UK the writers (like Hugh Bicheno) were unfair with the Scots Guards because they were 'Guards'.

Like Vázquez and me, La Madrid possessed a copy of *Razor's Edge* – but did not mince words about what he had read:

It is easy to understand that (Bicheno) he does not like the Army men of both sides. He writes badly about both of us. In some of the British parts he was not a 'fair player'. We know that you (the British) did not always perform well, just like us. Both Brigade Commanders did not co-ordinate properly and sometimes pressed Major-General Jeremy Moore in order to 'be the winner' of the war, that the Darwin battle was unnecessary in military terms and the Gurkhas were better trained than the Guards. But this does not mean the Guards did badly. They performed excellently and won the Tumbledown battle. I agree with your opinion regarding Bicheno's chapters about Tumbledown and think there are plenty of mistakes because his information was not from primary sources. And of course we have the same thoughts. It is time that a serving and veteran soldier reject some of his statements. Maybe we will never have again a battle like Tumbledown. We can say it was 'the romantic and gentleman's combat' and I am proud of being your enemy at that time and of your behaviour as well as mine. It was not easy and there were soldiers of both sides ready to die for their own countries, as many of them did.

It is not a problem for me to speak about that last fight. First because I am really proud of what my soldiers did, and secondly because I could feel their 'pressure' to command them soon and properly ... So I will try to tell you what I saw and what we did, and really want to help you in clarifying as much as possible. Why? Because as you know, I left behind some of my soldiers there, none of who were hit in their backs. They were killed in action by brave and well-trained soldiers and deserve to be recognised also in the UK. For me you are not an enemy. You are a comrade that once was my enemy who fought better than me and, because of that, won. You did this really well. Maybe there were some mistakes in the execution, but war is not a field training exercise because nothing will be as you have planned! Later I was a Lieutenant instructor at the Military Academy and used your actions in night combat as a model for my cadets. I am proud of myself ... but also proud of the Brits as well.

Known as Esteban La Madrid,[2] he was a twenty-one year-old cadet at the Military Academy in Buenos Aires at the beginning of April 1982. But after Argentina had re-taken the Islands, La Madrid and some others of his intake were promoted to *Subteniente*:

We were sent to combat units in order to train there with the new soldiers as a 'mobilised' unit ready to take over from those on the Islands. In fact six of my fellow cadets were sent with me to the 6th 'General Viamonte' Infantry Regiment in Mercedes City ninety-eight kilometres north-west of Buenos Aires. But the Regiment lacked two officers in its organisation, so one (Palazzo) joined HQ Company (as 2IC of the Communications Platoon) and I joined B Company to replace an NCO who was the platoon commander of my 3 Platoon.[4] As a brand-new Platoon Commander I had well-trained soldiers from the year before. For example Brigadier-General Jorge Halperín (the Commanding Officer of RI6 in the war) took them in 1981 to La Pampa province in the desert of the Patagonia and trained them for thirty days. My NCOs were excellent, especially my 2IC, 1st Sergeant Jorge Corbalán.

The other cadets were sent to the Training Garrison with the new conscripts. I was one of the lucky men. Can you imagine your unit going to the war, while you are left behind alone in the unit's Rear Party and training soldiers? We arrived in the Malvinas on 12 April.

He was one of 168 men in B Company which was commanded by Lieutenant Raúl Daniel Abella. Aside from 3 Platoon, the three other platoons were commanded by Second-Lieutenant Guillermo Enrique Corbella (1 Platoon),[5] Second-Lieutenant Aldo Eugenio Franco (2 Platoon) and Second-Lieutenant Guillermo Robredo (Support Platoon). The latter platoon consisted of twenty-seven men, and the three other platoons of forty-seven each, while Company HQ had ten. La Madrid also had an unusual UK connection:

My eighty-six year-old mum, Meryl Spencer-Talbois, is one hundred per cent English from Cumbria [...] (she) told me old family stories about the Talbois, the Pearsons (my grannie) and the Cummins (her grannie), her house in Chiswick (London) destroyed in the Second World War, her ancestor William Spencer-Talbois, Colonel in India in the nineteenth century, when my grandpa came to Argentina after the First World War, my uncle Doodles volunteered in the Second World War [...] and finally her son in the South Atlantic of 1982. She wrote a letter to me in April and told me not to listen to the Argentine news. She said, 'Be sure the British will come, so prepare yourself and prepare your soldiers. God bless you.'

Our Senior Operations Officer, Major Oscar Ramón Jaimet, was a brave soldier buried in the Regimental HQ located at the capital Puerto Argentino. At the beginning of the war when B Company was the helicopter reserve and training at Moody Brook, he began his recces which led him to believe that Two Sisters was a better place for our Company than Moody Valley. So we were segregated from the Regiment and sent to Two Sisters as a Brigade helicopter mobile reserve, with the Regiment receiving a replacement Company from the 1st Infantry Regiment (our 'Guards'). One day during a recce before the San Carlos landings and Darwin battle, Jaimet was with *General de Brigada* Jofre's 10th Infantry Brigade Chief of Staff. As the latter pointed from Mount Kent to Moody Brook, I overheard him saying, 'Sir, the British will come through here. And this is the air corridor.'

Now we know that he was right.

Because of this conversation, Jaimet was appointed as a reserve Commanding Officer for B Company, a helicopter platoon (one Puma and four Huey UH1H), an artillery observer and a Blowpipe missile section. Captain Palacios, a Staff College officer who deployed as Jaimet's 2IC, became the new Senior Operations Officer.

Initially the situation between Abella and Jaimet was not as good as it could have been. Both were Commandos, very self-confident and the types of people who thought they were always right. Abella was one of the best soldiers in the mountains. His radio nickname during the war was 'Leader' or 'Paul' (Paul Newman) – the blond, good-looking deep-blue eyed officer and a winner. But gradually they found a good way to speak together and Abella served with loyalty. Being both Special Forces soldiers before the war, they were *aficionados* of 'dynamic' activities and, as soon as we arrived on Two Sisters in May, they could not see us in pleasant activities and always gave us something to do: ambushes on Murrell Bridge, hundreds of patrols, observation posts and block points on Mount Challenger, Goat Ridge and Mount Kent. I received the order to prepare a recce patrol to Mount Simon in order to find information of the British movement to Teal Inlet. This was aborted, thank God, because that mission was given to the Commandos' 602 Company, and the result was the Top Malo House combat.[6]

Jaimet was a pusher. He stole weapons from everywhere. Because of that, he received twelve anti-air missiles (the Soviet SAM-7) in May. We fired the first one at a Sea Harrier. It was trying to find our field kitchen! After that we learnt more about the missile, but did not have those on Tumbledown. Maybe they were sent to the capital or to the air corridor. We also had a rocket from a destroyed Pucará ground attack aircraft nicknamed 'Albatross', but that was in the reserve on Two Sisters North under Jaimet's command. We did not have that on Tumbledown either.

At the beginning of June, Jaimet asked the Brigade to reinforce the position (they sent the 4th Infantry Regiment) because we were exhausted. We had left Mount Kent to the Commandos – and it was very clear that the Brits were going to come from there.

B Company had been positioned on the eastern side of Two Sisters North. But apart from its Support Platoon's three 81mm mortars engaging 3 Para in the latter's simultaneous attack on Mount Longdon, and rearguard action of Private Oscar Ismael Poltronieri who, as one of two machine-gunners in La Madrid's 3 Platoon provided covering fire to the Company's withdrawal down Moody Valley, B Company did not engage the Royal Marines 42 Commando during the latter's north-western assault on Two Sisters. At the eastern end of Moody Valley B Company ceased withdrawing, but had resulting weapon and ammunition deficiencies on their new position:

Robredo's Support Platoon had two 105mm anti-tank guns on Two Sisters. But the 'czekalkski' was a fucking awful weapon, slow to prepare and not easy to 'fire and go'. We were convinced that 'if you fire, your location will be identified by the enemy' and all the enemy artillery shells and mortar bombs will 'rain' down onto your head. B Company did not use these guns during the war and, at the end, they were sent to the Anti-Tank Platoon located in the Regiment's defensive position nearer the capital (thank God). I am sure Robredo had a shortage of ammunition for his three 81mm mortars after the Two Sisters battle. His platoon was re-positioned on the eastern saddle connecting Tumbledown with Sapper Hill. There were also two 120mm mortars sent by my Regiment which were located close to Mount William. But these were in support of the Wireless Ridge battle: and one soldier, Azcárate, was killed at that mortar position on the morning of 14 June.

We were placed in a sort of defensive position and our area of responsibility was Moody Valley. The boundaries were (left) Two Sisters and Mount Longdon, and (right) Wireless Ridge and Moody Brook. There were no Marines in this area, although I found positions and tents. During the war we had a camouflaged tent near each sangar, using the principle of 'fifty per cent on the position, and the other fifty as comfortable as they can make themselves'.

We were given two missions. The first was to be prepared to attack any British movement from our current position. The second was to reinforce Tumbledown's western end defended by the Marines. I had only forty-five men, not forty-seven, because on Two Sisters North Private Guanes had been killed [7] and Private Todde wounded. We could not prepare our positions properly because we did not have enough time. After the Two Sisters battle we were without enough equipment and military rations on Tumbledown. So on the night of 12/13 June an unauthorised section of my soldiers went back to Two Sisters and came back with a sleeping bag, plenty of rations, grenades and other items.

I was also observing Mount Longdon from Tumbledown North and saw our artillery, signallers and logistics guys withdrawing in order to avoid the fire from the British artillery. I thought, 'They're thinking that my soldiers and I are already dead ...'

So I prepared my soldiers to fight and asked them to sleep and rest before the last combat. A few of us prayed and asked that if our destiny were to die, then that be fast without wounds. Like all soldiers, none of us wanted to die alone. The British soldiers also fought bravely against a brave enemy. Unfortunately some authors on both sides, but especially in my country, questioned the 'costs' of that battle, not giving proper value to what the soldiers did [...] and that was unfair. But 'in moments of difficulty, people remember God and ask him to help the soldiers, but when they are not in danger anymore they forget God and the soldiers as well'.

Then Jaimet asked me for my MAG 7.62mm machine-guns in order to prepare a section in which all the machine-guns were centralised. He tried to give me a Lieutenant with twelve soldiers from the 12th Infantry Regiment who had come from Longdon. But I refused, not wanting to share the ammunition with them and being unhappy with a 'foreign' officer in my platoon. So I 'suggested' that he and his men be sent to another platoon.

During the following night on 13/14 June:

Jaimet was speaking with the Marine N Company Commander Lieutenant Eduardo Villarraza in his HQ (on the east end of Tumbledown) during the Scots Guards diversionary attack. Jaimet asked him about the situation and his defensive positions.

Villarraza told him, 'I've got a problem because I've authorised one of the platoon commanders to withdraw to another position, and now I have a "hole" in my defensive line.'

Jaimet answered, 'Can you order him to go back to his positions?'

Villarraza replied, 'Too late.'

That was when Jaimet offered him to reinforce his positions with one of (the B Company) platoons and called Abella on the radio to tell him, 'Come here, a friend needs to ask you a favour.'

Abella was in his HQ in a cave drinking tea and talking about the situation with his HQ and Second-Lieutenant Guillermo Enrique Corbella of 1 Platoon. When Abella arrived at N Company, Jaimet said to him, 'We have one of our boys being engaged, so send someone to help him in order to block the British penetration.'

I think the Marines that Villarraza authorised to withdraw was the Engineer sub-unit and he called them again. Maybe an hour or more passed while Jaimet: went back to his own HQ with Abella; decided on the (details of the) maneouvre and who would accomplish the mission; and called me to his HQ. Maybe for Jaimet it was a Company counter-attack. I do not know what request he received from Villarraza. He planned to send first my 3 Platoon as a left flank, secondly Franco's 2 Platoon as a right flank and keep Corbella's 1 Platoon in reserve.

Of course I heard and saw the combat on Tumbledown behind me, but this was only artillery and much more heavy fire than from rifles and machine-guns. He introduced me to the Marine Liaison Officer Sub-Lieutenant Waldemar Aquino (of the BIM5 Logistics Platoon) and gave me a short brief to follow the Marine officer and his NCO and be prepared for a confused and bad situation. I think (to answer Bicheno whose information is not clear) that Jaimet received the BIM5 request by radio or from Aquino, thinking that a platoon was enough to block a penetration. I know Jaimet very well. Be sure that in a combat situation, if he really knows what is going on, he will order a company attack. So when leaving the position I heard Jaimet giving his preparatory orders to the other platoon commanders. After that I prepared my soldiers and gave them my orders.[8]

His platoon would have to move one kilometre up and along Tumbledown's long north-east spur to Villarraza's HQ. This would take about an hour in the dark and was difficult going:

It was after midnight (local time) that 3 Platoon began deploying up to the east end of Tumbledown. But I do not remember exactly because of the adrenaline and did not check the time! It is amazing. In all combat training exercises the last action is, 'Check if you all have the same time'.

As I ran into the N Company HQ to be briefed by Lieutenant Villarraza (at 01.40 local time or 04.40Z),[9] Sub-Lieutenant Aquino told me that Miño was there. A platoon commander (Vázquez) of N Company was reporting a bad situation on the radio.

While Villarraza briefed me, Vázquez was shouting, 'I'm surrounded by the British and fighting in my positions!'

Villarraza answered him calmly, 'Resist! Don't give up!'

And he repeated several times, 'No one will withdraw!'

Then there was another message from Vázquez, 'The Brits are almost here, sir!'

And Villarraza answered, 'Hold on!'

Then he gave me orders for the counter-attack.

'Listen *Subteniente*,' he said, 'the situation is bad, but we will resist. Your mission is to block the British and break their assault. Let me tell you that if you come back, the reserve company will open fire. You are here to fight, understood?'

I think he told me that because he thought the Marines were still in the defensive line. But no one was there. He did not tell me to reinforce Vázquez's position or for Aquino to guide my platoon there (because I did not know the direction from where the Scots Guards were coming from).

The N Company Commander was very rude to me – anyway he was justified because the situation could not be worse. I am very British in my feelings and do not lose my self-control easily. So while stealing with my other hand a bottle of peach nectar, I answered angrily even when tired and not too confident about the mission, 'Sir, I have been sent here to fight!'

That is why I cannot believe that, after this situation, he withdrew his HQ from Tumbledown. However I did not have any communications with him because our PRC and TRC radios had no working batteries, although Jaimet did have radio contact with Villarraza via his excellent TRC 300 Thompson. So maybe he assumed in the end that my operation had been neutralised by the Scots Guards.

I left his cave and moved back to my platoon hating him and a little shocked. I had come from a position opposite the Wireless Ridge side of Moody Valley. There had been no recces of the area to be attacked, and no communications with the Marine mortars. Near the Company HQ my platoon were waiting for new orders. Their faces were illuminated by British mortar explosions. I could see their eyes and feel their thoughts.

'Hey young officer! Wake up! We're waiting for you!'

Sub-Lieutenant Osvaldo Colombo, N Company's 2IC, was with me there in the final moments and opened boxes of ammunition to re-supply my men. That meant they had more ammunition than I had originally thought. Furthermore Acting Sub-Lieutenant Miño was designated originally as my scout by Villarraza or Colombo, but Sub-Lieutenant Aquino[10] had asked if he could guide me to the top because he had been with me from the beginning.

So he turned to Miño and ordered, 'Follow me.'

But there was no chance of La Madrid accomplishing his mission because communications are the mother and father of command and control. Despite their crippling shortfall, it was time for La Madrid's doomed but courageous men to deploy. The criteria determined by Sun Tzu for decisive leadership was being met by their platoon commander who 'like climbing high and removing the ladder' gave his men no choice but follow him at this perilous moment. According to La Madrid's Army doctrine this particular operation was a 'limited attack', it being part of the 'dynamic of the defence'. They moved off in a southerly direction for 300 metres past Tumbledown's extreme eastern end where the two Marine field kitchens are still to be found. Then they turned westwards and moved along Tumbledown's south-east boundary for another 300 metres before cutting into its centre on a north-westerly course for 100 metres or so when they switched again onto a due westerly direction.[11] La Madrid:

> During our advance we found some abandoned positions and tents in which a few lost 4th Infantry Regiment soldiers were trying to rest. But we left them because they were exhausted and unable to fight. I did not want to mix them with my soldiers.
>
> I waited for the Scots Guards, who did not notice our presence, to enter the 'dead ground' in the small valley close to the 'Terrace'. The situation was unclear. No-one appeared to be there. I left my platoon (a big mistake) and moved forward with Private Arrúa and Miño trying to carry out a recce to contact the Marine 4 Platoon Commander.
>
> Suddenly when thinking we must be close to 4 Platoon, I heard voices. But they were speaking in English! Can you imagine? Alone, no rocks around me, in a small valley, with my troops about 100 metres behind me and thinking that I was about to co-ordinate with the Marine 4 Platoon Commander?

La Madrid had mis-appreciated his precise location because, in reality, he was still separated from Vázquez's position further to the west by at least one kilometre.[12] He had heard the first four of the seven Left Flank Company Scots Guardsmen who had climbed up Tumbledown's east summit. Their Company Commander, Major John Kiszely, was first to the top. La Madrid enlarged on that tense moment and ensuing combat:

We checked them out and saw three to four men in the dark.[13] Those Litton night goggles were excellent. But there was no good place to take cover or even be unseen in 'dead ground'. At that moment I lost contact with Miño and said to Arrúa, 'I will fire this rifle grenade over there and, when you hear the explosion, run to our platoon.'

It was a rifle anti-tank grenade shot at those guys speaking. Then I gave orders to someone else, and ran back to my soldiers. There was an explosion, British shouts and stones falling down. That was the moment we received fire not only from our front at a range of less than 100 metres, but also on our left flank at a range in excess of 100 metres

Sub-Lieutenant Aquino opened fire from our side first, shouting at my soldiers, 'Shoot those bastards!'

We all did the same, and surprise was lost. That was the last I saw of him. But his attitude gave me more courage. Aquino was a brave soldier.

Two days before I had experienced the withdrawal from Two Sisters, and therefore shouted at him, 'Don't be a silly fucking bastard, we were waiting for them to come!'

I was certain the Scots Guards believed my fire came from three lost Argies and did not know a platoon was there. That was when a 'rain' of bullets poured down on us. Moments afterwards a 'rocket rain' began too, landing twice extremely close to Horisberger's machine-gun. He did not speak at all, but simply fired. The Guards on the north-east summit were hit by luck because my gunner 'swept' this area by shooting from left to right, and he only saw them well when they returned fire.

Initially the combat was easy. I was with Horisberger and indicated the targets. The other machine-gunner, Poltronieri, was with Sergeant Echeverría and had not opened fire. I fired my 90mm rocket launcher for a few minutes. There were people, probably Miño's platoon, exchanging fire less than 200 metres to the south. But not too much came from the Argie side and not for long. We fired six 90mm high-explosive rounds, hand grenades (I kept one for my last self-defence) and also rifle explosive rounds named PDF (translated 'double-effect fragmentary explosive round' in that it could be used against machine-gun positions or an armoured personnel carrier).

When I saw my soldiers behind me, I thought they were firing in the wrong direction. We had only five magazines for each rifle, although some of us had more ammunition in our combat ration bags. At that moment I shot my two PDFs at the guys speaking English [...] and the situation remained almost the same because, on returning to my men after having understood my targets had been

British, I shouted at them, 'Stop shooting like that!'

I felt alone there with my soldiers. We were the only people still firing.

'Fuck,' I thought, 'I'm dead. These guys outnumber us.'

There were more and more weapons shooting at us. Incoming fire was on my left. But then more began arriving from the front, and then some from my right. Only a few minutes had elapsed before this change of direction. It was about 07.00 (10.00Z) and combat would continue another hour.

When the Guards moved on both flanks matters began to go really wrong. I could not move forward because of the effective British fire. The situation became worse, and we received a volley of machine-gun and anti-tank fire against my two machine-guns.

My worries increased. This was not due to the incoming mortar or artillery fire, but because of the Guards' shooting and fact my machine-gun fire did not find its targets well. I could see the Guards approaching and tried to shout in English so as to gain more time to indicate a target to Horisberger. I thought the firefight could still be won because I had located a British anti-tank weapon which had shot at us twice. Horisberger and González tried to load more ammunition into the machine-gun while it seemed as if all the Scots Guards were firing at us.

In a pause I shouted to Horisberger, 'Shoot there, fucking bastard!'

I ran across to him.

He was still lying motionless in cover. I tried to kick him so as to wake him. But González shouted at me in order to be heard above the shooting and explosions, 'Lieutenant, Horisberger is dead!'

Giving González the machine-gun, I pulled Horisberger close to me and found him to be alive still, even though with three or four 7.62mm machine-gun bullet holes in his chest. But I did not hear him breath. He died a few seconds later.

González moved with me towards the south-east, but not more than twenty metres. After that we returned closer to Horisberger's position. Assisted by Private Andreacola, González became the machine-gunner (with Horisberger's gun). But he was effective only for a short time because we lacked ammunition and the British fire did not make things easy for us.

I opened fire shouting, 'Kill these bastards, don't be afraid!'

González fired again, but the machine-gun was not working properly. The next problem was that we came under fire while trying to fix the weapon. Before the Guards' assault, machine-gun and rifle fire intensified against us. It included grenades and other shit 'raining' down onto us.

So without ammunition and the machine-gun operating worse and worse (Horisberger had experienced the same problem and had repaired it twice), González left the weapon close to Horisberger's body. Then Poltronieri moved with his machine-gun and my platoon's Support Section Commander, Sergeant Héctor Echeverría, some distance further to the south-east before firing again only twenty metres from me. But I did not see this. Echeverría's machine-gun was one of the last weapons shooting at the end of the combat. Poltronieri was the same machine-gunner on Two Sisters who covered the withdrawal there two days before, and was decorated by the Argentine Congress post-war.[14]

Maybe there is a perception we were organised then on Tumbledown. But the truth is that it was all the NCOs' and soldiers' own initiative. Towards the end the Scots Guards were looking for us, and I thought we must withdraw now. But they had virtually surrounded us and so I was unable to contact all in my platoon. What can a junior rank do?

Abandon his soldiers when I could hear some of them asking for my help?

Minutes later I could see that a few were still shooting amongst the dead ones: like Rodríguez who had been in the unauthorised section which, the previous night, had returned to Two Sisters in order to collect equipment and rations. Another, Torres, saw Rodríguez killed. The Scots Guards were very close to his section which was trying to withdraw. When at last they did that, Rodríguez then exclaimed, 'Shit, I forgot my bag with the rations stolen from the Royal Marines on Two Sisters!'

He ran back to his previous position and opened fire when trying to collect his bag. But machine-gun fire cut him down. Because Torres was providing covering fire for Rodríguez, he could not follow his Section Commander and was taken prisoner a few minutes later. The death of Rodríguez, a farmer from Lobos City, was very bitter. Clever as a fox, he had always laughed and joked in bad situations and, in fact, had been a sort of magician for us.

At that terrible moment with the Scots surrounding us, Bordón was shot at from his left while firing at a Guardsman to the north. When trying to return fire at this new target and then move to another position, he became involved in close combat with the first Guardsman assaulting his position. A nearby NCO thought the attacker had been wounded by Bordón. But this Guardsman had first shot Bordón who then died shortly afterwards.

When I saw Becerra firing his FAP in the automatic mode, he was also surrounded and changed his position twice to avoid the heavy Scots Guards machine-gun fire and Light Anti-Tank Weapons' rockets. But being involved in my own combat, I lost contact with him and do not know how he died. Luna was a mystery. He was a 1 Platoon soldier, but when we were called for a counter-attack he was together with his close friend Balvidares who was in my platoon. Instead of remaining alone, he accompanied Balvidares and fought with his section. But neither do I know the circumstances of his death which was in the close-quarter combat's last moments.

During all that confusion I sent my radio operator Disciulo to Villarraza. His task was to ask for more information. But he returned and said, 'Sir, no one is there.'

Was that the truth? Did he really go to Villarraza's HQ, or had he hidden behind a rock and then come back and lied?

I could not contact the other machine-gunner, Poltronieri, and only one NCO received my order to withdraw in the last twenty minutes. Only a few soldiers around me were able to receive my orders. Meeting again later those who had been captured, they told me that as prisoners during the combat pauses my shouts were heard. As Poltronieri behind us began firing, we ran again to the other side of the mountain and stopped there to organise some sort of defence. But it was impossible.

Meanwhile Jaimet and Abella with some men from Franco's and Corbella's platoons had been climbing up the north-east spur in order to reach Villarraza's Company. Both platoons were only at one third strength (twelve to fifteen men) because the platoon commanders did not have enough time to alert and wake their men. Their main responsibility was towards Wireless Ridge and some of their troops were required also to stop any possible attack coming from that front.

Jaimet had also centralised all four platoon machine-guns into one group. He understood I was not having much luck with my attack. With Corbella's 1 Platoon covering the rear, Jaimet sent Franco's 2 Platoon to close the line. But he had given Franco an unclear mission, there was no recce and so the latter did not pass through my area. It must be remembered also that after a battle on Two Sisters, a withdrawal from there, and one day on our next position, we still could not communicate by radio with each other and our Company Commander.

Keeping to Jaimet's axis of advance, Franco was north of me and had lost his way. Almost in the valley, he eventually moved his platoon onto the north-east spur. He stopped to give a short briefing to his section commanders because of the unclear situation. Then he saw some Scots Guards at a range of 200 metres and exchanged fire with them for a short period. But Franco did not engage in combat because he was sure my platoon was not there. Nonetheless armed with a machine-gun, Second-Lieutenant Robredo, an NCO and two soldiers did manage to reach my location. But they were too late and only attracted Scots Guards fire.

It is amazing how soldiers in combat feel that 'their world is the only world'. Many officers (junior ranks) from Tumbledown, Two Sisters and Mount Longdon told me, 'They left me alone' or 'I was the only one there' or 'I was the last out'. But when you read the 'whole' story that is not true. The real problem was that we were in 'nests' because of the distances and could not 'feel' the presence of other troops on the left, rear or right and be immersed in the confusion of such a violent environment which even the mortars and artillery support. On some occasions that was true. But in many it was just the feeling of the loneliness of command. That is why some platoons began their withdrawals earlier. It is not easy to contain fear in such moments. Thank God I had brave NCOs and soldiers to contain the fear … and panic!

When Jaimet realised that the Scots Guards Right Flank Company was the main attack, and not a penetration, it was too late for a defensive manoeuvre. He thought I would hold my position and therefore waited for more British actions before engaging his reserve (Corbella's 1 Platoon). We have a principle: the reserve is engaged always for success, to recover the initiative but never to repair a bad action, otherwise you will be lost and the battle will be over … and Jaimet was very clever to make such a mistake. Because of that he only sent troops to assist my withdrawal. It was all a big mess because the BIM5 Commanding Officer never noticed the main attack and thought the situation was under control. But when he realised the Scots Guards were on the east summit it was too late for a counter-attack.

I have no doubt one of my soldiers shot Guardsman Ian Morton. In the position from where he was hit I had one machine-gun from my Support Section and, commanded by an NCO, a section of another nine soldiers. Two were armed with FAP 'heavy' rifles, two with rifle grenades, and five with FAL rifles and hand grenades. I am so sorry Morton was wounded. Maybe one day I will ask his forgiveness and tell him of my pride in each Guardsman as much as my own soldiers. We were simply fighting for our countries. Five of my men had been killed on the Tumbledown. Of the nine wounded some were recovered by us, and some evacuated by the Scots Guards.

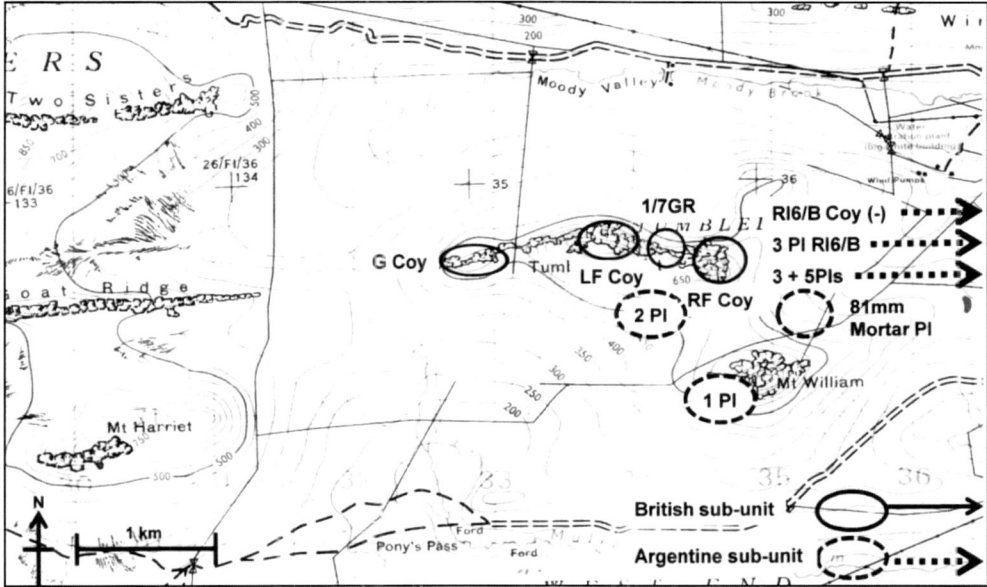

Map 6 (10.30Z-11.30Z) – 3 Platoon (BIM5) and then 5 Platoon (BIM5) withdraw to Sapper Hill, followed by 3 Platoon (RI6/B) and RI6/B Company (-). 1/7 GR moves onto Tumbledown.

With the Marines withdrawing from Tumbledown, Jaimet did the same as he was still worried about the perceived main enemy threat from Wireless Ridge. Dawn was about to break. 1st Sergeant Corbalán, Second-Lieutenant Robredo and Poltonieri firing their machine-guns, and a Mortar Platoon soldier were covering the withdrawal. They stopped fighting when it was thought no one had been left behind.

Also I had fired for a few minutes. Can you imagine me, an Argentine officer shouting in Spanish that dark night amid the explosions, rippling crack of rifle and machine-gun fire and bitterly cold wind? The only people who could hear me were the guys on my left and right. Then they passed the orders to the others a few metres away.

It was a situation of: 'Follow me and do what I do'.

We re-organised with the rest of B Company which lay spread out some 200 metres east of the abandoned N Company HQ. I had lost contact with at least twenty of my men and did not see Corbella, the 1 Platoon Commander, again. Exhausted and desperate at my inability to locate my missing men, I approached

Jaimet's Company HQ.

Jaimet saluted for a second, then tried to hug me while shouting, 'Son!'

I answered angrily, 'Son? Son of a bitch you are! Where did you send my platoon? You sent us to the dead!'

But that was my only negative feeling at that horrible moment after understanding this action had been a mistake. It was not easy for Jaimet to select a platoon to block a penetration. In fact without being falsely humble 3 Platoon was B Company's best prepared in terms of good morale. My men were very particular and had excellent NCOs.

Then I said, 'I'm sorry sir, but I've lost almost all my soldiers.' I wanted to rescue those missing, imagining they were either dead or wounded on Tumbledown and crying out for my help

I do not remember how long we stayed there, but the Scots Guards had taken over the summit of Tumbledown and our situation was becoming worse and worse. A few shots were fired at us from the summit and we returned fire. At that moment Franco returned from Tumbledown. So Jaimet sent a runner to contact the platoon commanders (we still had no radio communications because of the lack of batteries) and then issued new orders to us, 'Take the personnel you still have and be prepared to return to the Company rendezvous point. Our people coming from the other side of the harbour (Wireless Ridge and through Moody Brook) and from Tumbledown are waiting for our support.'

I was exhausted and confused. My main thought was of La Madrid now as a Platoon Commander loser. The Scots Guards were still firing at us from both sides of Tumbledown's summit. That meant my last minutes of combat had just occurred. To continue the fight meant, in reality, I would be killing my own soldiers.

So do you understand where I am coming from? was my silent question.

But my actual reply was only a meek, 'Yes sir.' I was a very junior rank to say the least.

The sun had risen and I could see troops from Tumbledown still withdrawing. My sympathy was with them, but Abella ordered us to prepare for a possible counter-attack on Wireless Ridge. Devastated and not ready for another such task, I did not answer.

We were about forty men who moved out in a north-east direction to the rendezvous point. This was about one kilometre away. Our objective was in a group of rocks near BIM5's logistic positions and the harbour between Moody Brook and Sapper Hill. The situation was extremely confusing. Danger abounded with continuous incoming artillery and mortar fire, light anti-tank rockets and other shit coming our way. The Scots Guards and Paras were also observing and occasionally fired at us. But in the daylight, thank God, either they were more preoccupied with re-organising on their objective, or did not want to engage in an all-out 'shooting pigeons' contest.

We were exhausted on arrival at our 'rocky nest' which was not big enough to accommodate any more seeking cover there. The position was prepared with Private Quaranta's machine-gun from 2 Platoon. I did not have my 90mm rocket launchers and only one of my two machine-guns. We had FAL rifles and two FAP automatic rifles per section, but further lacked rifle grenades PAF and PDEF.

To help our troops withdraw we resumed exchanging fire with British on Tumbledown's summit and Wireless Ridge for about an hour. A British paratrooper on Wireless Ridge has claimed that a machine-gun fired at his unit from the Water Plant in Moody Brook. But nobody was there at that time. The paratroopers had received this fire from Poltronieri. A retreat under pressure and heavy fire can never be well organised because all personnel cannot leave their positions simultaneously. As a result several more of my platoon arrived at our current location from the Tumbledown.

When we carried out the second phase of our withdrawal to Puerto Argentino, none of the Battalions (Marines or 7th Mechanised Infantry Regiment) were fighting. There was a perfect British artillery salvo fired from behind Tumbledown which exploded between my troops and the capital.[15] Many Marines were withdrawing still from Tumbledown and Mount William to Sapper Hill. But the story did not end there.

Minutes before, Echave had asked to borrow my 9mm pistol because he had no more FAL ammunition. As I handed it to him he said with a smile, 'Sir, if I have to die in close combat, then I want to do it when an enemy is with me and not alone!'

Then we moved on to another position close to the three-kilometre road leading eastwards into Puerto Argentino. Echave was twenty metres ahead of me and arrived first. While Balvidares opened fire on Wireless Ridge, Echave took cover behind a rock. But on arrival at their location I found them both dead. Echave had been shot in the neck and Balvidares in the chest.

At least they were together in their final moments.

I retrieved my pistol and hurried on quickly to avoid that efficient sniper. It was unclear if my two soldiers had been killed by the Scots Guards on Tumbledown or Paras on Wireless Ridge.[16] Jaimet told me that he thought the Brits at that moment did not want to kill more Argentine soldiers otherwise it could have been a massacre.

Close to the outskirts of Puerto Argentino, Jaimet (with Abella) met Robacio again. During their organised withdrawal Jaimet's Company used some hand grenades to destroy the 81mm mortars left behind by them, one jeep, a Marine communications truck and a helicopter which had landed close to Government House. After that they threw their machine-guns and heavy weapons into the harbour water. The long stretch from Moody Brook and Sapper Hill to the little capital was under heavy artillery fire, and there was a powerful detonation in a house which contained Sapper explosives. B Company was forced to make its withdrawal 'position by position and house by house' in order to avoid the effects of the shelling. However a number of soldiers were wounded, and so an Air Force truck was requisitioned to transport them to the hospital.[17] La Madrid:

I did not see all this because my withdrawal was close to the harbour and contact with Jaimet had been lost. At that moment I was just worried for my own life and lives of the few soldiers still with me. On entering the city I took off my helmet for the first time in two days and breathed deeply. I felt proud. My Sergeant Echeverría and Private Disciullo were still carrying their rifles ready to open fire [...] but a bastard in my country called them 'the kids of the war'.

I had visited Puerto Argentino only once before in May, having been sent there with a section of soldiers to take a bath. In the Upland Goose Hotel I asked the blonde daughter of the hotel's owner for a cup of tea with pie, but she gave me cocoa and biscuits. After that day I went back to the mountains. It was not easy being in the town when your soldiers are elsewhere.

But there is another story. Robert Lawrence (of Right Flank Company) and I shared the same combat, same number platoon (3), same rank, same age, and same birthday. But we had different luck. Post-combat while I was safe in the capital on my birthday, he was fighting for his life in a Field Hospital.[18]

La Madrid was justifiably proud of his men's battle performance:

You must understand that I did not teach Poltronieri or Horisberger how to manage a machine-gun. The combat was directed by Corporals Palomo and Fernández, 1st Corporal Zapata and the Support Section Commander Sergeant Echeverría. Remember that when the fighting started we had no radio communications, so it was their initiative and I do not want to steal their honour.

Bicheno or journalists writing about war and feelings of the soldiers or if the combat was easy or not, have probably never even boxed in a gymnasium! And yet you, Mike, are really trying to get direct, detailed information from the actors themselves. Thank you for 'pressing' me to remember those last moments [...] it is time for me too. We shared one night of combat. We are brothers in the blood left there, and tried to do as best we could – but you won because you were better trained. That is the secret. My soldiers fought with bravery. None of them were killed by a shot in the back, and all of them died by rifle and machine-gun fire. We had lost once again to the British infantry, and they are the best in the world – but on an isolated Island, without proper support and after three months, the effort of our infantry was simply not enough. We lost because it was the only result that the fighting could have had.

I am happy 3 Platoon did not kill any Scotsman in that battle. It was well executed by the Scots Guards because Lieutenant-Colonel Scott left the initiative to his Company Commanders and junior ranks. Their men followed them and did what they had been trained to do. For me, as an infantry officer, it was a great honour to have faced such a brave enemy. Close-quarter infantry combat is not easy. Killing each other is a serious and demanding job in war. It is done by soldiers with feelings. We are not super-humans and carry on our lives with those mementos in our minds. It is not a tale, but real life. There were some like Lieutenant Robert Lawrence fighting their wounds forever. And there are others like Horisberger's father who is proud of his son killed on Tumbledown fighting against a colonial country. It is that simple.

He was convinced initially also of his theory as to the identity of 'Pedro'. This was a nickname given by Islanders to an Argentine soldier who continued fighting on Tumbledown after the main battle had ended and until he was eventually killed.[19] La Madrid's flawed analysis is interesting, nonetheless, because it describes Argentine infantry minor tactics:

> The British story claims there was only one enemy machine-gun location. But there were always two machine-guns firing at different times. To avoid the excellent British fire, one machine-gun moved while the other was firing. Horisberger and his machine-gun were with me. But 'Pedro' was two gunners: Horisberger and Poltronieri. The British story states that 'Pedro' was killed near the 'Terrace' by a Lance-Corporal of Left Flank Company firing a 66mm Light Anti-Tank Weapon. But Horisberger was the only machine-gunner killed in action, and none other than Poltronieri was there. I have no doubt that Pedro was Horisberger, but the Pedro legend was finally completed (after his death) by Poltronieri's action.
>
> The Argentine infantry moved using the machine-gun like a rifle, firing like a rifleman two or three rounds per burst especially in offensive operations. We used to live behind the 'nest' of the machine-gun so we had another soldier with a rifle ready to fight. The machine-gunner moved as a soldier with a rifle between sections and, when he fired, he placed one leg to the rear otherwise the machine-gun could 'kick' him. Because of that, the machine-gunner is usually cleverer and stronger than the other soldiers. During the Tumbledown combat which, in our case, was done without a recce and in a confused environment, surprise is common because the direction of the enemy movement is unknown. For me it was not a defensive operation. That is why I kept one machine-gun between 1 and 2 Sections, and put the other machine-gun between 2 and 3 Sections. In that situation the machine-gunner only needs one soldier to supply him with ammunition continually, but he can open fire and move on his own.

I challenged La Madrid's Pedro theory by pointing out, 'Poltronieri survived the battle. So who was 'Pedro'?' He replied:

> I do not know my friend. Who do you think? Was someone else there at that moment? I only remember isolated tents and positions, some lost soldiers who did not want to fight with me when I asked them [...] and the Scots Guards surrounding me fast! What do you think? Who was Pedro? You just 'destroyed' my theory!

Whether it was Lance-Corporal Gary Tytler who killed 'Pedro' with a 66mm rocket or the following machine-gun fire did afterwards[20] is immaterial. The main point is that immediately prior to using the 66mm Light Anti-Tank Weapon against 'Pedro', Tytler was assisting Scots Guards casualties from the infamous mortar attack on loaded stretchers [21] midway between the north-east summit and west end of Tumbledown [22] at 12.04Z. This gives a much more accurate fix on the final location of 'Pedro' who must have been killed at about 12.30Z. Therefore all circumstantial evidence points to

'Pedro', who was dressed in an Army combat uniform, being a member of Vázquez's composite 4 Platoon.[23]

Like the remainder of the defeated Argentine forces on the Islands, La Madrid was swiftly repatriated to Argentina. He sailed with 551 officers and other ranks of the 6th Infantry Regiment on board the icebreaker ARA *Bahía Paraíso*, departing Stanley at daybreak on 20 June. Seasick the next evening while acting as the ship's Duty Officer, La Madrid and the unit finally arrived in the early afternoon of 22 June at the Punta Quilla Pier, a few kilometres from the capital city of Río Gallegos in Santa Cruz province. The two exceptions were the Commanding Officer, Lieutenant-Colonel Jorge Halperín, and Jaimet who had been put into the Special Category Prisoner group initially at Ajax Bay, and then on board MV *St Edmund* before being repatriated to Argentina on 14 July.

The combat of 1982 had a positive effect on RI6:

A year after the war Jaimet was still the Operations and Training Officer and he prepared a sort of 'own SOPs' (Standard Operating Procedures) for the unit training plan which included a lot of experiences from the war especially in night combat with the same hours as in the day. When we opened it there was a picture of a British soldier pointing a rifle 'at you', and he wrote something like: 'STOP – maybe tomorrow he will be in front of you [...] the better trained will win [...] and the other will be lying dead on the ground as a testimony' and, under that, 'So be prepared and train your soldiers. You are responsible for this and keeping them alive.' Cruel, but true my friend. It was a good year 1983.

But Jaimet disliked talking about the war. Despite many attempts, particularly by Eduardo Gerding, I failed to come into contact with him. His reticence is reflected in his relationship with RI6 war veterans as La Madrid commented to me, 'Jaimet has visited our Regiment only two times after the war (we all meet each year in the second Saturday of April).' However he would add later:

Jaimet was invited to the 6th Infantry Regiment in December 2010 and gave an excellent speech in the operations classroom. He was honoured by his name 'Oscar Jaimet' being given to the Operations Area and 'Exercise Room'. I think he feels like a soldier again. He told me that he will be happy if one day he could meet and speak to you and General Scott.[24]

During those intensive fifteen months I had enjoyed our cyberspace game of 'ping-pong' Q&A. So I asked Esteban La Madrid philosophically, 'So what were we doing all those years ago fighting each other?' He answered in a final e-mail flurry:

Even though there are many British families and their descendants here in Argentina, and also a long history of friendship between both countries – we two were professional soldiers and had to carry out the orders of our authorities to sustain their policies with our weapon firepower. So unfortunately we fought against each other. For me it was also weird because I had heard the English language at home, have a mother with a English name, had a daily English meal and breakfast with scrambled eggs, bacon and 'porridge' to strengthen my muscles (!), listened to English stories, ate my Christmas pudding, had a traditional wedding cake made with a six-generation recipe, and felt 'at home' there on the Malvinas not only because I am convinced that the Islands belong to us, but because of the language and people. I missed my cups of tea and scones!

As an infantry soldier, I learnt a lot from my comrades in the British Army and am sure after my UN tours of duty in the Middle East and former Yugoslavia that I have fought against the best soldiers in the world. The UK does not possess the best intelligence like the Israelis or the best equipment like the Americans, but it has the effectiveness of simple plans and simple actions carried out by excellent soldiers.

I wrote that the war was only 'my small war', but am now trying to get myself more familiar with the whole situation. And for me, I can do this 'normally'. But four years ago I did not feel ready to read, even to write, about the war. So I am acquiring more clarity about the situation because of you. I read in Spanish a few good books (but not with the detail like yours) on the war. Especially because we lost, most writers (with some exceptions) try to say, 'I did all that I could but [...] the logistics [...] the tactics never repaired the strategic mistakes [...] 'Miño, B Company and my CO abandoned me' [...] 'all my Battalion performed excellently, but the Company Commander and Jaimet left me alone ready to die against the Brits' [...] 'my soldiers were better than his' [...] and so on: a sort of justification of their actions.

Who then is the father of the defeat? Why did we lose all the battles? I am one of them, Mike. Soldiers of my platoon died because of my orders. So what I could do other than visit their parents and tell them how brave their sons were and how our life was during the war? I did that during the last few years and I wrote only when Brigadier-General Halperín told me, 'Who is going to write how your soldiers died? It is a moral obligation.'

Now I am ready to 'dig' deeper into their story and, one day, I will write it.

Lastly, I agree with you – the story of Silva and Vázquez moves one to tears like the stories of British soldiers I read. It is not easy being surrounded by a Scots Guards Company, abandoned (?) and fighting, instead withdrawing to a salvation close by. Who can see you in the darkness? [25]

But let me tell you something. As an infantry soldier, Custer in 1876 was a brave man, but directed his soldiers to their death as if he was a man possessed. British soldiers and Argies as well knew that they could die. They felt (like you and me) fear – but defeated it because they had a mission to accomplish and knew that behind them were comrades.

Esteban La Madrid's modesty precluded him from informing me that he had been decorated with the MVC for his courage on Tumbledown. His war on the Islands had lasted sixty-four days. The residents of the nearby small capital of 'Puerto Argentino' had endured seventy-four days of war. And one lady there updated her diary continuously during that extraordinary time.

Notes

1. *The Art of War*, Chapter 11 – The Nine Grounds.
2. At the time of this book's publication Esteban La Madrid was the Director of the Argentine Army PTSD Hospital in Buenos Aires. This was a facility where, he said, 'We try to help our veterans that are still fighting against the wounds of the '82 war'. La Madrid was also working hard to create a Joint PTSD Hospital for veterans under a new Argentine law from 2011 that also anticipates other problems (e.g. drug and alcohol addiction, family violence and depression). This was announced publicly to war veterans, politicians and senior military figures in the Casa Rosada (The Pink House), which is the official Buenos Aires presidential mansion of Argentina, by President Cristina Fernández de Kirchner on 7 February 2012. La Madrid and his wife Patricia, have one daughter, Eugenia, and a son, Augusto. In 2010 Augusto was a Lieutenant in the Argentine Army's 1st Infantry Regiment serving with the United Nations peacekeeping force in Haiti. His father possesses a good command of English. He and the author soon discovered a mutual interest for history which the former had taken to another level with his studies for a Masters degree.
3. But not 'de la Madrid' in *Razor's Edge*.
4. A sub-unit omitted in the Argentine Tumbledown order of battle in *Razor's Edge* (p. 289).
5. But not commanded by La Madrid, as stated in *Razor's Edge* (p. 289).
6. An intensive firefight took place on 31 May between a twelve-man section of the Argentine 602 Commando Company occupying Top Malo House, originally a deserted shepherd's house, and eighteen men of the Royal Marines Mountain Arctic and Warfare Cadre. The Argentines surrendered after forty-five minutes of fighting. Two Argentines were killed and six wounded. Three Marines were wounded and the building was destroyed by fire.
7. A 2 Platoon fatality on Two Sisters North is mentioned in *Razor's Edge* (pp 246-47). This was Guanes because Jaimet admitted later to his error of (incorrectly) marking Two Sisters and Tumbledown maps (probably for the authors of *5th Infantry Brigade in the Falklands*) with 2 Platoon instead of 3 Platoon.
8. *Razor's Edge* (p. 245) paints a far less nuanced and little flattering picture of this tense time: 'Jaimet, in turn, sent only one platoon under a green sub-lieutenant instead of ordering senior Lieutenant Arbella (the correct spelling is Abella) to lead a company attack, or better still leading it himself.' La Madrid's comment about this 'armchair' analysis was understandably negative, 'I do not agree [...] maybe at the end of the combat, but it is not necessary to be very clever to understand that this action would have been suicidal and stupid.'
9. War diary of Lieutenant-Colonel Eugenio Dalton, G3 (Operations), Argentine 10th Infantry Brigade HQ.
10. *Razor's Edge* (p. 298) muddles up Aquino with Midshipman Marcelo Demarco, Miño's artillery Forward Observation Officer, by incorrectly substituting the latter in Aquino's scout role.
11. *Ibid.* comments: 'De la Madrid says, "I spread my men out behind the men who were still fighting" in the Terrace area.' With the exception of 'in the Terrace

area', this statement had been extracted from Martin Middlebrook's book *The Fight for the 'Malvines': The Argentine Forces in the Falklands War*. Again La Madrid reacted (e-mail dated 4 September 2010), 'I did not say 'behind', I said to Middlebrook, 'left''. No wonder *Razor's Edge* (p. 298) puzzled over whether these (non-existent) men 'in the Terrace area' were either 'stragglers from Miño's platoon (unlikely)', or 'an unrecorded sortie by some of Villarraza's HQ Group'.

12. *Ibid.* incorrectly and illogically claimed: 'Braving the fire of two machine-guns and a 'missile-launcher' firing down from the summit, de la Madrid went forward until he heard English voices above and behind him.' La Madrid's comment (e-mail dated 4 September 2010) about this particular error was a blunt, 'I do not understand this.'

13. *Ibid.* incorrectly stated: 'He spotted a group of twelve men [...] ' Furthermore La Madrid replied, 'Yes, I agree' (e-mail dated 4 September 2010) to my conclusion that *Razor's Edge* (p. 298) had muddled Miño's counter-attack (on La Madrid's left flank) against the Scots Guards Left Flank Company 14 Platoon 'newly arrived to support Kiszely's tiny group' with La Madrid's lone rifle-grenade 'shoot' against the Scots Guards Left Flank Company Commander and his six Guardsmen on the Tumbledown's east summit.

14. The citation for Poltronieri's CMVC was:

> For combat deeds during the battle of Two Sisters, where as the operator of a machine-gun and unheeding the order to retreat he held the position all alone and by himself, thus facilitating the withdrawal of his fellow soldiers into safety while holding the enemy at bay by the fire of his lonely weapon and preventing the advance of the British attacking formation.

15. By this time the Gurkhas' B Company was advancing unopposed down Tumbledown's north-east spur. It is highly probable that this Royal Artillery 'shoot' was called down by B Company Commander Captain Lester Holley.

16. *Razor's Edge* (p. 309) has 'borrowed' and perpetuated the error from both *The Fight for the 'Malvinas': The Argentine Forces in the Falklands War* (p. 262) and *5th Infantry Brigade in the Falklands* (p. 200) that only Sergeant Eusebio Aguilar was killed in this incident. The other problem is that Aguilar was not a member of 3 Platoon (!).

17. War diary of Lieutenant-Colonel Eugenio Dalton, G3 (Operations), Argentine 10th Infantry Brigade HQ.

18. *Razor's Edge* (p. 325) contrived to muddle up Robert Lawrence with his father, John, in a brief reference to the former's 'harrowing account of his treatment' on return to the UK.

19. *Razor's Edge* (p. 34) introduces the story of 'Pedro' and a possible enemy machine-gun position (of Horisberger's?): 'On Tumbledown there is a rocky alcove, carpeted with old 7.62mm bullet cases, which looks out on the crest where Lieutenant Mitchell and two other Scots Guards were shot when incautiously admiring the view from the newly-won summit.' This gave nourishment to La Madrid's flawed theory of 'Pedro's' identity, even though *Razor's Edge* (pp. 309 and 310) states (correctly) that 'Pedro' was killed 'at least an hour after de la Madrid and the rest of the Argentine troops retreated'.

Furthermore the book *5th Infantry Brigade in the Falklands* (p. 202) describes 'Pedro' as a lone rifleman from Franco's 2 Platoon firing on 'at least three occasions [...] from rocks above the northern cliff face of Tumbledown'. The major error here is that no soldier in 2 Platoon was killed during the war (from La Madrid's e-mail dated 25 February 2011). *Razor's Edge* (p. 309) also (correctly) refers to the Scots Guards Captain Jeremy Campbell-Lamerton's attempt to persuade 'an Argentine officer to appeal to Pedro to surrender', but (incorrectly) concludes that this officer 'cannot have been Vázquez'. He was indeed Vázquez, and 'Pedro' also sniped in the direction of the Scots Guards Battalion Tactical HQ located at the west end of Tumbledown (see Chapter 10). Furthermore although the inference in *Razor's Edge* (p. 309) that a second Argentine officer had surrendered is correct, the traumatised (Officer B) was not the prisoner that Campbell-Lamerton had been interrogating when 'Pedro' fired at the Scots Guards Tac HQ. It was Vázquez.

20. *Ibid.*, p. 309.
21. Chapters 4 and 5.
22. *Razor's Edge* (p. 34) incorrectly states 'at the eastern end of Tumbledown'.
23. Discovered in 1983, the body of 'Pedro' was buried in the Argentine cemetery at Darwin with full military honours. His story continues to fascinate some Argentines. For example on 14 March 2011 a young history student undergraduate who was writing his thesis on 'Pedro' visited La Madrid in an unsuccessful attempt to ask for more information on the dead Argentine soldier. According to La Madrid, in an e-mail sent the following day, the student left the former's office 'desperate'!
24. E-mail dated 25 February 2011.
25. It had been planned that La Madrid and the retired Vázquez would meet for the first time on the evening of 9 November 2011 at the city of Pigue, home of the 3rd Infantry Regiment in the south of the province of Buenos Aires. The following day they would make presentations on their Tumbledown battle experiences at a leadership seminar for the 10th Infantry Brigade. But in an e-mail dated 14 November 2011 La Madrid informed the author that unfortunately the day of Vázquez's presentation had been changed to 11 November and so the two did not meet after all. The disappointed La Madrid ended his four-hour presentation to an audience of 600 with a few well-chosen words about Vázquez whose own presentation the following day to 200 junior officers was an emotional one:

> He was a brave young officer who fought the whole night against the Scots Guards on Tumbledown, had lost half of his soldiers and was taken prisoner on his position. His lessons learned will be unforgettable for you. I can tell you that he was alone there even when he asked for reinforcements twice. It is not important why the reinforcements did not arrive at his position. I can feel the loneliness he felt, but certainly that it is not easy to understand after the war. Be sure that the only thing we would feel would be a sense of 'betrayal'. I can understand him very well because he expected a counter-attack. I was lucky because my comrades reached me so I could withdraw and, because of that, had fewer casualties.

And so the superior military cuts down strategy.
Its inferior cuts down alliances.
Its inferior cuts down the military.
The worst attacks walled cities.

– Sun Tzu[1]

A person with a sense for local history, Rosemarie King married Peter King in the mid-eighties and lives now on Jeremy Moore Avenue in Stanley. She wrote to me, 'I am very much interested to read the full account of the battles on Tumbledown. As I look out of my window each day, it is almost inconceivable that such an event actually took place [...] but the sad reality is still in the forefront of my thoughts.'

Her address is appropriate. As a Stanley siege veteran of the war, Rosemarie spent the first six months of 2007 locating her 234 other fellow veterans still residing in the little capital. They were invited to join serving military veterans who had also been in Stanley on the night of 14/15 June 1982 for 'A Night of Reflection – 25 Years On'.[2] This hot buffet supper reunion held on 15 June 2007 in the Ross Road East Narrows Bar marked that night, precisely twenty-five years before, when Major-General Jeremy Moore put his signature to the Argentine surrender document.

But Rosemarie had done much more than that. In the immediate months post-war not only did she type John Smith's manuscript of his enthralling and definitive book *74 Days* about the Argentine occupation of 'Puerto Argentino' and another shorter account *Falkland Family at War* by Mike Butcher, but also typed the diary of her siege experiences which, twenty-five years later, was presented to the Stanley Museum. In agreeing that I could utilise key extracts from the diary, she emphasised that her decision was made because of the Gurkha representation of war:

> I have given this a lot of thought and decided that as the reputation of the Gurkhas actually held me and many others together throughout the Falklands War from when it was known they had landed, then I will indeed give permission for it to be included in your current book.[3]

Rosemarie's vivid writing also depicted the town as an extension of the Tumbledown battlefield in the war's final forty-eight hours. That year the twenty-five year-old (then Rosemarie Allan) worked as the PA to the Manager of the Falkland Islands Company Limited (FIC). At the time of the Argentine invasion on 2 April she lived in a flat with Peter King in the large white Church House situated just off Ross Road behind the Christ Church Cathedral and adjoining Parish Hall where Stanley Holloway presented shows to the West Yorkshire Battalion during the Second World War. This soon became a vulnerable area. Only twelve metres away was the Senior School – but soon converted into an Argentine communications centre. Protection for this high-value target comprised two 20mm Rheinmetall twin anti-aircraft cannon and a 105mm pack howitzer sited in the school yard. There were also Alsatian dogs and two machine-gun posts, each manned by three conscripts, in the alleyway between Church House and the school.[4]

The siege residents tuned into the BBC World Service broadcasts for news updates. However the situation in 'Puerto Argentino' deteriorated with news of the British Task Force's imminent arrival in the Total Exclusion Zone and, on 27 April, daily black-outs and an initial 5pm to 7am curfew came into force. The following day it was recommended that townspeople relocated themselves to 'safe houses'. So Rosemarie and Peter moved, on 29 April, to a 'safe' two-bedroom stone cottage at 39, Fitzroy Road in the next block directly south of Church House. This was the family home of Glad and Joey King (Peter's parents) and his brother Robert who was in the Falklands Islands Defence Force. He had been sent out on the night of 1-2 April armed with an SLR to defend the small capital against the unwelcome Argentine arrival. He was lucky. Others had to share weapons, there being not enough to go round. A few only had bolt-action Lee-Enfield .303 inch rifles and a single ammunition clip of five rounds. Yet peacetime thinking still prevailed in these hours of absolute crisis because the two boxes of FIDF 'pineapple' Mills L2 hand grenades were not issued. With their inventory item status they were deemed too expensive to replace.

Being twenty-one years of age, Robert was not so good at keeping to the strict curfew times and caused a few stressful moments to the others in the cottage. Also taking up residence here in the heart of 'Puerto Argentino' were Auntie Pud Stacey (*née* King), and the King family's best friends, Maud and Jack Sollis. There are five or six such cottages in this street, and all were full. But not everyone lived in the capital's twenty to twenty-five safe houses. Many stayed in their own timber houses and simply made a trap hatch down to the foundations. When required, they took shelter there. Rosemarie:

> We all had different daily chores. Mine included walking Auntie Pud (who was eighty-six years old) from her home at 23, Fitzroy Road to 39, Fitzroy Road just before curfew. She was amazing and never rushed no matter how manic the shelling and shooting. I was the only member of my large family of eight to be in Stanley for the war. My sister, Val, and her family were at Hope Cottage, Douglas Station, my brother Mike was a crewman on RRS *Bransfield* on which there was a near-mutiny involving Mike and Gerry Johnson plus several supporters in an attempt to blockade the Port of Stanley, my brother David was on a merchant vessel somewhere around New Zealand, and my parents and other two siblings were in England.

And like most people in 'Puerto Argentino' she was wary of Major Patricio Dowling, the notorious Intelligence Section commander of 181 Military Police Company:

> Whilst typing up my diary, I can think of many things not written about including several Major Dowling visits during the early days when we were ordered not to look out of the (Church House attic) window to the east (overlooking the Senior School). As tempting as it was, his was not a face you would wish to disobey!
> I was very aware when writing in my diary that it could well be picked up on one of the many Argentine 'visits' to our house and, with that in mind, many entries are very basic.

Initially Rosemarie wrote in her diary infrequently. Regretting this later, she wrote, 'I wish I'd started my messy diary on day one. Probably didn't as suppose I hadn't expected it all to last so long.'

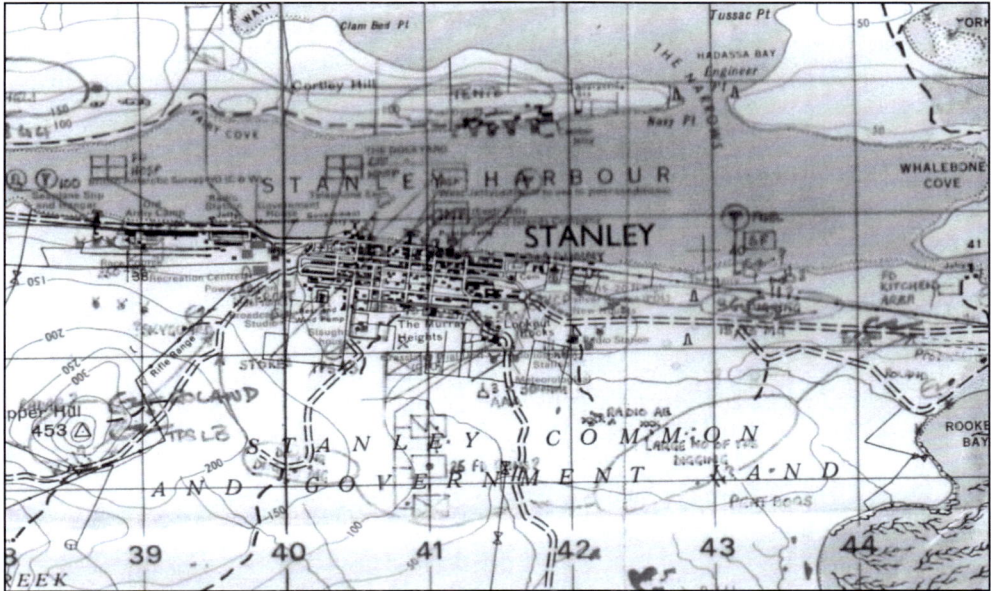

Map 7 – Original map indicating Argentine enemy positions in and around 'Puerto Argentino' (Stanley) according to intelligence received by the 1st/7th Gurkha Rifles when on board *QE2*, May 1982.

However on 21 May as the British landed at San Carlos eighty kilometres to the north-west as the crow flies, and the Argentine Air Force and its Navy counterpart then began slugging it out there against the Royal Navy, Rosemarie visited Church House. Her writing bloomed with expectancy:

A lovely day today – clear sky and no wind. [...] At the moment it is 1.30pm and nothing has yet happened in Stanley. I can see two vapour trails almost vertical, but didn't hear anything. This morning an Argentine jet flew over. The troops outside the office were busy washing clothes in a big tub at the back [...] Usually at lunchtime there's a lot more movement with troops, but today it's relatively peaceful. Quite a lot live here in the Parish Hall – at the moment there's a jeep here in the ally and a soldier is washing it out. There's a bunker here in the corner between the hall and the school [...] Have a feeling we're in for a dramatic weekend. Last night there was little activity in the vicinity of Stanley – I heard three crumps from 1am.

Not sure whether to have a bath or not – usually get in and they seem to start firing! [...] Last night we had three power cuts [...]

Reckon the British have a job on their hands getting through or rid of a supposed 12,000 Argentine troops. About the only place the troops have not dug or trampled is Arch Green [5] [...] The troops are always sweeping the roads and all over town are 'clean up Stanley' (Puerto Argentino) posters signed by Mario Benjamín Menéndez (Governor). The town is in such a mess except Ross Road, it'll be hard to see if a bomb has dropped! A lot of fences have been taken or burnt to keep the troops warm and used for cooking.

The majority of houses are empty. Most people are in safe houses or, should I say, stone houses which should prove safer from street fighting. This morning a soldier asked me to go and buy him chocolate, but I didn't – we only do for the fellas that are outside our flat. They're very young and are friendly – although I don't talk unless they ask for something to eat. They wanted tooth brushes the other day.

The following day, 22 May, was also the second of the Battle of San Carlos Water. Rosemarie tried not to become concerned about the ultimate worst-case scenario of fighting in the capital:

Today has been quiet. Horribly cold and windy though. [...] Quite a few groups of troops passed, but (they) looked quite dry for once [...] the Argies have pitched tents over our gardens down behind the Globe Store [6] We've a lot of carrots and cabbages there, but I guess they're eaten or flattened by now! [...]

Sitting in the kitchen with Maud and Jack we heard our first bit of shooting (at) 8.30pm. Just a short burst. [...] Slept on the floor last night thinking I wouldn't sleep so soundly, but remember dropping off at 12pm and woke at 9am this morning (having) missed all the shooting – blow it. Joey and Jack were the only two in the house to get their money's worth!

It was quite incredible yesterday afternoon watching aircraft over here. An Arg Mirage or Skyhawk aircraft crashed, it could have been one of each, as we watched a lot of smoke from the Yorke Bay/Surf Bay area (to the east of Stanley). The Skyhawk circled down at hill height and after two circuits we saw two fighters crash at the Airport vicinity [...] the pilots ejected and Robert witnessed two parachutes being folded up on Philomel Hill this morning when he left the house.

[...] It's hopeless trying to speculate as to what will happen when the British troops arrive in Stanley. The Argentines are quite (well) dug in. Last night and tonight the street lights have been kept on which is unusual as normally it's pitch dark [...] We usually put the blackouts up at 5.30pm and empty the ashes as, of course, it's not safe to leave the house or even open the door after curfew.

Rob, Pete and I sleep in the sitting room, Maud and Jack in the kitchen, Auntie Pud in Rob's room, and Joey and Glad in their room. Joey very rarely misses any action that takes place at night. He pulls the blackout down and looks out of the window. We always hope he'll wake us up, but he doesn't. He's built a bunker to the west of the house – it's good – and of course many bunker jokes are circulating. Hope we don't have to retreat to the bunker and it only becomes a tourist attraction or cat-house, but in these times of the unexpected one never knows!

[...] The Rediffusion radio is on all day until 6pm. Just music, no programmes, and odd announcement – like the ban on the use of motor-cycles, no water, etc.

The Argentine Navy Skyhawk which she witnessed crashing on 21 May had been piloted by *Teniente de Navío* (Lieutenant) José Cesar Arca. A short while before he had administered the *coup de grâce* on the crippled frigate HMS *Ardent* in Grantham Sound by putting at least one of his four 250 kilo Snake Eye bombs into her stern. However over Falkland Sound after escaping from a malfunctioning Sidewinder missile, Arca's aircraft was severely damaged by Sea Harrier 30mm cannon fire. No option was available other than to fly to 'Puerto Argentino'. But on an east to west approach to its airport, *BAM* (*Base Aerea Militar*) Malvinas, Arca was unable to make an emergency landing because of his Skyhawk's missing landing gear. In consultation with Air Traffic Control, he decided therefore to eject over the sea. Before doing this he activated the Skyhawk's auto-pilot: and so the empty aircraft went 'rogue', first flying towards its parachute-descending pilot, then 'Puerto Argentino', and then on to *BAM* Malvinas in an anti-clockwise direction. The 35mm cannon gunners there failed to shoot it down, but finally the doomed fighter from Río Grande ploughed into a beach. This was the only aircraft to crash near the capital that day. The rescue helicopter had a difficult time in rescuing Arca from the sea, actually putting a side bar into the water for him to grab. It succeeded on the second attempt.

On 25 May, the fifth and final day of the Battle of San Carlos Water, aerial activity around 'Puerto Argentino' and reciprocal ground action became more hectic:

> What a day – lovely, calm, little wind and a perfect sky of deep blue. As the water is off at 9am, [...] I strolled off to work at 9.40am just in time to witness the Argentine Governor and officials addressing a parade of a couple of hundred troops. I stood behind the barrier for some ten minutes before showing my pass and proceeding to the office. It was quiet at work, although the odd bangs: four being bombs on the Airport from, I expect, Harriers, and one bang being when one of the troops managed to shoot his own foot with his pistol!
>
> The Airport was again bombed at lunchtime. From early this afternoon until 5pm we were in and out like yo-yos. One Harrier was circling the sky above showing up well in the cloudless blue sky. A lot of firing from ack-ack and other artillery from the Arg started. Even guns of some sort were firing from the Senior School military zone [...] This Harrier circled around for, say, half an hour. A Pucará (aircraft) was at the same time buzzing up and down the harbour, hugging the sea-wall.

Two days later as British troops prepared to break out of their San Carlos beachhead in twenty-four hours for an exhausting overland near-100 kilometre advance to the capital, Rosemarie tersely noted two tragic incidents in 'Puerto Argentino':

> A cold, dull day [...] this morning jets flew over and the Arg retaliated with ack-ack fire. The guns were going off in front of Harold Rowlands' and I was at my office door – what a din. Firing could be heard to the west most of the day. An Arg soldier stood on a mine up by the 60-acre paddock (half-way along Moody Brook Road on the left, before the rise to Tumbledown) and was blown to pieces – sad. Also one drowned in his bunker outside of Harold's – also sad. Last night at 11.30pm we were all just about to doze off when one heck of a bang shook the

place. As usual we lay waiting for more but, alas, a quiet night followed.

Our water has been off all day [...] We've also had several power cuts since 4.30pm. In fact the water came on and I filled the bath. The power went off and so I had a hot bath in the dark!

On 30 May, the nocturnal Royal Navy bombardments and day Harrier air strikes around 'Puerto Argentino' intensified:

As I write this it is almost the beginning of this day. There's a heck of a din outside from Naval bombardment. I've been looking out of the front porch. The Airport and east in general is getting a hammering. It's pitch dark outside except for the huge flashes as the shells hit. The dogs are barking loud in town, but no shooting.

[...] it was a good night – finally finished at 4am. I'd say it was the busiest naval bombardment yet. Maybe worse tonight though! Today has been quite busy in the air. A lot of Harriers have been over, going around and being fired at by the Arg. At one stage we saw a thing like a missile whistling almost up the tail of a Harrier, but it couldn't have hit as no explosion; all reported as returned to base. The day has been crisp, ground frost – and the bluest of blue skies [...] It's 9.50pm and we can hear machine-gun fire outside – it could be a noisy night! There's been a lot of small arms shooting around town today.

Just (went) outside my house at one stage. The guard was poised to shoot. Still the bread cooked!

Next day, 31 May, the BBC World Service reported incorrectly that the 5th Infantry Brigade had landed. In fact the Gurkhas arrived at San Carlos on a clear 1 June day, and remainder of the Brigade on a foggy 2 June. Rosemarie was expecting almost immediate action in 'Puerto Argentino':

(I) went out this morning at 9am to driving snow, but by 10am all was clear and a crisp, clear day emerged. I had a good night last night – some shooting early. At 5.50am we heard Harriers flying over, a few minutes later came three mighty bangs which shook the house from all sides. In fact it broke panes of glass in Jack Abbott's garage and Willy McBeth's [...] Today Harriers have been evident for most of the day. The Arg fired like hell, missiles, rockets and ack-ack as the Harriers spun around and dropped bombs. The bombs were darn loud. We were standing outside Church House watching and you can sort of feel the pressure meet you.

The BBC has been reporting [...] that the *QE2* forces have landed 3,000 (est.) Scottish, Welsh and Gurkhas! Just hope I live to see one of these Gurkhas with his kukri.

We're sort of expecting to be woken and all hell let loose, but it could be another day or so yet. After two months of this another day or two is nothing [...] Today we helped clear Willie Bowles's house as the Air Force have requisitioned it – thirty of them. All residents on Davis Street had to vacate their houses today.

Robert King recalled that '[...] we were given about thirty minutes in which to remove what we could. We did not leave much and the shed was full by then. I think their washing machine was found up on Wireless Ridge after the conflict!'

On 1 June most of the Gurkhas were flown by Chinook helicopter 'Bravo November' to Goose Green, whilst Rosemarie witnessed the Sea Harrier of Flight-Lieutenant Ian Mortimer being shot down by a Roland surface to air missile due south of 'Puerto Argentino' on the coast. He ejected and, after eight hours in a dinghy was rescued, not by the Argentines, but a Royal Navy Sea King helicopter. Robert saw him come down too and, shortly after the war, met him at the Upland Goose Hotel. However there was no Argentine 'own-goal' that day:

> Today (is) crisp and cloudy. Last night proved quite quiet, some shelling but distant [...] saw not one Harrier today, but this afternoon the Arg shot down a plane right over Eliza Cove area [7] of course high up. I saw the plane explode and most others watched the pilot – after ejecting – floating down. A helicopter headed out and rumour has it that the pilot was picked up. Of course there is a chance it was an Arg plane!
>
> [...] The Arg hospital ship *Bahía Paraíso* is in the harbour. We're expecting 'crumps' tonight and praying our troops are OK. .

Despite a noisy night duel between the Met Station Argentine 155mm howitzer and Royal Navy, Day Sixty-Four of the Argentine occupation on 4 June was otherwise quiet:

> Jesus, it's another of these misty, drizzly damp days – not much action at all. Shelling began first thing this afternoon, first just periodically and then every minute or so but didn't last long. I remember lying in the bath this afternoon whilst the shelling was at its peak thinking, well this is it, then thought, Christ, I've thought that many, many times [...] the shelling died out and the evening has been silent except for the rain slashing the house and a blustery wind screaming around and into all corners.
>
> Poor Auntie Pud Stacey was the victim of yet another incident of entering her house (second night in succession no less) – the house was again fingered right through, groceries and valuables, i.e. bracelets, ring etc. taken. Tonight Captain Hussey has put a guard *in* the house.

Fluent English speaker Naval Captain Barry Melbourne Hussey was a member of the local Argentine Government, responsible for education, medicine and social matters. However one of his constituents, John Smith, was confined to bed by a stomach bug known locally as 'Galtieri's Revenge' from 5 to 7 June. Unfortunately this led to his book *74 Days* containing limited information for this particular period in 'Puerto Argentino'. However with its continued cocktail of domesticity and black-humour, Rosemarie's diary is a vivid surrogate for this local history shortfall during those seventy-two hours. 5 June:

> It's a lovely moonlit night [...] Earlier there were a number of crumps [...] Blow me,

wrote the last sentence too soon – just had some shelling, so guess the Navy are awake. In fact they're still shelling, but in moderation.

Early this afternoon I kneaded my bread in time with the shelling! Along the seafront the Arg were firing small arms (7.62mm rifles) into the harbour at gulls, quarks, loggers, etc. They have been seen making quark stews – wonder if it was tasty!

We're out of meat from the Butchery so hope they leave some quarks!

6 June:

[...] what a grotty Sunday, wet, windy and darn cold. Guess the weatherman took offence at the din during the night! We had hardly a minute's sleep when the shelling began. It started at about 3am. Some 2,000 or so shells must have been fired: sometimes they're hammered out every second for, say, bursts of fifteen, and sometimes every other second in bursts of eight. There were that many, some close, others very distant you'd never count them. We hear tonight on the BBC that the Gurkha, Welsh and Scottish Brigade are in the east and getting into position [...]

The heavy rain today has done a good job by washing the almost inch-thick mud off the roads. The troops use the kerb edges to 'relieve' themselves and chuck litter! It's painful in the mornings going to the shops as pathetic creatures loom up in front of you begging for you to buy food for them. In some cases people – including eight year-old children, have been threatened with guns (which are always carried by troops), if one refuses to get them what they want. Today wasn't too noisy, so let's hope the Admiral (Sandy Woodward) wants to sleep tonight!

There are a lot of Arg troops living in many town buildings [...] We still use the office from 9am and until 1pm. The West Store [8] and Co-Op [9] are open from 10am until 12am. Curfew is now from 4pm until 8.30am. (and) orders by the Arg are to be [...] adhered to. In front of our office is a barricade, and also there's one further towards the Globe Bar. No one is permitted to use this section of the street unless issued with a pass card by the Authorities, and then to restricted hours [...] Most houses on Davis Street have been looted, fences (back) chopped down and burnt, and poultry and cats killed and eaten. One cannot get up onto Callaghan Road as access roads have been blocked with notices to the effect that you'll get 'shot'!

What an amount of vehicles the Arg (have) brought in. Mostly big jeeps (Mercedes), lorries for transporting troops, diggers, excavators, etc. It was rumoured that a large trench was dug down at the cemetery to take 1,000 [...] They did start to dig bunkers in the cemetery, but were successfully stopped. There must be hundreds of bunkers and several ammo dumps in the town. The perimeter is surrounded, but of course we can't get to see it. You can see ack-ack guns around. There are still two machine-guns nests on John Street [...] The front of the Senior School is also well armed. On either side of the steps are another two machine-gun nests. In the alleyway there's an Alsatian dog. The Parish Hall seems to be housing top men, and a guard is posted outside.

We cannot go to our clothes line, peat shed, or litter bins as the dog makes such

a din and they have been known to break loose. So you don't feel too safe. Madge
Biggs's sweet shop is closed. She sold all her sweets to the West Store as the troops
kept breaking in and nicking them. The West Store is also designated as a safe
house – safe as you'll get sort of thing. About thirty locals live there from (the)
curfew [...]

7 June:

The troops were in luck today – [...] clear blue skies. Harriers took advantage (of
this) and soared across the sky. One Harrier dived down up west on Arg heavy
artillery, bombed it and shot off. Apparently the aircraft was a long way off when
the Arg ack-ack fire began. All day shelling or machine-guns and rifles have been
firing. From about 11.30am until well into the early hours. It was almost all
heading west and in great quantities. We spent a lot of time watching out of the
porch, some shots lighting up the whole town. It was a clear, bright night with a
full moon and no wind, so a perfect shelling atmosphere. As I write this tonight
the Navy is blasting shells hell, west and crooked – mostly west!

We hear via (the) BBC tonight that our Governor Menéndez wishes to go into
battle. He has stated that we're enemy, but as civilians we will be held in a safe
place – very considerate, I must say! Life in town has not really changed, but we
are expecting more restrictions and possibly all being housed into one building.
Just because Goose Green is free, the campers there seem to think it's nearly all
over – joke – and they make such bizarre statements and comments which could
have an adverse effect on peoples' well-being in Stanley. It would be an eye-opener
for most to see Stanley – it's like being inside a fort and the shelling and shooting
is that frequent that we'll miss it when it's all over. Mind, might feel one and end
up six foot under!

Today the water has only been on for two hours. Some parts of town have had
days of no water at all. During shelling the Filtration Plant [10] has taken a battering
plus subsidiary buildings further into the town. Rumour has it that the Arg troops
are bathing in our high level tank! Consequently all water has to be boiled in an
effort to avoid diseases spreading. A lot of the Arg troops have 'trench foot',
gangrene, hepatitis, exposure, etc. We have only two doctors, Mary Elfinstone and
Alison Bleaney, both inexperienced, so cannot afford to have outbreaks of any
kind. We do have an Arg Dr Mario helping out [11]   [...]

Every evening it seems the Arg authorities go to houses and check that all
people are present and no extras! Usually only a couple of houses are inspected [...]

8 June:

[...] We've had a pleasant day – almost spring-like [...] Let's hope the weather holds
for our soldiers [...] As I write this the shelling has again begun – it's 10.10pm. It is
fast becoming a daily and nightly occurrence this shelling and shooting. We
watched plenty of Harriers today, but two in particular were low and came under
heavy fire from the Arg guns in and around town. As is often the case, the Arg

took that long getting their range; the sky was a mass of exploding shells and the Harriers were miles off. It is fantastic to watch it, but always praying the Harrier can make it into thick cloud and then scream out of the other side. In last night's shelling, Evie and Tim Halliday's caravan was flattened. The Arg have a radar up by their caravan.

Today the residents of the Hudson Villas[12] were told to empty the personal effects from their houses as the Arg troops were moving in. Also the people at Stanley Cottage[13] were told not to live there at night time, so people are being squashed more and more into the town centre. Pete and I went for a walk up around Davis Street this afternoon – first time in about a month or more – what a mess with bunkers, troops and private houses (nearly all) with iron and wood over all windows, a bit like a ghost town and getting worse by the day.

I can't wait to see a Gurkha with a full bag of Generals' heads!

The Gurkhas *were* getting closer to 'Puerto Argentino'. Just north of Fitzroy, twenty-five kilometres from Stanley, our D Company had already been in action that day against the Skyhawks that bombed *Sir Galahad* and *Sir Tristram*. And more of our Battalion was flying up by helicopter to join D Company on 9 June:

Perfect Harrier sky today. A crisp, clear atmosphere but crippled by the constant din of shells being blasted off and rifle shots. This morning two Harriers flew in and came across from Fairy Cove[14] to attack positions to the west of the town. The Arg seem to have several 155mm guns which are a menace to the Brits. They're known as 'Big Bertha'. I don't reckon the Brits will have their assault on Stanley until these 155mm guns are put out of action. The biggest problem for the Brits must be the fact that the Arg heavy artillery is so close to the town – as one 155mm gun is up by our Power House (sub-station), and one up by the houses on Davis Street [...] I hear our Beaver hangar has been requisitioned – for the mortuary of all things, and is storing hundreds of bodies. The Beaver has been put outside. Action today has been to the south-west and north. We had a couple of hours of shelling last night and, alas, tonight's barrage has already begun!

[...] Even though I may get shot before this war is over, I'm darn pleased I stayed and witnessed things firsthand. Of course when we could leave we used to think, well, maybe it would be sensible to go, but now when we obviously can't leave and don't have to think about it, things seem different. Living here is such a contrast to what it was – it's gone from slow motion, peace and tranquility, to fast past, dangerous and mind-stretching! Where else would you see conscripts getting their first shooting practice in the middle of a main town, sitting and standing along the seawall shooting at wildlife and buoys in the harbour?

When the Harriers today bombed positions up by the School Hostel,[15] I was walking down the front road in front of Arch Green.[16] A din, like a heavy thunderstorm, screamed through the town and arrested me in my footsteps. I almost came face to face with a grotty-looking Arg soldier and we both looked up to see what was happening, saw nothing and seconds later the noise subsided. He went one way and me the other.

By 10 June the climax was near. Day Seventy of the Argentine occupation was also

Corpus Christi and the Argentine national Malvinas Day. The Gurkhas tabbed eastwards another twelve kilometres to Wether Ground and came under 155mm artillery fire in the late afternoon:

> Another crisp, bright and calm day [...] Last night there was quite a bit of activity – shelling and shooting, it seemed to stop at about 1.30am and then a lot of activity with helicopters flying over town. This morning I was whistled out of bed after 8am when several Pucará aircraft zoomed up the harbour, hugging the sea wall. They seemed to head in the Murrell area, dropped bombs of some sort, and then three returned to the Airport.
>
> You'd think the Airport would be unusable, listening to the BBC, but a couple of days ago three Hercules – Arg planes – landed in the dead of night. This evening an Arg Red Cross ship arrived in – *Bahía Paraíso* – which was here about a week ago. People of the International Red Cross are said to be on board, but I don't expect we'll ever know. Arg troops down by our rubbish dump still scurry through the litter bin contents as the carters empty the bins each day, retrieving apple cores, crusts, etc. [...]
>
> I don't think there'll be much left of Stanley at the end of this. We've had a lot of shelling and 155mm gun firing all day, and it's still happening at 10.30pm. Harriers over today. Again today the Harriers were in action. We were about to go into the Post Office [17] when all hell let loose. What a din – haven't yet found out what happened, but lots of smoke belched from the Murrell area. It sounded like Harriers, so let's hope it was and not the Arg planes.
>
> I'm feeling optimistic and tomorrow I'm going to buy some red, white and blue wool to make a hat for the first British soldier I see!
>
> The Argentine troops in town are waiting for the Brits to arrive, and have been in a state of full alert for weeks (at least two) now. We've been expecting hard times but so far nothing has changed thank goodness. I've spoken with a fair number (no Generals!) of the Arg garrison and have yet to meet one who wants to fight for the Malvinas. Most are pleasant home-loving folk and just want to go home. One soldier was here in the Kings' house tonight – he said that all the men born in 1962 were recalled to the military service, hence the reason he was here [...]

On 11 June 3 Commando Brigade was preparing for its night attack on the Argentine Outer Defence Zone of Mount Harriet, Goat Ridge, Two Sisters and Mount Longdon as the Gurkhas continued to be shelled that day and next by the 155mm howitzer behind Sapper Hill. The early-morning Harrier attack around 'Puerto Argentino' also included two missiles launched by a British Wessex helicopter at the Police Station. As Rosemarie noted, one hit its target:

> After a heavy frost last night, today has been perfect. Clear sky and no wind. Last night we again dropped off to sleep in the early hours to the Royal Navy vs. 'Big Bertha'. Shelling was fast and furious but nothing like the abrupt awakening I got this morning.
>
> At approx 8.15am all hell let loose. I zoomed out of bed to witness Harriers

being attacked from all quarters. Tracer bullets formed a patchwork effect in the air in front of the Town Hall, and over the harbour, rockets and missiles were swishing past – but all in vain. The Harriers bombed the Airport and other Arg installations around the Murrell and Camber areas[18] – what a noise. The glass in the windows rattled and some in our house took for cover. In all the action by the Arg to get the Harriers, a rocket went astray and finished off through the roof of the Police Station. The rocket left a large hole – approx forty-five per cent of the building was affected.

It's hard to concentrate as, at the moment (10.15pm), there's heavy firing going on outside [...] Lots of Harriers have flown today – the Arg have fired like mad, but thank goodness their accuracy hasn't improved with use and no Harriers were hit [...] it's a bit eerie looking out at night time as the town is blacked out and the shelling etc. echoes around the place.

The Arg have given the town a new look. The International Red Cross arrived, and today there's not a gun nest in sight or a bedraggled-looking soldier anywhere. Bet tomorrow's another story!

[...] I've been busy knitting tonight the hat for the first British soldier I see. Hope they're another month, otherwise I'll never get it finished! The Argentine Red Cross ship left this afternoon. For the past two days we've been lucky enough to get water all day. The shops have still not run out of any essentials. In fact I have run out of nothing except tomatoes! [...]

Today, Pete, Rob and I went for a walk around the town and included Brandon Road and Davis Street. What a mess to say the least, they're into every yard. Missile launchers, ack-ack guns and 155mm guns surround the perimeter of Stanley. And also in the town, for instance the Junior School yard, there's a missile launcher. The Senior School and Stanley House [19] also have heavy artillery. It's 1.50pm and there's quite a din outside [...] Hope the Brits know what they're doing, mind it's also saddening to see so many young Argentines being killed. Our plumbers saw hundreds (a figure of 800 was mentioned) being marched into the sea at the head of the bay and having to stand there whilst (I suppose) officers bombarded the water with rifle fire.

For what reason these conscripts were subjected to such treatment is not known. However the British missile attack on the police station was probably an attempt to target Rosemarie's *bête noire*, Major Patricio Dowling of the 181 Military Police Company. By first light on 12 June, 3 Commando Brigade had secured all its objectives. Judging by her portrait of the British artillery fire and Argentine return fire from within and around 'Puerto Argentino', the latter could rightfully claim now to be an integral part of the Tumbledown battlefield. These final seventy-two hours of the siege were the worst. Rosemarie:

A crisp, clear day with black ice covering the streets after a hard frost. No wind again. Today has been a sad existence. Sue Whitley and Doreen Bonner were killed last night. Mrs Mary Goodwin received severe cuts etc. on her arm and leg. Laurie Goodwin and Steve Whitley were also hurt. I have heard that a shell exploded close to John Fowler's house where the above, plus a lot of other civilians, were living. Seems the roof collapsed and shrapnel entered the house. I've had no first-hand account of the happening. Later today, about 11am, a shell flattened Danny Borland's house. He is in England, so it's empty. Last night and today have been fierce, shelling and shooting from approx 10pm last night until 5pm this evening. Thousands of shells zoomed over the town – close – and it is believed that it was one of these shells that struck Fowler's house. Other houses up at Ross Road West were struck by shrapnel.

At approx. midnight a lot of rifle shooting began, at that stage we vacated our normal sleeping places and lay under the window getting there at a fast pace. At this stage the power had died and was not restored until 11am this morning in our area; other areas still had no electricity this afternoon. All people living west of the monument were ordered to move into the town by 4pm today. Almost a hundred children are still in town and 600 adults, so the centre of town is quite crowded. Since 5pm we have only heard a few shells so are praying for a peaceful night [...]

Apart from last night and today, being a non-stop battlefield, the ice on the road proved a hazard to the Arg drivers and many fences were demolished completely or partially [...] Today eight Panhard armoured cars with 90mm guns were parked right up Villiers Street, so goodness knows where they are destined for tonight. [..] Back to the nineteen-hour battle. The shelling from the Navy seemed to be from the south-east and heading to the west towards Moody Brook. The small-arms fire seemed to be from the south – up in the paddocks behind here – north to the Camber area. Apparently Arg troops spotted a helicopter over towards the Camber and shot like hell in that direction for approx fifteen minutes. The noise was so loud it sounded like a street fight and pinging the house. Not a feeling you would want to repeat, but guess it's inevitable before long [...]

All day the Arg troops have been firing guns – 155mm jobs, one up at our Met Station, to Brit positions up on Mount Longdon and Mount Kent. They fired in that direction for hours. Shells were going off rapidly, sometimes two a second [...] sometimes eight in a row, and then a pause. A lot of Harriers have been over, criss-crossing in the sky. Wish they'd bomb these 155mm guns as they make such a din. They shake the house with every shell when fired from the Met Station area. When we went home today, it was obvious the (International) Red Cross had departed – all the machine-gun nests had been rebuilt and back on the road outside the Senior School. Bedraggled Arg troops were wandering the streets. Also saw Arg marines looking fresh – new uniforms – and apparently came off the Arg Hospital Ship [...]

On 13 June the Gurkhas flew eastwards up from Wether Ground to an area just south of Two Sisters. We were preparing for the second phase of the Divisional attack: this time against the Argentine Inner Defence Zone comprising Wireless Ridge, Tumbledown, Mount William and Sapper Hill. All these features were, at most, only five kilometres from 'Puerto Argentino'. Rosemarie's penultimate diary entry of the war is precise in recounting the intense British shelling that completely undermined Argentine morale:

Another crisp, icy, dry day although some snowflakes late this afternoon. The night proved not too bad, although at 7pm yesterday the Brits shelled Moody Brook and what a fire was still burning at midnight. They also blew up a radar installation by the Met Station which is full up with rockets. Today, about midday, a Brit shell flattened Wilfred Newman's house on Davis Street plus several sheds in the area. A rocket also damaged Derek Evans' house and went through Harry Milne's garage.[20] Also an Arg Chinook was hit at the Racecourse. A shell landed on Davis Street outside Pat McPhee's, made its mark, and broke the glass in Pat's house. A shell also landed at the top of Hebe Street.

This morning more fences are down where a lorry slid on the ice. One lorry went into an ELW warehouse[21] at the head of John Street. The streets around here are congested with crashed vehicles on the hills, others such as Marine three-tonners strewn across the roads after skidding. A dozen Mercedes Benz jeeps are parked along Fitzroy Road from Philomel Street to Hebe Street. A lot – we have some pieces – of shrapnel landed in the town. Shelling has been vicious today and is still going on, but by the Argentine troops and it's not so fast [...]

One incident today was remarkable. I was stirring a shortbread mix here at the Kings' looking out of the window and almost ducking as the shelling was flippin' violent and scary to say the least. OK inside, but shrapnel can be heard dropping, and so it's dangerous outside. Well, I couldn't believe my eyes, lots of Argentine troops came running down the back of the Kings' paddock and ended up on the back lawn. When we went out only two were armed, and one held a knife out of thirty soldiers. They said they wanted to surrender to Jack Sollis who was talking to them first. Of course he said they couldn't surrender to us, and so they had a rest for a few minutes saying how dangerous it was up on top of the town.

Shelling from the Brits today was widespread and, at times, I'd about convinced myself they'd gone mad and all were having a crack! Smoke shells were landing into the harbour over by the Camber, others spread through town, the Racecourse, Davis Street, Hebe Street and Cemetery Cottage area.[22]

It's 10.30pm and the 155mm gun is going off like a maniac, shaking the house and hard on the ear drums to say the least.

I finished the hat tonight.

Next day, 14 June, was the seventy-fourth of the Argentine occupation. It was also the day of the Argentine surrender when 'Governor B. Mario Menéndez' became a special category prisoner. Rosemarie's account of the night's outgoing Argentine artillery fire at the Scots Guards and Gurkhas on Tumbledown provides a compelling context to the fighting there:

Again a crisp, cold day. Sprinkling of snow on the ground. What a day, started with ten hours of fierce artillery fire. Last night was a hairy existence. We spent a lot of time looking from the front porch. Shelling was fierce from the Davis Street area by the Argentines and also the return shelling from the Navy. Flares were going off to the west, north and a couple down to the east [...] Most of the shelling headed west.

To the north, in particular the Camber Ridge from the Narrows Point[23] up, we could hear the rifles blasting off and watched tracer bullets zoom through the night. Shelling, especially from Args up Davis Street way, persisted throughout the night and, in fact, didn't stop until 10am this morning. We recorded a lot of the shelling and shooting last night. At one stage, whilst I lay on the floor trying to sleep, I counted fifty-six shells being fired in thirty minutes by the 155mm gun up on the top of Stanley to the east of this house. This morning the firing was twice that. Shells were blasting off at three, four, five a time. We had our doubts that the porch window panes would stick the pace, but they made it. We're not sure what's now going on as we're confined to our houses. We haven't been moved to a neutral zone as advised by the BBC media – said the Cathedral area, I think.

It is almost 11am, and out on Fitzroy Road hundreds or thousands of Arg troops are lining (or, should I say, taking up all?) the length of Fitzroy Road that we can see. Philomel Place alleyway is also a mass of sitting and waiting Arg troops. We have yet to find out what they're waiting for. We've no electricity or water. Several fires are evident by the belching of smoke [...]

At 2.10pm this afternoon Patrick Watts broadcast that there was a ceasefire at present. The Brits have advanced as far as the Battle Memorial, and so have taken Wireless Ridge and Tumbledown Mountain areas, and Mount William. The announcement said that the Generals from both sides are to meet at 4pm this afternoon to assess the next step. We are to stay indoors until further notice. Thousands of Argentine troops appear to be in town and, of all the things, we watched them pile up lots of their radio equipment and then set to and bash it up with pickaxes. This happened right here outside the Kings' yard. At approx 1pm we watched the *Forrest*, *Penelope* and an Arg patrol vessel go over to the Camber, pick up troops and bring them over here. We've been watching Arg troops – like straggling sheep, no marching army – gather over at the Camber from all along the ridge.

Sun Tzu's strategy of attack had worked perfectly for the British. They had cut down Argentine strategy and alliances, engaged the latter's military forces with conventional airpower, naval and artillery bombardment and infantry attack, but the final assault against 'Puerto Argentino' never came because 'the worst attacks walled cities'. It is also the least effective way of 'taking whole'. Rosemarie:

It's 2.50pm [...] I've just looked out onto the street and Arg troops are marching up Fitzroy Road heading west. It's snowing periodically today and so they're a wet, sloppy, looking assortment. Most have large capes on and a blanket around their neck. At one stage today about fifty soldiers passed chanting and singing, 'Viva the Argentine Nation'. Harold Rowlands called in a short while ago (3.15pm) and said that in places the road kerbs were laden with rifles and bullets. It will be interesting to hear just how many Arg troops are around and in Stanley. On the whole, so far, the town's faring quite well. With the snow it looks a bit cleaner and brighter.

Yesterday morning the butchery men, consisting of all odds and sods, delivered big slabs of Argentine frozen beef to the families in town. It has thawed out today and so Maud (Sollis) is busy making a large stew and curry. The Gurkhas are in luck if they arrive at the door tonight. I'm not looking forward to hearing how many casualties resulted from last night's battle [...]

On the BBC 5 o'clock news tonight we heard from an Argentine communiqué via London that 'Governor B. Mario Menéndez' has flown to Argentina, and a ceasefire has been agreed but not signed. Now we'll wait for an official notice from MOD to advise the exact position.

The Arg helicopters have spent hours this afternoon scouting the Camber Ridge and ferrying casualties to a Red Cross vessel which is in Port William. We could see the glow of the vessel out there last night, but the ship still hasn't appeared in the Harbour. Pete and Rob have just put up all the blackouts. Curfew is at 4pm and black-out supposed to be at lighting-up time – 5.15pm approx. [...] The water is again off. The electricity is again on, although it has been on and off a couple of times. I had the candles lit, but then the lights returned. Apparently we've now only one generator, so I guess it's a bit overloaded. The lights are not at 100 per cent strength.

It is now 9.30pm and I'm just going to sleep on the floor, but what a treat not to have shells screaming past, and not being sure if you'd be on the other end of the shell or not. We're all rather excited tonight, although (we) know things are certainly not finished with and haven't had a drink to (celebrate) today's events or felt it as total victory. Goodnight.

Alas, the Gurkhas could not accept Rosemarie's invitation to 'a large stew and curry' in what was no longer 'Puerto Argentino' but Stanley again. Most of us had to remain on the Tumbledown-Mount William battlefield until 16 June and fight against the wintry elements before being evacuated by helicopter back to Goose Green.

But Rosemarie's deep-rooted conviction of the Gurkhas' fighting abilities provides an opportunity to chronicle how our Battalion went about its business of preparing and operating in the war with those traditional and battle-winning Gurkha tools of *kaida* and *josh*.

Notes

1. *The Art of War*, Chapter 3 – Strategy of Attack.
2. The invitation contained a request: 'Whether just a paragraph or page, we would appreciate hearing your personal experience(s) of the 14/15 June to contribute to a document for the museum and the archives.'
3. E-mail dated 7 October 2008.
4. One was at the southern John Street entrance and the other against the fence adjacent and to the east of Church House.
5. By the Cathedral.
6. On the junction of John Street and Philomel Street.
7. Due south of Stanley on the coast.
8. By the Cathedral.
9. On the junction of John Street and Barrack Street.
10. At Moody Brook.
11. This Argentine doctor's assistance during the siege included an operation to

      remove a Stanley resident's appendix.

12. Terraced houses on Davis Street.
13. Situated across Ross Road overlooking Victory Green to the east of the Upland Goose Hotel.
14. On Stanley Harbour's northern shore opposite the capital.
15. Situated behind Government House.
16. The green is in front of Church House.
17. On Ross Road.
18. To the east of Fairy Cove.
19. This was the Stanley School Hostel on Ross Road adjacent to the West Store.
20. At Hebe Street.
21. Estate Louis Williams (ELW) warehouse opposite the Globe Store.
22. In East Stanley above the cemetery.
23. At the entrance of Stanley Harbour.

51.   *Teniente de Fragata* Diego García Quiroga in 1982 (larger image).

52.   Government House, Stanley, late June 1982.

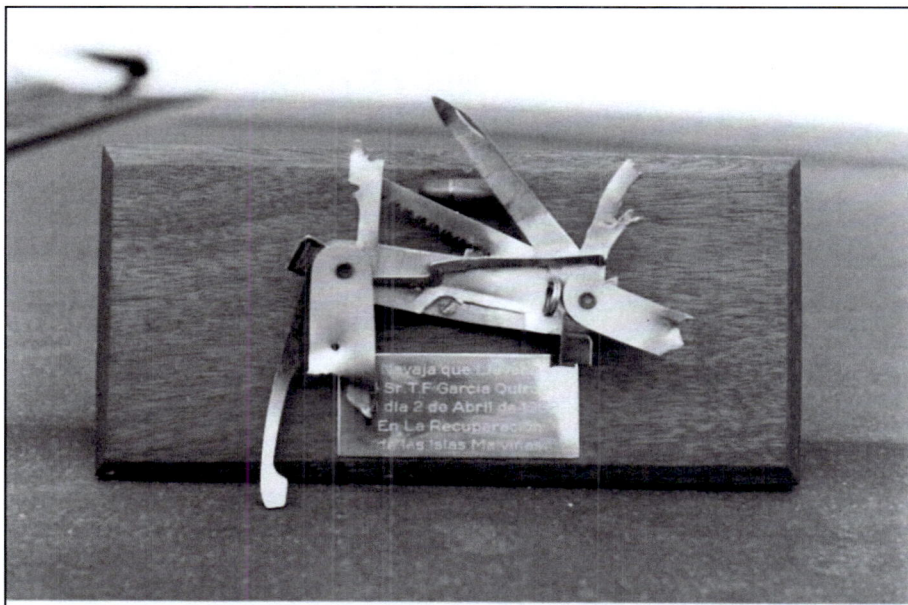

53.   Smashed by a Royal Marine Commando bullet, the Swiss Army Victorinox penknife which saved Diego García Quiroga's life outside Government House, Stanley, 2 April 1982.

54.   King Edward VII Memorial Hospital, Ross Road, 'Puerto Argentino' (Stanley) in late June 1982, where the badly wounded Diego García Quiroga was taken for initial treatment prior to casualty evacuation to Argentina.

55.   The author with the Villarraza family at their Buenos Aires home,
2 April 2007.

56.   Marines of BIM5 move through 'Puerto Argentino' (Stanley),
early April 1982.

57.   Argentina's hero of the Battle of Tumbledown, *Teniente de Corbeta* Carlos Daniel Vázquez (in 1981).

58.   The author with former BIM5 2 and 5 Platoon Commanders Marcelo Oruezabala (left) and Héctor Omar Miño (right), Buenos Aires, 28 March 2007.

59.   Part of the field of fire for Vázquez's 4 Platoon to the south-east, including (middleground left) Mount William's west shoulder.

60.   Part of the field of fire for Miño's 5 Platoon to the west, including (middleground centre) the rocky knoll and Goat Ridge, 15 June 1982.

61.   *Capitán de Navío* Carlos Daniel Vázquez (right) and his eldest son,
       Guardiamarina Carlos Horacio Vázquez.

62.   Carlos Daniel Vázquez: husband and family man.

63.   3 Platoon Commander (RI6/B), *Subteniente* Esteban La Madrid (right) after arrival at the *BAM* Malvinas Airport on 12 April 1982.

64.   La Madrid's platoon marches to 'Puerto Argentino' on 12 April 1982.

65.   La Madrid (right) and some of his men at Moody Brook, April 1982.

66.   The 3 Platoon, RI6/B camp site at Moody Brook, April 1982. Note (background) the abandoned Royal Marines' Moody Brook Camp.

67.   La Madrid (foreground kneeling) at the RI6 B Company HQ with Lieutenant
        Raul Abella (rear, fourth from left), 6 May 1982.

68.   La Madrid (centre) and members of his platoon at Moody Brook as the heli-
        reserve, 12 May 1982.

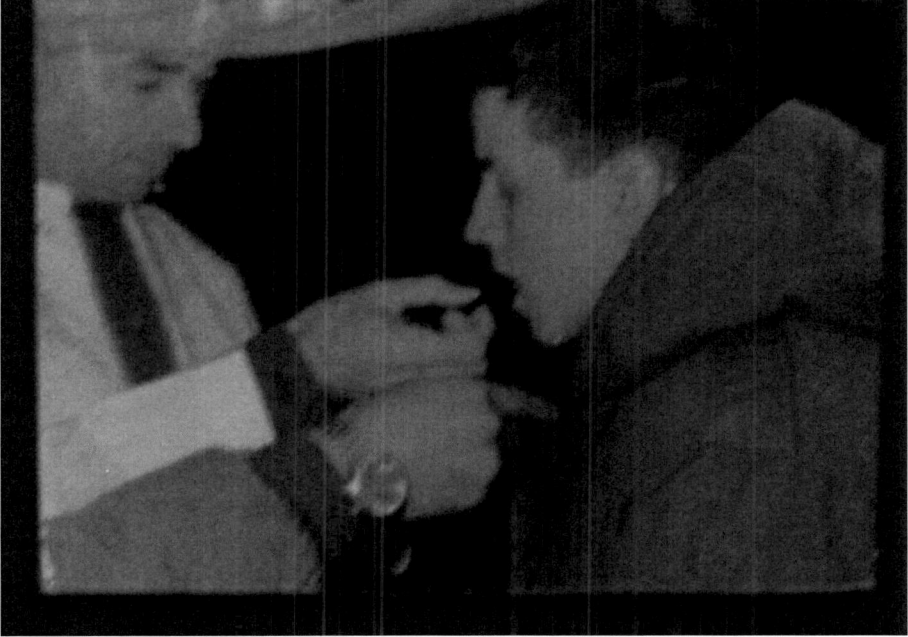

69.   La Madrid receives spiritual support.

70.   B Company, RI6 at Two Sisters North, May 1982.

71.   La Madrid at Two Sisters North on 20 May 1982, twenty-four hours before the British landings at San Carlos.

72.   La Madrid at Two Sisters North on 22 May 1982. Note the two rifle grenades which would be fired against the seven Left Flank Company Guardsmen after the latter had reached Tumbledown's east summit on 14 June.

73.   La Madrid (left) visiting 'the city' to get a shower, 25 May 1982.

74.   La Madrid (left) with his 2IC, 1st Sergeant Jorge Corbalán (centre), and Support Section Sergeant, Sergeant Héctor Echeverría at Two Sisters North, end of May 1982.

75.   The site (foreground) where La Madrid's machine-gunner Horisberger was killed and (middleground) Tumbledown's east summit.

76.   La Madrid, Sergeant Echeverría and Private Disciullo arrive at 'Puerto Argentino' on 14 June 1982 a few hours after the Tumbledown battle. The site at which they are passing by an abandoned Argentine Unimog vehicle is, ironically, where the Liberation Memorial now stands.

77.   La Madrid continues into the 'city' on 14 June 1982. Seven soldiers of his platoon have been killed and nine wounded during the battle and subsequent withdrawal. Another of his soldiers had been killed and a further wounded at the Battle of Two Sisters (11/12 June 1982).

78.   'The poetry of war is in the pity of it' – Wilfred Owen, First World War poet. Argentine fallen (two – foreground) at Tumbledown's east end, 15 June 1982.

79.   Nearly three decades later (in 2011) *Coronel* Esteban La Madrid (foreground centre) remains an active rugby player.

80.   Esteban La Madrid with his daughter, Eugenie, and wife, Patricia.

81.   Stanley, late June 1982.

82.   Digging in at 'Puerto Argentino' (Stanley), April 1982.

83.   Argentine Army Panhard armoured cars in the centre of 'Puerto Argentino',
May 1982.

84.   The Police Station in 'Puerto Argentino' just after the British helicopter
missile strike, 11 June 1982.

85.   An Argentine Army 'Big Bertha' CITER 155mm L33 gun located near the Met Station, 'Puerto Argentino', June 1982.

86. An Argentine Army OTO Melara 105mm pack howitzer on the Racecourse, Stanley, late June 1982.

PHASE IV
GURKHA *KAIDA* AND *JOSH* TO MOUNT WILLIAM VIA TUMBLEDOWN

13   Invincibility lies in oneself

Whose officers and soldiers are trained?
— Sun Tzu[1]

On Friday, 2 April 1982 as a recently seconded and naive Light Infantry officer to the 1st Battalion, 7th Duke of Edinburgh's Own Gurkha Rifles, I was approaching the end of my fourth week as the unit's Operations and Training Officer. The Battalion was part of a newly-formed 5 Infantry Brigade which possessed a NATO 'out-of-area' role with, theoretically, the world as its oyster. So in my Hampshire Church Crookham married quarter lounge as I watched that evening's BBC TV Nine O'clock News of the morning's Argentine invasion of the Falkland Islands, an uncomfortable feeling of disquiet grew.

'God, if this is "out-of-area" then I don't know what else is! We're going to get involved here without any doubt,' was my reflex reaction as the TV screen flickered with images of celebrating Argentine soldiers on amphibious vehicles that rolled along the streets of the tiny capital Stanley.

'You're just a born pessimist,' retorted Tove. My disbelieving Norwegian wife refused to be drawn into thinking about an immediate future with a worst-case profile.

Despite her ridicule of my alarmist reaction to the start of the Islands' seventy-four day occupation, my conviction our Battalion would be immersed sooner or later in this crisis remained rock-solid. As the mother of our two daughters, four year-old Victoria and Emily who was nearly two, Tove had every right to adopt such an attitude. But for anyone in a crisis management profession, military or civilian, thinking 'worst-case' is an obligatory skill. It is necessary to keep a constant finger on the pulse of an ever-changing situation. It implies a devil's advocate process of proactivity in trying to foresee events and devising possible alternative courses of action. And it forces continual use of the intellect and constructive thinking. There are three perceptions of a situation, or in any combination of these three – is, should, want. Worst-case thinking affects perception. But Napoleon Bonaparte got it right:

> At the moment war is declared there is so much to do that it is wise to begin preparation several years in advance [...] I calculate on the basis of the worst possible case [...] (When) it comes to planning a campaign [...] I purposely exaggerate all the dangers and all the calamities that the circumstances make possible. I am in a thoroughly painful state of agitation. This does not keep me from looking quite serene in front of my entourage; I am like an unmarried girl labouring with child. Once I have made up my mind, everything is forgotten except what leads to success.[2]

This particular event 'down south' was to change my life both in the short- and long-term. The knock-on effect immediately started an intensive eight-week Gurkha training enterprise prior to our landing on the Islands that would be unlike anything I had experienced in nearly fourteen years of British Army commissioned service. This had much to do with the Gurkhas' background and their culture. They had two Gurkhali words which already I heard often. '*Kaida*' dominated everything. It means method or rule, the way something works. Sun Tzu uses the comparative word '*Tao*' which 'is what causes the people to have the same purpose as their superior – thus they can die with him, live with him and not deceive him.' [3] This applied to the Gurkhas. Then there was '*josh*', meaning enthusiasm and which enables the mission to be carried out with supreme effectiveness. Hard facts of history speak volumes for these two words. Gurkha British officers, colloquially known in the Brigade of Gurkhas as BOs, have won thirteen VCs, Britain's supreme award for gallantry on the battlefield. But despite Gurkha soldiers only becoming eligible to be awarded the VC as late as 1911, they did not waste time. Two were won by Gurkhas in the First World War, ten in the Second World War, and one more in the Borneo Confrontation. Many other gallantry decorations have been gained by Gurkhas. For example, during the first two years of the 1948-60 Malayan Emergency there were thirty-seven awarded to them out of a total fifty-one despite the Gurkhas representing only a quarter of that country's security forces.

Yet the Gurkha and his culture are full of paradoxes: even the name 'Gurkha' means 'defender of the cows'. One who eventually went to war was Rifleman Dilkumar Rai. Number 21163278 was also the cousin of Rifleman Baliprasad Rai, also of the 1st/7th Gurkha Rifles and included in my first book. 'Dil' served in D Company as the 12 Platoon HQ radio operator:

> My father was in the British Army and had served with the 2nd/7th Gurkha Rifles. Unfortunately, he was killed during the Borneo Confrontation in Sarawak and I was raised by my mother in a village called Simpani – 9, Baksila, Diktel District in Eastern Nepal. I had always wanted to join the British Army as I thought that this would let me travel and see the world outside of my village. Also being in the British Army was perceived as being very reputable in Nepal.
>
> Following my dreams, I enrolled in the British Army as a seventeen and a half year-old boy in the Dharan Depot on 3 November 1979 and completed my basic military training in Sek Kong, Hong Kong. It was always a great desire for me to join my father's Regiment and I was fortunate enough to be selected for the 7th Gurkha Rifles.
>
> As a young soldier, I was determined to be successful in the Army. One thing which had always been on my mind was to go back home on long leave and meet my family, friends and relatives. But with my leave near, the Falklands War broke out. At that time I was on a Gurkha Higher Certificate of Education course, but in everyone's mind and conversation the only subject was the war.

My forthcoming task of co-ordinating and participating in the training programme would leave an indelible impression on me. The Gurkha training standards in the weeks prior to our entry into the Land Theatre of Operations at San Carlos, East Falkland became my benchmark in a later-life profession of a crisis management consultant and, not least, design, construction and delivery of different types of disaster exercises. There would also be one overriding lesson identified and learnt. To possess even a reasonable chance of coping with the unique extremes of battlefield or crisis stress, any preparatory training exercise, no matter its scope and size, must generate the maximum possible realism throughout.

This requires a detailed planning attitude and approach which, in turn, demands considerable investment in effort and time not unlike Sir Winston Churchill's preparations for those legendary wartime speeches in the House of Commons, i.e. for every hour of oration, thirty were required in preparation. My late Aunt Nancy, otherwise the Baroness Seear of Paddington and one-time leader of the Liberal Party in the House of Lords, would also follow Churchill's example. She was the first peer to make a speech whilst televised direct in the Upper House. Using a personal habit of a lifetime, it was done without notes. When asked afterwards by admiring peers as to how she had accomplished this twenty-minute effort, her reply was a crushingly simple, 'Thorough preparation!'

Likewise her brother Herbert, who was my father and Second World War RAF veteran of the longest siege in British history on the Mediterranean island of Malta GC, had a similar speech-making ability founded on the same principle. I was influenced by this family practice. The need to prepare thoroughly by acquiring basic knowledge of the organisation to be exercised through asking all the right questions, 'wrapping the wet towel around my head' in scripting a logical but testing crisis scenario and detailed inputs to ensure a near-perfect as possible crisis management exercise, and diligently capturing all lessons learnt in a thorough post-exercise report would become self-imposed professional standards. Years later this attitude, reinforced the hard way by my Falklands experience, would ironically also be my undoing.

But with the likelihood of a Gurkha deployment, training and exercising would assume an importance unsurpassed at any other point before in my life or since. It would also take place against an ever-intensifying international political process of finding a peaceful solution to this fraught situation. UN Security Council resolutions, US Secretary of State for Foreign Affairs Alexander Haig's peace shuttle, and UN, Peruvian and US peace plans, plus numerous other similar hopeful initiatives, bumbled on and on as an interesting but inconsequential backdrop to the main business of comprehensive Gurkha military training prior to going to war.

In the short period up to this South Atlantic scenario which had now crashed into our lives, the Battalion had been training intensively for air landing operations supporting the Parachute Regiment in *coup de main* or evacuation situations abroad. However the prospect of switching suddenly from the real possibility of air to sea moves, coupled with a complete change in tactics to match this potential Falklands scenario of an offensive 'light infantry' limited war, did not bother the Battalion as much as other British units because the Gurkha soldiers were flexible, already well-trained – and without their wives.

We were also in the Cold War's final decade. During my previous Army appointment as a junior staff officer working in the HQ 1st British Corps Exercise Planning Staff at Bielefeld, West Germany, I had witnessed first-hand just how much strategic and operational fixation had been the hallmark of the British Army since the Second World War. With the exception of Northern Ireland training and operations, the primary use of massive effort and resources to prepare and train the 1st British

Corps' four armoured divisions for the mobile defence of north-west Germany against a Warsaw Pact 'Orange' forces invasion had been pursued for decades. This perceived threat had become a dangerous and classic Sun Tzu *bête noire* of strategic fixation – which was now rocked on its heels by the thunderclap of reality booming from nowhere over the South Atlantic to cause the instant formation of the British Task Force.

Although the Battalion was not given its formal notice to deploy to the Theatre of Operations until 3 May, this did not prevent the Commandant (the 7th Gurkha Rifles official alternative for Commanding Officer), Lieutenant-Colonel David Morgan, from formulating a simple strategy in assuming 'worst-case' and acting in a proactive manner.[4] He had assumed command of the Battalion in October 1981 and, three months later at Stanford in Norfolk, his Gurkhas were participating in Exercise Green Lanyard. This had been designed by the Brigade Commander to train the Brigade in its new role. The exercise was memorable for Colonel David because of a question asked by his friend the CO of 2nd Battalion, Parachute Regiment, Lieutenant-Colonel 'H' Jones. His name would become, arguably, the most iconic of the Falklands-Malvinas War:

> I called him my friend because we were neighbours in Church Crookham, our families vaguely knew each other and 'H' and I were not only at Staff College together, but he looked after me for a few days during my initiation to Northern Ireland. He was most helpful to me as a new CO and I knew then he would be a star of the future, and the following exchange proved my point. The exercise was well into its third or possibly fourth day when I happened to be listening in to the Brigade net to hear this extraordinary exchange between 'H' and our august leader, Brigadier Tony Wilson:
> 'Hello 9. This is 2. Fetch Sunray. Over.'
> Brigadier Tony's voice came on the air: '2. Sunray listening. Send. Over.'
> 'Who the hell is running this fucking shambles?'
> Stunned silence.
> Having been a Lieutenant-Colonel for just three months at the time, for the merest moment I thought that this was perhaps the way one should normally speak to one's superior, but then I realised that you had to be someone really very special to get away with words like that, and I was nowhere near 'H's' league.[5]

But the relatively new Gurkha Commandant's training message now in early April 1982 was equally unambiguous. The political challenges of deploying his Battalion which comprised twenty British officers, 637 Gurkha officers and men from Nepal, and forty-three attached British officers and other ranks (known as BOs and BORs) were left to the British Foreign and Commonwealth Office (FCO) and Ministry of Defence in London to resolve. We had to kick-start our training and other preparations immediately for what, in the end, would be the Task Force's largest fighting unit. The Battalion's invincibility would now lie in the quality of our training for war. It was also important to maintain the momentum regardless of events, because the crucial assumption made at the outset by Colonel David was that we *were* going to be deployed *and* fight in the war. Also our enemy was *never* to be underestimated. His consistent leadership in these issues during this national crisis gave the Battalion confidence that its own environment was intact, trustworthy and predictable, and within which all the Gurkhas could apply their training exertions in a worthwhile manner. Such a strategy is also an important Sun Tzu principle: 'If one acts consistently to train the people, the people will submit'.[6]

The need to implement our training programme immediately had, in some respects, crisis management perspective for the next six weeks. We began individual and platoon basic training for two weeks at our Church Crookham camp seventy-two hours after the Argentine landings and as lead elements of the British Task Force, notably the aircraft carriers HM Ships *Invincible* and *Hermes*, departed from Portsmouth. Our immediate emphasis was on weapon training, zeroing weapons, 'hijacking' range allocations and facilities from other Aldershot area units not likely to be earmarked for the Falklands – and physical fitness. The Gurkha soldier is light years ahead of his British counterpart in fitness levels, and their daily running sessions, known as BIT (Battle Individual Training) continued. Helicopter and first aid training were also prioritised, as were briefings on Falklands' topography and climate, and our assumed enemy: the Argentine land and air forces. Unlike the later Gulf War, US-led Iraq War, and UN and NATO operations in the Balkans and Afghanistan, the potential air threat against us was considerable and our training also had to take this into account.

Time was not on our side however as the politicians and diplomats dithered on the perceived merits or otherwise of Gurkha involvement in Operation Corporate. Indeed the attitude of the FCO in London to the possibility of including Gurkhas in the British Task Force was one of always finding a reason not to deploy them in case this upset relations with other countries or, even worse, the Kingdom of Nepal. At the root of this seemingly inflexible cultural attitude was the perception held by many, also outside the FCO, that the Gurkhas were mercenary troops.

For the Battalion this was a 'battle' that had to be won on two fronts: in London and the Nepalese capital of Kathmandu. As the preparations for our going to war got underway, the FCO asked the British Embassy in Kathmandu for its views on the possible deployment of a British Army Gurkha Regiment with the Task Force. The Ambassador, John Denson, was of the old school, and maintained initially that it would be much better if a Gurkha Regiment was not included: the rationale being that the Embassy would then not find itself mixed up in any controversy. However by pure coincidence the 7th Gurkha Rifles already had 'its man in Kathmandu' located at the Embassy. This was the British Defence Attaché, Lieutenant-Colonel Keith Robinson, and his knowledge of the 'interface' protocol between the Nepalese Royal Palace and the country's Government Ministers and military would prove its weight in gold as far as our Battalion was concerned. It was also in accordance with the Sun Tzu principle of superior knowledge (in this case of Gurkha culture): 'Thus it is said, "Victory can be known. It cannot be made."' [7]

But first Colonel Keith took the initiative to have a discussion with John Denson in which the former not only emphasised the overriding necessity of the British Army being allowed to decide unilaterally on its force composition for the Task Force, but also the well-known points as to why Gurkhas should not be excluded from normal operations. However the Ambassador was still concerned that if Gurkhas were deployed then Nepal would not only find its relations with Argentina embarrassing, but also those with its powerful neighbour China which was backing Argentina. There seemed, therefore, little hope of any breakthrough to this impasse.

A couple of days later Colonel Keith was approached by the Royal Nepalese Army Director of Military Intelligence who was the conduit between Defence Attachés and Army HQ, and asked if the 7th Gurkha Rifles' officer could brief him on the Falklands crisis. Colonel Keith cleared this meeting with the Ambassador, but then decided to utilise his knowledge on Nepalese protocol and cleverly suggested to this officer, 'Perhaps I should also brief the Chief of Army Staff?'

The shrewd British Defence Attaché made this offer knowing that the Chief of Staff (COS), General Simha Pratap Shah, might then afterwards have to inform Nepal's absolute monarch His Majesty King Birendra Bir Bikram Shah Dev, who was also the Supreme Commander of the Royal Nepalese Army, of the conversation's content. The meeting with the General was agreed and it took place in his office on the appointed day. After providing his briefing on the current situation, Colonel Keith ventured to ask, 'What do you think the reaction of His Majesty's Government would be to the possible inclusion of a Gurkha Regiment in the British Task Force being sent to re-take the Falklands?'

The General replied in the context of the 1948 Tripartite Agreement between Britain, India and Nepal which regulates Gurkha service in the latter two countries, 'Under the Tripartite Agreement Britain does not require Nepal's agreement, but only that we should be kept informed.'

'Of course that is so,' was Colonel Keith's response, 'but we don't want to embarrass a very good friend if we can help it.'

'I can see no reason why Nepal should be embarrassed,' the General replied soothingly. 'I feel that Nepal would be quite happy for Britain to include Gurkhas in the Task Force that's being sent to the South Atlantic. So could I be kept informed of events as they unfold?'

It was a simple matter to agree to General Simha Pratap Shah's request. Colonel Keith also realised that all decisions of this nature required King Birendra's agreement and that the COS would now have to brief His Majesty accordingly. On return to the British Embassy he went to the Ambassador and reported on his conversation with the General and the latter's decision. John Denson was surprised at this outcome. Nonetheless he decided to explore belatedly his own political channel of communication and added, 'I'll ask the Nepalese Foreign Minister for his views.'

Not unexpectedly these turned out to be favourable as, without doubt and in accordance with Colonel Keith's gilt-edged assumption, the COS had already briefed the King before the Foreign Minister was granted his audience with His Majesty. Subsequently the Ambassador then informed the FCO that he could now see no reason why Gurkhas should not be included as Nepal had no objections. For his part, Colonel Keith kept his word and ensured that all telegrams coming into the British Embassy concerning the Falklands-Malvinas War, less obviously anything too sensitive, were copied to the COS. In essence therefore, both General Simha Pratap Shah and the Royal Palace were the recipients of whatever the British Embassy and Colonel Keith received.

There were also other 7th Gurkha Rifles assets still abroad. One was the Battalion's B Company serving on a six-month overseas tour of duty in Belize. They would arrive back at Church Crookham six days before we embarked on board *QE2*. Another was C Company in Cyprus on a training exercise which was terminated prematurely. After expensive civilian car indulgence freight, much to the owners' great irritation, had been unloaded from their Hercules transport aircraft to create more passenger space, the Company was flown back to the UK for the second phase of our 'work-up' training at Sennybridge in Wales. Then there was Captain Nigel Price, the Mortar Platoon Commander. He kept a 'pre-embarkation' diary and, twenty-eight years later, could recite to me an accurate tale of his exotic repatriation:

I had been pestering Major Bill Dawson, the Battalion Second-in-Command, to send me on the Jungle Warfare Instructor's Course in Brunei for ages and, finally, he did so. I flew from Gatwick on Monday 29 March via Dubai to Hong Kong, and so was there at the start of April preparing to fly onwards to Brunei for the course. On Saturday, 3 April I woke to find the papers full of news of the Argentine invasion. The next day I visited our 2nd Battalion at Lyemun Barracks and asked the Adjutant, Captain David Hayes, to send a signal to the 1st Battalion. I insisted that if the latter were going to the Falklands as part of the 5th Infantry Brigade, then they were not to leave me behind!

On Monday, 5 April ten members of 3 Para were taken off the course and returned to the UK. Two days later those of us remaining on the course flew to Brunei. The course began on 8 April. However, nine days into it on Friday, 16 April, after all the basics of jungle survival, navigation and immediate contact drills, I was halfway through a jungle navigation exercise when some news caught up with me. My section stumbled out of the jungle for a break in the exercise when the course chief instructor took me to one side and told me I was to return to the UK. The reason given was that my Battalion, a Royal Anglian Battalion (then the Spearhead Battalion), and 2nd Battalion, the Scots Guards were all to reinforce Belize lest the Guatemalans move against it in sympathy with Argentina! (Maybe this was just a cover story, but that is what I was told).

So, instead of returning to the jungle, I was driven back to TTB (Training Team Brunei) at Tutong, and the following day handed back my kit. On Sunday 18 April a car drove me from Tutong back to Brunei City and, at 7.30pm, I boarded a Cathay Pacific DC10 bound for Hong Kong. At Kai Tak Airport a staff car took me to HMS Tamar (the British HQ) where I spent two nights. On the Tuesday evening I boarded a British Caledonian DC10 to Gatwick, arriving there via Dubai early on 21 April.

A car took me to Church Crookham where I learnt that the Royal Anglians were indeed off to Belize, but that the Gurkhas, Scots Guards and Welsh Guards (in a re-constituted 5th Infantry Brigade) were bound for the Falklands! I had forty-five minutes to re-pack and then hitched a ride with the Regimental Signals Officer, Captain Kit Spencer, in one of his Landrovers to Sennybridge. At that point we were told that our *QE2* embarkation date would be on 5 May – a date which was to slip.[8]

It had taken Nigel four days to trundle economy class from the TTB jungle to Sennybridge Training Area to start preparing for war. However a Scots Guards Sergeant on Nigel's course travelling to the same destination and for the same reason was recovered much faster. His affluent Regiment bought a *first-class* ticket to fly him on a British Airways Concorde toute de suite from Kai Tak to Heathrow, thereby permitting a less stressful arrival at Exercise Welsh Falcon.

This 5th Infantry Brigade exercise had its focus on shooting, section and platoon live-firing exercises and a final four-day Brigade field training exercise. But the pre-training co-ordination conference had revealed a serious problem. Despite our requests, the Sennybridge training staff would not 'bend' the range rules and permit live-firing exercises at night. They were incapable of carrying out the considerable mental quantum leap required from their comfortably predictable world of 'peacetime' training rules and restrictions to our urgent 'wartime' requirement for optimal training realism and flexibility. We would be the ones going to war and fighting the enemy at night – yet, crazily enough, not be permitted to train on their ranges with such vital simulation exercises. Our men had to become ultra-confident experts in fire and manoeuvre, that basic of all battlefield offensive movements when one part of any attacking unit is moving into a final assault position while the other is providing suppressive fire to keep enemy heads down. It was essential such night exercises be carried out under conditions which would resemble accurately a Falklands battlefield by using live, not blank, ammunition.

The Confucious philosopher Lao Tzu, a contemporary of Sun Tzu, described this dilemma with precision, 'If you tell me, I will listen, If you show me, I will see. But if you let me experience, I will learn.'

Moreover the Battalion had received an augmentation of General Purpose Machine-Guns which doubled our GPMG arsenal to ninety-four guns. Our enemy did not possess the equivalent. This meant each rifle section of ten men now possessed two GPMGs, and new tactics had to be devised and practised using live ball and link ammunition by day and night. Our ultimate aim was to generate unbeatable teamwork and firepower to defeat the enemy on the battlefield. The prospect of going to war focused the mind and reinforced the fight against bureaucracy wonderfully. So the Nelsonian blind eye was turned to the problem, thus enabling the Gurkhas to train with live ammunition at night throughout this period at Sennybridge. At the end of the twelve days there the *ketaharu* (boys) could really claim they had lived up to their Gurkhali saying: '*Training ma pasina bagae larain ma khun joginchha.*' ('If you sweat during training, you can save blood during the real thing.')

But we never solved serious training ammunition shortages encountered during this period. For example, only six Very flares were allocated to the whole Battalion itching to practise its night-fighting skills. There was also just a limited amount of SLR 7.62mm tracer ammunition available, not enough 66mm anti-tank live rockets, and no Milan anti-tank live missiles. All these would be required for the decisive art of night fighting which would be employed predominantly by British land forces in the Falklands Theatre of Operations. A vital item which would require an improvised training programme was also delivered to Sennybridge to coincide with our arrival – the first batch of the new Clansman radio system to replace our antiquated Larkspur sets. Kit Spencer, also employed crisis management to issue Clansmen rapidly, withdraw Larkspur, and implement a signals training programme for all Gurkha radio operators on how to operate a system they had never seen before. But we were progressing and Nigel Price noted in his diary, 'The Gurkhas are quite serious now, the play gone from the exercise: God help anyone who gets in their way.'

The Brigade field training exercise began on 26 April. On the second day Nigel's Mortar Platoon took part in an impressive firepower demonstration together with other units' mortars, artillery, four RAF Jaguar and four Harrier GR3 ground attack aircraft, all filmed by the BBC and ITN. It was beautifully stage-managed, but the target area was at such an ultra-long range that binoculars were required to view this 'representation of war'. Afterwards I wondered how reality would be on the Falklands battlefield. The answer came in little more than six weeks. Next day, just before the Battalion's attack on a simulated 'Port Picton' capital, we received the General's visit which also rapidly developed into a crisis management situation for Colonel David:

> As a Commanding Officer one always dreaded visits from senior officers, particularly when you were given no notice. 'Don't make any arrangements, old chap [...] only with you for twenty minutes or so.'
>
> That sort of language usually spelt panic, but with the 'whocker-whocker' of the helicopter in the distance there was nothing much that could be done anyway. The visitor was Lieutenant-General Sir Frank Kitson – a small but powerful and influential Deputy Commander-in-Chief of HQ United Kingdom Land Forces (UKLF) with a fierce reputation and incisive pen in writing such books as *Low Intensity Operations* and *Bunch of Five*.
>
> At the time the Battalion was steadily picking up new equipment, new radios, more machine-guns and so on, so it would have been quite normal for additional reinforcements to appear out of the blue. Usually, however, the Commandant was pre-warned.
>
> The General arrived just as I was finishing an Orders Group, and said that he wanted to meet some Gurkhas. I thought that the easiest thing to do would be to take him to the mortar line that was sited some 100-150 metres away from the Battalion Headquarters. The walk to the mortars followed a well-marked track on top of a steep bank that led down towards a tree-covered stream.
>
> As we were walking along this slightly elevated path I suddenly smelt cigarette smoke and, knowing that the men did not smoke on exercise, looked about me. To my horror I saw that underneath me, on the bank leading down to the stream were about thirty-nine British Other Ranks (BORs) lying on the grass, shirts off and enjoying a smoke break. I had absolutely no idea who they were or where they had come from, and dreaded a question from the great man. Fortunately he was smaller than me and on my right-hand side, and fully gave me the impression that he had not yet noticed what I had just observed.
>
> Once we had reached the mortars, however, the question arose as to how to get back to the helicopter without the General meeting the Brits. Solution? Return along by the stream in the hopes that the trees would cover him from the BORs – and vice versa.
>
> Sadly, my great plan crashed around me. Walking along beside the stream we

turned a corner – only to find a very young British soldier sitting on a rock in the middle of the water. The subsequent conversation is burnt into my memory, particularly since the young man in question possessed a voice reminiscent of Private Pike in the BBC TV comedy series *Dad's Army*.

'Hello,' said the General.

'Hello,' replied the soldier without a trace of respect towards or recognition of 'senior rank' in his voice.

'What are you doing?' asked the General.

'I am sitting on a rock,' replied the lad.

'Why?' asked the General.

'Because my friends don't like me,' replied the soldier.

Needless to say whilst this riveting conversation was taking place I was busy tearing my hair out and trying to find someone in my team who knew what on earth was going on. But the General was not in the least bit fazed by the situation.

'I'm sure you'll be alright soon,' he commented, and moved on without another word.

He never said anything to me about the incident and, as his helicopter disappeared, I was told that the lad was Territorial Army medic and he had just arrived from Catterick to join us for the duration of the operation down south.

He and his friends were to prove their weight in gold later.[9]

But the exercise had revealed many shortfalls, not least the need to improve the system for tasking helicopters. Unfortunately the weather throughout maintained unrealistic tropical temperature levels as opposed to the Brigade Commander's desired Antarctic weather conditions that usually could be almost guaranteed at Sennybridge. And 'unrealistic' was also the only word to describe HQ UKLF's hope that one four-day field training exercise for a Brigade formed only five months before, and then have its original order of battle gutted by the early deployment of its other two infantry units, 2nd and 3rd Battalions, Parachute Regiment – only to be cobbled together again by inclusion of the 1st Battalion, Welsh Guards and 2nd Battalion, Scots Guards – would be enough in short period remaining before deployment. I believe a 'bad' exercise is, in reality, a really 'good' exercise because many shortfalls and lessons identified can be revealed *before* the 'live' event. A possibility existed to make corrections, even though these would have to be accomplished at sea. Also needed was a Brigade Command Post Exercise (CPX) involving all Battalion and minor unit HQ's during our eventual 'cruise' south.

Our stay at Sennybridge was extended with more section and platoon live-firing exercises. The climax was a Battalion defence and counter-attack live-firing exercise: the first training activity of its type to be held there since just before the 1944 D-Day landings. It took place, at last, in atrocious high winds, hail, sleet and snow. Just after 'endex', we heard the news from BBC World Service on our high-frequency Clansman radio set of the enemy cruiser ARA *General Belgrano*'s torpedoing and sinking. Then two staff officers arrived at our range to inform us the Brigade would become part of the Task Force. Only nine days remained before our embarkation on *QE2* at Southampton.

It was now 3 May, and another noteworthy event took place that evening in

Kathmandu during an Israeli Independence Day cocktail party held at the Israeli Embassy after the world had been informed of our forthcoming mission. The party's guest of honour was Prince Dhirenda, the brother of King Birendra. His Highness usually attended such social events, but broke with tradition to make an unexpected speech in which the main message was that Nepal fully backed the UK Government on its actions in the South Atlantic, and was proud that Gurkha soldiers were taking part in Operation Corporate.

'You could have heard a pin drop,' commented retired Lieutenant-Colonel Keith Robinson nearly a quarter of a century later. 'The Diplomatic Corps were astonished, but the British Embassy staff present felt a great sense of pride at that moment.' [10]

We had entered a sinister new phase. Our preparations would continue, but in the certain knowledge we *would* be going to war. But despite our Sennybridge exertions, we had never been able to simulate our ultimate challenge in the final twenty-four hours of the Falklands-Malvinas War: participation in a two-battalion night attack on two enemy objectives supported by eight 81mm mortars, three artillery batteries of eighteen 105mm Light Guns in support, naval gunfire from the two 4.5 inch Mark 6 guns of HMS *Yarmouth*, and single automatic Mark 8 guns of *Avenger* and *Active* respectively plus, in reserve, sixteen offensive air support sorties available from RAF Harrier GR3 ground attack aircraft armed with the Laser Guided Bomb. Indeed what infantry unit had simulated in training such an esoteric fire and manoeuvre attack plan using live ammunition and these external assets? Yet this was precisely what we would be confronted with on the East Falkland battlefield. No UK training area would have ever contemplated such an exercise scenario. And even Gurkha zeal for training realism was forced to bow to the Sennybridge staff's insistence that our final Battalion live-firing exercise had to commence at dawn. Range safety restrictions would have been violated if the exercise had taken place at night.

A passage from our post-operation report revealed the frustrations in having carried out the unique business of training infantry for a limited war 13,000 kilometres from the UK:

> The time has now come to realise that training must become more realistic. In order to mean anything to the soldier, training must be pertinent, relevant and honest [...] From now on safety rules within all training areas must be relaxed, in order to achieve the realism required. Correspondingly commanders must be prepared to accept casualties. For example, in all but the most basic drills, emphasis on the use of blank rounds must shift fundamentally in favour of the maximum firing of live rounds. Troops must be allowed to move much closer to artillery and SA (small arms) fire. The artillery firepower demonstration at Sennybridge whilst remaining within the safety rules was, frankly, a waste of time. (Finally) restrictions must be lifted on night training, and also on the use of live ammunition in fire and movement exercises by day and night. [11]

Back at Church Crookham, those final nine days were devoted mainly to the issue of Arctic clothing and equipment. But the sinking of HMS *Sheffield* by an enemy Exocet missile within the Falklands Total Exclusion Zone on 4 May persuaded even the few doubters in the Battalion we were at war as Nigel Price commented in his diary, 'Everyone was shocked and it seems it could now be a long, hard slog.'

Despite this, a morning of training was carried out next day for the benefit of numerous TV crews and journalists during a 'press-call'. Some of the participating Gurkhas were ordered by crafty Gurkha Quartermaster Captain Rambahadur Gurung, a combat veteran of the sixties' Borneo Confrontation, to sharpen their kukris on a millstone. The photographers gathered around them like bees in a honey pot and the resulting pictures, to our advantage, caused much more than just concern in Argentina and enemy units on the Islands. It was a great example, as Bernard McGuirk reminded me twenty-five years on, of representations of war which can *also* kill people. And nearly five years later retired Brigadier David Morgan also remarked to me:

> My impression now (after your Nottingham colloquium, really) is that this one incident had more to do with the breaking of Argentine morale, and therefore the will to fight, than anything else that happened in the whole war. It was no minor moment.[12]

The Battalion was issued at this late stage with six .50-inch Browning Heavy Machine-Guns. A Heavy Machine-Gun Platoon had to be formed from the Mechanical Transport Platoon and training began for these Gurkhas whose new weapon was one that none had ever seen before. The fifty-eight kilo Browning also illustrated the infantryman's dilemma in this war as this, like every other infantry weapon, had to be carried into position. The problem became an argument between the weight of fire advantage versus the weapon system's weight disadvantage. The Gurkhas' physical fitness, allied with their natural ability of carrying enormous loads over demanding terrain would be put to the test thoroughly. And history would show that they passed with flying colours.

A consignment of unfamiliar M-79 grenade launchers was also delivered to the Battalion and weapon-training commenced with these. On 6 May Nigel Price received two brand new 81mm mortars which brought his platoon's total up to eight. Although he had no trained men to crew them, these 'tubes' became spares and were packed into the Battalion Land-Rovers loaded on board the Brigade logistic ship MV *Nordic Ferry*. But the 'tubes' never saw the light of day until after the war. Due to no clear G (Operational) plan being issued, tactical loading was impossible to achieve at Southampton or Ascension Island. And for various naval operational reasons the *Nordic Ferry*, other Brigade logistics ship MV *Baltic Ferry* and *QE2* would never sail in close enough company to cross-deck cargoes and therefore fulfil the all-important tactical loading requirement. Furthermore the later air threat and lack of helicopters prevented the two 'tubes' from being delivered to Nigel's platoon during the land campaign.

But all that was in the chaotic future. Now, on Friday, 7 May in Church Crookham, Nigel wrote, 'There's a seriousness and sense of purpose in all our activities not present before.' Another batch of Clansmen radio sets had also been delivered. Kit Spencer had to ensure these were issued, the Larkspur sets withdrawn, and more signals training initiated. All these frantic preparations impressed Dil greatly and contributed to concerns of his own that weekend:

Before our deployment we were allowed an administrative slack day. I went out with two *gurujiharu* (senior soldiers) who were both married with a family. They seem worried as to how the war might affect their wives and children if something happened to them. For me, the question was when I would return to take my long leave and be reunited with my family, friends and relatives. If it had been an exercise then you would know when it will end and the return to barracks. But in a war the period of time it would last was uncertain, and no one could predict what would happen. I knew our deployment would be tough on my mother. She was on her own at home and, having already lost my father, was never ecstatic for me to follow in his footsteps. But she never discouraged me from pursuing my dreams. I guess doing something that involved less risk with my life would have been her hope for me.

Next Monday evening Nigel recorded more 'hot off the press' information:

The CO held an Orders Group at 5pm telling us we would be boarding the *QE2* on Wednesday morning and sail at 16.00 hours. He gave us the outline plan – two days at Ascension Island, reach the Falklands around 26 May, the Royal Marine Commandos to establish a beachhead, and us to be the break-out force.

Second-Lieutenant Jeremy McTeague was another member of the Battalion getting ready for the great adventure. A 3O who had been recently transferred from the 2nd King Edward VII's Own Gurkha Rifles (The Sirmoor Rifles), he was the Platoon Commander of D Company's 10 Platoon. It was now the day before departure to Southampton:

When we were in the final hours of preparing our packs before heading off to Southampton, I was struck by how incredibly heavy they were. Having recently completed the Jungle Warfare Instructors course in Brunei, I knew that we had to minimise weight because our ration packs, always less than generous in terms of quantity, were nonetheless horribly heavy. They also needed a lot of fuel for cooking. However in the jungle we had used Mee noodles a lot. They were light, tasty and quick to cook – an ideal supplement to the regulation fare.

Discussing this with my fellow platoon commanders and NCOs, we decided to buy them in the nearby town of Fleet. So accompanied by two Gurkhas, I motored off in my Fiat 129 to the supermarket and bought up all their stock. Time was short as we had a briefing to attend and I had no qualms about exceeding the fifty miles per hour speed limit.

About quarter of a mile out of the town I was pulled over by a policeman. After the preliminary, 'Hello, Hello, Hello, what's going on here then, Jackie Stewart?' patter, I explained with a soupcon of exaggeration that we had to return to barracks and attend a final briefing before leaving for Southampton.

The policeman immediately sprang to a sort of 'attention' and replied, 'Well, we'd better get moving fast then, sir!'

Then he jumped into his car, switched on his flashing blue lights and began racing towards Church Crookham. Regrettably my Fiat could not keep up. So after a short distance, he was forced to slow down in order to escort us at a sedate sixty-five miles per hour the remainder of the way to Queen Elizabeth Barracks.

On arrival at the Officers Mess and armed with his Mee noodles, McTeague would have read Colonel David's valedictory Battalion 'Special Order of the Day'. Published both in English and Nagari script,[13] its content threw the gauntlet down to the Gurkhas:

> Tomorrow we sail for operations in the Falkland Islands. During the voyage South we will have plenty of opportunity to train and prepare ourselves even further for what I expect to be a hard and difficult battle under severe conditions. These are the sort of starting rules that that we in the First Seventh revel in, and I am absolutely confident that we will acquit ourselves well. You must all be aware that the eyes not only of the Brigade of Gurkhas but the rest of the British Army are upon us, and be under no illusion that we are going into battle against a soft enemy. The Argentinians will fight hard and it will require all our skill, determination, courage and dedication to remove them … but remove them we will. The best of luck to you all. *Jai* Seventh.

Wednesday, 12 May had finally materialised. Dil:

> On the day of our deployment, the whole Battalion congregated on the parade square. There was a photo session in our small groups and we were seen off by all the civilian staff working in the camp and a rear party.

The Battalion travelled in coaches and busses. 'Schoolchildren with flags lined the streets, and on the drive to Southampton, lorries and cars seeing our convoy flashed their lights and waved,' commented Nigel. This was to be the largest troop embarkation since the Second World War. The liner lay at Berth No. 38 in Southampton Docks. There had already been much activity before the Battalion arrived. *QE2*'s gourmet supplies were enhanced by fifty lorry loads containing 350 tons of bar stores (18,500 cases of beer and 12,000 gallons on tap), twelve tons of chips, 100 tons of meat, eighty tons of flour and seventy-five tons of dairy produce. But out of the liner went 2,000 chairs, 1,000 sun beds, 500 deck chairs, 400 tables and a Himalayan pile of articles such as potted plants, fruit machines, television sets and statuettes, all of which were loaded on forty transporters. *The Daily Telegraph* newspaper reported:

> The Gurkhas were the last troops to arrive – from their base at Chuch Crookham, Hants – to a mighty roar from their Scots and Welsh comrades. Lt.-Col. David Morgan, the Gurkha Commander, confided that the only thing they were really concerned about was seasickness. But, he said, they had brought 'thousands' of seasickness pills and were going to have at least one curry (*bhat*) a day [...] Gurkha Captain Rambahadur Gurung's wife was with their son, Bishwar, 18, who is himself about to join the Gurkhas. 'I am really proud of him going to fight,' said Bishwar. 'They are doing their duty and they will win,' said Mrs. Gurung.

While the *Daily Mail* focused more on the Gurkha battle reputation:

> Gurkhas pressed to the windows of coaches bringing them through the shouting streets of Southampton. There was toughness about them, solid and disciplined. Their curved kukris, their knives, were sheathed at their sides.
>
> 'Go in quickly, go in first,' an officer commanded, and that was only to board the ship. You would think Galtieri would give up once he knew the Gurkhas were coming.
>
> CO David Morgan, 21 years in the unit, looked proudly at them. 'Nothing stops them,' he said. 'Nothing.'
>
> Fifth Brigade was boarded. 3,250 men with logistic support. It was in no mood to be fooled with. The American NBC Morning TV programme in New York opened live with the scenes in Southampton. 'They're going to love this,' the producer said.

And another national newspaper report contained Cunard Chairman Lord Mathews's colourful comment, 'Half of me wishes I was going with them. The other half tells me not to be such a bloody fool'.[14] Dil's anxiety also increased:

> Sailing from Southampton was my first experience of being in a ship. I found it to be an emotional as well as worrying moment; there were innumerable people gathered to send us off both on ground as well as on sea with small boats following our ship and blowing horns wishing us "good luck". On board, we took more photos on the deck and I can remember a British soldier on board receiving his girlfriend/wife's bra hooked in a winch.

'A day I will never forget,' Nigel wrote that night, while Colonel David made the first entry in his personal war diary:

> I left home at 07.50. and the Parade Square at 08.30. We got to Southampton an hour or so later, and embarked at 10.10 through a mass of press reporters. I gave lengthy interviews, but not to the TV cameras, then spoke to Mr John Nott (Secretary of State for Defence) and the CGS (Chief of the General Staff – General Sir John Stanier) on camera. It was a most emotional farewell. We stopped for repairs (off the Isle of Wight) at 21.00! Battalion Orders Group was held at 21.30. I got to bed late, but am very, very happy indeed!

Next morning emergency muster stations and lifeboat drills were held. This was not a simple matter because the liner was carrying more than double the number of her usual passenger load. Unsurprisingly the muster stations drill was an organisational disaster and had to be repeated three times before being executed satisfactorily. The mass of humanity and lack of space, where only five of the thirteen decks were available for training and advantages of the spacious Queens Room on the Quarter Deck were at a premium, created a 'time and space' challenge for my main task of co-ordinating the Battalion's training. This had to be resolved twice daily during the 'cruise' south. It began with my participation at a 14.00 hours Brigade training conference where the requirements of the three major units and ten minor units had to be co-ordinated, followed by a 17.00 hours Battalion conference where our sub-units were allocated training times and areas. That evening the first of my thirteen daily Battalion training programmes was published for the following day's activities. In his diary Colonel David was also contemplating the threat against *QE2*:

> I got up at 06.15 for BIT (Battle Individual Training). The weather was perfect, if a little choppy. The boat stopped – for repairs, but then got going again on two boilers (out of three) by about 10.00. The training facilities on board are extremely crushed. But the food is superb with a bottle of wine per meal. Everybody is worried about the submarine threat to this vessel – what a prize she would be, and what *would* UK's reaction then be if she was sunk?

There was also another dimension to such a possible event. With 3,200 troops on board there would not be enough lifeboats for all in the event of 'abandon ship' being ordered.[15] Therefore the hint of a potential *Titanic* disaster scenario also hovered over the *QE2*.

Notes

1. *The Art of War*, Chapter 1 – Appraisals.
2. *Napoleon on the Art of War*, Chapter X – The Operational Art, pp 132-33.
3. *The Art of War*, Chapter 1 – Appraisals.
4. David Morgan came from a seafaring family. His father was born at Tavistock, Devon in 1889 and enlisted in the Royal Navy at the age of fifteen. An Engineer Lieutenant at the Battle of Jutland in 1916, Geoffrey Morgan was on board HMS *Warrior* when she was hit below the waterline and sank. But he managed to escape with twelve out of the sixty-eight sailors in his Engine Room, and subsequently enjoyed a distinguished naval career to reach the rank of Engineer Rear-Admiral with eighteen decorations or medals. He died in 1957. His son, David Morgan, had been born in March 1939 on the Mediterranean island of Malta GC eighteen months before the arrival of the author's father and, as he put it, 'seemed to recall spending most of the first three years of my life largely underground'. Three of his homes were destroyed during the Axis forces' siege, but in 1942 he and his parents escaped on board an RAF Hudson bomber aircraft. Later educated at Cottesmore, Marlborough College and the Royal Military Academy Sandhurst, he was then commissioned into the 7th Duke of Edinburgh's Own Gurkha Rifles in 1959 and already had experienced active service in Northern Ireland, Malaya, and Borneo.
5. 7th Duke of Edinburgh's Own Gurkha Rifles Regimental Association Journal, 2007, No. 13, page 95.
6. *The Art of War*, Chapter 9 – Moving the Army.
7. *Ibid.*, Chapter 4 – Form.
8. E-mail dated 6 May 2010.

9.   *Ibid.* dated 14 June 2006.
10. From an e-mail to the author dated 18 July 2006.
11. *Op Corporate 1/7GR Immediate Debrief Points* dated 10 July 1982.
12. E-mail dated 24 November 2011.
13. This is an abugida alphabet of India and Nepal. It is written from left to right, does not have distinct letter cases, and is recognisable by a horizontal line that runs along the top of full letters.
14. *The Falklands War: Then and Now*, p. 167
15. In peacetime *QE2* could accommodate 1,995 passengers and 1,040 crew: a total of 3,035. During the voyage south in May 1982 there were 3,200 troops and 650 crew on board: a total of 3,850. The liner therefore carried 815 more souls on board than normal.

14   Knowing the other and knowing oneself

*And so one skilled at employing the army may be
compared to the* shuai-jan.
The shuai-jan *is a snake of Mount Heng.
Strike its head and the tail arrives.
Strike its tail and the head arrives.
Strike its midsection and both head and tail
arrive.*

– Sun Tzu[1]

I was also writing a first letter to my parents on the evening of 13 May in which there
was lodged a complaint about the liner's interior décor. It was probably because of all
the chipboard laid on the floors and covering the walls to protect the liner against
heavy Army boots and grubby hands:

> Well, alive and kicking aboard the *QE2*. Rather a disappointing boat for such a
> reputation, but anyway it's very nice to be aboard and sampling the good weather
> at the moment.
>
> It would appear that our first port of call will be Freetown, Sierra Leone before
> we move on to Ascension Island. Goodness knows how long we're going to be
> there. Should arrive at Freetown on Tuesday (18 May), but will not be going
> ashore. I have been taking photographs of the very hectic farewell we got at
> Southampton. No doubt you saw it on the box. It was really quite an astonishing
> atmosphere. More like a Cup Final than a troopship sailing to distant parts! I am
> sending a roll of photos back to Tove, so you should be able to see them in due
> course.
>
> I hear that they have knocked out another three Argentine planes yesterday. At
> this rate there won't be anything for us to do if (?) we get down there. I'll keep you
> posted on developments.

It was obvious from reading her daily letters that Tove was also battling with reality
and the 'is, should, want' perceptions of this frightening situation. Libby Stewart was
the wife of Major Rory Stewart, another Battalion seconded officer, and she had gone
to Southampton to watch *QE2*'s departure which Tove had deliberately avoided.
There was also a minor family crisis to handle. When I received the letter at Ascension
Island ten days later it made me homesick:

> I popped in to see Libby Stewart this morning who told me all about Wednesday
> (and *QE2*'s departure) [...] I hope you are 'happier' now that you're surrounded by
> fellow warriors – we're fine at this end. So far. There is a lot to be said for living on
> a patch and having other wives to share the worries with. I can't see us going to
> Oslo before mid-June, if then [...] Emily fell down the stairs again and was terribly
> upset. Really shaking and I had to hold and carry her for a long time [...]
>
> Lovely surprise: the ladies in the baby-sitting circle have decided to sit for us

'Falklanders' free! [...] I think that is very, very kind – they actually do help out instead of just talking

[...] The news here is that by Tuesday (18 May) we will know if there'll be peace or invasion – not hopeful about the former! Maybe your dates on the wall chart are a little too late?

Her battle would continue, but she was learning in a crisis that it is essential to focus on the 'is' perception of her situation – 'should' and 'want' are red herrings and unimportant. This was reflected in the lessons learnt from the previous day's disastrous muster drills. We took this most seriously, not least because the Gurkhas were accommodated on Deck Five in order to counter their vulnerability to seasickness. That was the area closest to the waterline and therefore rolled least. It led to the creation of a Gurkha drill that was repeated continuously during the first week on board as a consequence of the following crisis scenario: an air-launched AM-39 Exocet missile strikes the liner three metres above the waterline (and Deck Five's location) at a velocity of Mach 0.9. The subsequent explosion cuts electrical power, and therefore lighting, causing fires that generate thick, acrid smoke everywhere. Suitably briefed, half-platoon teams of Gurkhas would then be blindfolded with gas respirators on, and ordered to move from their Deck Five accommodation to their boat stations on the Boat Deck. A competitive element (always beloved by these Gurkhas) was introduced by making this into an orienteering competition. Sun Tzu's dynamic image of the *shuai-jan*, a snake of Mount Heng, provides an appropriately Asiatic illustration of our ambition-level. Other Brigade units were amused by our antics, but the relevance of this 'hands-on' training would be underlined by the mass casualties caused by the enemy air strike on the RFAs *Sir Galahad* and *Sir Tristram* little more than three weeks later. No one laughed then.

Meanwhile Jeremy McTeague, was becoming accustomed to the evening dinner ritual cocooned in the starched white linen, crystal and silver of the intimate low-ceilinged Queen's Grill, *QE2*'s first class restaurant, together with the five other young Gurkha British officers:

From the first evening, the sail down to the Falklands became an unexpected pleasure when we learned that the *QE2*'s wine cellar was to accompany us. The prices were happily tax-free and Palmer, Redding, Oates, McTeague, Spencer and Morris, who normally dined together, were so impressed by the Pouilly Fuissé that in a concerted effort they managed to drink the boat dry within a week. A feat never achieved in peacetime according to the liner's sommelier.

Absenting myself from the table one evening, I staggered into the first class restaurant's 'heads' to find a young waiter in tears being calmed by another.

'She's a bitch, a total bitch! She's flirting with everyone,' he wailed.

'I know, I know, she's a beastly bitch,' comforted the other.

Just then in came yet another young waiter who was promptly met with a hail of, 'You bitch, you bitch!'

Executing the only British retreat of the entire war, I returned somewhat 'educated' to the last of the Pouilly Fuissé.

Each training day begin at 06.30 hours and ended at 21.30 hours. It was limited to this time because of the thunderous noise generated by the continual thump of boots running around the Promenade Deck. This was the first Gurkha activity of the day: BIT running and also physical training on the Sports Deck from 06.30 to 07.30, followed by comprehensive weapon training. SLR and GPMG loading, unloading and stoppage drills were repeated *ad nauseaum*. Other subjects taught initially on board were signals, first-aid, winter combat survival, mines and aircraft recognition. Also included were enemy intelligence, Falklands topography, and Geneva Conventions briefings. Colonel David's diary continued for 14 May:

> This was a relatively quiet day on board the *QE2* with a low, slightly uncomfortable sea swell and overcast day. I attended the usual 17.00 Orders Group which gave a most depressing intelligence picture. Then I got mildly drunk at the Captain's Cocktail Party. I did not sleep brilliantly and apparently snore!

Dilkumar Rai was also becoming accustomed to the routines, but seasickness reared its ugly head:

> Travelling in a ship for me was a completely new experience and beyond my imagination; the size of the ship and the facilities; it was just like a small town. The routine of the ship commenced and one of the important things was the emergency drills. Apart from that, our routine included fitness training, weapon training, first-aid, map-reading, helicopter drills, live-firing, intelligence briefings and the Ship Captain's inspection. Seasickness was a killer amongst many people but, thankfully, I was never badly affected. It was so much that people were vomiting and unable to eat and work for several days.

To make the surreal nature of the voyage complete, our fifteen-hour training day for war became a bizarre cocktail when mixed with the daily 'cruise' entertainment of feature film shows, band concerts and cocktail parties. But this contributed to forming many cohesive teams of men who soon would have to fight for their lives. Such a total cheek to jowl environment provided the setting to hone our basic preparations for success as Sun Tzu once pointed out: 'Therefore, the victorious military is first victorious and after that does battle.' [2] But the Morgan diary entry next day not only reflected a bad start to 15 May, but also the socialising disadvantages:

> I got up early for BIT, but twisted my ankle badly on my first running circuit, but it is not serious. The Brigade Commander was supposed to visit Support Company at 09.15 – but he didn't arrive! A lovely day, it's beginning to warm up. The Navy is in whites. I went to a gambling party and lost £4. I had a good time, but got to bed late feeling lousy. Got up late. The clocks go back one hour.

Next day, 16 June, was also the Battalion's Regimental Birthday. It would be a chance for the *ketaharu* to let their hair down during that evening's planned Battalion party on the Sports Deck. Colonel David looked forward to a good Gurkha night:

Despite the Regimental Birthday this was a normal training day, but the ship's cooks baked us a huge birthday cake to be issued at our party tonight. There were masses of activity on board, but mostly of a training nature. The weather is warm, but cool with a strong breeze. A good day.

During the party at which the Pipes and Drums played constantly and the Gurkhas did their best to dance through the Sports Deck floor, not only did the Battalion receive the cake but also a framed picture of the *QE2* from her Master, Captain Peter Jackson to mark the occasion. Late next night Colonel David's diary reported on that event and its owner's continued nautical socialising:

> The party last night was *fantastic*! The morale of the Battalion is *beyond* control! I've never seen anything like it, and hope it never gets lower. This was a quiet day while moving along in reasonable weather – still fairly choppy and cool in the air. I felt ghastly all day – probably 'flu aggravated by drink, I think. I ended up at no less than three cocktail parties, including the Sergeants' Mess! I was in bed by midnight though.

On 18 May, *QE2* berthed at Freetown, Sierra Leone to bunker water and fuel. Our main training activity was to practise the drill for assembling in the large public Double Down Room located on the Upper Deck from the Gurkhas' Five Deck assault boat stations, and then move up to the specially constructed aft helicopter landing pad constructed two weeks before over the Lido swimming pool area. Our familiarisation with the Sea King helicopter was limited to climbing into its cabin for the first time in our military careers. It was a disadvantage not to fly because Sea King (and Wessex) helicopters would be important transportation assets during the campaign. Colonel David's diary provided information of other matters, including a 'left-over' embarrassment from the Regimental birthday party:

> I got up for BIT and did a lot – a very warm sweaty day. We saw land at about 9am, and docked in Freetown just before midday watched closely, and no doubt enviously, by a Russian trawler. Freetown is a ghastly dump. We sail at 01.00 hours tomorrow morning. The ship is fully darkened now – no light escapes at all. The GM (Gurkha Major) picked up this morning the presentation photo given to us from the Master of *QE2* on the 16th during the Regimental Birthday party. We had left it on the Sports Deck. Horror of horrors!

Back on the high seas next morning, there was SLR and GPMG live-firing off the liner's stern as well as Milan missile live-firing. The Gurkhas' Milan harmonisation equipment, which provided a means of zeroing and ensuring alignment before firing, had been loaded into a locked store. But prior to the training taking place, it was discovered that this vital kit had been stolen. The Battalion was not alone in suffering from this problem, indeed 5 Brigade's official logistics history of the campaign stated 'there was a widespread breakdown in simple honesty and [...] many people regarded stores as public property to be taken or used at will.' [3] Non-public property of many units was also vulnerable to theft. This included two Gurkha boxes of Regimental stores on board *Baltic Ferry* and *Nordic Ferry*. These boxes were also forced open and kukris, whisky, track suits, calendars and folders to the total value of £1,000 removed.

During the afternoon of 19 May, Colonel David was subjected to King Neptune's equatorial rituals:

> Today we crossed the Line and I, of course, was selected to be dunked (or given to the Bears present). Needless to say we were covered in muck and filth and it took ages to get clean. A calm day, but the evening brought in some higher seas and we were moving about a lot by late at night. I attended a cocktail party in the evening. It was grotty and a waste of time!

At Church Crookham, Tove had to juggle with following the daily news of events in the South Atlantic and family matters:

> One week down and endless numbers to go!
> [...] We're busy here with day-to-day matters. Today was a big day for Victoria because she came down to the big school with me [...] and put her name down (to start school) on 3 September. She held my hand tightly most of the time [...] I'm behaving (and) making plans for the future which implies that life will resume normally when you come back. Important things did happen to me however in those awful weeks before you left – but I have not got the strength to dwell on them. They are put away at the back of my mind. There are more important things to care about now, like you returning home safely and the girls suffering as little as possible by your absence [...]
> I'm absolutely dying for a letter from you – Victoria drew a round rainbow and our house for you – Emily drew something only she knows.

The Heavy Machine-Gun Platoon had also continued their weapon-training on the Brownings under the guidance of a British Army Small Arms Service Corps instructor. However on 20 May when the liner arrived in the vicinity of Ascension Island in mid-Atlantic, he was flown off. For the next forty-eight hours *QE2* circled below the horizon around the Island. With no sign of any Brigade HQ Command Post Exercise, a two-day Battalion table-top exercise was designed by Major Mike Kefford, the tough D Company Commander, and held for all our officers. Normally known as a TEWT (Tactical Exercise Without Troops), on the high seas it became a Gurkha TEWL (Tactical Exercise Without Land). The task of planning and executing a Battalion helicopter assault onto the north-east coast of East Falkland near Teal Inlet was a near-similar scenario I would be required to carry out twenty-four days later on. There was rising excitement on board, with everyone anticipating the British landings on the Falklands, but the Morgan diary entry that evening recorded laconically, 'A normal day. No excitements.'

I had a couple of necessary conversations in the next twenty-four hours with the sympathetic Welsh Guards chaplain Padre Peter Brooke about life, family and the situation we were approaching in the Falklands. He helped me greatly. Twenty-four years later Peter was a priority person to locate as I wanted him to participate in the

University of Nottingham's colloquium. Alas, a Guards source in London informed me that he had been killed in a 1987 UK motorway accident. Although this awful news had a vintage of nineteen years, I was despondent for the rest of that day. Wherever he may be now, I wish him well.

It was indeed the lull before the storm. Day Two of our TEWL on 21 May coincided with the British landings at San Carlos, East Falklands and start of the Battle of San Carlos Water in which the Royal Navy slugged it out against 121 enemy air strike sorties in the next five days. At Ascension Island the weather was warm, and McTeague's morale received a boost:

> One evening I was called by the Adjutant, Mark Willis, and told that the CO wished to see me in his cabin I immediately dreaded the worst of being sent to a technical platoon such as Signals, Battalion HQ or even Quartermaster's Platoon. Basically there were few British officers and these platoons needed good English speakers in order to communicate with the rest of the Brigade.
>
> David Morgan welcomed me in, and smilingly asked, 'How are you? Are you enjoying D Company?'
>
> My suspicions grew, and I was just about to ask him why he wanted to see me when he pulled out my confidential report. He told me it was great and to sign it, and then handed over a pair of combat jacket epaulettes emblazoned with the rank of Lieutenant. It was then I realised my promotion had happened on the way to war! This was the best feeling I had ever experienced, and my surge in confidence would see me through the periods of self-doubt that were to follow.

Colonel David's diary noted both the momentous external events and duller on board happenings of that day:

> I can claim separation allowance from today! The British landings at San Carlos took place today at 11.00 hours unopposed. Argentine reaction was swift and damage to our ships was expected. Twenty-one SAS men died when their helicopter crashed this afternoon – it was not hit by enemy action – but engine failure! I spent a quiet night drinking with the Company Commanders until about 1am, and then went to bed.

The Sea King accident within the Total Exclusion Zone also reminded us of the worrying lack of emergency drill training during our brief familiarisation with this helicopter type at Freetown. It was also impossible to disregard the loss of HMS *Ardent* and major damage inflicted on HM Ships *Argonaut* and *Antrim*. Meanwhile Major-General Jeremy Moore, Commander Land Forces Falklands Islands and his staff arrived on board by Chinook helicopter from Ascension. Our Battalion also received reinforcements of seventeen Gunners commanded by Major Mike Fallon from 132 Field Battery (The Bengal Rocket Troop) of the Royal School of Artillery. Colonel David's diary entry of 22 May contained an update of events 3,000 nautical miles southwards:

There was the usual BIT start to the day. By midday we had news of the continued air/sea battle. By 14.00 hours some twenty enemy aircraft had been shot down, but we had lost one ship, two seriously damaged and a further five damaged. Three soldiers have died, and twenty wounded. The numbers of enemy casualties are not known, but must be considerable. I saw a film in the cinema.

QE2 had also begun to move south again. For more than just a few on board, the liner had become a psychological pressure-cooker in which it became difficult to focus on training. The Gurkhas, with a fatalistic outlook on life (and death) founded on their Hindu religion and Durga, the Goddess of War, remained deeply concentrated in their training. To be given a chance of winning a decoration for bravery in combat and, if fate should so decree, be killed on the battlefield, was progress. Their Pandit (priest) was not on board because his high caste prevented him from eating English food, and facilities were not available for him to cook his own *bhat* meals. But life for the British chaplains became even busier. For example, by the end of the 'cruise' about half the Scots Guardsmen on board had sought out their chaplain Padre Angus Smith for one-on-one conversations regarding matters spiritual and existential. Others adopted a more collective approach to the situation and participated in the corresponding upsurge of church services that attracted larger and larger congregations. We had tried to learn on board about our prospective enemy. Now people were learning about themselves. It was an essential process for success in the strategy of attack as Sun Tzu had so perceptively remarked: 'Knowing the other and knowing oneself, in one hundred battles no danger.'[4]

Colonel David's diary entry that 23 May evening began with 'Sunday after Ascension':

> Correct! The clocks back an hour this morning which was very nice – an extra hour in bed. There was feverish activity all day in planning loads, ammo etc. I had supper with the General (Major-General Moore – Commander Land Forces Falkland Islands). He seems pleasant enough – I gather he is heavily decorated and a decent man. I *think* he was an instructor of mine at RMAS (Royal Military Academy Sandhurst). I went to bed late.

In reality, operational planning was gaining ascendancy on board *QE2*. For example, planning the trench layout of the thirty-eight man Battalion Tactical HQ was completed in this period. A total of four-three man trenches and thirteen two-man trenches would be required to house the entire HQ. The circular pattern layout would have the key five Battalion staff officers' trenches of the Operations Officer, Adjutant, Helicopter Operations Officer, Mechanical Transport Officer (Helicopter Operations Officer's Assistant) and Intelligence Officer positioned at the hub. The HQ had been reinforced by twelve British soldiers comprising a Forward Air Controller and two Signallers, Major Mike Fallon and four Gunners in his Battery Commander's party, and four Signallers from 30 Signals Regiment. Meanwhile news of HMS *Antelope*'s demise in San Carlos Water indicated that the air to ship battle there was continuing. Colonel David's evening diary entry reflected the new operational modus. His landing date on East Falkland was too optimistic however:

We were told this morning that we were all going to South Georgia to trans-ship and then head for the Falklands, aiming for a landing before 31 May if possible – but only the weather will be able to tell. We are due to land at San Carlos early on Thursday morning (27 May). Plans for our landing are in embryo form [...] a lovely and cooler day.

Next day, 25 May, the Battalion completed its first 'bombing-up' procedure with a formal issue of live ammunition for all weapons, a procedure never practised in peacetime. McTeague's 10 Platoon received items such as radio batteries and 7.62mm ball and link ammunition. Some of his Gurkhas were also 'making their own weapons such as knuckle-dusters and garrottes, copying some "warry" Scots Guards'. This was also a dreadful day for the Task Force with HMS *Coventry*'s demise by an enemy air strike and Cunard's SS *Atlantic Conveyor* becoming an Exocet victim. By the end of this day, the final total of British casualties in the Battle of San Carlos Water stood at fifty-seven killed and eighty-one wounded. On the credit side it had been reported that thirty-two attacking enemy aircraft were 'splashed', later pared down in post-war analyses to a more realistic nineteen. The loss of the two ships had not yet percolated through to us on board *QE2*. Instead Colonel David's diary indicated how rapidly plans were always changing:

Last night our plan changed: and we were told that, due to a submarine threat, we were now heading to Line A (a mysterious line in the middle of the ocean!). By 15.00 we were back to the South Georgia operation. It is much colder, windier and generally more murky, but the sun is out. Everybody is very keen to get off this ship and on with the job.

His pessimistic diary entry for the following evening on 26 May mentioned erroneously a third British ship sunk the previous day:

The weather is poor, but not as bad as expected. It is much, much colder now and we are back to sweaters despite the artificial air in the ship. We arrive for the transfer shipping tomorrow morning but do not expect to move until a.m. on Friday (28 May). Today, although we downed another three aircraft, we lost three vital ships including a stores ship containing helicopters, aircraft and tentage. We are now pushed – very pushed indeed.

After rendezvousing with the battle-scarred 'County' Class guided missile destroyer HMS *Antrim* to cross-deck onto her the advance party of HQ 5 infantry Brigade, we arrived a little later that morning off Grytviken on the island of South Georgia. The BBC World Service News broadcast on that 27 May evening was not good with reports of further enemy air strikes on the Ajax Bay logistics facility and San Carlos settlement. These killed another seven British servicemen and wounded twenty-six. As Brigade units began the lengthy process of cross-decking onto the cruise liner SS *Canberra* alias 'The Great White Whale', our modest P&O ferry MV *Norland* and the auxiliary vessel RFA *Stromness*, another letter was written to my parents:

Now at South Georgia, and I couldn't celebrate a stranger tenth wedding anniversary than at this place. It really has been a strange last two weeks, but now I think that the 'relaxing' time is over. On an operation of this complexity the plans have changed hourly, but I think that we shall be inserted onto the Falklands on or about the 30th at San Carlos. Not a very appetising thought, but I guess that I shall just have to shut my eyes and get stuck into the work.

I hear on the (BBC World Service) radio today that the Argentines claim to have sunk the *QE2*. Well, that couldn't be further from the truth. We are here now safe and sound. The only tricky bit is going to be to put us ashore at San Carlos.

Must admit that I have been a bit depressed about recent events, but I am now trying to square up to whatever situations are going to present themselves to us. It's better to be working together as a group than as an individual in these circumstances.

Hope you are both well. I know that it can't be much fun listening to all the TV and reading newspapers about this sorry mess. However we'll soon be out of this – heard the Paras and Marines are now generally advancing towards Stanley.

Please can you keep an eye on Tove and the children? I get worried about them. She (Tove) is a very strong girl, and I am sure that she is OK.

Meanwhile Colonel David's diary entry, begun the previous evening, was critical of the logistics operation:

We are due in South Georgia tonight. The weather is strange, calm, cold and misty. Birds have been seen.

Arrived after dawn – ship blackened out. Usual confusion on the ship as to what the loading/unloading plan is. I went to bed at midnight after A Company and our Advance Parties had trans-shipped to the *Norland*, a North Sea ferry.

Next afternoon the Gurkha and 16 Field Ambulance main parties carried out their cross-decking to *Norland*. She had already transported the 2nd Battalion, Parachute Regiment from the UK to San Carlos Water and, while under heavy air attack on 21 May, had disembarked her human cargo which would then land at Blue Beach 2, San Carlos. *Canberra*, *Norland* and the auxiliary ship RFA *Stromness* then weighed anchor in the early polar evening of 28 May to begin a four-day voyage to the Falklands. Colonel David's writing vented further frustrations:

The plan was for trans-shipping to start not before 09.00. By 11.00 B Company were still waiting to go. I changed the order and got Battalion Tactical HQ to go with C Company. Delays are mounting, but I am told that *Norland* is due to sail with all 1/7 Gurkha Rifles aboard plus the freight with vertrep (vertical replenishment by helicopter) at 18.00! It is very un-military in my view. Still, we'll see. We sailed at about 2300Z which wasn't bad.

His negative comments about the dubious logistics operation were justified. Insufficient time had been allocated to off-loading the Brigade's ammunition from *QE2*, and so she returned to Southampton with considerable quantities still aboard.[5]

However such serious matters could be overshadowed briefly by the receipt of personal news from home. For example Tove's 'is' perception of reality now dominated her letter written that night and which, fifteen days later, I would read on the eve of going into battle. It was a supremely surreal moment:

> Thank you so much for the beautiful roses which arrived this morning. It was in fact rather nice to receive them the day after – otherwise today would have been a bit of an anti-climax. Instead I've been able to say to everybody: 'Well, it was our 10th wedding anniversary yesterday!' And they (the other wives) all go, 'A-a-h!'
>
> Emily's speech is improving almost daily. She now strings words together into four to five word long sentences. The famous stubborn streak is also becoming more apparent – and she sulks! [...] Victoria has been drawing for you tonight. She was very pleased with the picture of *QE2* you sent. She is really very good – and has suddenly started to tell me out of the blue that she loves me. No doubt she is sensing a certain loneliness about me – she is definitely aware of your absence and includes you in all the family talk. We talk about all the things we like and it's always: and Pappa likes that too [...] or Pappa doesn't like it. Yesterday we had some pancakes, and she said that we had to save some for you. So we froze them! It's the right thing to include you in our little routine and it doesn't hurt [...]

But training *à la QE2* now ceased completely because a gale at sea blew up for the remainder of our voyage. Dil:

> The waves were very strong, as a result we received more sea sickness. Nonetheless I kept lucky. We had to practise drills in the event of air attack; taking cover under our own bed wearing a helmet. As we approached closer to the Falklands, the ship was completely blacked out.

Whilst swaying reciprocally with *Norland*'s north-west struggle through the big dipper South Atlantic waves, I listened to BBC World Service radio broadcasts being 'piped' on the ship's Tannoy with reports of the campaign's first land battle. This was 2 Para's fourteen-hour fight at the Battle of Darwin and Goose Green that ended in victory with the loss of eighteen men and thirty-six wounded. I thought about our Battalion training during the previous eight weeks. Had it been sufficient to cope with the rigours of battle on the Falklands? And, indeed, what would it be like to fight in such a battle? In sixteen days time, during the climax of our own combat experience, I came to the conclusion that training for battle would never be able truly to simulate the real event. For how can an exercise provide the stress-effects of fear felt on the battlefield that can negatively impact an individual's decision-making process?

The air threat against us increased as, correspondingly, the distance between *Norland* and the Falklands decreased. We had manned the top deck air-defence stations with two Blowpipe missile launchers, two Browning Heavy Machine-Guns and ten GPMGs ready for the Argentine Air Force's expected visitation. There was a yellow air alert that late afternoon as a report arrived about the tanker *British Wye* which had been bombed unsuccessfully by an Argentine Hercules transport aircraft fitted with wing bomb racks. Although this incident took place several hundred nautical miles to the north-east of *Norland*, it was nonetheless a timely reminder of the need to increase our preparedness. So training became more specific in countering the current threat and consisted of 'closing up' to defence stations coupled with muster stations and fire drills. Colonel David was concerned about the elements' effect on his men:

> By morning the weather was foul – a Force 8 gale and a lot of movement in the ship. Many lads are ill. We practised boat drill and also the assault drill – and I spent some time on the bridge. There was little else to do. I heard that 'H' Jones had been killed yesterday. What a terrible tragedy, and what a fantastic victory. 900 prisoners! Well done 2 Para.

I also wrote to my parents. But my remark in the following epistle about British 'light casualties' at the Battle of Darwin and Goose Green soon proved premature:

> This boat has twice been in San Carlos and is due to take us back there or near there. We should land on the night of 1-2 June. Apart from the submarine threat, we are also very aware of our vulnerability from Exocet. We pray to God that we are not the chosen blip on the radar screen.
>
> I know that all of you at home must be very worried and biting your finger-nails to the bone. At times the atmosphere gets a wee bit tense on board here as well. As we get nearer to the operational zone it is going to get even tenser. I assure you that we are going to be a lot happier when we set our feet on dry land again.
>
> I would not like you to tell Tove of the contents of this letter. Please keep it until I come home, and then we can all have a good laugh at it. I am trying to keep on an even keel, and be cheerful, although at times it does get a bit difficult (shades of Seear pessimism).
>
> However I guess today we've had our first good bit of news that 2 Para have taken out Goose Green/Darwin and have only suffered light casualties. That's very good news, because now we have an airstrip which can be put to very good use, and we have driven a very solid wedge between the Argentine forces on East and West Falkland.
>
> Our only lifeline with the outside world is BBC World Service radio, so if you could ask the family to write letters I would be very grateful. Mail becomes very, very important to us lads in the Task Force at the bottom of the world. I'll be writing again soon.

Next day we carried out a more comprehensive 'bombing-up' of sub-units than on *QE2*. McTeague's Gurkhas received amongst other ammunition types, high-explosive and white phosphorous hand-grenades, and 2-inch mortar bombs. Reality quickly hit home with the extra weight as he describes:

> I remember that it was fifty-five kilos (pack plus twenty-five kilos with weapon and webbing) and thinking it was ridiculous as this was much more than we normally trained with. So much for being light infantry! There were no complaints but quite a few gasps as we shouldered our packs on the *Norland* after bombing up.

There was also a rehearsal for moving all the fully-equipped and heavily-laiden Gurkhas from the upper decks onto the lower Car Deck where, at San Carlos, we would embark onto 3 Commando Brigade's landing craft. Apprehension rose considerably as we approached our entry into the Total Exclusion Zone around the Falkland Islands. The following was Colonel David's diary entry for 30 May. It upped the number of enemy prisoners taken:

> I heard that 2 Para had picked up 1200 prisoners at Goose Green/Darwin. A tidy haul, particularly when one thinks that the enemy was dug in and defending! This *must* mean an early advance on Stanley and resultant chaos for us on arrival. The seas are very rough. The old boat is tipping and turning all over the place – with a bad night as a result. Nineteen days at sea for us is really too long.

Tove's letter, also written that night, described similar pressures at home:

> I am now at the stage where I notice couples on the street and think how lucky they are to be together. Seeing lovers part on TV produces buckets (of tears), but then it always did. Now though I feel bitter [...] Emily was up for a long time in the night – she actually cried for you. Amazing, I thought she was too young, quite literally, to miss you consciously. Maybe you don't want to hear that – it might make you sad – but it also shows that you are much loved.

The penultimate morning on board was spent in carrying out a second rehearsal of moving the entire Battalion down to the Car Deck. Afterwards, in the afternoon, there were final sub-unit checks. It was then that a platoon commander's managerial crisis confronted McTeague:

> I wanted to do a last inspection of my platoon before the final D Company inspection that was to take place the next morning. While there was real tension on the faces of the men that evening, the kit inspection passed quickly with everything and everybody's equipment in good order.
>
> Just as I was about to dismiss the men, one of my Section Commanders, an old and definitely 'passed over' Corporal, stepped forward and said that he had been thinking about the role he was expected to carry out and had decided that he did not wish to remain in the platoon. He added that he did not join the Army to go actually into combat and that he had family responsibilities.
>
> I was very shocked by this and my Sergeant, Paulraj Rai, thinking quickly, stepped in and told the Corporal to remain behind and dismissed the men in the normal way. The Corporal made it plain once more that he did not want to go to the front. My immediate thought was that there was no way on earth that I wanted him to remain in the platoon. His entire section of eight soldiers had witnessed him stating his position and forcing him to soldier on would have been to their direct detriment. They needed to go into action with a Corporal they could rely on. Certainly I knew that my overriding requirement was to be able to count on absolute reliance from all three of my section commanders. After the very briefest

of consultations with Sergeant Paulraj it was clear that we were of the same mind.

I went to report this difficulty to Mike Kefford, and meanwhile Paulraj reported the event through the 'Gurkha net'. Mike understood the situation immediately and did not even try to talk round the Section Commander. The matter was quickly resolved, and a couple of hours later a real *burho* (old boy) Corporal from the Machine-Gun Platoon reported to me as a replacement. It was a stroke of good fortune as he had a wealth of experience, a 'can-do' attitude and great leadership qualities.

The positive effect on the men was immediate and palpable. By the time we disembarked both morale and equilibrium had been restored – not least my own since at the time I found it impossible not to interpret the Corporal's action as a vote of no confidence. In my view this was a superb example of the Gurkha '*kaida*' system working to ensure that the task at hand is addressed without compromise, but in the best interests of all concerned. I got what I needed – a strengthened platoon, the Corporal got what he needed – a place in the rear echelon, and the *burho* Corporal got what he needed – a chance to perform to his real potential: something he did most impressively. There were no 'waves', and nobody felt aggrieved or let down.

This incident remained a D Company 'in-house' matter and never reached the ears of the Commandant. Presumably, post-war and back in the UK, the Corporal concerned was eventually sent on pension at his due date and nothing more was said. But now on *Norland* there were two more challenges for McTeague. The first:

On board the Cunard liner RMS *Queen Elizabeth 2*, (the Battalion) received its warning order to land at Blue Beach 2, San Carlos Water on 1 June. The (subsequent) orders given to the Battalion, and down through the organisation (on) the night before the landing, were scant [...] My orders book clearly reports: 'Action on beachhead – no idea'.

This caused my Section Commanders and me real concern. We were about to enter a battle-zone and the plan to effect that act of entry was non-existent. A plan is always better than no plan, and while initiative is rightly a valued trait, it cannot and must not be relied upon as the sole factor/contributor to define courses of action. All officers and non-commissioned officers should be trained to understand why they should never use the words 'no idea' in formal orders.[6]

And the second:

With all preparations finally completed, it was time for some relaxation and the officers congregated to watch a video. It was the war film *Gallipoli* which I thought entirely appropriate in the circumstances. But others were vehemently opposed to it. One went so far as to order that the film not be shown to the other ranks (which I did agree with as I believed it would be natural that soldiers would judge their officers and compare their decisions to the idiocy so clearly portrayed in the film).

The 10 Platoon Commander had a point, but I did not dare attend the showing of the gory *Gallipoli*. However after that vetoed war disaster, I enjoyed *Chariots of Fire* – a patriotic British story in which ability and hard training were rewarded by success. It uplifted my spirits prior to the next two weeks of extreme mental stress, in which the second one often included demanding physical exertion. We were now well inside the Total Exclusion Zone and the air threat against *Norland* was considerable. It was the final night of fitful sleep in our cramped cabins aboard the 12,988-ton RoRo ferry of Amphibious Task Group 317.1.2. Shakespeare's Agincourt eve of battle speech for Henry V contained some pertinent lines for those 'protected' 8,000 nautical miles away to the north:

> And gentlemen in England, now a-bed,
> Shall think themselves accursed they were not here:
> And hold their manhoods cheap, whiles any speaks
> That fought with us upon Saint Crispin's day.

But Colonel David's diary, written later that night, reflected on other matters, not least the urgent need to terminate our three-week maritime existence:

> All day has been spent at sea. Everything is very fraught – serious, heavy seas and a constant threat of air attack. I am very keen to get our feet on ground. We are due to arrive at 09.30 tomorrow.

His fears nearly materialised when we arrived in San Carlos Water, aptly nicknamed 'Bomb Alley'. During our subsequent 1 June 'administrative' disembarkation procedure for the Battalion's landing at San Carlos which commenced at first light, a nail-biting red air alert was sounded. It was the first of fifteen we would experience during the war's final fourteen days and served to more than hasten our departure from *Norland*. The Battalion was transferred from ship to shore by two 'Landing Craft Utility' of 3 Commando Brigade. Ours reached Blue Beach 2 at 10.45 hours. But no Gurkha had ever seen a LCU before in their bid to reach the longed-for land environment. And Dil was ferried to land in a later daylight shuttle run:

> Sailing in a landing craft was somewhat scary. Standing with a bergen weighing over fifty kilos was not an enjoyable moment, but difficult and tiring. Finally, we stepped on the land of Falkland after a very long, tiring and risky journey. Although we were leaving behind all the facilities of the ship and getting close to the enemy as well as facing the severe weather condition, I was relieved when stepping onto the ground. I could imagine the risk of being hit by the enemy fighter (aircraft) while in the ship as well as on the ground. However if we were hit in the ship, we would have to face a significant loss of life and casualties, but the chances of surviving on the ground was obviously greater than in a ship.

While the Gurkhas in Rear Echelon began to establish themselves at San Carlos, the remainder of the Battalion moved about three kilometres south. We stopped and dug shell scrapes in order to wait for the landing of the only surviving Chinook helicopter from the Exocet-hit SS *Atlantic Conveyor*. 'Bravo November' would fly most of the Battalion south to the settlement of Goose Green but, on landing, turned out to be Darwin, a few kilometres *north* of Goose Green. The pilot's error (or mis-understanding or lack of communication or whatever) would become par for the course in the next fourteen days. It caused absolute chaos on the four-day old battlefield with many lost Gurkha sub-units and tempers.

But first I received a radio message of a second red air alert. That was child's play compared to the first on *Norland*. The reason was an enemy C-130 Hercules transport aircraft which, after taking off from Stanley's airport to return to Argentina, had been spotted by two Sea Harriers much further to the north of us near Pebble Island. One of them shot down the unlucky Hercules. Afterwards D Company started out on their deployment to the Sussex Mountains where they were to guard the southern flank of San Carlos. As they departed, the Chinook arrived. Then 'sticks' (loads) of seventy-plus Gurkhas at a time piled into the double-rotored machine's seat-bare cabin via the rear ramp and door prior to an immediate take-off. Meanwhile being the 14 Platoon radio operator, Dil carried a Clansman radio set in addition to his personal kit up Sussex Mountains:

> Our Company had initially walked on flat ground and climbed uphill to arrive finally at an abandoned defensive position. I felt my back pain at this moment when having to carry my heavy bergen and walking uphill [...] When there was an opportunity, I used to bend forward to rest it on my back. At that moment I had no idea about the whereabouts of the rest of the Battalion [...] We stayed in this defensive position for two or three days. I can remember my Platoon Commander, Lieutenant (QGO) Bhuwansing Limbu (later the Gurkha Major of 7 GR) always educating our platoon about the conservation of ration and energy. He told us that in a war situation, re-supply is not always possible due to the enemy threat and lack of transport. Everyone was advised to conserve rations in the event of an emergency. But there were some members of the platoon who did not take the advice seriously in eating every day's ration scale and finishing them. Like our Platoon Commander warned, we did not have any re-supply until we arrived close to Goose Green. This was a good lesson learnt for some members of the platoon.

The Commandant's diary summed up our first day on the Falklands:

> We arrived at San Carlos Water at 08.30 and ahead of schedule, but did not get off *Norland* until after dawn (at 11.00). We walked up to an Assembly Area some three kilometres from the jetty and dug in. By early p.m. we were being moved forward, and ended up standing in a Chinook helicopter that took off destined for Darwin and Goose Green. We landed at Darwin and I drove forward to Goose Green to meet (Major) Chris Keeble (of 2 Para). I sited the Battalion Tactical HQ in a dip about one and a half kilometres north of Goose Green and we dug in. It was a decent night weatherwise.

Our Tactical HQ's location was at Carcass Creek. The next day, 2 June, was quiet with some movement by 2 Para up and down the track connecting Darwin and Goose Green. While the Commandant became involved in planning the next phase of their operation which was a move further to the east, C Company were sent to the north of the Goose Green isthmus and, near Burntside House, began securing the start line for a Brigade overland advance. But after a full day of digging the Company was ordered back to the Goose Green area at 18.30 hours.

The reason why the fresh Gurkhas after their arrival were not deployed further along the coast and nearer the all-important goal of Stanley instead of 2 Para, was that the 5th Infantry Brigade Commander, Brigadier Tony Wilson, ordered the Battalion to remain in the settlement and defend it. At the time it was believed an Argentine unit with air assets was located on West Falkland. This particular unit, the Commandant was told, had the capability of launching a counter-attack to avenge the loss of Darwin and Goose Green and recover the strategically important Darwin/Goose Green isthmus. Against the background of such a threat, the Brigadier did not want to take the chance of leaving Goose Green lightly defended. In retrospect, however, the Gurkhas could have contributed much more to the war-fighting effort if we had carried out that exciting leapfrog eastwards.

Meanwhile Lance-Bombardier Alan Gibson, one of four Gunners in the attached artillery Battery Commander's party of Major Mike Fallon, began to forage with others for Argentine weaponry. A 20mm Rheinmetall twin anti-aircraft cannon was of interest:

After arriving at Goose Green, Bombardier John Batchelor (JB) and I went for a look around to see if there was anything we could procure for local defence. It was then that we found the 20mm gun very close to the water's edge. After checking for booby-traps or other visible signs of sabotage, we discovered that it was missing one of the breech-loading trays. This was found a couple of feet out in the water, cleaned and oiled and replaced in the gun. We managed to get one barrel working and dry-fired it to ensure the weapon functioned properly. Whilst JB was tinkering with the gun, I turned my attention to the ammunition which was stacked about ten metres away.

In Goose Green at the time was an unexploded bomb which was in the process of being made safe by a scruffy officer from the RAF. I think his name was Flight-Lieutenant Alan Swan, but I cannot be one hundred per cent sure. He sat astride the rear of the bomb with his hat on the back of his head and a roll-up dangling from his lower lip banging away at the fuse casing with a bloody great hammer. The whole area was taped off with mine tape to a distance of about three metres.

'Am I safe here, sir?' I asked.

'Yes,' he replied with a sardonic grin, 'as long as you stay behind the tape.'

I remember feeling very comforted by his expert advice and asked him, 'Would you mind casting an eye over the stacked boxes of ammo to ascertain as to whether or not they were safe to use?'

'OK,' he replied, 'I'll do that when I've finished my present task.'

About thirty minutes later he found us by the gun and, after a brief chat, bumbled off to check the ammunition. He was a great guy with the sense of humour you would expect from someone doing that sort of job. Five minutes later he came back with a bit of paper in his hand and a rueful look on his face.

'Go and check the signatures on those boxes,' he told me.

I did, and came back to be handed the piece of paper he had in his hand. On this he had scribbled his signature. He was not a happy bunny.

'Six weeks ago,' he said, 'I checked those boxes out of Newcastle. They were being shipped to France!' The signatures were exactly the same. It seemed that 2 Para had been shot at with our own ordnance.

The footnote to this tale is that after we fired a few rounds from the gun we were quickly surrounded by half a dozen extremely concerned Paras who thought it was a counter-attack from the Argentines. For some reason they became upset to find two very happy Gunners playing with their new toy.[7]

That night the Commandant summarised his day:

> I went to meet 2 Para and confirmed a plan to push them forward with our help acting as a reserve. They flew with a helicopter recce and found no enemy between Goose Green and Bluff Cove. They plan to move forward again tomorrow.

And about this time, under the title 'Battle news reaches Nepal', *The Times* newspaper reported on how news of the Battalion's deployment to the South Atlantic was being received in Nepal:

> One of the villagers could read English. He grasped the battered copy of *The Times* and people gathered around as he translated for them. Fingers jabbed at a map. Port Stanley has suddenly entered the vocabulary of a remote mountain people who could hardly be farther away from the remote Falkland Islands.
>
> Tauprasad Gurung looked up from the newspaper. 'It is always the same in a war, isn't it? Mothers are anxious, fathers are proud and old Gurkhas are remembering their own fighting days.'
>
> 'Of course, no one has heard of the Falkland Islands, or even Argentina, and no one really knows what this war is about. I have some education and I don't know. But ever since the Gurkhas were sent, people have wanted news. Many families have connections with Gurkha soldiers. I myself have an uncle serving, and also a brother by marriage, though I do not know whether they are in Falklands.
>
> 'I would not say people are worried, but mothers always worry, don't they? Fighting far away in strange places is a tradition for men from our mountains. A man who gets into the Army is considered fortunate. It is the best of jobs.
>
> 'You have to work to live and the Army is a good living, and when there is fighting it is do or die, isn't it? People here are used to it and they do not ask why there is a war, but they hope it will end quickly.'
>
> News travels quite quickly. People listen to the BBC in Hindi and English. The news is passed on and travellers take it to the far villages [...] As an integrated part of the British Army, Gurkhas do not fit the only (UN) internationally agreed definition of mercenaries. In Nepal there has been a barely noticeable protest

against the employment of Gurkhas in the Falklands – editorials in one or two small leftist papers and, in an isolated incident, the pasting of some posters by students near the Gurkha depot in Pokhara.

Back on the Sussex Mountains next morning, Dil was not aware of the helicopter shortage caused by the nine aircraft that had sunk aboard *Atlantic Conveyor*:

> Our Officer Commanding D Company (Major Mike Kefford, later CO of the 7th Gurkha Rifles) always used to say 'spend sweat to save blood'. We had heard that other Companies had reached Goose Green by helicopter. A helicopter move was too risky so where possible, moving on foot was always his preferred option. I do not know whether because of his plan or helicopters not being available, we walked all the way to Goose Green [...]
>
> There was one lad in our Platoon who struggled and cried. He was one of the newest intake soldiers in the war, quite a young town boy who had only spent a short time in the Battalion. Nonetheless the walking with the heavy loads without sufficient food, in cold weather conditions and difficult ground was quite a challenge for all.

Ten Snotrac vehicles failed to rendezvous with D Company, so the latter remained in a night harbour location to await helicopter transport next afternoon at 13.00 hours. The Battalion's next move was described in the Commandant's diary entry for 3 June:

> Moved forward from our dug out (I slept in a stable last night – it was very comfortable) and entered and took over Goose Green. 2 Para started to move out by a series of helicopter flights. My companies came in and, after a very good Orders Group, at first light moved into their locations to take over from 2 Para. I slept in the settlement shop.

The Battalion HQ was re-located in the Goose Green shop and we assumed responsibility for 471 Argentine prisoners of war corralled in the Goose Green sheep-shearing sheds. Meanwhile the helicopters destined for D Company failed to materialise and therefore these Gurkhas continued their march over the appalling terrain covered with a multitude of ankle-wrenching tussocks of grass. Fortunately two Snocat vehicles delivered rations to them and lifted their bergens to Burntside House which D Company then reached at 18.00 hours. McTeague described those thirty hours of exertion:

> After the Battalion landings at San Carlos, D Company proceeded to march at a stiff pace towards Darwin. (I don't recall hanging around for very long at all on the Sussex Mountains). Despite carrying even heavier loads than those we had during our final training in Wales, the terrain was so exposed that the men required little encouragement to move fast in order to reach our destination where shelter would be found or dug. We arrived two days later in a boulder field near Burntside House. By the water's edge in the dark, we all gratefully ate, rested and prepared for our next move.

It was not just the terrain that was appalling. The other negative factor was the weather which had been frightful all that day on 4 June with high winds and rain. 'The proof the pudding is in the eating' – and there was no doubt that the Falklands climate would play a significant role as to the success or otherwise of our imminent operations.

Notes

1. *The Art of War*, Chapter 11 – The Nine Grounds.
2. *Ibid.*, Chapter 4 – Form.
3. *5 Infantry Brigade on Operation Corporate – Logistic History*, Annex C.
4. *The Art of War*, Chapter 3 – Strategy of Attack.
5. *5 Infantry Brigade on Operation Corporate – Logistic History*, paragraph 11.
6. *Hors de Combat*, pp. 53-54.
7. E-mail dated 8 January 2008.

15 In sum, positioning the Army and scrutinising the enemy…

The ultimate in giving form to the military is to arrive at formlessness.
When one is formless, deep spies cannot catch a glimpse and the wise cannot strategise.

— Sun Tzu[1]

The Welsh Guards Recce Platoon was already in D Company's location, having been sent to recce a harbour area. But now they were ordered to stay because their Battalion's march from San Carlos had been aborted after only a few hours. Both Guards Battalions were simply not fit enough for a sixty-kilometre march westwards to Fitzroy, and it was obvious that any such a move would have to be made by sea because of the continued helicopter shortage. We put in a helicopter request to return the Guardsmen to San Carlos, and flew out fifty prisoners of war to Ajax Bay. The Commandant's diary highlighted the logistic activity:

> Overall a quiet day – but the daytime was, of course, hectic. Everything happens in about seven hours of daylight. There were massive helicopter moves of prisoners and with strangers coming in with general chaos everywhere. I went over to see local manager. Taj Lewis (C Company Commander) is staying with him. They are a nice, poor, honest, hard-working family. It was a good evening.

On 5 June Jeremy McTeague received an unexpected visit:

> The weather was clear the next morning when a sentry signalled the approach of about thirty men. It soon became obvious they were Welsh Guardsmen, and it was with pleasure I recognised the platoon commander from my Company at Sandhurst. I went over to meet him, cheerily waving. After a few preliminary pleasantries, he pulled me to one side out of earshot from his men and muttered the urgent question, 'By any chance do you know where the hell we are?'
>
> When I showed him on my map, the truth then all came out as he exclaimed, 'Ah! "They" must have dropped us in the wrong place!'
>
> Being mightily pissed off and concerned for morale and the boys' sensitivities to being thought 'second-class citizens', I then told the Guardsman, 'OK, here's the deal. I won't tell your men you're lost, if you don't tell mine that you had been flown the whole way here.'
>
> The proposal was accepted immediately.

Having established ourselves as the Goose Green garrison, we proceeded to mount a number of patrols in Lafonia to the south and elsewhere. Another 200 prisoners of war were back-loaded to Ajax Bay, but already various ideas were being considered for moving our Battalion up to the frontline forty kilometres eastwards. One of these was of putting back into service an enemy Coastguard patrol boat which had been damaged by two Sea Harriers in an air strike on 22 May and beached further up the coast at Button Bay. And another was of utilising the Falkland Islands Company's motor coaster MV *Monsunen* moored at the Goose Green jetty. During the Orders Group that evening we were informed, amongst other matters, that the Coastguard vessel would be examined by a Sapper search team. Later the Commandant's diary noted an example of the Gurkha patrolling and mentioned the 5th Infantry Brigade's ongoing advance eastwards:

> There is a major threat from a radar station which is supposed to be on Lively Island. Taj took three Scout helicopter loads out to Lively Island and checked that, Fox Point and the whole of the Choiseul Sound. NTR (nothing to report). The Scots Guards went up to Bluff Cove by a series of boats and arrived really in very bad order – with several cases of exposure!

On 6 June A Company provided a firing party of twelve Gurkhas and one NCO for the burial of Argentine dead at Darwin, while another group of 200 prisoners of war were flown out of Goose Green. As the Sappers had deemed the Coastguard vessel unseaworthy, it was decided *Monsunen* would be used next day. But the Morgan diary entry was primarily about that day's grim news: a Gazelle helicopter shot down (by a Sea Dart missile fired from HMS *Cardiff*) and the consequences:

> At 04.00 Major Mike Forge and Staff-Sergeant Griffiths of the Brigade HQ Signal Squadron were killed in a helicopter trying to get to a rebroadcast station on Mount Pleasant. Captain Belbahadur Rai took thirty men from C Company up to the mountain to check it out. It was a filthy day with very high winds and fine driving rain. Everybody got very, very wet. I am getting used to living in this abandoned shop now, but am really keen to get this wretched business over and done with. D Company will go forward to Fitzroy further up the coast tomorrow.

So D Company began to move southwards again at first light on 7 June. Dilkumar Rai:

> I think we spent a night in a house called 'Camilla Creek' before we reached Goose Green. On our way down to Goose Green, we saw the aftermath of the war: empty cases, destroyed houses, shot-down enemy aircraft, the enemy's helmets, kit etc. There was more travelling to do to reach Fitzroy which included sailing on board a ship named *Monsunen*. We were told that this was used by Argentine forces before the British landings, and British fighter aircraft tried to destroy the ship several times but it escaped being hit. Now it was our turn and we would hopefully be lucky enough to miss being hit from Argentine aircraft.

Concurrently Second-Lieutenant Quentin Oates, the Recce Platoon Commander was being deployed to Lafonia, south-west of Goose Green. He had instant success:

> My section flew to a farmhouse – Egg Harbour House – in a Scout. As we flew, probably   500 metres out, we saw a group of ten Argentines run out. We landed,

got out and observed, while calling in a reserve platoon of C Company from Goose Green. Seven of these guys were rounded up and my section stayed.

Dil was ambivalent to the forthcoming voyage on *Monsunen*. She departed from the Goose Green jetty at 18.00 hours:

> Again, travelling on a ship was quite risky and frightening because someone else would be in control of it. This is a different situation to being on the ground and able to run in any direction you thought was the best. However it was reassuring to be travelling at night and use the dark as cover to avoid enemy air attack [...] We had air defence cover from C Company [...] and my best friend from C Company was in the ship with his anti-aircraft gun system. It was the first time we had met since leaving the *QE2*.

Meanwhile the Recce Platoon's operation continued. Quentin Oates:

> At last light, with Gurkha eyesight being what it is, Lance-Corporal Sitaram Rai said he could see three to four armed men approaching. Of course I could not see a thing until, from our shell-scrapes, it was apparent that three Argentines were approaching the house. I sent two (Lance-Corporal Sukrim Rai, now pensioned off as CSM C Company – and Rifleman Budhi Limbu) around the back of the building. The Argentines came in. At a range of twenty metres, with safety-catches off and us lined up, they were told to stop and lie down. Lance-Corporal Sukrim eventually appeared and drew his *kukri* and, in Nepali, got quite angry with them. We held them over night and they were flown back next day. They were Air Force and part of a SAM-7 missile detachment: an officer and two equivalent airmen.

Obviously these Argentines had decided beforehand to surrender, but the Gurkha Lance-Corporal's anger was directed at the detachment commander who refused to lie down. One look at the *kukri*, and he joined the other two lying on the ground. At Button Bay *Monsunen* chugged past the beached Coastguard patrol boat GC-83 *Guardacosta Río Iguazú* which had been attacked by the Harriers sixteen days previously. On board *Monsunen* McTeague became interested in the stricken eighty-ton vessel and photographed her. Shipping on the exposed southern East Falkland coastline line was vulnerable to air attack. *Río Iguazú*'s fate was a portent of things to come for the British next day. But McTeague also would have been unaware of the historic nature of her action against the British jump-jets: it was the first-ever air to vessel combat engagement for any Argentine naval force. During the November 2007 Pilgrimage I met former Police Officer and then Justice of the Peace Andrew Brownlee. Together with his brother-in-law James, he had been a twenty year-old eye-witness of the engagement which occurred three kilometres from them. At the time they were drinking 'a good cup of English PG Tips tea (loose tea – not tea bags!)':

> Before sunrise I was on top of a hill just outside Walker Creek, along with my brother-in-law, a former Royal Marine, and noticed a small vessel moving in

Choiseul Sound in the area of Gull Island. It was a beautiful start to the morning, the sky was red, calm and dry. We then noticed two Sea Harriers (their shape is unmistakeable) high in the sky to the east of us.

The Harriers had obviously spotted the *Iguazú* and went into a very steep dive pattern down towards it and flew very close and low over it at high speed. Nothing was fired at this stage. They then banked and regained height and came back around and in from the east. On this pass the lead Sea Harrier opened fire. We saw streaks of red coming from the aircraft towards the vessel of which we now had a clear and unobstructed view and daylight was a little better. You could see that the vessel was being hit with just about everything the Harrier had. My diary states that only the lead Harrier fired. We could not see any sign whatsoever of any gunfire or tracer coming from the vessel towards the Harriers. After the attack run both aircraft regained height and did victory rolls high in the sky, then flew off in a westerly direction. Neither had any trails of smoke from them.

We could see a lot of smoke coming from the vessel which then went out of sight. I saw the vessel from a Gazelle helicopter on the morning of 17 June 1982 beached onto a small island in the Choiseul Sound, it could well have been Gull Island or its neighbour Sea Lion Island (not the famous wildlife reserve to the south of the Islands). She was listing right over to her port side. You could see extensive damage to the vessel – holes everywhere and signs that the surviving crew had slept on the beach. The helicopter hovered over the area for around a minute so that I could get a good view of it.[2]

Corporal Oscar Guzmán, one of the medics under Eduardo Gerding's command in 1982 at the Arsenal Azopardo in Azul, Province of Buenos Aires, was on board the vessel and received a medal in recognition of his actions that day from the Argentine Congress on 27 November 2007. He had to treat two casualties, one of whom had his leg severed by the Harrier's Aden 30mm cannon fire. Nearly twenty-one years later another story of determination and courage emanating from the *Río Iguazú*'s loss was published in the Argentine media. It further vindicated McTeague's curiosity:

He was a stranger to the sea. And still today, twenty-one years later, as he recalls diving in the frozen waters that surround the Islands, his memories are not about the icy stabbing of the water, nor about the fear. They are about the inhospitable scent of iodine and the pungent taste of salt.

At half past eight (11.30Z) in the morning of 22 May 1982, well into the war, Sub-Lieutenant José Eduardo Navarro was a novice officer. Aged 21 and born in Monte Caseros, province of Corrientes, he had graduated from the Military Academy hardly five months before the war, and still found it hard to come to terms with such an immensity of salt water as he swam for his life trying to reach the sticky surface of a small barren islet near Darwin. He had until then been travelling on board the *Río Iguazú* a coastal vessel run by the Argentine Coastguard, and she had just been badly damaged by two British Harrier aircraft.

'We had been commissioned to take two OTO Melara field guns to Darwin to support the Task Force put together by the 12th Infantry Regiment and C Company of the 25th Infantry Regiment. While attempting to load them onboard, we rapidly realised they were too large to be positioned safely for the passage as they were, so with the help of two Sergeant-Majors and the soldiers of my artillery battery, we took them apart to load them piece by piece. Our departure was delayed for four critical hours, for reasons that I still don't know.'

This delay was to prove fatal. Navarro, now Lieutenant-Colonel, was at that time serving in the 4th Airborne Artillery Battalion. He remembers that the Captain of the Coastguard vessel foretold the nightmare to him with the oracle's accuracy: their passage would demand eight hours, the main part of the sailing being carried out in daylight; when the Brits shot at everything that moved.

'At eight o'clock in the morning the air attack alarm went off, and ten minutes later there was a tremendous explosion, the lights went out and the bridge filled with smoke. The order to abandon boat was issued and as I made my way towards the bows I looked around and saw that most of the men were already in the water swimming towards the coast, which lay about thirty metres from us. At the same time I spotted one of the planes returning for a second strafing dive, this time along the beam. I dived into the water with the rest of my men and we reached land, though not on the mainland. We gathered on a small barren island of no more than 3,000 metres' diameter.'

The *Río Iguazú* had not given up without fighting back. Her artillerymen fired against the incoming Harriers. One of them died while firing his gun (a Browning) and an engine-room mate pushed his corpse away, manned the weapon and shot down one of the planes.[3] On land, Navarro and his men began to believe in miracles. 'Nothing dramatic had happened to my people, but we had two severely wounded Coastguard men. One of my men, Conscript Roberto González, told me that his throat felt sore. I inspected his neck only to discover a wound from which blood was oozing. I tried to open his jacket, but could not: a four centimetre piece of shrapnel had lodged itself in the metal zipper, rendering it useless but missing the flesh underneath.

'I then took a headcount and noticed that I was missing a man. Conscript Rodolfo Sulín had dived again into the water. He climbed onto the vessel and threw two life rafts overboard. He then loaded them with what rations, dry clothes and medicines he could find and returned to the island with both rafts. I think that saved us all dying from exposure.'

A helicopter rescued them about five on the same afternoon and took them to Darwin. The following day, Navarro returned to the *Río Iguazú*. A comrade, Sub-Lieutenant Juan Jose Gómez Centurión was with him. They had set themselves to accomplish a nearly impossible mission: the rescue of at least one of the disassembled guns, its transport to Darwin, putting it together and making it workable. The circumstances presented both a challenge and an advantage: the gun parts were underwater, in the hold of the semi-sunk ship, but Gómez Centurión was a trained diver.

'We spent all that day in the water. Gómez Centurión would dive and hand over to me the different parts and mechanisms that he had found and we would load them in the boat. After we finished we both let out a vow: "May God help us!" A helicopter picked us up and took us to Darwin. I remember it was hard to believe on realising we had recovered a whole OTO Melara in pieces …'

When the Brits attacked Darwin and Goose Green, the gun rescued from the sea was used to delay their advance. So were rocket launchers salvaged from the bodies of semi-destroyed Pucará aircraft, which were artfully rigged on top of a requisitioned tractor, until the order to surrender came on 29 May. Navarro was taken prisoner and learned of the surrender of Puerto Argentino while on board a British ship on 14 June. He landed back on the Islands still a prisoner, along with a group of comrades who – for one reason or another – had chosen to call themselves 'The Dirty Dozen'. But that is another story.[4]

Ten days after the Darwin and Goose Green battle, the remaining prisoners of war there were flown out on 7 June. That evening the Commandant's diary noted the patrolling results:

I haven't washed yet! A fairly dull day but the weather was fine and the wind high – so the boys dried out after the rain. A cold Captain Hombahadur Gurung was sent up to Mount Usborne (to the north-east of Goose Green) to try and find a suspected enemy observation post. But they had no luck. He is waiting until tomorrow morning to try again. Quentin Oates' insertion to Egg Harbour House produced seven prisoners and arms and equipment for a total of ten. Quentin is to remain on ground. We are to move up tomorrow.

We had been already looking at our maps in accordance with the intelligence provided to us on the enemy positions in the hills west of Stanley. Two 5th Infantry Brigade objectives were obvious: Tumbledown and Mount William. Both were occupied by Argentine Marines and, in particular, Mount William was reckoned as being a tough nut to crack. Options for attacking it were already being considered. One was a daring *coup de main* helicopter assault on this objective's steep southern slopes. The Intelligence Officer, Second-Lieutenant Paddy Redding, began studying contour lines and working on inter-visibility calculations. Most were relieved that he came up with a 'no go' result, but no one (thankfully) questioned or checked the precision of his deliberations.

Next morning the *Monsunen* and its load of 150 comprising D Company and 2 Para's Rear Echelon arrived at Fitzroy. McTeague:

This voyage successfully debunked the myth that Gurkhas and sailing do not mix. It was a rough, freezing passage with not a single case of sea sickness – something of a blessing since we were packed into the hold like olives in a jar and the only place to vomit was over everyone else.

[...] (at Fitzroy) a staff officer from 5 Brigade came aboard and, after giving Mike Kefford and a couple of other assorted fellow passengers a short briefing, we hurriedly disembarked as daylight was approaching and the likelihood of air attack was very high   [...] I was with Mike at Brigade HQ when the *Sir Galahad* arrived. The same staff officer advised the Welsh Guards Company Commander to disembark his men as soon as possible due to the serious air threat. The Guards Company Commander refused to disembark citing that his men were tired. While I was not witness to the discussions that followed, there was an altercation that Mike commented on to me at the time. He was critical of the Welsh Guards Major's reasoning, attitude and rank-pulling.

Dil:

> [...] we disembarked and slept in an old house which wasn't exactly a protective shelter. But what do you expect? This was war! In the early morning of the next day, we moved up to a high feature where we started to construct sangers. The Platoon's General Purpose Machine-Guns were mounted on louch poles and positioned covering almost 360 degrees.

D Company was in the hills above Port Pleasant. According to McTeague, they were 'awaiting further orders' and, by midday 'were all well dug in and enjoying the clear views'. The Recce Platoon was still deployed. Quentin Oates:

> I was out with two other sections on the West Coast of East Falklands and my particular task was to provide early warning of incoming Argentinian air attacks. As it turned out we saw the aircraft go across that subsequently attacked the *Sir Galahad* and *Sir Tristram* but, with (radio) HF communication being what they were, there was never going to be any real chance of alerting anyone in time.

Radio communications between our Battalion HQ in the Goose Green shop and D Company on the Battalion net was also non-existent. News of D Company could only be received on the Brigade net. Dil:

> Whilst the construction (of sangars) was under way, enemy aircraft flew past our position, but we were unaware that they were Argentine aircraft as we had no early warning. We thought it was our aircraft and, to our surprise, the aircraft bombed one of our ships. They came back for a second sortie and this time we had been ordered to open fire. All the GPMGs from our Company positions and other friendly positions opened fire, some even used their rifles.
>
> One of our *gurujiharu* (senior soldiers) jokingly claimed that he shot down the aircraft and he should be awarded a VC. I thought we hit the aircraft but there was no indication of the aircraft falling. I am guessing that the pilot accidentally did this in panic from all the weapon system being fired at them. But eventually the second ship was hit and thick smoke coming from it could be seen as it caught on fire. There were explosions coming from the ship and helicopters approaching to carry out casualty evacuation tasks.

McTeague:

> We received air alerts, a couple of which were false alarms. During or just after stand-to, two Argentine fighters were sighted approaching our position from the west. With barely a second to spare every machine-gun and rifle was firing at the

incomers. A veritable hail of fire was sent up by D Company. The aircraft were low and we only had to aim up about twenty to thirty degrees (if that). Their height was about 200 feet and they were silhouetted against the sky. We had no air sentries. I personally loosened off at least six rounds deliberate from my SLR.

Lots of noise, but tragically as it would turn out, to no effect. One fighter (nearest seaward) dropped its white fuel tank 100 metres from our position in a small valley, and I (along with everyone else) was certain that it was a bomb dropped on us to suppress our fire. It landed with a tremendous crash on the ground.

Our medic, a lanky lad from the Royal Army Medical Corps ducked down into the rocks with such force that he became our first man wounded in action. His panicked shouts of 'I'm wounded, help!' quickly abated when his level-headed colleague told him to shut (the fuck) up and apply a band-aid to the scratch on his little finger – the wound. In the meantime the fighters had succeeded in overflying the Scots Guards' positions which had also sent up a wall of fire, and we watched in wonder at their low, almost leisurely approach to Bluff Cove where they dropped a pair of bombs on the *Sir Galahad*.

The Scots Guards, alerted by the Gurkhas, then started firing at the aircraft as they passed over them some thirty seconds later. Initially we had no idea about the scale of the carnage caused by the attack, and it was with increasing disquiet that we watched a constant stream of helicopters flying in and out of Bluff Cove. There were two separate attacks but they were close together. We certainly witnessed other attacks during that day and at other times but did not and could not engage as the fighters were many miles beyond range.

History had been made that afternoon. D Company's firing of 4,000 rounds was the first occasion that Gurkhas had engaged enemy jet fighter aircraft in combat. Afterwards McTeague's platoon sat down together and discussed how far ahead the Skyhawks they had been aiming. Their *gora saheb* (white officer) platoon commander advised that aiming off at least twenty aircraft lengths was required in order to have a chance of a hit. But the Commandant's diary summed up that day of disaster:

Quentin Oates found the three prisoners. He came in rather late. This was another super day of weather. We are due to move out at 12.00 today [...] At the time of writing (14.30), I am worried about the condition of 3 Commando Brigade. There is still no news of an attack on Stanley and they must be getting nearer. I understand we must now be part of the major battle [...] There was a heavy air attack on Bluff Cove this evening. HMS *Plymouth* was sunk as were the two LSLs (Landing Ships Logistics). This caused over seventy casualties, presumably all Welsh Guards.

The fog of war swirled around his writing. No ship was sunk, but *Plymouth* was damaged and both LSLs severely damaged. The casualties, however, were double the Commandant's numbers. Meanwhile *Monsunen* had returned to Goose Green and the next load of Gurkhas, comprising B Company, Battalion Main HQ and A Echelon, embarked on board her to depart for Fitzroy after last light at 20.30 hours. At Little

Wether Ground McTeague was preparing for D Company patrolling operations:

> The next day (9 June) was spent resting, planning and in the routine of a patrol base because we were earmarked as the Brigade Patrols Company. Each morning we would watch in fascination as anti-aircraft missiles would be fired only to lock on to each other. Probably the most expensive fireworks display I have ever seen.

The Battalion was expecting to move by helicopter at first light – but did not. During the night *Monsunen* had to provide assistance to a badly-damaged LCU en route. This caused a delay and, with the current air threat, *Monsunen*'s voyage was aborted. She returned to Goose Green, arriving at 11.00 hours. The Commandant's diary was updated before our helicopter fly-out which would move us nearer to the front line:

> I got up early and was pressing for news: heard the Argies had 'moved west'. I hope so, they will make a good target. I planned to move A Company by boat (*Monsunen*) this morning, but now have changed my mind after having heard the BBC World Service news announce the task. Now they will move after dark. Tac HQ will fly. I must get the Recce Platoon in and poor old Captain Hombahadur Gurung off the mountain.

In the late afternoon A Company, Battalion Tactical HQ, and Mortar and Recce Platoons finally flew by helicopter to join D Company at Little Wether Ground. Next morning the Commandant's laconic diary entry registered success with the QGO's patrol and result of our helicopter flight:

> Eventually we got Hombahadur off Mount Usborne. He was cold, but proud that he had done his job. It was a very courageous effort in being up for two nights without rest. There were no casualties. All personnel are to move forward to Bluff Cove. The boat voyage for the mission is in one day [...] We arrived and dug in on the hill with D Company. There was no shelling and we had a peaceful night.

We had built sangars and peat houses on the Little Wether Ground ridge in anticipation of an uncomfortable night which turned out to be just that – very cold and wet. Meanwhile Battalion Main HQ and B Company remained overnight at Goose Green which was now being garrisoned by C Company. There was a scare there during that night with the reported credible threat of an enemy parachute landing nearby. But it was decided finally not to use *Monsunen* anymore due to the BBC World Service news compromise. The Adjutant, Captain Mark Willis, continued to write assiduously his daily notes for the official Battalion War Diary. His chronicle on 10 June detailed the complexities of moving the Battalion forward during a long and tiring afternoon and evening. This effort took us through Welsh Guards positions and nearer the imposing outline of Mount Harriet. This would be assaulted by 42 Commando in thirty-six hours. East of Harriet lay our already known objectives of Tumbledown and Mount William:

D Company moved before first light to GR2368 position ten kilometres further east (beyond 1WG), leaving packs behind for transport in Snocat. A Company and Tac HQ improving positions. Commandant to Brigadier's Orders Group at 10.00. B Company flew in by helicopter from Goose Green, followed by Battalion Main HQ and A Echelon. On the Commandant's return, moved D Company to new location 1 kilometre west. Battalion started march east approximately 14.00. Moved with packs except Heavy Machine-Gun Platoon and A Echelon who remained in location for helicopter lift. Marched approx. 7 kilometres over rough country. Through 1WG area. Took up position to the south of Wether Ground. B Company in rear, A Company right forward, D Company left forward. Tac HQ in final location at approx. midnight. Battalion Main HQ location near 1WG Tac HQ at start of road. Local protection for 29 Battery RA.

The Royal Artillery gun line was close to our positions. Also busy that night was the Royal Navy with its offshore bombardment. But Dil and his fellow Gurkhas were preoccupied with the enemy 155mm artillery:

We moved further towards Mount Harriet. Enemy artillery fired throughout the night; we were lucky that the rounds were landing away from our locations. I admit that the night was frightening and I feared for my life. One thing I can recall upon is the firing of enemy artillery which would create three sorts of sound one after the other; first it was a loud '*Twong*' (artillery fired) followed by a 'whistle sound' and the bursting of rounds on target '*Jhum*'. We were so familiar with this that we could work out how long it would take for a shell to arrive after it had been fired.

D Company had been tasked that night to mount a series of patrols in the area of Mount William. But alas, it did not turn out like that and eventually they had to withdraw and re-join the Battalion. McTeague:

Mike Kefford called me over to his trench that evening (10 June) and told me to prepare to lead a patrol. I was in some pain at the time with my knee as a direct result of long marches over tussock grass carrying a heavy pack. I knew I needed to rest it for a couple of days if I was to be able to function effectively in the forthcoming action. I told Mike this and he nominated Lieutenant (QGO) Hangseraj Magar (a future Gurkha Major) to lead the patrol. However the patrol was cancelled and we moved back to a new position where we dug in at Wether Ground near an artillery battery.

Also we had received our first taste of enemy 155mm shelling while moving through the Welsh Guards' position at Wether Ground that early evening. The Commandant had been with the Brigade HQ staff most of the day. Intelligence indicated that the enemy was located in considerable strength on the rocky knoll immediately west of Tumbledown (two machine-gun posts), Tumbledown (two rifle companies), on the saddle between Tumbledown and Mount William (one rifle company), on Mount William (one rifle company), due south of Mount William (one rifle company), and at Pony's Pass (one rifle company). It would seem that the mission would not be an easy one at all. However in reality this intelligence was flawed and overstated the enemy strength in the Tumbledown-Mount William area.

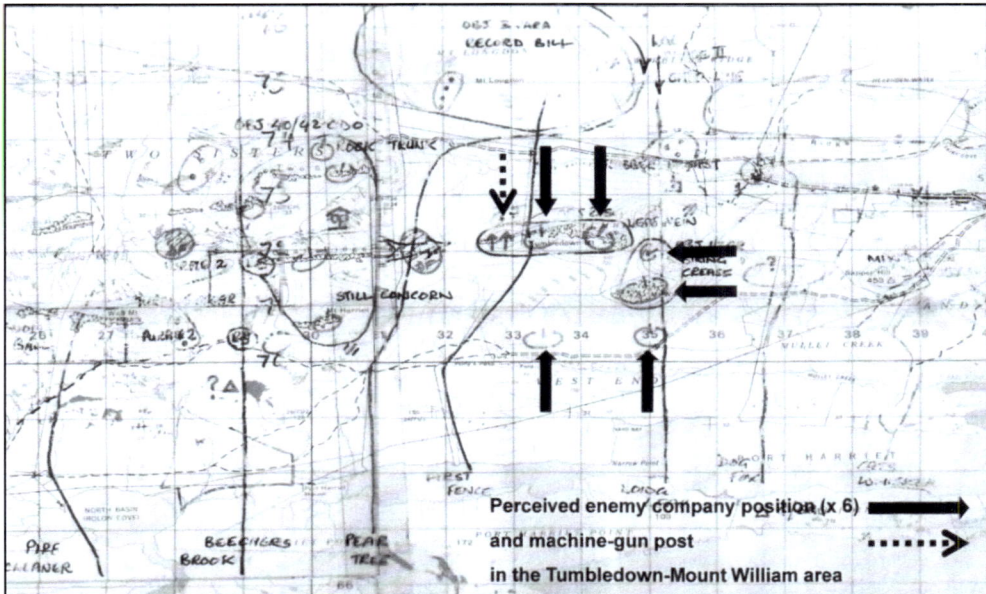

Map 8 – Original map indicating perceived enemy positions as at 17.00Z on 10 June.

The Commandant's diary took up the story from B Company's arrival and our advance out of Little Wether Ground. However the final remark of 'reasonably close' shelling was an understatement:

> All are now in their positions. We moved forward by daylight six kilometres to a position forward of the Welsh Guards. We came under heavy 155mm shelling all night. Next morning two shells landed in A Company Commander's (Major David Willis) and B Company Commander's (Captain Lester Holley) trenches, but fortunately both were out of them at the time. There were no casualties. Later three Gurkhas were wounded by splinters including Captain Dalbahadur (Sunwar) of B Company. We found a good position behind rocks for Tactical HQ. The shelling was reasonably close – but it was a good initiation.

In fact shrapnel had wounded four, not three, B Company Gurkhas. Mark Willis noted down the casualties' 'Zap' numbers (105, 111, 115, 520) from the Battalion Operation Corporate nominal role.[5] Dil:

> There were several movements of going backwards and forwards in the new area that we spent the first night, and we were lucky not to be hit by indirect fire. Unfortunately B Company's location and the Gun Battery location were harassed and hit. My cousin (21164257 Rifleman Baliprasad Rai) was in B Company and

suffered a head injury. Hearing all this was quite frightening and worrying, questioning maybe it would be our turn next?

Firepower in a battle plays an important part on the morale of a soldier on the ground. I cannot forget the weight of fire that our gun battery brought down on the enemy positions. It was really electrifying, encouraging and exciting to see the bombardment on Mount Harriet before the Marines mounted their night attack.

The enemy shelling impressed me. But strangely it did not have a similar effect on McTeague:

The 105mm guns would fire periodically which, on a couple of occasions, caused the Argentines to reply with erratic and pathetic counter-artillery fire. I remember thinking at the time as shells exploded quite near us that putting infantry next to active artillery was surely not the preferred bivouacking option.

During this sporadic enemy shelling, the remainder of 29 Battery's guns and ammunition were flown in by Sea King helicopters. But our A Echelon remained at Little Wether Ground. There was therefore no re-supply, and neither the 81mm mortar ammunition nor Heavy Machine-Gun Platoon was flown up to join us despite the many oft-repeated requests made by our Battalion Tactical HQ to Brigade HQ. All this led to unusually adverse comments about the latter in the Battalion's post-operational report. I agreed with them. Such a 'hands-on' experience taught me that operations and logistics must work seamlessly to ensure success as our post-operation report indicated:

It is believed that there were shortcomings in the organisation of Brigade HQ. Too often G (operations) and Q (logistics) decisions which involved movement by land, sea, and air, were made independently and without overall co-ordination. Junior watchkeepers seemed unaware of their responsibilities, and often appeared incapable of passing across the most mundane information to the relevant staff officer. Too often no officer of authority was available to make decisions or resolve priorities. A Brigade Deputy Commander of Colonel/Lieutenant-Colonel rank who was *permanently* available, would have resolved much of this vacillation. In addition the lengthening of watchkeepers' hours of duty would have provided greater continuity, and therefore improved the service to subordinate units.[6]

However in mitigation, members of the Brigade HQ had been working together for barely six months and therefore it was only natural that confusion reigned – and, of course, if that occurs at the top then in a war all hell lets loose lower down. After the Commandant's return he decided to hold a Battalion Orders Group. One of the many present was Quentin Oates:

It was at the O Group, held on the high ground overlooking Bluff Cove and in the rocks where Tac HQ was located, where David Morgan gave his orders for the Battalion assault on Mount William, when an amusing incident happened.

The O Group followed its normal course – despite that on this occasion it was very much for real and was the first orders for a Gurkha Battalion attack for some considerable time. As the O Group went on, the Argentinians started to fire their artillery. It was rather sporadic, and only a couple of guns were firing, but the rounds seemed to get progressively closer and closer to the O Group, whether by design (directed) or luck (they must have been aware we were in the area, but had no observers). As the rounds got closer, the pace of the O Group picked up – I am sure David Morgan did not appreciate it. The end of the O Group came as a round was fired. By this time there was a degree of tension amongst all of us, and we were perceptively keen to get going.

'Any questions?' – almost within the same breath – 'Good.'

At this point everyone was already up and moving, but stopped as they realised this particular round was going to be much closer than the others. Within the close confines of the rocky enclosure where the O Group was being held, everyone fell to the ground. There was no room for me, apart from being on top of another body. So I stood surrounded by, as it seemed to me at the time, a lot of senior officers taking cover while the round landed and exploded.

Everyone got up and there was a couple of sheepish looks as they saw I had stood through the incident. We moved back to our men to brief them.[7]

The successful (and exceptionally noisy) 3 Commando Brigade attack on Mount Longdon, Two Sisters and Mount Harriet took place that night of 11/12 June. During the next morning 155mm shelling on our positions continued and A Company had four bergen backpacks destroyed by shellfire. McTeague:

Information was scarce and we had little knowledge about what was happening during those days, so it was heartening next morning on 12 June to see a long column of (eighty-seven) prisoners being marched past us to the rear (and evacuated by helicopter).

His point about passage of information was most apposite. Indeed this was a major shortfall throughout the campaign which, again, our post-operation report savaged:

This has not been called the 'Mushroom War' without reason. From the outset all information concerning the enemy, friendly forces' moves, actions by supporting arms and adjacent units, and even future intentions were never passed on to subordinate units. Any information received was either inaccurate, or out of date by the time it reached Battalion level. This resulted in a total lack of confidence by subordinate commanders to senior command. Correspondingly rumours quickly spread in a vacuum generated by this lack of information. This consistent rumour mongering had a marked effect on morale, and could have been averted by resorting to the normal military practice of transmitting twice daily sitreps (situation reports).[8]

Our Battalion, according to Mark Willis's diary, had been 'expecting to move forward as a reserve' after the 3 Commando Brigade attack. This did not happen 'except for the Recce Group prior to the attack on Tumbledown and Mount William'. McTeague:

> We were flown forward onto (a ridge south of) Two Sisters with the other platoon commanders to recce our objective, Mount William. It was distressing to see the terrain, devoid of cover and dead ground. We saw a few Argentines moving around on the lower slopes, but it was clear that the bulk of the force was well ensconced in the rocks and boulders that completely dominated the upper reaches of the conical mountain. My appreciation was simple and lacking in any optimism: we had to cover about 1,000 metres of ground that swept gently upwards towards the enemy position. The enemy was well dug-in, their defences were in extraordinary depth and, with only a few exceptions, virtually hidden but with fantastic fields of vision and fire.
>
> We would have to attack at night if we were to have any chance, yet we knew that the enemy had superior night vision equipment. I sat with my Platoon Sergeant, Paulraj Rai, and discussed our options with him. This took about one minute as there really were none.

Mark Willis's Recce Group participation contained a culinary perspective:

> By the time Battalion HQ moved forward from Goose Green I was already beginning to tire of rice and curried *dhumba* (sheep), and at this time even compo (Army composite rations) was in short supply as all the helicopters were being used for the transport of troops and ammunition for the artillery, so rations were in a low priority. On the day when our 'O Group' went up to Two Sisters to make its recce for the forthcoming attack, a welcome opportunity arose. Our OP (Observation Post) was in amongst some former Argentinian defence positions, and a quick inspection revealed a number of part-used rations. I remember how these all included a little religious picture accompanied by a prayer or two, and sometimes a hand-written letter to 'our boys at the Front' from schoolchildren back in Argentina. There was also one type of ration pack that included a miniature bottle of spirits of some sort. Allegedly this version was for officers only! I came back from the recce with various confectionary items and biscuits, but the most welcome items were some tins of pasta with a spicy meat sauce – the Argentinian equivalent of 'Spag Bol' – which turned out to be surprisingly nice. It is funny how somebody else's rations always seem more appealing than one's own.[9]

The Recce Group returned to Wether Ground in one piece. Then late in the afternoon a Sea King helicopter landed near the Battalion Tac HQ's rocky outcrop. We were expecting a much-needed logistic re-supply, but instead the TV war correspondents Brian Hanrahan (BBC) and Mike Nicholson (ITN) together with their two cameramen, Bernard Hesketh and John Jockell, emerged from the Sea King. They had been dispatched from Brigade HQ at Fitzroy and (to use the term developed later in the 2003 international coalition forces' invasion of Iraq) were going to be 'embedded' with us for the attack. However on catching sight of these innocent media representatives, the Battalion 2IC Major Bill Dawson, went ballistic over the Brigade's prioritisation of media rather than much-needed logistics. The surprised arrivals beat a hasty retreat and maintained a smart tactical low profile after Bill's tirade by not appearing at the second Orders Group on Wether Ground when the Commandant gave out his formal orders for the attack.

But after the Heavy Machine-Gun Platoon and some rations had been flown in just before last light, I took pity on the war correspondents and decided to put on my secondary official hat as the Battalion Public Information Officer. They needed facts on forthcoming events so I wandered over to where they had set up bashas and were busy cooking food. After introducing myself I proceeded to give them an hour-long informal briefing on the Battalion's imminent tasks. On hearing this, Mike Nicholson wanted to be 'embedded' further with the Battalion Tac HQ, but I persuaded him that this was not a good idea. My fear was that these media professionals could get in the way during the stress of directing a Gurkha Battalion night attack on Tumbledown's north-east spur and, the main prize, Mount William. Moreover the darkness would preclude them from capturing images on celluloid of any Gurkha *kukri*-wielding assault which could prove to be a bloody affair. It would be better if the war correspondents accompanied Battalion Main HQ commanded by Bill Dawson. Come daylight this would give them an excellent grandstand view of proceedings while perched high up on the eastern end of Two Sisters South.

They agreed to my suggestion and Nicholson thanked me. It appeared that the TV team had not been treated too well during Operation Corporate. So maybe they were surprised that a Gurkha officer had been willing to assist them, in addition to volunteering much-needed information. Love or hate them, the media wield considerable power. They are also a main contributor to information warfare as the true significance of the *kukris* and millstone episode back at Church Crookham on 5 May would be revealed post-war. Better to get the media on your side, rather than endure a poor public relations feedback afterwards and downgrading of a military unit's reputation.

The result in the war's last forty-eight hours for the Gurkhas and TV team would be a 'win-win' situation. In the late-afternoon of 13 June some spectacular video film sequences would be recorded of Gurkhas under enemy artillery fire on Two Sisters South, and the Tactical Air Control Party co-located with Battalion Main HQ laser-marking enemy targets for two Harrier GR3 Laser Guided Bomb attacks. Another twenty-four hours later, recorded for posterity, would be that iconic 'bloody marvellous' remark from Bill Dawson after hearing on the Brigade radio net of a 'white flags over Stanley' report (which, although also announced in Parliament by Mrs Thatcher, never occurred). Indeed Bill's 'bloody marvellous' was only uttered in relief that there had been no more technical hitches or fluffing of lines at the end of a successful fourth stage-managed take. But there was a formal Argentine surrender at that day's end, and all those images were included in the final episode of the eight-part BBC documentary film series *Task Force South*.

The Commandant's diary entry of 12 June alluded to the intense planning which had been taking place during the previous seventy-two hours:

> We were supposed to have attacked tonight, but both Mike Scott and I complained that since we had neither got the right airlift nor the opportunity to see the ground,

we would walk into chaos. Fortunately the Brigade Commander agreed. We went up on the mountain and had a look with our officers. It is a hell of a long way away, but Stanley is plainly visible – a great sight.

Twenty-five years later he elaborated further on some of the problems (but not our logistics shortfalls) which caused a twenty-four hour delay to the Brigade attack, and how the double Battalion assault on Tumbledown and Mount William had been designed:

There were [...] three meetings; a formal 'O' Group to which the Press were invited (on 9 June); a follow-up 'O' Group at which I said (supported strongly by Mike Scott) that I could not keep to the timings laid down, and one with Mike and I discussing the detail [...] I remember very little of the main 'O' Group at Fitzroy (just goes to show how much attention I must have been paying at the time). I do recall that the Press were invited – TV and all, but were soon dismissed. (Brigadier) Tony Wilson then said, 'Right, now that they have gone, this is actually what we are going to do!' After 'H's' experience at Goose Green nobody trusted the Press [...]

What I do recall is the 'O' Group in the hills (on 11 June) with Mike Scott [...] That was when the two of us complained that we simply could not put in the attack to the timeframe he (Tony Wilson) laid down, and, after a while we (Mike and I) got the go-ahead to delay so that we could 'gird our loins' and could have a look at our objectives in daylight – the Scots Guards had had this privilege, but I had not [...]

Mike Scott was the one who persuaded Tony Wilson that it would be better to faint onto the south and produce a strong attack from the west [...] It is my recollection that my instructions were simply to 'take Mount William' [...] The question then was how are the Gurkhas going to get into the act and reach their objective at William?

The answer to me was to do what we did, namely to skulk around the north (of Tumbledown) [...] and dive down [...] with one Company [...] from behind the Argie positions, but it was Mike Scott and I who decided that – not Tony Wilson.

One should not confuse this quite complex attack with 'H's' one at Goose Green. For him it was simple. He had just his Battalion, and could have been as autocratic and complex as he liked. No one else was involved. As far as I am aware the Tumbledown/William attack was the only two-Battalion attack in the war, and was thus fraught with co-ordination problems which, of course, appeared.

I was at the time, and remain so, totally confident that one Company would take out resistance on Mount William supported as it was (like no other Battalion out there) by so much hardware – and A Company was to be the reserve if things had gone really pear-shaped. However I was equally sure that the battle would end up with close-quarter fighting – and there is no-one better than the Gurkha at that. I can also remember wishing that C Company was with us! [9]

As observed by Vázquez, the Argentine Marine 4 Platoon Commander, the Scots Guards' 'faint onto the south' at Pony's Pass would succeed in a most effective way by utilising the Sun Tzu *Tao* (way) of deception, thereby creating the all-important effect of 'formlessness'. Our post-operation report alluded to other important matters such as air photographs, rehearsals and, not least, time:

> Air photographs should be taken, and time allowed for their study. It should be noted that air photographs issued for this Battalion's attack on Mount William gave a reasonable coverage of Stanley Airport: but none of the intended objective. Furthermore men must be prepared and rehearsed, and ammunition brought forward. Many other seemingly minor, but nonetheless important tasks must be carried out: all take time, and this was the one requirement lacking in this campaign.[11]

McTeague attended the subsequent D Company Orders Group where Kefford explained his plan for the perilous assault on Mount William. Two of his platoon commanders were Nepalese Queens Gurkha Officers, while McTeague was the only BO platoon commander. There is nothing like a 'hands-on' experience of this gravity to concentrate the mind. And later in life he pointed out a major shortfall in his training at Sandhurst:

> What we do not normally have to face is a rapid escalation in the threat and to manage the realisation of its new enormity. At the Royal Military Academy Sandhurst we were not trained in how to deal with fear of a threat that was so large that one's death (and that of most of one's men) appeared (quite rationally) to be the only logical outcome. My orders book again provides insight into my thinking on the eve of the Battalion's battle, and the D Company attack on Mount William in particular. This was to be a frontal attack (on) two Argentine Marine platoons totalling approximately 110 men who were dug-in both on Mount William itself and just to the north-west of this objective. This enemy force equated in size to D Company.[12] The only hope of success was that the darkness of night would cloak us and our movement, and supporting fire from A Company's fire base of Browning heavy machine-guns, Milan anti-tank missiles, general purpose machine-guns in the sustained fire role, our Battalion 81mm mortars and the artillery would suppress the enemy whilst we were exposed in the open.[13]

D Company's attack plan can be best described as a scissors movement. First 12 Platoon would make a westerly right hook from Tumbledown to take the northern slopes of Mount William. They would then provide fire support to 11 Platoon's follow-up easterly left hook onto the southern slopes. Our post-operation report described the tactics to be used: with the 'throw away after use' shoulder-fired 66mm Light Anti-tank Weapon (LAW) being a potential Gurkha 'battle-winner' in the anticipated close-quarter fighting. Its limitations were also mentioned:

> It was planned that (the 66mm LAW) should be used to engage rifle fire at night. The shock of the explosion in the general vicinity of the enemy trench would allow riflemen, covered by further automatic fire, to close with the enemy. The noise

generated in such an enclosed rocky location as Mount William would also clearly add to the shock effect. 1/7 Gurkha Rifles carried four 66mm per section of eight men. This is clearly not enough for protracted operations [...] There is (also) a marked difference between the trigger pressure of a live rocket, and that of a practice round. Most 66mm rockets fired (in training) missed the target by a considerable margin because the soldier was simply not used to firing live rounds. It is obvious therefore that the annual allocation of live 66mm LAW is too low. The use of the 66mm is effective provided it is fired accurately. Accuracy comes with practice, and practice can only be achieved by firing more live rockets.[14]

Then Kefford arrived at McTeague's outline mission. The latter's 10 Platoon would be in reserve for the Mount William attack. This seemed simple enough in the circumstances. But his stomach slowly began to tighten when heard the details. The increasingly anxious subaltern jotted down his notes (in italics below) which steadily became a mounting list of operational dilemmas. McTeague:

> The scene is set with an uncertainty: *Phases 2 and 3 of the attack will be together, or one after the other?*
>
> Then the tasks: *11 and 12 Platoons will be the first attack platoons. 10 Platoon* (my command) *will initially be in reserve* (sigh of relief). But then: *10 Platoon will commit sections piecemeal to support 11 and 12 Platoons. And one section is to look after prisoners.*
>
> Then as a third task: *another section is to evacuate the wounded until it is committed for the assault* (this was verging on the impossible, since the section could be one kilometre to the rear at the time I was meant to be putting it into the attack. Also for the record: at this point all three of my sections had now been committed to various tasks!)
>
> Then it gets worse: *Carry extra ammo.* Ammunition is very heavy and carrying it for other soldiers when attacking, is like sending a boxer into the boxing ring in handcuffs.
>
> And even worse: *attached SF (general purpose machine-gun in the sustained fire role) has to go to A Company* so I had also lost my only integral fire support. I was then told that *the enemy artillery is very accurate and that we must re-organise ourselves after the attack under cover.* In effect this meant treating wounded, re-supplying and dealing with prisoners whilst under artillery fire.
>
> Finally Major Mike Kefford, my Company Commander and a man warranting great respect, advises that the fight is going to be *'man to man combat'.*
>
> Without overstating the case, this set of orders describes a desperately difficult set of circumstances with a level of complexity that was bound to result in massive casualties, if not outright failure. The level of fear and hopelessness I felt was shared by my men and it was palpable, yet there was full acceptance of my orders.[15]

There was every reason for the mounting concern. According to Sun Tzu a defending force always has the advantage over an attacking force. Therefore the Chinese General's maxim that 'attack and one is insufficient' was becoming acutely relevant to the current situation facing McTeague and the remainder of D Company.

But matters would also get much worse.

Notes

1. *The Art of War*, Chapter 6 – The Solid and the Empty.
2. E-mail dated 28 November 2007.
3. No Sea Harrier was shot down as Andrew Brownlee's eye-witness account clearly indicated. Furthermore two Argentine Air Force Observers, Ciano Zampieri and Julio Rotea, witnessed the attack on the *Río Iguazú* and also did not see any Harrier destroyed. But this myth has persisted in Argentina, not least in official publications, possibly to enhance the Argentine historic nature of this engagement. 'The rumour was probably spread by the Coastguard,' Eduardo Gerding informed the author (e-mail dated 10 December 2007). Regrettably not only did the author's first book (page 172) include the loss of a Harrier, but also that three, not two, of these aircraft attacked the vessel. The lesson was learnt. If possible, always consult with eye witnesses before putting pen to paper.
4. *Clarín* dated 1 April 2003: 'Malvinas: the history of a field gun rescued from the sea'.
5. The Adjutant is responsible for personnel matters. In war one of his essential tools of trade is a Battalion nominal role with a pre-allocated 'Zap' casualty number for each Battalion member. In transmitting casualty information over the radio, for security purposes the 'Zap' code is used as opposed to a soldier's name.
6. *Op Corporate 1/7GR Immediate Debrief Points* dated 10 July 1982.
7. E-mail dated 11 November 2006.
8. *Op Corporate 1/7GR Immediate Debrief Points* dated 10 July 1982.
9. 7th Duke of Edinburgh's Own Gurkha Rifles Regimental Association Journal, 2007, No. 13, p. 102.
10. E-mails dated 10 and 14 August 2007, and 24 November 2011.
11. *Op Corporate 1/7GR Immediate Debrief Points* dated 10 July 1982.
12. The author's later research and calculations (see Chapter 8) to establish the correct number of enemy who were finally on Mount William before they retreated to Stanley was 197 men – so, in fact, D Company were outnumbered by nearly two to one.
13. *Hors de Combat*, p. 56.
14. *Operation Corporate 1/7GR Post Operation Report – Part II* dated 27 July 1982.
15. *Hors de Combat*, p. 57.

On the day that orders are issued.
The tears of seated officers moisten their lapels,
The tears of those reclining cross their cheeks,
Throw them where they cannot leave –
It is the bravery of Chuan Chu and Ts'ao Kuei.
– Sun Tzu[1]

Nearly three decades later I was privy to an e-mail discussion between two former Sapper officers who were veterans of the war in which they held the rank of Major. One was Rod Macdonald (Squadron Commander of 59 Independent Commando Squadron attached to HQ 3 Commando Brigade), and the other Chris Davies (Squadron Commander of 9 Parachute Squadron Royal Engineers attached to the 5th Infantry Brigade HQ). They had differing 'perspectives' as to our forthcoming attack's necessity. Macdonald:

I was on Wireless Ridge for the attack which, building on previous experience, was the most professional I saw in the campaign. I met up with (Major) Chris Keeble and his (2 Para) HQ first then joined my forward Recce Troop. As daylight dawned I watched artillery fire come down on what I thought was Tumbledown but, by that time, we had outflanked all the southern objectives and had worked our way along Wireless Ridge to Moody Brook Camp. To the south and behind us, I saw many Argentinean soldiers fleeing in disarray. It was shortly after, and as we were moving down to Moody Brook, when a radio message came through that a ceasefire had been called [...]

The key and strategic ground was Stanley. The Argentine positions to the south were all outflanked and bypassed by the attack on Wireless Ridge which resulted in British troops on the edge of Stanley in a relatively short period of time. This brings into question why the attacks on Tumbledown and Mount William were required at all. I questioned this at the time when plans were being formulated, not least because these extra attacks caused the Wireless Ridge assault to be delayed twenty-four hours while others to the south prepared.

My conclusion at the time, which I think was shared by (Brigadier) Julian Thompson, was that the resultant Divisional plan was entirely understandable because everyone wanted a piece of the action. I am sure the Scots Guards are very happy to have this battle honour. Mike (Seear) knows how disappointed the Gurkhas were that the surrender came before they could go into their own assault. There is no doubt that the southern attack prevented any flanking counter-attack as we speedily moved across Wireless Ridge. However, whether those attacks and the resultant loss of life were really necessary to secure Stanley is something I have often thought about.

But then, at the end of the day it's a pointless debate; we won and that is what really matters.[2]

418

Davies:

'Perspective' is always interesting and our own is always driven by what we can see plus what we can only imagine about what we cannot see. Happily there is no 'action replay' or 'fourth official' with a video to remind us of what actually took place at the time or – at this distance in time – what we actually knew at the time. Maybe there is a Golden Gate and St Peter will show us the overall picture when we finally get there. In the meantime, old mate, we will just have to disagree on whether Tumbledown needed to be attacked at all.

I do not think it was a question of needing to get a slice of the action. I recall that the Commandos had the limit of exploitation of Tumbledown and William (perhaps even Sapper Hill – my memory is not reliable) if their attacks on Mount Harriet, Two Sisters, Mount Longdon etc. were successful. In the event, it was some time after first light when all objectives were finally secured and (most important) the land-based gunners were pretty well out of ammunition and at the limit of their range. The (Royal Marine) Commando Company I met on Mount Harriet certainly felt that they had done their bit and they had no inclination to carry out a follow-on attack. (I saw only one sentry and the rest were lumped together under bivvy sheets trying to keep warm and out of the pretty accurate shellfire we were experiencing – frankly, I could not blame them).

I felt strongly at the time (and I, with (Lieutenant-Colonel) Tony Holt – the CO 4th Regiment, Royal Artillery – prevailed upon (Brigadier) Tony Wilson to accept the view) that it would be madness to commit the Scots Guards to an attack on Tumbledown the night after the 3 Commando Brigade attack. They had not seen the ground, the guns were not far enough forward (and they only had about six rounds per gun anyway): it would have been suicidal to have attacked on the 12/13 June.

I may have been wrong but I felt that the Argies had less chance of substantially reinforcing the position, and that 3 Para, and 45 and 42 Commandos had a better chance of coping with the weather than the Scots Guards had of surviving if they had attacked that night. I know the Commandos were pretty scathing about the whole thing but, in their position, anyone would have been. Whatever the 'Green Machine' might think/have thought, I do not think 3 Commando Brigade would have carried all of the objectives by themselves.[3] It was necessary to have 5 Infantry Brigade there: the Argies did not know how dysfunctional it actually was and, if nothing else, the multi-directional attack certainly gave them some problems.

I am puzzled that you think that Tumbledown was an unnecessary attack. Given the shape of the ground thereabouts, it pretty well dominates Wireless Ridge. I think 2 Para would have had a very sticky time indeed if they had attacked Wireless Ridge without Tumbledown (and the artillery etc. in its support) had not been seriously preoccupied at the time. It would have been like attacking Longdon without doing something about Two Sisters at the same time. (B Company, 3 Para would have been completely destroyed by the enfilade fire from there if it had not had anything else to shoot at.)

But, old friend, we are getting into the realms of 'fighting corners' on what we believed to be the case at the time. Back to perspective. We were on different sides of the hill and it is entirely reasonable that we should have had a different view/ understanding of what the hell was actually going on. *C'est la vie.* Happily we survived to enjoy our differing perspectives. Sadly some we both knew well were not blessed with that option.[4]

I veer towards the latter's perspective. However perhaps this is due to my bias of being involved in the attack which would also include our B Company having to assault the long north-east Tumbledown spur. The esoteric value of this only two-Battalion attack mounted during the war was increased by its taking place at night without any prior rehearsal. Indeed when had there been a field training exercise last held in the UK that involved two infantry Battalions carrying out a night attack while using *live* ammunition? And, after the Falklands-Malvinas War, has there ever been held anywhere such a British Army live-firing exercise to practise the lessons that we were about to learn?

But back to Wether Ground on the morning of 13 June 1982 and only thirty-six hours to run before the ceasefire and eventual Argentine surrender. There was a sprinkling of snow on the ground as I got out of my sleeping bag just after dawn at 10.00Z. As usual there had been little sleep. But there would be none at all during the next thirty-six hours, the most mentally punishing of my life. The BBC and ITN reporters Brian Hanrahan and Mike Nicholson watched while their cameraman was busy filming the deployment of Lieutenant Mark Coreth's 4 Troop of B Squadron, The Blues and Royals in their two Scimitar and two Scorpion light tanks. Also I stood behind the cameraman watching with interest this troop's move eastwards past us along the Darwin to Stanley track prior to their participation in the coming night's bloody, but highly successful Scots Guards composite platoon diversionary attack on the enemy Marines' O Company position at Pony's Pass. One light tank crew member grinned at the cameraman and gave a 'thumbs-up' sign. There was no problem with his morale on the eve of battle.

A little later I would be preoccupied in organising the 'fly-out' of 467 Gurkhas by eight helicopters in a shuttle-run of sixty-four 'sticks' to a Battalion Assembly Area just south of Two Sisters. However the first to leave Wether Ground was the Commandant and Captain Mark Willis. The latter described what happened next and, in particular, a final co-ordination meeting with the Scots Guards CO Lieutenant-Colonel Mike Scott and his Operations Officer, Captain Tim Spicer:

I still have my little notebook in which I wrote notes for the War Diary. In this the entry for 13 June reads:

CO and Adjutant left early in a Gazelle (helicopter) for the recce of DOP (Drop Off Point). 1/7GR lifted out after 8.59. Drop did not go well due to lack of comms. with the helicopters. People dumped in wrong place, but finally sorted out just before last light. Intelligence Officer's (Second-Lieutenant Paddy Redding) party was mortared on landing. There was heavy shelling in the Assembly Area prior to landing (45 Commando also in this area). The mortar line was located to the south of Goat Ridge in the Scots Guards area. Confirmatory O Group was given at last light, 20.00 hours.

I do not remember being under fire myself at this time, though I suppose it is possible that some shells arrived somewhere in the vicinity whilst we were conferring (which would, no doubt, have caused us to move our position). Shells often seemed to land quite close by, whereas they were probably in reality miles away and just seemed close because the terrain was so open.

My main memory of this meeting (with the Scots Guards CO and his Operations Officer) is the uncertainty about the exact location of a minefield that was alleged to be somewhere along the north side of Tumbledown – hence a significant factor in our plan for the approach. Everyone had it marked differently on their maps. Actually this means marked in chinagraph pencil on their plastic/talc map-cases, inside which the maps tended to move around a fair bit. I felt that we ought to have spent some more time establishing exactly where the minefield was, but the COs did not seem to give it that much importance.[5]

Although the two COs had completed their co-ordination, the minefield issue returned almost immediately afterwards. The Gurkhas' Commandant explained:

A young 9 Para Squadron Royal Engineers Lieutenant by the name of Peter McManners and who was attached to the Scots Guards, came up to me and told me that my plan of sneaking 'under' the north face of Tumbledown and coming at Mount William from the north would be 'impossible'.

Indeed his actual words were 'You can't do that, sir!'

So I asked, 'Why not?'

He replied, 'The Argies have placed a minefield where you propose to go and it's bound to go right up to the rocks!'

I had two choices. Either feel my way around the minefield to the north, or cling to the rocks. I chose the latter for three reasons. First I had visions of being caught up with whatever was going on near Wireless Ridge. Second we could get lost. And, third, keeping to the rocks would be quicker.

So I made the decision and asked our own 9 Para Squadron RE party commanded by Sergeant Ron Wrega to lead. Later they did find booby-trapped hand-grenades in D Company's path further up on Tumbledown's eastern sector, rather than where I thought they were supposed to be. Was it Napoleon Bonaparte who once said something like 'Give me a lucky General over a good one every time?'.[6]

However the Commandant's perception of his luck was wrong. At the time of the latter's decision, Miño and his Marine Amphibious Engineer 5 Platoon were still located on Tumbledown's west summit. These defenders had a great field of fire overlooking the dummy minefield they had marked out and planned route of the Gurkha advance which would 'cling to the rocks'. The Commandant's lucky break came a few hours later when, well before the Gurkhas arrived at the 'minefield', Miño and his men withdrew to the Tumbledown's east end because of the 'overwhelming' attack that Miño had perceived from the tracer fire of the Blues and Royals Scimitar 30mm Rarden cannon on Wireless Ridge and, to a degree, at Pony's Pass with the Scots Guards diversionary attack.

In making his plan, Lieutenant-Colonel Mike Scott was influenced by what he had been told the day before:

> I remember, vividly, talking to Commandos who had taken Goat Ridge when we went up for a recce and they said, 'No problems, the Argentines merely fire off a magazine then come out with their hands up.' I therefore anticipated we would roll it up by midnight, especially when G Company took their objective virtually unopposed, thus leaving the Gurkhas to take William in what was left of the night but, having said that, it would have been a tall order if there had been real Argentine resistance on William.[7]

He had already prepared the ground from which to launch the Scots Guards advance:

> Goat Ridge was always north of our line of advance and was therefore on our left flank. The start line was theoretically the line of the fence marked on the map. This was for ease of identification at night. Although in actual fact the real start line was the top of the ridge of the saddle between Goat Ridge and Harriet. The Assembly Area was where we were flown into by helicopter to the west of Goat Ridge and Mount Harriet. The Forming Up Point (FUP), where we shook out into our attack formation, was the dead ground to the west of the top of the ridge separating Goat Ridge and Mount Harriet. This had been earlier laid out by my Second-in-Command and Recce Platoon.[8]

The Commandant's diary entry for 13 June gave details about the two Battalion COs' final co-ordination meeting:

> I got up at the normal time and was prepared to meet (the Brigadier) at 13.00 as ordered. I was called for earlier and told to go to meet Brigadier at the 500-ring contour. I did so with Mark Willis – but there was no Brigadier – and no radio. I spoke to Mike Scott ref. battle plans. This was most useful – indeed vital. I feel happier about tonight, although naturally apprehensive. I trudged over to the Battalion Assembly Area.

With all the Gurkhas flown up to the Assembly Area, it was Squadron-Leader Jerry Pook's dramatic GR3 Harrier Laser Guided Bomb attack on the rocky knoll adjacent to Tumbledown's west end which captured much attention. Quentin Oates witnessed part of it, but mistook the aircraft's target as Mount William:

> It was during (the) O Group (held on 11 June at Wether Ground) I had been told that the Recce Platoon was to be used as stretcher bearers and I would be attached to the Scots Guards as a liaison officer with their Battalion Tac HQ. I moved with one of my section junior NCOs – Lance-Corporal Sitaram Rai to tie up with Scots

Guards. I was not there for their formal orders for the attack, but arrived to hear orders for the movement and actions of the HQ itself. It was during this briefing that a fast jet appeared over the rocky hill tops. It was low and very suddenly there coming out of the sun, and therefore unidentifiable as to being friendly or not. Added to this, a large round black (silhouetted) object detached itself from the aircraft. There were immediate shouts from everyone at the O Group as they all attempted to get out of the way (of what turned out to be a 1,000 pounder from a Harrier – lasered on to Mount William). Once again I was confronted with a number of rather sheepish members of the O Group as they all got off the ground as I had stayed put.[9]

But this was only part of the second LGB mission flown that day. The first was flown by Wing-Commander Peter Squire [10] at about 14.00Z against 'a Company HQ position' [11] which was probably that of the Marine Amphibious Engineer Company HQ co-located with Robacio's Battalion Tactical HQ and Marine Logistic Support Area at Felton Stream. The first LGB fell well short, but the RAF claimed a direct hit with Squire's second attack. But also this bomb fell short – albeit by only 200 metres.[12] A cluster-bomb attack by the second GR3 on the western end of Tumbledown also missed the Argentine Marines' 4 and 5 Platoons. About two hours later Oates had witnessed a third GR3 flown by Squadron-Lear Jerry Pook rocketing in southwards from the Bluff Cove area and, covered by a fourth, releasing its first LGB. Directly below on the southern Two Sisters feature I was mesmerised by this aircraft flying momentarily beside its sinister bomb. The latter's stabilising fins flipped out and then it wobbled to lock onto the laser reflection from the target before disappearing rapidly to the east. The GR3 escaped westwards. Based on Pook's Forward Air Controller, Major Mike Howes's (callsign Red Dragon) radioed exclaimation, 'Green Lead, that was right on the barrel!', a direct hit three kilometres away was claimed on 'an artillery position at the base of Mt Tumbledown'.[13] But no artillery was in the target grid square of VC 3372 (which contains the western-centre end of Tumbledown) written in the subsequent combat report of the courageous pilot.[14] Only 4 and 5 Platoons were in the vicinity, but further along. Pook's LGB also missed both platoons. He repositioned his GR3 for a second attack, but 'the next bomb fell a bit short'.[15] So 13 June proved unlucky for the RAF.

One who had been an eye-witness to this LGB mission was Major Chris Davies at the 5th Infantry Brigade Tactical HQ:

I remember distinctly the Harrier launching the bombs from lower than we were and from behind us – on the rocky outcrop a midgeon north of Harriet. The bombs waggled over our heads until gathered by the Forward Air Controller's laser [...] I was almost next to him on the rocky outcrop which is slightly north but still part of the Harriet feature when the bombs were delivered. The first missed his aiming point and hit low down on the first knoll (of Tumbledown) – he said he flinched! The second bomb (later, but I could not say how much later) hit higher up the feature. They certainly made a bloody great big bang ... and we winced at the explosions. The pilot might have been told he was aiming for an artillery piece but he could not have seen one because – you are absolutely right – there was not one there. I think (Major Mike Howes) was aiming at what we thought was a platoon position (or maybe a machine-gun). Certainly, we could not see anything that looked remotely like a gun so I do not know where the pilot got this 'duff gen' from. Fog of war! [16]

Our post-operation report contained acid comments on the 5th Infantry Brigade HQ's use of the GR3 Harrier and LGB:

> The knowledge of the value and control of OAS (Offensive Air Support) was appallingly bad. Staff control of close air support was far too tight. Greater use of offensive delivery assets, particularly the Laser Guided Bomb, would undoubtedly have saved casualties on the Tumbledown feature. A total lack of staffing and communications contributed to this failure. Harrier pilots were at fifteen minute cockpit alert on HMS *Hermes* for a three day period towards the latter stages of hostilities. They were only given two missions on 13 June, and one mission on 14 June despite repeated mission requests by the TACPs (Tactical Air Control Parties). A total of eighteen sorties had been promised over these two days. The fact that the pilots were actually waiting for tasking was later confirmed by the Captain of HMS *Hermes* three weeks later whilst on a visit to Battalion HQ at Goose Green.[17]

There was also the dreadful intelligence which wasted Pook's LGB attack on the supposed enemy platoon or machine-gun posts on the rocky knoll adjacent to the west end of Tumbledown because, as Chris Davies pointed out, 'not only did we expect there to be at least a platoon on this feature, but it would certainly have made no tactical sense NOT to have had at least a platoon on this forward position.' [18] This was the objective of the Scots Guards G Company. The LGB attack might have forced a tactical withdrawal from it, yet Vázquez never indicated to me in our protracted dialogue more than twenty-five years later that he had ever placed men on the knoll. With the benefit of hindsight it was not surprising therefore that, during the Scots Guards platoon's highly successful diversionary attack later that night on the Argentine Marines' below-strength O Company at Pony's Pass, G Company took their objective unopposed.

It was nearing 20.00Z, the time at which the Commandant wanted to assemble his final confirmatory Orders Group. Soon we had to call in the Company Commanders from their positions located due south of us in the proximity of that exposed hillock known as the '500-ring contour', and others in the Battalion Tactical HQ snugly hidden in the rocky southern Two Sisters feature. But skiing accidents in the Commandant's youth had caused weaknesses in his shoulders and, despite a corrective operation, they were still vulnerable to being dislocated. The medical advice if this happened was 'find a chair, dangle the arm over the back of the chair and the arm will go back'. Such a situation now occurred at a most inconvenient time as he describes:

> After the Battalion had been sent on its march towards Tumbledown, I found myself sitting on the ground, miles from nowhere, trying to put on, or perhaps take

off, the waterproof galoshes that we had been issued with, and the effort of tugging at the wretched things pulled my shoulder out. I uttered the well-known cry of '*Shit!*', and started wandering around in the fog holding my useless arm looking, as I had been taught, for a chair. This performance startled Dilbahadur, my orderly, who was busy making tea, and on my instructions went off to seek the Doctor *saheb*.

Clearly he thought I must have lost whatever marbles I had because, when he arrived at the Regimental Medical Officer, he told him that I had just been bitten by a snake and could the Doctor *saheb* please come as a matter of urgency in order to save the Commandant's life?

In the meantime I had found, in some desperation I might add, a rock. Bending down I draped my arm over it and, Hey presto! The shoulder went back. So, by the time (Captain) Martin Entwistle and Dilbahadur had staggered back uphill through the murk I was as right as rain. Both must have thought I was truly 'out of it', but both were far too polite to say so. What I have never worked out is why Dilbahadur thought I had been bitten by a snake. Perhaps he thought that '*Shit!*' was my attempt at saying '*Samp!*' (Nepali for 'snake'). I do not suppose we will ever know.[19]

Amongst others were four key officers at the Commandant's Orders Group. As per our planned order of march towards Tumbledown, they were: Major David Willis (A Company), the Battery Commander Major Mike Fallon (Battalion Tactical HQ), Captain Lester Holley (B Company) and Major Mike Kefford (D Company). They and, indeed, all of us others, were about to be (according to Sun Tzu) thrown 'where they cannot leave'. The Commandant's final anxious sentence in his diary of 'I gave out the final Orders Group, then sat nervously getting colder and colder until the move off at 02.15' underpins the possibility of how such a feeling could suffocate forthcoming personal action. But this is not so (as Sun Tzu indicated by his example of 'the bravery of Chuan Chu and Ts'ao Kue'). Faced with appalling danger, a trained soldier's resolve to fight is stiffened.

So the three Company Commanders returned to their locations. Their next task was to prepare and give out their orders. A Company was to be the Battalion reserve Company providing fire support to the other two Companies and, according to David Willis, 'thereafter to join D Company at Mount William and exploit forward to the (Darwin to Stanley) road area'[20] due south of that feature. It was fortunate they never reached that far. The road area was heavily mined. His detailed plan was impressive:

For the final advance to Tumbledown and support to B and D Companies, A Company took under command the three 0.5-inch calibre Heavy Machine-Guns, six Milan (anti-tank missile) firing posts, three Mortar Fire Controllers, and seven General Purpose Machine-Guns in the sustained fire role (on tripods) plus an Engineer section to help clear any minefields encountered. 1 Platoon was detailed to support the B Company assault (on the north-east spur of Tumbledown) with two Heavy Machine-Guns plus two Milan firing posts and three General Purpose Machine-Guns in the sustained fire role, 3 Platoon was to support D Company (in its attack on Mount William), with 2 Platoon which led the move, forward in reserve [...] (The) fire support weapons [...] in B Company were to be tasked subsequently to relocate across to the south side of the top of Tumbledown to beef up the support for D Company which was to begin its attack after B Company's Captain Steven Crowsley (Heavy Machine-Gun Platoon) and Lieutenant John Palmer (Milan Platoon) [...] were certainly very active in getting forward to site their people.[21]

Others in the 5th Infantry Brigade Tactical HQ located on Mount Harriet had concerns. Davies:

> The important point, I think, is that the enemy we all faced should not be under-estimated. When the battle for Tumbledown started nobody expected it to be a pushover; and it was not. We all prayed that the Scots Guards would whistle up the hill, that the Gurkhas would romp through them onto Mount William and, then, the Welsh Guards would cut along to Sapper Hill and capture that before daylight was too advanced on 14 June.
>
> But life is seldom like that and it certainly was not on the day. Given what we expected the size of the enemy to be, there was a real fear (in the 5 Brigade Tactical HQ) that the Scots Guards would fail at their first attempt and a follow-on attack might be necessary the following night. This is why Tony Wilson asked me to be prepared to deploy my Squadron as an infantry company if such a second attack were necessary – a prospect I viewed without relish!
>
> Incidentally, there was never any doubt in the Brigade Commander's mind that Sapper Hill was the objective of the Welsh Guards. He made this quite clear in his orders and the Welsh Guards CO was clear about this. I was surprised, therefore, to read recently that (Brigadier) Julian Thompson had made this a Commando objective and, further, he accused the Welsh Guards of almost causing a blue on blue when his troops showed up in helicopters to find the Welsh Guards already there.
>
> It just gets curiouser and curiouser! [22]

Much other preparation had to be carried out prior to our advance onto Tumbledown and Mount William via Goat Ridge. For example the Mortar Platoon had succeeded man-packing loads in excess of sixty kilos per man, so there was full confidence that the Gurkhas physical fitness training would pay dividends when it was decided that three of our Browning Heavy Machine-Guns had to be man-packed by A Company 6,500 metres from the Assembly Area and over the appalling terrain near to the north-east summit of Tumbledown. This required the fifty-eight kilo weapon (including its tripod) be broken down into four parts. In addition 4,500 belted rounds per gun would have to be carried. David Willis:

> (We) were tasked to carry forward 100 rounds of 0.5-inch calibre ammunition each, to be collected from an ammunition point in the area (of the 500-ring contour) where pallets had been dropped. When the first few riflemen tried to shoulder this burden it was quickly realised the weight was quite impossible to

carry when combined with everything else we had (and) that the number of rounds were (then) reduced to fifty. Returning to the Falkland Islands in 1994 to visit a Company based there as garrison troops, I walked the advance route and found some pallets, empty of ammunition, still on the spot they had been dumped twelve years earlier. Extraordinarily, the holes left in the peat by the double front tyres of a Sea King helicopter were also clearly preserved.[23]

Slung around the shoulders as a bandolier, the extra weight amounted to seven kilos per man. The Gurkhas could cope with these heavy loads. But it also illustrated the infantryman's dilemma of 'weapon weight' versus 'weapon firepower' as our post-operation report mentioned:

> In general the aim was to bring the maximum weight of fire down against individual enemy positions, so that the enemy could be defeated in detail. All the weapons [...] had to be carried into position. The problem thus becomes an argument between the advantage of weight of fire against the disadvantage of the weight of the weapon system. Anything that can be done to reduce carriage weight, yet retain firepower will be of considerable benefit in future conflicts of this type.[24]

In contrast the Scots Guards relied on the easier option of locating and firing their six Browning Heavy Machine-Guns which had a maximum range of 6,770 metres and maximum effective range of 2,000 metres, from the western side of Mount Harriet. Years later Mike Scott described how these Brownings were used with the ranges to the west ends of Tumbledown and Mount William from these weapons being nearly two and three and a half kilometres respectively:

> We had converted our Anti-Tank Platoon to use them with instructors from Bovington when we were on the *QE2*. We moved them onto the forward slope (of Mount Harriet) after last light. They then fired one-in-one tracer which produced a stream of very comforting fire, which we could see, over our heads or to our right. They engaged the enemy on Tumbledown until the angle between their fire and our leading troops was too narrow, then switched to targets on William to prevent the enemy there engaging us or reinforcing Tumbledown. I had the Platoon Commmander (Captain Jeremy Campbell-Lamerton) in my Tac HQ so I could tell him immediately when I wanted the guns to lift or change target.[25]

Captain Nigel Price and his Gurkha Mortar Platoon also had to carry out comprehensive preparations, not least the stacking of 800 mortar bombs in their boxes beside Goat Ridge rock. He would advance with the Battalion Tactical HQ to Tumbledown leaving his men on the mortar line to operate the 'tubes':

> The Mortar Platoon consisted of three sections, each of two barrels – total six. Just before departure, I received two more, however I did not have the men to crew them and so took them to use as spares. They were packed and sent with (Second-Lieutenant) David Wright (on board MV *Nordic Ferry*), but never appeared until the

war was over. Of the six operational barrels (the 'old' ones, if you like), when we all moved up towards Stanley, I left one section (two barrels) with Major Taj Lewis and his C Company to defend Goose Green. So on my mortar line behind Goat Ridge I had just the two sections (4 barrels).[26] But it was only when the lads tried to feed a round into them that they discovered one had been slightly dented by a shell-splinter at Wether Ground when B Company and my Mortar Platoon harbours had been shelled by the 155mm gun, and just enough to prevent the round sliding down the barrel.

By measuring distances you will also see the problem I had with ranges and lack of augmenting cartridges for the higher charges (seven and eight). The basic range without them took my bombs out to only 3,440 metres. The augmenting cartridges took them the extra range out to the weapons' maximum of 5,660 metres. Working on the more basic range (which is all I could rely on) I could only reach the most forward targets on Tumbledown; and Mount William was even harder – only the forward slopes really, using the precious augmenting cartridges. All depth targets were down to Major Mike Fallon and the guns. You can also see there was absolutely nowhere else to site the mortar line and remain on a reverse slope: the most difficult circle for a mortar officer to have to square.

We had to be sufficiently below the crestline so our firing would not give away our position, but even so it was pretty easy for the enemy to guess where my mortar line was (and that of the Scots Guards further along from us) – hence the heavy Argie counter-battery fire fire that the mortar line was under throughout. It was shell splinters from that fire that dented a further two of my barrels – and gave my mortar crews an interesting time in the process! At the end of the battle I only had one barrel remaining in action and that was at the bottom of a sodding great hole it had dug for itself in the soft peat because of the recoil! [27]

It was a relief clambering across those treacherous stone runs illuminated occasionally by bursts of star shell to our Battalion FUP on the west end of Goat Ridge. Strenuous physical activity was far preferable than ultra-pessimistic brooding. So strong was my memory of this that I described it precisely twenty-eight years later in an article written for a high-quality Argentine magazine's special edition on the war:

Nine hours sleep out of the previous ninety was not optimal for being so near to going into battle. I was tired but also alert because of the adrenalin pumping through my body. The worst time was in those last few hours before moving out of our Assembly Area. I did much thinking while gazing at the bright stars in the night sky. Having been under sporadic artillery fire in the past four days seemed insignificant to what we were facing now: a battle with Argentine Marines on Tumbledown and Mount William. If death occurred, I prayed it would be quick. Then how would that journey to those stars be like? Thankfully I was also pre-occupied at this time in arguing with the 5th Infantry Brigade HQ about the location of the helicopter landing site for casualty evacuation. But fear ceased and my 'auto-pilot' kicked in as we moved out towards our start line. This was the benefit of training.[28]

Oates had already moved out of the same FUP a short time before:

> The Scots Guards Battalion HQ followed the lead Companies [...] along Goat
> Ridge which overlooked Mount Tumbledown across the other side of a valley. My
> role was to remain with the CO of the Scots Guards and liaise directly between the
> two COs (Scots Guards and 7th Gurkha Rifles). I had two radio nets; a radio on
> the Scots Guards Battalion Command Net (carried by me) and another on the
> Gurkha Battalion Command Net carried by Lance-Corporal Sitaram Rai. We got
> to the top of the rise between the red and green lights laid by the Recce Platoon
> of the Scots Guards. The battle had already started by the time Tactical HQ
> reached the summit in a position from where they could observe Tumbledown.
>
> I was not aware of the detail of the plan. A diversionary attack took place south
> of us. In the meantime artillery was coming down on Tumbledown and the lead
> Company was in contact on the lower part of the mountain. There was a
> considerable amount of tracer from both sides, with illumination, mortar, naval
> gunfire support and artillery fire.
>
> The weather was very cold, a very strong wind blew into our faces and it turned
> to snow. The Battery Commander was having difficulty with the guns; one was
> firing short and they were trying to work out which one it was. The guns were
> firing 'danger close' missions and the rounds from it were dropping short.[29]

Oates was an eye-witness to the Battery Commander's desperate attempts at crisis-
managing this artillery problem. It would be the cause of our agonisingly long delay in
advancing from west to east along the two-kilometre Goat Ridge plus a further one
kilometre before reaching Tumbledown's northern slopes. The resources of Major
Gwyn, the Royal Artillery officer in question, were simply not enough at the start of
the battle. But when Murphy's Law (inevitably) intervened, this exacerbated the
situation which (as Gwyn later described):

> was more critical than it otherwise would have been because of radio
> communication problems. I only had two FOO (Forward Observation Officer)
> parties but it was necessary to provide FOO facilities for all three Companies and
> also for the diversionary attack force. This was achieved by detaching NCOs from
> my own party but it left me with only one radio set instead of three. This set had to
> be on the Gunner net so I forfeited the preferred ability to speak directly with
> Major Kiszely direct and his own company net when Captain Nicol became
> separated from him. I did however have communications to the guns and to all of
> my FOO parties including Captain Nicol, but could only maintain this from a
> position about thirty metres away from the CO (Lieutenant-Colonel Mike Scott).[30]
> From choice I would have been directly next to him and would also have had one
> set on his frequencies and another spare set. The available resources did not permit
> this and so I was dependant on messages gleaned from the BG (Brigade Gunner)
> net by a succession of thirty metre dashes in the dark!
>
> At this stage all available guns were firing on the Tumbledown feature and
> Captain Nicol described the noise as deafening. He asked me to stop the guns

firing in his general area so that he could establish voice contact and rejoin the Company Commander. This he eventually did and then described Major Kiszely's problem. Captain Nicol's difficulty was that he, and I suspect everyone else, was disorientated in so far as he could not estimate how far along the Tumbledown feature he had progressed and was therefore unable to produce a safe grid reference for opening fire on the enemy positions to the Company's immediate front.

I therefore attempted to move the fire of a battery from a known safe grid (reference) progressively towards the Left Flank (Company) positions to a point where Captain Nicol could acquire it and then bring each gun in separately as close as he dare to the enemy positions. This proved unworkable as time and again we would reach a point beyond which the guns posed more threat to our troops than they did to the enemy. There was pressure on me from above to use more guns to break the impasse. To have done so would have undoubtedly caused an unacceptable level of own troop casualties and after a brief word of explanation to Lieutenant-Colonel Holt (the Artillery Regimental Commander) he accepted this.

It was decided to risk illuminating the area so that the fall of shot could be more clearly observed. It was then possible to see that the battery I had selected had one gun which was not firing parallel to the others. The battery was once again moved away from own troops and the rogue gun isolated by firing each gun separately under co-ordinated illumination whereby an illuminating round is timed to burst just before and above the HE (high-explosive) round. Captain Nicol then started to bring the remaining guns individually onto enemy positions using the special danger close procedure linked to the co-ordinated illumination. In Gunner terms it is difficult to conceive of a more demanding or hazardous test of technical ability.

The inaccuracy of the guns has been mentioned already and merits some explanation. Guns require a correction to the firing data to compensate for the current meteorological conditions. This data is normally provided by a small component of a Locating Battery which had been left out of the Falklands order of battle. This fact alone meant that the initial fall of shot in that climate could be up to 900 metres from the grid reference ordered. Guns also require a firm and stable firing platform to produce consistent accuracy. Firing from water-logged peat gun positions often caused guns to slide about on their platforms. It was an appreciation of these factors and awareness of the high risk to our troops which made me and my FOOs more cautious than we might have wished in the application of the available fire power.[31]

Scott had no doubt as to what would have happened if all these Gunner problems had not occurred:

I only know what happened from our own point of view. All the 5th Marine stuff was told to us afterwards by them (particularly at Nottingham of course) or written up by people who weren't there [...] The real point is that Left Flank were held by a combination of good shooting with excellent night-sights of the Argentinians and our own inability to get our artillery right. Had we not had the rogue gun, Kiszely would have been able to assault earlier with close-in indirect fire support.[32]

Naval gunfire support was also used intensively on Tumbledown, but even this could not shorten the ever-growing delay to the Gurkha attack which now would have to be carried out in daylight. It would be the worst-case scenario. Oates:

> During all this the Gurkhas waited for the Scots Guards to complete their attack to allow the movement around and attack on Mount William to commence. Follow-on companies of the Scots Guards moved in extended line past us, bayonets fixed, illuminated by all the flares from ships, guns and mortars. I was in touch with David Morgan and relaying to him the state that I believed the Scots Guards had reached. It was difficult to get information from the CO of the Scots Guards. He was obviously busy with his battle. It was then decided that the Gurkhas should move (although the battle with Scots Guards was nowhere near over) and then, suddenly, the Gurkhas arrived in single file. I asked the Scots Guards CO at this point to be released in order to rejoin my Battalion. I was desperate to return as I saw everyone walk past me. But permission was refused! [33]

David Willis:

> We were held somewhere around the saddle just south of Goat Ridge (and between Mount Harriet) [...] My notes give a time of 'No move before 0300' [...] as part of the orders. But at what time we actually moved because of the delay, I do not remember [...] we were all increasingly anxious about the passage of darkness as both B Company and D Company were supposed to have conducted night attacks. [34]

After a delay of nearly two hours, the 406 Gurkhas and attached British ranks started their single file advance from the west end of Goat Ridge just before 05.00Z. We moved excruciatingly slowly in stops and starts along the southern edge of Goat Ridge. It was just before 07.00Z that A Company arrived at the eastern end. At the end of the Gurkha 'snake' were D Company and Jeremy McTeague. He had been learning rapidly the tricks of the platoon commander's trade:

> No matter how long the time one has known the men under one's command, there will, in my experience, always be a change in the way they behave and in how one behaves as combat becomes imminent and the danger grows or, indeed, is experienced. We all react in different ways and, in many instances, I was surprised by how much and in what unexpected directions my men's behaviour changed. Interestingly it was not that the men's behaviour changed for the worse *per se* – it just simply became erratic and intense.
>   This presented problems in command and created the need to be super-understanding and empathetic on the one hand, and firmer and occasionally more authoritarian on the other – depending on the individual and specific circumstances. Vitally, it became clear to me that I had also to examine my own behaviour to ensure that this remained as consistent as possible. I should stress that this did not mean my pretending to be unaffected by the situation – just that

the manner of my being affected was consistent with the Lieutenant McTeague my soldiers knew from before. Being recognised as having a good sense of humour is invaluable in this respect.[35]

The previous afternoon he had experienced a 'quiet' helicopter flight to the Assembly Area where his platoon made final preparations which included five men writing letters of farewell to relatives in Nepal. The 10 Platoon Commander was entrusted with these letters which, after a worst-case scenario, would be sent onwards to their intended recipients. He described his platoon's initial advance towards Tumbledown:

> We stashed our packs, made last minute adjustments to our equipment and, as ordered, moved at night along the side of Goat Ridge and then onto Tumbledown in the wake of the Scots Guards who were clearing it of the enemy. We were then to cross [...] our Company Start Line (the location from which a company deliberate attack is launched) on the eastern end of Tumbledown [...] prior to dawn and under covering fire from artillery, mortars, aircraft and our Heavy Machine-Gun Platoon sweep through and capture Mount William.
>
> We started our approach in the dark. It was rough country and the going was slow. We could see tracer and explosions, and heard the fighting on Tumbledown and Wireless Ridge to the North on our left.

David Willis:

> I remember sitting at the back of (the Scots Guards) Tac HQ which was in a small cutting on Goat Ridge with a view forward, waiting for the word to go forward, listening to the Commanding Officer communicating with his forward companies and the Gunners in re-organising the fire plan and trying to co-ordinate a new assault, with the odd snow flurry illuminated by mortar flares in the distance washing over us all and streams of tracer from our side going across the valley. It was all very eerie and is still a vivid memory.[36]

Behind A Company was the Battalion Tactical HQ where I was located. We had ground to a tedious halt once again. Waiting to go into battle was a stress factor in itself. Maybe that is the reason in later life I get most impatient which rapidly increases to sheer anger whenever forced to stand in queues. And everything gets worse when there is a time deadline involved – just like that particular night at Goat Ridge where I continued to monitor the Brigade rear-link radio frequency. The seriousness of the situation was obvious from the content of the ongoing radio transmissions which mirrored Sun Tzu's crucial aim of 'doing battle'.[37]

This can be devastating to all if prolonged, therefore it must be quick.

Notes

1. *The Art of War*, Chapter 11 – The Nine Grounds.
2. E-mail dated 24 May 2010.
3. 'The Green Machine' is the Royal Marine Commandos' self-imposed nickname.
4. E-mail dated 24 May 2010.
5. *Ibid.* dated 7 August 2006.
6. Based on an e-mail dated 28 November 2011.
7. E-mail dated 19 October 2006.
8. *Ibid.* dated 21 October 2006.
9. *Ibid.* dated 11 November 2006.
10. Air Chief Marshal Sir Peter Squire (two decades later).
11. *RAF Harrier Ground Attack Falklands*, p. 159.
12. From the author's conversation with Carlos Hugo Robacio in Nottingham on 15 November 2006.
13. *RAF Harrier Ground Attack Falklands*, p. 160.
14. *With the Gurkhas in the Falklands,* p. 238.
15. *RAF Harrier Ground Attack Falklands*, p. 160. Published quarter of a century later, this excellent book written by Pook contained the comment (p. x) that Bicheno's *Razor's Edge* was 'stunning and venomous'. However this description did not apply either to Pook's first or second attack.
16. E-mails dated 24 and 25 May 2010.
17. *Op Corporate 1/7GR Immediate Debrief Points* dated 10 July 1982.
18. E-mail dated 24 May 2010.
19. *7th Duke of Edinburgh's Own Gurkha Rifles Regimental Association Journal, 2007*, No. 13, pp. 97-98.
20. E-mail dated 22 October 2006.
21. *Ibid.* and e-mail dated 1 October 2006.
22. *Ibid.* dated 25 May 2010.
23. *Ibid.* dated 1 October 2006.
24. *Operation Corporate 1/7GR Post Operation Report – Part II* dated 27 July 1982.
25. E-mail dated 21 October 2006.
26. But not six as depicted in *Razor's Edge* (p. 289)
27. E-mails dated 6 May and 31 July 2006.
28. From the Argentine magazine *El Pulso Argentino*, Edition 7, December 2010.
29. E-mail dated 11 November 2006.
30. *Razor's Edge* (p. 288) incorrectly stated that 'during the battle Gwyn lost radio contact with his forward observers'.
31. From the Charles Messenger draft manuscript.
32. E-mail dated 13 March 2009.
33. *Ibid.* dated 11 November 2006.
34. *Ibid.* dated 22 October 2006.
35. *Hors de Combat*, p. 55.
36. E-mails dated 1 and 22 October 2006.
37. *The Art of War*, Chapter 2 – Doing Battle.

Throw them where they cannot leave.
Facing death, they will not be routed.
Officers and men facing death,
How could one not obtain their utmost
strength?

– Sun Tzu[1]

It was busy on the Brigade rear-link radio frequency. The Brigadier Commander was constantly asking Lieutenant-Colonel Mike Scott of the Scots Guards for situation reports and making irritating suggestions as to how his Battalion might make headway with their attack. Scott was being unnecessarily distracted by this stream of suggestions. He was also aware of the presence of David Willis and the latter's A Company.

> There was a Gurkha Company, in waiting so to speak, to be called on if I needed it. I could not use it anyway due to the narrow frontage. (I think the Company Commander was with my Tac HQ and may have been the source of the story that I unplugged my radio from Brigade HQ!).[2]

There must have been a real fear running through the Scots Guards Commanding Officer's mind at that time of his Battalion being held by the Argentine defenders. What were the alternatives if the Guards had to withdraw at dawn? He and the Commandant had a dialogue. Apparently a request for direct Gurkha assistance to the Guards was refused. A Company had been allocated such a reserve role. But David Willis had 'no recollection of this being part of the plan, neither any written record in my notebook' [3] He and his men eventually continued their 'tab' (tactical advance to battle):

> across a flat bit of ground which included crossing one of the sheep fences before moving to the west end of Tumbledown and making our way along the north side of it, probably along the 450-foot contour (line). I remember getting very cross at the fence because the wire cutters, despite instructions, had been left behind with the bergens at the Assembly Area. As a result it was slow getting everyone over the fence. [4]

Meanwhile Oates was confronted with a minor crisis of his own:

> It was in the early hours that I wanted to speak to the Gurkha Battalion (Tactical) HQ but could not find Sitaram. I asked the RSM of the Scots Guards whether he had seen my radio operator. He then started to shovel around with his hands in the snow and unearthed Sitaram who had fallen asleep.[5]

Still at the rear of the Battalion file, 10 Platoon had reached the northern slopes of Tumbledown just past its western end. McTeague:

> After several hours of starts and stops, we came to a suspected minefield that had already had its entrance marked. We were moving in single file through it [...] when, suddenly, we came under heavy artillery and mortar fire that lasted nearly an hour [...] It was truly our baptism of fire and it took great discipline not to run for cover across the minefield [...] The standard operating procedure (SOP) in such a situation is to fall to the ground, seek cover and await orders. As the Platoon Commander, I was aware of my responsibility to get my men into safety. We could not just scatter, and yet to make an orderly exit, we would have had to keep close together in single file – a perilous action indeed in the context of the current situation. But falling to the ground was only a marginally better solution as we remained within the target area of the accurate Argentine artillery and mortar fire.[6]

It was about 08.00Z. The incoming enemy fire came down in an area 1500 metres north-east of the enemy DF PR26 (Goat Ridge). This area had been subjected to shelling at least once that morning at 04.00Z.[7] However if Miño and his 5 Platoon had remained on Tumbledown's north-west summit, then it was precisely at this moment he could have capitalised on his position's height advantage and severely complicated matters for the Gurkhas by raking them with accurate small-arms fire. The Commandant:

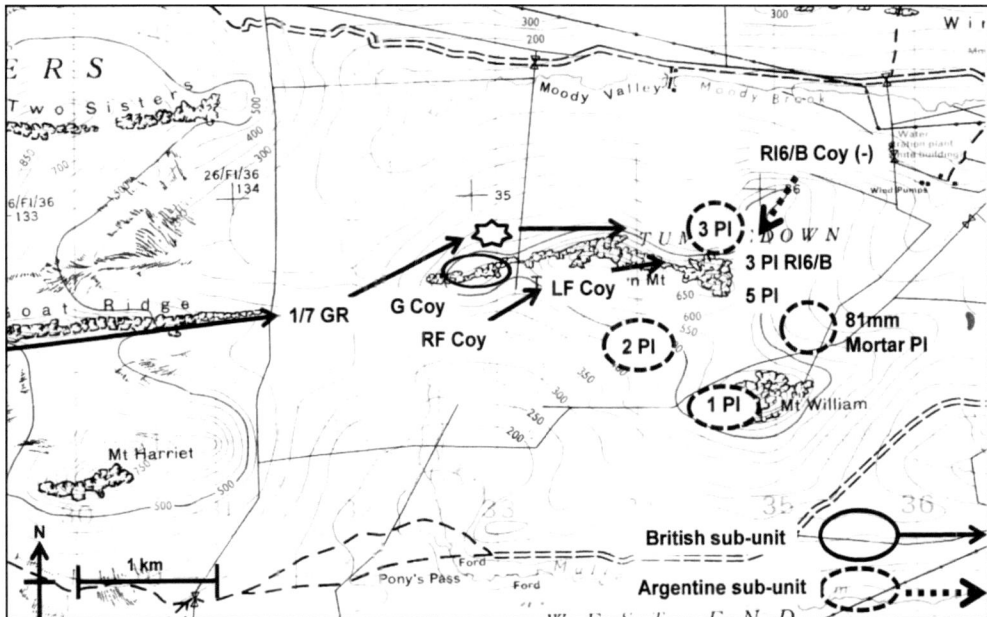

Map 9 (07.45Z-10.00Z) – 1/7 GR is shelled and mortared for one hour while advancing along Tumbledown's northern slopes. Afterwards 1/7GR continues its advance.

Just past Goat Ridge we were hit by a massive accurate artillery and mortar DF. Eight were wounded, two seriously. One shell landed eight feet from me and pushed me about six inches into the air – highly exciting! [8]

Seear:

(We) were ambushed in a ferocious Argentine artillery and mortar bombardment that lasted an hour. As the first rounds of the many that exploded around us 406 Gurkhas, I screamed into my radio handset to the Brigade HQ Tactical HQ on Mount Harriet and, hopefully, Brigade Commander, 'You should have been here!'

Such cheek from a junior officer (I was a Major at the time) seemed appropriate in that crisis. The world had gone crazy as the shells and mortar bombs crashed down amongst us. There was no cover. We lay on the frozen ground and hoped our ordeal would end soon. Two 105mm shells landed ten metres away from my Battalion Tactical HQ, but did not explode. They were duds. Luckily we took only eight casualties. Bleeding badly, some were helped past me to receive stabilising treatment before being evacuated to the rear. [9]

Price:

The moment we were caught in that intense artillery bombardment something happened. I was not aware of it at the time, of course; just of a hollow, empty feeling. But I suppose for me that was the moment when existential authority kicked in. It was as if I saw through – in one instant – the whole sham of civilisation with its artificial rank structures and carefully-maintained levels of society. Anyone can reach that point intellectually, but this was experiential. I can only liken it to the Buddhists' instantaneous realisation of *satori* (enlightenment) which comes in a flash and entails a complete psychological transformation, although unlike *satori* this experience was far from positive. Since then it has been difficult to be awed by authority. You realise we are all muddling along together, pretending. Hiding behind our ranks and status, all of it a mirage. Children at play in the garden. [10]

Dilkumar Rai:

I can remember seeing the friendly forces and enemy tracer rounds firing while we were waiting to move. It was two to three hours before the first enemy indirect fire hit our way. A Company were in front of us and received some casualties. A round landed very close to the forward elements of 12 Platoon (my Platoon), but we were very lucky that it did not explode. Everyone ran back completely in an uncontrolled manner but myself, Rifleman Jhandiram Rai (3868 – sniper) and Corporal Prithibahadur Rai (59794 – Section Commander) did not move.

David Willis:

We were shelled somewhere along the route and suffered several casualties at the tail end of the Company column. I sent the Company Second-in-Command, Captain Narainparsad Rai, back to deal with them. Fortunately the RMO (Regimental Medical Officer) was able to get there fairly quickly and saved them.[11]

Oates:

I was listening to the Scots Guards radio net. A lot of casualties were being called in, the weather was worsening, ammunition was low and the artillery had still not found the gun that was firing short. Then I started hearing more activity from the Gurkha radio net, in particular D Company who came under accurate artillery fire [...] I heard a radio operator from D Company, split up from everyone as they all dispersed under artillery fire – and then unable to recover in the darkness and snow. Major Mike Kefford, while trying to regroup his dispersed Company, then, in Nepali, calmed down the very excited radio operator and talked him back in to the main company body.[12]

McTeague:

Having decided that we should remain in cover, I was still without any other options and so felt powerless to protect my men further. In that situation the realisation there is nothing one can do, is not easy to accept, and one feels a corresponding overwhelming sense of inadequacy. Indeed for some time after this frighteningly intensive and prolonged bombardment had ceased, I worried that my men thought of me as being ineffective. This was a poor state of mind for a young officer preparing to participate in the launching of a deliberate Company attack on an enemy defensive position that had been prepared for sixty-seven days beforehand.

My message is crystal-clear It is simple to teach young commanders and soldiers alike that instances of powerlessness will occur on the battlefield. So merely having that knowledge in advance will allow soldiers in a similar position to deal appropriately with it.[13]

Four men in the Battalion Tactical HQ were hit. One of these was Lance-Corporal Gauriman Limbu who had received seriously shrapnel wounds in the chest and abdomen. The Battalion Intelligence Officer, Second-Lieutenant Paddy Redding, was just behind him. As the artillery and mortar bombardment continued, the 'rogue' Royal Artillery gun which had caused such problems for the Scots Guards also began to drop rounds on the Gurkhas. Redding observed Battery Commander Major Mike Fallon attempting to adjust this gun's fall of shot,[14] despite Bombardier Richard Bowley and Gunner John Williams in his BC Party having received shrapnel wounds to the right arm and head respectively. It was a situation that fell into the Sun Tzu category of when 'even death seems no disaster' and men become 'untuned yet disciplined'[15] everything becomes clear and immediate, with doubt and fear of the unknown instantly eliminated.

One of Fallon's two unwounded Gunners was Lance-Bombardier Alan Gibson:

Two of us, (I think JB – Bombardier John Bachelor – and myself) were sheltered down together trying to take cover from some pretty accurate mortar fire. We had been in this position for about half an hour and desperately waiting for a lull so as we could move to a safer, more sheltered position. As normal it was cold, windy and (snowing). We were cold, wet, tired and very scared.

I felt a tap on my boot followed by the words, 'Would you care for a drop of whisky chaps?'

Thinking it was someone taking the mickey I replied, 'I'd rather have a three-course meal and a shag! Now piss off!'

'That's no way to talk to the bearer of the Queen's Commission,' came the reply. 'Us Gurkhas are the only regiment left that gets a daily tot. Christ, even the Navy doesn't get this now. It should be rum, but we've run out.'

After profuse apologies on my part and the promise that if we survived I would be more than happy to face a court martial for my behaviour, we lay together and, rather surreally, drank whisky.

Should this ever be printed and Captain Kit Spencer reads it, I would just like to say 'Thank You' to him for helping me maintain my sanity through that particular incident. War is not only about the bad memories, but also about the things that for one reason or another stay in your mind. I sometimes tell some of these stories to 'civvy' friends of mine, and you can tell from the look on their faces that they don't believe you. But you can tell by the tears in my eyes that they are true.[16]

McTeague:

Thankfully only a few rounds landed close to us and we sustained no casualties in the platoon. The fire ceased abruptly and, with no fuss, the boys formed up again and we moved forward. I was struck at that time by their motivation and 'matter of fact' attitude. I really had expected that the NCOs would have had to cajole and shout to get them moving.

Dil:

Despite the dangerous situation and severe weather conditions, we dozed off for about ten to fifteen minutes. But when we woke up there was no one around us. It was a completely quiet moment of puzzlement and (a feeling of being) lost. But we managed to track down our platoon and re-grouped without any problem. The weather was very chilly so we got out our warm clothes but, within a short time, were ordered to continue our move and had to take the warm clothes off.

Oates:

My role now was over. I stayed with (the Scots Guards) Battalion HQ until they rejoined the forward companies on the top of Mount Tumbledown. The activities on Mount William are not for me to try and talk about. I rejoined the Battalion with Sitaram mid-morning.[17]

Six Gurkhas and the two British Gunners had received shrapnel wounds. One Gurkha was treated on the spot and returned to B Company. The other seven were placed on stretchers which the Recce Platoon had the unenviable task of carrying back to the Scots Guards Regimental Aid Post (RAP) on Goat Ridge. At last A Company was able to start their slow progress again along Tumbledown's northern slopes parallel to explosions and firing of the Scots Guards Left Flank Company which was securing Vázquez's main position on the southern side and moving further up to take the east summit.[18] First light was at 10.00Z. David Willis:

> We were all increasingly anxious about the passage of darkness as both B Company and D Company were supposed to have conducted night attacks. We were in the dark of the night until getting up to a point about (1.4 kilometres along the northern slopes of Tumbledown) where we stopped, probably just before or just as it started to get light. We could not have overtaken Right Flank in my view because we emerged onto the top of Tumbledown to the *west* of the uppermost Argentinian positions which Right Flank had had to clear [...] There is an escarpment along the north-east edge of Tumbledown to the east which makes it difficult, if not impossible, to gain access to the summit from that part of Tumbledown.[19] The simplest way up was through a grassy (?) break or channel through the rocks at the point where I established my Company HQ with the fire support weapons and platoons moving to their final positions from there and the rest of the Battalion going its separate ways. B Company and D Company of course had to conduct their operations in the full exposure of daylight [...]
>
> Although the Scots Guards were supposed to have re-grouped on the south side of Tumbledown, we came across the odd group in the dark on the north side and it was very alarming as often they claimed not to know we were coming along that route. Under a very large rock they had a couple of wounded men sheltering in sleeping bags. Returning in 1994 I recognised the spot and found a few 7.62mm rounds still on the ground.
>
> I doubt these men mentioned were from Right Flank. I think they were from the first assault company, the one (Left Flank) which took the western part of Tumbledown. The area I came across them was well to the west of the area Right Flank would have attacked, and I would expect Right Flank to have re-grouped on the southern/south-western area slope of Tumbledown.
>
> I saw no other Scots Guards personnel until well into the day when a monocled Major (Iain Dalzell-Job, the G Company Commander) came looking for a missing man [20] – who subsequently turned out to be a chap who disappeared during the battle and was found alive and well a few weeks after the war at some abandoned buildings. All the fighting was over by then, apart from the Scots Guardsman who subsequently shot and nearly killed the artillery Forward Observation Officer (Captain Keith Swinton) who was moving with our Tac HQ in what would now be called a friendly fire incident.
>
> The most poignant moment for me was the discovery of the body of a young Scots Guardsman just above our position who we think had been wounded but bled to death, undiscovered in the dark.[21]

There is little doubt that the dead Scots Guardsman was Lance-Sergeant Clark Mitchell of Left Flank Company. Meanwhile the Scots Guards RAP was dealing with our casualties from the shelling and mortaring two hours previously. Lieutenant-Colonel Alan Warsap was the Scots Guards Regimental Medical Officer:

> From the RAP on Goat Ridge on the morning of 14 June during hostilities, elements of the RAP staff and me went forward in a Navy Sea King helicopter to start the casualty pick-up. As we took off we crossed the Gurkha mortar line which were close by and preparing to fire on a forward target, probably Mount William. The mortars erupted, and at least one mortar bomb must have passed through the helicopter's rotor blade motion. We picked up, I believe, seven or eight Gurkha casualties. All were semi-comatose with sleep deprivation combining with the pain of their wounds. They were typically stoical, and we took them to the 16 Field Ambulance Advanced Dressing Station at Fitzroy. At this point helicopter evacuation formally ceased. Friendly-fire incidents, inevitable in war, take their own special toll in the misery of war – and we had been lucky to escape such a fate on this occasion.[22]

Warsap and his RAP staff had evacuated four of the Gurkhas and the two Gunners. But one Gurkha casualty was still on the battlefield. This was Corporal Gyanbahadur Rai of A Company who had serious shrapnel wounds to his back, chest, left leg and foot. The 'Teeny Weenie Airlines' [23] Scout helicopter pilot Captain Samuel Drennan, who had served in the Scots Guards, described how he and Corporal Jay Rigg, his air gunner and co-pilot, were then given the task of flying out from Fitzroy to evacuate Gyanbahadur and a Scots Guardsman from the side of Tumbledown:

> We went up to the RAP and went past that to Goat Ridge. From there we had a look, and on one side was the Gurkhas' mortar platoon, dug in in holes in the ground. Previously a Navy helicopter had got that far and the Gurkhas had put a mortar straight through his rotor blades without touching a blade. On that, the Navy gave up – they wouldn't go any further. They've got big helicopters, and without a doubt they would have been hit. We didn't go forward of the Gurkhas mortar platoon because they'd probably have scared us too. So we went round the other side and we looked over the ridge and Jay pointed out where the first casualty was. I realised that no helicopter had been that far forward on Tumbledown. The Argentinians then opened fire on us [...]
>
> The first one we stuck our neck out for was a Gurkha [...] We found the Gurkha and they lifted him into the pod. We were using pods, like coffins, on the side of the helicopter, so we could get more casualties in [...] I was watching all this activity conducted by Jay around the aircraft, helping the Gurkhas to get their injured mate into the aircraft. I was just looking round, and there was little puff of a shell landing here and a little puff there, and I thought, 'Christ, I hope there's not a little puff here soon.'[24]

Next they located the wounded Scots Guardsman in a minefield, loaded him aboard the Scout and:

then lifted off, turned round and went like a bat out of hell for the safety of the ridge behind Tumbledown [..] We went whizzing back to the MDS (Main Dressing Station) [25] where the two casualties went to the surgeons straight away.[26]

B Company had pushed on through A Company and then carried out an assault down the long north-east spur [27] along which Sub-Lieutenant Esteban La Madrid and his 3 Platoon had advanced up into the eastern end of Tumbledown during the night. The Gurkhas captured three enemy who had taken cover in a trench where there was found also the body of a fourth killed by shellfire, and took the spur unopposed.

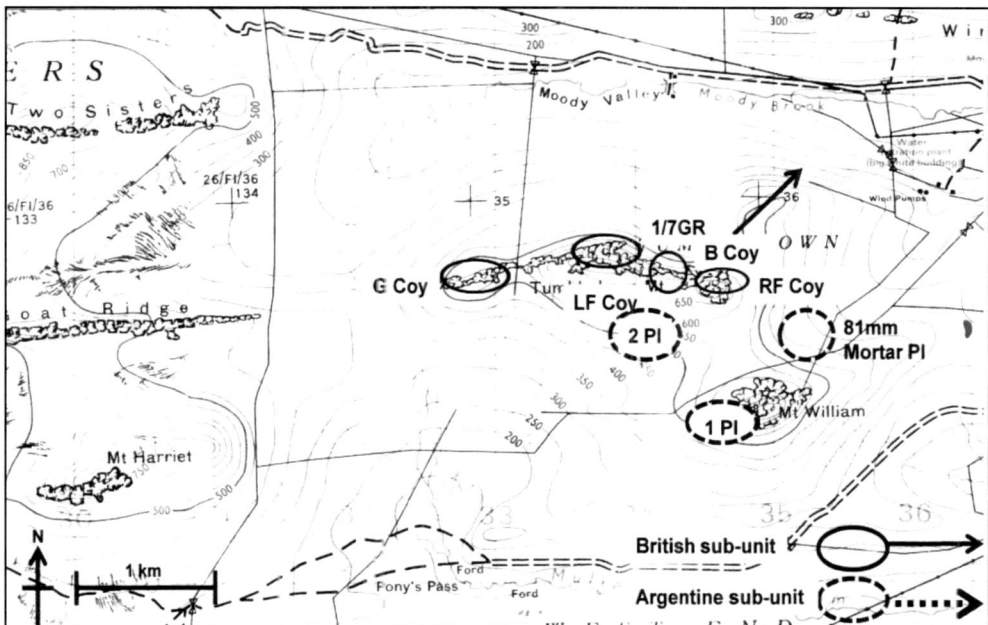

Map 10 (13.00Z) – B Company (1/7 GR) assaults Tumbledown's north-east spur.

Two decades later retired Rear-Admiral Carlos Hugo Robacio wrote to me about his perceptions of the Gurkhas' role in the attack on Tumbledown:

But the most important consideration I have to make [...] is that although the Scots (their attack concentrated on 4 Platoon) attacked obstinately, they would not have advanced or conquered Tumbledown had it not been for the direct action of the Gurkhas [...] Some of these [...] later took the rear cooking facilities of N Company. The effective Nepalese forces, very well led by their British officers, simply reached an inaccessible position by crossing a mined area, then climbed on in spite of our pre-planned (artillery) fire and pushed my Amphibious Engineers back, conquering the highest and most dominant part of the mountain. They grouped and efficiently fired their weapons on the rear of [...] 4 Platoon, causing it to collapse at that point of the defence.

(Acting) Sub-Lieutenant Miño (of the Amphibious Engineers) was able to see your men climb at the Wall (almost inaccessible in daylight, much more difficult by night) in order to reach a higher position. This was done in spite of his men's fire and the concentration of 106,6mm mortars and our own artillery. We tried an offensive reaction with men from the 5th Marine Infantry Battalion and with officers and regulars from B Company, 6th (Mechanised) Infantry Regiment, including Sub-Lieutenant La Madrid. This attempt was insufficient, for those of you who had succeeded in setting foot on that part of the mountain did not give way.[28]

The similarity with Robacio's description of the battle differs from ours in that we never engaged Miño's 5 Platoon, never took the west summit, never 'climbed at the Wall', never fired on the rear of Vázquez's 4 Platoon (executed by the Scots Guards' 13 Platoon), never engaged any Argentine Marines or Army sub-unit (executed by the Scots Guards' Right Flank Company), and most certainly did not take 'the rear cooking facilities of N Company' on Tumbledown's extreme eastern end (executed by Right Flank Company with Captain Bryden and Guardsman Morton in the van). Robacio had continued to muddle the true historical facts. However the bitter reality of defeat is softened if Argentine military history can credit his Marine Battalion with fighting two British battalions simultaneously.

Back on Tumbledown in 1982, D Company had also moved on past A Company while the Battalion Tactical HQ set up a new temporary command post behind A Company and slightly higher up amongst the crags of Tumbledown. McTeague:

As dawn broke, we found ourselves marching through a Scots Guards Company on Tumbledown that had just completed its mission. They were exhausted, silent and entirely withdrawn into themselves. They sat and lay in a manner that spoke of embarrassment, even humiliation at being seen and scrutinised by dozens of Gurkhas who were streaming by. Shocked, exhausted and dishevelled, they did not greet us, shout encouragement, or respond to greetings at all. They just sat on rocks with some eating. They were not sorting out their kit or anything. I really felt that they resented our presence greatly. Maybe it was grief, but to me they seemed to be communicating that they detested us seeing them as they were. I had a clear sense that by just looking at them we were invading an extremely private and personal moment and that we were seeing men as they would never wish to be seen. They had fought bravely and effectively and it was now our turn.

This group of Scots Guardsman must have been 1 Platoon (including Steve Cocks) of Right Flank Company. The disturbing image remained with McTeague and, years later, he elaborated on his observations:

War for the combat soldier is likely to be a humiliating experience. He is on an emotional roller coaster. He has to open himself up and prove himself to other men to such an extent that it can be, in retrospect, humiliating – rather like a teenage boy boasting or flexing his biceps in the vain hope of impressing a girl. His comrades see him terrified, hugely aggressive and even feeling guilty. Indeed they see him in a wider range of unpalatable emotional states than should his mother or wife. They witness his basest behaviour which, at its worst, is him having to kill another. The immediate reaction to such behaviour is normally positive and this can last for some time. But in the end, years later, feelings of shame and humiliation come to the fore as we judge our memories against the standards of the mature individual.

[...] In my own experience during our training we were told of the existence (on operations) of some of the more palatable emotions and even how to deal with a couple such as boredom and (vaguely) about apprehension. However the less palatable ones (such as lust, revelling in aggression and fantasising about killing/inflicting pain on the one hand and shame, anger guilt and humiliation on the other) were not even discussed, let alone dealt with in terms of us being given a better understanding of their causes or how to deal with them [...] Dealing with these emotions requires fortitude, and the worst thing is that they are unexpected. Forewarned is forearmed.[29]

The attack on Mount William was nearing. But first McTeague become embroiled in another problem:

It was now daylight and there was still at least one sniper on Tumbledown who had just shot our artillery FOO (Forward Observation Officer – Captain Keith Swinton). I did not prepare a section, just offered one to the CO in a flurry of bidding from Captain Steve Crowsley, myself and somebody else. It was a flash of a moment that struck me as humorous at the time. It must have lasted ten seconds before David Morgan told Crowsley to sort it. But the sniper was a Scots Guardsman. Swinton was wounded in the chest by a ricochet from one of the Guardsman's rounds.

Also standing nearby was the Commandant. Lucky not to be hit also from this 'blue on blue' incident,[30] he described the effects a few days later: 'I also got a bullet ricochet off my helmet – eyes and ears rang for ages!' [31] Dil's 12 Platoon was also affected:

In the morning, we could see the enemy moving towards Stanley and being hit by our indirect fire. Our FOO was hit by a sniper. He was then evacuated while we had to halt for several hours due to the sniper fire.

As a young soldier, I was unable to understand why our platoon (12 Platoon) most of the time was to take the difficult or more risky tasks (lead Platoon, OP – Observation Post – reconnaissance of the enemy position). It is only as time passed by that I realised our Platoon Commander was the most senior amongst the rest of the Platoon Commanders as well as the most experienced. Of course with his experience and intelligence, I believe that our platoon was always in this position (of doing such tasks).

Continuing to move on, we entered into an area nearer Tumbledown's eastern end where mines had been laid. We only found out after a section and 12 Platoon

HQ had crossed the mines. This was pure luck for 12 Platoon as no one stepped on one. After discovering the suspected mines, we were ordered to stay clear of the danger area and take cover as the area was cleared by the Engineer team.

The incident provoked a warning about infantry mine training in the Battalion's post-operation report:

> Whilst being irresponsible and in some cases in contravention of the Geneva Conventions, the enemy's use of mines proved to be the one major factor in this campaign that the British forces feared. The detrimental effect on morale, channelling of assault forces into ground of the enemies' choosing, and disruption of an attack, were all experienced during operations. There is a need to devise a well-practised drill for the extraction of troops, particularly those injured who are trapped in a minefield. Casualties in the Falklands would have been far greater had the enemy covered their minefields by fire. Used properly, it is clear that the anti-personnel mine is a most potent weapon. Generally the British Army is not fully mine and minefield conscious. Time is not spent in the infantry in learning to lay or lift mines during exercises. This skill must be introduced as a matter of urgency.[32]

McTeague:

> We were told to press forward to our Start Line and, by this time, I was seriously worried about our ability to take Mount William. As we formed up I passed on last details and words of encouragement and admonishments to take care of my Platoon HQ and Section Commanders.
>
> I shook hands with my section commanders half an hour before crossing the Start Line (now in broad daylight because of the delay imposed on the Scots Guards' attack by fierce enemy resistance), I wished that my training had included guidance on how to alleviate the obvious fear that we all felt. It was a really unpleasant final thirty minutes whilst we waited to move.[33]
>
> It was clear that nobody felt any more confident of escaping a bloodbath than I did. Nevertheless, I felt a great calm. I knew we were going to mount an attack in lethally adverse conditions and that there was no other option available to us or to the command. I felt terribly sad, but was proud of my men and myself (and a little relieved) as I knew with certainty that I would fight and not flinch.

D Company then came under concentrated enemy mortar fire. This and the other problems with mines caused the attack's start to be postponed until 15.00Z (12.00 local). McTeague:

> It was extremely unpleasant. Everyone went to ground immediately and, while close, the fire did not seem too accurate at the time although, of course, my personal fear was that it would be quickly and accurately corrected. The firing did not last for long at all and certainly nobody was adversely affected.

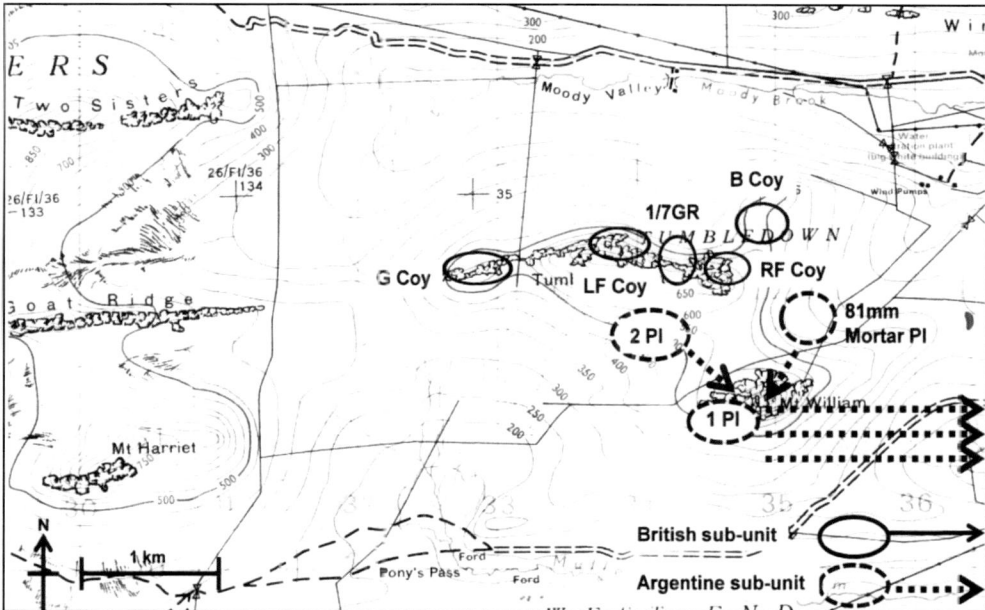

Map 11 (14.30Z) – 2 Platoon (BIM5) and 81mm Mortar Platoon (BIM5) withdraw to Mount William. Then, together with 1 Platoon (BIM5), all three platoons withdraw to Sapper Hill.

McTeague:

> At Company HQ Mike asked the platoon commanders if we were ready to go. We stood up and he ordered us to move across the Start Line. As Reserve Platoon Commander I was positioned close to the Company HQ so as to be able to take orders without having to rely on the radio. As we crossed the line we suddenly heard shots in the distance in the area of Mount William, but in no way could this be interpreted as fire on us. Within a minute we saw (what seemed to be) hundreds of Argentines clambering out of their trenches and running away.
>
> Mike was screaming into the radio that he wanted mortar fire on the enemy position and he wanted it 'Now!'

Major Chris Davies in the 5th Infantry Brigade Tactical HQ on Mount Harriet also had been in action:

> I had a very clear view (from Mount Harriet) of Mount William both on the afternoon before the battle and in the early dawn before the surrender. On the morning after the Tumbledown battle I personally asked for artillery fire to be brought down on the lower slopes of Mount William where I could see troops milling about in the open. When this fire ceased and the Argies decided they had had enough, I saw at least a Company's worth of men troop back over the mountain in the direction of Port Stanley. If this is what I could see then I do not think it would be exaggerating to believe that there must have been at least the

equivalent number that I could not see, either on top of the mountain or on the reverse slope.[34]

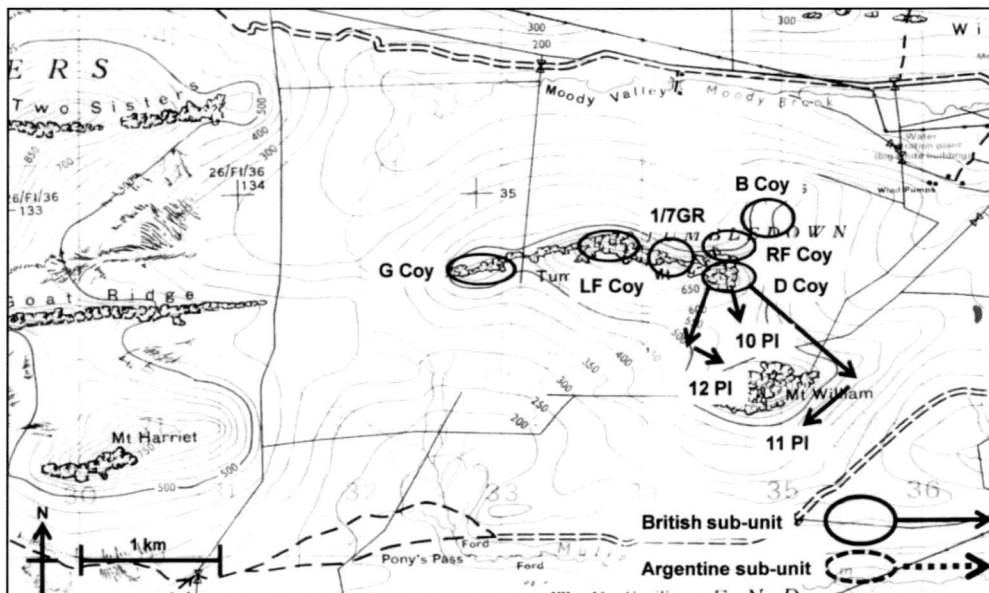

Map 12 (14.00Z-16.00Z) – D Company (1/7 GR) moves into position and then assaults (unopposed) Mount William.

This had to be exploited immediately. McTeague was also an eye-witness to the enemy withdrawal and D Company's reaction to take advantage of it. This complied with Sun Tzu's simple concept: 'When the enemy opens the outer gate, one must quickly enter'.[35]

> The Argentines were just moving in disparate and widely-spaced groups. Given the distance and the light we thought there were more leaving than we could see. They ran towards the eastern flank of Mount William, i.e. they moved away uphill diagonally towards the left and rear as we watched. .
>
> Suddenly Mike said that the Argentines had surrendered. He was still on the radio to Battalion Tac HQ and recounting his orders to us. In short, we were to continue the advance against Mount William, but we were only to open fire if fired upon. We walked slowly and deliberately across the wide expanse of tussock grass with the NCOs shouting continuously at the men to keep their spacing (some things never change) and the lead platoons still maintained a section fire and manoeuvre routine until they hit the boulder fields at the base of Mount William.

Dil's 12 Platoon had been, of course, tasked to launch the first phase of D Company's attack:

Before reaching our objective, there was open ground between Tumbledown and Mount William. It was at this time that, in between Tumbledown (and) Mount William, as the platoon radio operator I was informed about the surrender of the Argentines. During the clearing process (on Mount William) we found an Argentine soldier's dead body covered in a blanket. I think this was the time when the Platoon was told of the surrender of the Argentines. It was such a relief and excitement for everyone and I am assuming that our Platoon Commander did not disclose this news immediately to avoid slack drills at our objective and, more importantly, to ensure the area was clear of any enemy.

McTeague:

On arriving on the objective we cleared the area and secured it. The Argentines had all fled and were in disarray. There was one corpse. He was no conscript and was quite old (mid–late twenties), well-dressed and had an empty pistol holster. I searched him and pulled articles out of his pockets looking for maps and intelligence information. He was carrying photos of his family and looked relatively well to do. His home in Argentina looked a nice place. (I replaced the photos in his pockets). There was no blanket over him when we found him. He was wearing a Parka. I do not know if he was wearing a two-piece uniform or not and did not see any detail on his belt He was wearing a hood although it was not up covering his head or face very much. Later someone covered him up (there were plenty of Argentine blankets around). His rifle was shattered and a crater in the ground from a mortar bomb explosion told the tale of how he had been killed.[36]

The Argentine positions were appalling. The fire trenches were poorly constructed, waterlogged, and surrounded by personal effects, helmets, rubbish and weapons and ammunition. We were told to secure our positions for the night. Our packs were back at the FUP so the boys started to ferret through the trenches for food. The temperature had plummeted and everyone was seriously hungry. We had not eaten a meal since leaving the Little Weather Ground what seemed like days before. It was therefore with great glee that one of my corporals found a supply store full of cigarettes, tins of *paté de fois gras*, tea and other wonders. Other Battalion elements started to arrive and establish themselves while we awaited further orders. Their ferreting in turn found more supplies, and before long there was a veritable market with goods being bartered left, right and centre. It was therefore with a sense of horror that I discovered that one of my Corporals had bartered away most of the *fois gras* for some weird pasta. It was even more distressing to find that his section had opened the remaining tins of *fois gras* and were warming them up over a fire 'To make soup, *saheb!*'

Nearly twenty-nine years later Robacio died from a stroke in the Buenos Aires provincial city of Bahia Blanca on 30 May 2011. His testimony was published a few days later. It included an account of his unit's actions while the Gurkhas occupied Tumbledown and Mount William:

I commanded 700 men of my Battalion and about 200 Army troops with whom we faced the most critical and ferocious British attack. In spite of this last we had few casualties: thirty dead and 105 injured. We inflicted the highest number of casualties on the enemy, although this was not officially recognised by the British. In the area where BIM5 fought, the British lost 359 men.[37] Where did I get these numbers? The British themselves told me.

In the seventy-four days spent on the Malvinas, we endured forty-four days of sustained fire to which we were unable to respond. We had only four or five final days of real battle. I remember the last day, 14 June at 10.30 a.m (13.30Z). It was a very critical time. We were retreating onto Sapper Hill from Tumbledown and Mount William. I saw my Second-in-Command, Daniel Ponce falling, exhausted and worn out. The 2IC was a perfect example. When he fell, two recruits assisted him. He was not injured. He was exhausted and could not move on. Ponce ordered his men to withdraw. They answered, 'If we must die, then the three of us will die.' They helped him, lifted him and the three came out alive. I call this cohesion.

Everybody knew what was being done. I was deeply moved by Army Sub-Lieutenant Silva who was incorporated into my unit when 4 Regiment withdrew. Silva was a brave man. He came to me and requested to be sent where the combat was going to be tougher. This place was Tumbledown. He died with his four soldiers, fighting with utmost bravery. Then there were the Scots (very good men, like the British paratroopers) and the famous Gurkhas who were pure propaganda. They dropped like flies.[38] I also remember a conscript who disobeyed my orders. In a time of combat during which the British were repulsed, he ran after them without ceasing fire. I ordered him to stop. But he continued. He was hit by the enemy fire and fell dead. I buried him myself. He was 500 feet ahead of his assigned positions and surrounded by dead enemies. There were a lot of such acts of bravery, but not due to disobeying my orders.

I am neither brave nor bold, or anything like that. I am a common man. I feel fear when I cross the streets. But in the Malvinas I could not be afraid. I could not feel it because I believed that God would not let me feel it. I could not afford the privilege of being afraid because I had a great concern for my men who were all giving of their best.

Yes, I felt bitterness. I suffered the greatest bitterness of my life at two critical moments: one, when I had to order the start of the retreat to Sapper Hill, and the second that was terrible: when my Battalion entered Puerto Argentino marching with their weapons shouldered. That meant surrender. That broke my spirit. More than one saw me crying.

One of the strongest counter-attacks against the enemy took place on 14 June at 3 a.m. (06.00Z) on Tumbledown, along with the largest Army Company of Jaimet's. They were the ones that clashed with the famous Gurkhas.[39]

We had 150 men, while they were between 800 and 1,000. I concentrated there all the Army artillery fire (from Groups Three and Four commanded by Colonel Balza and Colonel Quevedo who supported me indiscriminately). According to the British General (Brigadier) Wilson of the Fifth Brigade with whom I talked while being held prisoner, only one third of the British forces remained alive. Now he denies it, but we really swept them aside.[40]

A whole regiment of British forces crashed against sixty or eighty of my men and the former were killed.[41] We stopped them. One of the questions I was asked was: Why did not I counter-attack if we had already broken them? I had the Company Mar ready to counter-attack. But the reality is that by the time when we could do it we had no ammunition. On the other hand we had already received the withdrawal order. Thousands of shells per hour fell on our positions besides the naval bombardment plus aircraft and helicopter fire. It was tremendous. Still, we could have fought back if we had some ammunition. But this would not have changed the course of battle. The die was cast. Of course the British did not know my real situation. They were waiting for my counter-attack. They told me that they prayed we would not counter-attack them. But … with that? When I told them we were a Battalion they could not believe it. I also remember that when I decided to do the counter-attack I called my staff officers and told them about my plan. I took out a paper and outlined the orders. They looked at each other. They said nothing. They simply obeyed. After 14 June I asked myself why did they look at each other? So one day I finally asked them. They told me they thought I was crazy. Once things were over I kept asking them, 'Even so, what would you have done, anyway? They answered. 'We would have carried out the order. Period.' That was BIM5. That is what counts. Confidence. But let me emphasise that in the Malvinas each man fought as he could, and with whatever they had. There were six or seven British casualties for each of our men who fell.[42] Now they know that we are not afraid, we are not Indians and that their soldiers will not come to a picnic.[43]

It is sad that Robacio's facts about the British forces were so totally wrong. Despite the language barrier, I had liked and respected him on the numerous occasions we had met in Nottingham and Buenos Aires: but regret the lack of a discussion which might have revealed and corrected all of these misunderstandings which he took to his grave. That he has also gone on a stage further in having them published also reflects adversely on his gullibility and inability (or unwillingness) to establish the correct facts. Indeed his blatantly misleading *proceso* figure of 359 British killed (the equivalent of more than half a British Army infantry Battalion) places this into a fictional category of the *desaparecidos* (disappeared) of Tumbledown.

In the late afternoon of 14 June 1982 the Gurkha Battalion Tactical HQ joined D Company on Mount William, while A Company remained on the eastern end of Tumbledown and B Company moved down to the western end. As everyone set up 'bashas' to shelter from the strong winds and snow, the Commandant summed up in his diary those final Gurkha twenty-four hours of participation in Operation Corporate:

We waited until 05.00 for the Scots Guards to do their attacks. They were terribly slow over very difficult country and against very good (comparatively) enemy. Eventually we moved off on our own. I met Mike Scott, and continued onwards on my side of the ridge. We were very heavily shelled, eight wounded and one shell missed me by inches. All were very shaken. We continued on in the snow. We got into an accidental fire fight with the Scots Guards. I got 'ear-winged', and our FOO got a ricochet in the chest. Silly buggers. Peace was unofficially declared at 16.00. Our plan was for the Scots Guards to take Tumbledown with 1/7 Gurkha Rifles to infiltrate through and behind them to take Mount William from behind. The sight of us in line outflanking the enemy position caused heavy artillery shelling, then withdrawal and final surrender. The Gurkhas were coming! We were in a minefield. But the risk proved worthwhile!

That night was cold. Battalion Tactical HQ, joined by Battalion Main HQ, had established itself on Mount William. Our normal routines were followed, including maintenance of a Duty Officer system to man the radio. Mark Willis:

Lieutenant (QGO) Chandra Pradhan, the Assistant Helicopter Operations Officer and (also responsible for) the Duty Officer roster was on 'stag' in the Battalion Command Post on Mount William (during) the night of 14/15 June after the ceasefire. In the middle of the night he went to wake up his relief for the next shift on watch. Shaking vigorously the (presumed heavily asleep) body of Kit Spencer, Mike Seear or someone, he got quite angry that the person would not wake up. Finally losing patience he lifted out his torch and shone it in the face of – a dead Argentine soldier! This unfortunate [...] was lying beside a rock close to our Command Post.[44]

Mark Willis also continued to write his staccato notes for the Battalion War Diary. These graphically illustrated the logistic challenges and requirement for bad weather endurance during those next twenty-four hours on Mount William and Tumbledown:

Weather conditions very poor. Bergens lifted by helicopter from FUP to most companies (less B Company and RAP). Also ration re-supply. (On 15 June**)** B Company bergens lifted by helicopter to Fitzroy (Brigade HQ) then to Goose Green when news received of 1/7GR's intended return to this area. Spent all day waiting for helicopters. Weather very bad – strong wind with snow. B Company lifted out to Goose Green at last light. Remainder returned to bashas for night. 1 x (A Company) medic casevaced by Scout (frostbite?) during evening.

Colonel David wanted to see the Battalion's wounded who had been evacuated to *Uganda*, the Task Force Hospital Ship. In his diary he noted the difficulties that the weather had on his Gazelle helicopter which arrived at Mount William: 'The wind was too high for it to land next to me, so I went 500 metres to it.' Eventually he 'landed up in Goose Green' where 'B Company came in complete' and there was 'a big village party'. Also the last of the Scots Guards flew out from Tumbledown by 20.00Z. But 12 Platoon remained on Mount William. Dil:

I was very curious to go around and seeing what war souvenirs could be found. I cannot remember if we were given any specific direction about the collection of enemy items but was aware from the Law of Armed Conflict lesson that we must not take any enemy property. Despite knowing that, we collected rations (rice and tinned food). I thought that rations and ammunition were acceptable items. Though the quality of rice was not that good, it was good enough just to be eating with the tinned curry. It was great!

One thing I was always curious about is what Stanley town was like; it could be seen from our location and was not far away. I still wonder what it was like and would love to visit it now but, at that point in time, it was impossible.

Next day Mark Willis jotted down in his notebook a description of those final agonising hours on a weather-beaten Mount William where frustration had turned to anger:

Mortar Platoon moved at first light by helicopter 'dedicated' to Battalion. Then after a long pause A Company lifted to Darwin with Heavy Machine-Gun Platoon, Anti-Tank Platoon and some medics to Goose Green. Another long pause and much radio traffic, then D Company lifted out to Goose Green. Another long pause, strong language on radio and then Tac HQ lifted out approx. 16.30.

McTeague and his 10 Platoon had endured those two days with fortitude:

The good feelings did not last long as we got progressively colder. The wind was constant and with it a wind chill factor of minus forty degrees centigrade. Many soldiers had wet feet and so, as it got colder, they started to suffer. Finally we were lifted off the battlefield by helicopter and taken to Goose Green where we were given the luxury of a sheep shed as shelter. Spirits rose rapidly and, after liberating a couple of bottles of sherry from the store, we were able to plan for the future.

Mark Willis's notes then described the Battalion's 'personal admin' after all Gurkhas had been recovered to Goose Green:

Some of A Echelon moved up by helicopter from Fitzroy (Brigade Administration Area). QM2 (Quartermaster No. 2 Captain Les Peacock) tried to sail from Fitzroy to Goose Green in LCU (Landing Craft Utility) with vehicles, but weather was too bad and had to return. SQMS Massey arranged central feeding for the evening meal (later discontinued due to lack of equipment and suitable rations).

Dil recalled Massey's efforts: 'After we re-grouped at Goose Green, we had a huge centralised feeding which was the first time I saw all the members of the Battalion since our disembarkation in San Carlos'; while Colonel David noted in his diary:

The remainder of the Battalion arrived during the course of the day after a fearful night on Tumbledown Mountain where it froze – there were four men with frostbite thanks to inefficient helicopter tasking. The Brigadier arrived as did (Lieutenant-Colonel) Tony Holt with no real news of the future. One must just sit and hope. I saw a film in the village hall this afternoon – *Flight of the Golden Goose*. It was absolute rubbish. Wrote to Bin (Belinda: his wife).

It was time for reflection. What were the major lessons learnt from those final hours of the war? They were obvious and would be included later in our pithy post operation report:

> The value of moving and attacking by night, proved to be invaluable: this skill being learnt well before the training period at Sennybridge. Generally night training is paid only lip service in the Army. This is mainly due to accumulated separation of family men, and the restriction placed on most night training areas in peacetime. The debate regarding the merits of day or night attacks will continue, however in the West European Theatre it is generally agreed that the operations will be fought on a twenty-four hour basis. Night training must now dominate this Battalion's future training since it does require continuous and detailed practice. However to achieve this aim successfully [...] it is therefore time for the following changes to be implemented: the easing of restrictions on night training areas: so at least one night per week can be set aside for additional training; the easing during the day of non-essential commitments, which will allow more time for night training; the issue of realistic illuminating ammunition scales, thus permitting night training to take place, e.g. on Exercise 'Welsh Falcon' at Sennybridge this Battalion was only issued with six one-inch Very cartridges for the entire training period; (and) the easing of restrictions on live firing at night, in order to allow fire and manoeuvre.[45]

And Chris Davies's keen war veteran's eye for history led him to assess the performance of those who had participated in Operation Corporate:

> The more I study the Campaign and, now that I have walked pretty well all of the important 'Ground' (Darwin, Goose Green, Harriet, Goat Ridge, Tumbledown, William, Sapper Hill, Kent, Longdon, Wireless Ridge) the more I am amazed at how awesome the victory was. The short-notice deployment, the weather, the logistic chaos, the set-backs, the distance from home base, the terrain etc all combined to make this as hard fought a campaign as any I can think of (ex-Chindits might take exception with this!). The sheer guts of the British Infantryman (plus their Gunners, Sappers, RHG/B (B Squadron of the Blues and Royals), Teeny Weenie Airways (Army Air Corps) etc.) who carried the whole thing off defy adequate description. It was awesome. What a privilege and pleasure it was to have been amongst it all. Not sure I would want to do it again! [46]

As for me, I would need considerable time to assimilate this life-changing experience. But it would take much longer than my initial post-war reflections. My first book and this, its sequel, are proof of that.

Notes

1.   *The Art of War*, Chapter 11 – The Nine Grounds.
2.   E-mail dated 18 October 2006.
3.   *Ibid.* dated 22 October 2006.

4. *Ibid.* dated 1 October 2006.
5. *Ibid.* dated 11 November 2006.
6. *Hors de Combat*, p. 55.
7. War diary of Lieutenant-Colonel Eugenio Dalton, the Argentine 10th Infantry Brigade HQ G3 Operations. Artillery and Mortar Defensive Fire – a reference point on the ground for pre-planned fire against advancing enemy.
8. From a letter dated 19 June 1982 written to the previous Commandant of the Battalion, Lieutenant-Colonel Tom Blackford.
9. *El Pulso Argentino*, Edition 7, December 2010.
10. E-mail dated 2 December 2011
11. *Ibid.* dated 1 October 2006.
12. *Ibid.* dated 11 November 2006.
13. *Hors de Combat*, p. 55.
14. From a conversation between Major Paddy Redding and the author during the twenty-fifth anniversary *Uganda* Falklands War reunion at Southampton on 20 April 2008.
15. *The Art of War*, Chapter 11 – The Nine Grounds.
16. E-mail dated 10 January 2008.
17. *Ibid.* dated 11 November 2006.
18. In the author's first book (page 264) it had been stated incorrectly: 'A Company could not wait, and *overtook* (the Scots Guards) Right Flank (Company) to begin establishing their fire base in preparation for D Company's assault.'
19. *Razor's Edge* (p. 290 – lower map) contradicts itself by incorrectly indicating that the Gurkhas had continued to advance all the way along the foot of these cliffs and, on arrival at Tumbledown's eastern end, turned due south to move onto Mount William. Not so. Mount William was only D Company's objective and, before this planned assault, the Battalion had climbed north up into a very steep Tumbledown re-entrant just before the cliffs but not, as *Razor's Edge* (p. 308) states, 'up the northern cliff-face'.
20. Mike Scott, the former CO of Major Iain Dalzell-Job, confirmed this was also the pattern of interaction between them in an amusing e-mail of 6 September 2006:
    Iain D-J was always looking for me or vice-versa. He was invariably late for any Group or conference, to the extent I never have to 'roll-call' if everyone was present; merely look for D-J and if he was there, everyone else must be!
21. E-mail dated 22 October 2006.
22. *Hors de Combat*, p. 37.
23. Nickname (TWA) for the 5th Infantry Brigade's 656 Squadron Army Air Corps (helicopters).
24. *Above All, Courage*, pp. 417-419.
25. 16 Field Ambulance's medical facility at Fitzroy was, in fact, an Advanced Dressing Station.
26. *Above All, Courage*, p. 419.
27. *Razor's Edge* never mentions the actions of A and B Companies on Tumbledown.
28. *With the Gurkhas in the Falklands*, p. 288. An extract from an e-mail sent to the author by Robacio in May 2002.

29. *Hors de Combat*, p. 58.
30. The description in *Razor's Edge* (p. 310) is a classic example of muddled chronology and incorrect facts which serve only to antagonise veterans who were there:

    > One of the forward observers with the Gurkhas, while moving along the cliff face and driving Lucero's platoon ahead of them, was shot in a blue-on-blue by a member of 2SG Reconnaissance platoon. The Gurkhas then had eight men wounded by Argentine artillery as they re-grouped below the Terrace, called in by the forward observer de Marco.

    Lucero's 3 Platoon was never on Tumbledown's western salient or north-east cliff face area. The Gurkhas were wounded much further back along Tumbledown's northern slopes and definitely not 'below the Terrace', an Argentine name given to the area known as the 'lodgement area' by the Scots Guards. On the map in *Razor's Edge* (p. 290) it is marked too far to the north.
31. From a letter dated 19 June 1982 written to the previous Commandant of the Battalion, Lieutenant-Colonel Tom Blackford.
32. *Op Corporate 1/7GR Immediate Debrief Points* dated 10 July 1982.
33. *Hors de Combat*, p. 57.
34. E-mail dated 24 May 2010.
35. *The Art of War*, Chapter 11 – The Nine Grounds.
36. The author's later research with Argentine veterans revealed that this man was probably Corporal Roberto Verdun of the 4th Infantry Regiment. He had withdrawn from Two Sisters forty-eight hours before.
37. Utter nonsense.
38. *Ibid.*
39. *Ibid.* It was the Scots Guards Right Flank Company who fought against Jaimet's Company.
40. *Ibid.*
41. *Ibid.* But this is also final confirmation that the Scots Guards' diversionary attack by a composite platoon on the BIM5 O Company at Pony's Pass was completely successful (see Chapter 5). It led to a series of incorrect Argentine decisions and fatally delayed the counter-attack on the west end of Tumbledown. Robacio's figures for O Company's strength in his testimony (sixty or eighty) contradict those given in his book *Desde el Frente* (p. 213) (*aproximadamente 100 hombres*) – and the correct figure of eighty-nine.
42. Utter nonsense.
43. From an Argentine website: **http://elrosaleniodigital.com.ar/2011/05/fallecio-el-contraalmirante-carlos-robacio**, published on 3 June 2011.
44. E-mail dated 7 August 2006. See note 35.
45. *Operation Corporate 1/7GR Post Operation Report – Part II* dated 27 July 1982.
46. E-mail dated 24 May 2010.

87. Gurkhas sharpening their *kukri*s prior to deployment, Church Crookham, 5 May 1982. (Photo by courtesy of *Soldier: Magazine of the British Army*.)

88. The result: Gurkha 'Cold Steel for Johnny Gaucho', *The Sun*, 6 May 1982.

89.   The media focus on the Gurkhas continues in the Queen Elizabeth II
Terminal at Southampton Docks, 12 May 1982.

90.   'Top Brass' (including UK Secretary of State for Defence John Nott) visiting
RMS *Queen Elizabeth 2* immediately prior to departure at 16.00 hours, 12 May 1982.

91.   *QE2* departs from Southampton on 12 May 1982. The liner possessed only one operative boiler out of three and had to be pulled out of her berth into the Solent by five tugs. Contravening Board of Trade regulations, she was seriously underpowered at seven knots. But the propaganda value of sailing on time superseded everything. Later that evening *QE2* anchored up overnight off the Isle of Wight for repairs to be carried out on a second boiler before proceeding to the South Atlantic.

92.   Gurkha General Purpose Machine-Gun weapon training on board *QE2*, May 1982.

93.   Gurkha early morning BIT (Battle Individual Training) on *QE2*'s Promenade Deck, May 1982. (Photo by courtesy of *Soldier: Magazine of the British Army.*)

94.   The 1st/7th Gurkha Rifles' Regimental Birthday Party on *QE2*'s Sports Deck, 16 May 1982. (Photo by courtesy of *Soldier: Magazine of the British Army.*)

95.   Gurkhas dancing at the Regimental Birthday Party, 16 May 1982.
(Photo by courtesy of *Soldier: Magazine of the British Army.*)

96.   Gurkha helicopter training on *QE2*'s aft helicopter landing pad at Freetown,
Sierra Leone, 18 May 1982.

97.   Crossing the Line and 'King Neptune's equatorial rituals', 19 May 1982

98.   Gurkha SLR live-firing into the South Atlantic from the stern of *QE2* below the aft helicopter landing pad, 22 May 1982.

99. Enemy aircraft and ship casualty list status (including the ongoing Battle of San Carlos Water) as displayed on *QE2*'s Quarter Deck, 08.00Z 23 May 1982.

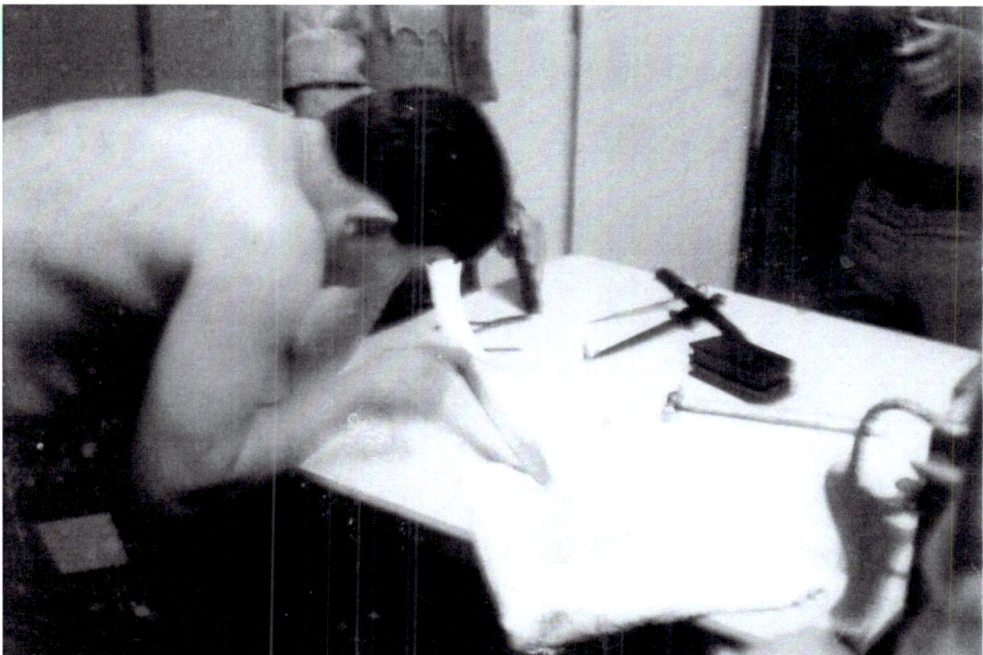

100. A Gurkha on board *QE2* preparing for war, May 1982

101.   'Next day, 25 May, the Battalion completed its first "bombing-up" procedure with a formal issue of live ammunition for all weapons, a procedure never practised in peacetime.' (Photo by courtesy of *Soldier: Magazine of the British Army.*)

102.   The 1st/7th Gurkha Rifles cross-decking from *QE2* to the P&O RoRo car ferry MV *Norland*, South Georgia, 28 May 1982.

103.   Approaching MV *Norland*, South Georgia, 28 May 1982.

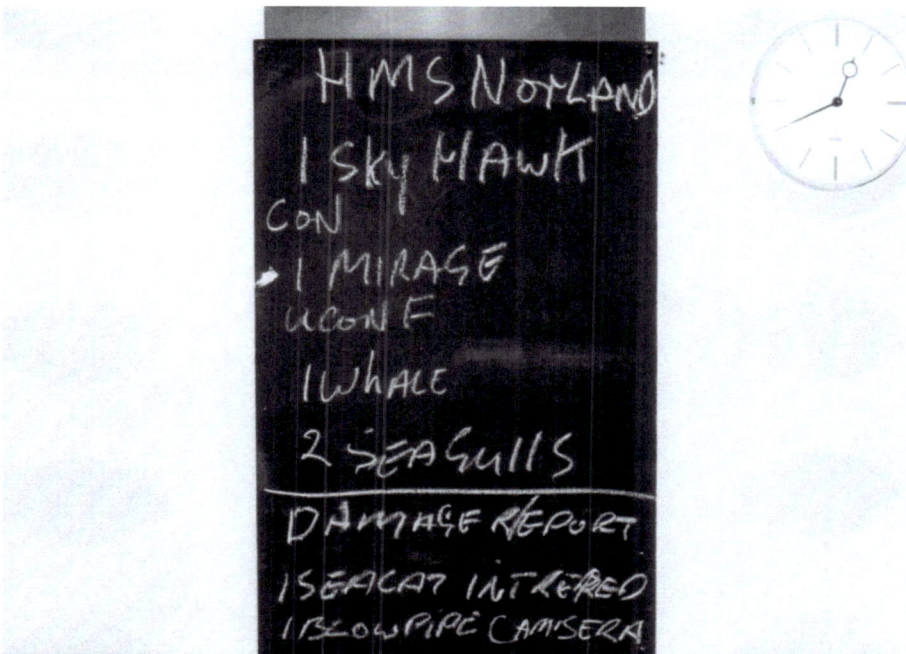

104.   The result of *Norland*'s ensuing participation in the Battle of San Carlos Water after landing 2 Para at Blue Beach 2 (as depicted on the dart blackboard in the Officers' Wardroom), 28 May 1982. Note 'HMS' instead of 'MV' and conviction that *Norland* had shot down an enemy Skyhawk fighter aircraft and (unconfirmed) a Mirage (Dagger) aircraft, in addition to the demise of a whale and two seagulls.

105.   Defence stations are manned on board *Norland* during a yellow air alert en route to San Carlos, 29 May 1982.

106.   Nearing the Total Exclusion Zone, 30 May 1982.

107.   The first ongoing red air alert in 'Bomb Alley'/San Carlos Water at 10.00Z 1 June 1982 just one hour before disembarking *Norland*, (l. to r.) Captain Mark Willis (Adjutant, 1st/7th Gurkha Rifles), Corporal Chris Aslett (Signaller for the Operations Officer, 1st/7th Gurkha Rifles) and Captain Graham Stewart-Smith (Paymaster, 1st/7th Gurkha Rifles).

108.   The second red air alert and 1st/7th Gurkha Rifles Battalion Tac HQ after the landing at Blue Beach 2, San Carlos, 1 June 1982.

109.   Gurkhas emplaning the Chinook helicopter 'Bravo November' at San Carlos,
1 June 1982.

110.   The burnt-out remains of an enemy Pucará twin piston-engined ground
attack fighter on the Goose Green air strip, 1 June 1982.

111.   RSM Karnabahadur 'One-Ton' Rai (foreground) leads a Gurkha patrol armed with SLRs from the settlement of Goose Green.

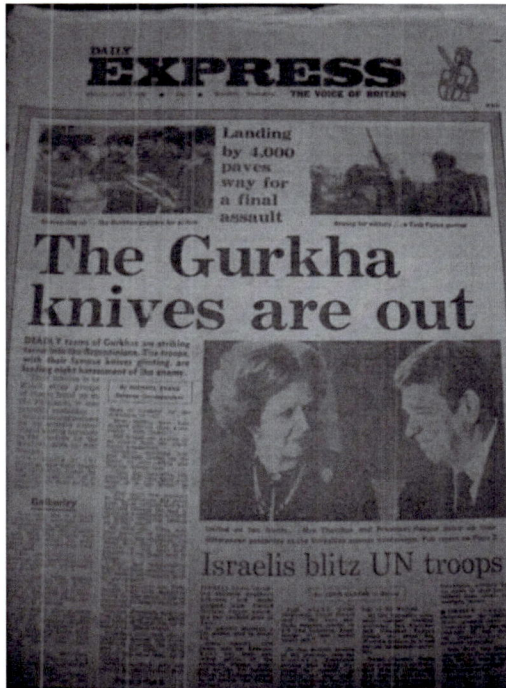

112.   The *Daily Express* headline (edition dated 5 June 1982) after a US peace plan had been presented on 3 June to the UK Prime Minister, Mrs Margaret Thatcher, prior to the opening of the eighth G7 summit at Versailles, France.

113.   MV *Monsunen* at Goose Green, June 1982.

114.   The beached enemy Coastguard patrol boat GC-83 *Guardacosta Río Iguazú* at Button Bay, Choiseul Sound.

115.   A Wessex helicopter deplaning some of the 1st/7th Gurkha Rifles' Battalion Tac HQ at Little Wether Ground, 9 June 1982.

116.   B Company 1st/7th Gurkha Rifles under enemy 155mm artillery fire at Wether Ground on 11 June 1982 viewed from A Company's position. The Battalion Tac HQ is sited behind the rocky outcrop (middleground right). The shell explosion can be seen just on the left and further to the rear of the outcrop.

117.   'During this sporadic enemy shelling, the remainder of 29 Battery's guns and ammunition were flown in by Sea King helicopters.'

118.   'Information was scarce and we had little knowledge about what was happening during those days, so it was heartening next morning on 12 June to see a long column of (eighty-seven) prisoners being marched past us to the rear (and evacuated by helicopter).'

119.   Captain Nigel Price, the 1st/7th Gurkha Rifles 81mm Mortar Platoon Commander with a dawn (11.00Z) 'brew-up' at Wether Ground, 13 June 1982.

120.   Some of the 1st/7th Gurkha Rifles' Battalion Tac HQ at Wether Ground on 13 June 1982, (second left) the author and (third left) Captain Mark Willis.

121.   The 1st/7th Gurkha Rifles' Milan Anti-Tank Platoon at Wether Ground waiting to be flown out to the Battalion's Assembly Area south of Two Sisters, midday 13 June 1982.

122.   Three A Company Gurkhas with a 'brew-up' prior to flying out from Wether Ground to the Battalion's Assembly Area. Note the Gurkha rifleman's basic weapons (foreground right): the SLR and *kukri*.

123.   Riflemen of 10 Platoon, D Company, 1st/7th Gurkha Rifles amongst the stone runs in the Battalion Assembly Area due south of the 500-foot ring contour, late afternoon, 13 June 1982.

124.   The final pre-battle co-ordination meeting between the Scots Guards and 1st/7th Gurkha Rifles, (l. to r. seated) Captain Tim Spicer (Ops Officer, Scots Guards), Lieutenant-Colonel Mike Scot (CO Scots Guards), Lieutenant-Colonel David Morgan,(Commandant, 1st/7th Gurkha Rifles) and Captain Mark Willis (Adjutant, 1st/7th Gurkha Rifles), at the Assembly Area south of Two Sisters, late afternoon, 13 June 1982. (Photo by courtesy of *Soldier: Magazine of the British Army*.)

125.   Tumbledown's northern slopes viewed from Wireless Ridge.

126.   Lieutenant Jeremy McTeague, Platoon Commander of 10 Platoon,
D Company, 1st/7th Gurkha Rifles.

127.   Mount William (background) and the saddle (foreground and middleground) viewed from Tumbledown's eastern sector.

128.   Some of the 1st/7th Gurkha Rifles' Battalion Tac HQ under enemy mortar fire on Tumbledown, 12.00Z 14 June 1982.

129.   The Commandant of the 1st/7th Gurkha Rifles, Lieutenant-Colonel David Morgan, is informed on Tumbledown of the *de facto* ceasefire at 15.00Z, 14 June 1982, (left) Second-Lieutenant Paddy Redding.

130.   Riflemen of A Company, 1st/7th Gurkha Rifles in their fire base on Tumbledown's south-east slopes at 15.15Z 14 June 1982. Note the Browning Heavy Machine-Gun 0.5-inch fifty-round belts of ammunition slung around the shoulders of five of these Gurkhas. One belt weighed seven kilos.

131.   The 1st/7th Gurkha Rifles' Mortar Platoon's 81mm mortar bomb ammunition stacked up by the southern side of Goat Ridge at 15.15Z, 14 June 1982. Note the Sterling submachine-gun (foreground left). (Photo by courtesy of *Soldier: Magazine of the British Army.*)

132.   'At the end of the battle I only had one barrel remaining in action and that was at the bottom of a sodding great hole it had dug for itself in the soft peat because of the recoil!' (Photo by courtesy of *Soldier: Magazine of the British Army.*)

133.   The 1st/7th Gurkha Rifles' Battalion Tac HQ examining Argentine grenade booby-traps placed out on the ground at Tumbledown's east end at 15.45Z, 14 June 1982.

134.   A BIM5 N Company bunker on Tumbledown's east end at 15.50Z, 14 June 1982.

135.   The 1st/7th Gurkha Rifles' Battalion Tac HQ on Tumbledown's east end looking east towards Stanley at 16.00Z, 14 June 1982.

136.   The Scots Guards and Gurkha Battalion Tac HQs meet on the saddle between Tumbledown's east end and Mount William at 16.15Z, 14 June 1982.

137.   Lieutenant Jeremy McTeague on Mount William, late afternoon,
14 June 1982.

138.   Two D Company Gurkhas occupy an Argentine position on Mount William,
late afternoon, 14 June 1982. Note the abandoned Argentine Para FAL rifle.

139.   D Company, 1st/7th Gurkha Rifles on Mount William at 16.45Z,
14 June 1982.

140.   The Commandant, Lieutenant-Colonel David Morgan, on Mount William,
late afternoon, 14 June 1982.

141.   Waiting for helicopters to land at Mount William while enduring the snow blizzards, 15 June 1982, (l. to. r.) Captain Martin Entwistle (1st/7th Gurkha Rifles Regimental Medical Officer), unknown Gurkha and Captain Kit Spencer (1st/7th Gurkha Rifles Regimental Signals Officer).

142.   The 1st/7th Gurkha Rifles A Company Commander Major David Willis (white gloves) with two Gurkhas on Tumbledown's east summit, 15 June 1982.

PHASE V
POST-CONFLICT CULTURES

Now battle for victory, attack and attain it.
But if one does not follow up on the achieve-
ment it is inauspicious.
One's fate is 'wealth flowing away.'

Thus it is said –
The enlightened ruler contemplates it.
The good General follows up on it.

– Sun Tzu[1]

Sun Tzu's exhortation for 'the good General' to 'follow up on the achievement' of victory cannot be underestimated. In the chaotic conditions of the immediate post-war Falkland Islands, this action was carried out to the letter by the Gurkhas with their assistance in the clear-up at Goose Green and other settlements where they were billeted. They found differing post-conflict cultures in various places. But one place that the Gurkhas did not stay at initially was in the battered but liberated Stanley. Rosemarie King updated her diary with an illuminating picture of the culture and outright relief that now existed on 15 June, the first full day of no siege:

> Our first day out after a peaceful night. We first of all went for a sight-seeing tour of Hebe Street, Davis Street and Callaghan Road. The mess was indescribable – debris just littered the town – mainly the Callaghan Road area which has been out of bounds for a couple of months. Yesterday (14 June) Wilfred Newman's house was shot down with a couple of shells. Jim Lellman's old peat shed was set on fire. George Butler's house burnt to the ground. I went to Pud Stacey's to face the mess of yet a third break-in. Walked up Ross Road and saw the PWD yard still belching smoke. Next we walked to the football pitch area and watched helicopters land (British of course). It was quite dramatic to me as the fellas that emerged from the choppers were my first sighting of British soldiers. It was a first class sight after waiting ten weeks. I felt so relieved I nearly cried. A weird feeling to say the least.
>   We moved home today and in the evening enjoyed the company of two helicopter pilots until 3.30am in the morning. The stories were non-stop from both sides. Graham Bound brought them as they were living at the Bounds'. Both pilots are based at Teal Inlet where a base was established.

Her diary entry on 16 June described the informal celebrations:

> What a hive of activity. Today has been excellent. British troops like flies (good flies). Argie prisoners like rats! The contrast difference is unbelievable. Our men, even after the long trek, look well-kept and fit to fight. The Argies on the other hand are filthy, licey and so dejected to say the least. The Arg officers are in perfect condition though!

Well tonight we, Elizabeth, Simon, Robert, Pete, Lewis and I went for a night out to the Globe Hotel. For the first hour drinking was by candlelight and then the power came on. The place was packed with British troops. Of course there were a lot of familiar faces. Phil Shuttleworth, Keith Rugby, Pete Ramft, Jack Hunter, Tony Gibson, Geordie Gill etc. that I can think of. Some of the soldiers asked Pete for permission to 'sniff my hair' as they wanted to smell a woman – acceptable I suppose under these circumstances! After the Globe we had quite a party here in the flat. Four Marine officers have moved into Church House so they joined the party. This ended in the early hours – after millions of questions and answers. Some mind-boggling tales.

But at Goose Green Colonel David's frustrated 17 June diary entry reflected the opposite:

I held a large Orders Group this morning to plan for the future. I can't do anything until, and unless, we get helicopter support. But none, apparently, is available. I am very angry about the sheer lack of support from all resources. Once orders had been given I had very little to do. The weather is bad – wet, chilly and very muddy. I made plans for the disposal of companies and a general clean up of this place. Then I saw another film – it was a Bob Hope one which was very funny. I couldn't sleep. I wrote to Bin.

He was not the only one who had insomnia. Mine lasted nearly three weeks. Frustration also featured in a letter from my wife after the Argentine surrender:

There is no communication at all from the camp in Church Crookham. The officer in command of the Gurkha Rear Party has just gone on leave to Greece. Beat that! Jane Pearson told me today that the Battalion had suffered ten wounded in the last battle for Stanley. If that is all, then I suppose you were lucky [...] Surely the mail should be getting into a regular routine soon, so we don't have to wait too long? I rush downstairs every morning to make tea – grab the paper and turn on the 8 a.m. news on the radio. I only wait for voices to say that the whole Task Force is coming back – no more hostilities – with all the papers signed!

The Battalion's deployment plans were for B Company to move to North Arm on the southern tip of Lafonia, and C Company to Hill Cove on West Falkland. It was A Company, however, which was the first Company to leave Goose Green by returning to their original base at the tiny settlement of Darwin. Much effort would be devoted to clearing up the battlefield by back-filling Argentine trenches. David Willis:

We had little contact with the settlers other than Brooke Hardcastle (the Falkland Islands Company Manager) who actually lived at Darwin and was the only person in that settlement. I think relationships were always warm wherever the boys were as they are so naturally polite and self-effacing.

This contrasted with Rosemarie King's more lively existence in Stanley:

Today (17 June) has been super. Still no water. We got electricity though. I went down to my office today. British troops have established a Headquarters Interrogation Centre in my office area, so there is no work. I've been getting the house sorted out – made bread etc. Electricity was on at half power, so not very successful. I have had quite a day carting water, shopping, etc. The Major (Richard Dickson) we have in the flat across the passage is in charge of 450 to 500 Marines. His three other officers also live here. They are all excellent characters.

Last night riots broke out in town with the Argentine prisoners. This resulted in the Globe Store and Squash Court being set on fire. A lot of houses were looted and the Post Office – well, hopeless to try and describe the state of the Post Office. Human excrement smeared the floor and the walls!

Sir Bedivere, HMS *Plymouth* and *Canberra* – were three of the ships today in the harbour. What a day of activity with ships, helicopters, vehicles, Arg and British, plus thousands of troops. Arg prisoners are cleaning the town under British supervision. The prisoners are picking up the gash by hand so it is a sight. Graham and Robert were around for a yarn and drinks. General Galtieri resigned.

And on 18 June:

A lovely sunny day. The town is looking better already. Huge mounds of debris sit on corners, in yards and against prominent buildings. The Globe Store is still smouldering – well, what's left. All that stands are the stone walls.

Tonight I cooked a large junk of beef, potatoes, cabbage and peas and invited the four officers in for supper (Major Dickson, Pete Ramft and Dutchy, but can't remember the name of the other). It was their first meal in ten weeks so they thoroughly enjoyed (or said they did). We enjoyed a good evening in their company. Rob and Graham were also in plus Phil Shuttleworth and another marine. The electricity went off for a while tonight. Lewis was in for a while. His water is on so I'm going up for a bath tomorrow!

Prince Andrew is in town today – he was in the Secretariat and other buildings.

Back in Goose Green an irritated Colonel David noted in his diary on 18 June progress with resolving the settlement's congestion problems by B Company's night departure:

General Moore and the Brigadier are due to visit us today – perhaps they want to warn us that we will be the garrison! We'll see. We were visited by VIP swanners today: 1 Commander, 3 Captains (RN) and the Brigadier – but no help! I saw another frightful film. B Company sailed for North Arm on the good ship *Monsunen* thus relieving the pressure here a fraction. Tomorrow I'm going to fly over to the *Uganda* to see our wounded with (Major) Mike Fallon and the GM (Gurkha Major).

The outstation deployment plan was also changed. D Company would go to Fox Bay and C Company to Port Stephens: both settlements being on West Falkland. Next day (19 June) Major Mike Kefford, the D Company Commander flew to Fox Bay for a recce, but discovered that Royal Marine Commandos were occupying it. Only my third day in Goose Green after being evacuated by helicopter from the snow blizzards ravaging the Tumbledown and Mount William battlefield, I was still coping with the effects of the so-called 'blue period' when, minus my usual adrenalin diet, anti-climax had set in and my mind was re-calibrating itself. Also I had a forty-eight hour bout of influenza. But twenty-eight years later, after my telling the Norwegian Professor Lars Weisæth about this, he remarked it had not been influenza, but the effect of my body *also* re-calibrating itself to a relatively normal life. Like many others, I was enduring the effect of PTSR (post-traumatic stress reactions). Other symptoms included sleeping difficulties (already mentioned), a heightened sense of alert, irritability and occasional apathy. They would continue a few more months, but then gradually fade.[2]

Thoughts and emotions about the final twenty-four hours of the war were still raw. They appeared in an unbalanced letter written to my parents that day. Facts and figures regarding time: 'We set off at about midnight (and) it took us some three hours to reach our Start Line'; Argentine unit strengths: 'there were at least two enemy platoons on Tumbledown (and) Mount William [...] was held by a company, with another two companies on the main road leading into Stanley'; and Scots Guards casualties: 'six dead and four wounded' – were wildly inaccurate because of, despite cessation of hostilities, the still-pervading fog of war. As for the shelling on the Battalion my letter also indicated that 'I escaped death three times in as many minutes' and, once on Tumbledown: 'I heard over the radio preliminary orders for 5 Infantry Brigade to take out Stanley. Fortunately we were never used.' My final remarks included a description of how the 'blue period' affected me: 'I feel drained, and really somewhat bemused by what has happened in the last week [...] At least now we have a relative period of peace and quiet. We all need it.'

Meanwhile Colonel David continued to endure the unknown regarding his Battalion's future and its postponed unaccompanied seven-month tour to Belize because of the Operation Corporate deployment:

> I woke up and got up earlier today. My tummy was much more settled. I had a shower and changed at Eric Goss's house. I went to Darwin to see David Willis – but he was absent on walkabout. The Brigadier arrived for tea this morning with no news other than the fact that we must be prepared for a long, dreary stay here in the Falklands. What about Belize? Are we to go there after this battle? A confirmation is required. I will be attending the Memorial Service in Stanley tomorrow. A massive amount of mail and newspapers arrived today.

And Rosemarie provided a description of that day in the small capital:

> I woke up this morning at about 10.30am. Last night's session lasted until 4.30am, so a short night. I have been busy today sorting out accommodation. Scrubbed out No. 1 flat here and this afternoon three more officers moved in. There are now seven officers in the house. British Forces are spread throughout the town but, of course, it is impossible to house so many. We've still lots of prisoners here. The *Canberra* today arrived in Argentina with the first 4,200 prisoners. *Norland* also is heading to Arg with 2,000-odd prisoners, so we're a few less thank goodness.

We went to the airfield for a look tonight – not nearly as bad as I'd envisaged. Whilst at the airport we picked up three SAS men, and so had a good yarn with them. They've been in the hills in the Islands for two months. They live on a ship at San Carlos and flew in by helicopter for an hour. We drove them into town to the football field. After that we went for a spin up the Darwin Road.

In a postscript she remarked 'we have photographs taken on this day of a dead Argentine lying on the Darwin Road close to Sapper Hill.'

Next day was Sunday, 20 June. Accompanied by thirty-nine members of Battalion HQ, Colonel David's visit to Stanley gave a significant boost to his morale:

The clocks went back a full hour today. I wandered around for most of the morning waiting for a helicopter to arrive at 11.30. I flew to Stanley via Fitzroy for a Memorial Service. The Cathedral was packed solid – the most moving service I've attended for years. I took the GM (Gurkha Major) and Sergeant Yambahadur with me. They were instantly popular with locals who took photos etc.! I found some Argie dry rations, bought some horribly expensive whisky and pinched a few spares for my Argie Mercedes staff car! Several people told me that the Argies surrendered because we were coming. It's great to win a victory without fighting!

There was no mention of the Memorial Service in Rosemarie's diary for that day, but she painted another vivid picture of hectic activity in other parts of Stanley:

Today has been muddly. I've been cooking bread for the officers in the house. We've had quite a lot of visitors. Also the officers were in for drinks. In the evening we went up to Goss's for a drink and to see Charlie Cork who is staying with them. I've seen a lot of prisoners filing down the Public Jetty to embark on the *Forrest* and be transferred to one of the Task Force vessels. The harbour is extremely busy – twelve quite large vessels in the harbour and another thirteen I hear are visible around Stanley waters – haven't got around to counting them yet! Helicopters are like gulls in the sky – just pray that none drop on the town. A lot of people are being flown in from the Camp. All of the food left by the Arg is being given to the public. The Drill Hall for instance, was full up with tinned foods, sacks of flour and potatoes. There was plenty of food in Stanley in the past week which had arrived off the Red Cross vessel. Most of the prisoners have left thank goodness.

The following day, one week post-siege, she noted another British national event and a semblance of normalcy returning to Stanley:

Princess Diana gave birth to a boy today at approx 9pm. I've had my first day at work. The office is occupied by British troops – approx thirty sleeping and others working. The Interrogation Centre and Logistics, I think, have been set up. The chaps are very pleasant. It's not so convenient though without electricity and water but we're getting by.

The electricity is off in the day but luckily on at night in Church House. Today

Lewis, Rob, Pete and I enjoyed champagne to celebrate the birth. Later we were joined by Major Dickson and Pete Ramft. In the middle of our celebrations we heard a hefty bang – on examination saw a fire up on Callaghan Road so the party broke up whilst it was investigated. It was gas cylinders exploding which were stored in my Dad's old hen house I hear.

The shops opened today on new hours – 1pm until 3pm at the West Store. We're working from 9am through to 2pm. Today I sent a telex to my family to let them know we still exist. Got a letter from Muz – chuffed pink I was.

That day I wandered around the settlement at Goose Green. This included a sightseeing trip to the adjacent air strip that had become a local rubbish dump for the breathtaking amount of Argentine weaponry which came in all shapes and sizes. Not least there were a multitude of stacked-up boxes containing napalm bombs, artillery shells and other types of ammunition, while the sea of ball and link 7.62mm small arms ammunition strewn over the ground made one's eyes water. It was also Colonel David's wedding anniversary on 21 June, and he entertained more VIP visitors at Goose Green. But his diary entry also registered more frustration:

Well, we had Generals and Captains (RN) and Brigadiers all here today. General Moore stayed for a long time and left just enough time to move down to North Arm to see B Company. B Company are all well. I gather that we will now all move over to West Falkland and stay there for the duration. God knows what and when will (be) move(d). What a wedding anniversary! God, I wish Bin was here.

This mood did not apply to Quentin Oates and his Recce Platoon which was attached to B Company:

The Recce Platoon was 'housed' in a house next to the area used to slaughter sheep and cattle; hence what looked like the killing fields outside the back door with skulls and bones littered around. We shot a large number of geese to supplement rations and spent time helping out constructing ranges with B Company (400 metres, Close-Quarter Battle, Grenade etc). We had a very good rapport with the inhabitants. Our alcohol allowance (daily ration) was saved and consumed in one 'binge' party with the locals who loved these events.

There was activity on 22 June as A Company's 3 Platoon deployed to Lively Island for forty-eight hours to search for a suspected enemy airman (that would only result in a find of kit), and C Company helped Eric Goss, the Goose Green Manager, to fight and extinguish a gorse fire. But Colonel David's diary entries for that, and the following day, summed up a dreadful forty-eight hours when his D Company deployment plan of utilising the Falkland Islands Company motor coaster *Monsunen* was wrecked and the 5th Infantry Brigade HQ vetoed Plan B of moving the Company by helicopter:

D Company will sail to Fox Bay today and we move temporarily to their vacated accommodation, thus relieving the shop. Cheers will ring out all around the settlement! (Later) But D Company did NOT sail although we planned that they should. I flew to *Uganda* to see the Gurkha patients. All are very happy including our most serious, Corporal Gyanbahadur and Lance-Corporal Gajabahadur. All will be back to UK soon. I spent the evening (and night) with the Goss's. It was very comfortable [...] (23 June) This was probably the most useless day for ages. Nothing that I wanted to do succeeded. All my plans to move D Company by the *Monsunen* failed, ending in the Royal Navy just walking away. Brigade HQ were, as always, their usual helpless selves. *Nothing* was done to help us, and I'm bitter about it. It was a waste of a day really. Brigade HQ has broken up (for holidays).

On 24 June the Gurkha Pipe Major and another Gurkha piper played their pipes at the 2 Para memorial service on Darwin Hill where a simple cairn with a cross had been erected by the Islanders. But it would be a grim day for our Battalion as Colonel David registered in his diary:

Today whilst filling in an enemy trench 21161666 Lance-Corporal Budhiprasad Limbu was killed when his shovel hit an explosive device thought to have been an M-79 grenade. He will be buried tomorrow. I went to North Arm and then to Fox Bay, and saw Garjuman and KB respectively. The Brigadier arrived late in the evening. NAAFI stores arrived tonight!

The last three digits of Lance-Corporal Budhiprasad Limbu's regimental number were prophetically ominous. Rifleman Dilkumar Rai had been also engaged in the same task as Budhiprasad on the northern section of the battlefield at Burntside House:

We had been ordered to fill in enemy trenches in the Goose Green area. Not long after we started filling the trenches, we heard a very loud bang in the area of Company HQ. Unfortunately it instantly led to Lance-Corporal Budha's (61666) death and two others received injuries caused by the explosion of a grenade. It was decided no longer safe to run this task so we had to stop everything and return to Goose Green. With everyone still relieved that the war was over, the sad news was given to us. I knew them all personally, Lance-Corporal Budha in particular.

I wrote another letter (on 6 July) to my parents describing my involvement in the crisis management of this 255th and final British forces' fatality of the war:

Life is slowly returning to something akin to normal at the settlement here. We are very well looked after by the locals – their hospitality is quite remarkable to say the least. It has been snowing here the last couple of days, and we've got at least six inches on the ground. At least everyone is living under a roof, and there are no trenches to dig!

I'm afraid that we suffered our first fatality of the campaign last week. One poor Gurkha who was filling in an Argentine trench accidently hit an unexploded grenade with his shovel. The thing exploded, took half his head off, and wounded two other men in the legs. I was on duty in the Ops Room at the time. God, did I have to work quickly. Ordered up a casevac (casualty evacuation) helicopter, diverted another which was landing at our heli-pad, whipped the doctor up to the scene of the accident, contacted the CO who was in mid-air at the time, and briefed Brigade HQ. I was really shaking at the end of a concentrated half-hour piece of work.

I cannot rely on the Gurkha signallers in the Ops room and thus tend to double my workload. I don't speak their language, and they haven't exactly a wonderful command of English either. Consequently I tend, in occasions of stress, to get very short with them. However, they are a very *faithful* lot, totally unlike British soldiers. It has taken a lot of time even to begin to learn their strange ways and customs.

We should be back in the UK on the 26 July, if all goes well. See you then – with a few stories to tell.

The somewhat unfair criticism of the Goose Green Ops Room Gurkha signallers should be viewed in the context of my final Northern Ireland tour of duty. During the second half of 1979 I was a watchkeeper at the Lisburn-based 39th Infantry Brigade HQ that had Belfast as its tactical area of responsibility. This underrated job had taught me the immediate action drills and skills for handling incidents on the ground: a most useful experience prior to becoming a Battalion Operations and Training Officer. Consequently on 24 June 1982 my reactions had been faster and more proactive than those of the Gurkha signallers.

However Colonel David's diary for 25 and 26 June had better news concerning D and B Companies' deployments:

I went out to North Arm today by helicopter to see (Captain) Lester Holley and continued my otherwise interrupted trip yesterday. All was very well. I came back for the 1666 funeral which went off without a hitch, except I forgot to salute. (Major) Bill Dawson (the Battalion 2IC) was sent by me to CLFFI HQ to fix helicopters and crew for *Monsunen*. This was done well. The crew arrived and will sail tomorrow [...] (26 June) A quiet day except that the Chinook for D Company arrived at 08.30 to take them to Fox Bay, but we were told 09.30. Not to worry, all went extremely well. C Company sailed at 13.30 for Port Stephens, and is due in there at 09.00 tomorrow. New *dhobi ghat* (laundry) arrived. The Officers Mess is now a goer. However it needs a Clansman (radio).

After his arrival with 10 Platoon into the post-conflict culture of Fox Bay West, Jeremy McTeague described what happened next:

We were flown over by helicopter and given the brief of helping 9 Para Squadron Royal Engineers clear the minefield that had been laid around the settlement by the Argentines. We were warmly welcomed by the settlers and set about helping them clean up the mess left behind by the Argentines. This meant collecting mines, ammunition and weapons and putting them into a makeshift compound. In turn the settlers literally killed the fatted cow and provided many of us with Wellington boots to replace our now entirely useless DMS boots.[3]

We were billeted in a series of small houses and sheds and I promptly put up a sign on the Platoon HQ that proudly read 'Supreme Allied Commander, Fox Bay

West'. While we were able to wash, the water was generally cold as the boiler was for a small family house and peat-fired. It was impossible to wash anything other than socks and underpants.

The Farm Manager complained that an Argentine had taken his tractor and driven over a mine by mistake. The tractor was now blocking the main track out to the pasture lands. I went and had a look at it and knowing that there was no possibility of getting a heavy recovery vehicle in the Falklands (full stop), I devised a plan to blow it up into small pieces. My signaller, a couple of other riflemen and I started to pile up land mines below the tractor. Adding about two kilograms of plastic explosive to the mass allowed me to use an ordinary detonator. I set it for five minutes and we all retreated the 100 metres calculated to be a safe distance in a ditch.

On time it detonated. The tractor flew dozens of feet into the air and, according to plan, shattered into a thousand pieces. The noise was awesome and smoke incredible. Mud and small debris rained down on us (thankfully without causing injury). Deafened, we staggered around in circles for a couple of minutes before stopping to admire the enormous crater I had blown. Ears ringing, we started to walk back towards the station when we saw our two 'liberated' four-wheel drive Argentine Mercedes racing towards us. They were carrying the Farm Manager, his wife and a gaggle of other excited people who had heard the noise from over a mile away and wanted to know what had happened.

On 27 June Captain Mark Willis led a foraging party to recover Gurkha lost kit at the 500-ring contour near Mount Harriet. They also brought back Argentine equipment. In Goose Green Colonel David's diary entries for the next four-day period encompassed visits, waiting, bad weather and, at last, good news:

A day of rest I suppose, but we had quite a busy one really. We were visited by the Brigadier and the Director of Public Relations who had been sent by the CGS (Chief of the General Staff) himself to find out what we did and how we did it. I think/hope that I impressed him with our part in the battle [...] (28 June) A miserable day from the weather point of view. Took off in rain and fog for North Arm and made it. Talked to Lester and saw B Company. All was fine. I flew on miraculously to Fox Bay and saw Mike Kefford and Bhuwansing but could not fly down to see Taj Lewis at Port Stephens. I will see him hopefully tomorrow if all goes well. We have three Gazelles here for the night! [...] (29 June) This was a truly foul day – with heavy fog, persistent rain and really very chilly wind from the east. A large mail delivery was made by a brave Sea King helicopter which arrived through the fog. I went for walk in the rain and found some Argie keys [...] I will have to reply to all the letters tomorrow. Went to bed early after humour on TV [...] (30 June) Our fifty-eighth day separated from our families. I wonder how much longer we'll have to endure this? I saw Taj Lewis at Port Stephens and Mike Kefford at Fox Bay today. I went also to Port Howard en route to Goose Green. The Brigadier stayed for supper. It is now decided that we are due to sail back to the UK on 14 July. Plans are made and a very drunken evening ensued. I decided (Major) Bill Dawson must go home with the Advance Party due to leave on 3 July by air.

Back in Fox Bay Dil enjoyed himself – apart from one episode:

> 10 and 12 Platoons stayed in Fox Bay West and Company HQ and 11 Platoon in Fox Bay East. This place was occupied by the Argentine forces during the war but I had no idea about the actual effect of the war on the people of this settlement. On our arrival, I witnessed the rifles that were dumped in the settlement we lived in. Our stay was very pleasant; we were given a house to live in. I shared a small room with Corporal Kumar Limbu and Rifleman Bhimraj Rai (63894), 10 Platoon's radio operator. It was very relaxing and I even got time to write to my mother and brother for the very first time after arriving in the Falkland Islands.
>
> I remember eating fresh steak prepared by Lieutenant McTeague *saheb*. During our stay there, Bhim and I also prepared curry from a leg of pork. By mistake we forgot to take off the pig's toe nails. Cleverly enough, whoever discovered this did not disclose it until after we had finished eating. Although the curry was delicious, we could not help but be disgusted about it.

On 1 July the Mortar Platoon was moved by Sea King helicopter to the settlement of Chartres on West Falkland. Colonel David's diary entries of 1-3 July logged the effort of gathering the Battalion's vehicles together, rumours about our return home, more visits, fickle Falklands weather and (not least) delays in delivery of mail to the UK:

> This was a frustrating day as we tried to bring all people and vehicles in to Goose Green. *Monsunen* sailed on time (to Stanley) with all vehicles, including the Argentine Mercedes land rover, for loading onto the *Baltic Ferry*. We're unlikely to succeed but we're going to try. The QM came back with dismal stories of Stanley. The Advance Party is due to leave tomorrow. It is unlikely for us to sail to UK on 14 July [...] (2 July) All sorts of rumours running around about the Advance Party and Main Party move. Needless to say we don't believe any of them. A cold, sleety day but no real snow yet. (Major) Rory Stewart came for supper at the Goss's house – slides were shown again. There was a massive mail delivery. Two letters from Bin, neither very up to date but fabulous nonetheless [...] (3 July) It snowed terribly all over the place. I flew by helicopter to see the Companies and platoons 'in camp'. I saw (Captain) Hombahadur Gurung at Lively Island, Lester at North Arm, Amaraj and (Second-Lieutenant) Tim Morris at Port Stephens and went with Tim to Weddell Island, having dropped off Rory and his adventure training party at New Island. I ended up seeing (Major) Mike Kefford at Fox Bay. He has a bit of work to do, but is coping well I think. I had supper in Mess [...]

While Colonel David was out flying, Royal Navy Captain Linley Middleton and his Padre from the aircraft carrier HMS *Hermes* visited Goose Green. They paid their respects at the grave of Sea Harrier pilot Lieutenant Nick Taylor whose aircraft had been shot down by fire from a 35mm Oerlikon cannon located in the settlement on 4 May. Unfortunately the snow covered the flowers around Taylor's grave. They had been planted by some Gurkhas, a good example of their thoughtfulness. Elsewhere a mobile digger was now being used for back-filling Argentine trenches, while another problem arose with Brigade HQ's initial insistence of 'no helicopters on Sundays' regarding the Advance Party's move to Stanley. This nonsensical diktat was eventually overcome as Colonel David's diary entry indicated for 4 July:

> This was a freezing day with snow both during the night and again in the morning. An element of the Advance Party left Goose Green, led by Bill Dawson, for Stanley and hopefully the UK today. Sunny weather arrived, followed by snow, followed by rain – quite attractive really. It has been a quiet day. *Monsunen* arrived with NAAFI goods. Letters were sent to Bin. I got four back in today's post. She is *still* not getting mine.

His final complaint was also reflected in a letter from my wife about the continuing information vacuum. Her writing was also a snapshot of her roller-coaster emotions – interrupted by two family incidents:

> No letters today either. It's been two weeks now and I know the old ones by heart almost [...] I feel fairly low, I'm afraid. It's such an anti-climax to watch all that elation and triumph and still not have you home! [...] I have just had the chance to cry over some TV film – cried for more than I should, it was just so nice to open up the flood-gates. Pathetic really, there isn't much left of your brave wife [...]
>
> Poor Victoria fell off her bike in a big way today. For the first time! But, dear oh dear, she's a mess in the face – top lip cut both under and over – bruises and grazes on cheeks and chin ... one front tooth was bleeding and might turn black [...] I just cuddled her for hours.
>
> [...] Emily is playing with water in the kitchen sink at the moment – so she's quiet and happy. Yesterday at the lunch table she suddenly announced, 'Pappa Falkland Island' – and I nearly fell off my chair! Amazing – I didn't even know she could say the words, let alone have picked up that piece of information. I don't have tears from Victoria any more – she seems to have accepted the situation. That doesn't mean we have stopped talking about you, though. You're still verbally included in all we do.

As well as assisting Falkland settlers in clearing up, the Gurkhas had started training again. Most Companies built their own shooting ranges which they used to good effect. The Mortar Platoon also carried out field firing at Chartres on the afternoon of 4 July in order to trial new base nests. They were determined to find a possible solution to counter the soft peat ground which had caused such a serious sinkage problem to their base plates during the firing of their 272 mortar bombs in support of the Scots Guards' attack on Tumbledown and, prior to D Company's attack, on Mount William.

Colonel David's diary entries of 5 and 6 July continued to chronicle the ongoing uniqueness of the Battalion's activities. These included the Pipes and Drums musical 'cruise' on board the *Monsunen* to all settlements which housed a Gurkha presence:

> It was a cold start today. The forecast is minus four to zero degrees centigrade. The snow is drifting to about six feet. I flew off to see Chartres, Mike Kefford at Fox Bay and Darwin. Mike's posting came through. I don't think he will be very

pleased. I went to Chartres and Fox Bay, and had a super lunch at the latter. Mike is OK. We need more information on his posting really. The press will arrive on Friday and for our party on 10 July. I will have to think of something to say. The vehicles arrived from D Company – but were the wrong ones! [...] (6 July) Deokumar arrives and will stay until 19 July. It is a lovely day, snow and sun, but very few showers. I slept like a log last night, nice and warm. Pipes and Drums rehearsed well today for the 10th. I pulled and carried a 105mm shell from under the sheep-shearing shed this morning with Paddy and D.B. *saheb*. Fortunately there were no problems! God knows how. In pulling the shell to the dump I walked back into a pile of bombs. Knocked 'em for six and swore!

Meanwhile one Islander, Tim Miller, was helping to host a week-long visit by a Gurkha party from Fox Bay to Dunnose Head farm on West Falkland. Two months previously it was suspected that there had been an enemy air-drop on Dunnose Head. Therefore on 23 May four Harrier GR3s from HMS *Hermes* had attacked the farm's air-strip. But there was no Argentine presence there, and Tim had been wounded by an explosion during the attack. He had to wait a considerable period of time for treatment but eventually, on 13 June, arrived on board *Uganda* to undergo an operation which removed a piece of shrapnel from his right eye. Unfortunately its vision could not be restored. The Gurkhas had been sent to clear up the mess at Dunnose Head from late June to early July. Tim:

> The Gurkhas were always very popular especially out on the farms. I guess in some ways we and they empathise with a similar type of rural life in some respects. But they did not like the cold and wet of winter as you will well know! Upland Goose *baht* (Gurkha curry) was very good. However I remember their surprise when watching me butcher a lamb – 'But you use saw and not *kukri*?!'
>
> We had a game of football with them – we were only three civilian lads, so we mixed up and had, as they called it, old party and young party teams! The first half was thirty minutes. The second went on for a lot longer and was fine for the fit Gurkhas, but we three Bennies were knackered! I recall a young Corporal narrowly missing goal and saying, 'Oh, I am unlucky bastard!' – which amused us all.
>
> They were a great bunch. We took them all out one day to see some penguins, which fascinated them, and they made the curry (not a penguin though: wild upland geese).
>
> On a trip to Stanley two days after the surrender to see my parents and let them know I was alive (they knew I had been wounded in the air attack), I picked up a couple of live 66mm anti-tank rocket launchers that were lying dumped (as one did in those crazy days) and took them back to the farm on the helicopter. Very rightly the lads were a bit concerned about us having them on the farm, so we built a big pile of driftwood and rubbish and had target practice under tuition. I am very glad they were there as, in hindsight, it would not have been a very good idea to fire one without knowing how to!
>
> The Farm Manager and his wife, his being the only house left habitable, was where we all ate and bathed. He was presented with a *kukri* set mounted on a piece of wood when they left.

We asked, 'Wouldn't you get into trouble for "losing it" as it was Army issue?' The comment back was, 'No problem, I tell Stores it lost in Falklands War!' [4]

Colonel David's diary entries written on 7 and 8 July explained the Pipes and Drums entertainment programme, but pulled no punches regarding the 5th Infantry Brigade HQ:

> The Pipes and Drums Beat the Retreat in Fox Bay East and West. It was seemingly successfully. They move down to Port Stephens tomorrow on the *Monsunen*. I spent all morning talking to two scientists who wanted to know what went on. It was all terribly boring. I was told today that we are unlikely to leave before the 20th at the earliest. If this is the case I'll keep the platoons *out* in their locations longer. I went for a good walk. There was a lovely sunset [...]
>
> (8 July) The Pipes and Drums are to Beat the Retreat in Port Stephens today. We were visited today by 1 x Brigadier and 1 x Admiral. Both arrived unannounced, but both seemed fairly happy. The Admiral arrived in a Sea King! The press party is due in today, but still no sign of it by 12.00. Taj Lewis was visited by the Brigadier unannounced. The latter told Taj that he would be going in two hours. News to me! God, this Brigade organisation is *crap*!

The Gurkhas' Milan Anti-Tank Platoon had no opportunity to fire any missiles during the war, so a special field-firing day was organised for them at Fox Bay. I had no bad conscience in writing off six perfectly serviceable and highly expensive Milan missiles because of so-called 'war shrapnel damage' so that the platoon could launch these on a specially constructed 1,400 metre range against a rock and peat Gurkha-built bunker with full overhead protection. Colonel David's diary for the next four-day period mentioned this 9 July event as well as a hijacking of the *Monsunen* which the Falkland Islands Company decided unilaterally to repair at Port San Carlos:

> The Pipes and Drums are to Beat the Retreat at North Arm. Or at least that was the plan! I went out to Fox Bay West via Chartres to watch a Milan firing display. It was most instructive and a report will be written in due course. I saw seals ten feet from us while waiting for the boat to cross to Fox Bay East. Lunch was at Fox Bay East. I returned to be told that *Monsunen* had been hijacked by Royal Navy. I blew my top! She arrived at San Carlos late less our poor Pipes and Drums [...] (10 July) The Pipes and Drums to Beat the Retreat and a party at Goose Green tonight. I spoke to the Manager Falkland Islands Company at the Hardcastles' home at 8 a.m. this morning. It is clear that he had ordered *Monsunen* to return to San Carlos without my permission or clearance despite the fact that the Pipes and Drums were on board. Man management – 0 ex 10. I am worried about tonight. But there was no reason to be. All went tremendously well. A super Beat the Retreat and Party which went on until 03.30 with HE (His Excellency: the FI Governor Rex Hunt) present all the time [...]
>
> (11 July) It was very cold. I got up with a splitting head and went off to Darwin to see off the Brigadier, HE and General. All were happy, but all had thumping heads. I went for long walk today covering a considerable distance in the snow. I

was very tired on return. I wrote to Bin again. Tomorrow David Willis and I leave on a Brigade Battlefield Tour! [...] (12 July) We expect to cover San Carlos, Goose Green and other places of interest today, and expect also to spend the night at Stanley and have a dining-in night at Brigade HQ. (And later in Stanley) It was a fair day. A bit of a bore really, but the weather was fine. Orders Group was the usual crap: but good news – we return to UK on the *Uganda* leaving on 15 July. There was a good night's party afterwards.

The North Arm Beating the Retreat performance had to be postponed *sine die*. Meanwhile at Goose Green a Brigade Warning Order was received on 12 July that 253 Gurkhas would embark MV *St Edmund* on 17 July and, three days later, 397 would embark MV *Norland* – a total of 640 men. However in accordance with the standard Falklands-Malvinas War pattern of plans being forever changed, this double-ship solution was altered in the late afternoon to a single ship. The entire Battalion would now embark *Uganda* on 15 July and our Rear Party would handover on 19 July prior to their return to UK by air. Next evening (13 July) Colonel David's diary mentioned briefly the Brigade Battlefield Tour and its final day:

> I slept at Stanley in a very nice house with good bed and breakfast. I shared a room with Mike Scott (Commanding Officer, Scots Guards). I spent the day on the Battlefield Tour which, because of the snow, I was not much involved in (with explaining the Gurkha role) and it became a wee bit boring. I returned to Goose Green just before dark in a Chinook and gave a lengthy Orders Group. Tomorrow we must fly C Company in, and then prepare for the big move to *Uganda* tomorrow (our forty-fourth day on the Falkland Islands).

His diary did not allude to the infamous accident at Stanley Airport that morning involving a Welsh Guards fatigue party which had been clearing snow and ice from the runway to enable RAF Hercules transport aircraft to land from Ascension Island. The party was ordered off the runway because a Sea Harrier Combat Air Patrol was about to take off. However one of the two Harriers accidently fired its two Sidewinder missiles which hit and badly injured eight Guardsmen. The Commanding Officer of 16 Field Ambulance, Lieutenant-Colonel John Roberts, who was also a participant on the Battlefield Tour, was called to assist with the casualties. Afterwards he stuffed his combat uniform pockets with field dressings and morphine before rejoining the Brigade Battlefield Tour party on Tumbledown. He wanted to be well prepared for all eventualities because the Royal Engineers in the 5th Infantry Brigade HQ had advised the Brigadier not to hold the Battlefield Tour because of the danger of Argentine mines. Roberts was used to dealing with such matters. Prior to deployment on Operation Corporate, he had been told that surgeons would not be required in his unit. His successful resistance to such a wildly unimaginative view of the 'worst-case' was vindicated by the surgeons' work in the Fitzroy Advanced Dressing Station after the Brigade attack on Tumbledown. He resigned his commission after returning to the UK.[5]

But focus was now on implementing the plan for embarking the Battalion on *Uganda*, officially re-designated as a troopship with her white funnel and its red cross painted over by a boring matt yellow and her last patients (the Welsh Guardsmen) flown off on 14 July. The Pipes and Drums were flown that day to North Arm to carry out their final Beating the Retreat, while at Goose Green a tree was planted in memory of the late Lance-Corporal Budhiprasad Limbu. Colonel David's diary entries described other 14 July activities and, on a foggy 15 July, the first phase of our move off the Falklands:

> Things seemed to go remarkably well certainly up to lunchtime. C Company and the Assault Pioneers flew in on schedule and we are all packing up like mad ready for the mass exodus tomorrow. A small party was held by locals for us in the Church Hall. We are due to leave these shores on Saturday, possibly Sunday and I think the journey will take about three weeks [...] (15 July) Well, of course, the weather was foul, and the first Chinook arrived only after I had stood everyone down at 11.30. Thereafter things went really very smoothly ending with our thirteen underslung loads at about 16.00. *Uganda* is a funny ship. Lots of Royal Navy, Marines, Nurses, 16 Field Ambulance and Gurkhas are aboard. We sail tonight for Fox Bay to take on B and D Companies – a total of 311 personnel.

The potential for disaster was ever-present during the numerous landings on *Uganda*'s small flight deck. The rear exit of the Chinook helicopter 'Bravo November' was not only precariously protruding over the sea in Grantham Sound, but as many worried passengers' eyes witnessed on board *Uganda*, chocks had to be applied to the helicopter's wheels because of its total absence of brakes. But Colonel David's initial diary entry on 16 July prior to the embarkation of the remainder of his Battalion was wrongly pessimistic:

> I woke up to fearfully bad weather. It was cold, wet, foggy and miserable. I doubt if we'll get 'em all on board today. We are due in Stanley tomorrow morning. However we got all aboard without any fuss by 15.00 thanks to some superb flying by 18 Squadron RAF. The weather was lousy – and the seas were rough around South Lafonia. *Uganda*'s thirtieth birthday drinks party was held at 19.15. I went to bed fairly early.

Despite the slippery flight deck the entire Battalion was now at last on board and on the move towards our final goal in the Falklands – Stanley. Colonel David's upbeat diary described the next forty-eight hours even though there was sense of *déjà vu* with the bad weather:

> We arrived in Stanley at about 08.00 after a frightfully rough night. We immediately went alongside a water tanker and filled up with *pani* (water). We also shipped off the sick men and one or two others. We are due to sail at 17.00 tomorrow provided we get all our kit together. I rang Bin this evening – must have been about 23.30 her time. It was marvellous to hear her voice after all this. She really is a fantastic girl. What would I do without her? [...] (18 July) Oh joy of joys, I found a piano today and made my radio work so that I got some music at long last. I've never been so music-starved before. It rained heavily last night through my open

windows! It was a lousy day today with a Force 8 gale and rain. We sailed at 10.15 to rendezvous with a re-supply ship to our north. The Stugeron seasick pills are actually not too bad – there is a gentle rock to the ship. There are nine days to Ascension Island, eleven to UK, and one day at Ascension to come.

This was going to be a long and tedious three-week voyage beck to Southampton at a pedestrian average speed of seventeen knots. But in retrospect it would also provide an effective psychological 'Third Location Decompression' for this large group of Gurkhas after their war experiences on the Tumbledown battlefield and elsewhere in the Falklands.[6]

Notes

1. *The Art of War*, Chapter 12 – Attack by Fire.
2. The Norwegian disaster psychiatrist, Dr Pål Herlofsen, with whom the author developed a professional association later in life within crisis management training, provided a informal definition of PTSR to the author (e-mail dated 28 November 2011):
   > PTSR is well defined, i.e. a certain amount of symptoms. But some strive with anxiety and depression, not a full PTSR, which will tend to freeze in the sense that some symptoms stay on, decreasing in intensity. PTSR will, for the most part, pass over in months, and only a few will develop PTSD which is indeed a disorder.
3. The British Army DMS (Direct Moulded Sole) boot was of appalling quality and leaked like a sieve. It caused many cases of trench foot during the war.
4. E-mail dated 20 October 2008.
5. From a conversation between Lieutenant-Colonel John Roberts and the author during the twenty-fifth anniversary *Uganda* Falklands War reunion at Southampton on 20 April 2008.
6. The term 'Third Location Decompression' (TLD) has only been developed officially since 2005. It represents the start of the post-operation winding-down process whereby those soldiers who have been deployed to an operational theatre move out of the theatre to an intermediary location for some days before returning to their peacetime home base. In other words 'troops who fight together begin to unwind together'. Troops from Afghanistan, and formerly Iraq, stop off in Cyprus for thirty-six hours in order to relax. But this does not even begin to compare with the TLD of the Gurkhas and other troops on board *Uganda* in 1982! Source: *King's College Centre for Military Health Research: A fifteen year report, September 2010*, p. 33.

Pwun-pwun. Hwun-hwun.
The fight is chaotic yet one is not subject to
  chaos.
Hwun-hwun. Dwun-dwun.
One's form is round and one cannot be defeated.
— Sun Tzu[1]

No collective stress debriefings, such as the concept of Trauma Risk Management[2] pioneered much later by the Royal Marines, took place on board *Uganda*. Perhaps subconsciously I needed that, hence my writing draft one of a book manuscript on board which would be published twenty-one years later after eleven more drafts. However, would the fatalistic Gurkhas with their different culture have benefited from stress debriefings? Nigel Price, a far more experienced Gurkha British officer than me, articulated this 'non-issue' as follows:

> Somehow, I suspect there is not a big PTSD problem with the Nepalis. This will sound utterly brutal, but I think that by the time they enlist, the hill boys have been so inured to hardship from birth, that they are considerably more emotionally and psychologically robust than their western counterparts. Also, when they go back, they cannot rest on any laurels or rely on any welfare state – barely even the most rudimentary medical system. In a way, that is when the real hardship begins! Life existing day after day in an unforgiving environment, made even worse now by the Maoist insurrection. It might make life in the cocoon of the regiment seem a past wonderland – even (dare I suggest) in a war environment. I do realise that could sound callous in the extreme, but it is their mindset. I also suspect there is a Nepali-style *macho*'ness (bad word, but you know what I mean) whereby there could be a degree of *sharam* (shame) in admitting the 'weakness' as they could perceive it of PTSD. They are probably quite Victorian in that respect.[3]

When combined together with their inate fatalism, their close family support, their pride in the Regiment and comradeship that I had observed and which is so strong in a Gurkha unit, all these factors seemed to have had the effect of containing or, arguably, even preventing the PTSD problem. So apart from one Gurkha in D Company who, out of the blue, completely broke down on 29 July and remained under medical observation all that day, Nigel's judgement about the Gurkhas and PTSD appeared to be accurate. According to Jeremy McTeague, the Gurkha in question was one of the keenest and brightest young soldiers in the Company and was well-known for his charm and diligence, but he never really recovered from this particular episode. However Dilkumar Rai had no traumatic stress problems. On the contrary his psychological 'decompression' was an enjoyable affair:

> The day we were waiting for a long time finally arrived, I was very excited and could not wait to arrive at Queen Elizabeth Barracks (in Church Crookham) and

take my long Nepal leave.[4] The environment on our journey back home was of course completely different to going to the Falklands. Everyone was thrilled to be going back and more relaxed as we made use of the large entertainment facilities in the ship i.e. cinema, Nepali Culture show, inter-Company water polo competition and many others.

Nineteen year-old Clive Jefferies, the 16 Field Ambulance medic who had survived the Argentine air strike on *Sir Galahad* and then went on to work in the Ajax Bay 'Red and Green Life Machine' Field Hospital [5] from 9-20 June before returning to Fitzroy, was already on board *Uganda* when the Gurkhas embarked. His Grandfather had served with the Gurkhas in Palestine during the First World War, but this was Jefferies first close encounter with them. He described how their 'decompression' included improvised play:

> There was almost a feeling of relief amongst our unit that we were taking the journey home with such polite, civilised, accommodating and agreeable people who I had heard so much about from my grandfather. I was struck by their incredible cheerfulness and engaging and outgoing friendliness that seemed totally at odds with their fearsome reputation [...] A couple of days out from Stanley, *Uganda* hit a big storm (and) the crew battened everything down including all the hatches. Unable to sleep that evening we went to the stern of the ship which was used as a recreation room. Several Gurkhas were also there and appeared to have [...] definitely gained their sea legs. So regardless of culture and race, and because we were all teenagers, it was soon discovered that if you waited until the ship got to the top of its pitch and then jumped as the deck fell away, you suddenly found yourself six feet in the air. The actual feeling was like being eight feet up. Almost weightless, we then all crashed onto the deck simultaneously amidst spontaneous laughter.[6]

However a few Gurkhas had not embarked *Uganda*. And at least one of them, Jeremy McTeague, suffered by not being exposed to such a 'decompression' because he encountered some difficulties in re-calibrating to normal life for the first three to four days once back in the UK:

> We had spent three weeks in Fox Bay West recuperating, our only worry being how to stop one of the Islanders in his constant attempts to 're-liberate' one of the Mercedes.
>
> It was, in retrospect, an important time which allowed us to talk together about our personal experiences in an unstructured, and yet safe and comfortable way. Yet this was not the purpose of the exercise, which was to clear up the mess left by the Argentines and to mark out and clear minefields. I sometimes wonder what the effect on us all would have been if we had been taught how best to use such a period of respite? [7]
>
> Finally our orders came through to return to the UK. I was tasked to be in the Rear Party – something I was less than chuffed about until I saw the smile on Mike's face as he explained that the rear party would be flying back and would

therefore arrive home long before the Main Party. The latter departed and, as ordered, I made my way back to Stanley to meet up with Captain Kit Spencer and the doctor, Captain Martin Entwistle. We were billeted overnight in an abandoned semi-detached house near the Airport and spent a couple of days buying postcards, being interviewed by journalists and drinking heavily (NAAFI stores had arrived!).

We were told we would definitely be on the next morning's flight and should report at 11.00 hours. So after an extraordinarily massive liquid supper and long night's boozing, we headed for the Airport on 20 July. On reporting in, we were disdainfully informed by rather spruce RAF dispatcher that it would be a twenty-four hour non-stop flight. Kit asked him why he was so clean. As we waited mulling over the idea of the long flight without as much as a magazine to read, the Doc then had a brainwave and handed us each a sleeping pill out of his medical sack. Knocked back with the last dregs from our respective hip flasks we proceeded to stare down all the newly-arrived REMFs who were curiously eyeing us as we slouched filthy, ragged and pallid against anything solid enough to support us.

The line of men was growing long and snaked its way outside the dispersal building. As young officers we knew it was our lot to be the last on board. The Hercules transport aircraft started to fill up and men were being sandwiched in around a massive internal fuel tank, the size and shape of a water bowser. As the last three passengers we were called on board, given a paper lunch bag and told to sit on top of the fuel tank. The flight took off and we spent those next twenty-four hours medicated to the eyeballs trying not to sleep as we clung on to the slippery rounded surface of the fuel tank. Unfortunately for the poor souls sitting below us, we were not entirely successful in this tedious endeavour, and for the first three or four hours kept falling onto them.

On landing at Brize Norton the three of us were walking towards the terminal building in the warm morning air looking for a Gurkha driver when Kit, spying some waving civvies, asked if I thought anyone from my family would come to meet me. I replied emphatically that there was no way my family would come down from Scotland, particularly when the flight schedules were so arbitrary. His family came from Cumbria and so he agreed (with a sigh of relief shared by me) that we could get back to Church Crookham, clean up, rest and then take some well-earned leave – preferably in the constant company of a gorgeous and impressionable woman. No sooner were the words out of his mouth than a chorus of, 'Kit, Kit!' and 'Jeremy! Jeremy!' went up as we turned the corner into the main concourse. Our entire families had come to meet us. With tears and smiles (but unsurprisingly somewhat limited hugs) we were welcomed back by those a minute ago we had so cockily denied. The outflow of emotion stopped as fast as it erupted when we realised the presence of the other family and them of us. In what is probably best described as a 'British moment' everyone was introduced, polite enquires into health made, and gentle congratulations given.

Major Bill Dawson then stomped up and immediately put the collected company at ease with his easy smile and firm, but friendly (and most welcome) order to us to take one week's leave. Then I departed in the family car which, after a mile, was speeding through the country – with all windows down.

My parents had arranged that we would all stay with old family friends near Winchester on route back to Scotland and as we drove, they outlined their plans. I suddenly felt very uncomfortable, anxious and a sense of wanting to be left absolutely alone. I did not want to talk about my experiences, not out of any sense of painful memory, but because I knew immediately that my family would not be able to comprehend my experiences and thoughts. I felt in many ways (and still do) that to have witnessed humiliation is in itself humiliating, and even recounted second-hand, an element of it is likewise communicated.

Meanwhile training quickly had gathered pace during *Uganda*'s voyage back to Southampton. Gurkha BIT became most unpopular with the ship's crew as the latter were constantly woken early in the morning by the crashing of Gurkha boots onto the deck. We kept ourselves busy with other matters on board. For example there were five Gurkha educational courses and an Inter-Platoon Sports Competition. Colonel David was in daily contact via Marisat (maritime satellite telephone) with Bill Dawson and the latter indicated that the Battalion, after its UK arrival, would have to march through the local town of Fleet. Colonel David's diary entry of 21 July indicated the opposition to such a proposal, 'I spoke to him (Bill) ref. the march through Fleet. It's most unpopular with everyone. He'll try to get us off if he can.'

But Bill failed, much to the chagrin of the Gurkha British Officers who felt that the Battalion had not been involved operationally enough in the war to warrant such an embarrassment. Meanwhile the four Company Commanders were debriefing themselves collectively and presented their 'think-tank' findings of sixty-eight points on 26 July to Colonel David. This resulted in an update to the *Op Corporate 1/7GR/Immediate Debrief Points* written on 10 July in Goose Green. Twenty-four hours before our arrival at Ascension Island on 28 July my editing of *Operation Corporate 1/7GR Post Operation Report – Part II* took all day to complete. Back in the UK all that past week McTeague had been contending with domestic issues:

Re-entry to family life was hard. They were generous, thoughtful and bent over backwards to give me a hero's welcome. My sister, a student reading law at Edinburgh had decided to stay over in Glasgow for my leave. My old and good friends in Glasgow likewise gave me great support, but still I had an overwhelming sense that everything they discussed, planned and did was immaterial, superficial and just not important. What did it matter whether my mother wanted to know if she should buy yellow or blue curtains for the dining room? Getting enough to eat, and being in a constant state of readiness to face any threat – these were the important matters. Also I became reasonably depressed by what the future would hold. It just looked so flat and pedestrian.

Things came to a head quickly. The women in my mother's office had kindly held a collection and had sent a huge parcel of chocolate, cigarettes and other luxuries to my Gurkha platoon. This had never arrived: nevertheless my mother asked if I might go into the office and thank her colleagues. I was happy to oblige and after a round of pleasantries one old lady finally came up to me and demanded sternly as to how many Argies I had killed.

Decidedly taken aback by her directness and, frankly, blood-thirsty attitude, I could not coherently respond. She gave a harrumph! and marched off.

A little distressed and depressed I was relating the story to my family over dinner that night when my younger sister burst into tears, stood up and proceeded to give me the firmest talking to I had ever received. Not only was I self-absorbed, arrogant and rude, but I had no right to act in such a superior manner towards everyone. And did I have any idea of the worry that my family and friends had had for me?

She went on to relate how my father had driven from Glasgow through to Edinburgh on business and had decided, as a surprise, to visit her at her flat. Blissfully unaware of the effect this was about to have, he had knocked on her door. On opening it, she saw my father and immediately knew that he had come especially to break terrible news about me to her. My younger sister, safe at home in Edinburgh had, in one dreadful moment, had a worse experience of war than I ever had. This recognition sparked a sharp change in my attitudes and behaviour. I realised that I had to make a positive and active decision to regain my balance, my respect and consideration for others and to start thinking ahead to the future – not just my own but of those whose lives were interwoven with mine.

He returned to Church Crookham to welcome back the Battalion at Southampton on 9 August, and then marched through Fleet that same day. Dil:

We arrived at the same Southampton port but, this time with happiness and excitement. As we were approaching, there were small boats and ship coming our way to welcome us and thousands of people (friends, families and dignitaries) waiting to welcome us. Before we arrived at Queen Elizabeth Barracks, we were dropped off near the Fleet train station and marched along the planned route via Fleet town. Fleet local people were standing on the both sides of the road to welcome us home. Field-Marshall (then General) Bramall and some important person (I believe, a Fleet Councillor) were taking the salute.

Despite the march's unpopularity with the Gurkha BOs, Colonel David was also caught up in the heady atmosphere as his closing diary entry described:

We are due in UK at 11.00 hours. The march through Fleet is due at 16.00. I was up at 05.00. A lovely morning, but by 07.00 it was clouding over. There is great excitement of those on board. All the sailors are behaving like children – but the Gurkhas all take it in their stride! [...] Our reception was fantastic and the sort of thing that I will never forget. Our march through Fleet was amazing. I can't believe I have seen so many happy people.

Dil's final comments concerned his return to Nepal:

The arrival at Queen Elizabeth Barracks was truly exciting, followed by post-operational tour leave and the long-awaited Nepal leave. When I finally got to see my family, friends and relatives, I was very proud to talk about the war and tell them what exactly we have done and happened to us. One interesting thing I heard from my mother was that rumours reached her that I was injured during the war with my cousin Rifleman Baliprasad Rai. It was a worrying time for her, but she was relieved after receiving my letter that I sent from Fox Bay. I think it was a more jovial time for my mother and brother than me when I came back home.

On the whole, it was really a challenging as well as frightening time, but when I returned home unhurt with bags of experiences and stories to tell, I was really proud and all of it was rewarding. I think I did a good job as a young soldier, particularly as a platoon radio operator.

My post-Falklands War Confidential Report in summary reads: 'Rifleman Dilkumar Rai is a trustworthy soldier, who puts his duties before his own personal interest. An outstanding Rifleman who should make a good leader in the future.' [8]

The Battalion took a month's leave. The experience of McTeague's return to 'civilisation' and family struck a chord with that of Price's:

> I similarly felt glad to see parents and sister and family friends, but most wanted to be completely alone, or with fellow 7th Gurkha Rifles mates. My family put on a party and someone – a complete stranger – thanked me! In great embarrassment I wondered what the hell for!
>
> It all seemed very silly, but because their sentiments were all sincere and genuine I also felt that I was being thoroughly ungrateful. I quickly flew to West Germany to stay with my sister and her husband who lived in Munich and, with a pack, went off alone to walk in the Alps – which was wonderful and restorative. My brother-in-law apparently said to my sister that he felt he simply could not talk to me. I was morose and uncommunicative. It was totally my fault, not his. And their friends were very concerned for my safety as I had gone off to climb the Zugspitze completely alone. I was fine and did not give a toss, either about my fate, or about their concerns. It was all thoroughly selfish, I accept. I am sure that I came across as a stuck-up, self-centred prig. And I was. [9]

My young family went on holiday to Corfu, but once there I continued to write my book manuscript. I was tense, irritable and impatient with most. On our return to the UK and after leave was over, the Battalion resumed normal training. My writing obsession continued by getting up at 04.30 daily to write for three hours before work. In October I became the A Company Commander in command of 150 Gurkhas and, during that same Autumn, Colonel David gathered a postscript to his Operation Corporate experience. It was about an unholy mix-up:

> In the euphoria after the victory in the Falklands in 1982, some of us were lucky enough to be asked to go to dinner at No. 10 Downing Street. I was asked to attend at 7 for 7.30pm dressed in Mess Kit, and my wife was asked for 10.30pm for coffee. So that got us off to a good start.
>
> I did as was told and turned up with about seventy others all dolled up in our finery, and soon found myself talking with the Reverend David Cooper whom I had met down South. He was the famous 2 Para Chaplain and trainer of their Regimental snipers. All the much more important people were also there;

Generals, Admirals, Foreign Office Mandarins, Lord Mayors and members of the Cabinet led, of course, by the redoubtable 'Iron Lady'. I just knew that it was going to be an unforgettable occasion.

We were issued with a drink and engaged in small talk before suddenly we were led into a large room where the Prime Minister Margaret Thatcher was ushering us into position for a photograph – everybody dancing like schoolchildren to her calls of, 'No, General, more to your left!' and 'Come on, Admiral, we haven't got all day!' Eventually, when she was satisfied, the photograph that I still have on my study wall, was taken

We had a superb meal, great conversation, and enjoyed a notable speech by the Prime Minister which impressed at the time but which has since disappeared from my memory. Afterwards the girls arrived to round off a splendid evening that included a guided tour of the house by the Prime Minister. But all too soon the evening came to a close, and we lined up to make our farewells. As we were in the queue a young man approached me and asked me my name. I told him, and thought no more about it.

When it came to our turn I said to our hostess, 'Prime Minister, thank you very much indeed for a truly excellent evening.'

'Yes,' chipped in my wife, 'and thank you for including me!' At which point I seem to recall treading gently on her toe.

The Prime Minister looked at me resplendent in my Seventh Gurkha Winter Mess Kit, and remarked, 'Do you know, I was reading the works of the Reverend Smith only the other night. I never realised how much work he had done for the volunteer army in London in the 18th Century'.

This statement left me completely nonplussed, and my mouth opened like a gormless fish out of water. My mind raced ...

What on earth was she on about? What could I say?

There then followed what is generally called a 'pregnant pause' which was ended by the PM. 'Never mind,' she said, 'the world marvelled at that sermon you gave in Stanley!'

To this day I still wonder what she said to David Cooper.[10]

It was important that Gurkha lessons learnt in the Falklands-Malvinas War be not forgotten, so the Battalion's two-month Exercise Trumpet Dance at Fort Lewis in Washington State, USA during January and February 1983 provided a good environment for post-war training.

But ending the book with this would be too bland. What about the long-term effect that war leaves on those who have fought in it? My father with his customary understatement had told my wife just before the Battalion's return from the South Atlantic, 'When men come back from war they can be a bit difficult and want to make babies!' I proved no exception. The Battalion was posted to Hong Kong in April 2003 and, five months later, our third daughter, Kristina, was born at the British Military Hospital in Kowloon. She had severe Down's syndrome and four holes in her heart. Father was also clairvoyant in his emotional reaction to the news of her birth by remarking, 'This'll break them.' And eventually it did just that.

Perhaps not unsurprisingly I failed to shine as a 7th Gurkha Rifles officer during those fourteen months in Hong Kong, two of which were spent on an A Company overseas training exercise in Malaysia. Kristina had been suffering from frequent bouts of pneumonia and, whilst I was on this exercise, complications were detected with her heart. My Gurkha secondment ended in June 1984, but somehow I secured my dream job as a logistics staff officer in the NATO headquarters at Kolsås just outside Oslo, Norway. En route we transitted via my parents' West Sussex home where an unwelcome brown envelope from halfway round the world finally caught up with me. It contained a final unimpressive confidential report that covered my last three months of Gurkha service in Hong Kong. A few additional adverse comments had been written by a Brigadier who did not know me and whom I had never met. While gazing at those words of this so-called Senior Reporting Officer I decided there and then that Norway would be the final port of call in my military career. Fifteen homes – with another two coming up in Norway – in twelve years of marriage had been enough. And I vowed that similar remarks would be never written again about my work performance.

So the next three and a half years were excellent professionally. A previously reserved person by nature, I noticed the beneficial effect of Falklands' post-traumatic growth. But matters continued to be fraught privately with Kristina undergoing two open-heart operations in successive years. My posting had been scheduled for two years only, but her problems enabled me to gain an eighteen-month extension at Kolsås to January 1988. However, informed that my next posting would be to Blackpool and the 2nd Battalion, Light Infantry as the HQ Company Commander, i.e. boss of the cooks and bottle-washers, this news merely hastened my desire to retire from the Army. I was forty years old and spoke Norwegian with passable fluency but with plenty of room for improvement. My challenge was to find a civilian job in Norway. The lucky break came in October 1987. One day while reading the national daily newspaper *Aftenposten* I noticed a job advertisement for the position of a Scandinavian Airlines Security Manager in Norway. As the only Brit of the 120 persons who applied, I was most surprised to be offered the job after three interview rounds.

Two weeks after joining the airline at Oslo's Fornebu Airport in early 1988, another major task was added to my job description: emergency response planning. I rejoiced. What could be better for a recently retired war veteran? With fourteen SAS air stations dotted up and down Norway the scope was immense. This also became a subconscious second bite at the 'Falklands-Malvinas apple' which might, I hoped, rectify a nagging unhealthy perception that I held of my performance during that war. But it would be not until two decades later that Alan Gibson (the former Lance-Bombardier in the Gurkha Battalion Tactical HQ) sent a veteran peer support message that had the effect of a balm being applied:

> You said that you felt you under-performed in your role. All I can say to this is that it was never noticeable from where I stood. We can all look back on parts of our lives and say that 'I could have done better here', or 'I made a mistake there' but we do as we do and nothing can ever change that.
>
> Just a thought for you, did you know that it is impossible for a human being to make a wrong decision? That is one hundred per cent absolutely true as every

decision we make, given the facts at the time, is the correct decision *at the time we make it.* If it was not, we would make the other one. It is only with hindsight that we realise it was wrong. Hindsight is a commodity that nobody has at that time. During a war that amount of time is compressed and taken away by many other factors, fear not being the least.

Trust me Mike, you did not under-perform. When you think of the amount of responsibility you carried and the scope for making very large cock-ups, you will see that none of us did a bad job from the top to the bottom.[11]

Little had been done in SAS Norway for operational security and emergency response planning, so my work started from scratch. There were also the additional tasks of acquiring greater fluency in Norwegian, getting to grips with a new culture, and becoming acquainted with new colleagues and civilian work environment. I was motivated and on leaving SAS nearly nine years later, plans, procedures and a trained emergency response organisation of nearly 300 persons had been built up. In addition to the operational work, a leaf was taken out of the Gurkha book with training receiving a high priority. This included the design, construction and delivery of nine two-day security courses, forty-six one-day station emergency response courses (for 580 personnel), fifteen two-day emergency response seminars, ten station input-response simulation exercises, and lecturing on sixty SAS Flight Academy and nine SAS global security courses.

I enlisted two well-known disaster psychiatrists of the Office of Disaster Psychiatry in Oslo, Doctors Lars Weisæth and Pål Herlofsen, to lecture in the seminars. They taught me, in an enlightening yet simple way, the theory of traumatic stress and psychosocial support after my 'hands on' experiences from the Falklands-Malvinas War. The knowledge they gave me was a powerful tool. Post-traumatic growth intensified and manifested itself into ultra-ambition and work levels combined with a surge of energy, dynamism and self-confidence over a sustained period. Unlike the 'bad news story' of post-traumatic stress disorder which the media often writes about in exaggerated terms,[12] PTG is scarcely mentioned in the public domain because of its 'good news' quality. But, as I was to discover, if not reined back in a non-post-conflict culture it can lead to disastrous personal consequences. While stretching myself to the limit and expecting others to do likewise, I was also displaying considerable existential authority (EA). Such a condition is frequent in war veterans; even Homer's *Iliad* depicts EA affecting the soldier who has returned from the perils of war. Jeremy McTeague's definition was spot on:

I have found recently that my ability to accept authority has weakened considerably. This may be tied up to natural ageing but, since my return from the conflict, I recognise that I internally question the right and qualifications of each of my superiors to tell me what to do. It is very simple. They have never had to manage under the circumstances that I have experienced, and I am convinced (wrongly I am sure) that they know little about *real* management of people other than what they have been taught on courses. They have not had the ultimate hands-on experience of exercising high-stakes leadership.[13]

This PTG-EA combination became my ticking time-bomb spiced with an Homeric combat veteran's long return 'voyage home' undertone.[14] I was also burning the candle at both ends. The problems with Kristina increased and sleep at night was a rare commodity. In 1990 came the first separation from my wife. We reconciled – only to be followed by two more separations. Finally I collapsed while on a long weekend visit to my parents at Easter 1993. On return to Norway pain manifested itself everywhere in my body. This included terrible headaches, an inability to lift my arms above shoulder level and, worst of all, no energy. For example, driving the car just 200 metres became an impossible task and my chest felt it was imploding when I attempted to work on my office computer. This was a breakdown of the much under-estimated link between body and mind when the former refuses to do what the latter demands. Unable to comprehend what was happening, I was admitted to hospital for five days. Tests were done but, somatically, nothing amiss was discovered. But at least there was a diagnosis, and 'chronic fatigue syndrome' resulted in six months of sick leave.

I made a gradual recovery and returned to work. SAS were losing money and, as a result, major changes were made to the top management in Stockholm. My original boss (a professional in terms of security and emergency response) was inexplicably replaced by a person with no background in these twin disciplines. There was a hidden but important strategic signal here that I failed to pick up. Personnel working in these disciplines were unpopular with those who had power and wrestled with airline financial budgets.

Then on 3 November 1994 a Bosnia War refugee hijacked flight SK347 just after take-off from Bardufoss in North Norway. There had been no security control of passengers or their hand baggage in line with the bizarre cost-savings policy that the Norwegian civil aviation authorities had at that time. Allegedly armed with a hand-grenade concealed in a pocket of his coat, his ultimate demand after landing at Bodø was that the aircraft be flown to Gardermoen Airport, north of Oslo and then onto Sarajevo as a political protest against the war. Having just returned from a debriefing of my civil aviation crisis management exercise that had been designed, constructed and delivered to Norwegian Government's crisis information group the previous week, I was appropriately prepared to deal with this unexpected challenge and personally activated the SAS Norway emergency response plan and its organisation.

Another SAS McDonnell Douglas MD-82 aircraft of the same internal configuration as the hijacked MD-82 was flown to Gardermoen so the police anti-terror unit could exercise a possible storming of the hijacked aircraft. After landing, the hijacker requested to speak to the police negotiator into a secure voice system, but this was not available as it was still being transported to Gardermoen from Oslo. The police could have used a land-line plugged into one of the eleven points available on the aircraft's fuselage or wings. There was enough cable available for the negotiator to have been out of sight to the hijacker. This was a secure system and all equipment was available, but it was not used. The result was that negotiations with the hijacker were conducted on an Air Traffic Control open radio frequency which the Norwegian commercial TV2 station then tapped into and broadcast. And strangely no experienced SAS pilot was incorporated as a liaison function into the police crisis management organisation. His knowledge would have been invaluable in this situation.

The hijack would only last for a total of only eight hours and was terminated peacefully that evening without any injuries. There had been numerous weaknesses revealed with the plans I had written, but the airline's overall emergency response succeeded. Like the immediate aftermath of the Falklands-Malvinas War, my personal reaction post-incident was enduring five successive nights of insomnia. But unlike in the post-war episode, a sleeping pill eventually solved the problem.

I attended a police debriefing and spoke briefly about the SAS emergency response. An aircraft hijacking is a rare event for any airline. Lessons learnt had to be captured immediately, so I spent six weeks writing a forty-five page post-incident report which concluded with nineteen findings and recommendations. In the New Year I staged a full-day debriefing for nearly 100 people from SAS, Civil Aviation Administration and police. With the benefit of hindsight, perhaps at some point that day the latter were irritated by my EA. This debriefing was followed up by a half-day version presented at the SAS Head Office in Stockholm. But the only formal reaction from my Swedish masters was a poorly-written three-page executive summary report. Devoid of analysis it only described the hijack and then highlighted in two sentences the need to refine SAS Norway's contingency plans. Maybe that PTG-EA combination had a grating effect. I knew too much about everything and everybody: and probably was perceived now as a 'threat' to the system.

As ordered, I amended my emergency response plans radically before the arrival of 1996 – my *annus horribiis* plus. On 23-24 April that year I attended a working group meeting of Civil Aviation Administration, police, fire service and airline representatives to discuss the emergency response planning for Stavanger Airport in southern Norway. An aggressive debate ensued between the young police officer responsible for this contingency plan and Civil Aviation Authority representatives who wanted to amend some of its contents. After two hours of listening patiently, I chipped in by pointing out that the current plan obliged airline personnel to become involved with dead and injured passengers after an aircraft accident. This placed an unfair burden of responsibility on such personnel as they did not have the relevant training. Also I highlighted other aspects of the plan which were problematic. The police officer did not like my intervention. Prestige was at stake. He absented himself from the following day's deliberations and, instead, reported me to the SAS Station Manager at Stavanger for disagreeing with his plan. Next day, back in Oslo, I received a summons to report to my boss at the SAS Head Office in Stockholm. Twenty-four hours later he showed me the yellow card and insisted that the police must not be irritated in future, even if their emergency response planning was flawed. The matter had become an illogical political issue.

Fate had already determined what would happen next. On 22-24 May I attended the bi-annual European Civil Aviation Conference on security at, of all places, the Queen Elizabeth II Conference Centre in central London. There were 400 civil aviation security delegates present and an opportunity existed to ask questions after each presentation listed on the comprehensive programme. There was no media present. During the first day a Lufthansa pilot spoke about his experiences of an aircraft hijack in 1993. It motivated me to probe further. So I received the microphone at the end of his presentation and asked two questions relating to the airline's lessons learnt and need to amend emergency response plans post-incident. To illustrate this I mentioned the SK347 hijacking and requirement to re-write my plans post-incident after major weaknesses had been identified, and that there had been communication problems with the police without providing further details. But the pilot's response was without substance and I ceased my polite inquisition.

My life had spun on a five pence piece during those two short minutes. Also present was a Norwegian senior police officer who had been responsible for directing the authorities' response to the SK347 hijacking. Two days later, at the end of the conference, I was informed that the Norwegian policeman had so disliked my remarks in open forum that he was going to report me to the SAS Head Office at Stockholm. Five minutes later I stopped him on the way out of the conference centre. He merely confirmed his disagreement and forthcoming intention – and strode on. My heart sank into my boots. The red card was about to come my way.

However describing effect, not cause, is my prime aim with this bizarre story. As promised, the Norwegian policeman's complaint was duly received by the bearded Danish SAS Senior Vice-President of Station Services. Summoned to the SAS Norway Personnel Department on 31 May, I was informed that my ejection from the airline would occur on 1 August and that re-location to an 'outplacement' company would assist me in acquiring a new job. The Norwegian policeman had got what he wanted. Seear was to be sacrificed on the altar of political expediency.

This was a personal disaster. I continued to work as normally as possible. But throughout June I had to endure either no sleep at night, or waking at 02.00 in a cold sweat unable to fall asleep again. Headaches, apathy, isolating myself from others, depression, extreme anxiety, repeated self-blame for this situation and often a sense of being on high alert, all contributed to make this a most uncomfortable experience. Some of these symptoms, I told myself, indicated a form of PTSR, but *not* PTSD. Meanwhile work continued as well as making scheduled trips to Tromsø, Bergen and Stockholm. On 19 June a second meeting took place with the Personnel Department. Midway I walked out in protest at the unlawful dismissal process taking place. Despite a SAS Norway Head of Department's offer to me of another job, the bearded Dane must have intervened because the Personnel Director refused later to endorse such a move. Whatever the cost, my removal from the airline was to be prioritised.

The month ended with a family holiday in Egypt from 28 June to 7 July. Unsurprisingly it proved no success. My alarmed wife's observation of her husband's depression and deteriorating condition was endorsed by a friendly female SAS company doctor on our return to Norway. So she made an appointment for me to see a psychiatrist which was repeated another three times that month. This was a 'first' for me. So was the next of becoming a member of a trade union, SAS Management Forum (SMF). My father would have turned in his grave if he had known. But it was an extraordinary time in my life which required extraordinary measures.

I returned to work in the middle of July and carried out my final training activity – an emergency response input-response exercise at the North Norway SAS station at Alta before the 1 August 'execution day' arrived. But although my job as the Security and Emergency Response Planning Manager was gone, the airline still formally employed me. My wife's brother was a lawyer and he provided legal assistance. The Personnel Department was obliged to accede to his demand of providing me with another office. I moved into this on 2 August, but spent the next ten days twiddling my thumbs doing nothing. This was a tactic to 'freeze' me psychologically out of the system. It was the most humiliating time of my life: partially offset later by the satisfaction of learning, via a third party, of the bearded Dane's irritation with my intransigence.

SMF disputed vigorously (God bless them) the Norwegian policeman's assertion that it would be a provocation if I continued to deal with security. Alleging my dismissal from the airline was in violation of *Arbeidsmiljøloven* (The Working Environment Act), SMF offered to fund further legal assistance and set up a meeting with a lawyer specialising in employment disputes. An hour-long discussion with him resulted in an assessment that I had 'more than a fifty per cent chance' of winning any eventual court case. But was I interested in such a potentially draining matter? Even if successful, what job would be given to me by an unwilling employer? My Falkland-Malvinas War experience and civil aviation qualifications provided me with the ultimate motivation of continuing to pursue a career in emergency response planning and training. It was my niche in life. I could not contemplate anything else professionally. So the bearded Dane got what he wanted and, on 12 August immediately prior to another psychiatric consultation, I terminated my employment by signing the execution order to become a *desaparecido* of SAS. With hindsight I was in no fit condition to take such an important decision. Nonetheless next day I re-located to the outplacement company, but was told immediately by the Managing Director to take a fortnight's break.

So Seear's 'Homeric voyage home' continued, including a few more psychiatric consultations during that 'holiday' period. My wife and her family could not understand my 'over-reaction'. But how can civilians understand how it is to fight in a 'normal' war and then, as a combat veteran, be confronted fourteen years later with another where such underhand methods had been employed? Years later I explained in *Hors de Combat*:

> My second bite at the '(Falklands-Malvinas) apple' had turned rotten completely crushing my professional ego. Refusing to accept the fact that, in reality, I had grown out of my job, this event also proved to be that much talked-about war veterans' 'trigger in later life' which re-awakens past battlefield traumas. I endured a prolonged sense of powerlessness, just like that on the last night of the war when we came under intensive enemy artillery and mortar fire behind Tumbledown.[15]

My depression deepened even more. At the end of August I began 'work' at the outplacement company as an unemployed 'candidate' who had to be taught how to increase my chances of success with job applications. But I continued to cut myself up mentally in the most brutal fashion. My thoughts turned back to the Falklands-Malvinas War. A lightning-fast death on the Tumbledown battlefield would have been better than the events of this long, hot summer of 1996. Such a postulation bred an even more dangerous one. Perhaps suicide would be the best way out of all these problems? Winter Norway can be harsher than austral winter Falklands. At times savagely cold with double-digit sub-zero temperatures and chill-factor dangers, Norway's inhospitable subarctic winter environment could complete 'the job' efficiently. I played with the thought of wandering out alone, not into *fjellene* (the mountains) and their deep snow, but into a dense forest situated in an isolated *dal* (valley) where the climatic phenomena of inversion creates much colder temperatures. Only my soul would exit the forest again.

At this stage I lived isolated in the cellar of my home. Eating ceased to be important and consequence of this would be a loss of eleven kilos of weight in the next four weeks. Going to bed with clothes on was a common occurrence – and a classic symptom of a severe depression. Concurrently the tempo of psychiatric consultations was increased significantly. There were another twelve in all that month. During several of these I had to fill out a formal psychological test questionnaire which would provide a reading on the expected improvement in my mental well-being. But when these were completed, the result always edged up higher than the previous one: indicating increased anxiety and pessimism. By the middle of the month my test score stood at sixteen points. Next time in the discussion chamber it had increased dramatically to twenty-six. The threshold for prescribing an anti-depressant was thirty, therefore as a pre-emptive strike, my conversation partner issued me with a prescription for my ammunition: the anti-depressant Tolvan. But this, Seear's first encounter with *lykkepillen* (the happiness pill), did not bring any smile. On the contrary, it was totally ineffective. So a week later a tactical switch was made to more ammunition affording a bigger punch: Seroxat. Yet as imminent events were to prove, this *lykkepillen* type would also fall into the same category as the first.

There was also another side of the coin in that awful month. My 'work' at the outplacement company included frequent meetings with the Managing Director. These always contained great optimism about the prospects of my acquiring a new job and assurances that the average time 'candidates' required for acquiring a new job was about five to six months. But in six months I would be fifty, was my overriding thought, and who gets employment at that age? So the effect of these get-togethers wore off after only a couple of hours, and I allocated them the appropriate Norwegian name of *surstoffmøter* (oxygen meetings). The Managing Director, who was a well-meaning man, became quite irked when I told him. Also his contingency plan, I added, for dealing with such an extreme 'candidate' as me needed a revision. I offered my services to do the job, but he never gave it to me. Afterwards the remainder of my day was spent in one of the company's quasi-offices for us 'candidates' where gazing for hours out of a window contemplating defeat in the war and my SAS *desaparecido* fate became my sole (in)activity. Could this have been how many Argentine troops felt after the unconditional surrender had been signed in Stanley?

Some of the other 'candidates' observed the British war veteran's odd behaviour and became quite concerned. On Fridays we would be invited to eat *bløtekake* (cream cake) and witness a successful 'candidate' or two bounce a ping-pong ball into a large glass gold-fish bowl half-full of other ping-pong balls. This was to celebrate their escape from 'jail' by their productive networking which had landed them a new job. But in my depressed state of mind no opportunity existed at all of my taking aim at that elusive target.

Finally, D-day arrived on Friday 27 September in the psychiatrist's office. Hyperventilating, I could not stop myself. The dam suddenly burst and I cried for half an hour.

Flashback. I was back on board *QE2* with Padre Peter Brooke of the Welsh Guards and thirteen days to run prior to the Gurkha landing at San Carlos.

The psychiatrist became frightened and a box of Kleenex was pushed in my direction. It was obvious he had never treated a war veteran before.

'*Ta deg selv sammen!* (Pull yourself together),' he ordered eventually; but then shortly afterwards in a softer tone when referring to my waterworks display, '*Jeg tror at du trengte det.* (I think you needed that.)'

He decided that my nervous (emotional?) breakdown was so severe that it would become my compulsory three-week entry ticket into Blakstad Hospital under the aegis of Section 3 of the Norwegian Psychiatric Health Care Act. This was a unique event: for which other member of the 1982 British Task Force has been consigned to such an institution in Norway?

The anxious psychiatrist made a phone call to my wife. Eventually she arrived and the situation was explained. He gave her a taxi requisition order. 'It'll be the safest way of getting him to the hospital,' he told her.

But we ignored his instructions and she drove me in our car to this well-known psychiatric hospital. I tried to rest in the front passenger seat, but battled against a strange whistling sound that swirled continuously in my ears. On arrival we were ushered into a small room containing just a bed and a chair. After a while my wife left. I collapsed on the bed, an exhausted heap of humanity. Shortly afterwards a female psychiatrist, Dr Wenche Løbben, entered. She was accompanied by a male nurse.

Also her security guard in case I attacked her? I thought.

This was the most appalling state of affairs for a former British Army officer.

But Dr Løbben's first words were even more shocking.

'*Planlegger du å ta ditt eget liv?* (Are you planning to take your own life?)'

I took her point immediately. The question had the desired effect and initiated a deep train of thought about my predicament. I managed to deduce that 'planning it' was in a totally different league from just 'thinking about it'.

We had a conversation in Norwegian while she wrote notes. There were more questions: and then she left the room with her 'security guard'.

I could not help thinking in those next six hours that passed in this 'casualty department' before my transfer to Ward 2B that my British Army past held much missed comforts and securities as well those occasional terrors. And so began, next to the Falklands-Malvinas War, the strangest experience in my life which I would come to label as my 'time-out from life'. A male nurse showed me my patient's journal and provided a standing invitation to record my thoughts in it. So next evening I obliged:

> I find the staff pleasant, but intellectually find myself rather like Robinson Crusoe on the proverbial desert island. I find little inclination to stare at the television set which is continuously switched on from early morning to late at night. In other words there is a real danger of this particular patient becoming intensely bored with this existence. My problem is depression brought about by a series of problems caused basically by myself and no one else. I find myself in a complete cul-de-sac in my life at the age of forty-nine – soon fifty. It is little surprise that I blame myself for the reasons that I am placed in here.

The treatment regime at Blakstad contained the classic components of conversation, drink, food and a bed to sleep. Indeed these were the same provided to me for a fortnight in the home of Keith Baillie, the Postmaster of Goose Green, after the Gurkhas had returned from the Tumbledown and Mount William battlefield. But in Blakstad this was reinforced by my intake of Seroxat (anti-depressant) and Imovane (sedative). I slept badly and suffered from such a severe depression that even participating in the patients' gentle daily morning physical exercise session or joining in the silk painting group proved impossible. It was more comfortable to isolate myself in my own room during the afternoon and evening. On Sunday, my third day 'inside', I talked to Wenche Løbben who would be in charge of my treatment. She wrote in my journal:

> I have talked a lot with the patient at the weekend and he provided a good contact.(I) have a Mike (here) with a great need to be seen, heard and tell his 'story'. Says he thinks it is easier to talk to female staff about his situation.

There was also a daily patients' meeting at 10am which obviously attempted to re-introduce a degree of structure to the lives of those who attended. I was passive at my first meeting but afterwards, and in accordance with my request, a shuttle of six female nurses, Turid, Hege, Liv, Gunn, Tanya and Lotte, began to get me talking. However it would be Lotte Rosenqvist, a Thai-born Swede, who was assigned eventually as my regular nurse point of contact. This Florence Nightingale was dedicated in her task with the Falklands-Malvinas War veteran. We agreed that all our conversations would be in English, while Norwegian would be used with all the other staff. On Day Five Lotte noted in the journal:

> He is in the grieving phase, sits a lot and thinks about his life situation, what has happened and why. Active with nurse contact, tells openly about his feelings and weaknesses. Has a heavy head and not motivated for anything. Trembles a little, side-effect of the medicine? Tired, has slept during the day. The patient has been more open and is beginning to see situations and consequences of them. He thinks a lot about the reasons for this depression.

I was brimming with anxiety and at times felt like two persons: a professional one and a Mike which was very frustrating. Worried about an inability to sleep and not looking forward to that night, I asked for and received an increased dose of Imovane. My Seroxat dose also followed suit. But despite my predicament there was also a gradual awareness that other patients were worse off than me. One girl was a rape victim and suffered from PTSD. There was a teenage girl who tried to commit suicide by slashing her wrists. And on another occasion a newly-admitted patient was brought screaming into the ward during the small hours. Occasionally an alarm would sound in the middle of the night indicating help was required in another hospital ward. Slowly a degree of equilibrium began to return. The support of the staff was invaluable. One told me in no uncertain terms that I had displayed 'a healthy reaction to an unhealthy society'. And another that 'it was only the best who were admitted to the hospital' and 'don't let them break you'. But in retrospect, my situation did not even begin to compare with that of Miguel, the Argentine Malvinas War veteran in Vicente Zito Lema's play *Delirium Teatro*.

I became more active at the daily patients meeting, making improvised speeches on different themes: the patient's role, the disadvantages of *lykkepillen*, the nurse's facilitator role, and the service provided at 'Hotel Blakstad' which was 'far superior to any Radisson SAS Hotel'. Despite the beautiful Autumn colours outside, I remained inside and used my opportunity to talk and talk (or debrief?) inside the hospital about what had happened and my current situation. My wife started to visit me regularly as from Day Six which contributed to an increasingly better mood and form with positive future-orientated thoughts. On Day Seven Lotte updated the journal. Her entry, in effect, described my PTG consequences:

> The patient seems to have a bad conscience about himself and the situation he is in. Thinks a lot about the past and what can have caused the different conditions. He says that work influenced negatively the possibility to create a good family atmosphere when his job demanded much and left family time to nil. He will try to get a balance in the future between job and family. The treatment period is confirmed to be about three to four weeks where leave was mentioned as a possibility in the future.

My improvement continued and on 7 October (Day Eleven) I was transferred to Ward 4-1, having been judged now as 'no suicide danger'. Lotte wrote in the journal:

> He is in an incredibly good mood. Wants to be out in the ward with other people and not sit alone in his room. Seems both positive and future-orientated with his condition, is worried a little about work in the future. He feels that he is a little 'different' than other patients on the ward. Realises that in reality there are people who have lifelong problems and thinks about himself as being fortunately able to get better. He says from the start that he is very thankful and that he looks forward to leaves during the coming weeks.

Blakstad was under the westerly flight approach path for aircraft landing at Oslo's Fornebu Airport. And it was in my room in this new ward that I became aware of these aircraft, including those from SAS, flying high above me. Why were there not any red air alerts? I thought while my mind created images of circling SAS vultures. Perhaps that was why the following night and day were more problematic as my journal entry indicated:

> I decided not to take my sleeping pill last night. The result: no sleep and sweated right throughout the night. Conclusion: take the sleeping pill tonight! Fairly 'down' the first part of the day today, but came up again in the second part of the day (sorry – very poor written Norwegian!). Had a little more social contact with the others this evening plus a long chat on the telephone with my wife. She was rung up by a colleague from SAS and was informed that I am very much missed at my old job. It is both sad but also good to hear.

I saw a job advertisement next day on 9 October in the national newspaper *Aftenposten* and decided to apply for it. The first task was to write a CV, but panic slowly grew as my writing amounted to only three lines in four hours. Despite the whole exercise turning out be only of therapeutic value only as nothing would materialise from my eventual application to the potential employer, it nonetheless gave a positive lift in my mood during that weekend at home on my first leave. But the mistake was to use much time in drafting the application which caused, understandably, much irritation with my wife. I slept badly (without Imovane) and returned to Blakstad on the evening of Sunday, 13 October. Lotte's journal entry next day noted my improvement:

> He is in good form after the weekend leave at home (and) is seriously preoccupied with writing a job application to an advertisement from Thursday. All the morning and day he has been out in the ward with others. Sits and talks together about the weekend with others. Feels to be in form and is ready to go on leave as from tomorrow (Tuesday, 15 October). Thinks a lot about these few weeks in the ward, how much he has learnt to get nearer to his life situation and be able to tackle it in the correct direction.

There was also one more tactical change of *lykkepillen* type that day as I moved on from Seroxat to yet another: Fevarin. The following evening on 15 October I returned home for a second forty-eight hours of leave. That day had started well with a patients meeting where, according to my journal, I 'had participated with engaging enthusiasm when there was talk about stress and steadily more demands about making workplaces more efficient'. By now I was getting fed up with the anti-depressant and sedative diet and, on return from leave, also indicated my desire to be discharged from the hospital next day. My mutiny was countered by a furious Lotte who exclaimed, 'You're stupid! Take your medicine!' and later wrote in my journal:

> (He) has not slept well last night because Imovane was not taken. Patient refused at first to take his morning medicine, but took them after being persuaded of the importance of continuity of medicine intake. Is somewhat uncertain and anxious as to how he should mention his admittance to Blakstad in relation to an interview for a job. Humour-wise he is stable and focused on the future, family and work. Is happy and extrovert.

But there were still mood swings as Wenche Løbben's journal entry later observed:

> He seems tired and sad all the afternoon, but then got a bit better during the evening. Says he has had an exhausting day, and had slept badly the previous night.

Next day on 19 October, I returned home for my final forty-eight hour leave. Back at the hospital I attended the 10 a.m. patients meeting on 22 October, and said goodbye to those who had helped me before being discharged. Lotte even remarked, 'It was fun to work with you!' However my twenty-six days as a Blakstad patient would not bring an immediate end to the stress, so I had been given a supply of Fevarin to assist me in coping with 'normal' life. But a week or so after being discharged from the hospital, I flushed the lot down the toilet at home. Lotte would have been more than furious with me; on the other hand I had taken an independent decision which made me more than happy. I was going to survive on my own without any artificial support. Despite this patently unwise action which made me groggy for twenty-four hours because of my sudden *lykkepillen* 'withdrawal', it nonetheless represented a proud little victory.

Unemployment would continue for another nineteen months. My day consisted of ringing companies to find out if I was of interest to them, searching the newspaper for possible jobs, and drinking countless cups of coffee. Then my marriage inevitably broke down in the August of 1997 and I moved out of my home into a thirty square-metre basement flat much nearer Oslo. Depression attacked me again, but this time there would be no psychiatrists, no anti-depressants, and no sedatives. Struggling through this would be done alone. But there were also hidden positive opportunities which explain Sun Tzu's contention that 'one is not subject to chaos' although 'the fight is chaotic'. I was determined there would be no defeat because my response now would be without confusion. In this regard time was my ally. So to claw myself out of the *yin* of this deep black hole back up to the *yang* of normal life, I embarked on a six-year cathartic re-write of my book manuscript on the Gurkhas and Falklands-Malvinas War which had been drafted during the first two post-war years. The aim was to improve its quality to such an extent that it could be published.

Eventually life did change for the better. I lost my unemployment status in April 1998 and re-married, two years later. My new wife, Else, was also Norwegian. Further jobs and tasks in emergency response both nationally and internationally materialised as my book-writing continued. My search had already begun for one particular Argentine veteran, Nicolás Urbieta, whose unposted letters from the battlefield featured in the manuscript. The country's national newspaper *Clarín* had published a full-page story about us in 1997. Nicolás had been located, but he refused to meet me after an Argentine TV channel offered to fly me out to Argentina. Nonetheless the *Clarín* article attracted considerable attention and important contacts. It led eventually to my first visit to Argentina at the end March and beginning of April 2002 when I met a number of veterans.[16] These rewarding encounters created an excellent platform for possible future expeditions into the country. I lost no time because the act of reconciliation was not only therapeutic in itself but also with oneself.

In December 2002 I made a second visit to Argentina accompanied by Lars Weisæth. This eminent psychiatrist with a glittering global reputation on traumatic stress had become a good friend. He had given me moral support in the long-term aftermath of my unlawful dismissal *proceso*, and we had continued to collaborate professionally on crisis management training and other matters. Lars was the perfect travelling companion with a mutual interest in wanting to become acquainted with Argentine war veterans and their 1982 experiences. Also he possessed a keen interest in military history.

Before the visit I had established a further Buenos Aires contact in addition to independent TV producer, political analyst and Gurkha friend Alberto Peralta Ramos. This was Eduardo Gerding who arranged a meeting with eight veterans. I was intrigued to learn that two of them had been through similar unlawful dismissals as me. As a result they were still unemployed. I tried to encourage them by sharing my experience. It was a rewarding session of active veteran peer support. There was a survivor there from the Royal Navy's deadly torpedo attack on the cruiser *General Belgrano*, and a few had been at the Darwin and Goose Green battle. But those two without jobs as a result of their PTG-EA combination condition were experiencing a most difficult time. Veterans' long-term unemployment and resulting depression is an underrated suicide cause, so I tried to emphasise that there was 'always light at the end of the tunnel'.

As in my first visit, Lars and I travelled on to Córdoba province and the General Roca home of Marisa Clausen de Bruno. Regarded by many as the 'Mother of the Malvinas War veterans', she had helped me come to terms with myself in our letter exchanges when I was at the bottom of my post-Blakstad 'black hole'. She invited another six veterans to meet us. We discovered that one of them had problems and Lars was quick to assist by writing a medical prescription. My only regret was that Nicolás had not been among Marisa's guests, but I came away from this second experience with more constructive thoughts:

> The exchange was most positive, and I became convinced that veteran peer support is a most effective concept for assisting veterans who continue to suffer with traumatic stress reactions. Indeed I thought then, and still do, that a potential opportunity has been squandered by government and experts alike in not attempting to organise a unique bilateral project between Argentina and the United Kingdom on Falklands-Malvinas combat veterans' issues. Focus on the concrete challenges of humanity rather than the abstract notion of sovereignty might have brought the two countries closer together on the Falklands-Malvinas issue.[17]

Early in 2003 I informed Marisa about the July publication of my book *With the Gurkhas in the Falklands: A War Journal*. It would mark the end of my re-calibration to normal life. She replied with the news that her latest book *Entre tu mano y la mía* (Between your hand and mine) describing her initial contact with me, subsequent exchange of letters and first meeting in Argentina would also be published shortly.

Also the Córdoba City Book Fair was taking place in September. So could I return to Argentina at that time to make a joint book presentation at the Fair?

Notes

1. *The Art of War*, Chapter 5 – *Shih*.
2. TRiM: a new popular system of peer support and risk assessment carried out by trained unit personnel themselves, thereby making it better suited to military culture. From the *King's College Centre for Military Health Research: A fifteen year report, September 2010*, p. 33.
3. E-mail dated 23 December 2005.
4. The standard Gurkha six months leave in Nepal after continuous British Army service for a period of three years.

5. So named because it was a 3 Commando Brigade Field Hospital whose 'owners' and those who worked in it wore either green (Commando) or (Para) red berets. Many of the hospital's patients were also Royal Marine Commandos and paratroopers of the Parachute Regiment.

6. Clive Jefferies provided the author with this anecdote during the twenty-fifth anniversary *Uganda* reunion at Southampton on 20 April 2008. He retired from the British Army in 1993, but his admiration for the Gurkhas was undiminished. Four years later as a qualified state registered nurse he made the first of four trips to Nepal (over an accumulated period of twelve months) where he met many retired Gurkhas. His later visits to the country included voluntary work at the Tansen Mission Hospital in Sarurah, Chitwan district.

7. *Hors de Combat*, p. 59.

8. Dilkumar Rai continued to serve with D Company, 1st Battalion, 7th Duke of Edinburgh's Own Gurkha Rifles (which later became the 2nd Battalion, Royal Gurkha Rifles) and eventually became the Company Sergeant Major. He married Prashanna during his third Nepal leave in June 1987 and was granted married accompanied service at that point. In 1994 he was promoted to Lieutenant (Queens Gurkha Ofiicer) and left his 'home' of D Company to serve in various appointments within and outside the Battalion. Apart from Falklands, Dilkumar served on operational tours of duty in East Timor, Sierra Leone, Bosnia and Northern Ireland during his twenty-eight year British Army career. He was awarded the Long Service and Good Conduct Medal and Queen's Jubilee Medal, and eventually reached the rank of Major (QGO) in 2006 to become Second-in-Command, 2nd Infantry Training Battalion at the Infantry Training Centre in Catterick, UK. He retired from the Army in October 2008 and is now working in Nepal as a Gurkha Area Welfare Officer. His son, Diwas, and daughter, Pradita, became UK University undergraduates in 2009. Dilkumar summed up his philosophy of life as follows: 'I am a great believer in luck, God, hard work, friends and family support.'

9. E-mail dated 1 December 2011.

10. *Ibid.* dated 15 June 2006.

11. *Ibid.* dated 2 January 2008.

12. Professor Simon Wessely, Director of the King's College Centre for Military Health Research in the UK, carried out a study in 2010 on what, post-deployment, had happened to troops who had served in Iraq and Afghanistan between 2005 and 2009 in addition to those who had not been deployed. Unlike newspaper reports which were expecting a tsunami of PTSD cases, Wessely's research revealed that the rates of PTSD remained stable among regular Armed Forces at between three and four per cent. Alcohol problems were a much greater threat. – *Defence Focus* magazine, Issue 242, July 2010, page 19.

13. *Hors de Combat*, p. 60.

14. American psychiatrist Jonathan Shay has argued 'convincingly' in his book *Odysseus in America: Combat Trauma and the Trials of Homecoming* published in 2002, that Odysseus' decade-long and critical event-filled voyage home with returning veterans from the battle of Troy, 'is actually a metaphor for the considerable time

it may take for a combat veteran to become a civilian citizen again'. – From an essay entitled *Post-Traumatic Stress Reactions: A Hindrance or Facilitator to Peace?* by Lars Weisæth and Trond Heir in the book *The Genres of Post-Conflict Testimonies: Studies in Post-Conflict Cultures 6*, p. 325.

15. *Hors de Combat*, p. 11.
16. *With the Gurkhas in the Falklands*, Chapter 25.
17. *Ibid.*, Epilogue.

> *Therefore, one hundred victories in one hundred*
> *battles is not the most skilful.*
> *Subduing the other's military without battle is*
> *the most skilful.*
>
> – Sun Tzu[1]

I attended my first 7th Gurkha Rifles Regimental Association Reunion at Netheravon on Saturday, 13 September 2003. It was an enjoyable event and also provided an opportunity for me to sell a few copies of my book published two months before. Already I had received a number of letters which confirmed my writing efforts had not been in vain. For example, Reg Woollard of Lutterworth, Leicestershire:

> The first book I read about the Gurkhas was *Bugles and a Tiger* by John Masters. I was captivated by his powers of description and love of those gallant loyal warriors. (*With the Gurkhas in the Falklands*) conveys some of that magic – just the word 'Gurkha', is enough to stir the hearts of men and put fear in the enemy. Such a book is difficult to put down.

But more important was my return to Argentina for a third time to make a formal presentation of the book at the Córdoba City Book Fair and, secondly, thank those Argentines who had assisted me in my writing. So forty-eight hours after the Gurkha Reunion, I boarded my late-evening British Airways flight to Buenos Aires via São Paulo. After my fifteen-hour journey, a surprisingly cold winter's day of four degrees centigrade greeted me at the Argentine capital's airport. A taxi drove me quickly to my usual haunt of the Imperial Park Hotel in central Buenos Aires, little more than a stone's throw from the Plaza de Mayo and *Casa Rosada* (the pink building) Presidential Palace from where General Galtieri, the Head of the Military Junta, harangued tens of thousands of excited Argentines there in those dramatic April days of 1982. Lunch was followed by an interview with freelance journalist Guadalupe Barriviera who wanted to write an article for a well-known weekly magazine. She had interviewed me eighteen months before, and her article in *Clarín* attracted considerable interest. In the evening I met my old acquaintances from previous visits, Alberto Peralta Ramos and Eduardo Gerding. Both had provided me with useful contacts and information that were included in the book.

The following day, on 17 September, I contacted Colonel Peter Reynolds, the Defence Attaché (DA) at the British Embassy. He was also a Royal Marine Commando and Falklands-Malvinas War veteran, so it was most appropriate to provide two copies of the book to him and the British Ambassador, Sir Robin Christopher. I was privileged that evening to enjoy another three marvellous surprises provided by the irrepressible Alberto. He was acquainted with many high-ranking officers in the Argentine Army, including Brigadier-General Mario Benjamín Menéndez, former Military Governor of the Malvinas' Islands and Commander-in-Chief of the Argentine Land Forces garrison on the Islands in 1982. We met on my first visit to Buenos Aires when I had promised him a copy of my book. If ever one Argentine should learn the truth of what the Gurkhas did during the war and afterwards then it had to be him. Alberto had arranged this second meeting in the same Buenos Aires restaurant as before.

On arrival I shook hands with the retired Brigadier-General. His face continued to bear a slightly haunted look and, after we sat down, he immediately recalled gravely in good English, 'The war was a war of principles for both sides.' Over a cup of coffee we soon settled into animated conversation and he thanked me profusely for the book and five of its illustrations in the form of watercolour prints drawn by my mother. We spent twenty minutes together as Alberto took a number of photographs. 'My son was an officer in the 5th Infantry Regiment at Port Howard on West Falkland during the war,' he informed me, 'and was most displeased that I had surrendered to the British.' Soldiering was in his family's blood because he added proudly a little later, 'My great-grandfather, grandfather, father, three uncles and five cousins have all served in the Army.'

There is a twinge of pride whenever I recall that unique little meeting. Next stop was at the apartment of retired Lieutenant-Colonel Tommy Fox. Many in the 1st Battalion twenty-one years before would have recalled the effect of those 155mm shells that sporadically hit us on Wether Ground during the period 10 to 12 June. It was Tommy who directed this fire as the artillery Forward Observation Officer for the Argentine 'Big Bertha' 155mm gun located by Sapper Hill. He was perched on top of Mount Harriet, having been entrusted with the task of making our lives as unpleasant as possible. The abiding memory I had of Tommy from my first Buenos Aires visit was his graphic English description of coming under Royal Navy 4.5-inch gunfire, an experience he will never forget. But now a second promise was kept as I presented him with his copy of the book. Unfortunately there was hardly time to drink our tea or eat the cakes that Tommy gave us because Alberto had to usher me onto the 197th Regimental Birthday Parade of the 1st 'Los Patricios' Infantry Regiment, the oldest regiment of the Argentine Army.

This unit was permanently based in Buenos Aires and its history included a successful defence of the capital in 1806 against 10,000 British redcoats commanded by Lieutenant-General Whitelocke who had landed at Montevideo, crossed the River Plate and advanced on the town with the intention of seizing it as a trading base.[2] Much pride was evident during the parade on that 2003 September evening. It was staged against a backdrop of an enormous Argentine national flag illuminated by spotlights and which hung from the front of a building overlooking the parade square. The entire Regiment was drawn up in a hollow square formation and patiently listened to the inevitably long speeches given by two officers. Spectacular mounted cavalry then made its entrance past a small contingent of the Regiment's war veterans of 1982 also on parade. The latter were from A Company deployed to Stanley, which had one man killed during the war. Dressed in drab civilian clothes, in stark contrast to the remainder of the Regiment's colourful Napoleonic ceremonial uniform of black knee-high boots, white breeches, scarlet waist sash, dark-blue tunic, white cross-belts, and compact black top hats adorned with a vertical long white feather, these veterans were the last to march past. A standard bearer marched in front and they received rapturous applause from the large number of spectators.

Afterwards we withdrew into another building to enjoy a sumptuous cocktail party that included food for the many guests. Here I met not only Brigadier-General Menéndez again, but also the retired white-haired Lieutenant-General Diego Soria, former Commanding Officer of the 4th Infantry Regiment during the Battle of Mount Harriet. Alberto then revealed one more surprise that evening. It concerned Nicolás Urbieta whom I had researched and written about in my book, but still had never met. But now the Brigadier-General had intervened. To my delight Alberto informed me that he had managed to acquire the authorisation for the air flight to Buenos Aires of this ex-4th Infantry Regiment Malvinas' War veteran from his current unit, the 24th Mechanised Infantry Regiment based 3,500 kilometres in the south at the town of Río Gallegos.

Thirty-six hours later I set out on a six-hour bus ride through the grassy pampas countryside to Marisa's home. It was to be here that my meeting with Urbieta would take place after my hunt for him had begun in 1997. She was a retired school teacher who had taught her pupils emphatically that, '*Las Malvinas son argentinas*! (The Malvinas are Argentina's!)' Also a local Peronist politician and vehement supporter of the Malvinas' War veterans' cause, Marisa had been an outstanding facilitator for me during my previous trips to Argentina. Well-acquainted with Brigadier-General Menéndez, it was her idea of flying Urbieta up from Río Gallegos. At next morning's breakfast in her kitchen we two war veterans met for the first time. As well as Marisa, also present were her husband Roberto and three neighbours: Natalia, who always acted as my interpreter at General Roca, Ligia who had translated my letters to Marisa, and Marcelo the pleasant local police chief who provided the security. In an emotionally-charged atmosphere Natalia burst into tears whilst interpreting the initial conversation after Nicolás and I had embraced. To the casual reader this latter action might appear strange. However, although on opposing sides, we had shared the experience of having fought on the Falklands-Malvinas battlefields – and it was this that prompted such spontaneity.

Reconciliation can be a powerful game-changer as Nicolás described later:

In 1983, five (of my) letters [...] which had never made it to their destination arrived at my billet, shipped by the International Red Cross. Until fourteen years later, I never got to know who had taken the trouble to get these letters back to me. The fact is that it had been Mike Seear who, after those fourteen years, had cared to look into whether I had made it back from the Islands and how I might, eventually, be doing. He even brought back to me some of my personal gear that I had left behind, an act which filled me with happiness. I have treasured it, as I have treasured his great generosity, ever since.

It is because of him, because of this 'British Officer Mike', that I then also began to recover some of my history. Even when he travelled to Argentina, I still refused to meet him. However, he then met other veterans and even made friends with some of them.

Nevertheless, he insisted on meeting me, and this encounter was finally made possible through the intervention of Señora María Isabel Clausen de Bruno, who arranged things so that we could meet each other at her home and during a presentation of their books at the Córdoba City Book Fair. Her book *Entre tu mano y la mía* was written for the veterans, and I was happily surprised when reading its contents and found that much of the experience and many of the feelings of the veterans were synthesised there.[3]

Contrary to what I had written originally in my book, Nicolás had been decorated with his Army's second highest award for gallantry, the medal *Abnegación y Valor* (Self-denial and Valour), in recognition of rescuing Lieutenant Jorge Pérez Grandi, his badly-wounded platoon commander, from the battlefield of Two Sisters. Even though our conversation continued to be carried out via Natalia, after only five minutes I sensed the stockily-built small Argentine could be relied upon in a crisis. He was a Warrant Officer now and had served twice with the United Nations in Croatia in 1992 and 1996. On his first tour of duty there he served alongside not only a Nepalese Army infantry battalion from which he had acquired a *kukri*, but also British Army logistics and medical units. I attempted to prise more information from the modest Nicolás about his war, but he did not want to talk too much about the details. Perhaps this reluctance of verbalising traumatic experiences mirrored that of other Malvinas' War veterans, and which exacerbated psychologically the majority's current unhappy situation in which seventy per cent were unemployed and a plethora of suicides among them. However he did reveal that whilst his sub-unit, C Company, was located in defensive positions on Wall Mountain during May 1982 as part of Task Force Monte Caseros, its officers had told the men about our Battalion's deployment. The ensuing rumour quickly spread that Gurkhas cut off their enemy's ears in combat and he also confirmed that this piece of information kept 4th Infantry Regiment soldiers well awake whilst on night sentry duty in the East Falkland khuds.

A few days after the surrender Nicolás had embarked on board SS *Canberra* and was subsequently repatriated to Argentina as one of many prisoners of war who disembarked at Puerto Madryn. Together with the other soldiers in his regiment, they experienced a difficult time back in their barracks at Monte Caseros in the province of Corrientes. Defeat was painful to accept. Most suffered from depression and they also had a tendency to isolate themselves from the outside world in those immediate post-war months. In other words, they suffered from classic post-traumatic stress reactions – which, it should be added, are normal after an abnormal event. Collectively one great lesson was learnt from the war – a conscript army starts with too many disadvantages when pitted against a regular one. This was one of a number of reasons why military conscription in Argentina was eventually suspended in 1995 and replaced with a voluntary military service.

There was also a practical matter to resolve after twenty-one years. By chance I had brought to Argentina Nicolás's training manual, photographs of his section and himself training and travelling in Argentina after mobilisation prior to being flown to the Islands, an order of battle for his Company that he had written on a mud-encrusted sheet of paper, and his section's names and addresses written on a piece of toilet paper. All these were the remnants of that souvenir hunt a few Gurkhas had embarked on at Mount Harriet and Two Sisters led by the Adjutant, Captain Mark Willis. All these items had been utilised in writing my book and tracing Nicolás. He thanked me, and then took out his war file and placed these new artefacts in it. Although good to return them, there was also a little sadness. I had held them in my possession for so long and they had given me my initial clues which finally led to this unexpected rendezvous.

Later that morning Marisa, Nicolás and I visited the town's modest waist-high Malvinas' War Memorial. Also accompanied by Natalia, we stood before it for a few moments of silence in respect to those who had fallen on both sides. An Argentine Army helmet was mounted on top of the white-painted concrete block. Underneath the latter had been buried a piece of the Islands' peat. A short aluminium flagpole was also incorporated into the memorial and, being an ardent Malvinist, Marisa had designed the official flag of the Malvinas' War Veterans comprising a dark-brown motif of her beloved Islas las Malvinas superimposed on the pale blue and white Argentine national flag. This was hoisted annually on 2 April. Back at her home she also showed me *Entre tu mano y la mía*, her recently published 135-page third book of the war's aftermath. The first two had been about the Argentine Malvinas' War veterans and Marisa hoped that all her books might help the veterans tackle their difficult life situation better.

Her initial anger about the Gurkhas and me, fiery passion for the Malvinas and Argentine war veterans, and yet a paradoxical willingness to assist me had been powerfully juxtaposed in the book's opening chapter. It was also a snapshot into a much aggrieved post-conflict culture:

It was 1997.

All the noise of the class was interrupted by the sound of an old bell.

One by one, my students left their desks to enjoy the school break.

The classroom was left filled with only silence, the board and chalks.

But suddenly, I heard steps behind me and a voice told me: 'Look. This is for you. It's an article from the *Clarín* newspaper about the Malvinas. When I read it, I kept it for you.' (It was Delia, my school headmistress)

The Malvinas! My hands always tremble and my heart beats faster with anxiety when something about them appears!

I started reading it but [...] what a high price I have to pay for not studying English before! I couldn't understand anything. But María Belén, the English teacher, said: 'OK. I can help you.'

In the middle of innocent laughs of the children, between their games and shouts, this simple story started to take shape.

Then the bell indicated that the break was over.

My decision was already taken. I would write to this man, this English officer!

I love my Malvinas, even further than my reason.

Neither nothing nor nobody can ever make me understand they are not mine. And thinking they are lost forever or killing this love towards them is just impossible. They are a piece of land that grew inside me, with me, as my body did.

I am the Malvinas and the Malvinas are me. Because we are both Argentine. It was our destiny to be Argentine.

I could live anywhere in the world, but this would not change my identity and my sky-blue and white mind.⁴

British and Chilean people live in the Malvinas but they will never take them away from our country.

Feeling all this [...] a far away resentment made me decide to write my first letter to that English gentleman, a kind of robber to me, and a bit cheeky, who wanted to have contact with an Argentine soldier.

It was Christmas time in 1997. I was writing cards with greetings and wishes to my friends. A folded draft copy appeared among other papers. It was to be sent to Norway but the paper stayed sleeping in my lack of decision.

My hand, trembling with anger, emotion and uncertainty, I started to write letter by letter.

Mr Mike Seear,

I hope you are well, happy with your family. I know this letter will be mysterious and a bit cheeky.

In fact, a long time ago, when an article from the *Clarín* newspaper came into my hands, I decided to write to you. But then time passed by [...]

Now that we are near Christmas and New Year, I believe this is the right moment to write. I wish that God blesses you, and forgive you if you feel guilty for anything.

I am a primary school teacher who organises in my small town of General Roca, Córdoba, the annual Act (of Remembrance) by the Department for the Malvinas Veterans. Their return was not easy for them.

I want to ask you if you could send me one of your books so as to clarify some doubts that hurt my Argentine heart. And I also want to tell you that, if some day you want to come to Argentina, (which sounds difficult) I offer you my house. It is humble but open for you.

You know, the Argentines did not go to war against the English, but I would like to recover our Islands and plant my flag there.

Our soldiers went there to recover their country, and they went with their bodies, minds, hearts and young lives.

Did you (the English) come here to kill? Why did you come?

Because I know that military men study how to defend their countries. I do not understand those who fight only for money. Is that the case of the Gurkhas? What's the reason? What for? Is that a simple job for men?

Is it contempt for humanity? Is it that they don't respect their own lives and others' lives?

Is it a challenge against God's commandment 'You must not kill'?

Your behaviour gets me confused. You seem to be a good person since you have sent those letters (of Nicolás Urbieta) to the International Red Cross. Did the letters interest you? Their content? Now you want to write a book. Why? Do you feel any affection towards an unknown person or is there anything that makes you identify with him?

What did you feel being a military expert with an enemy aged eighteen to twenty years old?

Did it wake up your anger?

Did you fight feeling the ideal of patriotism?

We were not less guilty than you.

Many people at that moment closed their eyes and did not live the war, the reality. It was not so in my case. But I was one in a hundred.

Today, after fifteen years, our Malvinas Boys suffer from the peoples' indifference. In our town we have a small monument which has a flagpole and soul (earth) from the Malvinas.

There we raised the flag. The cloth represents our country. The Islands because they are part of it. The Sun is made by the hands of some veterans. It represents the idea that we do not renounce the Malvinas.[5]

Why am I telling you all this? Because I think that any veteran, any Argentine would not renounce Malvinas patriotic rights.

If a foreign person enters your house, what would be your reaction?

If another country comes and takes a part of your loved country, would you cross your arms or would you fight for it?

What would you do as an Englishman and as a Gurkha?

Can you understand our attitude in 1982?

As I read in *Clarín*, Nicolás does not want to have any contact with you. It is simple: there is much pain and he cannot forget.

Why am I writing to you? I do not know exactly. Maybe to tell you that if nobody wants to receive you in my country, then I will.

I think you are, apart from an Englishman, a human-being.

I want to believe in your human heart, I want to think the Gurkhas are not killing machines (as it was said).

Although many people do not understand my opinion I thank God for all those who came back from war, despite the triumph or defeat.

Looking forward to your answer.

María Isabel Clausen de Bruno.

P.S. None of my questions are insults to you. They are curiosities about a person, his story and feelings. Because the Malvinas were, are, and will be Argentine. Because this is what we feel here. We have them in our minds and hearts, and nobody can change that.

After writing this, positive and negative feelings shook my reason. The pain was too much and it ended in tears.

I prepared an air mail envelope for the letter, wrote the address and walked to the post office as a person in love, waiting to recover a love.[6]

More than a third of *Entre tu mano y la mía* consisted of my letters to Marisa – a daunting fact, but one that I had agreed to. Translated into Spanish, these had explained the background of the Gurkhas, their role in the war and how life, for one particular British veteran, became somewhat tangled afterwards. A three-hour launch of her book had been organised in the local school's assembly hall during that evening of 20 September. In addition to invited people from the town, half a dozen war veterans from the local area attended this emotionally draining event in which reconciliation was the theme. With his rich Spanish voice, Marcelo was the logical choice for compère. There was a strong Argentine cultural flavour to the programme which included canned music, speeches, songs, tango dancing, solo guitar-playing and poetry readings. In her long dress, the blonde Marisa possessed an Evita-like presence as she made several speeches, distributed her book to many called up onto the stage and also recited poems she had written about her initial meetings with Nicolás in Río Gallegos and me in the Plaza de Mayo. I also presented him with a copy of my book after making an impromptu speech to the large audience. It included three local TV reporters and camera crews who interviewed us afterwards. The prologue of *Entre tu mano y la mía* pointed out what had been achieved:

> I am not a writer of technical studies, so maybe this book and others only 'seem' to be books in shape but they are not good books.
>
> I am a person who wants to show her feelings or cover empty sheets of paper with a message from the soul, with a passion some people consider to be ending: patriotism.
>
> I am sure I am one of the few idealistic persons in the world.
>
> I believe that true love, the love which is around many things, is never ending. It is always with us, in any part of the Universe.
>
> Anyway, this is my opinion.
>
> And I thank God because He showed me the tools so as to allow myself to love my country, its Islands and the Malvinas veterans, because they are my country and my treasure.
>
> I know I belong to a place. And that place belongs to me.
>
> I never studied English, only for the exams at Secondary School. But today I regret. Sometimes life takes you to unbelievable situations: I was totally anti-British and now, I am the friend of an Englishman.
>
> Fate! [7]

Marisa, Roberto, Nicolás, Natalia, her future husband Gabriel and I departed General Roca early the following morning to travel 300 kilometres north-west to Córdoba City and the Book Fair. En route we passed through the town of Oliva and stopped there at the National Museum of the Malvinas War. Outside were assembled three Argentine aircraft from the war – a Pucará twin piston-engined ground attack fighter, an A-4B Skyhawk jet fighter and Canberra bomber. The latter happened to be one that participated in the final air strike on British forces. I also noted that truth remains a casualty from the war. On the port side of the Skyhawk's fuselage below and in front of the cockpit was painted a red silhouette of the Royal Navy's Type 21 frigate, HMS *Avenger*. The date of the attack, 25-05-82 (not without coincidence Argentina's National Day), was also painted in red alongside, indicating that the pilot of this particular Skyhawk from V Fighter Group based at Río Gallegos had claimed the sinking of the frigate. However on that day the Argentine Air Force had only attacked HM Ships *Broadsword* and *Coventry*, the former being slightly damaged and the latter sunk. And in a final Argentine Super-Étendard bomber raid east of the Falklands, the aircraft transport containership SS *Atlantic Conveyor* was hit and fatally set on fire by an Exocet AM-39 missile strike.

But *Avenger*, however, did not arrive in the eastern sector of the Total Exclusion

Zone until twelve hours later direct from the UK. During the remainder of the war she was used extensively in coastal bombardments, firing more than 1,000 rounds from her 4.5 inch automatic gun. Our Battalion, dug in at Wether Ground on East Falkland, heard this gun firing its 156 rounds from the Stanley southern gunline in support of 3 Para's Mount Longdon night attack on 12 June and again during the Battle of Tumbledown on 14 June from the Berkeley Sound northern gunline. This case of mistaken identity displayed at Oliva is a neat example how the fog of war can persist decades after a war. A pity, too, there was no time to visit the museum.

Two hours later we arrived at Córdoba City to stroll around the Fair which had been open for the previous two weeks, and then enjoyed a late lunch of juicy steak and excellent Argentine Malbec red wine before presenting our books. The event was sponsored by a local cultural association with the colourful name of *La Solapa*. A 'walkabout' TV cameraman recorded some of the proceedings that would, we were told later, be broadcast nationally. The room was packed with at least seventy people and included, seated in the front row, three stern-faced Argentine Army officers in full Service Dress. Another Argentine officer in civilian clothes came up to me before our presentations began and, in good English, introduced himself as Colonel Sergio Fernández, the Deputy Commander of the Argentine Army's 4th Airborne Infantry Brigade, who had been stationed at Port Howard during the war.

However there was little time to talk as two female *La Solapa* representatives began an elaborate introduction of how the two books came to be written. Afterwards Nicolás was asked to say a few words. Then it was my turn. Usually I do not speak in public using notes, but this occasion was an exception in deference to Natalia who was my interpreter. The theme of my forty-five minute speech (which, underestimating the time needed for Natalia's interpreting, proved far too long) was reconciliation. The following extracts from the speech are proof of my amateur attempts at diplomacy in a somewhat tricky situation. This included using the name 'Malvinas' throughout and mentioning the Argentine 'landings' on the islands as opposed to 'invasion':

> Two centuries ago the great French General Napoleon Bonaparte told his staff officers before one battle, 'Ask of me anything but time. I will lose a man, but never a moment.' Like Napoleon I have a similar problem – too much to tell and a lack of time in which to do it. Therefore I must be effective. There is a profound yet wonderful irony of being here.
>
> 'So why is this?' you might rightly ask. It is because I am not just presenting my book in public for the first time but, more importantly, doing this in the country I once fought against. Recently an Argentine freelance journalist asked me if I felt that I was betraying my country by doing this in Argentina. My answer was a definite 'no' because the book is a universal story about a soldier before, during and after a war. I have also discovered a further awful common denominator between the combat veterans of both sides of this war. No fact is so striking as the suicides that have, and still are, occurring in both countries. Last year the conservative figure of 264 Malvinas War veteran suicides in Argentina was published whilst, at the same time, it was made known in Britain that more than 200 suicides have been committed there by Falklands War veterans.

The latter figure will probably soon exceed the number of 255 British servicemen who were killed in the war.[8] This is an epidemic where it does matter if the victims have been on the losing or winning side. Surely therefore this humanitarian matter is the common ground between Argentina and Britain, and which transcends a territorial dispute?

This is now my third trip in seventeen months to Argentina, a country that continues to impress me. The most valuable natural resource of any country is its people and, as always, I am overwhelmed by the friendliness and hospitality displayed by all Argentines I meet. My research carried out in Argentina last year and subsequent assistance by the Malvinas War Veterans' Medical Coordinator, Doctor Eduardo Gerding, meant that I could also expand and complete the absolutely essential Argentine perspective to the book. This was built on the original information I had acquired from Nicolás Urbieta. He was an Argentine soldier of the 4th Infantry Regiment from Corrientes and some of his letters he had written during the war had come into my possession at Goose Green. My aim was to show that Argentina possessed brave and capable soldiers in the war, and I believe that the subsequent detailed and unique stories of Nicolas Urbieta, Tommy Fox and Jorge Pérez Grandi prove this point.

Midway I had also provided some background information about myself and experienced a momentary, but unintentional, frog in my throat when I mentioned my mentally-handicapped daughter Kristina born in the aftermath of the war. Natalia was also trapped in a tearful moment and had to stop briefly to catch her breath. Guilty of causing her a similar embarrassment, I put a supporting arm on her shoulder. Then to this Englishman's complete surprise, the remaining ninety-odd Argentine occupants of the room reacted with a spontaneous outburst of applause.

'It is our way of showing that we Argentines suffer with you,' I was told later.

Marisa then presented her book. When she had finished, there was a chance to ask questions. A lady immediately stood up and spoke earnestly. The room fell silent. My nil knowledge of Spanish prevented me from comprehending what was happening, but then Natalia whispered excitedly in my ear, 'This lady has introduced herself as the mother of Jorge Pérez Grandi and she's come here this evening to shake the hand of the man who saved her son's life!'

Pérez Grandi's mother had never met Nicolás before. Appearing overwhelmed, the combat veteran from the Battle of Dos Hermanas (Two Sisters) walked out to embrace both her and her husband. My writing had at least achieved something positive by making such a meeting possible. The conclusion to this remarkable evening included some hectic signing of Marisa's book and a few of mine, shaking hands with Pérez Grandi's tearful parents, and one of the *La Solapa* ladies who, employing her exceptionally limited English with optimal effect, made a stout declaration to me of, 'I love you!'

As I packed, one of the Argentine officers seated in the front row also approached me and, in halting English, introduced himself by saying, 'I am a Malvinas War veteran of the 4th Infantry Regiment and was taken prisoner in the war by some Gurkhas at Port Harriet House.'

Initially a mystery, I realised later that this officer must have been one of the eighty-three enemy who had been captured during the Battle of Mount Harriet in the early hours of 12 June. Afterwards, in daylight, 42 Commando had handed these POWs over to our D Company who then escorted them to our Battalion Tactical HQ location on Wether Ground prior to their helicopter flight back to Ajax Bay. But just to confirm there was absolutely no doubt of his conviction, I asked, 'Are you certain they were Gurkhas?'

'Yes, of course,' the white-haired veteran replied firmly, 'because I saw they had *kukris* attached to their belts!'

Unfortunately lack of time prevented us from conversing more. But at least Colonel Fernández had bought a copy of my book. He also asked, 'Could you return to Córdoba on another occasion to make presentations about the war to Argentine military units in the area?'. With an eye to the future we exchanged e-mail addresses. This appeared to be an offer of dialogue and further reconciliation, falling in line with Sun Tzu's most famous thought of all that sees battle in the context of victory and ends with the phrase 'subduing the other's military without battle is the most skillful'.

As I moved out of the building more Argentines stopped me. One introduced himself as a representative of a local Malvinas War Veterans' Association in Córdoba. In halting English, he continued. 'We collect books on the war for our library. Is there a possibility we could have a copy of your book?' I could not refuse such a direct request, and he immediately started to flick through the pages of his newly acquired gift.

After a relaxing beer at an outdoor restaurant, we travelled back to General Roca that evening to arrive late at night. Before dawn the following morning on 22 September I had to say farewell to my hosts and climb aboard the bus back to Buenos Aires. There was time to sleep during the journey before arrival in the capital at lunchtime. In a nearby restaurant I ate my final Argentine steak, and then took a taxi to the *Monumento a los caídos en Malvinas* (Monument for the fallen in the Malvinas), located near the city centre at the Plaza San Martin. Colonel Peter Reynolds had already confidentially tipped me off that the then British Chief of the General Staff (CGS), General Sir Michael Jackson, was on an official visit to Argentina that week and, at two o'clock that afternoon, would lay a wreath at the memorial.

I arrived half an hour early and sat down on a bench to enjoy the tepid sunshine of that second austral day of Spring and also observe the contrasts. As my thoughts inevitably spun back twenty-one years to 1982's eventful second quarter and those extraordinary events in the South Atlantic that changed so many lives, a few blissfully unaware people continued to sit on the adjacent grass bank. I gazed at the long, slightly elliptical pink-stone memorial and its eternal flame guarded by two Argentine Navy sentries clad in dark-blue uniforms and armed with bayonet-fixed rifles. It was far more impressive than the simple rectangular square light-grey stone with the engraved names of the British dead of the war which is to be found in the Crypt of St. Paul's Cathedral, London. Perhaps the sheer size of the Argentine monument is an expression of how much more deeply the war affected Argentina.

A dark-suited civilian nearby who was obviously connected with the security arrangements, spoke almost continuously into his mobile telephone as a cleaner swept away some cigarette ends and rubbish from the memorial steps. Then two 1st Infantry Regiment soldiers in their eye-catching Napoleonic uniforms appeared. They were carrying an enormous wreath and positioned it carefully nearby as a simple guard-changing ceremony took place, the incoming naval sentries taking up position in front of the memorial with a low-key goose-step march. The Buenos Aires' traffic continued its tirade of hooting and whirlwind speeding by as, escorted by a uniformed Colonel Peter Reynolds, Sir Robin Christopher and some high-ranking Argentine officers, the red-bereted CGS arrived to carry out the simple ceremony. The watchful DA nodded at me as they walked up to the memorial to lay the wreath and salute whilst a 1st Infantry Regiment trumpeter blew the Argentine equivalent of *The Last Post*. With a reflex action of one who, in his youth, had been exposed to the vociferous teachings of Guards Sergeants for many months on the Old College Drill Square at Sandhurst, I stood immediately to attention as the first notes were sounded. Afterwards I became a trifle taken aback as the CGS was ushered across in my direction and promptly introduced to me by the DA. As we shook hands, it was satisfying to realise this must have been the first occasion a British Paratrooper, Commando and Gurkha, all from regiments profoundly associated with the Falklands-Malvinas War, had met at this ironical venue.

General Jackson looked back sombrely at the striking memorial which displayed those 649 names of Argentine servicemen who had died in the war. Perhaps 'Jacko', as he was known to his officers, was also thinking about the more than 1,100 Argentines who had been wounded, as well the 255 British dead and 746 wounded whilst, almost to himself, he remarked quietly, 'Well, it's been twenty-one years that have now gone by ...'

The former Parachute Regiment officer whose forty-one years of service as a soldier that outstripped by far my puny twenty-one years, then swung round again towards me to ask in his gravelly baritone voice, 'So what are you doing here? Just passing through?'

'No sir,' came my respectful correction to the fifty-nine year-old General who was three years my senior and also, like me, a Northern Ireland veteran. 'I came to Argentina to make a formal presentation of a book I've written about the war at the Córdoba City Book Fair.'

This former Commander-in-Chief of NATO ground forces in Kosovo in 1999 and contributor to the British Government's decision-making process to participate in the invasion of Iraq six months previously did not appear to register on my literary explanation. But his growled response, 'Then what were you doing in the war?' indicated an incomplete briefing on my background.

My reply was deliberately short, but to the point. 'I was with the Gurkhas, sir, as their Operations and Training Officer – on Tumbledown.'

'Jacko' blinked. His craggy face adorned with those trademark heavy eye bags twitched from benevolent relaxation into instant curiosity at my terse reply. However I refrained from adding, 'And may I recommend my book if you want to know more?'

But his time was up, and the stressed DA quickly ushered him back to his waiting car – leaving me to gaze at the memorial and think that this was a fitting way to end my third visit to Argentina. The circle was finally closed. Back in my hotel that evening came the perfect postscript – a third meeting with the former 4th Infantry Regiment platoon commander of the war and now successful Buenos Aires lawyer Jorge Pérez Grandi. He was more than happy to receive the twelfth complimentary copy of the book I had given to Argentines during the past seven days.

Mission accomplished, I flew back home to Oslo via London the following afternoon. Life as a Falklands-Malvinas War veteran blossomed. My book became a door-opener for making presentations on the Gurkha role in the war to the younger generation at the military academies of Norway, Denmark and Sweden and other Norwegian military training establishments. It gave me satisfaction to explain lessons learnt and advise audiences how to avoid my mistakes made in war. Additionally with regard to modern expeditionary warfare, there was an esoteric spin-off as I found myself providing considerable input, much of which was about family support and use of unit chaplains, to Lars Weisæth's enlightening 2006 military psychiatry paper entitled *Operational Mental Health: A NATO Programme for the 21st Century*. But on the coin's dark side there remain dangerous traps. I know them too well. So does Jeremy McTeague:

> When we subsequently returned to the United Kingdom, much of our excitement of being at war had worn off. In particular, we no longer experienced such a range of emotions. Nevertheless I was still experiencing intense emotions and mood swings. These quickly diminished, but in recent years I find that a pattern of behaviour has re-emerged. Common balanced emotions, such as irritation, can flash into anger with little provocation, a negative question or statement can be interpreted as an insult, causing strong reactions of insecurity, aggression or even the behaviour associated with victimisation. Feelings of low personal esteem also surface with some intensity.[9]

His explanation helped I was not alone. But veteran peer support comes in many forms, like that of Nigel Price's. Not only did he provide professional advice, but also his war experiences and two of his own high-quality poems – *Before Battle* and *On The Surrender of Port Stanley: 14 June 1982* – for the manuscript of my first book. So there was a major sense of *déjà vu* when I read his third poem in a gold nugget of a letter sent on 14 December 2005 and received just after my initial visit to Bernard McGuirk at the University of Nottingham: [10]

Staring Into Space

How easy to define oneself by it all
And wear the tag of *veteran* like designer shades
Basking in the pats of praise
Fair payment,
But for what?
Being young and a bit of a lad
Thinking our thoughts bold
Pretending to be brave
Only confessing to a fashionable terror
After the event,
Adding to the kudos
Adding to the lie.
And the truth?

Harder by far to make a marriage work
Harder by far to leave the lad behind
And learn to make of women's tears
Something nobler than a war.
Harder by far to budget for the bills
Pay the tax, earn the bread
Tab the hills of civvy-street
Pack and rifle ever felt in empty hands.

The dupe of Life –
To think our dead
Full settlement of the account.
To think
We sailed beyond them,
Home in feted ships
As they descended into soil and sea.
We didn't know so many more
Would take their leave,
Not fizzed and pinged and shot at
In the snow's fierce purity,
The wave's insistent crease,
But cornered by the passing years.
Sullen rooms drove them in upon their guns.

For harder by far to feel the years encroach
And wonder still what happened then
To set us spinning
Like a needle that's attained the Pole
But rations gone and no way back
An end achieved and we the cost
Tokens kept like pornography
In a cloth in a box in a shed
Mine, a jagged shard of shell
Hotter than hot-potato hot
When prised from the earth beside my face
Rusted now, like so much else.

And easy to croak over a pint
About the youngster face-up on the hill's bleak crest
Where livid splinters tested the air's flesh.
Muzzle-down in peat,
His rifle tinkled dog tags from the trigger guard
Name become slighter than chimes,
His shocked and open face
Boring holes in the snow-filled sky
Soft flakes coining blank the dead retinas.

But harder by far to live the winded panic of his Dad
Staring deep into the empty garden
Stilled of his boy's shouts
Slippered feet set parallel before his chair
Silent hands tightening
As he heard of the brigade's attack
The move into a frosty bay, the bomb-summoned flame
Envisioning a spirit dead
Longing to be gone
Shot of its torn body
Pissed with life
Dreaming of a garden and a lost embrace.

And harder, harder by far to look upon my sleeping son
And pray and beg and plead that wars will cease
Before my boy awakes and finds himself a lad –
And know my hope forlorn.
The world will turn and ignorance survive
And flesh and shell compete
And gardens empty of their shouts
Decanted, frantic, or to hills and cratered plains
In a tracer-shredded dark that no one grasps
Except the old men we become
Fearful for our sons, still and staring into space.

Nigel's delicately-crafted work immediately reinforced my motivation to write this book sequel. My only disappointment was the original neutral title: *Twenty Years On*. But the excellent substitute arrived with Nigel's concise explanation.[11]

However I had missed a trick. *Staring Into Space* that completed his trilogy should have been recited in open forum at the University of Nottingham's colloquium eleven months later. Those Falklands-Malvinas War veterans enjoying Bernard's unique 'academic forum' reconciliation initiative would have greatly appreciated Nigel's lyrical reflections. The latter and this book are pertinent also for those servicemen who have returned from the twenty-first century wars in Iraq and Afghanistan because 'the world will turn and ignorance survive' while wars go on 'and gardens empty of their shouts'.

Notes

1. *The Art of War*, Chapter 3 – Strategy of Attack.
2. Also engaged in fighting the British was a naval infantry battalion, predecessor of today's Argentine 5th Marine Infantry Battalion which, in the 1982 Falklands-Malvinas War, was amongst the opposition of 2nd Battalion, The Scots Guards and 1st Battalion, 7th Duke of Edinburgh's Own Gurkha Rifles on Tumbledown and Mount William. Ironically the Gurkha motto '*Kaphar Hunnu Bhanda Marnu*

Ramro Chha' (It is Better to Die than to Live a Coward) has a strikingly similar sentiment to the Argentine Marines' *'Pugnams Pereror Per Patriam'*(Fighting I Die For The Fatherland). The latter's predecessors in 1807 also defeated Brigadier-General Robert Crauford and his 2,000 redcoats at the Battle of Plaza del Mercado in Buenos Aires to complete the two-year struggle against the British which is recalled proudly by Argentines as 'The Defence'.

3. *Hors de Combat*, p. 17.
4. Relating to the blue and white colours of the Argentine national flag.
5. A locally made Argentine national flag with a brown symbol of the Malvinas Islands superimposed on the flag's centre.
6. *Entre tu mano y la mía*, pp 15-19.
7. *Ibid.*, p. 11.
8. A *Sunday Times* colour supplement published in November 2010 indicated that the official figure for Argentine suicides stands at 480, and unofficial figure at 620. However after the author e-mailed Eduardo Gerding on 16 August 2011 for more information, he replied, 'There is no serious official statistical data on suicides on either side, just estimates and, if I may say, reluctance as well to know the precise figure [...] According to a remarkable book most suitable for the Pulitzer Prize entitled *Hors de Combat* you may read on page 66 that the latest estimate was 350, and such a figure was published in *La Nación* on 28 February 2006. Of course there have been more suicides since, but the trend is curving down.' It was estimated in 2007 by the South Atlantic Medal Association 82 that at least 300 British veterans of the war had committed suicide.
9. *Hors de Combat*, p. 59.
10. The letter read:

> Here is the poem I spoke of. I wrote it last year, about the time of the D-Day commemoration in France. I watched all those wonderful old boys in the sun, blazers with regimental crests, sunglasses and battered old berets. It was so right that they should be feted like that, but I nonetheless felt a certain unease. For yes, big chunks of war are unimaginably awful, but for many of the veterans, it was the defining experience of their lives and nothing since has measured up to it. They all refer to the comradeship of those times, and have rarely found anything since to compare. But the people who really suffered were not present at the commemoration because – of course – they are long gone.
>
> I recall my mother commenting how, on hearing the news that 5 Infantry Brigade had been on the *Sir Galahad* and *Sir Tristram*, my father sat and stared into the garden, not knowing for several days what had become of me. A friend of his came and sat with him. The image of these two men (then just a little shy of sixty years old), never really struck more until I had a son of my own. I watch him now, playing in the garden with his best friend, the two of them whooping and shouting, and can barely imagine what my father went through. (An American chap who works for our company has a son in the US Marines about to be sent to Iraq. So it goes on and on, a never-ending tumble of generations.)
>
> I heard through the Royal British Legion of a young man (Falklands

veteran, I think – but I might be wrong) they found living rough in a wood, like a prolonged military exercise. They set him up with a flat and some cash to get him restarted in life.

Then there are the horrific suicide figures, as in the article I sent to you the other day. You will doubtless recognise many of the references in the poem.

At the Pole, I understand, a compass needle spins round and round. Many a veteran reaches his own Pole, similarly to find there is no way back. Thereafter their needles spin, losing direction. In the poem I used Scott's Antarctic expedition as a metaphor, the compass needle spinning when they reached the Pole, signifying both the attainment of the goal, but also a lost sense of direction. Rations gone, no way back. The end achieved, but at the cost of the dead and many of the veterans who failed to put their lives back together again. For those who died in the battles, there was literally no way back – both British and Argentine. But for many of the others too, there was no way back to the men they had been before. Everything had changed for them – and, consequently, for the families they returned to. Lots of people were left 'staring into space', not just the dead. People like your Scots Guards contacts.

Finally the tokens in verse four are the things we bring back, like the piece of shell splinter I retrieved, but the tokens are also the veterans themselves. The last line of the poem of course refers equally to the father and the son.

11. This second letter read:

Staring Into Space is significant in several ways. It is the closing phrase of the whole poem. It is the dead soldier staring into space, but also the imagined father, staring into the space of the garden, 'emptied of his boy's shouts.' But beyond that, it is also us, the survivors. It is the thousand-yard stare of the veteran. And it is staring into the space of the future as we all venture forward, retreating ever further and further from that formative and life-changing experience. Staring into the space of the future and, ultimately, death [...]

I am glad you like the poem title. I felt it had been lacking this, so hope this resolves the issue. The phrase seemed to capture so much of it. Those ten weeks were defining moments for all of us – some more than others, I suppose. The Falklands War will remain a pivotal experience of our lives. It is something I will never regret having taken part in – but then I came back in one piece, so it is easy for me to say that.

143. Argentine munitions gathered up on the Goose Green air strip, 21 June 1982.

144.At the 1st/7th Gurkha Rifles' farewell party in Goose Green, 10 July 1982, (l. to r.) Major-General Jeremy Moore, Brigadier Tony Wilson, unknown female settler, Lieutenant-Colonel David Morgan and Falkland Islands Governor Rex Hunt.

145.   Gurkha 'Third Location Decompression' on board SS *Uganda* during the
Inter-Platoon Tug-of-War Competition, July 1982.

146.   SS *Uganda* arrives at Southampton, 9 August 1982.

147.   The 1st/7th Gurkha Rifles march through their home town of Fleet, Hampshire, 9 August 1982.

148.   Retired *General de Brigada* Mario Benjamín Menéndez (former Argentine Military Governor of the Malvinas in 1982) and the author, Buenos Aires, 17 September 2003.

149.   The author and Argentine Army war veteran *Teniente Coronel* Tommy Fox in the latter's Buenos Aires home, 17 September 2003.

150.   After meeting for the first time – Argentine Army war veteran and serving *Suboficial Mayor* Nicholás Urbieta and the author in Marisa Clausen de Bruno's home at General Roca, Córdoba province, 20 September 2003.

151.   The local Malvinas War Memorial at the town of General Roca, Córdoba province.

152.   A Pucará ground attack fighter is inspected by Nicolás Urbieta and the author at the National Museum of the Malvinas War, Oliva, on 21 September 2003. It was the first time that the author had seen an undamaged Pucará.

153.   The joint presentation of *Entre tu mano y la mía* and *With the Gurkhas in the Falklands: A War Journal* at the Córdoba City Book Fair meeting sponsored by *Asociación Cultural La Solapa*, 21 September 2003.

154.   *Monumento a los caídos en Malvinas* (Monument for the fallen in the Malvinas) at the Plaza San Martin, Buenos Aires.

During recent years the British search for oil in the vicinity of the Islands has generated fierce Argentine reactions and demands for a solution to the ongoing territorial dispute. In the immediate period leading up to the publication of this book and commemoration of the war's thirtieth anniversary, Argentine President Cristina Fernández de Kirchner has led a considerable ratcheting up of tension between the two countries by demanding an immediate UN-facilitated resolution of the dispute. This has been firmly rejected by the United Kingdom's Prime Minister David Cameron. But what are the thoughts of 1982 war veterans about this issue? This was Jeremy McTeague's response to *The Guardian* national UK newspaper in February 2010:

> I served on the Islands with the 7th Gurkhas during the war, though my contribution was minor in comparison to many others'. From bitter experience we must surely have learnt by now as a nation that it is the responsibility of the victor to ensure a sustainable peace. While your assertion that the politicians in both countries need to 'grow up' resonates well, I believe a call for action to resolve this issue must first be directed at the war's veterans – especially in Britain. It is only they and their families who can allay British politicians' fears that a political settlement may be a 'betrayal' of those who fought in 1982. This will provide politicians with the latitude they need to deal with this issue in a straightforward manner. Once policy-makers have been given the freedom to frame sensible policy, they should be allowed to do so without unwarranted interference.

And his e-mail to Eduardo Gerding on 19 March 2010:

> I share with you your despondency at this time. Clearly there are those who were involved in the Malvinas/Falklands war who cannot see past the issues of self-justification, or self-congratulation or more honestly, the memory and honour of comrades lost. They misunderstand wilfully or not, the need for peace and harmony, and so seek a voice and even self-aggrandisement through the continuation of governmental or societal posturing. But we should not be surprised – few men wish to admit that the results of actions they took as young men are now perhaps redundant. Moreover, if they suffered any kind of trauma or humiliation they will not let go their memories as they are central to their persona, their character and reputation and may even be a prop upon which they can lay blame for all the other ills and inadequacies in their lives.
>
> I feel that those of us who can learn to recognise that our behaviour may be skewed by the way we deal with our experiences, can quickly and constructively compensate for it. A critical step forward is to be able to dispose of personal prejudice and entrenched attitudes (such as 'if you're not with us then you're against us'). I believe that politicians and opinion-formers can, and in some cases are, abusively manipulating people who do not recognise that their behaviour and attitudes are skewed. I think that this is what we are having to deal with today.
>
> I am contemptuous of the political posturing and the political posturers – yet I

feel compassion for our comrades who are drawn into the behaviours you describe and believe we need to find a way to help them come to terms with the past. We need to help them for their own good and also for the good of our countries. But how?

Diego García Quiroga wrote an article entitled '1982, the oil, our emotions and our children' which was published on 25 February 2010 in an Argentine electronic newsletter entitled *Periodismo de Verdad* (*No-bullshit Journalism*), an offshoot from the former family-owned newspaper *La Gaceta* in Tucumán. The newsletter is currently very much a reference point for commentators who do not adhere to the current political leadership. It is somehow right-wing in its opinions, widely circulated and often quoted in other media:

> True, the official reaction to the British oil industry's outpost can be labelled, if one chooses, as 'symbolic'. But no less 'symbolic' is the avalanche of repudiation acts, marches, fiery tirades and denouncing publications that countless 'pro-Malvinas' associations carry out. As a participant of the warlike confrontation of 1982, I have the dubious privilege of being listed as a mail recipient with too many groupings and associations related to the subject, and so it is that for me every morning begins with the routine of erasing from my inbox a pile of scandalised declarations and calls to action that never venture beyond the 'need to demand immediately'. Using the same grandiloquent vocabulary that has stuck with us I believe, from the first military Argentine Government, the signers of these incendiary harangues call for the pacific mobilisation – a neologism of unclear meaning to me – against, in support of the denial, in defence of [...]
>
> Had we not fought in the way we did, I would just feel fed up. But we fought, and therefore this continuous whining after justice for the rape of our presumed virtue plunges me into deep sorrow. Years ago a term was coined: '*malvinizar*'. Out of ignorance, I assume that it means to create – or maintain awareness of the ideas that drove us into the confrontation in 1982. I cannot fathom what good this could bring us, taking into account the sorry circumstances that Argentina has seen for years in all fields of economic, moral and political development. It would be simply another anachronism; it would be – once more – to turn and look behind us, to deny the possibilities that lie ahead, to condemn our children to travel the same obsessive, populist path; to urge them to adore the same golden calf of the defence of our tramped virtuous nationality and the permanent denunciation of the implacable abuse to which the supposedly powerful ones – over whose table we vomit whenever we are invited to dinner – inflict upon us.
>
> It is absolutely true that England does not have any right to do what it is doing. But in this game, the right is not an absolute moral value, accessible to everyone. It needs to be earned, is necessary to deserve it. England, with all its deficiencies, is a nation deeply involved in processes of much greater global importance than the Malvinas, processes on which our world's stability and the well-being of innumerable people depend. The effective exercise of that responsibility endows that country with high standing and a singular weight at the time of thinking on

jeopardising its stability. In other words: to think it possible that the consensus of nations will significantly press England over the Falklands issue is like believing in Donald Duck. The existence of England, and its smooth functioning, is too important for worldwide stability. This may not seem ethical, nor may it be morally defensible and it could certainly be argued that the right is on our side, but the truth is that the civilised world cannot cheat in the luxury of doing without a powerful and well-working England.

But can the civilised world do without Argentina? Unfortunately and with increasing regularity we give evidence that yes, it could, that our participation in the questions which have to do with the progress of civilisation, the building of a sustainable world, the improvement of life conditions for the majority, is not part of our agenda. The peace missions in which our Armed Forces join continue being – aside from the excellent human and professional quality of the personnel who man them – exercises that do not represent any real sacrifice to the State (rather to the contrary). It is, as I have already mentioned, as if we were 'outside the world'. Peculiarly, this attitude defines us today as nation, to be denied by the individual efforts of each hard-working Argentine – and there are many of these – working in our country or from abroad in search of a better future.

Let us think about this issue of Malvinas oil: one suitable answer to the possible exploitation of these resources by other nations could be to launch a national campaign of serious, extensive scientific education, aiming to reach a leading position in the research and development of alternative power sources within a determined timeframe. Would it not be wonderful to see our country – for once in these terrible fifty-odd years that I have seen it bleed – turning its energies towards objectives of universal meaning instead of crying like nuns over spilled milk?

The alternative chosen by the 'pro-Malvinas' organisations that I know seems regrettable: this continuous complaining about the injustice inflicted upon us by a world that the most simplistic among us label as 'the powerful ones', and which is made up of countries that risk in ventures of aggressive development to improve the world in which we all live, that look beyond their limitations and dare to dream goals that require a common consciousness about which we do not seem to have the faintest idea and which is the key to progress and subsistence.

We could think about Brazil and its Brasilia as a valid example. Brasilia, a city nobody thought possible and which took five or six years to build, with the participation and effort of almost all the country. Could our Argentina do something similar in scale, at least? Because this was not only about the city itself: Brasilia was the dream of Kubischek to reclaim a hidden Brazil, to develop a rightful country, more democratic, more including. Unfortunately not everything worked the way he had planned it, but at least it offered an example to the world, it showed that Brazil could also move in that direction, that it could stop being feudal, that it too could have a voice as a truly participative country.

I do not believe that we need a Brasilia more than we needed a Viedma, but there are innumerable urgencies that call us. The Chaco calls, the eternally flooded coastal populations where life is a permanent uncertainty calls, the education system that collapses at every minute calls, the public health system calls, the industry calls. The list is enormous. But to recognise our shortcomings and plug the holes before the boat definitively sinks, it is necessary to take our eyes from that sort of Creole microscope that prevents us seeing what happens around and that makes us, among other things, to continue focusing on the Malvinas issue solely as a personal affront, isolating it from all the context that we cannot see but which is exactly the one that interests the rest of the world, and by which 'our problem of the Malvinas' carries for others so little importance.

We want the civilised world to pay attention to our rights and to enforce at any cost the respect for the laws that all of us have created and accepted by consensus. But we ourselves, when it fits us better, do not honour those laws: let us not mention once more that scandal that was the debt default; it has no possible defence. But neither do we honour our commitments in human rights, to mention something that is obvious in the legal aberrations that the Kirchner regime implements, to take revenge over its enemies. It is like asking justice from a court we do not respect when it is our turn to obey the law.

And we do not add, it is essentially this, we do not add. The internal status of Argentina – its moral, social, ideological and political status – is unacceptable for any observer who knows the value our culture and our history. We have given the Malvinas a priority that helps us not to look at, as if we were ostriches, the much more serious problems on which our future as a country depends. The voices that indignantly urge to fight and denounce the 'persistent iniquity of Albion' should be aware that those who fight and die while fighting do it for reasons that are nameless. They do it for things like affection, or deep love, or for a smile that they remember and belongs to somebody very dear; or because of the brotherly pat that a comrade gives them in the shoulder, or for the confidence they felt after the glance of a superior or a subordinate, notwithstanding that they might not have known each other; for the pride of proving themselves able, for the peace born out of being sincere and for all those things that have nothing to do with the military objectives, but find in action the opportunity of being recognised.

Those reasons are the same currency with which we can build, raise hope, educate and offer support. The islands are just that: Islands. But the effort we made and the fight we fought were expressions of an Argentine unity of which we must be proud. Let us honour the courage and devotion of those who fought, but let us understand for once and for all that they did it out of self-respect. There is no 'vain struggle', nor 'useless sacrifice'. We all fought for each other, for our idea of life, for the things we want and against the things we did not want. The 1982 fight cannot die as having been solely an obstinate endeavour, forever attached to the Islands. It cannot be left there; that objective is circumstantial and even forgettable. Nations are formed by the consensus of ideas and wills; a piece of land is not enough.

If we truly want to honour that fight, let us revive in us the will to fight for our ideas of honesty, of justice and order. Instead of mobilising to 'show or despise', let us look a little towards ourselves. Let our efforts be spent on giving universal reach within our country to the ways in which we Argentines face and enjoy life, and let us defend the rights of others to achieve the same possibilities. Let us work to regain the standing we have lost. Let us stop clowning.

And finally an extract from the author's presentation to the Association of Hispanists of Great Britain and Ireland's annual conference at the University of Nottingham on 11 April 2011:

It might have been noted that I am using the unconventional expression 'Falklands-Malvinas'. The 1982 hostilities between Britain and Argentina are known in the United Kingdom as either the Falklands conflict or Falklands War. Nearly three decades afterwards, I am convinced it is more precise to describe it as the Falklands-Malvinas War. I do this out of respect for my former enemy.

The Islands' sovereignty is an abstract issue. It is also pitted with minefields. Fighting in the war of 1982 caused me afterwards to read extensively about the Islands' history. As on the battlefield when the fog of war swirls around the combatants, so does an eternal dispute shroud around the Islands' sovereignty issue based on equally diffuse historical facts. During my most recent visit to Argentina in 2007 I was asked by a female TV reporter for my views on this. The red air alert klaxon rang in my head as I wrestled to answer her reasonable question. My analogous reply related to a ten year-old British schoolboy asking his geography teacher, 'Excuse me, Miss. In my atlas it shows that the Falkland Islands are 8,000 nautical miles from Britain. Yet they are less than 400 miles from the Argentine mainland. So why do the Falkland Islands belong to Britain?'

In doing this I did not directly answer the interviewer's original question, but commented instead, 'I could understand the pupil's confusion and his question. His teacher probably would have had great problems in providing a coherent reply since British ownership stemmed from an accident of history. Since then the United Nations has been created with its Charter containing the right of self-determination.'

Such subjects are not taught in British schools. Why should they be? The British people do not have the passion for the Falklands compared to Argentines whom, in their childhood, are taught at school all aspects of the Malvinas.

Any Briton viewing this particular TV interview might perceive that I was skating on thin ice. This would certainly be the case for the Islanders. But my reply was reinforced by having witnessed in Argentina many times the absolute conviction all Argentines possess of their right to claim sovereignty over the Islands. I respect this, but disapprove strongly of the method Argentina used in recovering the Islands. International disputes must be solved peacefully around the table and the military must not be used in any alternative option to this process. Yet in 1982 no other option remained for Britain other than to use force in the South Atlantic. History knows what happened next.

When visiting the small Córdoba province town of General Roca in March 2007 I gave a presentation about the personal after-effects of the war together with my good Norwegian friend, Professor Lars Weisæth. Our audience consisted of nearly 150 town inhabitants and twenty-five war veterans. I was overwhelmed by the reception given to me by these latter men just before going on stage to lecture. Shaking hands with each one, we met with reciprocating smiles, laughter and a flood of goodwill that produced an unforgettable moment. In my presentation I told the audience about the Nottingham colloquium and remarked, 'It was a success because no politician was present!' The comment generated intense applause.

It helped reinforce my belief that Government-sponsored reconciliation between veterans of the war is a vital prerequisite to any more political initiatives being launched on the Falklands-Malvinas sovereignty issue.

0.5-inch Browning Heavy Machine-Gun – US-manufactured M2 air-cooled belt-fed heavy machine-gun with a rate of fire of 450 to 635 rounds (calibre 0.50 BMG/12.7mm NATO) per minute and effective range of 1,800 metres. It was used by both British and Argentine forces in the Falklands-Malvinas War.

2IC – Second-in-Command of a military unit or sub-unit.

2 Para – 2nd Battalion, Parachute Regiment.

3.5-inch *Lanzacohete* – M-20 rocket launcher.

3 Para – 3rd Battalion, Parachute Regiment.

9 Para Squadron – 9 Parachute Squadron, Royal Engineers.

20mm Rheinmetall twin anti-aircraft cannon – Germain-manufactured anti-aircraft weapon designed to engage low and very low approaching enemy aircraft in order to prevent them from firing their weapons or delivering their ordnance on an Air Force installation.

66 – US-manufactured M72 portable one-shot 66mm unguided anti-tank weapon which is fired from the shoulder. The rocket has an effective range of 200 metres and the empty canister is thrown away after use.

81mm mortar – British-manufactured LI16 81mm muzzle-loading mortar with an effective range of 5,675 metres and rate of fire (manual) of fifteen bombs per minute. The US M252 version was used by Argentine forces in the Falklands-Malvinas War.

84 – Infantry platoon Swedish-manufactured two-man team (gunner and loader) man-portable 84mm Carl Gustav recoilless rifle classified by British forces as a medium anti-tank weapon (MAW) with effective ranges of 400 metres (moving targets) and 700 metres (stationary targets), and rate of fire of six rounds per minutes. It can be manned by one man, but with a reduced firing rate.

105mm Light Gun – Used by the Royal Artillery in the Falklands-Malvinas War, the British-manufactured L118 Light Gun is a 105mm towed howitzer. It has a crew of six and maximum range of 17,200 metres.

105mm OTO Melara pack howitzer – Used by the Argentine Army 3rd and 4th Artillery Groups in the Falklands-Malvinas War, the Italian-manufactured 105mm OTO Melara Mod 56 has a crew of four and maximum range of 11,100 metres.

155mm CITER L33 gun – An Argentine-manufactured 155mm gun which was used by the Argentine Army in the Falklands-Malvinas War. Four were flown to the Islands in the final weeks of the war. Three were used, with two being positioned in 'Puerto Argentino' (Stanley) and the third behind Sapper Hill. The gun's effective range was twenty kilometres.

AAA – Anti-Aircraft Artillery (Triple-A).

Adjutant – Battalion Commanding Officer's staff officer for personnel and discipline matters.

Advanced Dressing Station – Battle casualties from a Battalion Regimental Aid Post (RAP) are evacuated to an Advanced Dressing Station where further stabilisation of the casualty can occur.

A Echelon – Part of the Battalion Rear Echelon's organisation responsible for logistic re-supply to an infantry Battalion's sub-units at the frontline.

ARA – *Armada de la República Argentina* (the equivalent of HMS).

Assembly Area – This is a secured area on the ground where an infantry Battalion assembles in order to carry out final battle preparations.

Bantam Missile – The Swedish-manufactured Bantam (Bofors Anti-Tank Missile) is a wire-guided missile and has a maximum range of 2,000 metres.

Basha – A waterproof groundsheet with eyelets on its perimeter which can be set up, camouflaged and used as a shelter.

Battalion – An infantry Brigade sub-unit that comprises three Rifle Companies (four in a Gurkha Battalion), Support Company, HQ Company and Battalion HQ. It totals 650 men (1,000 in a Gurkha Battalion) and is commanded by a Lieutenant-Colonel.

Battalion Main HQ – Once deployed in the field, 1st/7th Gurkha Rifles Battalion HQ split itself in two. 'Battalion Tac HQ' assumed command and control, while 'Battalion Main HQ' only monitored operations. If 'Tac' was 'blown away' on the battlefield then 'Main' would take over 'command and control'.

Battalion Operations and Training Officer (Ops Officer) – This function is responsible for the co-ordination of the unit's operational tasks and assisting the CO in planning. The Ops Officer is also responsible for co-ordinating the unit's overall training.

BBC – British Broadcasting Corporation.

BC – Artillery Battery Commander.

Bergen – British Army generic term for a military-type rucksack.

BFBS – British Forces Broadcasting Service.

BIM5 – *Batallón de Infantería de Marina No. 5* (5th Marine Infantry Battalion).

BIT – Battle Individual Training (Gurkha Battalion terminology for physical fitness training).

Blowpipe – British-manufactured man-portable surface to air missile used by both British and Argentine forces in the Falklands-Malvinas War.

Blue-on-blue – Accidental clash between forces of the same side which causes a 'friendly' fire incident.

BO – British Officer (in a Gurkha Battalion).

BOR – British Other Rank (in a Gurkha Battalion).

Canberra bomber – This was an Argentine Air Force two-man English Electricmanufactured light bomber aircraft. Eight used bombers had been purchased from the Royal Air Force, and were used in the Falklands-Malvinas War.

Casevac – Casualty evacuation.

CGS – Chief of the General Staff.

Chinook – US-manufactured Boeing CH-47 double-rotored transport helicopter capable of transporting forty-four men in peacetime and nearly double that number in wartime (by removing the seats). Used by both British and Argentine forces in the Falklands-Malvinas War.

CHVC – *Cruz 'La Nación Argentina al Heróico Valor en Combate'* (the Argentine Nation's Cross for Heroic Valour in Combat).

CID – Criminal Investigation Department.

Clansman – A British infantry Battalion radio communications system which had been issued to the 5th Infantry Brigade only a two or three weeks prior to its deployment to the Falklands-Malvinas War.

CLFFI ('Cliffy') – Commander Land Forces Falkland Islands.

Cluster bomb – The Royal Navy Fleet Air Arm used the BL755 cluster bomb which could eject 147 sub-munitions (mini-bombs) which exploded on contact with the ground.

CO – The Commanding Officer of a major unit (e.g. infantry battalion, artillery regiment etc.) with the rank of Lieutenant-Colonel.

Commandant – The 7th Gurkha Rifles' alternative title for the Commanding Officer.

Company – This is an infantry Battalion sub-unit comprising three platoons and a Company HQ. In the British Army this totals about 100 men and is commanded by a Major. Smaller-sized units of other arms are known as Squadrons (Engineers, Signals, Transport etc.) and Batteries (artillery). Argentine Army and Marine infantry Companies are much larger.

CPX – Command Post Exercise.

CSM – Company Sergeant-Major.

Dagger – Israeli-manufactured Argentine (multi-role) fighter-bomber aircraft.

Dassault-Bregeut Super Étendard – This was a French-manufactured strike fighter aircraft which carried the AM-39 Exocet air to surface missile.

DCM – Distinguished Conduct Medal decoration.

DF – Defensive Fire. This is a pre-recorded and adjusted target on the ground for artillery or mortar fire. A series of DFs can be plotted by a unit or sub-unit in a defensive position and utilised quickly against attacking enemy forces.

DFC – Distinguished Flying Cross decoration.

DMS – British Army Direct Moulded Sole boot.

DSO – Distinguished Service Order decoration.

EA – Existential Authority.

Endex – British Army colloquial expression for 'end of exercise'.

Exocet – This is a French-manufactured medium-range anti-ship missile which can be fired from the air (AM-39) and surface (MM-38). Its maximum range at sea-skimming height is seventy kilometres travelling at 315 metres per second.

EXPAL – Explosivos Alaveses, a Spanish company that develops, manufactures, integrates and maintains products, systems and services for defence and security systems.

FAC – Forward Air Controller for Harrier GR3 ground-attack aircraft.

FAL – *Fusil Automático Liviano* – This was the standard Argentine Marine and Army Belgian-manufactured FN (*Fabrique Nationale de Herstal*) light automatic assault rifle. It fired a high-velocity 7.62mm round and had an effective range of between 200 to 600 metres.

FAP – *Fusil Automático Pesado* – The Argentine heavy automatic (assault) rifle.

FCO – Foreign and Commonwealth Office.

FIDF – Falkland Islands Defence Force.

Field dressing – A sterile pad with attached bandages for emergency first-aid on the battlefield.

FOO – Artillery Forward Observation Officer (usually with the rank of Captain) who accompanies front-line infantry and brings down artillery fire onto artillery targets.

FUP – Forming Up Point (a point on the ground where an infantry Battalion moves to from its Assembly Area before moving out to its start line for an attack).

Gazelle helicopter – The Westland Gazelle is a British-manufactured (under license to the French company Aérospatiale) utility helicopter which can carry five passengers.

GC – George Cross decoration.

GM – Gurkha Major, the most senior (Nepalese) Queen's Gurkha Officer in a British Army Gurkha Battalion.

GP – General Practioner (Doctor)

GPMG – Belt-fed 7.62mm General Purpose Machine-Gun.

GPMG(SF) – General Purpose Machine-Gun in the sustained fire role. It was mounted on a tripod which enabled the weapon's range to be increased from 600 metres to 1,800 metres.

Harrier – Hawker Siddeley Harrier jump-jet capable of vertical/short take-off and landing (V/STOL). The Sea Harrier (SHAR) variant was a naval air strike/air defence fight. The Harrier GR3 variant was an operational close support and reconnaissance attack aircraft.

H-Hour – The time by which a unit crosses its final start line immediately prior to mounting an attack on an enemy position.

Hispano-Suiza 30mm twin anti-aircraft cannon – A French-manufactured anti-aircraft weapon.

Huey UH1H – The Bell UH1H was a utility helicopter used by Argentine forces. Nine of this helicopter type were used in the Falklands-Malvinas War.

Infantry Brigade – This is a formation comprising (normally) three infantry Battalions, supporting artillery, cavalry, engineers and logistic units, and Brigade HQ and Signals Squadron. The formation has a strength of about 3,000 men commanded by a Brigadier.

Inner Defence Zone – The Argentine Inner Defence Zone was located just to the west of Stanley and incorporated Sapper Hill, Mount William and Tumbledown. The Outer Defence Zone included Mount Longdon, Two Sisters Mount Kent, Mount Harriet, Mount Challenger and Wall Mountain.

IO – Battalion HQ Intelligence Officer who is responsible for gathering, compiling and providing intelligence (information of value) on the enemy.

ITN – Independent Television News.

IWS – British Army Individual Weapon Sight.

Kelper – Nickname for the Falkland Islanders (derived from the kelp seaweed).

KIA – Killed in action.

L42 sniper rifle – This was the last Lee Enfield rifle to see active service in the British Atmy, the L42A1 was a manually bolt-operated 7.62mm sniper rifle with a ten-round magazine. It was fitted with a telescope sight and had a maximum range of 1,000 metres plus.

Larkspur – A Battalion radio communications system that was the predecessor to the Clansman system used in the Falklands-Malvinas War.

LCU – Landing Craft Utility.

LGB – A Laser Guided Bomb is a guided bomb that uses a semi-active laser homing to strike a designated target with greater accuracy than an unguided bomb. This requires a laser designator unit to mark or illuminate the target. In the Falklands-Malvinas War such a laser designator was manned by a four-man Tactical Air Control Party (TACP) on the ground.

Light weapons – These are, broadly speaking, weapons designed for use by two to three persons serving as a crew, although some may be used and carried by a single person. They include, inter-alia, heavy machine-guns, hand-held under-barrel mounted grenade launchers, portable anti-aircraft guns, portable anti-tank guns, recoilless rifles, portable launchers of anti-tank missile and rocket systems, and mortars of a calibre of less than 100 millimetres. This definition was adopted by the UN General Assembly on 8 December 2005.

LMG – Light Machine-Gun. British forces in the Falklands-Mavinas War used the Bren Gun with a 7.62mm .barrel. The weapon had ammunition magazines rather than link belted ammunition, and a effective range of 600 metres..

LSL – Landing Ship Logistics.

M2 high-explosive hand grenade – US-manufactured fragmentation grenade known as a 'pineapple' grenade because of its shape and structure.

M-79 grenade launcher – This weapon is a single-shot, shoulder-fired, break-action grenade launcher that fires a 40mm round. Its effective range is 350 metres and rate of fire is six rounds per minute.

MAG – *Mitrailleuse d'Appui Général* – This was the standard Argentine FN (*Fabrique Nationale*) 7.62mm General Purpose Machine-Gun.

MAPCO – Map Code used for encoding grid reference numbers.

MBE – Member of the British Empire award.

MC – Military Cross decoration.

Mexeflote – A landing raft used to move cargo and vehicles between ship and shore.

MFC – Mortar Fire Controller is an 81mm Mortar Platoon forward observer who can correct the fall of mortar bombs on a chosen target.

MID – Mention in Dispatches decoration.

Milan – Infantry wire-guided anti-tank missile. Manned by a two-man team, the launch unit weighed fifteen kilos and had a maximum range of 2,000 metres. It was successful in attacking Argentine bunkers during the Falklands-Malvinas War

Mills L2 hand-grenade – This is a British-manufactured high-explosive anti-personnel grenade based on the US M-26 grenade. It contains 170 grams of explosive giving a lethal radius of ten metres. Its fuze gives a time delay of 4.4 seconds.

Mirage – Dassault Aviation Mirage III French-manufactured supersonic multi-role fighter aircraft flown by the Argentine Air Force. It was used mainly in the air defence and escort role during the Falklands-Malvinas War.

MM – Military Medal decoration

MVC – *Medalla 'La Nación Argentina al Valor en Combate'* ('The Argentine Nation's Medal for Valour in Combat').

NAAFI – Navy, Army and Air Force Institute.

NATO – North Atlantic Treaty Organisation.

NCO – Non-Commissioned Officer.

NGS – Naval Gunfire Support.

NHS – National Health Service.

OAS – Offensive Air Support.

OBE – Order of the British Empire award.

OC – Officer Commanding a Battalion sub-unit.

O Group – A Commander's formal Orders Group where operational orders for a specific mission (e.g. an attack) are given out to subordinates. These orders are then passed on down the chain of command.

OP – Observation Post.

Panhard armoured car – The Panhard AML is a French-manufactured light armoured car with a permanent 4x4 drive for mobity. It has a 90mm quick fire gun and a crew of three. Twelve Panhards were deployed to Stanley in the Falklands-Malvinas War, but hardly saw any action.

Para FAL – *Fusil Automático Liviano* – This was exactly like the standard-issue Argentine FAL rifle but with a hollow collapsible stock.

PDF – An Argentine double-effect fragmentary explosive round.

Phantom – A US-manufactured McDonnel Douglas F4 Phantom all-weather supersonic jet intercepter/fighter/fighter-bomber was used for two decades by the Royal Air Force as a deterrent force (four aircraft) based at the post-war built Mount Pleasant Airport on East Falkland.

Platoon – An infantry company sub-unit comprising three sections and a Platoon HQ. A British Army platoon's strength is thirty-five men. The strength of an Argentine Army platoon (*sección*) was forty-five men. An Argentine Marine Infantry platoon had fifty-five men.

PM – Prime Minister.

PNA – *Prefectura Naval Argentina* (Argentine Naval Coastguard).

PoW – Prisoner of War.

PTG – Post-Traumatic Growth.

PTSD – Post-Traumatic Stress Disorder.

PTSR – Post-Traumatic Stress Reactions.

Pucará – Argentine twin turbo-prop ground-attack fighter for close air support operations.

Puma helicopter – The French-built Aérospatiale SA330 utility helicopter was used by Argentine forces in the Falklands-Malvinas War. It can carry eighteen passengers.

QE2 – Cunard Line's RMS *Queen Elizabeth 2.*

QGO – Queen's Gurkha Officer (Nepalese).

RA – Royal Artillery.

RAP – A Battalion Regimental Aid Post where wounded are assessed, stabilised and prepared for evacuation from the battlefield.

RAPC – Royal Army Pay Corps

RE – Royal Engineers.

Rear Echelon – Split into A (front) and B Echelon (rear), this is an infantry Battalion's organisation responsible for logistic re-supply to the Battalion's sub-units at the frontline.

Recce Platoon – The Battalion Commanding Officer's forward 'eyes and ears' sub-unit responsible for gathering information on the enemy by carrying out reconnaissance patrols and manning forward observation posts.

REME – Royal Electrical and Mechanical Engineers.

REMF – British Army colloquialism for 'Rear Area Mother Fucker'.

RFA – Royal Fleet Auxiliary.

RI6 – *Regimiento de Infantería 6* (6th Infantry Regiment).

RN – Royal Navy.

RSO – Battalion Regimental Signals Officer.

RSM – Regimental Sergeant-Major

RV – Rendezvous Point.

SAM-7 – Soviet-manufactured shoulder-held surface-to-air missile,

SAMA82 – South Atlantic Medal Association 82.

Sangar – A small temporary fortified position built above the ground with a breastwork (in the Falklands-Malvinas War) of rock and peat. The term was used by the British Indian Army on the North-West Frontier and comes from the Persian word *sang* (stone).

SAS – The Special Air Service (also Scandinavian Airlines System!)

Scimitar – British Army Combat Vehicle Reconnaissance (Tracked) light tank armed with a 30mm Rarden cannon.

Scorpion – British Army Combat Vehicle Reconnaissance (Tracked) light tank armed with a 76mm gun.

Scout helicopter – The British-manufactured Westland Scout helicopter was a general purpose light helicopter used by British forces in the Falklands-Malvinas War. It could carry three passengers.

Sea Dart – A Royal Navy medium range surface to air missile which was effective in engaging targets at altitude in the Falklands-Malvinas War.

Sea King helicopter – This was a British-manufactured Royal Navy helicopter deployed in the Falklands-Malvinas War. The Westland Sea King performed anti-submarine search and attack, and also replenishment, troop transport and special forces' insertions into the Islands. It could carry twenty-two passengers. Argentine Forces also used the Sea King.

Section – A platoon sub-unit comprising eight to ten men commanded by a Corporal. An Argentine Army section (*grupo*) comprised thirteen to fourteen men. An Argentine

Marine section had seventeen men.

Sitrep – Situation Report.

Skyhawk – The US-manufactured Douglas A4 Skyhawk carrier-capable ground-attack aircraft was used by the Argentine Air Force and Navy extensively in the Falklands-Malvinas War. Forty-eight aircraft were deployed in the war and half of these were lost. The Skyhawk inflicted considerable damage on British shipping.

SLR – The British Army standard-issue 7.62mm self-loading rifle used in the Falklands-Malvinas War. It had a twenty-round magazine and an effective range of 300 metres.

Small arms – These are, broadly speaking, weapons designed for individual use. They include, inter-alia, revolvers and self-loading pistols, rifles and carbines, submachine-guns, assault rifles and light machine-guns. This definition was adopted by the UN General Assembly on 8 December 2005.

Snake Eye bomb – This is a US-manufactured aerial-dropped 250 kilogram Mk 82 Snake Eye bomb which employs retarders or parachutes so that the aircraft delivering the bomb can escape the detonation in low altitude attacks.

Snotrac – A Royal Marine Commando tracked supply vehicle used in cold-weather climates.

SOP – Standard Operating Procedures.

Spearhead Battalion – This was the principal high-readiness infantry battalion in the British Army with a mandatory seventy-two hours notice to move. Since the Falklands-Malvinas War this has now become the Spearhead Lead Element (SLE) of the British Armed Forces comprising a Battle Group based on a light infantry battalion and focus on joint operations with other arms.

Start Line – A natural feature on the ground which marks the start line for a Battalion to cross at H-hour in order to carry out an attack on an enemy position.

Sterling submachine-gun (SMG) – British-manufactured 9mm submachine-gun with a folding shoulder stock. The weapon's curved box magazine contained thirty-four 9mm calibre rounds. Its effective range was 200 metres.

Stick – A group of troops comprising eight to ten men embarked on board a helicopter.

Tab – Tactical advance to battle.

Tac HQ – Battalion Tactical Headquarters.

TACP – Tactical Air Control Party (see Laser Guided Bomb).

Teeny Weenie Airways – The nickname (TWA) for the 5th Infantry Brigade's 656 Squadron Army Air Corps (helicopters).

TEWL – Tactical Exercise Without Land (Gurkha *QE2* variant of a TEWT).

TEWT – Tactical Exercise Without Troops.

Tigercat – This was the British-manufactured land version of the Seacat, an optically guided surface-to-air missile. The Tigercat was used by Argentine forces in the Falklands-Malvinas War.

Total Exclusion Zone (TEZ) – A 200 nautical mile exclusion zone which was put in place by the UK Government around the Falkland Islands. Argentine forces (ships, submarines and aircraft) were not permitted to enter the TEZ. If they did so, then UK military force would be used against them.

TTB – Training Team Brunei.

UK – United Kingdom

UKLF – United Kingdom Land Forces.

UN – United Nations.

UNITA – *União Nacional Para a Independência Total de Angola* (Portuguese) (National Union for the Total Independence of Angola).

VC – Victoria Cross decoration.

VIP – Very Important Person.

Warsaw Pact – This was a mutual defence treaty between eight Communist countries in existence during the Cold War from 1955-91.

Wessex helicopter – The British-manufactured Westland Wessex helicopter was used by British Forces in the Falklands-Malvinas War for troop transport, and moving fuel, ammunition, artillery and Rapier missile systems. It could carry ten passengers.

XO – Executive Officer

Royal Navy	British Army	Argentine Navy (including Marine Corps)	Argentine Army
Admiral	General	*Almirante*	*Teniente General*
Vice-Admiral	Lieutenant-General	*Vicealmirante*	*General de División*
Rear-Admiral	Major-General	*Contraalmirante*	*General de Brigada*
Commodore	Brigadier	*Comodoro* [1]	*Coronel Mayor* [1]
Captain	Colonel	*Capitán de Navío*	*Coronel*
Commander	Lieutenant-Colonel	*Capitán de Fragata*	*Teniente Coronel*
Lieutenant-Commander	Major	*Capitán de Corbeta*	*Mayor*
	Major (QGO)*		
Lieutenant	Captain	*Teniente de Navío*	*Capitán*
	Captain (QGO)*		
Sub-Lieutenant	Lieutenant	*Teniente de Fragata*	*Teniente Primero*
	Lieutenant (QGO)*		
	Second-Lieutenant	*Teniente de Corbeta (Acting Sub-Lieutenant)*	*Teniente*
Midshipman		*Guardiamarina*	*Subteniente*
Warrant Officer	Regimental Sergeant-Major	*Suboficial Mayor*	*Suboficial Mayor*
Chief Petty Officer	Company Sergeant-Major	*Suboficial Principal*	*Suboficial Principal*
	Colour-Sergeant	*Suboficial Primero*	*Sargento Ayudante*
Petty Officer	Sergeant	*Suboficial Segundo*	*Sargento Primero*

Leading Hand	Corporal (Guards: Lance-Sergeant)	*Cabo Principal*	*Sargento*
	Lance-Corporal	*Cabo Primero*	*Cabo Primero*
Rating	Private	*Cabo Segundo*	*Cabo*
		Marinero Primero	*Soldado de Primera*
		Marinero Segundo	*Soldado de Segunda*

[1] Honorary rank.
[2] QGO – Queens Gurkha Officer.

7th Duke of Edinburgh's Own Gurkha Rifles Regimental Association Journal 13 (2007), p. 102, The Falklands Gourmet – Little Wether Ground.

Arthur, M. (1985) *Above All, Courage*, London, Cassell Military Paperbacks.

Bicheno, H. (2006) *Razor's Edge: The Unofficial History of the Falklands War*, London, Weidenfeld and Nicolson.

Bramley, V. (2009) *Two Sides of Hell*, London, John Blake Publishing.

Brown, D. (1987) *The Royal Navy and the Falklands War*, London, Leo Cooper.

Clausen de Bruno, M. (2003) *Entre tu mano y la mía* (*Your hand in mine*), Córdoba, Imprenta Corintios 13.

Conway, A. Review of Mike Seear: *With the Gurkhas in the Falklands: A War Journal. 7th Duke of Edinburgh's Own Gurkha Rifles Regimental Association Journal* 9 (2003), pp 106-7.

Dalton, E. Unpublished war diary of member of G3 (Operations), Argentine 10th Infantry Brigade HQ.

Demaria, C., and Daly, M. (eds.) (2009) *The Genres of Post-Conflict Testimonies*, Nottingham, CCCP.

El Pulso Argentino, 7, December 2010 (an Argentine high-quality periodical), p. 43-45. LA GUERRA Y LA POSGUERRA SEGÚN LA MIRADA DE UN SOLDADO INGLÉS – "Lo que viví en Malvinas los políticos y los gobernantes no lo polrán entender jamás" – LA BATALLA FINAL.

Falkland Islands – Report of Census 1980 (taken on 7 December 1980).

Falklands 25: The 2007 Pilgrimage (British Forces Broadcasting Service DVD).

Falklands Islands – Census Statistics 2006 (taken on 8 October 1986).

Falklands Islands – Report of Census (taken on 16 November 1986).

Freedman, L. (2005) *The Official History of the Falklands Campaign: Vol. II – War and Diplomacy*, London and New York, Routledge.

García Quiroga, D., and Seear, M. (2007) *Hors de Combat: The Falklands-Malvinas Conflict Twenty-Five Years On*, Nottingham, CCCP.

García Quiroga, D., and Seear, M. (2009) *Hors de Combat: The Falklands-Malvinas Conflict in Retrospect*, Nottingham, CCCP.

Green, P. *Falklands War Diary: My own view from HMS* Yarmouth *2 April to 28 July 1982* (**http://www.twogreens.co.uk**).

Hutchings, R. (2008) *Special Forces Pilot: A Flying Memoir of the Falklands War*, Barnsley, Pen and Sword Aviation.

Jolly, R. (2007) *The Red and Green Life Machine*, Saltash, Red and Green Books.

King, R. Unpublished war diary by resident of Stanley, Falkland Islands.

King's College Centre for Military Health Research: A fifteen year report, September 2010, p, 31, Section 5, How is psychological trauma managed in the armed forces?

Luvas, J. (1999) *Napoleon on the Art of War*, New York, The Free Press.

Macdonald, I., Rought-Brooks, H., and Wilson R. (2005) *The Gurkhas: The Forgotten Veterans*, Kathmandu, GAESO.

McGuirk, B. (2007) *Falklands-Malvinas: An Unfinished Business*, Seattle, New Ventures.

McManners, H. (1987) *Falklands Commando*, London, Grafton Books.

Messenger, C. Draft manuscript for an unpublished Scots Guards regimental book.

Middlebrook, M. (1989) *The Fight for the 'Malvinas': The Argentine Forces in the Falklands War*, London, Viking.

Naylor, M. (1995) *Among Friends: The Scots Guards 1956-1993*, London, Leo Cooper.

Nicholson, M. (1992) *A Measure of Danger: Memoirs of a British War Correspondent*, London, Fontana.

Op Corporate 1/7 GR Immediate Debrief Points, 10 July 1982.

Operation Corporate 1/7 GR Post Operation Report – Part II, 27 July 1982.

Pugh, N. (2010) *White Ship, Red Crosses*, Ely, Melrose Books.

Ramsey, G. (2009) *The Falklands War: Then and Now*, Old Harlow, Battle of Britain International.

Robacio, C., and Hernández, J. (1996) *Desde el Frente, Batallón de Infantería de Marina No. 5 (From the Front Line – 5th Marine Infantry Battalion)*, Buenos Aires, Editorial Solaris.

Scots Guards Briefing to the UK Staff College, 26 May 1983.

Scots Guards Commander Diary Narrative (Army Form C2118) 7 May-10 August 1982.

Seear M. (2003) *With the Gurkhas in the Falklands: A War Journal*, Barnsley, Pen and Sword Books.

Smith J. (2002) *74 Days: An Islander's Diary of the Falklands Occupation*, Old Basing, Quetzal.

Soldier, Magazine of the British Army 63, 6 (June 2007), 'We did our job', p. 5.

Sun Tzu. (2002) *The Art of War: The Denma Translation*, Boston and London, Shambhala.

Supplement to *The London Gazette.* 8 October 1982.

The Guards Magazine: Journal of the Household Division, Spring 2007, p. 5, Face to face with the enemy.

Van de Bijl, N., and Aldea, D. (2003) *5th Infantry Brigade in the Falklands*, Barnsley, Leo Cooper.

Vaux, N. (1987) *March to the South Atlantic: 42 Commando Royal Marines in the Falklands War*, London, Buchan and Enright.

West, N. (2002) *The Secret War for the Falklands*, London, Warner Books.

B

C

D

E

F

O

P

S

T